International Sport Management

Ming Li, EdD

Ohio University

Eric W. MacIntosh, PhD

University of Ottawa

Gonzalo A. Bravo, PhD

West Virginia University

Editors

Human Kinetics

Library of Congress Cataloging-in-Publication Data

International sport management / Ming Li, Eric W. MacIntosh, Gonzalo A. Bravo, editors.
   p. cm.
 Includes bibliographical references and index.
 ISBN-13: 978-0-7360-8273-0 (hardcover)
 ISBN-10: 0-7360-8273-5 (hardcover)
 1. Sports administration--Cross-cultural studies. I. Li, Ming, 1959- II. MacIntosh, Eric W., 1977- III. Bravo, Gonzalo A., 1959-
 GV713.I585 2012
 796.06'9--dc22

                2011004871

ISBN-10: 0-7360-8273-5 (print)
ISBN-13: 978-0-7360-8273-0 (print)

The web addresses cited in this text were current as of February 2011, unless otherwise noted.

Acquisitions Editor: Myles Schrag; **Developmental Editor:** Katherine Maurer; **Assistant Editor:** Steven Calderwood; **Copyeditor:** Bob Replinger; **Indexer:** Michael Ferreira; **Permission Manager:** Martha Gullo; **Graphic Designer:** Joe Buck; **Graphic Artist:** Denise Lowry; **Cover Designer:** Keith Blomberg; **Photographer (cover):** Pedro Ugarte/AFP/Getty Images; **Photographer (interior):** Photo on page xvi © zuma/ICON SMI; page 70 © Sport the library / Photosport; page 218 © Xinhua/Imago/Icon SMI; page 300 © Sport the library / Photosport; and page 392 © Sport the library / Presse Sport; **Photo Asset Manager:** Laura Fitch; **Visual Production Assistant:** Joyce Brumfield; **Photo Production Manager:** Jason Allen; **Art Manager:** Kelly Hendren; **Associate Art Manager:** Alan L. Wilborn; **Illustrations:** © Human Kinetics, unless otherwise noted; **Printer:** Sheridan Books

Printed in the United States of America   10   9   8   7   6   5   4   3   2   1

The paper in this book is certified under a sustainable forestry program.

Human Kinetics
Website: www.HumanKinetics.com

United States: Human Kinetics, P.O. Box 5076, Champaign, IL 61825-5076
800-747-4457
e-mail: humank@hkusa.com

Canada: Human Kinetics, 475 Devonshire Road Unit 100, Windsor, ON N8Y 2L5
800-465-7301 (in Canada only)
e-mail: info@hkcanada.com

Europe: Human Kinetics, 107 Bradford Road, Stanningley, Leeds LS28 6AT, United Kingdom
+44 (0) 113 255 5665
e-mail: hk@hkeurope.com

Australia: Human Kinetics, 57A Price Avenue, Lower Mitcham, South Australia 5062
08 8372 0999
e-mail: info@hkaustralia.com

New Zealand: Human Kinetics, P.O. Box 80, Torrens Park, South Australia 5062
0800 222 062
e-mail: info@hknewzealand.com

E4794

Contents

Foreword   vii • Preface   xi
Acknowledgments   xv

Foreword

Earle F. Zeigler, PhD, DSc, LLD

The opportunity to write a foreword for a book titled *International Sport Management* presented a challenge I am pleased to accept. I congratulate the editors sincerely for their professional zeal. Given the breadth and scope of this text, as well as the names of those scholarly professionals who accepted writing assignments in this wide-ranging volume, this publication will undoubtedly have an influence on the profession.

This book will help prospective sport managers understand what competitive sport has become in the world. In addition, it will help them understand why many of its promoters are confronted with a dilemma. I believe that sport—as well as all other social institutions such as politics—will face many troubling and difficult decisions often ethical in nature. These decisions will have to be made as professors of sport management seek to prepare professionals who will guide sport into becoming an increasingly responsible social institution. The fundamental questions facing the profession are these: What kind of national and international sport experience do we want to promote, and what kind of world will be shaped as a result in the 21st century?

It is fascinating that, during the course of the 20th century, sport and physical activity have become one of the important societal institutions and an ever-more-powerful social force. Among those institutions are societal values, the type of political state in vogue, the economic system, and religious beliefs and systems. To these longstanding institutions I have added the influence of forces such as education, science, technological advancement, concern for peace, and now sport itself (Zeigler, 2009). Of these, human values, and the accompanying norms that are developed, form the strongest social institution of all. The following is a list I developed with H.M. Johnson; we present some of the personal values that are fostered through the promotion of the right kind of sporting competition:

1. Health
2. Making a contribution regardless of actual success—the value of effort itself
3. Actual achievement, including excellence
4. Respect for opponents
5. Cooperation (i.e., one's ability to subordinate the self to the attainment of collective goals)
6. Fair play (i.e., respect for the rules of competition, which are ideally universal)
7. Orderly procedures for settling disputes
8. Grace in intensely competitive situations (including magnanimity in victory and the ability to accept defeat gracefully, then try to gain victory the next time)

Similar to other professions today, the burgeoning profession of sport management is striving to cross what has been termed by Borgman (1992) as the postmodern divide. It is argued that Western society is being stubborn in its refusal to move beyond practices that are unconscionable when the future is contemplated (e.g., the primitiveness of archaic religions and a waste caused by a throwaway society that is destroying the environment). Postmodernists now form a substantive minority that supports a more humanistic, pragmatic, liberal consensus in which highly competitive sport, *if uncontrolled*, may also be viewed as an increasingly negative influence on society.

The fundamental values of a social system will eventually have a strong influence on the individual values held by most citizens in that country. If a country is moving toward the most important twin values of egalitarianism and achievement, for example, what implications does that have for competitive sport in that political entity under consideration? The following are some questions that should be asked *before* a strong continuing commitment is made to sponsor both national and international sport through government or private funding:

1. Can it be shown that involvement in competitive sport at one of the three levels (i.e., amateur, semiprofessional, professional) brings about desirable *social* values (i.e., more value than disvalue)?

2. Can it be shown that involvement in competitive sport at one of the three levels brings about desirable *individual* values of both an intrinsic and extrinsic nature (i.e., creates more value than disvalue)?

3. If the answers to questions 1 and 2 are both affirmative (i.e., that involvement in competitive sport at any or all of the levels provides a sufficient amount of social and individual value to warrant such promotion), can sufficient funds be made available to support or permit this promotion at any or all of the three levels?

4. If funding to support participation in competitive sport at any or all of the levels is not available or such participation is not deemed advisable, should priorities—as determined by the expressed will of the people—be established about the importance of each level to the country based on careful analysis of the potential social *and* individual values of the society and its citizens from such participation in competitive sport?

Having stated that "sport" has become a strong social force internationally, there has been some ambiguity about what such a simple word as *sport* means. In essence, what we are describing here is an athletic activity requiring skill or physical prowess. It is typically of a competitive nature as in racing, wrestling, baseball, tennis, or cricket. For those involved, sport is often serious, and participants may advance to a stage where competitive sport becomes a semiprofessional or professional career choice. For many others, however, sport is seen more as a diversion, as a form of recreation, and as a pleasant pastime. Here the horizon is expanded to include the experiences and opportunities provided to humankind by friendly competition among all nations of the world.

Viewed collectively, however, at present the totality of sport appears to have become a strong social institution. Yet it appears to be one that is without a well-defined theory whereby it could be determined, for example, to what extent international sport contributes to world peace. This lack is recognized increasingly in some quarters. Nevertheless, at this point the general public, including most politicians, seem to believe that the more competitive sport we have, the merrier—but they don't know why! However, we who might serve internationally

in the sport management profession can't disregard the need to answer such questions as these: What purposes has competitive sport served in the past? What functions is sport fulfilling now? Where does sport seem to be heading? How should international sport be employed to serve all humankind?

In response, I believe that sport can function in the following ways:

1. As an organized religion (for those with or without another similar competing affiliation)

2. As an exercise medium (often a sporadic one)

3. As a life enhancer or arouser (puts excitement in life)

4. As a trade or profession (depending upon one's approach to it)

5. As an avocation, perhaps as a leisure filler (at either a passive, vicarious, or active level)

6. As entertainment for spectators

7. As a training ground for war (used throughout history for this purpose)

8. As a socializing activity (an activity where one can meet and enjoy spending time with friends)

9. As an educational means (the development of positive character traits, however described)

As I review this list, I find it most interesting that I listed sport as a developer of positive character traits last! It may well be that sport is contributing significantly to the development of what are regarded as social values: teamwork, loyalty, self-sacrifice, and perseverance consonant with prevailing corporate capitalism in democracy and in other political systems. Conversely, it may also be that there is now a great deal of evidence that sport is developing an ideal that opposes the fundamental moral virtues of honesty, fairness, and responsibility in the competitive experiences provided (Lumpkin, Stoll, and Beller, 1999). This disturbing evidence presents a challenge to international sport, because it is telling us that sport is being used more for promoting socioinstrumental values than for promoting moral values. Such a development presents a distinct challenge to the various professional associations for sport management that have sprung up worldwide.

Certain changes will have to be made to reverse this development. Those in power internationally along with international sport managers, as well as citizens themselves, will have to be convinced that there is a developing problem worldwide and then figure out what steps to take to rectify the situation. Such change won't occur overnight. The solution to this problem is simple or complex depending on what is done, how and where it is done, and under what circumstances it is done. This is the interesting, perhaps ridiculous, aspect of the development of sport—an aspect of life that has grown so disproportionately important during the 20th century of humankind's presence on a speck in the universe known as Earth.

As is the case with so many facets of life, a social development can be used for the subsequent improvement or detriment of humankind. We are using sport well in some ways, but we are also abusing it badly in others. In the case of commercialized competitive sport, perhaps we have reached a stage where the world could in the foreseeable future be doing more harm than good with it. One might say that the greater the amount of overt commercialization that exists in sport, the greater the danger for more harm than good resulting. International sport managers simply must promote the development of enforceable codes of ethics as well as work tirelessly to control the use of drugs and other doping techniques.

I am not arguing that what I call the proper use of sporting activities throughout the earth's affairs could be a panacea for all of the world's ills, the elixir that would create a heretofore unknown era of goodwill and peace worldwide. I *do* believe that, when wisely employed, it could enrich lives healthwise and recreationally for many more mil-lions than it is doing currently. I believe also that sport could be significant in the promotion of world peace. What I am arguing, therefore, is that, employed properly, sport as one of a number of vital social forces (e.g., nationalism, ecology) could contribute significantly to the improvement of the current world situation. In this text, the editors and authors provide the information and insights so that students can envision sport from this ideal perspective.

Additionally, and fundamentally important because of the overarching influence of values on the social structure, I believe that the active use of competitive sport worldwide to promote what have been called moral values and attributes, as opposed to socioinstrumental values, would create a force of such strength and power that humankind might be saved from the social and physical devastation looming ahead. At the very least, I believe such active promotion would delay to a considerable degree the onset of problems in what promises to be a difficult century for humankind.

References

Borgman, A. (1992). *Crossing the postmodern divide.* Chicago: University of Chicago Press.

Lumpkin, A., Stoll, S.K., & Beller, J.M. (1999). *Sport ethics: Applications for fair play* (2nd Ed.). St. Louis: McGraw-Hill.

Zeigler, E.F. (2009) *Sport and physical activity in human history: A persistent problems analysis.* Bloomington, IN: Trafford.

Preface

The genesis of this book took place over 12 years ago at the University of Massachusetts with the advent and the development of a course titled "International Sport Enterprise." The idea behind this elective course was to present content and a context for upper-level undergraduate and graduate students interested in Olympics and international sport. A central objective of this course was to challenge the prevailing U.S.-centric view of sport and sport management often held by American students. At the time, there were no texts that dealt with topics and issues in international sport in any systematic way, so professors interested in teaching in this area of the sport management curriculum were left to develop their own materials gleaned from an assortment of articles, books, and personal experiences. Over a full decade later, this situation has not fundamentally changed despite a growing base of literature in the field of international business and management.

The first sport management program was established at Ohio University in 1966. Since the early 1990s, sport management programs in North America, Europe, Oceania, and Asia have rapidly proliferated, supported by professional associations such as the North American Society for Sport Management (NASSM), the European Association for Sport Management (EASM), the Sport Management Association of Australia and New Zealand (SMAANZ), the Asian Association for Sport Management (AASM), and more recently the Latin American Association for Sport Management (ALGEDE) and the African Sport Management Association (ASMA). Topics addressing transnational, cross-cultural issues in the functional areas of sport management are beginning to emerge more consistently at sport management-related conferences. Trade journals, such as *Sports-Business Journal* and *Sport Business International,* are focusing on international sport issues and are being used as supplemental course materials in sport management programs. Despite these developments, only modest growth has occurred in the sport management literature focused on international sport management issues as evidenced by new works in the areas of international sport governance (Chalip, Johnson, & Stachura, 1996; Thoma & Chalip, 1996), international sport law (Wise & Meyer, 1997), and sport sociology (Maguire, 1999). Recent sport management introductory textbooks have generally included at least one chapter on international sport issues (Masteralexis, Barr, & Hums, 1998; Parks, Quarterman, & Thibault 2006), but a single chapter cannot cover the full range of critical points in depth.

This text is a response to the absence of any book like it in the field. It is intended to introduce the principles and practices of the business and management of international sport, although the authors make no pretense that a single text can provide adequate depth and breadth in all key functional areas of managing and doing business in a global context. The emergence of international business and management as a field of study within the broader confines of academic programs in business and management indicates the potential of international sport to become a new subdiscipline of study within sport management.

International sport management is an emerging field of study that focuses on the organization, governance, business activities, and cross-cultural context of sport. Sport itself has become a prominent vehicle of the international exchange process. Rarely does any management decision in any field of business and management escape the influence of global events. Thus, without education in the global context of sport, managers are susceptible to naive views of international politics, cultures, economics, law, marketing, ethics, monetary policies, and foreign competition. Understanding and applying "the rules of the game" are crucial to determining winners and

losers relative to a company's or organization's bottom line in the international arena.

A goal of this book is to awaken greater awareness and understanding that an array of intercultural competencies is needed to function effectively and appropriately in a multicultural work or event environment. Specifically, the book provides relevant theoretical and practical insights from which an undergraduate student in his or her third or fourth year of study or a first-year graduate student can develop a broader understanding of the real world of international sport organizations and business. Ultimately, this book provides a student, professor, or practitioner with critical insights into the practice of business as it intersects with the practice of international sport. This text strives to incorporate the relevant theoretical advances in international business and organizational management literature and pedagogy in a manner that is easily comprehended by either undergraduate or graduate students in sport management. Most important, this text strives to integrate the practical and theoretical issues presented in the various chapters through a strategic management and total quality management framework. This approach allows students to select from a broad range of issues and challenges found within the enterprise of international sport management and to be able to apply a strategic process grounded in ethical practices to analyzing and finding solutions to complex problems. This text is intentionally written for use by students in sport management programs from throughout the world and is not limited to a North American perspective.

Each of the book's 22 chapters includes several case studies or sidebars that illustrate a multitude of real-world examples of organizational and business issues in international sport. The case studies are drawn from primary industry sources, newspapers, and journals and are intended to provide the student with the opportunity to apply concepts outlined in the chapter to real-world situations. In addition, each chapter is organized to assist the student through the inclusion and highlighting of chapter objectives, key terms, learning activities, and review and discussion questions. This text includes extensive bibliographies and reference sections to help support the work of practitioners in the field.

Each chapter is written by academics and practitioners from throughout the world who are recognized within their respective disciplines. A distinctive feature of this text is that it was consciously developed with a global perspective, not a U.S.- or Euro-centric viewpoint.

International Sport Management has been arranged into five distinct sections. This structure creates a helpful progression to build students' understanding of international sport management issues and allows the text to be used in a modular fashion to support other courses, such as sport marketing, sport law, sport economics, sport business and finance, or other required and elective courses typically found within a sport management curriculum. The five distinct parts introduce the issues associated with international sport management, examine sport from a global perspective, and introduce the student to the structure of international sport governance before investigating issues and strategies essential to international sport management.

Part I: Issues in International Sport Management

This section lays the foundation for the sections and chapters that follow. Its three chapters introduce critical issues and concepts in international sport, describe the role of strategic management in international sport, and delineate the cultural competencies necessary to be a successful international sport manager. This perspective focuses on looking at international sport within specific geopolitical environments while dealing with the critical contexts of nationalism, regionalization, globalization, and internationalization. This section introduces the essentials of how to manage in an international sport business and organizational environment, providing a relevant framework and context for the chapters to come.

Part II: Field of Play in International Sport

This section gives students a broader and more in-depth understanding of how the world of international sport operates within different geopolitical environments and cultures throughout the world. This section is organized into six megaregions including North America, Latin America, Europe (including Russia), Africa and the Middle East, Southeast Asia and Oceania (including the Indian subcontinent), and Northeast Asia. As more production of sport products is outsourced to nations with emerging economies, as sport teams and leagues build international fan bases, and as the World Cups of football (FIFA), basketball (FIBA), and cricket (ICC) and the Olympic and Paralympic Games seek new locations in Asia, Africa, and

South America, an international sport manager must have a fundamental cultural understanding from which to operate with appropriate sensitivity to local customs and practices. This section also includes maps of each region and lists of key sport figures and events.

Part III: Governance in International Sport

This section expands on the more traditional treatment of Olympic or professional sport in the sport management literature by including the significant perspective of other international sport federations and the Paralympic Games. Professional sport leagues, tours, and organizations are examined within the contexts of more popular-based sport systems, such as school-based and club-based sport systems. This section also explores current topics and controversies in international sport such as the attempt to control action sports from an event, media, and sponsorship perspective, as well as issues of gender and disability discrimination surrounding the Olympic Games.

Part IV: Management Essentials in International Sport

This section separates this text from all others in the field in that it is the only international sport management textbook that examines the principles and practices of the business and organization of international sport from a strategic management perspective. The five chapters in this section provide a primer for students on international trade and economic integration, macroeconomics in international sport, legal aspects and institutions that govern organizations and businesses, corporate responsibility, sustainable international development in emerging economies, human rights, and managing service quality in a cross-cultural environment.

Part V: International Sport Business Strategies

Building on the core principles and cases outlined in the chapters of section IV, this section explores five primary international sport business strategies as encompassed in the traditional segments of sport marketing, sport media and information technologies including sport broadcasting, sport facilities and design, and sport event management including sport tourism. Within the context of each chapter in this section, critical issues are explored, such as the use of mass versus customized marketing strategies in different parts of the world to promote both traditional and nontraditional sporting enterprises and events and the expansion of broadband and wireless technologies as they intersect with the expansion of different sports.

Acknowledgments

First and foremost, we would like to acknowledge the many individuals who made contributions to this book and who played an instrumental role in its creation. This book is a product of all the contributing chapter authors who provided their diverse expertise, wisdom, and global insightfulness. Further, it would not have been possible to complete this project without the patience and relentless support of the editorial staff at Human Kinetics.

Of paramount importance to this book is the conceptual outline developed by Ted Fay. His incisive points of view on topics and issues pertaining to international sport management have formed a solid foundation for the success of this book. We are truly indebted to him in this regard.

We would also like to acknowledge the help provided to us at various stages of the process by colleagues and friends working in academia as well as the sport industry around the globe. These people made it possible for us to have access to resources that are not always available on the web or in the libraries.

Finally, we express our gratitude to members of our families, Wan Chen, Madison Li, Holly Li, Jaclyn Smith, Gretchen Peterec, Sebastian Bravo-Peterec, and Sara Bravo-Peterec, for their encouragement while we were working on this project.

Part I

Issues in International Sport Management

NBA star Baron Davis signs autographs for young Chinese students during a visit to the Beijing GuangAi Primary School. Over the past decades, the NBA has steadily expanded its brand around the world, including numerous partnerships and investments in Chinese markets.

Key Concepts and Critical Issues

Michael E. Pfahl, PhD
Ohio University, USA

Chapter Objectives

After studying this chapter, you will be able to do the following:

- Understand the importance of globalization and its effect on the sport industry
- Be familiar with the terminology and key concepts related to the globalization of sport
- Appreciate and understand the issues that sport managers might face when they begin international operations
- Understand the basic competencies and skills required to manage a sport organization in an international environment

Key Terms

The international nature of modern sport requires sport organization personnel to modify their personal and management practices in order to remain effective and competitive as they seek to secure and develop fans. Given the ever-expanding sport and entertainment options available to the average fan, this is no easy task. Although modern sport has always had an international element to it in events like the World Cup and Olympic Games, numerous forces have given rise to a greater diversity in sport coverage, events, and participants. Technological changes have transformed broadcasting revenues, creating more sport entertainment options for fans and more revenue streams for organizations than ever before. Capital investment has moved with great speed, creating new stadiums, teams, and merchandising opportunities. Athletes are perceived (and oftentimes act) like entertainment celebrities. As discussed by Dr. Zeigler in the foreword to this book, determining whether these transformations are good for global society is beyond the scope of this text. But approaching modern sport management with an international focus from the outset will better serve sport managers in the development of their sport or sport organization. This chapter is intended to help sport managers develop an understanding of the critical issues and concepts of managing sport business around the world.

In the first section of the chapter, key concepts are defined to prepare a foundation that will aid in understanding the issues to be discussed later regarding the global nature of modern sport. The terms and concepts discussed in this chapter are complex and contested but offer a solid underpinning for the deeper discussions of international sport issues found in later chapters.

The second section explores cultural, political, social, and economic elements within the critical contexts of internationalization and globalization that affect a sport manager's ability to manage his or her organization effectively. This examination provides a clear picture of the major issues that sport organization personnel must address when operating in the international environment, irrespective of organizational size. Sport managers who have this knowledge will be better prepared for the inevitable intercultural and ethical dilemmas that they will face when engaging in international operations.

The third and final section of the chapter explores the personal and professional competencies neces-sary to be a successful sport manager. Although no person can be expected to excel at everything, a sport manager who engages in a discussion about these competencies and learns about ways to incorporate them into daily living will become adaptable and sensitive to the nuances of sport culture and practice across the globe. In doing so, he or she can continuously work to develop skills and abilities in these areas.

Key Concepts

In this section, key concepts are defined to aid in understanding the terminology used in the international sport world. These terms help to contextualize the study and practice of international sport. At the same time, they provide (or perhaps clarify) important terminology in constant use in international sport. These terms include globalization, internationalization, regionalism, nationalism, glocalization, and localization.

Globalization

For more than 20 years, a key topic across social, economic, political, business, and numerous other fields of study has been the concept of a global economy. No single word generates more passion, divisiveness, and confusion as **globalization**. As a heavily contested word, *globalization* has gone through a number of definitional iterations over the course of its existence. It is a broad concept encompassing many elements and characteristics of life in the postindustrial era. When globalization began is difficult to pinpoint, but as Hargreaves noted, some believe that "while contemporary globalisation constitutes a unique order, a new era, globalisation as such is not new and various attempts have been made to periodise its development" (Hargreaves, 2002, p. 26). In other words, globalization has been going on for thousands of years as humans moved across the earth interacting with each other. Yet in the early 21st century, it has become common for people to try to place a starting point for globalization to come to terms with the changes currently taking place. The Age of Exploration (European explorers), the Industrial Revolution (development of capitalism), post–World War II (blocs of allied nations grounded in ideologies), and the fall of the Soviet Union (a single superpower, the United States, remaining) are all recent examples of such starting points for globalization. In actuality, outcomes from all these occurrences seem to have come together to create the set of economic, political, and social concerns that loosely define globalization.

Many definitions of globalization begin with economic concepts (capitalism, market economy), although the term is inextricably linked to political and social issues (such as power and poverty), especially those arising from the post–World War II era when the cold war began, international economic systems were revamped, and technological changes altered cultural interactions (Hargreaves, 2002). Many believe that globalization entered mainstream public consciousness at the end of the cold war in the late 1980s and early 1990s (Sklair, 2002). The end of the cold war resulted in numerous outcomes, one of the most important being that a single superpower remained, the United States, a nation that promoted a capitalist agenda of open markets and free trade. Based on this outcome, globalization has been used to describe ideologies of consumerism and capitalism. A corporation can now successfully operate in countries around the world (Naisbitt, 1994). Thurow observed (1996), "Shifts in technology, transportation, and communications are creating a world where anything can be made anywhere on the face of the earth and sold anywhere on the face of the earth" (p. 9). The steady development of **consumer culture** suddenly gained momentum as it spread across the globe. Consumer culture is the term used to describe the capitalist, or market economy, ideology whereby individuals aspire to ever-higher standards of living and material consumption. With the end of the cold war and the outcome of a single dominant superpower in the United States, this ideology became prominent, although in some form or another it has dominated many countries since the Industrial Revolution.

Others, however, take a broader, more culturally focused view of globalization and articulate concerns over the interrelationships between social, political, and economic issues, oftentimes clashing with the conventional, capitalist and consumerist globalization ideology (e.g., Nederveen Pieterse, 2003; Ritzer, 1993; Tomlinson, 1999). For example, Maguire (1999) argued, "Globalization can therefore be understood in terms of attempts by more established groups to control and regulate access to global flows and also in terms of how indigenous peoples both resist these processes and recycle their own cultural

products" (p. 93), with control coming in the form of economic policy as much as any other. The result is a tension between heterogenization (maintaining differences) and homogenization (making similar) (Maguire, 1999). An interesting example of this tension occurs in relation to food. For years there have been discussions, jokes, and even protests about the proliferation of American fast food around the world. Many of these arguments discussed culinary cultural issues in relation to losing identity to the likes of McDonald's (Ritzer, 2007). In response, a movement developed in 1989 has come to be known as the slow-food movement, whereby people are encouraged to grow their own food and eat and share with others. Although some elements of this movement now encompass environmental issues and social justice concerns, the original impetus was the fact that people around the world (and even in the United States) saw fast food as a homogenizing force and wished to keep alive local and national variety and identity (heterogenization).

In sport, globalization has been described as being driven by economic considerations more often than not, although cultural elements play a role. The balance between the two is difficult to find. A search for such a balance can be seen in the emphasis that the International Olympic Committee places on culture as part of its governing ideology. The demonstration of cultural uniqueness through hosting the Olympic Games (i.e., Opening and Closing Ceremonies) and through the local efforts for disseminating broader Olympic values through Olympic Day all speak to cultural elements within the globalization of sport (Olympic Day, 2010). Rather than allowing money to be the sole driving force behind the Olympic Movement, the International Olympic Committee and related national Olympic committees strive to use educational, cultural, and athletic experiences to facilitate social development and change.

Yet the economic incentives of hosting an Olympic Games are touted as a primary reason to bid for them. Although the economic and cultural elements are often seen as being in conflict with each other, the International Olympic Committee strives to show how they can be combined for the betterment of all the world's peoples.

Since international sport is being "driven by the West, and since America in so many ways leads the West, it should come as no surprise to learn that globalised sport is highly Americanised" (Hargreaves, 2002, p. 32). This conceptualization of international sport does have some merit, but it is flawed because it renders non-American, non-Western influences that are also part of globalization less important and fails to address the nuances that define Westernization or Americanization (Bairner, 2001; Maguire, 1999). In other words, a narrow, Western-centric view of international sport ignores the various local, regional, and national cultural elements that contribute to sport around the world, including within the West (Blanchard, 2000).

Despite the importance of culture in globalization debates and in sport, economic considerations do play a significant role because of the need to expand markets and drive profits by (inter)national companies using sport as a sponsorship platform (Coakley & Donnelly, 1999, in Horne, 2006). The economic impact of sport can be felt in the areas of media, the aforementioned corporate sponsorship and influence, branding and celebrity culture, and the general sense of commercialization of sport (Horne, 2006).

When sport managers are driven by the search for diversification in assets, capital flows, and new markets to enter with existing products or product associations, changes to sport occur. For example, corporate sponsorship and influence have moved beyond supporting sport, and corporate entities can now be found in the offices of current sport ownership where interest in controlling sport organizations is increasingly falling to those who have amassed the largest fortunes. To illustrate, AC Milan (Italian Serie A), one of the largest and most popular football clubs in the world, is owned by prime minister and telecommunications tycoon Silvio Berlusconi; Chelsea (English Premier League) is owned by Russian billionaire Roman Abramovich; Manchester United (English Premier League), another successful and globally popular football team, is owned by American Malcolm Glaser, who also owns the Tampa Bay Buccaneers (National Football League); Aston Villa (English Premier League) and the Cleveland Browns (National Football League) are owned by Randy Lerner, son of financial tycoon Al Lerner; and Manchester City (English Premier League) is now owned by the Abu Dhabi United Group after being owned by former Thai prime minister Thaksin Shinawatra. The result is the need to recoup the initial investment through

actions to accumulate profit (in the interest of the owners), perhaps at the risk of fielding competitive teams or pursuing championships (in the interest of the fans).

Sport ownership also can contribute to a company's global expansion. Recently, the Cleveland Cavaliers (National Basketball Association [NBA]) signed an agreement with an investment group from China for 15 percent ownership in the team (other deals and collaborations have been signed with the New York Yankees and other sport franchises) (Withers, 2009). The involvement of Chinese ownership groups further opens the Chinese market to the NBA and the Cavaliers, along with various attendant merchandising, broadcast, marketing, and sponsorship opportunities. This move solidifies the NBA's quiet work for "an international group to become involved in ownership on a minority level" (Withers, 2009, p. 7), part of its decades-long move toward creating a global market for its products. For over 15 years, the NBA has been slowly making inroads with its brand around the world. The NBA has hosted international tournaments, played exhibition games outside America, and welcomed numerous international players to its teams. In terms of unusual international marketing, in one instance a referee, that most controversial of sporting entities, became a product endorser. Pierluigi Collina, one of the great football referees in the world, was hired to do product endorsements by sport apparel and equipment manufacturer Adidas in 2002 (Collina, 2003).

Internationalization

Although the term *globalization* has become more popular in recent years, the **internationalization** of sport gained momentum following World War I. Internationalization is a term used to describe the worldwide dissemination of sport, driven, in part, by the development of the 20th-century consumer culture. In addition, the term refers to the movement of athletes around the world in the pursuit of work (Magnússon, 2001). This trend occurred despite "sport not being controlled or produced in a single country" (Keys, 2006, p. 187), unlike manufactured products. Sport, as an element in the internationalization of cultures, could be claimed by nations (both politicians and citizens) as "an expression of intrinsically national characteristics" (Keys, 2006, p. 188). Coakley (2003) identified

> ## CASE STUDY

Development of Formula One's Global Reach

Formula One is the world motorsport championship that began in 1950. Steve Matchett, former Benetton Formula One team mechanic and current color commentator for the Formula One broadcasts on Fox's Speed Channel in the United States, said the sport "has grown to become one of the leading sport businesses in the world, a colossal multi-billion-dollar industry" (2005, p. 22). With even the smallest components costing substantial sums and the race prize amounts kept relatively secret, Formula One is built on mystery, excess, politics, and glamour (Pfahl & Bates, 2008). "Formula One cars are the most exotic automotive machinery in the world, built to the highest standards and specifications" (Matchett, 1999, p. 19). In years past, the championship was run primarily on European race circuits, although a handful of races were run in countries such as Australia, Brazil, South Africa, and the United States (depending on the year). The teams operated from

bases in England, Germany, and France, although the drivers were from all over the world.

By the 1990s the sport had grown in popularity, and the governing body, the Fédération Internationale de l'Automobile (FIA), and the marketing entity for the sport, Formula One Management (FOM), began to set eyes on emerging global markets. The driver of this expansion was the broadcast rights sold by FOM across the world and the increasing sponsorship money that followed the massive international broadcasting and fan base of the sport. FOM pushed for new tracks to be built in rising economies such as those of Malaysia, Turkey, and China. By 2009 the championship boasted a 17-race schedule that ran from March to November and raced in 16 countries (including, for example, Italy, Bahrain, and Hungary). Although some have questioned the viability of the FIA and FOM's strategy, Formula One remains the top motorsport competition in the world.

---

three main areas that paved the way for the internationalization of sport: market economies, changing demographics including increased disposable income and greater leisure time, and large-scale capital investment by public and private sources. Although these elements could not, and cannot, be found in every country in the world, they do indicate the driving forces behind the last 100 years or so of growth in the popularity of sport, participation in sport (and athletics and exercise in general), and the **commodification** of sport and athletes. In this case, commodification refers to the influence of economic forces on the structure and practice of sport. Although sport has never been pure or free from these forces, the last 20 years or so have shown a distinct shift toward sport as "a commodity governed by market principles" (Sewart, 1987, p. 172) with an overt profit motive.

As sport is internationalized, it carries with it cultural elements from the hearts and souls of people in local communities to people around the world by television, radio, and computers. For example, the English Premier League is one of the most popular football leagues (domestically, regionally, and inter-

nationally) not only because of the quality of play in the league but also because of the associated English cultural elements broadcast around the globe with each match (e.g., language, fan culture). These elements are evident in the United States where, for example, the official supporter organization of the Columbus Crew (Major League Soccer) has adopted the chanting and singing of songs during match play, an international occurrence, but one with special connections to British football. British hooliganism (see Giulianotti, Bonney, & Hepworth, 1994) has even found its way to Columbus, Ohio, recently as 100 Crew supporters, ironically named the Hudson Street Hooligans, clashed with 30 or so supporters from the English Premier League side West Ham United during a friendly match (Leonard, 2008). Although this image is not the one that English football would prefer to present to the world, it does show that the cultural characteristics of the British version of the sport find their ways to other communities through the internationalization of sport.

The internationalization of sport has increased opportunities for fan involvement and enjoyment, and has provided exposure to cultures from around the world, because of developments in television, satellite, computer, and computer-mediated technologies. For example, American fans of the Italian Serie A football league can watch league matches from the comfort of their homes on the Fox Soccer Channel, and Thai fans can wake up early in the morning to watch live broadcasts of the American National Football League games by satellite television. Many major sport teams around the world have multiple-language websites (e.g., Spanish, Japanese, Chinese, Portuguese) that offer unique content for fans in different countries to maximize sponsorship and marketing opportunities, especially merchandise sales.

Regionalization

Within the framework of internationalization lies regionalization. Blocs of countries or market areas within a specific geographical, cultural, or economic condition have developed in the modern era. Although groups of nations have come together for various purposes throughout history, in the era of globalization formal entities such as the European Union, the Association of South East Asian Nations, and the Non-Aligned Nations (Baghdadi, 2009) have developed in response to various forces of globalization and internationalization. In the world of sport, regionalization has also taken hold as governing bodies for various sports have created confederations and regional tournaments in addition to the larger, global ones run by international federations such as Federation Internationale de Basketball (FIBA).

For example, the Union of European Football Associations (UEFA) is the powerful European football confederation that runs the UEFA Champions League and other competitions that are broadcast worldwide. These events receive almost as much attention as the World Cup itself. Although the competitions draw from European domestic leagues (e.g., England, Italy), the tournaments themselves are broadcast around the world. Fans are able to cheer their teams at an entirely different level of competition than in the domestic leagues. For the sponsors, the championships are an important advertising platform, although not quite at the cost level of the Olympics or World Cup. Although other regional confederations host similar tournaments (e.g., African Nations Cup, Asian Champions

League), none generate the excitement that surrounds the European championships.

Regionalism, based on a geographical area (e.g., Southeast Asia) made up of a set of countries with similar characteristics, plays an important part in international culture, specifically in sport. Regional competitions and teams maintain an international presence at a lower cost of operation than large, international competitions. Thus, they can be run more frequently and have the benefit of generating neighborhood rivalries among countries or communities. Examples of regional sport include the Southeast Asian Games and the Pan American Games. Regionalism can also include local regions within a single country (e.g., Northeast), but for the purposes of this chapter, it refers to the previous definition. But anytime that international cultural flows (of any kind) move through countries or regions, the possibility exists that not everyone will understand and accept the inherent diversity of ideas or practices. Despite the global nature of modern sport, at its heart, sport remains locally centered.

Nationalism

As the various forces of globalization developed, expanded, and exerted their influences over local cultures, a countermovement developed with the intention of retaining or promoting a national identity (nationalism). **Nationalism**, or a shared sense of what a country stands for or is composed of, is a **socially constructed** concept with ever-changing rituals, practices, and historical foundations (Horne, 2006). Nationalism is socially constructed because its elements (e.g., patriotic duty, value systems) are communicated, discussed, and debated by various members of the society until a general or mainstream account of each element is created. Nationalism is closely linked with individual and community perceptions of national identities, although nationalism takes many forms (e.g., civic, ethnic) (Bairner, 2001). The most common form of nationalism is promoting the characteristics of the nation-state itself. For example, although what it means to be an American varies by person, there is a mainstream, some might say hegemonic, version of being an American, which includes loyalty to family, country, and religious or traditional values. Additionally, a common expression of nationalism includes language that refers to *we* or *us* used in relation to an other, a *them*.

Naisbitt (1994) characterized the tension between local and global as a paradox in which "the more universal we become, the more tribal [local] we act" (p. 131). By tribal, Naisbitt is referring to the local cultures of communities, which include the nation (Maffesoli, 1996). Bairner (2001) views globalization and nationalism as opposite sides of the same coin whereby increased knowledge of other cultures helps to raise awareness and understanding of local cultural elements: "The most popular form of nationalist behavior in many countries is in sport, where masses of people become highly emotional in support of their national team" (Kellas, 1991, p. 21 in Bairner, 2001, p. 17). The most visible of the connections between national team and nationalism is associated with the World Cup football tournament. Countries with long, sometimes violent, histories with each other—for example, England and Argentina, Japan and Korea, and Germany and Poland—tend to see a rise in nationalism ahead of an actual match as media references to the history and other memories are dredged up (Maguire, Poulton, & Possamai, 1999; McCormack, 2002).

The pressures of globalized cultures can weigh heavily on local cultural elements. Individuals and individuals within communities must negotiate the tensions inherent within a web of local, national, and international connections. Local cultural traditions and the need to retain cultural identity can clash with increasing capitalist ideals (wealth, status, stardom) (Friedman, 1990). Sometimes, the outside cultural forces are rejected, sometimes they are embraced, and other times hybrids of both are accepted. Hybrid forms are known as **glocalization**, or "the combining of global and local themes" (Horne, 2006, p. 133), which creates a new entity out of one or more cultural elements. In New Zealand, for example, the 20th century saw the rapid development, spread, and popularity of rugby after its introduction to the country in the 19th century. The country used the national team as a springboard to encourage social integration, culminating in the All Blacks Rugby team, through which "distinctions between social classes, between town and country, between regions, between colonisers and colonised, were both dramatized and bridged" (Perry, 2005, p. 159).

Localization

Closely related to glocalization is localization. **Localization** is the adaptation of nonlocal elements to the local context (e.g., language, rules). "Local culture should be seen in terms of the global cultural flows of which it is a part," (Appadurai, 1990; Wakeford, 2003) meaning that the interconnectedness of global and local communities influence each other and require knowledge of both to understand each. For example, a computer software program essentially runs the same way in any country, but the interface, colors, or the language of use can be adapted to fit local or regional needs. Language localization is common in business contexts. For example, product labels and commercial advertisements can be translated from one language into another in an attempt to keep a message consistent, if desired. On the other hand, organizations and companies that operate in multiple countries have found that tailoring messages (e.g., advertisements) to local cultures can be effective as well. Most major sporting teams and leagues have links on their main websites to specific language websites (e.g., Chinese, Japanese, Spanish). Slowly, these entities are also producing exclusive content for these local sites rather than merely translating what was presented on the main English (or Italian or Korean) page. Mobile telephony, computer-mediated communication, and wireless devices have redefined *local* to mean a focus on individual preferences to content, and websites such as Twitter and YouTube allow users to generate their own content such as news and reports. Although developments such as YouTube might be driven by profit motives and used to attract additional sponsorship monies, they also speak to the tightening of global ties that are a part of internationalization and globalization discussions.

In sum, within the duality of global and local, sport organization personnel must make strategic decisions to establish a brand presence in local markets while identifying ways in which to establish or increase an international presence. Differences in global, national, regional, and local communities make this task a challenging one. The sport managers responsible for making the strategic, cultural, political, and economic decisions for sport teams or organizations must be prepared for the challenges of the new sport landscape. They must be equipped with skills, abilities, and worldviews that are inclusive yet can differentiate cultural elements. Certainly, this is a challenge. After describing the various contexts in which sport operates, the next section of this chapter examines elements that play an influential role in the operations of sport organizations.

Sport Management Issues in the Global Sport Environment

The previous section explained the fundamental concepts affecting the modern international sport world. This foundation was developed by exploring specific issues affecting the performance of sport organizations and sport managers. This section examines how international sport is significantly affected by cultural, political, social, and economic elements. Grounded in social norms, values, expectations of various cultures, the issues examined here must be understood and addressed when operating in the international sport environment, no matter the size of the organization, because they are grounded in cultures of various communities (local, national). This knowledge will help sport managers identify the key skills and competencies needed to address the intercultural and ethical dilemmas that they will face when operating internationally (discussed in the third section of the chapter).

A note of caution will be helpful here. When discussing cultural differences, it is easy to become trapped in **binaries** by examining cultures against each other rather than simultaneously analyzing each on its own merits. Binaries in this sense are black and white distinctions between issues, in this case, cultures. We may tend to say that *we* do something right and, because *they* do it differently, they do it incorrectly. One way to avoid such narrow thinking is to ask many questions because intercultural issues have many shades of gray. The answers that you find provide information that can lead to an understanding of why a person in a particular culture follows a certain practice or takes a specific action. This approach lessens the chance of allowing stereotypical images or concepts to cloud understanding. Finally, however, we need to recognize the difference between understanding why something is done and accepting or agreeing with it. Reconciling deeper issues such as philosophical, religious, and other differences among cultures is always a tough task, one that binary thinking only exacerbates.

The elements that affect international sport include issues of politics, law, economics, finance, communication and language, time, technology, religion, and the environment. Although aspects of these issues can be barriers to effective performance, they are not insurmountable. Rather, they are elements of the intercultural complexities of international sport and are based in cultural differences and practices in communities around the world. In addition, while they are treated as distinct entities for the purpose of this discussion, each element is influenced by and influences the other elements. In other words, they are an interconnected whole of distinct parts.

Politics

As with most international activities, politics plays an important role in sport. Within the term *politics* are variations on what constitutes political activity. National governments set policies that affect sport, especially when governmental interests intersect with sport federations and governing bodies (Flyvbjerg, Bruzelius, & Rothengatter, 2003). Acknowledging that politics is a part of the activities of sporting federations and governing bodies, this section constrains itself to the influence and effect of politics at the international, national, state, regional, and local levels.

Sport and Political Agendas

The governance of countries, regions, and cities inevitably affects sport in wide-ranging ways. How sport serves political agendas and policies "depends upon their responsiveness to control" (McHenry, 1980, p. 239); that is, the extent to which a government can control sport determines the usefulness of sport to political aims. In other words, oftentimes sport and sport policies are perceived as "a means to an end, rather than an end in itself" (Horne, 2006, p. 101). Hargreaves (2002) argued,

> Political elites in the constituent states of the new world order have, for some considerable time tended to intervene in and to promote sport as an important instrument for the creation of a sense of national identity and as a way of enhancing their state-nation's prestige and influence internationally. (p. 32)

National governments set agendas, including many related to sport, and are important regulators and financial bodies for the development and maintenance of sport and sporting infrastructure, although this is not a desirable situation for all (McHenry, 1980). State, regional, and local governments are also heavily involved in the development of sport infrastructure and seek to host sporting events to encourage tourism, investment, and development. High-profile sporting events (megaevents) such as the Olympics are seen as highly desirable because of the real or perceived benefits that they bring with them (Dolles & Söderman, 2008; Horne, 2004).

In the buildup to the Beijing Olympic Games, IOC President Jacques Rogge announced, "The world would be watching China and Beijing with great expectation" (Dolles & Söderman, 2008, p. 147). This statement was made in Tiananmen Square, site of violent conflict between protestors and the Chinese military in 1989. Rogge's statement is complex and can be read in several ways depending on one's view of China and its political activities. Such complexity perfectly illustrates the relationship between politics and sport. Oftentimes, governments justify investment in sport, infrastructure, and megaevents by fluctuating economic and social benefits. "Economically it [sport or sport event] promises to operate as an industry around which cities can devise urban regeneration strategies" (Horne, 2006, p. 111), and socially it can help develop local communities such as by fostering community engagement, reducing crime, or increasing healthy behaviors (Chalip, 2006; Gratton, Shibli, & Coleman, 2005; Ohmann, Jones, & Wilkes, 2006). The same arguments can be and are used in relation to social change and economic development on an international level.

Thus, sporting events, especially the megaevents, are now showcases for countries and cities, with the attendant nationalism and patriotism, highlighting cultural, economic, and political positions in the international arena. Houlihan (1991) believed that the potential of these positive elements is what moves national, regional, and local governments to "humble themselves before the IOC and FIFA (Fédération Internationale de Football Association) governing bodies through lavish hospitality and the strategic deployment of presidents, prime ministers, royalty, and supermodels" (p. 194).

Political Systems

Adding to the complexity of politics and sport is the actuality that political systems and actors are not the same around the world. Different values, goals, governance mechanisms, and even stability make creating, financing, and hosting sport events or building sport infrastructure a difficult sea for sport managers to navigate. Broadcast rights, for example, are constrained or enabled by governmental communication agencies for both international and domestic events (Amara, Henry, Liang, & Uchiumi, 2005; Horne, 2006). In regard to regulation, for example, in the United States, although the national government has become involved in drug-testing issues (ESPN.com News Services, 2009), national and state governments are empowered to regulate sport agents (Shropshire & Davis, 2003; Willenbacher, 2004).

Coplin and O'Leary (1983) developed an initial political risk assessment tool to explore, understand, and interact with these differences. It examined issues such as key individuals, the potential for political instability, and the various parties that could come to power over the long interval that passes between initial planning and the actual commencement of some sporting events (e.g., the World Cup). However, this tool does not explicitly address issues such as currency and financial contexts, terrorism, or the potential for external events to influence a government. Even so, Coplin and O'Leary's initial work reflected the importance of understanding political systems in relation to sport. "The resulting tie-up between sport, national identity and nationalism" (Hargreaves, 2002, p. 41) underlines the importance of sport to governments.

Political activities in and through sport have been around for many years. The next section examines the effect of economic issues on sport organizations, an issue closely related to politics and policy (Simson & Jennings, 1992).

Economics

Closely linked with governmental policies and regulations, the economic environment that a sport team or organization operates in can enable and constrain the actions available to sport managers. Economics in relation to sport is defined as the way in which sport organization personnel manage resources in the face of fluctuating consumer demand and consumption patterns coupled with inconsistent access to resources (e.g., revenue, equipment). The last 20 or so years have seen the growth in the popularity in sport at the same time that global economic crises have had important effects on all levels of the world's economy. Significant international economic crises in 1987, 1997, and 2008 have made it crucial for sport managers to be aware of economic

CASE STUDY

Use of Sport for Political Purposes in Tanzania in the 1960s and 1970s

An example of how knowledge about political activities helps to understand their relation to and use of sport can be found in Tanzania more than 30 years ago. In his examination of Tanzanian politics and sport, McHenry (1980) examined the interplay between the Football Authority of Tanzania (FAT), the Tanzanian government, and citizens. Tanzanian football was in disarray. Fan rivalries turned into fights and social disturbances, referees were assaulted at matches by fans who disagreed with the calls made, and players were as eager to fight on the pitch as the fans were in the stands (McHenry, 1980). The FAT and the local law enforcement agencies did not take action to prevent the violence or to punish the players' incivilities (McHenry, 1980). The embattled FAT faced years of undisciplined behavior at matches, and the government criticized "not only players and fans, but sports organizations for their failure to control them" (McHenry, 1980, p. 242). The government had been vocal in its criticism saying that "national interests were being hindered" (McHenry, 1980, p. 243) because of the situation. Previous years saw the FAT under different government ministries—sometimes education, sometimes sport. In 1967 the National Sports Council (NSC) was developed to bring control of sport under one, consistent administrative structure (McHenry, 1980). The NSC struggled to bring order to the domestic sport landscape.

Yet while the confrontations continued on domestic pitches, Tanzanian officials were helping to build an ultimately successful coalition of allies to end apartheid in South Africa and attempt to bring about African unity through the use of sport (McHenry, 1980). The government could not control activities on the pitch, but it could control the participation of Tanzanian international teams in various competitions. This tactic was used to bring about foreign policy changes, specifically the end of apartheid

(minority white rule) in South Africa. Using sport as a platform to raise the apartheid issue (e.g., at the Olympics), Tanzania developed a skillful foreign policy tool through sport. Another context in which sport was used was the effort to build unity among the postcolonial countries in Africa. This endeavor was unsuccessful compared with the campaign to end apartheid mainly because "competitions often did not take place where they might have been expected to improve relations between countries" (McHenry, 1980, p. 255). In some cases, the organization of sporting contests created negative situations where friendly relations had previously existed.

Tanzania's government also used sport for internal policy development. Two goals were developed for domestic policy (and to retain hegemonic control): national integration and communal behavior (McHenry, 1980). The Tanzanian government wanted to use sport to bridge cultural divides existing in the country at that time (e.g., life in the capital city versus life in the provinces) as well as to suppress individual needs and wants in relation to the greater good (i.e., wealth and status issues). The government failed in both quests because sporting contests between city-based and provincial-based entities created disagreements and power struggles over funding issues and political posturing among the various sporting and government personnel. In addition, the attempt to quell individualism failed because individual football club owners saw the power of bribery and corruption in player salaries and bids for the best ones. Players even began to leave Tanzania for other countries in search of greater paydays, a trend that did not help to promote the greater good. Many years after this instance, issues of race and violence in sport and life still exist despite political and social efforts to bring about change, reminding us that continued effort and vigilance is needed when sport and politics intermix.

---

fluctuations, issues surrounding the financing of sport operations, and the fan base. Financing sport, specifically the construction and hosting of events, is briefly examined here but is covered more extensively in the next section.

Economic Fluctuations

The size of the international sport industry is difficult to calculate, but conservative estimates begin in the billions of dollars. Economic fluctuations, however, alter the sport landscape and affect the costs and revenues associated with managing teams and events. The effect of these fluctuations on a sport team or organization depends, in part, on where in the world the team or organization is located. In countries with growing economies that are susceptible to large economic fluctuations, a downturn in the local or global economy can have disastrous results. In a larger, more robust economy, teams and organizations might be able to weather the events easier (but not necessarily easily) with less negative effect. Thus, a sport team, league, or organization will be affected differently depending on its location when fluctuations in the business cycle occur.

Public Financing

Recent trends in the economics of sport show an increasing use of (and debate about) public financing for private stadiums and other facilities. One of the arguments justifying the use of public funds is that positive economic impacts occur on the surrounding community (e.g., an aging downtown area). Siegfied and Zimbalist (2000) argued that governments provide subsidies to sport teams, leagues, or events to gain social benefits of community and shared identity, status for the city or country, economic benefits (e.g., urban renewal, increased leisure traffic), and political incentives (e.g., political goodwill in the community, tax revenues). But the validity of such arguments is uncertain (Horne & Manzenreiter, 2004). Even if the reasoning is correct, variations in economic conditions in a given area have significant effects on a local community. Stadiums and other development projects are easier to implement in good times when money is plentiful, but not so easy in economic downturns. Further, a project begun in a strong economic climate may have dramatically reduced support in an economic downturn because perceptions might change as to its usefulness or the accuracy of the economic impact studies used to initiate it in the first place. When difficult economic times come, questions often arise about the merit of massive spending on sport when cutbacks in services (e.g., police, aid to the poor) are being made.

Sport Fans

Sport fans and their ability to pay for attending or watching sport events as well as buying ancillary items such as merchandise is an important component of the financial picture for a sport manager.

The global and local economic forces that affect sport organizations also affect the fans and their ability to maintain interest, spending, social interaction, and many other activities in relation to sport (Leys, 2001, in Horne 2006, p. 133). It has been argued that "the cost of being a spectator or a fan of professional sports have been rising much faster than the rate of inflation" (Horne, 2006, p. 28). Such a situation causes individuals and families to be more aware of their spending habits on leisure activities (including sport), if not more cautious about how they spend their discretionary income. A typical team or sport fan base is made up of people with varying levels of ability and willingness to purchase sport experiences and merchandise. A sport manager must be able to gather information about the different communities that compose a team or event's fan base and use that knowledge to maximize revenues from them. For many managers, this task involves significant investments in market research to understand issues such as consumption patterns, demographic information, income levels, interests and leisure-time activities, and so on. Sport managers cannot gather all the information possible from every member of the fan base; thus, they have to make strategic decisions based on imperfect information. The level of imperfection is, in many ways, driven by the choices made in gathering customer data and information.

Take, for example, Manchester United, one of the most popular sport organizations in the world. How can the organization speak to all fans and individual fans at once? The most obvious way is to create content in various languages. Although the team cannot do this for every language, they focused on Arabic, Chinese, Japanese, and Korean. If you said to yourself that these are not the languages I would have expected them to focus on, you probably were not thinking of the *fans*. The languages listed represent some of the strongest fan bases of Manchester United, and unlike football fans in Italy or Spain, these fan bases have weak domestic football leagues. The fans in these countries also do not have easy access to Manchester United game tickets and must rely on televised matches and web-based interactions to satisfy their fandom. The sport managers at Manchester United made a conscious choice to target these markets and develop the fan bases there in ways similar to the ones closer to home (through fan clubs, interactive website contents, video and mobile applications). Although Manchester United has begun the process of identifying fan behaviors in these countries, simply having language options is not enough. The team must continue to interact with and learn from these fans, especially when the team plays off-season exhibition matches in those countries. Only then can Manchester United develop unique and individualized content (by culture and by person) to strengthen fan loyalty to the team.

The next section identifies select important internal and external financial elements that influence the effectiveness of sport organizations.

Finance

The financial elements of sport manifest themselves in many ways. For teams and leagues, finance involves player salaries and the leaguewide balance of power between the richest and poorest organizations. Issues such as revenue sharing from broadcast rights or merchandising among league members (in the National Basketball Association, for example) are debated and discussed as part of collective bargaining agreements and international and domestic marketing and merchandising negotiations. For the international sport manager, however, other aspects of finance are of great concern. These areas of concern are built around aspects of managing sport organizations internal operations (budgeting), securing external revenue streams (sponsorship), and financing sport infrastructure (stadiums).

Internal Operations

Internal team or event operations are critical areas for sport managers and can account for a majority of daily activities. Financial management revolves around a sport manager's ability to allocate financial assets (in addition to other organizational ones) in a way that accomplishes organizational goals while simultaneously working to reduce costs. Further, as the immediate financial needs are in play, time and effort must be spent identifying ways to procure additional financial resources for various team activities (e.g., revenue streams, loans). Although not as glamorous as the buying and selling of players, the financial aspects of operating a sport entity are equally critical to the continued existence of the firm.

Sport side issues such as stadiums and player salaries are important cost components for a team and can often be at odds with business-side efforts

to manage revenues and expenses. Typical costs for a stadium include the operations of the team, taxes, maintenance and revitalization (e.g., environmentally friendly upgrades), debt payments for venue construction, and, depending on the context, international currency fluctuations. Further, the logistics of travel and lodging for sport teams can be significant depending on the frequency and length of the trips. Player salaries have been growing in line with the growth in the popularity of sport. Spending on facilities, players, and team operations in the course of competition can cause significant financial complications for teams and organizations (Condie, 2009; UPI, 2009b). The symbiotic relationship between the player personnel and business operations sides of sport teams or organizations might divide a sport manager's attention, but continued vigilance on both fronts will help to ensure financial returns and stability for the organization.

The finance issues faced by individual sport leagues are also connected with global economic patterns. In England, the Premier Rugby league, the top-level league in the country, considered reducing the league's salary cap, among other options, in the aftermath of the 2008 economic crisis (Jenkins, 2008). Individual teams announced that the high costs required to remain competitive, including salaries, were driving them into debt. A new television contract offered some assistance, but in the immediate term, teams began to take economic hits at the gate in terms of revenue from individual ticket sales and corporate suite sales (Jenkins, 2008). The immediate future for the teams and league is uncertain, but to ease the pressure, a special help center was created to work with teams to address their financial issues (English Rugby, 2009).

External Revenue Sources

Given the escalating costs of fielding and housing sport teams or events, external revenue streams must be generated and maintained to drive organizational strategy. Numerous revenue streams exist to provide a foundation for an organization. Sometimes referred to as incremental revenue sources (Stewart, 2007), important revenue areas include concessions, parking, ticket sales (season and gate), corporate sponsorship (including in-kind), media and broadcast rights, suite and premium seat sales, additional venue events (if owned and operated by the team or organization) as well as naming rights, publications and media, booster and support organizations (e.g., high school, college), loans, official merchandise sales (including those negotiated at the league level), and, although of limited use, financial shares (e.g., Green Bay Packers). Sport organizations develop, package, and utilize these elements in customized ways to maximize revenues and attain or maintain profitability.

The latest development in large-scale revenue generation involves technology. Technological changes in Internet and wireless technologies are revising notions of corporate sponsorships and fan experiences as methods to generate revenue (e.g., e-tickets, auction websites, fan sites) (Zwick & Dieterle, 2005). Monetizing, or generating revenues from an asset, virtual spaces requires a keen sense of customer and sponsor needs and wants as well as creative ways of leveraging the relationships once developed. The virtual spaces offer new advertising platforms and engagement opportunities linking team or organization, sponsor, and fan.

These platforms have given managers in organizations that use sport as a marketing platform the ability to speak to various communities of fans within the fan base of a sport property. Sponsors can use technologies such as wireless applications or websites to engage fans of a particular sport organization no matter where they live in the world. More important, these engagement experiences can be customized to a greater extent than ever before. For example, Vodafone, a global telecommunications firm, uses technology to work with fans of the Vodafone Warriors, a New Zealand rugby team. The activation of the partnership begins with the Vodafone One Tribe fan website and continues through numerous experiential opportunities at matches as well as online engagements such as fantasy rugby, forum areas, contests, and text updates.

Despite the increase in revenue-generating opportunities from international sport through television, live events, and virtual spaces, the growing influence of corporations on sport through broadcast advertising and other sponsorship has become worrisome. Corporate sponsors have increasingly put pressure on sport organizations of all types (e.g., International Olympic Committee, local teams) for a variety of reasons (e.g., return on investment, exposure, forced change) (Matsuda, 2010; Reuters, 2001). The large-scale commodification of sport reflects many of the negative characteristics associated with

the global nature of sport, especially when viewed as a hegemonic force of American corporate power and influence (Horne, 2006). A sport manager must be able to balance the need for corporate revenue throughout the organization's operations with the requirements, power, and influence of corporate and media organizations.

Despite the numerous creative options for generating revenue, sport is still beholden to actors who are significantly affected by global and local economic conditions. Sport managers must continually monitor economic conditions to gauge the effect that they are having on revenue sources and react with appropriate strategies to ensure the long-term success of the team or organization.

Sport Infrastructure

Sport infrastructure has been a significant area of debate for the past 20 years. In that time, private sport entities have been relying more and more on funding provided by local communities and governments. Under the auspices of economic growth and development and social well-being and community, teams have extracted massive concessions for building or refurbishing stadiums. As noted earlier, this spending significantly affects not only the organization but also the surrounding community, which bears the burden of the costs whether the event is a local team or a one-time international event such as the Olympics. In the United States, for example, an estimated "US$21.7 billion will be spent on . . . stadiums and arenas built or planned since 1990" (Siegfried & Zimbalist, 2000, p. 95). China's famed Bird's Nest stadium, built for the 2008 Beijing Games, cost around US$500 million, an amount similar to that for Japan's Nippon Stadium, built for the 2002 World Cup, which cost US$557 million (Egan, 2008). But these are relatively inexpensive prices compared to Montreal's "fiscally controversial stadium for the 1976 Olympics . . . paid off only in 2006" (Egan, 2008, p. 3), which had an estimated cost of US$1.4 billion, mostly from interest payments, or the recent refurbishments made to London's Wembley Stadium, which came in at US$1.5 billion (Egan, 2008). Such an expenditure on a new stadium would draw massive public ire in most countries around the world. As the Montreal example highlights, items such as interest payments can continue to exist long after the venue has been used, constraining operations because of the need to continue to finance the debt instruments used to build the venue in the first place. Further, loans taken out in foreign currencies can significantly raise (or lower) the cost of the investment depending on currency movements.

As a result of the massive corporate presence in sport and the spiraling costs of constructing sport venues and operating teams, oftentimes through the use of public financing, citizens have taken action to voice their opinion and positions about stadiums financing and construction (e.g., www.nolandgrab. org, www.fieldofschemes.com). Continuing to sustain such massive outlays in infrastructure, coupled with rising operational costs, player salaries, and ticket prices will be a challenge for future sport managers (and taxpayers). The options available to sport managers to operate under these conditions is enabled and constrained by international and sport law and governance.

Learning Activity

Visit a website such as www.worldstadia.com or www.worldstadiums.com and explore the differences in stadiums and venues around the world. Pay specific attention to location, size, estimated cost, and aesthetics. Look for revenue generation elements such as signage, naming rights, and corporate or luxury seating. What do you find?

Law

Sport managers are beholden to numerous legal requirements, opportunities, and constraints as they operate in local communities and across the world. They must not only navigate the law governing whatever land they are operating in but also understand and navigate the equally difficult world of sport governance (i.e., sport federations and sanctioning bodies). Laws create a structure for a society to live together, prescribe acceptable behaviors, and create a socially constructed set of limitations to freedom and actions. Each nation has its own legal framework (e.g., Carpenter, 2000). This section examines the differences between international law and sport law and the influence of governing bodies.

International and Sport Law

International law and sport law have fundamental differences. "International law deals with relations between nation-states. International sport law therefore can be defined as the principles of international law applicable to sport" (Foster, 2005, p. 3). A key point in this definition is that sport is not a nation-state, which means that various bodies establish laws that exist beyond the boundaries of national law, creating a law unto themselves.

The legal structure of each country views sport law differently. For example, the Swiss give the IOC, based in Switzerland, special status, but do not offer the same to other international organizations (e.g., FIFA). The American court system views the IOC as "an equal international personality" (Foster, 2005, p. 54) after legal action was taken following the 1980 Olympic Games in Moscow. The British courts "do not recognize international, continental, or national sports governing bodies as having the status of governmental or quasi-governmental organisations" (Wise & Meyer, 1998, p. 1478, in Foster, 2005). Thus the interplay between local, national, and international law, in conjunction with laws enacted by governing bodies and federations, makes commencing international activities difficult for sport managers and organizations. Critical to the strategy development processes that sport managers engage in when considering international operations will be their understanding of how national and sport law rules and regulations are enforced (e.g., tax law, drug testing, personal injury) and how litigation procedures are conducted.

Unlike international law, numerous sport law statutes have roots in the Olympic Movement, the foundation of the Olympic ideology, because numerous organizations subscribe to its principles. Although separate from IOC membership, the Olympic Movement "has spawned an extensive array of regional Olympic organizations each officially recognized by the IOC" (Thoma & Chalip, 1996, p. 24) (e.g., the Olympic Council of Asia). These organizations "share common administrative or regional concerns to discuss matters of policy and, where possible, to formulate shared positions on issues of governance" (Thoma & Chalip, 1996, p. 25). Foster (2005) believes that sport governing body regulations are now equally or more important than local or international law because they are independent of government regulation and oversight. He stated, "The globalization of sport has moved the focus of legal regulation increasingly into international sports federations" (Foster, 2005, p. 1), which are not nation-states.

Role of Sport Federations

Although most sport law is grounded in the construct of the Olympic Movement, "a more structured pattern of international administration and dispute resolution" emerged over the past 20 years (Nafziger, 1992, p. 489). Federations such as the Fédération Internationale de Natation Amateur (FINA, swimming) can utilize national law but also create their own regulations that govern individual sports. Such a position raises the highly contentious question: Is sport law truly autonomous from national and international laws (Foster, 2005)?

Not really, because the governing network of nongovernmental organizations, governmental organizations, and governing bodies that has emerged is "still rather fragile. Enforcement depends on principles of reciprocity and good faith" (Nafziger, 1992, p. 493). When a dispute arises, individuals and sport organizations have, depending on the context, different bodies with jurisdiction over the conflict. In addition to a nation's court system, sport disputes can be settled in an arbitration court. The Tribunal Arbitral du Sport (Court of Arbitration for Sport; www.tas-cas.org), or TAS, established in 1984 in Lausanne, Switzerland, has jurisdiction over nontechnical issues and is "not competent to resolve disputes involving technical questions, such as may relate to the ground rules of competition in a particular sport or the logistics of organizing events" (Nafziger, 1992, p. 507). TAS can "facilitate the settlement of sports-related disputes through arbitration or mediation by means of procedural rules adapted to the specific needs of the sport world" (Tribunal Arbitral du Sport, 2009, p. 1). TAS is overseen by the International Council of Arbitration for Sport, which has more than 300 arbiters from over 80 countries (Tribunal Arbitral du Sport, 2009). The law that governs the arbitration process is at the discretion of the parties unless they cannot agree, in which case Swiss law becomes the foundation.

Communication and Language

One of the most significant barriers to effective organizational operation is that of communication, and more specifically, language. Communication is a process by which meaning is created between people through a combination of behaviors, symbols, or signs. Meaning is not abstract or objective but is created between individuals as they share experiences, information, and perspectives. But the communication process can be interrupted or interfered with by variables within a communication context (e.g., noise). Thus, communication is a constant process of sharing, learning, and understanding oneself and others.

Most interpersonal social exchange occurs through language. Numerous languages exist across the globe. Some are dying away as fewer individuals within a culture follow traditional practices, such as the Amurdag language spoken by one man in the Northern Territory of Australia (Noble Wilford, 2007), whereas others are dominant in the sense that they can be found in most places around the world (e.g., English). Language is associated with power in the sense that language can be used to persuade (even manipulate), to inspire, to enlighten, or to punish others. Cultural elements are (co)created, contested, and shared through language. For example, media coverage or arguments can be used to perpetuate one belief or another. Consider how the term *female racing driver* packs a great deal of information into three words. Women are racing in motorsport formulae all around the world, but oftentimes they are referred to not as racing drivers but as female racing drivers. This label takes away from the relatively level playing field of motorsport, in terms of gender effect, as opposed to other sports (e.g., American football). Cultural practices, shaped in dialogue (language) by cultural members over the years, contribute to the power of language and the types of language used or not used (acceptable or not acceptable).

Communication and Social Issues in Sport

In the world of sport, communication and language are key points to effective performance. Mass communication technologies such as television and the Internet have the power to communicate various messages, which shape individual perceptions and attempt to encourage social change or reinforce existing beliefs or practices. Communication and language issues in sport and sport organizations are highly complex. The complexity increases when language issues are not adequately dealt with, especially in relation to social issues such as religion, gender, or race. Sport is replete with messages that, although language or symbols, place cultures in opposition to each other. Sport mascots are such an instance. For example, during the 1995 World Series, the Cleveland Indians and Atlanta Braves saw protestors raise awareness of the image symbols (Chief Wahoo), nonverbal gestures (tomahawk chop), and language used (the Indians, the Braves) by each team.

Racism has reared its head across the sporting landscape for many years, but recently the world has seen an increase in racist behaviors in and through sport (Reuters, 2009) because of the in-stadium messages, taunts, and signage at games (Bairner, 2001) targeting players and coaches. For example, FIFA, the official governing body of football, declares its mission to be to "develop the game, touch the world, build a better future" (FIFA, 2009, p. 3). As part of this mission, FIFA actively campaigns against racism in the game, using signage, player appearances around the world, and symbolic gestures before matches to communicate a message of tolerance and racial harmony.

Further, FIFA's activities also symbolize the power and **hegemony** inherent in intercultural communication and exchange. Hegemony is a term used to describe the methods that ruling powers use to maintain their status and position. FIFA's antiracism messages are frequently in English despite their being placed on football pitches around the world. FIFA's website is in English, although it has a link to German, French, Spanish, and Arabic sites. The choice to use the English language might be interpreted by some as a continuation of the Western, specifically English-speaking, dominance in world affairs, or at the least, a privileging of or bias toward Western values. But FIFA's choice to operate primarily in English, despite being a world governing body based in Switzerland, reflects the importance and shared acceptance of English as an official medium of communication in world football. This, however, does not mean that local cultures and other languages are unimportant. Rather, the opposite is true because FIFA actively promotes local cultures and spends significant time highlighting the cultures of the host countries for all its tournaments, especially the World Cup. What FIFA demonstrates is a way for global and local to coexist—in a context where

a dominant language is used to further understanding of heterogeneous cultural differences. Although certainly not without difficulties and opposition (e.g., imperialism, Western bias) (Maguire, 1999), the global sport arena represents a context in which dialogue can take place among cultures through a common culture and language. It is hoped that such a system encourages people to come together, share with each other, and learn together through the common love of sport.

Language Barriers

At the micro level, sport teams and managers face the challenge of selling their products and services to media outlets and fans around the world. Simple issues such as negotiations for television rights deals, website information and exchanges, or translations of books or magazines into local languages pose challenges to sport managers. These challenges extend to athletes and coaches as well. If an athlete or coach arrives at a team without much knowledge of the native language, socialization into that organization becomes more difficult. Athlete or coach interactions with the media, a primary source of fan knowledge and information, are also problematic because interpreters would be needed and misunderstandings about statements because of language issues would need to be addressed. Sport organizations run a fine line between making members feel at home and conducting efficient operations in relation to language and communication. For example, in the National Hockey League (NHL) several teams implemented an English-only policy to improve communication among team members from all around the world, and some teams imposed fines for not adhering to the policy (O'Donnell, 2001). "Teams fear that it [multiple languages] can cause a cliquish clubhouse where players only mingle with other players who speak their language" (O'Donnell, 2001, p. 7).

Sometimes attempts to manage language issues cause more trouble than good. The Ladies Professional Golf Association (LPGA) toyed with the idea of an English-only policy for its tour. The policy stated that players who "have been on the tour for two years can be suspended if they fail an oral evaluation of their English proficiency" (DiMeglio, 2008, p. 5), although the LPGA would provide language tutoring and materials to assist in language education. The ultimate goal of the rule was to help

Learning Activity

Using www.world-newspapers.com, compare and contrast the elements, reporting, topics, and other items of sport sections across major and minor English language newspapers. If you have another language competency, compare the English newspaper content with that of the language that you speak. What are the similarities and differences? You could also do this with team websites from around the world.

international players, who had recently been winning many tournaments, better interact with the media and sponsors. The legality of the rule was challenged in Florida, and the LPGA ultimately decided against implementing it. For more details, see the case study on page 66.

Language, and more broadly communication, poses numerous challenges to sport managers in the modern sport context. Because media channels allow global distribution of matches, merchandise, and brands, sport managers must navigate their way through language barriers that affect communication. Language and communication issues are just one potential barrier to sport managers and sport organizations.

Time

Time is another issue related to the issues affecting international sport organizations. Cultural approaches to time vary across the globe. Time is socially constructed by the members of a culture, but it is also "so fundamental that people in any culture regard their conception of it as simply an immutable part of reality" (Bluedorn & Denhardt, 1988, p. 300). Thus, they may take their view of it for granted, especially in relation to other cultures. This section begins by examining different views on time. Second, it examines effects of time on sport activities.

Views on Time

In many Western cultures and corporate organizations, time is considered a resource not to be wasted. Arising from the early scientific management movement and capitalist ideology (Taylor, 1911), time

has come to be a measure of efficiency "when it [a task] is accomplished with the smallest expenditure of energy and time" (Doob, 1971, p. 349). In other words, time is money. Compare this with a temporal orientation from a culture, such as that of Thailand, that views life as a constantly changing path (i.e., reincarnation), sees relationships as elements to be cultivated over time, and, although the pursuit of wealth through moral and legal means is fine, believes a person should not be "attached to I, infatuated with it, or enslaved by it" (Payutto, 1998, p. 67).

Researchers have attempted to describe the various cultural views of time. Despite general cultural conceptions of time, not everyone in a particular culture might ascribe to the culture's particular viewpoint. Nevertheless, the similarities in perception within cultures are sufficient to warrant investigation into perspectives on time. Edward Hall, an anthropologist, created the concepts of polychronic and monochronic time orientation (Bluedorn & Denhardt, 1988; Hall, 1983). Hall's original conception of polychronic and monochronic time was limited to European cultures, but his descriptions of them allow them to be applied in many cultural contexts. Polychronic time means that involvement or participation in several activities can occur at one time, and in monochronic time, activities are scheduled one at a time (Hall, 1983). Subsequent research has expanded Hall's original concepts to make them more nuanced and less binary so that they can refer, for example, to the exactness or relativity of time in relation to people's habits (Harris, Moran, & Moran, 2004). Even nuanced perspectives, however, can lead to stereotypes about time, such as when describing punctuality (e.g., Germans are precise, Thais are laid back). If examined appropriately, however, temporal orientations can explain certain behavioral characteristics.

Effects of Time

Time affects budgeting, planning, travel, logistics, and many other facets of life, sport or otherwise. Like language, time significantly molds cultural practices and can pose special problems when conducting sport business. For example, in the United States, sporting events follow a relatively common television schedule built around the working lives of people. Different times are scheduled for local broadcasts as compared with national broadcasts to maximize coverage.

A Failure in Planning

The 2009 Malaysian Grand Prix, held in Sepang, Malaysia, was asked to change the traditional 2 p.m. start time of the race to accommodate the European audiences who would otherwise have to wake up in the early morning hours of Sunday. The race start time was moved to later in the day, closer to 5 p.m. Malaysian time. Several important elements played a part in what happened in the race. First, the race is held during the rainy season in Southeast Asia, usually making the Malaysian race a wet affair. Second, in the late afternoon, the sun begins to set, darkening a track that does not have lights. Third, Formula One races have a two-hour time limit to run. During the race, the rains came and soaked the track. The race was stopped for over an hour, bringing the loss of daylight into play as well as the time limit. As the rains eased, drivers were concerned about visibility and did not want to race in the twilight. The race was ultimately red flagged after only 32 laps, ending a miserable day for many fans, viewers, and race and track personnel. To add further insult to the day, "When the race was stopped, lightning struck the circuit" (UPI, 2009a, p. 6).

In addition to the critical role played by traditional conceptions of time in operations, travel, and interpersonal relationships in sport, new concepts of time are developing. Besides applying to match and broadcast schedules, various conceptions of time need to be an important part of a sport manager's perspective. The advent of technological changes such as digital video recording and the Internet have shifted time in relation to traditional conceptions of it (e.g., 24-hour day). In other words, a sport manager must recognize multiple constructs of time (own culture, another culture, Internet) to maximize all sport operations.

When the Internet, digital video recording, and websites that archive audio and video material are factored into the equation, time means that the experience of sport does not necessarily have to take place when the actual event does. In fact, an event can be reexperienced as long as it is accessible. This situation only complicates cultural issues because, for example, translation of content from a match has to be completed and added to a website in a reasonable interval (time again!) to satisfy audience demands. For sport managers, this circumstance also means that changes occur in intellectual property laws, broadcast and marketing strategies, and the nature of a fan's experience. The nature of media relations changes as traditional media members (e.g., newspaper reporters) compete with new media reporters (e.g., bloggers) for space at events, story leads, and team and player information.

Whether monochronic or polychronic, punctual or late, time is part of a sport manager's daily existence, and it influences the nature of sport.

Although technology is driving some of the changes discussed earlier, it also contributes significantly to many other changes that are occurring in the world of sport.

Technology

"Where sporting events were once localized affairs, news of which barely filtered through to neighboring villages" (Maguire, 1999, p. 144), today's sporting events and team activities have become widely accessible, mainly through technological advances. Although technology has also had a major influence on the equipment used in sport, this subject is outside the scope of the chapter. This section examines the creation, production, and dissemination of various elements in a sporting event (e.g., ticket sales, broadcasting), the effects of emerging technologies, technology in relation to organizational operations, and the growing influence of corporate and media organizations.

Technology and Dissemination of Sport

Technology in terms of the creation and dissemination of sport has been a significant issue for over 100 years. Sport was a popular spectator event for many years before the advent of radio. But in the 1920s, as radio technology advanced around the world, sport began to take a central role in planned programming. Boxing was one of the first sports to embrace radio, and during the early 20th century it became one of the most popular sports, especially in North America (Gems, Borish, & Pfister, 2008).

Horseracing and baseball were also favorites of the radio audience.

By the 1950s television began to replace radio as the primary media source for entertainment. Sport embraced the new technology, and so did fans as the cost of television sets declined (Gems, Borish, & Pfister, 2008). Not surprisingly, corporations seized upon the new medium, and as its reach expanded, companies increased their use of it as an advertising platform. Corporations accelerated their sponsorship of sport events and teams to reach mass audiences (e.g., Amis & Cornwell, 2005a). In contemporary international sport, corporate sponsorship has become global. Global sport sponsorship is defined as "investment in an individual, event, team or organization with the expectation of achieving certain corporate objectives in multiple countries" (Amis & Cornwell, 2005b, p. 2). Companies such as McDonald's, Coca-Cola, Red Bull, Fosters, Vodafone, and many others are significant global advertisers. Through televised sport, the athletic event became a spectacle (Beck-Burridge & Walton, 2001). Some of the most viewed television programs of the 20th century include American Super Bowls, the World Cup, and the Olympics, all of which are broadcast internationally. Formula One, the world motorsport championship, draws tens of millions of viewers for each race. Domestic football leagues (e.g., English Premier League, Italian Serie A) have a substantial international presence and following because of the broadcasting of their matches on television channels around the world, especially through satellite television (Amis & Cornwell, 2005b).

Access to fans by broadcasting of events by teams and sport organizations has revolutionized broadcast revenues and advertising rates, driving an escalating cycle of money and power in a quest for an international presence (e.g., the Opening and Closing Ceremonies of the Olympic Games) (Tomlinson, 2002). The influence of the Games on corporate sponsorship and strategic goals means that the mass appeal and sizable audiences of the Olympics allow corporations to justify the heavy expenditure for advertising time and event sponsorship (Tomlinson, 2002). For example, late in 2008 the 2010 Vancouver Games had reached US$735 million in domestic sponsorship, 97 percent of its total, and expected an additional US$200 million through international sponsorship (Vancouver Olympic Games, 2008, p. 3). Companies that spend

Learning Activity

Visit the websites of major sport sponsors from around the world (e.g., McDonald's, Shell, Pepsi, Vodafone, Ford, Toyota, Red Bull). To what extent is their involvement in sport a part of their web presence? Do these companies discuss the sponsorships that they use in different countries? If so, compare their sponsorship activities to determine what organizational messages they are using and whether these messages transcend cultures (one message to all countries) or are customized to specific cultures.

this much in advertising and sponsorship believe that the expenditure is justified given the wide reach and large audiences generated by the Olympic Games, and they expect to be granted privileges for their sponsorship.

Building on the success of television, corporate and sport organizations alike are coming to terms with emerging computer-mediated media such as the Internet and various wireless technologies. Although team and event websites are now commonplace, teams and organizations are working to understand ways of monetizing their web presence and engaging fans, sponsors, governments, and other interested parties through mediated means. For some this is an environmental move to reduce costs of paper and printing by going to virtual business operations. For others it is a way of establishing interactive platforms to enhance fan engagement and corporate partnership opportunities. Team-driven social network sites such as Planet Orange (Phoenix Suns, www.planetorange.net) or CavFanatic (Cleveland Cavaliers, www.CavFanatic.com) are proving hugely popular with fans because of their exclusive content, interactive and social nature, and general inclusion of the fans' voice by the teams.

Technology and Organizational Operations

The changes in technology over last 60 years has meant that sport managers must remain vigilant and informed about what opportunities exist for their organizations and fans in relation to technological developments.

First, technology aids in the recruitment, retention, training, and utilization of new employees. For example, a person joining a new organization would go through various processes to obtain organizational information, interview and enter the organization, exist within it, and possibly exit at some point (Feldman, 1976; Jablin, 1985; Jablin, 1987; Jablin, 2000). Technology affects the human resources activities of sport organizations including training new organizational members (Flanagin & Waldeck, 2004), using online recruitment and management methods (Baker, DeTienne, & Smart, 1998), and using electronic human resources systems (e-HRM) (Stone, Stone-Romero, & Lukaszewski, 2006) to manage hiring processes. People are increasingly using technology sources (e.g., websites) to find organizational and career information (Cober, Brown, Blumenthal, Doverspike, & Levy, 2000).

Sport managers who understand the influence of technology (e.g., the Internet) on employees' prehire and posthire behaviors, expectations, and subsequent satisfaction with their work can strengthen and develop existing practices. A further challenge is the need to integrate operations with employees, volunteers, and other entities when operating internationally. Differences in technology levels affect each area discussed earlier, especially in terms of human resources where finding limitations to e-HRM systems might occur because of context-specific difficulties (e.g., limited access to e-mail and the Internet in a country). With increased knowledge about technology, sport managers can make better decisions regarding its use.

Second, in sales and marketing, teams are using online sales methods including instant messaging and live chat with representatives and virtual ticketing options (i.e., paperless ticketing). A team's web presence has also become an important strategic element because it serves as a marketing tool to fans, an information source for media members, and a partnership platform to increase corporate sales revenues. A web presence for a sport team or event requires a balance between local, national, and international interests. Many teams across the world with multilanguage websites include specific content for that area or language group (e.g., Spanish, Japanese) not available elsewhere.

Athletes have also taken advantage of the new media platforms to enhance personal brands. Although some athletes have a web presence (e.g., www.tigerwoods.com), others have used new media to develop revenue sources off the playing field. For example, Rio Ferdinand (Manchester United) launched a virtual lifestyle magazine as an extension of his existing web presence (www.rioferdinand. com), and environmentalist racecar driver Leilani Münter promotes her activist racing brand through her website (www.carbonfreegirl.com). Increasingly, team-operated social network sites are contributing to these three areas as well (e.g., Swarm City by the New Orleans Hornets, The Shed for Chelsea FC). The virtual space offers teams an additional area to capitalize on their media presence outside traditional broadcast means (e.g., television, radio) and monetize the virtual spaces to add new revenue streams to team operations. But complicated intellectual property issues arise in this environment because user-generated content and demand for sporting content create a market for accessible material, be it a past event or current team news.

Although sport teams continue to come to terms with modern technologies and their ability to influence various audiences, the nature of sport as an important cultural entity continues to grow. Some might argue that in the quest for monetary gain and the need to win to attract the maximum sponsorship money, sport has become almost religious.

Religion

Religion has far deeper cultural roots than sport, yet the two have become linked over time in ways that can contradict the foundations of each. "Both are bathed in myth and sustained by ritual; both reward faith and patience; both thrive on passion tempered with discipline" (Baker, 2007, p. 2). Whatever the origin of the connection between the two, it is now inextricable.

A religious system is one that provides "meaning and motivation beyond the material aspects of life, that is, the spiritual side of a culture or its approach to the supernatural" (Harris & Moran, 1991, p. 212). The reverence with which sport is treated around the world (e.g., football in Brazil or England, American football in the United States) incorporates religion through ritual and practice. Like religion, sport offers individual and communal experiences that move us beyond ourselves and enable us to

Learning Activity

By yourself or in groups of three or four in class, examine the presence of religion in sport. Compare past religion or spirituality to sport experiences that you or the group members have had. What do you believe is the role of religion in sport? You can go online and search for examples of the intersection between sport and religion from around the world or examine books such as *God in the Stadium: Sports and Religion in America* by Robert Higgs, *With God on Their Side: Sport in the Service of Religion* by Tara Magdalinski and Timothy Chandler, or *Playing With God: Religion and Modern Sport* by William Baker.

become consumed with the experience, forgetting all other aspects of life, even if only temporarily. Obvious tangible similarities exist between the two including rituals such as the inclusion of overt and subtle spiritual actions (e.g., prayer), and the fierce devotion and evangelicalization elements found in spiritual religions (Magdalinski & Chandler, 2002). A player may point to the sky, kneel in prayer, or remove a jersey to reveal a religious message on a T-shirt underneath (Goldenbach, 2007). Players gather for pre- and postgame prayers. Fans and athletes pause for invocations or prayers as part of rituals associated with the event (e.g., Indianapolis 500). Sport has sacred spaces (locker rooms), shrines (halls of fame), symbolic ritualistic elements (playing equipment), guiding texts (rulebooks), fierce devotion of the faithful (fans), and deities (superstars).

For example, ritual and practices can be seen in the Super Bowl as a religious experience. In addition to its political rituals (e.g., national anthem, military plane flyover), the game reflects religious processes and beliefs (Price, 2001). One of these is the sacred nature of the field (i.e., place of worship) and discussions of great heroes of the past (i.e., canonized saints). A more personal, but nonetheless telling, example is the thread of evangelical Christianity that is found in sport. In the late 1970s, Pete Brock, a lineman for the New England Patriots

who had recently converted to Christianity, noted, "I now approach Sunday afternoons as a worship service. . . . God has blessed me with a large body, great strength and the ability to play this difficult game" (Hoffman, 1992, p. 111). For fans around the world, sport and religion are linked in ways that can contradict each other but still affect the game, the players, and the fans in important ways, such as creating or maintaining elements of their identity.

In addition, sport can be a mask or magnifier for religious, class, and race differences manifesting themselves in fan identity and on-field war between ideologies. Such spiritual and sport conflicts can be seen around the world. For example, in Ireland and Scotland, the off-field differences between Catholics and Protestants find their way to the football pitch (Finn, 1991, 1994). The same can be said of interfaith tensions in Israel surrounding an Islamic football league (Sorek, 2002). In another instance, the mixture of cultural elements, especially religious and political, created a sporting event that means far more than sport. The America–Iran match in the 1998 World Cup is such an instance. Iran defeated the United States, knocking them out of the Cup and ending a difficult stretch for an American team with high hopes. "The victory was Iran's first in World Cup history, and it came over the team that represents a country routinely referred to in Iran as the Great Satan" (Obejuerge, 1998, p. 11). More than a decade later, the tumult caused by this match might have been mitigated had the American national team played a proposed friendly match against Iran (Associated Press, 2009) in the run-up to the 2010 World Cup. Although the match never happened, should the two countries play, the renewal of sporting contests between the two could have political, commercial, and religious ramifications.

Sport and religion are also used as opportunities for understanding of or resistance to hegemonic practices within both contexts. For example, Dagas and Benn (2006) examined the participation by young Muslim women in England and Greece in school physical education classes. Issues of cultural homogeneity and heterogeneity emerged as the British students noted that traditional approaches to their education did not consider their religious requirements. In the Greek community, the schools offered mixed physical education courses taught by male teachers, which caused concern among some Muslim parents. In another instance, Walseth

(2006) examined the life histories of a group of young Muslim women who immigrated to Norway and participated in physical education courses in school. For them, cultural notions of femininity were challenged by participation in sport. Although health and fitness are important parts of the Islamic faith, sport participation raised issues counter to Islamic cultural norms (e.g., attracting attention to oneself, showing aggression, spending time away from home) (Walseth, 2006). For these young women, the balance between being accepted in the new culture (Norwegian) often ran counter to expectations in their family culture and heritage. This circumstance led some women to have difficult relationships with their families over these issues. Although studies of these athletes have been conducted in Muslim communities outside of primarily Muslim countries, the use of sport to make statements about religion is significant.

Although sport does share elements of the spiritual world, it is also located in the terrestrial one. Sport and the environment are inextricably linked because many sporting events are played out of doors and the simplest of athletic actions (e.g., running) can have wide-ranging consequences for the natural environment.

Environmentalism

Recent years have seen sport organizations around the world begin to reexamine their athletic and management practices in relation to the environment. This section highlights the relationship between the natural environment and sport, and examines steps that sport organizations are taking to work within and with the environment.

Although environmentalism is not a new idea, it has emerged in the world of sport as a major issue in the 21st century. Events held at stadiums, fields, golf courses, and other venues all have an effect on the environment (water usage, traffic, food and power consumption). The influence of the environment on sport is as important as the effect of sport on the environment because "deteriorating environmental conditions make the playing of particular sports more difficult; sometimes the necessary land or water conditions simply no longer exist. In addition, air and water pollution put the health of athletes [and local residents] in jeopardy" (Maguire, 1999, p. 142). "Even as sports promote health, they can also degrade the environment upon which good health

depends" (Schmidt, 2006, p. A286). Sporting organizations are swiftly moving to address these issues.

Various organizations involved in sport have issued and sponsored studies, guidelines, and analyses related to environmental practices when organizing sport events (Chernushenko, van der Kamp, & Stubbs, 2001; Stahl, Hocfeld, & Schmied, 2004). One example is that the FIA and other motorsport organizations around the world have introduced rule changes that reduce the environmental impact of racing, and they are campaigning to reduce the environmental impact by automobiles (FIA, 2009). In Japan players in the Nippon Professional Baseball league have pledged their support to environmental efforts by reducing the length of games (AFP, 2008), and sponsors have found ways to leverage their environmental efforts with those of the league (JCN Newswire, 2008). Even the major professional sport leagues in America have taken steps to address the environmental effects of their sports. An example of this occurred in April 2009 when the NBA held its first Green Week (http://nba.com/green). Teams had green-themed promotions, and players wore warm-up shirts made from recycled materials. New sponsorship ventures were created to link corporate environmental messages and efforts with those of the NBA, and existing efforts by teams were highlighted to local fans (e.g., recyclable cups and utensils).

In terms of reach, the Olympic Games have few peers when it comes to taking an activist role in promoting environmentalism across the world. Some have argued that the environmental efforts of the IOC constitute a third pillar of the Olympic Movement, after sport and culture) (Cantelon & Letters, 2000). The 2008 Beijing Games generated

Learning Activity

Visit the following professional sport team and organization websites and examine their environmental activities: www.sabres.nhl.com, www.netsgogreen.com, www.philadelphiaeagles.com/gogreen, www.fia.com, www.vancouver2010.com, and www.london2012.com. Pay close attention to specific actions, goals, and sponsorship and partnership opportunities.

numerous discussions about China's environmental record and its potential effects on the athletes and the Games in general. The Games brought to light issues of air quality and other concerns and the steps taken by the Chinese organizers to address the situation, including removing over one million automobiles from the road and closing many factories near the events (Watts, 2008). Although these actions offered only a temporary fix to a large and persistent problem, the Games are an example of how the pressure of international events can help raise awareness of environmental issues and work to bring about change. Host cities are making substantive and public relations efforts to ensure that the Games are as green as possible. For example, the organizing committee in Vancouver, host of the 2010 Winter Games, said they "integrated environmental, social, and economic sustainability as part of its Games planning" (*Championing*, 2007, p. 9). Like Vancouver, London, the next Olympic host city, integrated environmental initiatives into its planning processes from the outset. For the organizers,

> Being "sustainable" means providing for peoples' current and long-term needs, improving quality of life while ensuring a healthy thriving natural environment. As the most high-profile event in the world, the Games gives us a chance to show how changes to the way we build, live, work, do business and travel could help us to live happy and healthy lives, within our planet's resources. (Sustainability, 2009, p. 1)

Olympic Games are closely watched, and their environmental impacts are assessed to determine whether their goals were met. Results from Beijing 2008 and Vancouver 2010 were mixed in terms of environmental issues (Dowd, 2010; Gronewold, 2009; Vancouver Olympics, 2010a; Vancouver 2010b). The IOC needs to continue to revise its environmental guidelines to ensure a strong showing in subsequent Olympic Games to give credibility to its message and be a source of environmental change for other sporting organizations, especially because true understanding of the environmental impact of an event might not be known for years afterward.

The most important lesson from the IOC, sport team, and league activities is that environmental variables are important components of strategic planning for any sport organization. Whether the decisions are about purchasing soap or electricity

management, the sport world needs to embrace sustainable and environmentally sensitive practices and define methods of incorporating them in daily activities (Lindsey, 2008). Given its unique cultural placement, sport can be a steward in the global movement to change human behaviors and help people live better within and with the environment.

Each of the topics discussed in this section of the chapter—politics, economics, finance, law, communication, time, technology, religion, and environmental impacts—are important to international sport managers. The sport manager of today needs to help define and develop an understanding of each area as it relates to his or her organization as well as how it relates to sport in general. The various functional positions in sport (e.g., marketing, human resources, finance) need to have a solid understanding of these issues, and organizations need to integrate them into the training and socialization of new members for them to be productive in the international sport world. Failure to do so might severely constrain economic, social, and sport options available to sport managers. To this end, the third and final section of this chapter is devoted to identifying and exploring the various competencies that will integrate the issues discussed earlier with sport manager and sport organization practices.

International Competencies for Sport Managers

To this point, the chapter has covered many areas and raised numerous issues that present-day (and future) sport managers must understand. Although this chapter is not comprehensive and can provide only a glimpse into the present (and future) international sport world, it does reflect the importance of highly skilled, knowledgeable, and aware sport managers to the future success of sport. But it has been argued that many people do not recognize the amount of information and knowledge needed to understand (broadly speaking) and function within the world of international sport (Thoma & Chalip, 1996), in part because it is both experienced and learned (Dewey, 1916; Kolb, 1984; Thoma & Chalip, 1996). Although this chapter has introduced numerous aspects of and influential elements relating to international sport, engaging in them is different from speaking about them. Putting this knowledge into practice requires international and cultural understandings and interpersonal skills. Hanvey (1976, p. 2) identified five main areas that influence international sport understanding:

1. Perspective consciousness (understanding differences)
2. State of planet awareness (understanding global issues)
3. Cross-cultural awareness (understanding cultural diversity and similarity)
4. Systematic awareness (operations of international organizations)
5. Options for participation (conducting sport business)

This section builds on this framework and integrates skill sets that have emerged in the years since Hanvey developed his awareness structure. These skill sets are what sport managers will need to understand in order to work within the modern sporting landscape. These skills are experiential (Kolb, 1984), in that experience will teach them as much as discussions regarding theoretical skill sets will. The skill sets include personal reflexivity, sensitivity to cultural differences, and a flexible expertise.

Personal Reflexivity

First, sport managers need to be **reflexive** about themselves, their actions, and their worldviews. Reflexivity describes the state of being self-critical or analytical. It encompasses personal reflection on attitudes or actions to understand why they came about and what outcomes they produced. Why should a person examine the self when the goal is to understand others? Primarily, a person needs to be able to gauge where he or she stands on issues and what knowledge is known versus inferred. As social beings, humans are a balance of self and other, (co)constructing life each day. In other words, we are individuals within communities of other individuals who interact and share ideas to create understandings of the world around us. As George Mead (1934), the father of modern sociology, noted, "No individual has a mind which operates simply in itself, in isolation from the social life process in which it has arisen or out of which it has emerged and in which the pattern of organized social behavior has consequently been basically impressed upon it" (p. 222). Further, nothing in this world is

absolute, isolated, or permanent because we are all linked together in some way, especially with our natural environment (Pfahl, 2002; Plamintr, 1994).

When we take the time to learn more about ourselves, we can learn about our relations to and with others and even about other people in deeper and meaningful ways. In terms of sport, you might be a person who cheers for the underdog at a sporting event and considers such an action a part of who you are or something you value. This behavior is associated with cultural values from the community in which you were raised. Learning this lesson about yourself helps you to gather information from others (e.g., dialogue, observation) and begin to understand how they view the world, or in this case, a sporting event between a top performer and an underdog (e.g., New Zealand versus Italy in the 2010 World Cup). Of course, new experiences and lessons mean that changes can occur to existing beliefs or value structures, but this is only natural (and probably useful for sport managers working within international sport). The self is social and socially constructed, yet a person takes her or his own journey, one-on-one with the environment. Thus, to understand others, we must begin by understanding the self because understanding ourselves provides ways of understanding others. This process also helps us to see that we do not have all the answers and fosters a sense of curiosity as to how others might see an issue or topic. Example questions to begin this process include the following: What issues are important to me? Have I ever watched a sporting event from outside the United States? Do I seek out information only to confirm my position? Self-examination is an individual effort without end, schedule, or other constraints placed upon it.

Sensitivity to Cultural Differences

Second, sport mangers need to be receptive and sensitive to cultural differences (Harris & Moran, 1991). Most people are aware of the legislation against discriminatory hiring or promotion practices as well as the more severe laws against racially or ethnically motivated hate crimes. Sport managers face a more subtle challenge in relation to cultural sensitivity, one that usually places one set of cultural values at odds with another. For example, National Basketball Association teams' use of Spanish language on jerseys can be seen as a sincere outreach gesture to an excited but underserved fan community. But the action might be insulting to others, who view it as using culture to sell tickets without a sincere interest in Hispanic culture.

Another example comes from the 2010 World Cup and the infamous vuvuzela horn. The vuvuzela is a descendant of a traditional cultural musical instrument found across Africa. Many observers in the media and football fans called for the horns to be banned, mostly because of the high levels of noise that they produce, which could endanger a person's hearing with prolonged exposure and interfere with broadcast commentary. FIFA president Sepp Blatter squashed all notions of banning the instrument, saying, "I have always said that Africa has a different rhythm, a different sound. . . . I don't see banning the music traditions of fans in their own country. Would you want to see a ban on the fan traditions in your country?" (Baxter, 2010, p. 2). Blatter's decision lay at the intersection of cultural traditions in one community and standards of behavior in another (most negative complaints and comments came from Western or Caucasian corners). If Blatter banned the horns, he risked having the move being viewed as racially motivated or, at the very least, culturally insensitive, especially because the event was the first World Cup held in Africa (and one that he championed). Yet even his comments, however positive, can be interpreted in another way because he praises the difference of Africa, a continent with numerous cultures. This account illustrates the complexity of culture in international sport.

As described earlier, culture has been broadly used in this chapter. It might mean traditional conceptualizations of cultures (e.g., nations), or it might mean cultures within cultures (e.g., surf culture, sport management majors). In any case, sport managers must balance the notions of difference and similarity; homogeneity and heterogeneity; and local, regional, national, and international. As shown in the examples, many gray areas are involved when it comes to cultural values. Choosing not to use racist language in a ticket advertisement is an obvious and easy decision for a sport manager to make. But for many sport managers in the international arena, perceptions are actuality, and sport managers cannot please everyone. What they can do is incorporate perspectives and decision-making processes that consider cultural issues and work

to find the best balance available. See chapter 3 for more information.

With such a vast world and numerous cultures, how can this be done effectively? Newspapers, magazines, journals, mediated programming, and other sources provide constant access to international issues in sport and beyond. In terms of direct industry practice, sport managers can examine the methods that sporting events and teams around the world use to engage fans, to market themselves, and to exist within different cultural realms. Such an investigation will provide a solid base from which to reexamine practices in one's own organization or industry and adapt them to international contexts in a culturally sensitive way.

Flexible Expertise

Third, a sport manager requires a flexible expertise. Understanding oneself and others and then communicating with them involves a fundamental worldview that values flexibility and adaptation. Opening up oneself to other cultures, influences, and knowledge requires a level of risk. This risk involves challenging personal (and perhaps deeply held) beliefs or practices, finding information that runs counter to belief systems, or learning something not previously known. Sport managers who maintain flexible and adaptable behaviors and practices will be better placed to seize opportunities, create them where they have not been capitalized on, and manage challenges to operations. Sport managers who can understand contextual elements of a situation and personal differences among fans, colleagues, or players will be well placed to move with the changes of the market, environment, or situation.

Sport managers, then, must develop operational expertise, communication expertise, and systems and critical analysis expertise that are grounded in technical, human relations, and conceptual skills and the principles of learning organizations (Katz & Kahn, 1978; Senge, 1994), although they differ slightly in size and scope. Operational expertise involves knowledge of marketing, sales, finance, accounting, economics, and personnel management—the foundations of business practices. The combination of the foundations with integrated strategic thinking (i.e., systems and critical analysis expertise) is the ultimate expression of operational expertise. Remember, however, that these skills are gained through education *and* experience. Effective sport managers must have communication expertise to be able to communicate thoughts, ideas, and concepts from around the world or from their own backyard. Finally, international sport managers need well-developed systems and critical analysis expertise to see the interrelationships among various organizational and market variables as well as the ability to balance macro and micro perspectives within a given issue.

The first component to flexible expertise is operational expertise. To some extent in a market system, operational expertise is understandable and translatable across cultures. But some nuances must be addressed. Examples include understanding accounting and financial regulation across different countries or regions (e.g., European Union), approaches to sales and marketing that vary along a continuum of relationship, and perhaps most difficult, the challenges of working for or managing people from other countries or cultures. Many books, articles, and other materials have been created to address intercultural management and business issues. Central to all of this is an open mind, a questioning or curious attitude, and a willingness to understand when a personal change is needed (e.g., a change in perspective).

A second expertise was introduced in an earlier section: communication expertise. Communication involves the knowledge of oneself and how to communicate various messages because the world is (co) constructed among individuals within communities (Baxter & Montgomery, 1996). Communication expertise can be thought of as communication competence, or the "ability to effectively exchange meaning through a common system of symbols, signs, or behaviors" (Bourhis, Adams, Titsworth, & Harter, 2004, p. 28). Communication competence is difficult to achieve because others have different perspectives, sense-making processes, and goals. Understanding and developing strong communication skills allows sport managers to interact with others to make sense of the world and communicate with others in their organization to achieve goals and make change. Cultural and international differences such as distance, language differences, and cultural practices (e.g., silence, relationship development) create *noise*, which affects the ability to communicate with others. A sport manager can develop communication skills to deal with these issues by using a systems approach—one that simultaneously under-

stands person, culture, and context (Hersey, 1984). For example, the National Football League (NFL) has several international websites (Canada, China, Japan, Mexico, United Kingdom, and NFLLatino. com). To overcome distance issues (time, too, because NFL games are shown in the middle of the night or early morning in some of these countries), each site is complete with videos, broadcast schedules, local news and information, and community content (e.g., user-generated content) to keep the game alive within each community. The Chinese and Japanese websites are created using a template that accounts for stylistic needs for the characters in each language. Creating websites in this manner shows that the personnel at the NFL understand the importance of integrating cultural practices into their marketing and information efforts. Although they cannot overcome all barriers, cultural and otherwise (e.g., time), this example demonstrates the importance of cultural sensitivity in sport business practices.

In another example, think back to the National Basketball Association teams that use Spanish names on their jerseys (e.g., Los Mavs). Speculating about how a Spanish-speaking audience feels about a team or this practice is different from knowing how they feel. Such a situation calls for dialogue and research into various communities of fans rather than only fans as a general body. Yet, there are limits because not every person in a community can be understood to the same level. Thus, relationships with cultural community members can help to develop cultural understandings and messages that ring true to members of the community.

A final flexible expertise component is systems and critical analysis expertise—the ability to see micro and macro issues simultaneously, make sense of the

Learning Activity

The chapter discussed the importance of communication and communication competence. Reflect on recent interpersonal or group interactions that you have had yourself or witnessed with others in terms of interactions with people from another country. Are you able to identify interactions that were not effective? Why? Can you identify ones that were effective? Why?

information available, and act within situational enablers and constraints. By viewing the world as an interconnected system of subsystems, sport managers can learn to appreciate the complexity of their positions. The complexity of international sport (e.g., language, time, distance, cultural practices) means that today's international sport manager has a great deal to handle each day. Thus, by examining issues (an event, a game, or a marketing campaign) from multiple perspectives and not being afraid to learn more about an unfamiliar issue or cultural practice, sport managers can develop better judgment and decision-making processes. The example of the NFL international websites for China and Japan being constructed in a way to make reading the content easy for the fans is a perfect demonstration of the extent to which critical analysis should go. Coupling that attention to detail with solid local knowledge and relationship efforts that speak with the fans versus to them will allow sport managers to cross cultural barriers with less difficulty and form engaging relationships with local fans and communities.

In conclusion, developing all three expertise areas is a never-ending process. The journey is the key to the development of a sport manager. Throughout this journey, sport managers have numerous opportunities to use these expertise areas in relation to the issues explored in this chapter and throughout the book.

Summary

In conclusion, the concepts and current issues within the world of international sport discussed in this chapter and the competencies necessary to work within and among them are of supreme importance to sport managers. Dr. Zeigler's opening comments about sport being a social force are crucial. Sport managers who are able to understand and work with the numerous social forces affecting sport will be able to play important roles in creating the future of international sport.

Issues such as globalization, regionalism, and localization place a burden on sport managers to reach across country and cultural borders and learn about other people and communities. Enabling and constraining these efforts are complex issues including politics, economics, laws, and cultural beliefs and practices. Communication, then, becomes a significant key to success. Time, patience, open mindedness, and a willingness to learn and develop personal skill sets will all serve a sport manager well in the international sport world. The remainder of this book is dedicated to building on the issues discussed in this chapter. By the end of the book, the reader should have a better understanding of the complexities inherent in the modern sport landscape and a deeper knowledge of his or her place within the international sport world.

? Review and Discussion Questions

1. How does globalization influence sport today?
2. Describe the tension that exists between homogeneity and heterogeneity in terms of sport and culture.
3. What are the differences between global, international, and regional sport? Provide examples of sport in each.
4. Discuss the effects of corporate sponsorship on modern sport.
5. Explain how sport and the environment are connected. How can sport managers create social goodwill and new revenue streams by integrating sustainable practices into strategic decision making?
6. In what ways can sport managers integrate themselves into the international sport world and learn more about culture, sport practices, and other elements involved in it?
7. What is the relationship between sport and religion or spirituality?
8. What are three competencies needed by international sport managers? Provide examples of each.

Strategic Management in International Sport

Sharianne Walker, PhD
Western New England College, Massachusetts, USA

Minoo Tehrani, PhD
Roger Williams University, Rhode Island, USA

Chapter Objectives

After studying this chapter, you will be able to do the following:

- Identify motivations for sport organizations to enter the global marketplace
- Explain the concept of comparative advantage as it relates to the globalization of sport
- Explain the strategic management process as it relates to global market entry and management
- Identify global strategies for expansion into foreign markets
- Discuss trend analysis in the sport industry and identify those environmental factors that facilitate and serve as opportunities or barriers to global expansion
- Discuss ethical dimensions of global market entry and social responsibility guidelines for multinational operations

Key Terms

During the past two decades, globalization of the sport industry has continued to expand. Professional and amateur sport teams, sporting goods manufacturers, sport facilities, sport services companies, tour sports, and a myriad of other sport organizations are seeking to compete in the international marketplace. Although organizations are choosing to operate in foreign markets for a variety of reasons, they face several challenges. The sport manager must determine the optimal location for expansion. He or she must then decide what form the expansion will take. Should the expansion be a strategic alliance? Should it be foreign investment? Should it involve creating franchises on foreign soil? Many options are available to the sport manager who wishes to expand internationally, yet there is clearly no one best approach for every organization or every country.

Those sport organizations that seek to compete globally must recognize that entry into the global marketplace requires careful planning, financial investment, and a commitment to succeed. Internationalization must be based on careful strategic planning and procurement of resources required for its successful implementation. The organization must have a clear strategic purpose for entering into the global marketplace. A strategic plan along with clearly articulated goals and objectives serves as the cornerstone of a successful global expansion. Strategic planning helps the sport manager determine not only when and where to internationalize but also how to penetrate a particular foreign market.

In this chapter, the concept of comparative advantage will be used to provide a theoretical context for the identification and discussion of the factors that have both encouraged and restrained the globalization of the sport industry. Using a strategic management perspective, this chapter identifies and examines both the opportunities and the challenges faced by international sport managers. Strategies used to expand sport organizations' markets across geographical borders are identified and examined. This chapter introduces various cultural, political, legal, economic, ethical, and logistical factors that continue to influence sport organizations seeking to succeed in the international marketplace. Key ethical issues faced by international sport managers are explored, and guidelines for managing a socially responsible multinational sport organization are provided.

Reasons to Enter the Global Marketplace

Sport organizations seek to operate in different nations for a variety of reasons, including access to new markets and the subsequent development of new customers, resource acquisition (personnel, facilities, technology, financial resources), enhanced marketing opportunities, sport and brand growth, and profit generation. Many sport managers believe that the potential for long-term growth and stability can be realized through international operations.

For many sport organizations, globalization is the result of stagnant or declining home markets. Sport managers may think that the sport itself or the sport product has reached its growth potential at home. Slow, declining, or stagnant growth may be due to competition in the marketplace, lagging interest in the sport or sport product, or a change in the economy or in consumer tastes. The organization's managers are involved in ongoing assessment of the marketplace. Because of their research, they may arrive at the conclusion that sales have reached capacity for a particular market or that no more customers are available in the market. Sport managers, seeking to counter these effects and jump-start growth, see international markets as an opportunity to reenergize sales or grow the brand in new markets. Diminishing market share or stagnant growth in existing markets often triggers efforts to gain access to new markets and develop new customers. Globalization offers the promise of new markets and a seemingly limitless source of new customers.

Another reason that sport organizations consider global market expansion is that they seek to acquire resources in international markets. For example, global expansion for some sport organizations might mean access to human resources including talented international players. Global initiatives could result in bringing top athletes together to compete in a world-class competition, or this strategy could simply be viewed as a viable approach to increasing the available player pool. Similarly, global alliances might bring together the best minds in sport marketing, sport manufacturing, or sport facility and event management. For some organizations, entry into the foreign marketplace means access to a cheap labor force that can support low-cost global manufacturing. For some sectors of the sport industry, such as golf and auto racing, global initiatives result not only in a deepening of the talent pool that brings together top athletes in the sport but also greater access to existing global facilities that enhance the quality of the tour experience and make events more attractive to competitors and spectators alike. For sport product manufacturers seeking to do business overseas, access to established manufacturing plants on foreign soil may be extremely attractive.

In a similar way, technology resources in foreign markets may drive international expansion. Such technology may be valuable as the sport organization seeks to enhance marketing, sport broadcasting, or product development initiatives. Technologically advanced broadcast system infrastructure, for example, might serve as an incentive to companies that are considering foreign expansion.

Lastly, some sport organizations may seek to acquire additional financial resources through global expansion. Given a situation in which economic conditions in a local market are uncertain and international exchange rates are favorable, a sport organization may choose to expand into a more stable market to shore up its operations or take advantage of exchange rates through foreign investment. For example, professional golfers have benefited from the international expansion of the golf industry and the addition of international events. These events not only provide professional golfers with new opportunities to make money but also to gain international exposure that may result in new sponsorship opportunities.

Sport managers might also seek to enhance marketing opportunities through global expansion. Footwear, apparel, and sporting goods companies provide a good example of how companies leverage global marketing opportunities. In recent years Adidas and other footwear companies have been particularly aggressive in seeking international marketing opportunities. In 2008 Adidas announced a long-term partnership until 2018 with the Russian Football Union (RFU). Adidas is the official sponsor and ball supplier of many high-profile football tournaments and teams. Adidas has many existing global partnerships with sport organizations in Argentina, China, Denmark, England, France, Germany, Greece, Italy, Japan, Nigeria, Spain, South Africa, and elsewhere (SGB, 2008, November). For Adidas, global expansion means putting the Adidas product in a variety of international markets and

developing both endorsement deals and advertising opportunities with individual football stars such as Steven Gerrard, Lionel Messi, David Beckam, Kaka, and Raul.

For the National Football League (NFL), global expansion is driven by a commitment to grow the sport and the brand. Besides playing preseason and regular season games overseas, the NFL's foreign broadcast initiative features 125 broadcasters from 231 countries and territories carrying nearly 200,000 hours of programming (Brown, 2008). For the NFL, international broadcast exposure is intended to increase the popularity of the sport and raise brand awareness of the sport and league. League officials also expect that such global brand development will result in increased profits. For individual franchises as well as for the league itself, the expectation is that global expansion will translate into real revenue gains in licensing and merchandising deals, sponsorships, rights fees, and in some cases online services.

All sport organizations considering global expansion must not only understand what is driving the desire to enter international markets but also articulate clearly the desired outcomes. The setting of clear, measurable, and realistic goals is the precursor to successful entry into foreign markets. Managers must articulate those goals in quantitative terms. For example, managers must base their plan on tangible outcomes, such as a 20 percent increase in sales in six months, 50,000 new online merchandise transactions from the targeted country in one year, or the securing of $1 million of new sponsorship money within three years of entry. Clearly articulated goals and objectives that focus on specific areas such as access to new markets, development of new customers, and acquisition of a variety of resources as discussed earlier provide sport managers with a defined set of targeted outcomes. These desired results provide not only purpose but also accountability to internationalization initiatives. Sport managers must always keep the vision of anticipated results as the guiding factor in strategic planning and management efforts.

After the outcomes are defined and envisioned, the next step is to set the course for internationalization efforts, that is, to identify specific strategies and actions for achieving those outcomes. At the core of this process is the understanding of comparative advantage.

Global Expansion and Comparative Advantage

After a clear understanding of the purpose and desired outcomes of international expansion is in place, the sport manager must undertake an analysis of the environmental factors of the host country or countries that can best contribute to the realization of the goals and objectives of the organization. Environmental factors that can create unique opportunities by a specific host country make up the comparative advantages of that country.

In the context of international expansion, **comparative advantages** are the environmental factors along with the sociocultural, political, legal, economic, technological, and geographical dimensions of a nation that compare favorably with those of other nations. For example, some of the comparative advantages of the United States along the sociocultural factors are the size, diversity, educational level, and disposable income of the population. Historically, the United States has been seen to be a highly favorable market for a variety of products. In addition, the democratic and well-developed economic system, abundant natural resources, highly educated labor force, and sophisticated infrastructure for distribution of goods and services (airways, waterways, roads, electronic communication infrastructure) are some of the other comparative advantages of the United States that attract foreign goods and services. Technological sophistication and favorable geographical location are additional factors that have made the United States attractive for operations of foreign companies.

Countries with abundant cheap labor and less restrictive environmental and labor laws such as Singapore, Vietnam, Korea, and Mexico have been attractive places for global expansion of numerous foreign corporations, including sporting goods and sport footwear manufacturers. Other sport organizations have found the sizable market potential and changing cultural and political landscape of countries like Russia, India, and China to provide a comparative advantage over other nations. Cultural factors, such as knowledge and appreciation for a particular sport, might also provide a comparative advantage, as is the case with rugby, which is embraced as part of the culture in England, New Zealand, Australia, and several European countries. Broad cultural acceptance and fan avidity in these countries create fertile opportunity for sport organizations that offer rugby-based products or services. Conversely, such companies might avoid global expansion to countries where rugby is relatively unknown.

Marketing Foreign Players

An examination of global expansion efforts of professional sport leagues and tour sport also demonstrates the importance of understanding comparative advantage. For many of these sport organizations comparative advantage has sprung from an understanding that the signing of foreign players to strengthen the home franchise roster translates into global expansion opportunity. Professional leagues around the world have quickly adopted this strategy.

For example, an examination of 2008–09 NBA opening-day rosters showed that close to 15 percent of NBA players were considered to be of foreign origin (NBA.com). Players making NBA rosters represent a variety of countries including China, Brazil, Spain, Argentina, Turkey, Serbia, Lithuania, Germany, and France. The NBA has sought to expand its presence in these countries through marketing, the Internet, and broadcasting initiatives.

Note that companies in the athletes' home countries concurrently seek to leverage the popularity of players competing elsewhere. They do this by creating corporate partnerships that enhance sales in local markets as well as help them reach new international markets. Each of the parties involved in these deals—the athlete, the franchise, the league, and the athlete's home country corporation—share the common objectives of enhancing brand awareness and recognition while developing new markets and subsequent revenue streams. A good example of this type of partnership involves Yao Ming of China, the Houston Rockets, the NBA, and a Chinese brewery. The Rockets, after signing Yao Ming, sought sponsorship agreements with Chinese companies immediately after his signing. The league was also exploring sponsorship, licensing, and broadcasting deals in China, and the athlete was seeking endorsement opportunities in his homeland. In 2003 the team signed a hefty sponsorship agreement with Chinese beer company Yanjing (Lombardo, 2003). With this deal the Rockets and the NBA were able to capitalize on the global popularity of Ming both in China and beyond. The Yanjing deal placed the player in ads in China and other Pacific Rim nations. The goal of the beer company was not only to generate sales in China but also to reach new international markets in targeted Pacific Rim nations.

In recognition of the strength of the connection between the foreign athlete and the home-country market, some sport organizations such as the National Association of Stock Car Racing (NASCAR) have purposefully and aggressively recruited international athletes in an effort to create a comparative advantage. Drivers including Columbian Juan Pablo Montoya, Scotsman Dario Franchitti, and Jacques Villeneuve, a former Formula One race car driver of French Canadian descent, have been signed to NASCAR teams with the intent of helping to grow the popularity of the sport in international markets.

Other Sources of Comparative Advantage

The NFL, which has few players not born in the United States, has launched expansion initiatives in Europe, Mexico, and Canada with varying degrees of success. The Mexico and Canada connections are based not on the foreign player home-country approach but rather on geographical proximity. Franchises in Southern California, Arizona, Texas, Chicago, Buffalo, Wisconsin, and Minnesota have facilitated interest in Latino and Canadian markets through international broadcasting as well as playing games in foreign cities. The NFL's presence in Europe was initially driven by an interest in creating a player development business beyond the U.S. collegiate system while building the NFL brand and opening up European markets to U.S. professional football. In 2007 the league announced that it would shut down its NFL Europa League, which was launched in 1995 as an all-European competitive league. The NFL announced that it would switch the focus of its international business strategy to presenting the NFL to the widest possible global audience through media visibility and staging international regular season games (*NFL Europa Closes*, 2008).

Still other professional leagues and teams have created global partnerships that have enhanced marketing opportunities, created value for both franchises, and grown revenue streams. An example of one such successful joint initiative is the 2001 strategic partnership between two of the most powerful professional sport organizations in the world, Manchester United and the New York Yankees. Together, they developed a strategic alliance to share market information, develop sponsorship and joint promotional programs, and sell each other's licensed goods. The deal essentially represented multibillion-dollar international opportunities for both organizations. When Manchester United issued a statement about the deal, its shares leapt by 9 percent within one hour on the London Stock Exchange (*Joining Forces*, 2001).

The story of Major League Baseball (see the case study) illustrates the five basic approaches that pro sport teams, leagues, and tours have demonstrated as part of their internationalization strategy. They include broadcasting, licensing and merchandising, playing exhibition and formal competitions, marketing foreign athletes, and grassroots programs (Gladden & Lizandra, 1998).

Cultural and Political Obstacles

For professional sport organizations, the major issue in penetrating targeted foreign markets has often been dealing with cultural or political barriers and overcoming tactical difficulties. In some countries, because of established tradition and cultural norms or attitudes, women are discouraged or not allowed to engage in public sport. Such a barrier is likely to be insurmountable for a women's sport organization that seeks to operate in such a nation. In other instances, cultural sport preference may present a barrier to successful entry. When a sport has become an elemental component of a country's identity and tradition (e.g., hockey in Canada, cycling in France, football in Italy), an entering sport or organization will likely be met with some resistance. The challenge for the sport manager is to introduce the sport into the culture and sponsor activities that will cause the culture to embrace the sport.

Although cultural barriers can often be problematic, political obstacles proved to be the major hurdle for the World Baseball Classic. The U.S. government initially refused to allow Cubans into the United States to participate in the event and threatened to halt the entire tournament. As was the case in this instance, political barriers may take the form of restrictive laws that govern entry and exit of people or products across borders. The Olympics are especially challenged by political

Major League Baseball Goes Global

Major League Baseball teams in the United States, which have a growing percentage of players from Central America and Japan, have identified those markets as having great potential for successful penetration. Central America and Japan are considered to offer a comparative advantage over other potential foreign markets because of their ability to offer a fertile new customer base that already demonstrates an interest in and understanding of baseball. Both Japan and Central America have established baseball leagues, an established baseball tradition, and a demonstrated interest in America's national pastime. Sport managers have traditionally taken advantage of the "hometown boy" phenomena (such as Japanese baseball hero Ichiro Suzuki of the Seattle Mariners and Dominican baseball slugger Albert Pujols of the St. Louis Cardinals) to drive international fan interest in U.S. league and teams. Back in their hometowns and home countries (Japan and the Dominican Republic, respectively), fans follow their countrymen as their national stars compete in the United States. The presence of international players has also spurred new interest in ethnic markets within the United States. Major League Baseball and many individual major league teams have hired directors of ethnic marketing who are responsible for the development of strategies to grow the popularity of the game within local Asian or Latino markets. Baseball historians attest to the fact that ethnic marketing is not a new strategy by any means. Baseball heroes such as Jackie Robinson, Joe DiMaggio, and Hank Greenberg were important figures in popularizing the game within African American, Italian, and Jewish communities in the United States.

Translating their most recent globalization strategy to action, Major League Baseball (MLB) not only encourages game broadcasts to local and foreign Latino and Asian markets in native languages but also has taken professional teams to play in Mexico, Japan, and Puerto Rico. MLB sent the Boston Red Sox on a preseason tour of Japan in 2008 in part because the Red Sox had signed one of Japan's top players, pitcher Daiske Matsusaka, along with Japanese pitcher Hideki Okajima. The Red Sox were already broadcasting games in Japanese as well as selling licensed products in Japan. MLB holds all international licensing and merchandising rights and sought to broaden that market through the goodwill tour. MLB also hoped to expose its product firsthand to Japanese fans to strengthen the MLB brand and build affinity for MLB leagues and teams. Besides playing exhibition games as part of the tour, players made public appearances and hosted clinics for Japanese youth. The idea was not only to increase interest in the game but also to build sales in these markets, increase audience, develop potential player interest, and court potential sponsors in Japan.

According to Paul Archey, MLB senior vice president of international business, 20 years ago MLB's international business was largely defined by operations in the Dominican Republic and Costa Rica, homelands to the majority of foreign-born players in MLB (Britcher, 2002). Today, however, nearly half of current players are born outside the United States. The challenge for the league has been to take advantage of the connections to MLB players' home countries and to grow the game globally. In 2006 the league launched the World Baseball Classic (WBC) as part of its efforts to create one global market for baseball. The tournament featured games in the Far East, Caribbean, and the United States and showcased some of the world's best baseball talent. For MLB the alliance with foreign teams meant further exposure to global fans and placed MLB on the international stage.

The 2009 version of the WBC featured 16 teams in world venues including sites in Canada, Japan, and the United States. Among the notable outcomes of the 2009 WBC was China's first WBC game victory, the Netherlands' two wins over the Dominican Republic, and the final between Japan and Korea becoming the first nationally televised WBC game in China. According to MLB officials, sponsorship revenues were up 50 percent for the tournament (Lefton, 2009).

The 2009 WBC continued to display the quality of baseball talent around the world, yet internal logistical and philosophical issues with MLB owners and team general managers affected MLB player involvement in the WBC. Attendance and fan support were uneven for the event, prompting MLB commissioner Bud Selig to encourage MLB owners to put aside provincial club interest for the good of the game (Thorne, 2009). Given the low attendance at many U.S. venues, the league will need to do a better job of marketing the event in its own home markets when planning future WBC events.

The 2009 WBC also shed light on issues that are challenging efforts to globalize the game. Although MLB is interested in attracting the best baseball stars to its league and grow international fan bases, foreign countries may be concerned about the defection of its best baseball talent and the effect that it will have on growing the game at home. Additionally, issues related to political systems and anti-American sentiment in countries such as Cuba and Venezuela threaten to cut off access to MLB for some foreign citizens who wish to sign with MLB clubs. Clearly, all these issues, both foreign and domestic, will continue to surround the WBC and MLB's efforts to globalize the game for its own strategic purposes.

---

barriers because nations seek to play out political agendas on the world stage.

Although the sport manager can often do little to overcome longstanding cultural, political, or religious attitudes and behaviors, sport organizations continue to try to introduce new sports and new sport products. Development of a sport in a culture begins by educating fans about that particular sport. Such educational programs take a variety of forms and may include exhibition games, youth clinics, media penetration, and educational programming. In the past, the introduction of a sport to new fans has been particularly problematic for non-Olympic sport organizations because inclusion in the Olympic Games guarantees at least some level of international exposure. For non-Olympic sports, education of fans in a country that has virtually no exposure to the sport must often start at the most rudimentary level with an introduction to the history and rules of the sport. The NFL ran into this problem repeatedly when introducing football to Europe, where the game had relatively little exposure. As part of its fan education strategy, the league undertook a broad-based program to introduce fans to the rules of the game.

Sport managers have come to realize that there is no universal understanding of the variety of sports that they represent. Rugby, cricket, football, curling, American football, softball, golf, auto racing, tennis, baseball, skiing, synchronized swimming, and so on are not universally understood or played around the world. Adoption is predicated by education. Brand strength and recognition vary greatly around the world for both individual sports and sport companies. Where a sport is known, a comparative advantage may exist. Where a sport is virtually unknown, the challenge is to educate potential fans and bring about adoption of the sport. The development of an awareness of and passion for a new sport or new sport company in a culture is a long, arduous process. Cultural norms and behaviors change slowly, and in fact, changes may never occur.

With the understanding that adoption of a sport in a culture takes a long time, most sport organizations have come to recognize the importance of reaching out to young potential fans and consumers. As a result, sport managers have focused strategies on educating young consumers and developing brand recognition at a grassroots level. **Grassroots strategies** involve creation of youth sport programs in host countries, staging of exhibition games, visibility at local festivals and celebrations, sponsorship of local youth tournaments and facilities, game broadcasts, licensing, corporate partnerships, creation of online sport information sites or communities, and media interviews by athletes and coaches who also host local clinics or competitions. Sport managers recognize that future consumers must be exposed to the sport, must understand how the game is played, and must develop a personal interest in the team, league, or player before they will attend, listen to, or watch a game, or purchase licensed products or related sport equipment.

Other sport organizations that have employed grassroots strategies as part of global market entry include the National Basketball Association (NBA), National Hockey League (NHL), National Football League (NFL), Association of European Rugby (FIRA–AER.), and Indy Racing League (IRL). The NBA, NHL, NFL, FIRA–AER, and IRL have all hosted or sponsored youth-related events including clinics, exhibition games, and youth championships. Some organizations sponsor youth equipment giveaways to facilitate sport adoption. Other activities designed to speed adoption include offering foreign language broadcasts of events, securing regional sponsorships of activities, promoting a hometown athlete hero, and offering multilingual websites and online sport interest communities. Each of these activities is designed for the purpose of reaching and educating new young consumers, and the ultimate goal is to hasten sport adoption.

In determining comparative advantage, the sport manager must recognize that although grassroots and other initiatives may overcome some barriers to entry, other challenges to entry may be insurmountable. Factors making entry difficult often take the form of logistical or tactical barriers. For example, the realistic problems related to doing business across multiple time zones, lack of transportation infrastructure, language barriers, scheduling problems, inadequate technology infrastructure, financial limitations, unfavorable tax or labor laws, and lack of acceptable facilities can make expansion in a particular country impractical. Unwieldy regulation, political instability, and even difficult terrain or climate may make foreign operation impossible. Although some challenges of foreign entry and operation may be overcome, others simply cannot be surmounted. The sport manager must identify and weigh each of these factors carefully and must ultimately assess time and financial costs versus realistic potential return.

For sport organizations, the importance of assessing comparative advantage is clear. Sport managers must look carefully at the whole spectrum of environmental factors—sociocultural, political, legal, economic, technological, and geographical—before determining a strategy for entering a nation's borders. Any manager seeking to compete internationally must carefully assess each of these factors, considering both potential benefits and potential challenges, and then determine whether existing conditions are favorable in comparison with operating at home or in some other nation.

Strategic Management Process

Comparative advantage is a critical concept to understanding the globalization of sport because it provides a theoretical explanation for where and how sport organizations seek to compete in the global marketplace. In effect, the determination of comparative advantage fuels the strategic planning process, which dictates not only where and when entry into the global marketplace occurs but also how it occurs—the form and shape that the global initiatives take. Therefore, to devise an appropriate global strategy, sport managers need to identify relevant environmental factors and assess them as either opportunities or threats in relation to their organizational goals and objectives. Based on this analysis, companies can then determine the appropriate strategies to take advantage of the opportunities in that targeted nation.

Organizations that seek to compete globally without a well-planned strategy and proper implementation are doomed to fail, whereas firms with an appropriate and thorough strategic plan and implementation strategies are more likely to penetrate new markets successfully and reap the full benefits of the globalization of the sport industry. The **strategic management process** is a set of decisions, activities, and plans of action that are necessary for an organization to survive, compete, and perform successfully. The process of strategic management includes the following steps:

1. Establishing the organization's direction
2. Analyzing the situation (environmental analysis)
3. Developing strategy
4. Implementing strategy
5. Evaluating results

International expansion is a complex enterprise that requires setting vision, mission, goals, and objectives that are suitable to the organization's resources. It involves assessing external environmental factors in the global marketplace and looking closely at both internal organizational factors and the state of the industry. It requires a careful synthesis and analysis of all this information and the identification of both existing opportunities and challenges to the organization's foreign market entry. The strategic planning process must account for all the various environmental factors and then translate them into strategies that can best accomplish the stated goals and objectives of competing globally.

Step 1: Establishing the Organization's Direction

A clear and compelling sense of direction is the starting point of the strategic planning process. Management is responsible for giving the organization this sense of its own enduring purposes. The vision and mission statement are the most common tools for translating organizational purpose into compelling language that can then be communicated to stakeholders. Vision serves as a starting point for the mission statement, which is a written summary of what business the organization is in or seeks to be in. The mission statement often includes a statement of the organization's philosophy and values. The statement provides insight into the organization's long-term vision—what it wants to be and whom it wants to serve. Beyond describing the business that the organization seeks to be in, the mission statement should also articulate the organization's basic beliefs, values, and priorities.

Step 2: Analyzing the Situation (Environmental Analysis)

In terms of the strategic planning process, even organizations with a clear vision and mission often get so caught up in the day-to-day business of their organization that they fail to recognize what is going on around them. Sport managers must realize that they do not operate in a vacuum. Monitoring changes in the environment, in the industry, and within the organization itself is critically important. As part of the strategic planning process, managers must analyze the situation carefully before they plan a course of action or strategy to support the mission.

The environmental or situation analysis component of the strategic management process highlights the strengths, weaknesses, opportunities, and threats that an organization needs to address. In strategic planning, this phase is referred to as the **SWOT** (strengths, weaknesses, opportunities, threats) **analysis**.

The environmental analysis undertaken as part of the global market strategic planning process begins with the identification and examination of the general external environment. The general environment includes macro environmental factors that deal with the external environment, including the sociocultural, political, legal, economic, technological, and geographical factors. In the global market strategic planning process, the manager must look at the external environments of both the home country and prospective targeted nations. As discussed earlier in the chapter, this external environmental analysis of prospective targeted nations serves as the starting point for determining comparative advantage among countries. Comparative analysis ultimately helps to drive the selection of the country or countries for global market entry.

Environmental analysis also includes the assessment of the micro environmental factors, commonly called the organization environment. This area involves the evaluation of the internal assets and resources of the company in all areas—finance, human resources, information, knowledge, and productivity. This microlevel environmental analysis will also indicate strengths and weaknesses of the organization itself. For the sport management student seeking to secure an internship or employment internationally, a microlevel environmental analysis can be an important decision-making tool. For example, through this process the student will learn about the organization's financial stability, its personnel practices, and whether appropriate resources are in place for the student to succeed. With this information, the student can make an informed decision about the internal working environment and assess whether the organization and the situation are a good fit to her or his interests and long-term career goals.

Lastly, an industry analysis is undertaken. The analysis of the industry, commonly called the task environment, provides information regarding customers, suppliers, industry characteristics (e.g., number of competitors, stage of the life cycle, government rules and regulations pertaining to the industry), profile of competitors within the industry, competition from other industries, and the key success factors for the industry. This assessment highlights the opportunities and the threats that managers need to consider in the strategic decision-making process. As part of the industry analysis, the organization seeks to discover industry trends that will influence foreign operation. Industry trends for the sport industry and global expansion are discussed later in the chapter.

Step 3: Developing Strategy

In the next phase of the strategic planning process, the organizational vision, mission, goals, and objectives are measured against environmental analysis

Levels of Strategic Options

Corporate-Level Strategy
- Merger and acquisition
- Retrenchment

Business-Level Strategy
- Differentiation
- Cost leader
- Focus

Functional-Level Strategy
- Production
- Accounting and finance
- Research and development
- Marketing
- Public relations
- Human resources

outcomes to identify the course of action that an organization needs to take to minimize threats and maximize opportunities that emerge in the environment. The strategies that an organization selects must reflect its mission, the opportunities and threats in the environment, and its own strengths and weaknesses. The process of developing strategy helps the organization find its best fit among the three sets of forces. The various levels of strategic alternatives are listed in the sidebar.

Corporate Level

Corporate-level strategy deals with the alternatives that a company or organization explores as it conducts business across several industries or markets. At the corporate level, strategy deals with an organization's decision about either to expand or retreat in general or from industry to industry. A useful approach is to think of corporate-level strategy in two distinct terms: either getting bigger or getting smaller.

Merger and acquisition are corporate-level strategies that represent the organization's intent to grow. Merger and acquisition strategies involve the combination or purchase of business entities to increase the size or capacity of the organization. Global merger or acquisition is seen as a solid corporate-level growth strategy. Retrenchment is a corporate-level strategy that represents the organization's interest in becoming smaller or downsizing operations to a smaller scale. These strategies can be adopted to achieve more efficient operations by eliminating divisions or areas that have become ineffective or unnecessary. The NFL adopted this strategy by its closure of NFL Europa.

Business Level

The second level of strategy deals with an organization or corporate business unit operating in a single industry and is known as a **business-level strategy**. The purpose of defining a business-level strategy is to give the organization an advantage over its competition. Business-level strategies define the strategies for each major product line or business unit (industry) of the company. Business-level strategies include differentiation, cost leader, and focus. For example, Nike's market development strategy for its footwear business unit encompasses differentiation of its products from its competitors based on perceived quality (product differentiation) and diverse marketing and advertising campaigns to create a unique image (marketing differentiation). Evidence of Nike's business-level differentiation strategy is the hiring of top-level professional athletes to promote its products. In the case of international golf superstar Tiger Woods, his endorsement deal with Nike led to the introduction of Nike into the golf industry and the eventual creation of a line of golf products. Evidence of Nike's differentiation strategy as an industry leader can also be seen in its international marketing efforts. For example, Nike always affiliates itself with the most prestigious and influential world sporting events such as the Olympics and World Cup. Note that business-level strategy may differ across units. Therefore, Nike might adopt different strategies for its Nike/Bauer division, Nike golf division, and Nike footwear division.

Cost leader strategy is implemented by companies that strive to produce goods or services at the lowest cost in the industry, thereby enabling them to offer the lowest prices. Some footwear companies such as Converse have sought to position themselves as affordable footwear and have adopted the cost leader strategy by keeping production costs low while providing acceptable quality and affordable products. Companies seeking to enter countries where average income is low must consider the cost leader strategy in their entry plans.

Focus strategy targets a particular customer or geographic market or follows a strategy that specializes in some way. To carry out this strategy, New Balance has employed a focus strategy by producing products for high-frequency users such as aerobics instructors and by offering an extensive width sizing. Another footwear company that follows this strategy is Adidas, which has focused its efforts on the football market. Adidas has sought international football stars to endorse its products and has become a visible brand in premier leagues throughout the world.

Functional Level

After corporate- and business-level strategies are set, the third level of strategy, **functional-level strategy**, is devised. Appropriate production, marketing, R&D, accounting, finance, and human resources elements define the type of functional strategies that an organization needs to achieve successful implementation of its strategic decisions. For example, the types of facilities, technologies, and employees' skills differ in implementing a cost leader strategy as opposed to a differentiation strategy. In a low-cost environment, mass production, low labor costs, automation, and standardization are major components of the functional strategies. For an international sporting goods company that follows a cost leader strategy and wishes to deliver a relatively inexpensive piece of equipment, a country that offers ample manufacturing capabilities and low labor costs would be essential. Meanwhile, competition based on differentiation may require a high-caliber, innovative workforce, unique marketing and advertising campaigns, and high R&D expenditures, among other factors. A sport media company, for example, wishing to follow a differentiation strategy that involves the creation of new cutting-edge technology products or software would seek an environment where a highly skilled and innovative workforce is available.

Therefore, the allocation of resources to different functional areas should fit the competitive position that an organization is trying to achieve. Functional-level strategies must link across departments and units. For example, the footwear company's marketing office, public relations office, finance office, human resources office, and so on must all work together to carry out and support the organization's global expansion efforts.

Step 4: Implementing Strategy

As important as it is to develop strategy at the corporate, business, and functional levels, strategies become effective only when they are translated into action. The organization's structure must be tied directly to its strategy; that is, structure follows strategy. The structure of an organization represents a pattern that emerges from the division of work in an organization. This pattern indicates the lines of command, authority, and communication. In a low-cost environment, an organization needs to implement a flat structure that enhances lower cost, centralizes control, and eliminates duplication of effort. On the other hand, decentralized organizations that allow for independent decision making, innovation, and creativity provide a more suitable work division for implementation of differentiation strategies. For example, a health club franchise engaged in international market entry that has chosen to implement a low-cost strategy may employ few staff members, have a single authoritarian manager, and feature services or programs to members that require few financial or human resources. This relatively flat structure supports the organization's strategy of being a low-cost price leader in the market. On the other hand, a club that wishes to differentiate itself in the market as offering an upscale, high-quality product may have a more vertical structure with several managers and employee teams made up of fitness experts who share responsibility for developing and maintaining a variety of high-quality and innovative programs and services.

As mentioned earlier in the chapter, strategy is always related to environmental analysis. The savvy manager will always rely on his or her understanding of both the operating environment and the organization's strengths and weaknesses. The health club manager who has selected an appropriate strategy based on these analyses will implement a structure that will best support the strategy in particular market conditions. For the sport organization competing globally, structure will always need to facilitate the unique needs of international communication and transportation. For the health club organization doing business internationally, structure might reflect global operations through the establishment of a European operations division and a Pacific Rim operations division.

After appropriate strategies have been selected on the corporate, business, and functional levels and structure has been set in place to support strategy, the manager must successfully implement these strategies across the organization. Implementation is the final phase of the strategic process. In this phase the manager ensures that the selected strategies are not only consistent with one another but also support the organization's overall mission and goals. Implementation requires managers to coordinate activity across the firm while securing the necessary support required by organizational units to assure that the strategies are executed successfully. Implementation means translating strategy into operational plans with specific activities and timetables for action established. For example, a professional league seeking to enhance global expansion must set a specific schedule for international matches. Teams must be set. Ticketing and sponsorship plans must be developed. Facilities must be secured. Travel plans and accommodations must be made, and an international marketing and broadcasting plan must be created.

Step 5: Evaluating Results

The final phase of the strategic management process is the continuous monitoring and evaluation of the activities and performance of the organization. The performance evaluation of an organization along the traditional financial measures (e.g., return on sales, return on equity), satisfaction of stakeholders (e.g., customers, employees, suppliers, management, community), and the value of the investments of the firm, past and present, in different areas (e.g., technology, human resources) will provide a comprehensive view of the performance of the organization. The results of the performance evaluation act as feedback throughout the strategic management process for necessary changes and adjustments to the various components of this process. In the international environment, establishing and agreeing on acceptable performance requirements and metrics appropriate to the particular market are critical. For example, an acceptable performance goal might be a near sell-out series of World Cup matches in Europe, but was that an appropriate goal for South Africa? For the United States? Performance standards need to be adapted to the international context.

Global Strategies in the Sport Industry

As sport organizations engage in the strategic planning process, they may determine that entry into foreign markets is critical to implementing their corporate-, business-, and functional-level strategies. At that point, focus must be directed to determining market entry location through comparative analysis and then selecting market entry strategy. Quite simply, the challenge for managers is to determine the most appropriate form or shape of the international expansion effort. Several strategies for operating in a foreign market are viable. Selection of the appropriate strategy is guided by the statement of purpose and goals, information gleaned through the strategic planning process, and careful consideration of comparative advantages. The challenge to sport managers is to select and implement a strategy that best leverages comparative advantages and effectively supports the organization's purpose, goals, and strategic direction. Entry into foreign market can take place in the form of foreign direct investment or strategic alliances.

Foreign Direct Investment

Controlling assets in another country, managing foreign activities, finding new markets in foreign countries, and searching for additional supply sources for existing markets represent an organization's **foreign direct investment** (**FDI**) activities. The reasons for choosing FDI can involve demand- or supply-related activities. Reaching new markets, jumping over trade barriers, having a local presence, understanding social values, and being able to compete locally are factors that can enhance demand for the products of a company. Therefore, any one combination of these factors justifies engagement in FDI because of the desire to increase the demand for the products. Organizations also engage in foreign direct investment because of supply considerations. Lower production costs, better access to raw material, lower delivery costs, and multiple sourcing (procurement of supply sources from different locations) are among the factors that can lower the cost of operations and motivate organizations to enter and invest in foreign markets. Table 2.1 provides examples of sport organizations' FDIs across the globe.

Table 2.1 Examples of Foreign Direct Investments (FDI) in Sport Industry

Sport organization	FDI activity
Skechers	Retail stores in 120 countries
AEG	Stadium and facility design in Asia
NBA	Creation of NBA Goodwill and clinics tour in India
Arizona Diamondbacks	Financial support of baseball leagues and field construction in Mexico
U.S. investors George Gillett and Tom Hicks	Purchase of England's Liverpool Football Club

Greenfield development is a prime example of foreign direct investment, incorporating both demand and supply reasons in implementing global strategies. Greenfield development is often the most labor intensive and costly strategy of the foreign direct investment activities. Rather than acquiring an existing company in a foreign market, **greenfield development** involves the creation and construction of foreign-based facilities, as well as marketing and distribution channels.

Although foreign direct investment for demand and supply reasons is a key consideration in the globalization of the sport industry, it represents a high-risk, high-cost involvement in international competition. Other avenues allow organizations to expand their customer and geographic bases with a lower degree of risk, cost, and involvement. These strategic initiatives can take the form of strategic alliances.

Strategic Alliances

Strategic alliances are ways in which organizations collaborate with each other to enhance their control over their industry and competition and to share the costs and risks of global expansion. In the sport industry these alliances are carefully constructed. Each sport organization is mindful of the serious political, cultural, ethical, logistical, economic, and other considerations that must be identified and negotiated.

Some of the major forms of strategic alliances demonstrated in the sport industry are joint ventures, sponsorship and licensing agreements, franchising, and outsourcing. Organizations enter into **joint venture** activities to complement or supplement each other's skills and expertise. In this strategy two or more companies (or in some cases, a governmental entity) come together to contribute resources and expertise to develop a product or service. Managerial functions such as marketing, management, research, finance, and facility development are often shared. Each partner contributes to the initiative. Both the home organization and the host-country-based organization share the risks and costs of the venture.

Joint ventures in the development of new technology, product development, and marketing activities are among the most common forms of alliances in the sport industry. On the international level, joint marketing ventures are prevalent. What would the Olympics be without international sponsorship? Joint ventures in technology or marketing include the establishment of a new entity, either temporary or permanent, by two or more parent firms to achieve special objectives, such as the development of new technologies or development of a marketing campaign or promotional activities for new products (Roberts & Mizouchi, 1989). Engagement in these types of alliances enhances new product development, contributes to brand recognition, ensures access to state-of-the-art technology, eases the recruitment of a high-caliber workforce, lowers the cost and the risk of new development, and raises the capabilities of the joint venture partners to compete effectively in their industry.

Corporate sponsorship or partnership programs represent a strategic alliance that allows both the sport organization and the sponsoring firm to create unique opportunities that support each other's business goals. Sponsorships take myriad forms including title sponsor, presenting sponsor, naming rights, promotional and sales collaborations, hospitality opportunities, and so forth. Sponsorship alliances are a driving force behind international sport. As companies seek to break into foreign markets or cement their operations internationally, sport has become one of the most powerful vehicles to achieve international business goals. Sport is a common language and a bridge between all cultures. Many corporations have successfully leveraged existing international sporting events to enhance their international success.

Another form of strategic alliances common in the sport industry, the licensing agreement, allows a licensee the legal right to use a technology or market a product. Through engagement in these types of alliances, organizations can reduce operating costs and offer a lower-priced product that in turn enhances the partners' competitive positions in the industry. One of the benefits of this strategy to sport organizations is that they are able to enhance brand recognition and build market share through a third party (licensee). Such licenses can often provide significant revenues to sport organizations through the creation of "officially licensed" products and sponsorship programs. The beverage category includes many interesting examples of how sport organizations create valuable alliances through the "officially licensed" designation. Beverage companies have successfully used this approach to generate sales of products like Coca-Cola and Gatorade in international markets.

Franchising is a form of strategic alliance that extends the legal right to use the name, the pattern of conducting business, and an array of products to a franchisee. Franchising is an effective way for a company to expand its business ventures without extensive disbursement of capital, high cost, and the risk of market development. Franchising is a type of strategic alliance frequently employed in retail management. For example, in the last 10 years, many sport organizations such as U.S.-based Ajay Sports, Inc. and its subsidiary, Pro Golf

International, developed a strategic alliance with the Pro Shop, Ltd. of South Africa to develop and create Pro Golf franchised retail stores in South Africa (Sporting Goods Business, 2000). This type of retail alliance has also helped to facilitate entry into third-party foreign markets. An example of this approach is U.S.-based L.L. Bean, which has developed and operates retail outlets in China through a joint venture with Korean-based partners (SGB, September 2008).

Alliances based on **outsourcing**, the procuring of products and or services from an outside supplier, can also lower the cost of operations, reduce the size of the workforce, and lessen the amount of expertise needed for completion of a product. In turn, outsourcing can enhance the cost position of the organizations in the industry. Outsourcing can be a combination of strategic alliances or FDI. Both sport and nonsport companies commonly seek low-cost labor in countries such as Mexico, Indonesia, and South Korea for components and parts.

The overall objectives of engaging in these types of alliances is to enhance the ease of access to new technologies and marketing channels, take advantage of international resources or expertise, expand the customer base, and broaden the geographical base of the organizations without significant cost to any single firm. Engagement in various strategic alliances is an effective way to penetrate foreign markets while sharing the cost and risk of development, ultimately enhancing the partners' competitive position in the industry. Some examples of strategic alliances may be found in table 2.2.

The phenomenon of the globalization of sport may be best understood from a strategic management process perspective. Sport organizations

Table 2.2 Examples of Strategic Alliances in Sport Industry

Sport organization	Activity	Strategic alliances
Starter–NBA	Legal right of merchandise sales internationally	Licensing agreements
Ricoh–FIS World Cup (Nordic disciplines)	Event sponsorship Technology provider	Joint venture marketing
Nike–Chinese Government	Manufacturing facilities in China	Joint venture
Samsung–Chelsea F.C.	Financial support of International Football in the Community international tour—coaches program and youth clinics	Joint venture, grassroots marketing
Sports Direct International, PLC (U.K.)–ITAT Group (China)	Retail store development	Joint venture

seek to compete internationally because managers believe that doing so will allow them to achieve specific organizational goals and objectives, which may include increasing market share, reaching new markets, enhancing organizational image or brand, accessing specific resources, lowering costs, or increasing profits. For this reason, engagement in global strategies through FDI or alliances must be carefully matched with an organization's goals and objectives. In effect, globalization strategies must be carefully devised and implemented to provide the organization with its best opportunity to meet its stated goals and objectives. Essentially, there is no one best strategy for globalization. Success of international initiatives can be evaluated on only their ability to meet the organization's stated goals and objectives.

The downside of engaging in alliances is that the company must protect its exclusive technologies and trade secrets. For example, one of the major challenges to international licensing is unauthorized or inappropriate use of licensed logos, names, and images. The Olympic Games are often beset with problems related to the illegal use of athletes' images, official logos, slogans, and mascots on unlicensed products. Companies seeking to capitalize on the name recognition or image of a sport property may illegally use a slogan, logo, or image within a marketing campaign without securing the proper license. Maintaining control of these properties through official licensing programs continues to be a major challenge for sport managers, especially given recent advances in technology that have facilitated illegal duplication, use, and distribution of sport-related logos, trademarks, and properties. The proliferation of new media such as personal telecommunications devices and Internet-based technologies such as YouTube and social networking sites has made it almost impossible to control unauthorized use of sport logos, images, highlights, and video footage.

In addition, international patent, copyright, and trademark laws regulating the use of such intellectual property and proprietary images vary widely and are often difficult to enforce in the international arena. The sharing of ideas, processes, marks, logos, and images involved in strategic alliances, such as licensing, outsourcing, and franchising, is generally nonexclusive. Because the purpose of these alliances is collaborative in nature, protection of

Learning Activity

Think about major international sporting events such as the Ryder Cup, World Cup, Tour de France, and the Olympics. What companies come to mind as sponsors for these events? What do you think motivates these companies to become involved in international sporting events? Discuss how these companies might use international sporting events to meet their international business objectives. You may wish to visit the websites of those companies to learn more about their international sport alliances.

intellectual property has not been a primary concern. Unfortunately, because of varying laws and regulation and the ease with which this information is copied and shared, control of unauthorized use in the international marketplace is difficult at best. Managers involved in these alliances recognize the financial cost of this lack of control and continue to struggle with finding ways to capture related lost revenues. Along the same line, for any investment in a foreign market, understanding the legal and political system of that market is extremely important for protection of the organization's investment. Hence, the management of organizations must seek to engage only in foreign direct investment or strategic alliances that are legitimately purposeful in their ability to advance the organization's goals and objectives.

Trend Analysis in the Sport Industry

To understand why sport organizations continue to seek out foreign market entry, we must recognize that the last two decades have brought about a unique confluence of macroenvironmental factors—sociocultural, political, legal, economic, technological, and geographic—that have facilitated business and cultural integration among nations. Each of these factors is a key element in a business environment that has become increasingly conducive to elevating the importance of strategic management in the globalization of sport.

Sociocultural Factors

As discussed earlier in the chapter, the sociocultural dimension concerns issues related to a particular population and consists of an understanding of the demographics, lifestyle, and social values of a nation. Demographics (e.g., the size, age, level of education, disposable income, and diversity of a population), the lifestyle of the population (e.g., the size of households, the leisure versus work orientation of a society), and the social values of a society (what it considers good or bad at a given point in time and its tastes and preferences) have tremendous influence on the activities of sport organizations. The characteristics of the sport product or service, marketing and advertising, and pricing strategies differ based on the sociocultural characteristics of a society.

For example, a sport scoreboard company may have recognized a few years ago that foreign sport markets and fans were significantly different from those in the United States, which has well-developed and varied professional, college, and university markets. The demand for sophisticated scoreboards and scoring products at the time was likely not significant outside the United States, and therefore the company would have decided to move forward slowly with global expansion plans. As sport facilities across the world were built and fans' tastes changed, the company might have ramped up their business in targeted countries where large amenity-laden spectator sport facilities were being built.

For other sport-facility-related companies, cultural variations in fan behavior are paramount. For example, sport fans in many nations view the sporting contest as a spectator event only. They attend the event and are fervent supporters of their teams, but they drink and eat before or after the game rather than during the contest. For sport food service companies and facility managers, cultural behavioral norms may limit revenue streams in food and beverage service. One of the most difficult sociocultural barriers to international expansion of football (soccer) in the United States has been an American cultural norm that values American football over all other sports. Conversely, the popularity of football (soccer) has been a major hurdle faced by all American professional sport leagues seeking to penetrate markets outside the United States.

Language barriers have also created challenges for companies attempting to introduce their products into foreign markets. There are many noteworthy and sometimes humorous anecdotes of U.S. companies' failures to overcome language and translation issues. One legendary story concerns Nike, which ran a commercial with people from nations across the globe supposedly saying the corporate slogan "Just Do It." After the commercial aired worldwide, Nike officials were surprised to learn that one Samburu tribesman featured in the ad was not saying "Just Do It." Literally translated, his message was, "I don't want these; give me big shoes" (Daft & Marcic, 1998).

Political and Legal Factors

The political and legal factors in a nation consist of the regulatory environment; the entities that have the legal right to establish laws, rules, and regulations (e.g., congress, courts); and political groups that, although they do not possess legal power, can influence the regulatory environment (e.g., unions, environmental groups, lobbying groups). Political stability, low trade barriers, and favorable regulations are among the factors that have enhanced globalization of sport organizations. A changing international political and legal scene has also opened up new markets to sport organizations in some previously closed nations such as the former Soviet Union. For example, in 2002 U.S.-based SFX Sports formed a joint venture with Russian political consultant firm Novocom to represent Russian athletes, including tennis, football, and basketball stars (Kaplan, 2002). Such a partnership would not have been possible under the previous Communist government. Additionally, economic integration pacts such as the European Union (EU) that allow free movement of goods, services, and people, and organizations such as the World Trade Organization (WTO) that have lowered global trade barriers, are among the factors that have further increased growth and intensity of competition in sport industry.

Although a changing political landscape may open up opportunities for sport organizations, governmental control of sport (especially amateur sport), trade barriers, and a strong presence of political groups (e.g., unions, environmental groups) continue to present challenges to sport managers. Many governments have specific policies for transfer of funds or strict foreign exchange regulations. Some rules restrict cash from leaving or entering the country. Tax regulations, exchange rates, import and export laws, ownership regulations, and copyright protections, all of which are under the purview of host country governments, significantly affect the terms and conditions of international initiatives. Sport organizations seeking to engage in international operations must be well versed in local laws and regulations. They must shape their business plans to account for variations between nations, especially in regard to laws that pertain to ownership, legal protections, financial transactions, and tax policy. Organizations that fail to consider these important factors and create plans to overcome the resulting barriers to operation will sabotage their efforts for international expansion.

Sport managers must also consider regulations of international and national governing bodies as well. For example, European club football regulations have restricted participation of non-EU players. By limiting the number of Africa-based players, particularly in France, regulations have prevented talented young African footballers from gaining European competitive training and experience. The regulations have been adopted in an attempt to favor local players and to secure more opportunities and roster spots for EU-born players, but they have had the resultant effect of limiting player development efforts among many African and EU-based clubs.

Economic Factors

Economic factors such as supply and demand, the labor profile (e.g., size, cost, productivity, level of education), availability and cost of capital, availability of natural resources, and adequacy and cost of infrastructure (e.g., waterways, railways, roads, airways, and electronic networks) are important variables in sport organizations' decisions to expand beyond their geographical borders. For example, in the late 1990s the increase of gross national product per capita and personal leisure time in Taiwan and a subsequent trend toward interest in personal fitness precipitated the entry of many foreign sporting goods companies into that country (Chen, 1999). Sportswear and sporting goods manufacturers are examples of organizations that may be motivated to expand globally in an effort to enhance their bottom line by securing less expensive foreign labor.

Technological Factors

Advancements in new products and processes are considered important technological factors in enhancing globalization of sport organizations.

Innovation in information technologies and broadcasting has tremendously enhanced live communication and eliminated communication barriers. Satellites, computer networks, the World Wide Web, cell phones, and digital technologies are making it possible for people around the world to witness events, share information, conduct transactions, and do business in real time.

In the world of sport, games, highlights, scores, and sport news are broadcast worldwide in seconds and made available to billions of consumers in hundreds of nations.

The evolution of transportation technology has also played an important part in overcoming geographical and logistical time boundaries. Improved transportation systems and technologies now make it possible for sport organizations to transport and exchange resources around the world in a few short days, if not overnight. New technologies not only help sport organizations operate more effectively and efficiently but also, by enhancing organizational speed and flexibility, have broken down geographical and time barriers to competing in the global marketplace.

New revenue streams, marketing opportunities, and educational resources that have been developed through new technologies provide additional opportunities for sport organizations. For example, because of the creation of international broadcast networks, professional leagues and tour sport organizations ranging from figure skating to rodeo are now able to sell international broadcast rights and leverage sponsorship deals through the creation of global audiences.

Geographic Factors

The geographic location, climate, and ease of access to a country are other factors that can give rise to environmental trends that must be considered in the strategic management process. Geography and climate shape managerial decisions such as selecting a country for sport activities, determining methods of transferring goods and services, deciding whether and where to relocate, and choosing event sites. For example, geographical factors including ease of access are important in the selection of sites and training facilities for the Winter and Summer Olympics. In some sports athletes have traditionally relocated to train based on geography and climate. For example, many participants in the Tour

Learning Activity

Select a sport that you are familiar with. Make a list of sociocultural, political, legal, economic, technological, and geographic factors that would affect future trends in that sport. What do these trends mean for the international growth of the sport?

de France temporarily relocate to France to train because of the terrain characteristics, climate, and proximity to the event. Long-distance runners have been known to relocate to geographical locations where high elevations provide the added component of thin-air training. For professional baseball players, off-season training camps and leagues located in Latin America provide a climate conducive to baseball. Training camps in Switzerland, Italy, and Austria provide facilities and conditions ideal for downhill skiing.

A sport manager involved in international operations must engage in ongoing trend analysis to help the organization respond effectively and efficiently to changes in the dynamic world marketplace. Trends may be long term or short lived. They are of varying strength as well as varying duration. Trends may exist in a variety of dimensions including sociocultural, political, legal, economic, and technological. The common denominator is that trends are constantly changing and shaping the business environment in which sport organizations operate. The challenge for the sport manager is not only to identify these trends but also to find meaning in them and to translate that meaning into organizational action.

Social Responsibility Guidelines

Although a trend analysis for today's sport industry indicates that myriad opportunities are available to companies seeking to compete globally, a variety of challenges or barriers stand in the way of successful entry into foreign markets. Cost, excessive regulation, lack of necessary resources, limited fan interest, language and cultural barriers, nationalism, and political barriers all present challenges for companies seeking to compete globally. For some

sport managers, cultural sensitivity and ethical operation is lost in the pursuit of organizational or individual goals. Their approach may be best described as ethnocentric because they believe that their culture and way of doing things are superior to that of the host country. Therefore, they need not concern themselves with local culture, mores, or standards. Their own organizational objectives supersede any local concerns or considerations. Such an approach can lead to exploitation of local workers or the environment. Because of such practices, sport organizations around the world face growing concerns over unethical practices in sport management. All organizations must strive to integrate principles of fairness, honesty, and respect in cross-cultural management. Many sport organizations seek not only to establish and apply international management standards but also to contribute in a positive manner to the quality of life in the host country.

The codes of conduct for multinational organizations, or international business ethics, encompass business conduct and the morals of these organizations in their relationship to all people and entities with whom they come into contact. To ensure just and fair conduct by organizations in dealing with the public, devising social responsibility guidelines for the corporation and training all employees along these guidelines are of the utmost importance. The sidebar provides a list of social responsibility guidelines for multinational organizations. Issues of corporate social responsibility and human rights are discussed in more detail in chapter 16.

Varying international standards for behavior complicate the ethics dilemma. For example, fears over the increasing use of drugs in sport have led to an international outcry about athletes who try to gain an unfair advantage in competition. Recent Olympics and international competitions have demonstrated that concerns over the regulation of drug use are real. The World Anti-Doping Agency continues to seek to develop and enforce a unified international drug use code and has taken the lead in addressing this important issue despite that fact that not all countries or all governing bodies agree with their approach. This example helps to illustrate the complexity of managing international interests and establishing accepted standard codes of behavior for international sport integration.

Multinational organizations operating in emerging countries face many obstacles in trading with

Social Responsibility Guidelines for Multinational Corporations

- Appropriate products and technologies
- Appropriate marketing practices
- Protection of customers
- Protection of physical environment
- Enhancement of employee education and training
- Honesty in employee relations
- Protection of employee health and welfare

- Sensitivity to minority and women's issues
- Corporate philanthropy
- Honesty in external relations
- Keeping out of local politics
- Formulation of specific ethical codes
- Reduction and elimination of inequalities
- Enhancement of human rights
- Not making profit from human misery

---

these countries. Technological problems, low levels of skill and education in the workforce, lack of capital availability, cultural differences, political instability and corruption, poorly developed transportation infrastructure and communication facilities, and limited availability of energy are major issues of concern for multinational organizations.

On the other hand, the presence of these organizations in emerging countries can create problems. Corporations may offer inferior technologies and products, contribute to class differences, interfere in local politics, contribute to corruption, widen the wealth gap between the rich and the poor, exploit labor, and fail to protect the physical environment. Footwear companies and sporting goods manufacturers continue to deal with the ethical challenges to their practice of foreign manufacturing. Critics have historically focused on conditions in foreign factories, use of underage workers, and sexual harassment and corporal punishment of workers (Tedeschi, 1997). Despite the ongoing debate over China's human rights policies, its low production costs and high technical skills combined with a commercially protective political policy has created a rather compliant workforce, and China has quickly become the

world's largest producer and exporter of footwear (RNCOS, 2008).

The selection of global strategies must be based on a deep understanding of the culture and respect for the host nation and its people. Successful foreign expansion often depends on the ability of an organization to balance sound business decisions with cultural sensitivity. To succeed, sport managers must be culturally aware and flexible. They must be able to abandon ideas based on ethnocentricity—the belief that one's own country and culture is superior to others and offers the one best way of doing things. For a sport manager to integrate successfully into a different culture, he or she must develop an understanding and sensitivity to the laws, regulations, values, norms, and standards of behavior and business operations within the host country.

Future Trends in the International Sport Industry

Advancements in communication and transportation technologies, economic integration pacts that eliminate geographic barriers among countries, availability of international capital, and increasing membership in trade organizations that reduce trade barriers and at the same time protect property rights are among the factors that have created sophisticated and complex market opportunities for the sport industry. The sport industry is not only a provider of various products and services but also the provider of passion. No other industry can create so much passion across nations and peoples. The FIFA World Cup and the Olympics are prime examples of sport events that can get millions of

Learning Activity

Research a sporting goods, apparel, or footwear company that outsources production. Evaluate how this organization has managed its operations in terms of guidelines for socially responsible management.

people focused passionately on the products of this industry.

To address the complexity and intricacy involved in successfully operating and managing an organization in the sport industry, in-depth knowledge of the sociocultural, economic, political, legal, and technological environments is a necessity. Rapid transfer of technology, the interconnectedness of international financial markets, the diversity of stakeholders (e.g., customers, employees, managers, agents, sponsors, and suppliers), and the activities of cable, Internet, and television companies create a tremendous challenge for the planning and operations of sport organizations.

The IOC's granting of the Olympic Games to Beijing for 2008 and China's rise to prominence in the footwear industry will likely further enhance the opening of Asian markets to a diverse array of sport goods and services. The increasing appetite of Chinese people for Western culture along with low costs and high skill levels will continue to facilitate foreign alliances. The fastest growing markets are likely to encompass South Asia and Central Asia, the Middle East, and Central and Eastern Europe. Although economic development in these countries and the availability of goods resulting from freedom of movement across these countries has increased, the proliferation of communication technologies will continue to feed consumption of sport brands that are often perceived as an important symbol of social status. In South Africa the hosting of the 2010 World Cup has further opened this market to the international sport industry.

Although professional baseball is well established in Japan and Latin American countries and has seen growth in Israel through the creation of a new league, Asia, Europe, Africa, and Latin America still consider football (soccer) the supreme sport. With ever-increasing emphasis on soccer in U.S. schools within the past two decades, and some growth in public awareness of the U.S. professional soccer league, the U.S. soccer market may provide a remarkable opportunity for future growth and expansion.

Corporations around the world will continue to use sport as a vehicle to market their products both nationally and internationally. International companies and teams will seek strategic sponsorship alliances with U.S. sport organizations as a way to enhance brand image, increase product sales, and build market share in the United States, and U.S.-based companies and leagues such as McDonald's and the NFL will continue to use sport sponsorship and exhibition matches as vehicles to support international market penetration.

As a whole, the sport industry has a bright outlook. Tremendous global growth opportunities are available across a diverse array of sport goods and services and related industries. Opportunities for growth, however, are likely to be tempered by economic conditions and world politics. As previously discussed, the knowledge and expertise necessary for managing and operating in a complex environment have created an enormous challenge for managers of sport organizations.

Summary

Sport organizations around the world seek to secure the benefits of doing business beyond the borders of their home countries. By entering the global marketplace, sport organizations may seek to achieve a variety of business goals such as enhancing their brands, reaching new markets, and increasing sales. International expansion is most likely to be successful when companies use the strategic management process to drive globalization. Through this process, organizations can ensure that they are moving into countries that offer a comparative advantage and provide environments that are conducive to achieving their stated goals.

The strategic management process also helps the organization select the optimal corporate, business, and functional levels of strategy for expansion. In effect, the strategic management process drives not only where to expand globally but also how to expand. Such strategies may include direct investment, joint ventures, outsourcing, merger, acquisition, or strategic alliance. In every situation, the sport manager must be mindful of environmental trends and forecasts and understand how the dynamic international marketplace continually provides both opportunities and barriers to expansion. Recognition of the set of complex legal, political, environmental, economic, and ethical conditions that affect operations in a foreign country is essential to the long-term survival and prosperity of sport organizations seeking to do business in the global marketplace.

? Review and Discussion Questions

1. What factors in recent years have led professional team sports to seek to expand in foreign markets? Which league has been most successful? Why?

2. Compare and contrast the various global strategies for international expansion.

3. Explain the strategic planning process.

4. Look up statistics and basic information on the sport industries in China, India, or Australia (or all three). Based on the information that you find, what strategies should sport managers consider when entering those markets?

5. Why should sport organizations choose to operate in a socially responsible manner when this approach often appears to undermine short-term profit objectives?

Intercultural Management in Sport Organizations

Eric W. MacIntosh, PhD
University of Ottawa, Canada

Gonzalo A. Bravo, PhD
West Virginia University, USA

Ming Li, EdD
Ohio University, USA

Chapter Objectives

After studying this chapter, you will be able to do the following:

- Describe the concept of intercultural management
- Identify characteristics of national cultures that can affect sport organizations and management
- Understand the concept of organizational culture
- Discuss ways in which managers can socialize employees into an intercultural organization
- Identify the various ways in which a manager can promote a sense of community in a diverse workforce
- Work more effectively in an intercultural environment

Key Terms

The plethora of sporting opportunities today that involve multicultural, multilingual, and diverse exchanges is far greater than ever before. Mega sport events, major athletic competitions, and minor global exchanges require people from different backgrounds to work together to operate and run successful competitions and businesses. Yet working with people from different backgrounds is not an easy matter. Understanding oneself is difficult enough, but having an appreciation for different ways of seeing the world, organizing, managing, and communicating is a substantial challenge. Arguably, intercultural management is one of the most important and timely topics in the world of sport management today. Reconciling various management dilemmas requires a deeper appreciation for oneself, the organization, and the entire picture.

The purpose of the chapter is to develop an understanding and appreciation for cultural differences and diversity that exist within a global business environment. Thus, throughout this chapter, concepts considered important within the process of understanding intercultural management are discussed. This chapter provides sport management examples to highlight the various ways in which today's workforce must consider differences and diversity, and incorporate them into daily organizational practice. Although few universal principles of management are germane to all situations, we have attempted to identify ways in which an intercultural manager or employee can embrace the myriad of differences that exist in sport management today.

Why Intercultural Management Matters

As the movement of people between countries becomes more fluid and the power of the Internet continues to blur operational boundaries for organizations, the appreciation of intercultural management becomes ever more important in sport management. The world of sport is at a crossroads. The next 10 years should be extremely interesting as professional sport continues to expand into new areas, as the Olympics and youth Olympics come under further public scrutiny, and as business networks evolve and strengthen globally. Intercultural management is a concept that requires careful consideration and deliberation, and its application is highlighted in many chapters of this textbook.

Today's sport leagues around the world are filled with coaches, players, and even team owners from various backgrounds (Maguire & Bale, 1994; Maguire, Jarvie, Mansfield, & Bradley, 2002). Although this sport labor migration is highly evident in the more developed sport markets like the United States and Europe, it is also occurring at a fast pace in many other areas around the world where qualified and skilled professional sport workers are needed. To illustrate, tables 3.1, 3.2, and 3.3 provide examples of coaches, players, and owners who have worked or continue to work abroad. Their movement reflects the *trend of increased global mobility* within professional and amateur sport and highlights the need for effective intercultural management even further.

The expanding phenomenon of sport employees working abroad is changing the landscape of many professional and amateur sporting systems and has clear implications for management of these organizations. Sport labor migration raises a series of challenges not only for the sport system that embraces the migrant athlete or coach but also for the home country that loses qualified sport personnel to more attractive and financially stable sport markets. Among other challenges, host leagues must integrate these athletes into a new culture through socialization and training. For their part, athletes must adapt and have fair expectations.

Intercultural management in sport affects multiple layers of the organization, such as human resource practices (e.g., recruitment, training, labor laws), communication (e.g., languages, media handling), financial, marketing, and communications, to name but a few. For example, in the area of marketing and consumer research, Chun, Gentry, and McGinnis (2004) noted that fans' identification with a sport is built not only through connection to the players or the team but also through symbolic meanings attached to the sport, which are shaped by cultural values and beliefs. The researchers suggested that the way in which Americans and Japanese fans experience baseball is strongly marked by specific cultural differences. Thus, baseball in the United States has been typically associated with a return to the past and a rural experience. In Japanese culture, however, baseball evokes a path to modernism.

Table 3.1 Selected Coaches Working Abroad (2008–2009)

Name	Sport	Country of origin	Team	Host country
Carlo Ancelotti	M-Football	Italy	Chelsea FC (EPL)[1]	England
David Blatt	M-Basketball	USA	Dynamo Moscow (EL)[2]	Russia
Fabio Capello	M-Football	Italy	England National Team	England
Igor Grinko	Rowing	Russia	China National Team	China
Guus Hiddink	M-Football	Netherlands	Russian National Team	Russia
Irina Illiashenko	W-Gymnastics	Ukraine	Brazil Women's National Team	Brazil
Jim Lefevbre	Baseball	USA	China National Team	China
Bora Milutinovic	M-Football	Serbia	Iraq National Team	Iraq
Carolina Morace	W-Football	Italy	Canada National Team	Canada
Manuel Pellegrini	M-Football	Chile	Real Madrid CF (SLL)[3]	Spain
Lang Ping	W-Volleyball	China	U.S. Women's National Team	USA
Preki Radosavljevic	M-Football	Serbia	CD Chivas USA (MLS)[4]	USA
Frank Rikjaard	M-Football	Netherlands	Galatasaray SK (TSL)[5]	Turkey
Ulf Samuelson	Ice hockey	Sweden	Phoenix Coyotes (NHL)[6]	USA
Joel Santana	M-Football	Brazil	South African National Team	South Africa
Pia Sundhage	W-Football	Sweden	U.S. Women's National Team	USA
Luis Felipe Scolari	M-Football	Brazil	FC Bunyodkor (UL)[7]	Uzbekistan
Otilio Toledo	Boxing	Cuba	Brazil National Team	Brazil
Giovanni Trapattoni	M-Football	Italy	Republic of Ireland National Team	Ireland
Bobby Valentine	Baseball	USA	Chiba Lotte Marines (NPB)[8]	Japan
Louis Van Gaal	M-Football	Netherlands	FC Bayern Munich (DFBL)[9]	Germany
Arsene Wenger	M-Football	France	Arsenal FC (EPL)[1]	England

[1]English Premier Football League; [2]Euro Basketball League; [3]Spanish La Liga; [4]Major League Soccer; [5]Turkish Süper Lig; [6]National Hockey League; [7]Uzbek League; [8]Nippon Professional Baseball; [9]Deutsche Fußball-Bundesliga

The critical value of the role of culture in conducting sport business is also illustrated by Sofka (2008), who noted that business practices that are successful in the United States might fail in China. He noted that franchise apparel companies like Adidas and Nike have decided to end their traditional retail strategy in China because most retailers tend not to follow multinational standards and directives from a foreign company. Instead, these multinational companies have moved into a vertical model of expansion by taking total possession of their businesses through their company-owned stores. In a similar vein, Lombardo (2010), when discussing the state of the NBA in China, pointed out that although the market in China for sport business presents numerous opportunities, it also presents great challenges not only because of the protectionist role and direct involvement of government but also because a completely different business culture is in place. Marc Ganis, a sport executive who has done business in China, stated, "The expectation of walking in with a great business card and a battery of attorneys may work in the U.S., but it doesn't work in China" (cited in Lombardo, 2010, p. 43).

A similar example that illustrates the complexity of doing business in China is shown in the documentary *Bird's Nest: Herzog & de Meuron in China* (Schaub & Schindhelm, 2008). The film shows how two distinct cultures clashed when dealing with the construction of a landmark building for China—the Olympic Stadium for the Beijing

Table 3.2 Selected Athletes Working Abroad (2008–2009)

Name	Sport	Country of origin	Team	Host country
Bobby Abreu	Baseball	Venezuela	L.A. Angels of Anaheim (MLB)[1]	USA
David Beckham	M-Football	England	L.A. Galaxy (MLS)[2]	USA
Yossi Benayoun	M-Football	Israel	Liverpool FC (EPL)[3]	England
Zdeno Chara	Ice hockey	Slovakia	Boston Bruins (NHL)[4]	USA
Francesc Fabregas	M-Football	Spain	Arsenal FC (EPL)[3]	England
Ruslan Fedotenko	Ice Hockey	Ukraine	Pittsburgh Penguins (NHL)[4]	USA
Manu Ginobili	M-Basketball	Argentina	San Antonio Spurs (NBA)[5]	USA
Hamed Haddadi	M-Basketball	Iran	Memphis Grizzlies (NBA)[5]	USA
Mauricio Isla	M-Football	Chile	Udinese Calcio (SA-LC)[6]	Italy
Avery John	M-Football	Trinidad and Tobago	D.C. United (MLS)[2]	USA
Ricardo Izecson dos Santos Leite (Kaka)	M-Football	Brazil	Real Madrid CF (SLL)[7]	Spain
Kaloyan Mahlyanov	Sumo	Bulgaria	Japan Sumo Association	Japan
Javier Mascherano	M-Football	Argentina	Liverpool FC (EPL)[3]	England
Hideki Matsui	Baseball	Japan	New York Yankees (MLB)[1]	USA
Yao Ming	M-Basketball	China	Houston Rockets (NBA)[5]	USA
David Ortiz	Baseball	Dominican Republic	Boston Red Sox (MLB)[1]	USA
Alexander Ovechkin	Ice hockey	Russia	Washington Capitals (NHL)[4]	USA
Sidnei Sidao Santos	M-Volleyball	Brazil	Trenkwalder Modena (LP-SA)[8]	Italy
Ichiro Suzuki	Baseball	Japan	Seattle Mariners (MLB)[1]	USA

[1]Major League Baseball; [2]Major League Soccer; [3]English Premier Football League; [4]National Hockey League; [5]National Basketball Association; [6]Serie-A Lega Calcio; [7]Spanish La Liga; [8]Lega Pallavolo Serie-A

Olympics in 2008, or the Bird's Nest, as the Chinese media renamed it. The movie documents how a Swiss firm dealt with the challenges involved in putting in place such a monumental architectural masterpiece in a foreign culture. Throughout the construction process, the firm has to reconcile and tactfully negotiate all sorts of challenges with the Chinese authorities, ranging from dealing with a reinterpretation of their original ideas, to the building, to applying various criteria to reduce construction costs (Dawson, 2008).

The understanding of culture also plays a critical role in sport television commercials, as shown by Jackson, Brandl-Bredenbeck, and John (2005), who found that violence related to sport advertisements took on different meanings for people in Germany, New Zealand, and Japan. An advertisement that showed a prominent cricketer with a chainsaw was not interpreted as violent by people in New Zealand, but those from Germany and Japan thought that the commercial contained a high degree of violence. Conversely, an ad that showed a well-known football player competing with all sorts of evil forces during a football match was not perceived as violent by Germans, but it was considered violent by people in New Zealand and Japan. Findings of this study suggest the importance of recognizing not only the critical role of culture but also the popularity of particular sports in different cultures. The bottom line, then, is that a commercial from a multinational that uses sport must always consider the cultural context in which that ad will be shown. This simple illustration displays just one way in which sport managers must be knowledgeable about the environment in which they operate.

Intercultural management is concerned with the various ways in which people from diverse

Table 3.3 Selected Foreign Owners and Main Investors in Professional Sport Teams (2008–2009)

Name	Sport	Country of origin	Team	Host country
Roman Abramovich	M-Football	Russia	Chelsea FC (EPL)[1]	England
Abu Dhabi United Group Investment and Development Limited	M-Football	Saudi Arabia	Manchester City FC (EPL)[1]	England
Ali al-Faraj	M-Football	Saudi Arabia	Portsmouth FC (EPL)[1]	England
Mohamed Al-Fayed	M-Football	Egypt	Fulham FC (EPL)[1]	England
George Gillett and Tom Hicks	M-Football	USA	Liverpool FC (EPL)[1]	England
Malcolm Glazer	M-Football	USA	Manchester United FC (EPL)[1]	England
Yasuaki Kagami	M-Football	Japan	Plymouth Argyle FC (FLC)[2]	England
Stan Kroenke and Alisher Usmanov	M-Football	USA and Uzbekistan	Arsenal FC (EPL)[1]	England
Randy Lerner	M-Football	USA	Aston Villa FC (EPL)[1]	England
Mikhail Prokhorov	M-Basketball	Russia	New Jersey Nets (NBA)[3]	USA
Antonio Cué Sánchez-Navarro and Jorge Vergara Madrigal	M-Football	Mexico	CD Chivas USA (MLS)[4]	USA
Ellis Short	M-Football	USA	Sunderland AFC (EPL)[1]	England
Straumur-Budaras Bank	M-Football	Iceland	West Ham FC (EPL)[1]	England
Carsen Yeung	M-Football	Hong Kong	Birmingham City FC (EPL)[1]	England

[1]English Premier Football League; [2]Football League Championship; [3]National Basketball Association; [4]Major League Soccer

backgrounds can work together in an efficient and effective manner. Sport managers must come to understand and appreciate intercultural management in part by reflecting on how their personal value system shapes their attitudes and behavior. This skill, personal reflexivity, is described in chapter 1. Further, understanding how things are done in an organization plays an important role in fostering a successful intercultural environment. For instance, expectations about punctuality, leaving early, working late, working from home, and work attire are ways in which work environments may differ from country to country, yet all are important ingredients to successful integration into an organization. Understanding these elements, combined with some cultural research and sensitivity training, can go a long way in promoting positive intercultural relationships.

One of the most important elements to consider when working within an intercultural setting is the notion of avoiding **ethnocentric** behavior. A person who is ethnocentric evaluates people of a different race or culture by criteria that are specific to his or her own. Hence, assuming that one's own way of doing things is the correct way has the potential to cause serious conflict and misunderstandings when working in intercultural settings (Chaney & Martin, 2004). Indeed, this type of behavior can cause people to resent their new colleague's way of doing things. Poor working conditions and failed projects are often the outcome.

Therefore, one key aspect of working in diverse settings is to avoid ethnocentric thinking. The talent pool of athletes, trainers, and coaches from different countries integrating into one organization or team can create many types of conflict. The false notion that there is one best way to do things can certainly impede progress. One of the worst things that managers or employees can do is to believe that their own ideas, ways of doing things, and answers to questions are the only right way or right answer to accomplishing tasks. Indeed, such ethnocentric views can create an inordinate amount of conflict and misunderstanding between colleagues. Evaluating people from different cultural backgrounds based on one's own specific beliefs, or lens, may be the most detrimental aspect to intercultural management other than outright

> ## Tips for People Working Within an Intercultural Environment

1. Keep an open mind in all situations; avoid ethnocentric behaviors.
2. Know your personal strengths, beliefs, attitudes, and preferences for behavior.
3. Be patient when working within a new context and fully engage in listening.
4. Know how to leverage diversity and potentially different opinions.
5. Be able to put yourself in the other person's position when making decisions.
6. Ask open-ended questions (e.g., who, what, why, where).
7. Ask closed questions (e.g., invite a yes or a no response).
8. Be observant of how things operate, be curious, and be sensitive.
9. Clear up any misunderstandings right away.
10. Do not jump to hasty conclusions about a new person and her or his culture.

Adapted from Carte & Fox (2004) and Rabotin (2008).

deceit and fraudulent behavior. The sidebar shows additional tips for working in an intercultural environment.

Sport business organizations and sport governing bodies that are multicultural and conduct multinational operations (e.g., Nike, Adidas, Rawlings, Reebok, IOC, FINA, FIFA) face challenges such as language differences (written and oral), business laws, taxation laws, immigration laws, and regulatory impediments sanctioned by local or regional trade organizations. Multinational organizations are also influenced by local customs and idiosyncratic factors (Dunning, 1989; Samiee, 1999). Thus, the challenge of a multicultural workforce wherein personal values and ways of doing things may drastically differ complicates matters of integration, socialization, and daily work life. What may be valued and work in one country may fail in another. Making business deals through technology is one example. In some areas of the world it is considered important to make decisions face to face, whereas in other areas it is common to do things over the phone or by e-mail. Hence, the value associated with one-to-one communication and interpersonal feelings may be more important in one country than in another.

National Culture

Although the concept of a **national culture** is different in many important ways from the concept of organizational culture, it is nonetheless an important consideration because it can inform general business understanding in foreign markets for newcomers. A systematic investigation of a national culture within a discrete set of variables will not describe the whole picture of a country, and in some cases it may not apply at all. Yet for the intercultural manager or employee set to embark on new relations, examining the national culture is a good starting point toward learning about what he or she may see and experience. This investigation is an important mental mapping exercise before leaving for a new place of work or study. The seminal work of Geert Hofstede (1980, 1991) provides an informative basis that can add to the understanding of expectations before working with a colleague of a different culture in a new setting. Hofstede's research indicated that countries can be understood based on the following value dimensions:

◆ *Power distance*, or the level of acceptance regarding the distribution of power in an organization, is a key aspect of national culture. A high power distance score indicates organizations where persons of lesser power accept and expect decision making from positions of authority (e.g., India, Mexico, and Brazil). A low power distance score indicates organizations where authorities foster a close working relationship with subordinates and include them in decision making (e.g., Austria, New Zealand, and Denmark). Knowing the power distance can inform newcomers of potential organizational practices or management strategies that they may encounter.

◆ *Uncertainty avoidance*, or the extent to which people are comfortable or uncomfortable dealing with unstructured situations. For instance, having a low uncertainty avoidance score indicates that there is greater acceptance to having less rules, laws, regulations, and change (e.g., Denmark, United Kingdom, and the United States). Another way to view this dimension is the propensity or intolerance for uncertainty and ambiguity in society. For instance, places with a high uncertainty avoidance score (e.g., France, Japan, and Chile) prefer rules, laws, and regulations, want to minimize risk taking, and are less tolerant for uncertainty and ambiguity.

◆ *Individualism–collectivism*, or the extent to which individual effort and success is valued within a country (e.g., Australia, Canada, and the United States) versus a broader focus and loyalty to the group (e.g., Greece, Indonesia, and Mexico). This dimension highlights the propensity by which people are integrated into groups (e.g., collectivism sees high levels of group integration). The drive for success and how that is defined can differ between people of various backgrounds when examining this dimension.

◆ *Masculinity–femininity*, or the extent to which achievements that are valued have more masculine or feminine qualities (extent to which typical "male" roles characterized by assertiveness and competitiveness, e.g., Italy and Japan, are distinguished from typical "female" roles characterized by nurturing, modesty, and caring, e.g., Denmark and Sweden). Thus, masculinity versus femininity exhibits the degree of assertiveness and competition versus modesty and caring.

Later, a fifth dimension was added, long-term versus short-term orientation (Hofstede & Bond, 1984). This dimension refers to an individual's preference to focus and prepare primarily for future events with a longer time frame attached (e.g., Hong Kong and Japan) or to concentrate on the present and the fulfillment of current obligations (e.g., France and the United States). Having a short-term orientation is more representative of fulfillment of social obligations and protection of one's "face" (Hofstede & Bond, 1984).

Knowing that organizational culture can be influenced by the national culture in which it operates, the employee new to an organization in a different country should become acquainted with the national culture and embrace the differences

that exist. The case study on page 60 illustrates how values at the national level play a key role in the management of sport events and how in certain countries the ways of doing things may be much different from what a person is used to or would expect.

Learning Activity

Consider what *best practice* means to you and reflect on the professional criteria on which you base your everyday management activities. Analyze how many of these activities may be based on your own culture and expectations. How would these criteria differ if you were based in a different culture? How would you adjust if any of them changed suddenly?

If you intend to work successfully on an international stage, you will need to develop a particular sensitivity to the culturally based factors that you usually take for granted but that will change, often subtly, depending on the culture in which you are currently immersed.

Shenkar, Luo, and Yeheskel (2008) noted that the cultural distance metaphor has popularized culture as a research variable but has also forced the phenomenon into what they coined a methodological and theoretical straightjacket that has proved to be counterproductive for understanding culture in international management. For instance, the premise that a culture clash based on predefined ways of thinking will occur when East meets West in the conduct of business is not always true. Such a simplification has played a central role in the descent of international management scholarship from the already limiting ethnocentric research.

With that said, the ready intercultural manager should be knowledgeable of several aspects of international business based on national customs and include them in her or his repertoire: handshakes, bowing and greetings, dining etiquette, the physical space of offices, gift exchanging, punctuality for business meetings, business attire (casual, formal), meeting expectations (sensitivity

Time Is of the Essence

Stephen Stuart, PhD, University of Ottawa, Canada

Imagine the scene: You are the senior manager responsible for organizing and delivering the Dubai-based regional press launch of a major international sporting event, intended to encompass each of the five continents during the course of the following year. Previous launches have taken place, without a hitch, in other major cities around the globe, and your team is comfortable with the task of working together.

This launch is particularly important to you and the organization because of the number of high-profile sponsors and potential sponsors residing in the region who want to promote an upbeat and positive image of the contemporary, world-class facilities of the emirate.

In conjunction with your regional partners, and following best practice, you have meticulously prepared and planned this event over the past few months. You have in place contingency plans for every eventuality that you could anticipate, and everyone is on standby alert in case anything untoward should arise. For example, you have secured the most appropriate location available— the presidential suite on the 15th floor of an international hotel (and Dubai is full of such amazing locations)—and put in place all the media and hospitality facilities that you need to satisfy a highly demanding audience. You have arranged for local and international media journalists and broadcasters to be present and catered to their technological requirements. You have facilitated the arrival and hospitality needs of your international partners, and you have satisfied the corporate needs of your local sponsors.

As the hour of the launch approaches on the day of this major event, all the key players are ready to deliver their well-rehearsed, finely tuned, and approved performances. Everyone from local royalty to corporate dignitaries and governmental functionaries, from sport stars to journalists and broadcasters, arrives at the destination. You are ready to press the "go" button when suddenly the entire city suffers its first major blackout in 20 years.

This is one eventuality that you have not prepared for. Of course, the hotel has backup generators in place to kick in automatically when the power fails, but their priorities are the air conditioning units, the fire and security services, and the elevators. The generators are not hooked up to the power circuits supplying electricity to nonemergency lighting and other services, such as those needed by the media to record and broadcast the event.

So what would you do? You would revert to survival mode and do what you have to do to save the event from becoming the most high-profile disaster of your career. Therefore, you would take control by sending most of your team out to locate the hotel's engineers and summon them to your suite, where you would persuade them to divert power and resolve the situation. Meanwhile, you would deploy the balance of your people to placate the high-powered and often volatile people who are in your care. After the engineers arrive, you would patiently explain the problem to them and request that they rectify it "now." The engineers duly smile and nod agreement that the situation is, indeed, serious, and that, "Insha Allah," all will be resolved.

At this point the clash of cultures occurs, and therein lies the core issue. For the engineers, mostly from countries on the Indian subcontinent, the overall problem (the loss of power) was not of their making, so they could do little to resolve it—hence their reply, in a borrowed Arabic phrase, that loosely translated means "If it is God's will." In this instance they hoped that the situation would be resolved at some time in the future, but they did not see what they could do in the present. The study of chronemics, how people perceive, structure, and react to time, indicates that the conception of time, particularly "now," is culturally defined; that is, there are major differences in perception between cultures. The manager in question was using his Western perception of "now" to mean something immediate. The engineers used a combination of Arabic, Indian, Pakistani, and Bangladeshi perceptions to arrive at a meaning of "soon, but at some point in the future."

The situation could have been further compounded had the manager resorted to the often-used but ill-advised tactic of becoming impatient, or raising her or his voice, in an attempt to overcome this cultural barrier. But the manager, despite increasingly irate colleagues and clients, patiently explained the complete scenario to the engineers—that all the people present had converged on the suite for the sole purpose of a one-hour media launch, that if the power was not rapidly connected, the opportunity would be lost forever and the cost of establishing the event would be completely wasted, and that the result would be a loss of credibility in the region for the organization and consequently the loss of sponsorship for the international sporting event. Subsequently, the power was quickly rerouted, and the launch went ahead successfully as planned.

Learning Activity

Write a paragraph about stereotypes that you may encounter when working with someone from another country, such as Japan, the United States, France, Canada, or Mexico. How would you ensure that you do not fall for these stereotypes?

to time), idle conversation at work (acceptable topics), conversations deemed acceptable, and a number of other issues.

Although typical practices and behaviors vary from country to country (e.g., handshakes in North America, bowing in Japan), and the behaviors (e.g., firm handshake versus weak handshake) can send mixed messages, managers need to remain open to these types of greetings at all times in a business environment. People value common courtesy and manners regardless of lines that appear on a world map.

An interesting example that illustrates differences between cultures is the case of presenting a business card (Chaney & Martin, 2004). The practice in the United States of glancing at the business card and promptly putting it in the pocket is considered rude in countries like Japan and China, where the card is often accepted with an attitude of interest and respect. The Japanese and Chinese often take the card in both hands, hold it in front of them, and carefully examine it while making a comment upon its acceptance. Chinese also believe strongly in maintaining a person's status in the most flattering light. Thus, the concept of "face" is important in making a good impression in business dealings. The exchange of business cards is one simple illustration.

Dining practices also vary considerably between cultures. In many parts of the world, such as Spain and Mexico, the main meal is partaken around lunch (2:00 to 4:00 pm), but in the United States and Canada the main meal occurs later in the day, such as at 6:00 pm, or at "dinner time." Ultimately, this difference can influence a person's natural biorhythm and ability to adapt to another time zone (a luxury or plight of international travel). When people are accustomed to eating should not be taken for granted. People need to prepare themselves and perhaps even excuse themselves from a meeting to eat a snack.

Another illustration of differences can be witnessed in the consumption of alcohol. Chinese enjoy alcohol with their meals and are known to hold informal meals before having a more formalized business meeting. Having alcohol with business meals is common and accepted in many parts of China. In contrast, business meetings in many Western countries do not include alcohol, particularly during the lunchtime hours and during preliminary meetings. But business people in Western countries do enjoy "happy hour." Business practices in China tend to become more social in nature over time compared with practices in many Western countries, where business relations tend to remain professional in nature. This difference may illustrate the collective versus individual attitudes noted by Hofstede. Discussion points during business relations in China may include personal information regarding the family, personal feelings, and aspirations. Although these elements can be discussed in Western countries, they are often not encouraged as part of business relations, thus highlighting another difference in business practices. In the United Kingdom, keeping business life separate from personal life is much more common, similar to what may be expected in Canada.

Another example is the role of the company mission statement. In many Western countries the mission statement is acknowledged as an important and potentially binding element of workforce life. In Canada and the United States, the company's mission statement is often used to promote a sense of common understanding and purpose for an organization. Clues to "how things are" in an organization can be found in its mission statement. But there is not a universal buy-in to the importance of having a mission statement. Although the North American workforce is often shaped by the mission statement and employees take the mission to be a serious measure of work, workers in other countries do not. A clear and simple mission statement is one way to come to know about an organization. But a mission statement makes up only part of the picture.

In addition to the aspects of culture immediate to the conduct of business, religion is another aspect that sport managers must take care to respect and accommodate. Although this subject can be difficult to breach, particularly in an intercultural setting where religious rituals and beliefs may present real ramifications to relationships, maintaining an open mind and accepting each person's right to religious freedom are critical when working in a shared environment and space. In some cultures more than others (e.g., Indian culture), discussing religious beliefs is important and is often part of getting to know one another. Embracing family heritage and background is often done in the first meeting with a new person. In many other cultures, however, religion is not openly discussed. Such a topic is breached only after much time and trust building.

Organizational Culture

A shared meaning of work or purpose in any organization is an important way in which people gain a sense of belonging, and this aspect should inform intercultural management practices. The phenomenon of organizational culture is thought to be one of the most important areas of attention for leaders of companies. Generally, **organizational culture** comprises values, beliefs, and assumptions that help guide decision making and describe why an organization is what it is (Martin, 1992; Schein, 1985).

Many scholars believe that organizational culture is a fundamental determinant of behavior. Whereas lower creatures are largely governed by instinct, humans mainly learn their behavior. Given the enormity of different backgrounds within the global sport industry, learned behavior obviously varies a great degree from country to country. For instance, a focus on what is good for the group is an early learned behavior in Japan that is different from the mentality of a focus on what is good for the individual, as found in the United States. Thus, we may expect to see some notable differences in organizational life between Japanese and U.S. organizations based on the differences in learned behavior that occur early in childhood.

A new person (coach, athlete, or staff member) working within an organization for the first time can find ways to understand "how things are done around here" that can inform his or her business behavior. For instance, a person can observe the physical surroundings and the way in which people dress to become informed about whether a business is "casual" in nature or "professional." A person can learn about an organization's culture by observing and ultimately understanding a wide array of symbols, actions, and meanings that take place within the organization. Schein (1985) noted that organizations can be understood based on three progressively deeper levels: artifacts, values and beliefs, and basic assumptions (adapted from Schein, 1985; MacIntosh & Doherty, 2008):

◆ *Level 1:* Artifacts are the most visible manifestations of organizational culture, including such things as dressing norms, stories, informal codes of behavior and conduct, rituals, ceremonies, company awards, jargon, banter, and jokes that members of the company would appreciate. Some common characteristics are the following:

- Visible signs
- Organizational structures
- Organizational processes

◆ *Level 2:* Values and beliefs are composed of organizational strategies, goals, philosophies, mission and vision statements, and the general direction of the organization. Some common characteristics of this level are the following:

- Company strategies
- Company goals
- Company philosophy
- Espoused justification of existence

◆ *Level 3:* Basic assumptions are the underlying assumptions of the organization:

- Unconscious, taken-for-granted beliefs
- Habits of perception
- Thoughts and feelings (ultimate source of values and actions)

Accurately deciphering an organization's culture can take time. Initial inspection at the level of artifacts can provide a general idea about the company, but values form the central aspect of the culture (MacIntosh & Doherty, 2008). "Values are social principles, goals, or standards accepted by persons in a culture. They establish what is proper and improper behavior as well as what is normal and abnormal behavior" (Chaney & Martin, 2004, p. 46). In an intercultural setting, the values are important to understand for several reasons, not the least of which is to have a more complete understanding of what is most important to the organization. Consider the differences between a culture that focuses on the group versus a culture that focuses on individual achievement. Such values tend to focus decision making. As a result, working in an intercultural setting can be a challenge to a person's basic assumptions about what is the right focus of attention and what is the wrong focus of attention.

If you encounter problems in understanding the culture of the organization or the ways of doing things within another country, ask someone who understands the local culture. Using this commonsense approach is an excellent way to gain an appreciation for the ways in which business works in the environment and a way to build a network through establishing a relationship with a mentor.

Organizational culture can also be shaped by geography. For instance, in some Latin American countries, having a siesta is common practice because of the uncomfortably hot afternoon temperatures. Allowing workers to rest and modifying working hours to accommodate this felt need can

alter the common work environment. Further, religious customs can change the manner of work. For instance, Muslims have an afternoon prayer session when all work stops for a time to conduct the religious ceremony. These two examples constitute practices that would not be adopted in every country because they are shaped by tradition or climatic factors specific to certain areas of the world.

Culture Shock and the Role of Human Resources

In the world of elite sporting competition, both professional and amateur sport organizations are interested in developing and enhancing various skills to enable athletes and teams to compete and win important events. The importation of skill, expertise, and knowledge is common in sport. For instance, within the amateur sport system, Canada's Pierre Lafontaine is a person whose skill in swim coaching has been sought in Australia, where he spent time working with elite amateur athletes. The acquisition of Lafontaine's skills related to swimming is an example of the transferring of technical expertise, which is becoming common in today's sport environment (e.g., in rowing, football, and ice hockey). The challenges of working and living in another country affect sport managers and other sport organization staff working internationally. Moving to another country (e.g., Canada to Australia) or even within a country to a different province or state brings with it a set of unknowns that need to be addressed. Table 3.1 in this chapter (p. 55) illustrates many examples of coaching expertise "on the move" globally.

Indeed, the aspect of **culture shock** is a real phenomenon that the sport manager, coach, athlete, or employee must consider when engaging in any intercultural management setting. Smith (2008) indicated that "culture shock may be viewed as travel anxiety, and it is nothing more than the experience of dissonance brought about by unfamiliar people and environments" (Smith, 2008, p. 42). Smith (2008) suggested that people could avoid culture shock by studying the country using such tools as Google Earth to help visualize it; by developing an understanding about the history, climate, and monetary system; and by using Mapquest as a resource to detail their new destination. These simple strategies help a person not only develop a mental map of the new place but also manage the anxiety that typically arises when going to a place where life is not exactly the same as it is in the place of origin.

In this regard, the critical role of the **human resource manager** (**HRM**) cannot be overstated. The HRM, who is responsible for managing and overseeing the personnel department of a sport organization and is involved in such tasks as personnel recruitment, training, and evaluation, needs to have an appreciation for the individual, the organization, and the interaction with the external environment. Consequently, this person needs to have a sophisticated communication skill set that includes knowledge of how to integrate and socialize people (coaches, players, new employees) into a new culture. Typically, the HRM is involved in a number of activities designed to ease the transition for the new person.

Within an intercultural management context, the HRM must recognize that what works within the organization in the home country in terms of procedures, laws, and other elements may not work the same way in another setting. The HRM must have a global mind-set to succeed in the international marketplace (Chaney & Martin, 2004). Language, sensitivity to time, motivation, and emphasis on goal orientation are many of the important elements to consider related to work life.

Employee Socialization

Allen (2006) noted that socialization tactics enable organizations to equip new employees with the proper tools and knowledge of the important values needed to succeed in their work. Strategies such as predeparture training (see earlier example) give new people a sense of what may be expected in moving

CASE STUDY

International Development Through Sport in Action

Commonwealth Games Canada (CGC) operates International Development Through Sport (IDS), a program that (1) provides opportunities for young Canadians to work and learn within an international setting and (2) provides support to Commonwealth countries in an effort to advance various social and educational initiatives. This type of programming is an example of intercultural management in action.

The IDS unit of the CGC recruits young Canadian university graduates and places them within various participating host countries (e.g., Zambia, Trinidad and Tobago) for an 8- to 12-month internship. The objectives are to advance various social and educational initiatives and increase sporting capacity. Social development in areas such as basic education, HIV–AIDS, health, gender equity, capacity building, child protection, and basic nutrition is part of the focus of the IDS programs (company documentation, 2009). Sport is used as a tool to bring people together in a forum that promotes physical activity. Educational instructions related to these social goals are delivered before games, during breaks, or after games.

A key element of the CGC-IDS programs involves what is known as *predeparture training*. Here, all interns engage in intercultural management workshops before leaving for their host organization to begin their internship. Preparing the interns for culture shock is important in creating their feelings of readiness before leaving and in alleviating some of the stress associated with working in an unknown country.

The training consists of three to four days of various workshops designed to enhance the interns' understanding of their own preference for behaviors, cultural adaptation strategies, cultural norms of the host organizations, health and safety abroad, job-specific details, and other important issues. This important process of the internship cycle is designed to educate interns about the **acclimatization period** (the period of socialization into a new culture) and aspects of the host organizational culture such as dress code, customs of business-related activities, and other details of the country itself (common foods, local health services, key contact information, and so on). Religious beliefs, formal and informal business practices, the role of family, and how time is spent in social settings are all part of the training received by interns to prepare for working in a new cultural setting.

to a new country to perform work. Indeed, we know from research that well-implemented programming at the front end of a new experience can influence turnover at the back end through job satisfaction. Three important stages mark the **organizational socialization** process for new employees: (1) anticipatory socialization (occurs before organizational entry), (2) encounter or accommodation (the newcomer enters the organization), and (3) adaptation or role management (the newcomer adapts and settles into the job). Knowing these three important stages and the importance of organizational culture, HRMs can use particular strategies to promote the message. The following activities are potential tools that management can use for these purposes (Cable & Parsons, 2001):

1. Collective socialization helps provide a common message about the organization, role clarity within various jobs, and appropriate responses for the new employees to be aware of. These elements are instructive right from the beginning. This activity helps reduce uncertainty concerning roles and can lead to a greater sense of shared values among people within the organization.

2. Formal tactics help provide a consistent message to new recruits and signal the importance of adapting to the new organizational environment, which may lead to shared values and reduce uncertainty about the job.

3. Sequential tactics provide information on the sequence of learning activities and experiences, which also help reduce uncertainty surrounding job tasks and responsibilities. Newcomers desire to establish routines and a sense of personal control. Thus, this tactic can reduce the anxiety and stress associated with adjusting to a new environment and a different organizational culture.

4. Fixed tactics help provide information on the timing associated with completing each socialization stage. This tactic is similar to sequential tactics in that it can reduce anxiety about the job as well as help newcomers develop a sense of control over their new environment.

5. Serial tactics provide experienced organizational members as role models or mentors who can help newcomers make sense of their environment and provide resources that they can turn to when in need of assistance. This tactic can help newcomers attain a sense of competence and task mastery.

Learning Activity

Discuss whether it is fair for an international sport organization to require all athletes to speak the same verbal language. Do they already share all the etiquette and rules of the game? Do you think that the inclusion of foreign athletes in professional leagues (e.g., the English Premier League in England or the National Basketball Association and the National Hockey League in the United States and Canada) hurts a league or makes it stronger?

6. Investiture tactics provide newcomers with positive social support from experienced organizational members. An important aspect of newcomer adjustment is gaining a sense of competence and confidence. Tactics that invest in newcomers by providing positive social feedback may help newcomers develop this sense of competence.

In essence, these tactics can provide common messaging and communicate the critical values and beliefs that shape organizational culture. Using such management strategies can ultimately lead to a better fit between the person and the organization. Further, when experienced organizational insiders are used in the socialization process as role models or mentors, turnover can be reduced. Including such tactics into the socialization process of new members can help the intercultural manager or employee avoid culture shock.

Summary

Today's sport managers need to understand the various ways in which people from different countries and diverse backgrounds can work together in an efficient and effective manner. As a result, when working with foreign personnel, sport managers must first strive to understand who they are and what values they hold. The sport manager involved in human resources, coaching, or instruction of any kind must demonstrate a genuine sense of appreciation and sensitivity for the person who, while bringing superb technical skills, might also bring a set of values that challenge the status quo.

CASE STUDY

LPGA Requirement of English Test

The increasingly global appeal of sporting events and rapid advancements in communication technology have made the sport phenomenon more global and less local. As a result, an athlete's popularity extends beyond his or her country of origin to a global audience. Within this global scenario, the influx of foreign athletes has certainly expanded the business potential of leagues that now can benefit from viewers and sponsorship from throughout the world. Yet this scenario of increasing numbers of foreign players in sport leagues has not been exempt from challenges. One of these challenges has been the ability of these athletes to adapt to the new culture and to communicate effectively with the media, fans, coaching staff, and teammates. Although the true language in the world of sport is communicated by athletes' capacity to kick, throw, pass, or shoot a ball, athletes are seen not just as gifted individuals with superb athletic skills but also as celebrities and commercial products that are crucial for the success of a much larger entertainment industry.

One of the most controversial policies regarding foreign athletes surfaced in August 2008 when the Ladies Professional Golf Association (LPGA) decided that foreign players who had been in the league for two or more years had to pass an oral English test. Failure would result in revocation of their membership. The LPGA, an American-based organization that in 2008 included 121 international players from 26 countries, including a large contingent of Korean players, believed that the proposed language policy was in the best interest of the

league, players, and fans. The LPGA executives stated that in their business what really mattered was the player as a whole, not just the athlete. Accordingly, the LPGA claimed that if players were not able to communicate effectively in English with sponsors, media, and amateurs who paid big dollars to be with them during the pro-am tournaments, the entire business of the LPGA would suffer.

Critics pointed out that no other professional sport had implemented such a rule. Moreover, LPGA sponsors, such as insurance company State Farm and Choice Hotels International, openly condemned the measure (Wilson, 2008). For many, the success in high-performance sport was to be accrued by merit of pure skill in the sport and not by any other means. After weeks of hot and controversial debate with lawmakers, sponsors, and other stakeholders, and after recognizing that a public relations disaster had occurred and that civil rights groups might sue, the LPGA overturned its original plan. Instead, the LPGA proposed a plan to provide and expand its cultural support to players who could not effectively communicate in English. As a result, in 2009 the LPGA collaborated with KOLON to implement a cross-cultural development program to train non-English-speaking golfers in the use of the English language as well as improve their communication skills. Since then, the KOLON program, in conjunction with the Indianapolis-based Language Training Center (LTC), has conducted a variety of intercultural initiatives for all players. In 2010 a seminar on cultural communication was required for all 2010 LPGA rookies (LPGA.com, n.d.).

Consequently, sport managers who are involved with an international workforce need to have sophisticated communication skills in order to work well with others.

Although people make the difference within organizations, it is also true that the culture of every organization is built from an array of influences not always directly initiated by people within it. Influences include various institutional forces that have been shaped over a long period not only within the organization but also from the wider environment. Because organizational culture is essentially made up of the values, beliefs, and assumptions about why

an organization is what it is, it plays a critical role in informing intercultural management practices. By simply observing how things are done in an organization, a new employee can obtain valuable information about what is appropriate and what is not in terms of business behavior. In addition, knowing that an organizational culture is also influenced to some degree by the national culture, the new employee working overseas should become acquainted with the national culture to learn how it might influence the way that business is conducted in that country (e.g., greetings, meetings, socializing outside of work, general values).

Rawlings, the Official Baseball Supplier to Major League Baseball

José Moncada, PhD, Universidad de Costa Rica

Rawlings has been the official baseball provider for Major League Baseball (MLB) in the United States since 1977. The factory in Costa Rica opened in 1987 because of political instability in Haiti and perhaps helped by the Caribbean Basin Initiative (CBI) proposed by the U.S. government in 1982 to develop strong economies in the region (Breitenecker, 1992; Stempler, 1991). Rawlings executives visited other countries in the Central American region, but compared with Haiti, Costa Rica was considered a paradise because of its political stability. It was the oldest democracy in the region, was strategically located near the Panama Canal, had well-established social security and labor rights, and was friendly to American culture.

The region where the plant is located is called Turrialba, a rural community in the province of Cartago near the Atlantic Ocean about 40 miles (64 km) from San José, Costa Rica's capital city. Turrialba's economy is diverse, the population is close to 80,000, and tourism is one of the major sources of income. Some international analysts have estimated that Costa Rica has better social security policies, labor administration, and unemployment insurance than the United States does. The countries have similar legislation with respect to child labor and minimum wages, but the United States is far ahead of Costa Rica in occupational safety and health issues, labor inspection, vocational training, and maternal leave (Hall & Leeson, 2007).

The Rawlings plant opened in Costa Rica with only 30 employees in a rented warehouse. Of those 30 employees, 10 were female Haitians who trained the locals in the art of sewing a baseball. Sewing balls was the only process performed in the plant in 1987. Currently, Rawlings Costa Rica does the entire process of making the ball from the inside out (four layers of winding, leather cutting, sewing, and stamping). Sewers now working in the Rawlings plant earn about 8 percent more than the official minimum wage for this type of worker (the base salary is 40,116 colones per week, or about US$72.28). Other incentives based on individual productivity are given to employees.

In 2011, four fully conditioned warehouses were part of the plant. Rawlings has expanded its business by making baseball uniforms for minor league teams and universities in the United States and may extend production in the near future to sports such as lacrosse. Hence, the Rawlings organization is an example of intercultural management. In an interview regarding how Rawlings views the expanding global market of baseball, Mr. Cotter, the general manager, noted that understanding culture plays a key role in the management of the company:

> There are and will always be cultural barriers, not only the language but also different mentalities in doing business. For instance, China may provide higher quantity of a product at a cheaper price; however, physical distance is a shortcoming and it may be preferable for companies in the U.S. to do business with companies in Central America, which is considered today a "hot region" for doing businesses. In our context, our plant in Costa Rica may meet the required quantities of a product at an acceptable price and delivery time.

Mr. Cotter went on to add that the company uses a lean-manufacturing approach popularized by the Japanese, an approach that

> produces in a shorter time, the exact quantity (not more or less), with the least inspection possible (do not over inspect), taking into account the employee as a person. Most world-class plants have successfully used this approach. In Costa Rica, other companies such as Intel use this approach.

Further, he noted the importance of creating "long-lasting relationships with our clients and providers" and that it is important to "show our partners the working conditions with our employees." Mr. Cotter went on to add, "We have open communication about our quality control and do not hide anything because that would impact our production."

For the Rawlings executive, the sharing of knowledge is key to learning how to operate at a more efficient rate.

> I have visited several plants not only in the United States but also in China and other countries. We learned from different cultures not only how to communicate to each other, but also regarding specific steps in the process of making a baseball. We take some aspects of their culture and integrate them into ours.

Overall, Rawlings recognizes the importance of working within a diverse business setting and takes the time to understand and share knowledge with their intercultural partners regarding their processes and operations.

Intercultural management practices can also be facilitated through a series of socialization tactics, which typically occur in three stages. By including formal tactics of socialization within the overall strategy of intercultural management practices, sport managers can significantly help new employees become better acquainted to the new environment. Socialization tactics can reduce stress and culture shock and facilitate a better fit between the employee and the organization.

Carte and Fox (2004) noted that misunderstanding and conflict between people of different cultures and between compatriots occur when people focus exclusively on their own agendas and do not consider others in their decision making. Sport managers who travel to foreign countries to do business knowing that they will encounter misunderstandings and communications challenges can alleviate some unnecessary conflict. Being alert to interpersonal obstacles can make or break a business transaction. Successful people, whether in business, industry, government, or science, know that in their relations with other cultures no specific values or behaviors are universally right. A successful global sport manager must remain flexible and open to accept differences in values, beliefs, and ways of doing things. In addition, she or he must be sensitive to verbal nuances and nonverbal signals, and be knowledgeable about religious, business, and social practices of other cultures. These and other steps will assist the sport manager in reducing the frictions, challenges, and confusion that typically emanate from poor intercultural management practices.

? Review and Discussion Questions

1. What factors does a sport manager need to consider when involved in an intercultural management setting?

2. Describe what is meant by ethnocentric behavior?

3. Define national culture and organizational culture. In what ways might these two types of culture overlap in a sport management setting?

4. Which aspects of organizational culture can be readily identified as describing what is valued within an organization?

5. How can a human resource manager ease the transition of a new person (e.g., athlete or coach) into the organization?

6. What strategies might you consider using if you are to host a new employee who has relocated from another country?

Part II

Field of Play in International Sport

New Zealand's Charlotte Harrison goes down in the tackle of Australia's Kate Jenner during the women's field hockey final at the 2010 Commonwealth Games in New Delhi, India. This quadrennial multisport event brings together members of the Commonwealth of Nations, most of them former colonies of the British Empire. 2010 was the first time that the Games were held in India.

Sport in North America

Willie Burden, EdD
Georgia Southern University, USA

Anthony G. Church, PhD
Laurentian University, Canada

Chapter Objectives

After studying this chapter, you will be able to do the following:

- Identify differences as well as similarities between U.S. sport organizational structures and those in other countries

- Explain differences and similarities among sport leagues within the United States and identify five types of decisions about league structures that teams in a sport must make

- Discuss innovative strategies employed by some contemporary sport organizations to protect against challenges from governmental interference as well as market forces

- Identify the main organizations involved in providing and regulating amateur sport in the United States

- Discuss the current issues faced by Canadian intercollegiate athletics departments

- Describe what role the state has in delivering and influencing sport in Canada compared with the United States and other countries

- Understand the advantages and disadvantages of the current structure of the sport delivery system in Canada

- Discuss the role of commercial and professional sport within the Canadian sport delivery system

Key Terms

Key Events

NFL Super Bowl. The preeminent sporting event in the United States. The 2010 Super Bowl (XLIV), played on "Super Bowl Sunday" in Miami, Florida, had the highest viewership of any American television program in history.

Major League Baseball World Series. The Fall Classic is a series of at least four games that ensures it as the highest-grossing annual championship event worldwide (Schwartz, 2010).

Summer Olympic Games (Atlanta, Georgia, 1996). At its time perhaps the most commercialized Games in history; it generated substantial corporate sponsorships; and its commercial success resulted in the Games making a profit of US$10 million.

2011 Masters Golf Tournament in Augusta, Georgia. Hosted since 1934 as an invitational at Augusta National Golf Club in Georgia, it is the first of the four major

tournaments on the PGA Tour. The 2010 event gave ESPN the highest U.S. audience ever for a golf event on cable television (Dobuzinskis, 2010).

2010 Vancouver Olympics and Paralympics Winter Games. Held on February 12 through 28, 2010, in Vancouver, British Columbia, this event attracted 10 thousand media representatives, 3 billion television viewers, and 75 million online media visitors worldwide (Olympic.org, 2010).

2010 Stanley Cup Playoffs attracted the largest television audience for professional hockey in North American history. Ice hockey is Canada's most popular spectator sport, and the broadcast of the 2010 Olympic game between Canada and the United States was watched by 21.5 million people in Canada, 64.3 percent of its population (Condotta, 2010; NHL.com, 2010).

Key People

Roger Goodell, commissioner of the NFL, named in 2006; the league's third commissioner since 1960.

Mark Emmert, PhD, executive director of the NCAA, named in 2010; the organization's fifth director.

Larry Probst, United States Olympic Committee chairman since 2008.

George Bodenheimer, president of ESPN, Inc. and ABC Sports, one of the world's premier business brands.

David Stern, commissioner of the NBA since 1984.

Mark Cohon, commissioner of the CFL since 2007.

Michael A. Chambers, former president of the Canadian Olympic Committee from 2001-2010.

Richard Pound, former president of the World Anti-Doping Agency (WADA) and former IOC vice president. Known for his investigation of the Salt Lake City Olympic judging scandal and outspoken views against performance-enhancing drugs.

"Made in America" is a familiar phrase in the United States. When discussing the evolution of sport in the United States in her article "National Sports and Other Myths: The Failure of U.S. Soccer," Collins (2006) contended that, in America, the sport culture developed sufficiently differently from other nations to create an identity and brand that could only be labeled as "American." So, beginning with the period of its introduction, sport in the United States has been uniquely different, distinctive, and remarkable in terms of magnitude and influence (Hums & MacLean, 2004). The effect has been profound for an assortment of reasons comprising its capacity to unify a community, region, or the entire nation; produce accomplishment and pride; generate a wealth of publicity; and probably most important produce windfall revenues (Nelson, 2005). Collins (2006) stated that most industrialized nations were developing sport cultures during the 60-year period beginning around 1870 and ending in 1930. So, while Canadians, Australians, and continental Europe were identifying with the British, the United States was spurning British bourgeoisie and culture to establish its own position and cultural direction in terms of sport. Popular British sports like football, which had been adopted by other countries throughout the world, became victim to U.S. efforts to attain its own identity (Collins, 2006). Just as American football is different from football in the rest of the world and baseball is different from cricket, sport structure in the United States is fundamentally different from that in other parts of the world, particularly Britain (England, Scotland, Wales, and Northern Ireland) and European countries where most sports in the United States originated.

The assortment of sports available in the United States is offered through diverse sport delivery systems. Shilbury (2000) suggested that sport delivery systems are complex infrastructures that exist to cater to participation in sport at all levels and in all forms; these systems possess the managerial expertise or ability to stage events. Thibault and Harvey (1997) stated that the notion of sport delivery system implies the involvement of a number of organizations, operating at different levels and participating in a coordinated fashion to achieve their goals and objectives. Sport delivery systems are certainly organized to accomplish the mission, goals, and objectives of the organization, and frequently they provide programs that emphasize participation and competition. The sections that follow examine sport delivery systems in the United States, beginning with an overview of the economic impact and distinctive characteristics and complexity of U.S. sport. Later sections examine the historical development of both professional and amateur sport as well as the current organizational structures of professional and amateur sport in the United States.

Economic Impact of U.S. Sport

Nearly all teams in the United States, amateurs and professionals, play in leagues as an economic necessity. The demand for games that are part of a championship schedule vastly exceeds the demand for games that determine nothing more than the identity of the winner of a particular game (Noll, 2003). For example, data from the National Collegiate Athletic Association (NCAA) website revealed that the average home attendance for all schools (330 total) in NCAA Division I men's basketball for the 2008–09 season was 5,185. The average home attendance for the 28 independent (not affiliated with a conference) colleges in Division I men's basketball for 2008–09 was only 768 (NCAA.org, 2009).

College conferences as well as individual major college programs thrive off sponsorship and advertising revenue. For instance, the University of Connecticut recently signed one of the richest multimedia contracts in the country with IMG College worth US$80 million over 10 years (SBJ Report, 2008). The NCAA signed one of the largest television contracts in U.S. sport history, a US$6 billion deal over 11 years through 2014 for its basketball championships (Epstein, 2008). The same holds true for commercially oriented professional sport. According to McAllister (2010), U.S. sport has profoundly embraced commercialism given its extraordinary entertainment value and viewer interest. Professional football, as the broadcast sport generating the most advertising revenue, broke the US$2 billion barrier in 2003 (McAllister, 2010). The National Football League's US$3.7 billion television broadcasting deal with CBS, Fox, NBC, ESPN, and DirecTV went through the 2010 season. Major League Baseball's contract with Fox, TBS, and ESPN runs through 2013 and is worth over US$700 million. Worldwide sponsorship spending on sport was nearly US$38 billion in 2007, and US$14.9 billion of that was spent on U.S. sport sponsorship.

Structure and Governance of Sport in the United States

A diverse range of sport delivery systems operates in the United States. One way to categorize them is as public or private depending on the funding source of the organization. Public sporting organizations are funded by governmental taxes at the local, state, or national level and are usually nonprofit. Private sport organizations are funded by investors or contributions of a private nature, and a main objective is to make a profit. The two types are not mutually exclusive. An organization such as a local private fitness club is a for-profit enterprise, even if it does not make a profit. On the other hand, the local public Young Men's Christian Association (YMCA) may not be for profit, but it could generate a surplus.

Such institutions have to turn a profit, or surplus, to ensure their survival (Chelladurai, 2001). All these characteristics influence the governance of sport organizations.

Governance and policy in sport organizations relate to the membership, regulations, programming, and organizational structure. The structure determines the regulatory power of the parent organization, and governing bodies possess this sanctioning power to various degrees. For example, the National Federation of State High Schools Association (NFSHSA) sets and enforces competition rules, but Major League Baseball's authority goes further; it can levy luxury taxes on teams whose payrolls exceed a certain amount (Hums & MacLean, 2004).

Professional Sport in the United States

Nearly all professional sport teams in the United States play in leagues, which are private-sector sport organizations. The two alternatives to league organization are independents and barnstormers. An independent is a team that does not belong to a league but creates an annual schedule of matches with other teams. Most teams in team sports began as independents, but few, if any, true professional independents exist today. Barnstorming teams were popular in the United States in the early 20th century but are no longer common. Professional basketball's Harlem Globetrotters, one of the most popular and successful barnstorming teams ever, is one of the few that carries on the tradition. The next section describes the historical background of professional sport leagues in the United States.

Historical Background of Professional Team Sport Leagues in the United States

Major League Baseball (MLB), the National Basketball Association (NBA), the National Football League (NFL), the National Hockey League (NHL), and Major League Soccer (MLS) are the five dominant professional sport leagues based in the United States. In 2007 these five organizations accounted for 149 sport franchises. A sport **franchise** is the privilege or right of ownership of a team in a league as well as the obligation to follow the policies and procedures of the league. The organizational design,

Professional and Amateur Sport in the United States Compared With Europe

Note: Europe was chosen for comparison because its influence on sport all over the world, particularly in the late 20th century, has been enormous. Also, most modern sports in the United States, besides basketball, had their origins in Europe (ICN Sportsweb .com, 2010; *Popular Culture,* 2005).

- Most teams in the United States are members of a single league. In Europe, teams commonly have membership in multiple leagues.

- In the United States, sport is organized into both individual and team sports. Primarily team sports consist of a hierarchy of leagues. The major league of each sport sits at the top of the hierarchy. Next are the **minor leagues**, or lower-division teams, that compete in less urban venues, often in smaller cities or towns. U.S. professional baseball has the most levels, consisting of five classifications—Major, AAA, AA, A, and Rookie leagues (Fort, 2000; Noll, 2003). In other parts of the world, notably Europe, sports such as football may have as many as 10 levels.

- The major leagues in the United States are closed, having a fixed membership that can be changed only by a formal vote of the membership to expand or contract. European leagues allow the best teams from a lower league to be promoted to the next highest league; the weakest teams are demoted to a lower level.

- The league competition format in the United States differs from that in other parts of the world.

- Fort (2000) described two additional distinctions between European and American sport structures besides the system of relegation and promotion: (1) European teams play both nationally and internationally and therefore require two oversight organizations (e.g., the Football Association and FIFA), and (2) funding is passed down from premier high-level, high-revenue organizations to the lower levels, a redistribution that does not occur in the United States.

- The United States has far more experience than Europe does with the relocation of professional teams.

- In the United States, colleges serve as the minor leagues for professional teams and feed talent upward; in Europe and other countries, lower-division clubs feed the upper divisions.

- American intercollegiate sport has four divisions for American football and three for other sports. In Canada, college teams compete as members of the Canadian Interuniversity Athletic Union, the counterpart of NCAA Divisions I and II (Danylchuk & Maclean, 2001). In the United Kingdom, British Colleges Sport (BCS) organizes the largest competition structure for college students and offers competition at the Elite, Performance, and Participation levels (British Colleges Sport, n.d.). Elite students, however, develop their talents primarily through the club system.

- The sports of basketball, volleyball, skateboarding, and snowboarding were created in the United States. Lacrosse is a Native American invention, and surfing originated as a Native Hawaiian sport.

- Baseball, football, basketball, and the Olympics have captured the nation's interest since at least the turn of the 20th century (Nelson, 2005). American football is the most popular sport in the United States; football (soccer) is the most popular sport in the rest of the world.

---

leadership practices, polices, rules development, enforcement procedures, and so on for these leagues (as well as leagues in other sports in the United States) are based on those of professional baseball, which was the first sport to develop as a professional league (Masteralexis, 2009). The following sections describe the early development of Major League Baseball in the United States and its influence on the structure of other professional sports.

Rules of the Game

The game of baseball was played in America in the early part of the 19th century. The earliest known newspaper account of a baseball game in the United States was published on September 11, 1845, in the *New York Morning News,* which described the game played the previous day between the New York Knickerbockers Club and the New York Club (19cbaseball.com, 2008). Team sport structure in the United States can be traced to the date when Alexander Cartwright developed a set of baseball rules for his team, the Knickerbockers Club of New York. The rules were broadly adopted. Versions of baseball had been played earlier throughout the northeastern United States in the form of a children's game known as rounders or townball (MLB.com, 2008; McLean, Hurd, & Rogers, 2007).

The Knickerbockers Club became the model upon which all early clubs were organized, and their set of rules became the foundation of modern baseball (19cbaseball.com). A formal single set of rules that all teams could play under brought more organization and dignity to the sport and helped set the standard for the professional league sport model. By the latter part of the 19th century, by acquiring the best franchises and best talent available, baseball had established itself as the one and only major league, meaning that all other levels of competition were something less. Baseball organized into two divisions that played a round-robin season and ended in a national championship, an arrangement still common today in baseball and among the other professional leagues in the United States (Starr, 1999). In terms of governance, baseball established a commission, which evolved into a commissioner, to oversee the rules and regulations of the organization (Noll, 2003). League rules respecting franchise and player movement were also adopted. No other sporting institution has influenced American professional sport culture as much as baseball has.

Barnstorming: Early System of Sport Delivery

Since the late 1800s America has always had at least one favored national sport. The first was baseball. Fans could watch their favorite teams play during the regular baseball season and then watch some of the best players play exhibition games between seasons, a practice called **barnstorming**. Barnstormer is the name given to a team that has no regular home field and travels the country playing exhibitions. Barnstorming was popular among fans and players in the late 19th century until the mid-20th century. Most top professional teams were then located in the Northeast and Midwest, so fans in most parts of the country could never have seen high-level pro baseball had it not been for the barnstorming teams (Center for Negro League Baseball Research, 2006; Hinkley, 2003). The players received salaries from

their regular teams, but this amount was not enough to live on year round. They had to find off-season jobs, or they could barnstorm. For many of the players the barnstorming schedule was more financially rewarding than the salary that they received from their professional teams (Hinkley, 2003). This arrangement also satisfied another interest of fans and players because barnstorming teams played a wide range of opponents that included Negro League teams, professional teams, semipro teams, other barnstorming teams, local town teams, and industrial league teams (Center for Negro League Baseball Research, 2006; Hinkley, 2003). At a time when there was no television, radio, or Internet and limited print coverage of baseball, people in small towns outside the league sphere were happy to pay at the gate to see professional baseball players in person (Hinkley, 2003). Barnstorming allowed high-quality baseball games featuring the game's biggest stars to be played and watched in virtually every part of the country (Center for Negro League Baseball Research, 2006).

Ownership also paid basketball players to barnstorm across the country. The first professional basketball league in the United States was formed in 1898, and professional basketball included teams traveling and playing games with no set season or schedule (Nelson, 2005; Robinson, 2005). The opponent was sometimes another barnstorming team that traveled with them. The leading example was the modern Harlem Globetrotters basketball team and their traveling opponents, the Washington Generals (Noll, 2003). Fan travel to ball games in the late 1800s was facilitated by the emergence of railroads, which made travel economically and geographically feasible. This evolution in transportation had an even greater effect on the traveling teams that had previously suffered through long, grueling road trips in the early years of barnstorming baseball (Center for Negro League Baseball Research, 2006). Fan demand for barnstorming games remained strong through the middle of the 20th century until league franchises became located throughout the country, more games were broadcast on television, and players' salaries increased substantially because of free agency.

MLB: The Original Professional Sport League in the United States

In terms of league competition, in 1871 the National Association of Professional Baseball Players was formed (Reiss, 1998). The National Association lasted until 1876, when some of its members helped to form the National League. The eight-team National League, organized by William Hulbert, was North America's first professional sport league (Barr, 2009; Robinson, 2005). It had evolved into an organization of clubs rather than an association of players. The National League essentially is Major League Baseball today.

At the turn of the 20th century baseball was the only professional league in the United States. The Western league, a minor league circuit that later became known as the American League, came into existence and competed with the National League for players and spectators. In 1903 the two leagues combined to create the Major Leagues, each recognizing the reserve clause. The reserve clause obligated a player to one team for as long as the team desired (Masteralexis, 2009). A national commission was established consisting of the president of each league and other members agreed upon by both leagues. This alliance led to the creation of a professional baseball championship, the World Series, in 1903, a tradition that continues today as the winners of the National League and the American League face each other in the ultimate playoff.

Structure of Modern Professional Sport Leagues

A classification of teams based on similar characteristics and following the same rules allows all teams to be competitive and have the opportunity to contend for a championship. Teams in a sport must make at least five types of decisions about league structure: (1) format—the method for scheduling matches to determine the champion; (2) hierarchy—the relationships between leagues of lesser and greater quality; (3) multiplicity—the number of leagues at the same level of the hierarchy; (4) membership—the conditions under which a team enters and exits a league; and (5) governance—the methods for deciding and enforcing league rules and policies. The sections that follow describe how U.S. professional leagues have handled these decisions. Other important decisions include developing playing rules and controlling aspects of the economic behavior of league members (Noll, 2003).

Format

In his article on the organization of sport leagues, Noll (2003) stated that teams form leagues in part

because the players, coaches, and owners enjoy contesting for a championship. Also, a league maintains a level of fan interest and support throughout a season, resulting in greater financial consequences. The coordinated scheduling format helps control travel costs and allows the league to market a game both as the contest itself and as one of a series that leads to a championship, creating even more fan and media interest. In a round-robin format, every team plays a predetermined number of games, and the games can be played home and away. The team with the best winning percentage is the champion and earns the highest seed for tournament play. Round-robin play helps to eliminate teams in leagues with a large membership. This format is used in most United States professional and amateur sport leagues because they benefit from both systems. The economic advantage of tournaments over round robins is that the best matches are saved for the final rounds and the demand for the games intensifies with each succeeding round (Noll, 2003). This format is also common among leagues in other countries. For instance, England's Premier League, Spain's Liga BBVA, and Australia's A League have similar scheduling formats. Each football club plays the others (home and away) during the regular season, points are awarded based on performance (e.g., three points for a win and one point for a draw), and at the end of the season the club with the most points is crowned champion. Final rankings may be determined by the leagues' tie-breaking systems (Noll, 2003).

Hierarchy

The draft system for acquiring talent is a way to maintain competitive balance and the way that players move between leagues of higher and lower quality (players, not teams, move between leagues). The current format for acquiring talent in American professional sport leagues has been developed through the collective bargaining agreement. The players unions of professional leagues and the leagues themselves have agreed to a draft for younger incoming talent. Each year, each team selects from the available list of prospective players in this system. The incentive for veteran players to agree to this provision in their union contract is that they are released from the restrictions placed on them under the old reserve system. A reverse-order draft scheme is justified by appealing to the importance of competitive team balance among a league's members (Siegfried, 1995). The supply of talent comes through the club system in other countries.

In the United States, colleges serve as the minor leagues for professional sport. College teams are supplied by the high school talent pools, and the high schools get their players from middle schools and grassroots community recreation programs or little leagues. All the major league sports with the possible exception of MLB have a similar system. MLB does draft college and high school talent, but the organization emphasizes player development through its long-established farm system (since the 1930s). After an athlete is drafted and signed to a contract, the parent club assigns the player to a farm club within its system based on the player's talent level (MLNSports.com., n.d.). Farm clubs are designated AAA, AA, A, and Rookie. AAA clubs are the level of competition immediately below the majors.

Multiplicity

American professional sport, unlike sport in many other countries, has multiple leagues or divisions at the top of the hierarchy. For example, in Europe each country has one league at the top of the hierarchy. In the United States, professional basketball, football, and hockey each has a single major league but two distinct conferences and then divisions within each conference. Major League Soccer in the United States is divided into two divisions. Divisional standings in the leagues determine qualifications and seeding for a postseason tournament. For example, the National Football League's postseason tournament culminates with the Super Bowl game, which pits the champion of each conference against each other. The event has become the most watched sporting event in the United States (Robinson, 2005). Teams have some interleague or interconference matches that count in the standings, but the schedules are unbalanced (Noll, 2003). In an unbalanced schedule teams play some opponents more than they do others. In Europe balanced schedules are the norm (Noll, 2003).

Membership

United States sport leagues have a fixed membership structure as opposed to the promotion–relegation system practiced by European team sports (Noll,

2003). Promotion–relegation leagues change their membership by replacing the weakest teams in the top-tier leagues with the best teams in lower leagues. The membership of United States professional leagues is permanent. U.S. leagues change through expansion or by granting franchises permission to relocate to other cities (Noll, 2003).

During the decades of the 1970s and 1980s professional sport leagues and franchises emerged as rival challengers to the establishment. Many eventually faded, but the strongest were merged into the NFL, NBA, or NHL. Between 1970 and 1997 the number of professional sport franchises increased from 95 to 118 (Cousens & Slack, 2005). An owner who is granted membership obtains a well-defined home territory (Masteralexis, 2009), which usually encompasses an entire metropolitan area. No other franchisee can hold contests or broadcast their games within another franchisee's home territory without first obtaining permission. This policy protects the franchise from local competition. The franchisee also receives revenue-sharing benefits consisting of a portion of various leaguewide revenues (expansion fees, national television revenue, gate receipts, and licensing revenues) (Masteralexis, 2009).

Movement Professional leagues have policies that govern the movement of teams from one location to another. Because of financial pressure, geographic shifts in the U.S. population, and threats of lawsuits, professional teams in the United States have tended to move more often than those in other countries (Nelson, 2005). Because leagues have a keen interest in protecting franchise territories and limiting movement, many proposed relocations have been rejected in past years. An optimal number of teams helps the leagues maximize their income and increase the teams' market valuation (Nelson, 2005). In U.S. professional sport, the Chicago Cubs, founded as the White Stockings in 1871, remain the team with the longest tenure in the same location (Cazeneuve, Habib, Menez, Syken, Woo, & Schecter, 2004; Reiss, 1998). Some proposed moves are highly controversial (Noll, 2003). When the NFL's Browns announced their move from Cleveland to Baltimore in 1995, the city of Cleveland and Browns fans were upset, lawsuits were filed, the U.S. Congress became involved, a protest was held, and team sponsors withdrew support (Sutton, McDonald, Milne & Simperman, 1997).

Expansion Substantial changes in the number of major league teams have been common only in the United States and North America. Since 1951 the four divisions of the English Football League have had the same number of members, 92 (Noll, 2003). On the other hand, in the early 1990s the NHL added 9 franchises to increase the total to 30 teams (Cazeneuve et al., 2004; Cousens & Slack, 2005). Between 1953 and 2003 MLB expanded from 16 to 32 teams, the NFL from 12 to 32, the NBA from 8 to 29, and the NHL from 6 to 30. (Football, or soccer, had none because there was no major league). This growth came through expansion or by merger with competing leagues (Cazeneuve et al., 2004; Noll, 2003).

According to Masteralexis (2009), the NBA, NHL, and MLB allowed cross-ownership (owning a team in another sport) until 1997. Football (soccer)

CASE STUDY

NFL Expansion and Relocation

The National Football League is the richest, most popular sport organization in North America. It evolved by aggressively expanding its market and fan bases and acquiring stadium-financing deals, sponsorships, and advertising dollars (Cousens & Slack, 2005; Noll, 2003). Because of its immense popularity, NFL expansion or franchise relocation has seemingly always been an interesting topic of conversation for fans of American football. The United States, Europe, Mexico, and Canada have all been mentioned as potential locations for the next league expansion. The latest franchise in the United States that was granted entry was the Houston Texans in 2002. Los Angeles, the number two television market in the country, remains the most viable market for the NFL; every other major U.S. market has an NFL franchise.

Fan markets in Germany and Mexico have been tested through exhibition contests. The NFL's effort to establish a feeder league in Europe between 1991 and 1997 failed because of low attendance and financial losses in the millions of dollars (Sandomir, 2007). But after this disappointment, the latest international focus has been Toronto, Canada's largest city. Toronto's potential is almost too glaring to ignore. The NFL has a large fan base north of the border. American professional teams such as MLB's Blue Jays, the NBA's Raptors, the NHL's Maple Leafs, and MLS's Toronto FC are popular in the Toronto market, so why not the NFL? If acquired, Toronto would be a top 10 market for the NFL and a city where sponsorships and stadium advertising deals could be maximized (Millson & Sekeres, 2008; Ralph, 2002). The NFL has already received interest from investors capable of acquiring the franchise (Brunt, 2009; Millson & Sekeres, 2008), and the US$1 billion expansion fee would fatten the

league's pockets. The NFL is currently investigating. An arrangement with Rogers Communications of Canada for US$78 million has allowed the NFL to play several exhibition games in Toronto. Also, a regular season game was played there in 2009 and 2010 and more are scheduled through the 2012 season. All the contests have featured the NFL's Buffalo Bills, a franchise primed for relocation (Masters, 2010).

Before the NFL moves forward, a few issues would have to be resolved. Toronto's Rogers Center has little on-site parking and holds only 53,000 fans for football, which is too small for the league's mandated minimum capacity of 65,000 seats. Stadium attractiveness and size are important because income from ticket sales, television deals, and merchandise revenue is shared with the league. Stadium sponsorship money, suite sales, and naming-rights revenue goes to the individual team. Another issue is the resistance from the CFL and resentment of CFL fans who view the NFL as a threat and the Bills' games in Toronto as a forerunner to a more permanent NFL presence in Canada (Millson & Sekeres, 2008). CFL commissioner Mark Cohon may seek the assistance of the Canadian government to block the NFL's move. Canadian fans loyal to the CFL have threatened to boycott games as well as any sponsors of the NFL in Canada. Attendance at NFL exhibitions and regular season contests at the Rogers Center has been less than capacity, even though thousands of free or reduced-price tickets were distributed for the exhibitions (Masters, 2009). In addition, if the NFL added Toronto by expansion rather than relocation, it would have a 33-team league that would require a more complex schedule. So far, everything is speculation. The NFL has said that it is not moving into Canada just yet.

club ownership does not violate this policy because investors in MLS invest in the league as a single entity, not in individual teams. The NFL and MLB prohibit a single owner from possessing interest in two or more franchises in the same league (Cousens & Slack, 2005).

Governance

According to Chappelet and Bayle (2004), sport has historically been managed by associate organizations that belong to the sport. Contemporary sport industry structures in the United States have evolved over the past 150 years (Croset & Hums, 2009). Structure, such as the flow of information, coordination, collaboration, and allocation of power and responsibility, helps the organization respond to the situations in which it operates. MLB's National League, an owner-controlled league in which the players were employees, set the precedent for all U.S. professional sport leagues. Many of the governing practices set forth by the National League are still in effect in all professional sport leagues today (Hums & MacLean, 2004). Governance structure and policies (franchise movement, territorial rights, reserve clause, and so on) ensure the viability of the league and its member teams (Berry, Gould, & Staudohar, 1986; Masteralexis, 2009). **Territorial rights** grant a team in a particular media market a line of demarcation that other league teams cannot encroach on in conducting business.

The U.S. model of sport governance is more economics (business) driven than the European model. According to Kaburakis (2008), European policies place more emphasis on the inclusion of the social, educational, cultural character, and contribution of sport. Governance structure features a single representative federal body, which is characteristic of the pyramid models used by professional football, the one major professional sport in European countries. The pyramid merges professional and nonprofessional sport into a hierarchy. The model features four levels of competition that has the community clubs at the base, the regional federations at the next level, the national federations at the next higher level, and the European federations at the top. A primary function of this pyramid structure is to facilitate an equitable distribution of revenue among the constituent sport clubs to encourage mass participation and competitive balance among clubs (Nafziger, 2008).

Commissioner MLB was the first professional sport organization in the United States to establish a single commissioner, the most visible individual in the governance structure of professional sport. The Black Sox scandal of 1919 had a significant effect on the structure of baseball. Eight Chicago White Sox players were indicted by a Chicago grand jury for conspiring to fix the outcome of the World Series that year. From that time forward, the governance of the league was placed in the hands of a single commissioner (Judge Kenesaw Mountain Landis was the first), a person outside the organization that insiders and outsiders had confidence in. The commissioner was given absolute authority to act in the best interest of the game (Masteralexis, 2009; Robinson, 2005).

Generally, each of the major professional leagues in the United States has a commissioner (Robinson, 2005). The role of the commissioner is to run the league office and the day-to-day operations of the league. The power within the leagues is with the owners. The owners hire the commissioner of the league and determine the commissioner's duties, responsibilities, and compensation. Therefore, the commissioner's first responsibility is to protect the owners' interests. Powerful committees consisting of team owners develop rules and rules changes, make decisions regarding league expansion and franchise relocation, negotiate media contracts, and negotiate with the players unions (Robinson, 2005)

Through the governance structure of professional sport, which recognizes and empowers the players unions, the players also have a voice in league policy decisions. Collective bargaining led to the end of the reserve clause in baseball in 1975, which greatly affected baseball and all professional sports (Galant, Renick, & Resnick, 2005; Masteralexis, 2009; Robinson, 2005).

Team League Structure and Antitrust Law The biggest professional leagues are almost always monopolies. Teams have a strong incentive to organize leagues in a fashion that reduces competition among themselves in both input and output markets (Noll, 2003). But an organization of teams that restricts or limits competition violates U.S. **antitrust laws** established through the Sherman Act of 1890, which made monopolies illegal. For professional teams to structure their operations and policies as efficiently as possible, they had to obtain an antitrust exemption, either in a statute or through collective bargaining (Noll, 2003). The U.S. Congress has

Learning Activity

Think of an American sport league or organization that you think would benefit from a change of structure. Research the organization to identify what aspects of their current structure need to be addressed and why.

allowed Major League Baseball an exemption from antitrust legislation since 1922 (Nelson, 2005).

A more recent trend has been for emerging leagues such as the Women's United Soccer Association (WUSA), Women's National Basketball Association (WNBA), Major League Soccer (MLS), and Arena Football League (AFL) to establish themselves as **single entities** to avoid antitrust liability and to create centralized fiscal control. A single entity is a centralized organization of league investors rather than a group of independent team owners. Personnel issues such as trades and staffing require league approval. The MLS structure has withstood an antitrust challenge from MLS players, who argued that it was a sham created for the purpose of restraining competition and depressing player salaries (Masteralexis, 2009). MLS's organizational structure is more innovative than those of the other emerging leagues. Potential investors in MLS can own teams, not just a share of a league as specified under the single-entity concept. MLS's structure allows owner–operators of teams, which means that the shareholders are members of the league's board of directors and also have the right to operate a team. Through their board positions, shareholders have some, but not total, control over negotiations of player contracts, assignment of players to teams, sales and trades of players to teams in other leagues (notably, to teams in first-division European leagues), sales of national broadcasting rights and product licenses, and the negotiation of stadium leases. MLS pays the costs for players and stadiums, and in return teams give the league half their revenues (Noll, 2003).

Professional Sport Circuits and Tours

Individual professional sports generally involve a professional tour of events, meets, or matches. The United States has professional tours in men's and women's golf, tennis, ice skating, bowling, skiing, and other sports. Competition also occurs in indoor football (soccer), lacrosse, roller hockey, auto racing, professional boxing, and horse racing (Robinson, 2005). Countless professional sporting events are staged in individual sports, including action sports, fencing, racquetball, running, and track and field. Examples of well-known individual sport tours in the United States are the National Association for Stock Car Auto Racing (NASCAR) Nextel Cup Series, Professional Golfers' Association of America (PGA), and Ladies Professional Golf Association of America (LPGA). These organizations have been fixtures on the American sport scene since the 1700s (Robinson, 2005). Circuits or tournament-style competition is popular in the United States (Noll, 2003).

Looking at the evolution of golf helps us understand how professional sport circuits and tours have come to be organized in the United States. From a historical perspective, the first U.S. Open golf event was held in 1895. The PGA's constitution, by-laws, and rules were modeled after those of the British PGA and were completed in 1916. In 1921 the PGA named its first commissioner, Albert R. Gates (Masteralexis, 2009). Today the PGA is the most popular and successful tour in America. Professional players became interested in tournaments and tournaments began to thrive after organizers persuaded corporations and communities to put up prize money. Sports like boxing and baseball depended on gate receipts and concessions to make a profit. Golf, however, was perceived as an "upside down" sport in which the participants paid to play. A new idea was developed and promoted in the 1930s by Fred Corcoran, who decided to sell the event. Therefore, celebrities, politicians, charities, manufacturers, or products gained exposure by being a part of the event (Masteralexis, 2009). Through prize money and exposure, professional players could be persuaded to participate. Corcoran enticed communities to guarantee the purse and convinced community leaders that the revenue generated by visitors and professional golfers attending the tournament would triple their investment. Also, Corcoran matched celebrities and touring pros together in exhibition matches (celebrity pro-ams) that preceded the regular tournaments. These events raised funds for charities and proved to be tremendously successful. This model became important because sponsors such as equipment manufacturers could use their association with golf to sell products, celebrities could enhance their fame or reputation, politicians could gain political influence, communities could generate revenues, tournaments could be promoted as effective advertising mediums, and the increased audience helped enhance the popularity of the sport (Masteralexis, 2009).

In circuits and tournaments, participants normally go through qualifying competitions to participate in some of the major events. Other events are invitational only, and some are open. For example, one of the ways that PGA professionals qualify to compete in tour events is to finish within the top 25 at the annual Qualifying Tournament (PGA.com, 2008). Track and field runners and auto-racing teams have to accomplish similar qualifying standards. Sometimes tours or exhibitions are created for athletes by their sport agency firms and by television and cable networks for programming purposes in action sports (ESPN's X-Games and NBC's Gravity Games), golf (ABC's Skins Game), and other sports (ESPN's Outdoor Games) (Masteralexis, 2009).

Amateur Sport in the United States

Participation in amateur sport is the most popular form of recreation in the United States. Benefits for children and adults alike are numerous and include skill development, self-discipline, motivation, sportsmanship, and physical fitness. Participation in sporting activities continues to rise. According to a survey by the National Sporting Goods Association, overall youth participation increased by 9.3 percent between 1998 and 2008 (NSGA.org, 2010).

The two major organizational categories that fill the developmental role of youth in the United States are school-based programs and community-based efforts. The community-based efforts consist of agency-sponsored programs, national youth service organizations, club sports, and recreation programs (Weiss & Hayashi, 1996). Service delivery is in the form of organizations such as the Amateur Athletic Union (AAU), Young Men's Christian Association (YMCA) and Young Women's Christian Association (YWCA), Little League, National Collegiate Athletic Association (NCAA), United States Olympic Committee (USOC), International Paralympic Committee (IPC), National Intramural-Recreational Sports

Association (NIRSA), and civic clubs. Amateur organizations such as these focus on the performance of their missions, not financial returns. Their specific management framework consists of voluntary work by those at the head, a democratic method of functioning, and a nonprofit basis of operation (Chappelet & Bayle, 2004). Although these organizations are voluntary, amateur sport clubs employ some paid staff members. For example, the premier governing body for U.S. major college athletics programs, the NCAA, has approximately 350 paid employees (Hums & MacLean, 2004).

United States Olympic Committee

The United States Olympic Committee (USOC) governs, manages, promotes, and communicates within and outside the United States for all activities of the Olympics, Paralympics, and Pan American Games. In 1978 the U.S. Congress passed the Amateur Sports Act, which was amended in 1998. The act specifically mandated the USOC to govern all American activities for the three major Games. The USOC is the self-professed "premier sports organization" in the United States. It is composed of a group of individuals and organizations whose common goals are athletic excellence and achievement on the world stage and promoting nation building through the achievement of athletes (Hums & MacLean, 2004, p. 268).

The USOC has an extensive membership. Research by Hums & MacLean (2004) identified 78 member organizations divided among seven categories including Olympic sport organizations, Pan American sport organizations, community-based multisport organizations, affiliated sport organizations, education-based multisport organizations, and the armed forces. The organization is structured such that elected officers, a board of directors, an executive committee, and various other committees help provide direction that the staff implements.

From a worldwide perspective, the International Olympic Committee (IOC) sits at the top of the Olympic organizational structure. Below the IOC are two branches, the national Olympic committees (NOCs) and the international federations (IFs). The NOCs are responsible for the development of the Olympic Movement in each country. The NOC for the United States is the United States Olympic

Committee (USOC). The USOC is responsible for the representation of the United States at the Olympic Games as well as the regional, continental, and world competitions patronized by the IOC. The IFs are the organizations responsible for the administration of individual sport competition on a worldwide basis. For example, Fédération Internationale de Basketball (FIBA) administers rules, competition, and sanctions for basketball. The national governing bodies (NGBs) fall below the IFs and follow the guidelines set by their respective IFs for their sport and country. USA Track and Field is the national governing body that selects U.S. track and field athletes for world competition (Fairley, Lizandra, & Gladden, 2008).

The 1896 Games in Athens reestablished the Olympics and provided organizations that participated in athletics with an arena for the allocation of international prestige (Nelson, 2005). The first Olympics held on American soil was in St. Louis in 1904. Los Angeles was the next U.S. host city, in 1932. Eight Olympic Games have taken place in the United States. Atlanta, Georgia, served as the most recent host city in 1996 (Nelson, 2005). The athlete selection process has changed over time. In the late 19th century and early 20th century, an entire team from one of the amateur competitions was often selected to represent the United States in the Olympic Games. Therefore, the best athletes did not make up the Olympic team; instead, an intact team from the YMCA, an AAU league, or college was sent.

The current process of selecting athletes for Olympic events requires the athletes to meet certain standards and successfully survive the selection process established by the sport's national governing body. For example, in the United States, USA Track and Field (USATF) holds trials for all track and field events. Athletes must meet minimal Olympic qualifying standards. The top three finishers (and one additional athlete for relays) in each race category go on to represent the United States at the Olympics. USATF maintains offices at the local level, and the national office maintains associations with colleges, schools, and clubs throughout the nation. Athletes may be recruited from their school track team or a club if they meet the standard. USATF posts the qualifying standard for each Olympic event on their website. The conditions under which the standard must be set (USATF-sanctioned meet and facilities,

Learning Activity

Discuss how you would categorize Olympic sports in the United States. Should participants be considered amateurs or professionals? Why?

fully automatic timing, acceptable wind speed) are also published. There are some exceptions to the regulations. For instance, a track and field athlete is eligible for automatic qualification into the Olympic Trials if he or she has earned an individual medal in an Olympic Games or in an IAAF World Indoor or Outdoor Championships during the four previous calendar years, or in the previous year won an individual USA Outdoor Track and Field Championship event (USATF.org, 2010). Individuals must meet requirements related to age and citizenship.

National Collegiate Athletic Association

The National Collegiate Athletic Association (NCAA) is a nonprofit educational association that has annual operating revenue of US$661 million. It is the largest and most influential governing body for intercollegiate athletics in the United States. The NCAA is organized to administer college sport and promulgate and enforce the rules agreed to by its more than 1,000 member schools. Back in the mid-1800s intercollegiate sport was steadily gaining popularity. Competition was being held in crew, baseball, track, and football. By the 1880s some events were drawing as many as 40,000 spectators (McLean, Hurd & Rogers, 2007).

In America, but almost nowhere else, identification with local universities creates a distinct demand for college sport that has relatively little competitive overlap with professional sport. The first documented intercollegiate athletics event was in a crew race pitting Harvard against Yale in 1852 (Smith, 1990). Athletics competition between institutions of higher learning expanded to include baseball in 1859 and American football in 1869, when Princeton and Rutgers competed in the first intercollegiate game. Shortly after colleges started competition in American football, the organization of college athletics that ultimately led to the formation of the NCAA began to take shape (Barr, 2009; Noll, 2003; Smith, 1990). Students, who initially ran intercollegiate athletics, recognized the need for increased governance and stricter rules, particularly with American football, and therefore formed the Intercollegiate Football Association in 1876. Problems persisted, however, and many injuries and even deaths occurred in American football, so the faculty took charge. Princeton University established the first faculty athletics committee in 1881. In 1895 the Intercollegiate Conference of Faculty Representatives (currently known as the Big Ten Conference) was formed because of the need for more legislative action concerning college football. Ultimately, discussion ensued about a university government structure to develop consistent rules that all institutions would follow (Barr, 2009; Noll, 2003; Smith, 1990; Robinson, 2005). The effort to reform college football led to the formation of the Intercollegiate Athletic Association of the United States in 1906. In 1912 the name was changed to the National Collegiate Athletic Association.

Currently, the NCAA has a constitution that consists of its mission and operating by-laws. An executive committee has representation from all three NCAA divisions (Divisions I, II, and III), but the majority of the board comes from Division I institutions (the most elite athletics division). The NCAA has an executive director and a national office that is not involved in the legislative process but rather works for the membership to host championships, conduct educational workshops, educate the membership on rules, and investigate rules violations (NCAA.org, 2008).

In terms of competition, the NCAA is organized hierarchically as divisions consisting of four divisions for American football competition and three for other sports. The National Association for Intercollegiate Athletics (NAIA) provides another division below NCAA Division III, except in basketball in which the NAIA has two divisions (Noll, 2003). The NCAA's top football category, known as the Football Bowl Subdivision (FBS) (formerly Division IA), has 120 teams divided into 11 conferences (plus a few independents). The six conferences that dominate the sport sponsor the Bowl Championship Series (BCS), which consists of five postseason bowl games involving the six league champions plus four other highly rated teams. One BCS game matches the two most highly rated teams to determine the

Learning Activity

Are the trends in NCAA athletics moving the athletes and events more toward professionalism? In what ways could the NCAA change its structure to ensure that its participants and sport competitions remain amateur in nature? Discuss what you think would be the best approach to these issues.

national champion. The lower football divisions and other intercollegiate team sports in all divisions have national championship postseason tournaments involving league champions and other highly rated teams (Noll, 2003).

Collegiate Intramural Sport

Intramural sport can be documented as one of the original forms of physical education and athletics competition in American colleges and universities. The desire of students to participate in informal athletics activities led to the beginning of collegiate intramurals (Kinder, 1998). Although intramural sport was unstructured, it achieved tremendous popularity in the early years. In 1859 Yale University formed intramural boating clubs that later evolved into interclass crew competition. In 1865 Princeton University formed intramural baseball teams, and within a decade numerous East Coast colleges had similar teams. The student-controlled intramural programs had to be centralized under the auspices of faculty supervision.

James Naismith, a teacher, coach, and minister from the YMCA founded basketball in 1891 to give young men something to do between football and baseball seasons. Naismith was under orders from his boss, Dr. Luther Gulick, head of physical education at the School for Christian Workers, to come up with an idea that would grab the attention of his disorderly physical education class. Basketball could be played indoors during the harsh Northeast winter months (Granatstein & Hillmer, 2000; Washington & Ventresca, 2008). By 1916 about 100 institutions had established intramural programs. In relation to athletics and physical education, intramural sport had the lowest priority, and this circumstance lasted until after World War II.

The National Intramural Recreational Sports Association (NIRSA), a professional, not-for-profit organization for intramurals, was established in 1950 when Dr. William Wasson convened a meeting of 22 African American men and women from 11 Historically Black Colleges and Universities at Dillard University in New Orleans. The organization has a nine-member board that includes the current NIRSA president and NIRSA executive director and governs the NIRSA Foundation (NIRSA, 2008). Outside North America, sport scholarships and college sport on the North American model do not exist, so the distinction between college and intramural sport has no relevance.

The success of intramural sport programs in U.S. colleges depends on the establishment of well-balanced leagues and teams. Club teams can compete with other clubs off campus. The intramural sport director is responsible for administering all phases of the intramural program in harmony with the college or university philosophy, objectives, and policy.

Interscholastic Sport

According to Hums and MacLean (2004), high school sport is a large segment of the sport industry, involving thousands of schools and participants. High school sport is primarily a North American phenomenon. In the rest of the world, athletes of high school age compete for club teams in their local communities. Around the turn of the 20th century the early form of interscholastic competition was student centered. As with American colleges, commercialism, poor sportsmanship, and cheating in athletics were the rationale for the creation of high school sport leagues and state athletics associations in the United States (Robinson, 2005).

Over 17,000 high schools are members of the National Federation of State High School Associations, and approximately 10,000,000 male and female athletes compete in interscholastic competition. In his review of high school programs, Robinson (2005) stated that the governance of interscholastic athletics competition involves four dimensions: the individual school district in which the school is located, the athletics conference in which a school athletics program competes, the state athletics association that governs a particular state, and the National Federation of State High School Associations that oversees high school athletics in this country. As early as 1924 all but three states in

the United States had started a state athletics association. The state associations establish rules; regulate competition between schools; enforce eligibility rules so that competition is fair; set standards for the registration, training, and evaluation of officials in all competitive activities; and provide other services such as the organization and administration of region and state championships.

Much like the NCAA, state schools are divided into classifications according to size. The state is divided into regions, and schools compete with other schools their size within their region. Some events are held as statewide events open to all schools, and some events are held on an elimination basis whereby regional winners advance to compete in state events in the various classifications (GHSA.net, 2006).

Community and Youth Sport

In their study of youth sport in the United States, De Knop, Engstrom, Skirstad, and Weiss (1996) divided youth sport into two organizational categories: (1) community-based programs and (2) school-based programs (other programs may be commercially based). Universally, community-based programs serve as many as twice the number of youth participants as school-based programs do, in part because of rapidly evaporating resources in the public schools and fewer people being qualified to coach. In contrast, community-based programs depend on parents and other volunteers to administer activities and coach children and youth in a variety of sports (De Knop et al., 1996). Note that in the United States intramural programs are rapidly becoming extinct at the middle and high school levels because legislation has drastically cut funding for them. In response to the evaporating outlets for youth who are not skilled enough to make varsity teams or who prefer less intense levels of play, programs sponsored by agencies such as local service organizations and affiliates of national youth organizations have emerged to fill the void (De Knop et al., 1996).

Community-based programs can be subdivided into various groupings based on service delivery such as agency-sponsored programs, national youth service organizations, club sport, and recreation programs (De Knop et al., 1996). Parks and recreation departments are the most common structure for delivery of services, but police, social services, health organizations and hospitals, public housing, and youth boards are other sponsoring agencies

(McLean, Hurd, & Rogers, 2007). Little League Baseball is an example of an agency-sponsored program. The Boys and Girls Clubs of America and the YMCA are examples of a national youth organization (De Knop et al., 1996; Edrington, DeGraaf, Dieser, & Edrington, 2002). The YMCA and YWCA systematically supply the needs of children, young adults, and older members with recreation, education, and service activity programs (McLean, Hurd, & Rogers, 2007).

As more participants specialize in sport, the popularity of nonschool clubs in the United States is trending upward at an accelerated pace. Nonschool clubs can serve as a farm system to high school or college sport and as a legal outlet for year-round participation in specific sports (De Knop et al., 1996). For example, national tournaments such as the AAU Leagues (AAUsports.org, 2008) and Nike Invitational Tournaments are readily available for nonschool clubs that are often made up of members of regular high school teams. College scouts routinely attend these tournaments and games in search of top prospects.

The foundation of community athletics participation has been city recreation departments (De Knop et al., 1996). Many local recreation programs across the country are capitalizing on the adult and baby boomer generation (estimated at 76 million). Adults have a range of interests, fitness levels, and needs for recreation programming (Gillion, 2008). Some programs are even customized to fit the demand of participants with special needs. For example, the adult program of the city of Palm Bay, Florida, includes activities such as tennis, adaptive tennis, aerobics, boxing, karate, belly dancing, and fishing in addition to baseball and softball leagues and tournaments (Palm Bay Parks and Recreation, 2010). Also, according to a 2007 survey by the National Sporting Goods Association, nationwide nearly 53 million adults aged 45 to 54 are participating in exercise walking, exercising with equipment, camping, hiking, working out at a club, and boating (NSGA.org, 2010).

Structure of Sport in Canada

This section describes participation in organized sport by Canadians and the sport governance structures in place in Canada. In addition to outlining the various sport organizations and structures in place—including high-performance sport, interscholastic sport, intercollegiate sport, community sport, and commercial and professional sport—these sections explain the various roles played by different levels of government, national sport organizations, and the relevant public policies.

Historical Background of Sport in Canada

Sport has a long and rich tradition in Canada. Many of the most popular sports in North America were first played in Canada and by Canadians. The games of the Native Peoples, such as lacrosse, had been played long before Canada was established as a nation and continue to be played and celebrated in communities across the country. As Europeans came to North America, they brought their favorite games with them. Other games were quickly adapted, often because of the realities of the new environment (Cox, Noonkester, Howell, & Howell, 1985).

Many sport clubs were established in the second half of the 19th century. Montréal served as the hotbed for organized sport in Canada. Although early Canadian sport had been mostly an experience for the upper classes, the growing industrialization and urbanization of Canada led to increased free time for the working classes (Metcalfe, 1987). Sport served as a popular diversion for many men and eventually for women as well. The Young Men's Christian Association (YMCA) played an important part in the dissemination of new games and in the provision of the space and facilities needed for many of the most popular sports (Johnson, 1979).

Up until the mid-20th century, sport had been mostly a recreational activity pursued by interested participants, wealthy benefactors, and, at the higher levels of competition, by those able to afford the costs associated with many sporting pursuits. In 1961 the federal government of Canada passed bill C-131, the Fitness and Amateur Sport Act. This formal piece of legislation identified sport as a legitimate concern of the federal government. This legislation and the programs and policies that followed rapidly transformed the Canadian sport system into a state-financed and state-controlled organism (Macintosh, Bedecki, & Franks, 1987).

Role of Government

In Canada, aside from ad hoc subsidization decisions made by various levels of government (federal, provincial, or municipal), professional sport is mostly outside the purview of the state-funded sport system. When considering the constituent parts of the Canadian sport system, an understanding of the basic tenets of Canadian federalism is necessary. In a general sense, the provincial governments are responsible for recreation, education, and health care—those sectors typically responsible for sport and physical activity (Simeon & Robinson, 2004).

The provincial governments have given municipalities (or regional governments) responsibility, for the most part, for the service delivery of education through local school boards, and of recreation through municipal parks and recreation departments. With that being said, the federal government also plays an important role in ensuring basic service delivery across the country by transferring funds to the provincial governments to support these services (Houlihan, 1997).

Sport is not specifically identified in the Constitution Act, but after decades of arguing between the provincial and federal governments over who had responsibility for sport, an understanding has been reached whereby the federal government has primary responsibility for high-performance sport and the provincial and territorial governments oversee recreation (Church, 2008). Therefore, the Canadian sport system is essentially another segment of the government bureaucracy.

The Canadian sport system (see figure 4.1), like the systems in most countries, is influenced greatly by the international sport community. The Canadian **national sport organizations** (NSOs) oversee most aspects of their individual sports, but much of what they do is dictated by the standards established by international federations and organizations who act as governing bodies for major games and other international competitions. Although control over the rules governing sport in Canada is mostly determined by international interests, the majority of the funding and support for the individual NSOs comes from the public sector (Church, 2008).

Sport Canada is the federal government organization that oversees most of the funding, programs, and policies relating to sport in Canada. It is a branch within the International and Intergovernmental Affairs Sector of the Department of Canadian Heritage. The director general of Sport Canada reports to the assistant deputy minister of International and Intergovernmental Affairs, who in turn reports to the associate deputy minister and the deputy minister of the Department of Canadian Heritage. Each of these positions is occupied by a member of the civil service, whereas the current

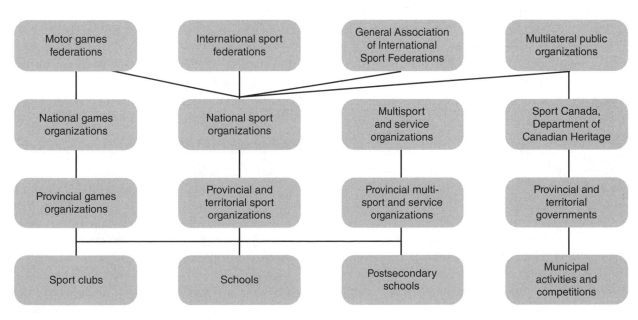

Figure 4.1 The structure of the Canadian sport system.

Courtesy of the Department of Canadian Heritage. Reproduced with the permission of the Minister of Public Works and Government Services, 2010.

government of Canada has an elected member of parliament (MP) serving as minister of State (the department that includes sport) and another as minister of Canadian Heritage and Official Languages. Both positions are federal cabinet positions.

Perhaps the most significant recent development in the Canadian sport system is the development of the Canadian Sport Policy. In 2000 Sport Canada initiated a process that would lead to the 2001 National Summit on Sport. The summit was intended to be a broad collaborative effort that would allow all sport stakeholders from across the country to have their voices heard as part of a process to develop a national policy on sport. The resulting Canadian Sport Policy, released in 2002, identified four principles upon which the Canadian sport system would be based: enhanced excellence, enhanced participation, enhanced capacity, and enhanced interaction. The policy also established a vision of "a dynamic and leading-edge sport environment that enables all Canadians to experience and enjoy involvement in sport to the extent of their abilities and interests and, for increasing numbers, to perform consistently and successfully at the highest competitive levels" by the year 2012 (Canadian Heritage, 2002, p. 4).

Following the release of the policy, the federal and provincial governments also established the Federal–Provincial/Territorial Priorities for Collaborative Action 2002–2005 and later the Federal–Provincial/Territorial Priorities for Collaborative Action 2007–2012. The priorities serve as strategic initiatives through which the different levels of government work together on common goals in sport. Shortly after the release of the Canadian Sport Policy, the federal government released in rapid succession a new piece of sport legislation and a half dozen new policies related to specific aspects of the sport system.

Currently a great deal of discussion is ongoing about the Canadian sport system. Without a doubt, the most pressing issue is the question of funding. Recently, certain stakeholders, led by the Canadian Olympic Committee, have become much more organized in their efforts at lobbying government and the private sector for increased funding. The federal government and the private sector have increased funding to support high-performance sport in hopes of achieving better international results, particularly with the attention on Canada as

host of the 2010 Olympic Winter Games (Priestner, Allinger, & Allinger, 2004). But with the dramatic cost overruns associated with hosting the Games and the international spotlight moving on to the next host country, the private and public sectors will again evaluate the importance of funding high-performance sport.

The discussion of the state's role in high-performance sport funding is becoming increasingly relevant, because a disturbing reality is the rising rate of obesity in Canadians, particularly in young people, and the declining rate of sport participation (Ifedi, 2008). Many advocates of public funding of sport are beginning to argue for diverting the funding from high-performance sport to increasing access for all to physical activity and sport opportunities. Still others are arguing for increased funding across the board for all sport (Leitch, Bassett, & Weil, 2006). With the Canadian sport system so dependent on public financing, managing a sport organization can be trying, because funding is closely tied to the whims of the government of the day.

Professional and Elite Sport in Canada

Although sport in Canada was originally founded on the British ideals of amateurism, over time professional sport has emerged to become the most pervasive form of sport in Canada. With three national all-sports television stations, multiple all-sports radio stations, sports sections that dominate national and local newspapers, and millions of people clamoring to consume as much sport as possible, the Canadian professional sport landscape has come to resemble that of the United States.

Commercial Professional Sport

Private entities have opportunities to gain their piece of the sport GDP pie, which is 1.2 percent of the entire Canadian GDP (Bloom, Grant, & Watt, 2005). Although participant-focused enterprises such as private sport clubs do generate a great deal of revenue, professional sport is most prevalent in the Canadian sport landscape and represents a large portion of the national sport GDP. Although professional hockey (both major and minor leagues) is the most popular sport, the largest leagues in Canada are the National Hockey League (NHL), Canadian

Sport Matters Group

Ian Bird is a former high-performance athlete who represented Canada in field hockey at two Olympic Games and the Commonwealth Games. He retired from competition after the 2000 Olympic Games in Sydney, Australia, and immediately set out to become a leader within the Canadian sport system. His leadership roles have included executive director of the Canadian Professional Coaches Association and chair of Athletes CAN, the Canadian association of national team athletes. He was also a catalyst in the growth of Esteem Team, Canada's first national athlete role-model program. In 2003 he was the winner of the Canadian Athlete Leader of the Year Award.

Since September 1, 2005, Ian Bird has served as senior leader of the Sport Matters Group (SMG). Although he identifies Sport Matters as an "open-source sport policy community" (Sport Matters Group, 2009), the fact is that much of what he and the SMG have undertaken over the past few years has been sport advocacy and lobbying of government bodies and officials. Essentially, the SMG is a collection of sport leaders and organizations who are working together to promote sport and strengthen the sport system in Canada, often through attempts to influence public-sector decision makers.

Although a great deal of what the Sport Matters Group does is informal cooperation and interaction between members, the organization has become much more organized and influential in the development of Canadian sport policy. SMG has chaired all candidate meetings for sport representatives from each political party to attend before federal elections, has facilitated local sport organizations' involvement in provincial elections, has regularly appeared before government heritage and finance committees to extol the virtues of sport, and organizes ongoing consultations throughout the country. Mr. Bird has frequently accessed decision makers at the highest levels, and civil servants and elected officials within the federal and provincial governments often listen to what he has to say. As Ian Bird and the Sport Matters Group continue to build legitimacy within the public sector, future sport policies in Canada will be increasingly influenced by what Mr. Bird and his voluntary group of sport leaders have to say.

Football League (CFL), the National Basketball Association (NBA), Major League Baseball (MLB), and Major League Soccer (MLS).

Besides those leagues, the National Football League (popular in Canada but based in the United States and without a Canadian franchise), mixed martial arts (popular in Canada but banned in many parts of the country), and automobile racing (National Association for Stock Car Auto Racing, Formula One, and the Indy Racing League have all held events in Canada) are professional sport organizations that have fans who attend events, purchase merchandise, and watch televised events.

Although each professional sport organization faces unique management issues, all share a number of concerns. Aside from the CFL, all the organizations previously listed are controlled primarily by international stakeholders. The United States is home to the head offices of the professional sport leagues and a great majority of the franchises. As such, many of the management concerns faced by professional sport in Canada are shared by the franchises in the United States. But issues relating to funding, Canadian content, and doping are more pertinent to Canadian sport organizations than to other international sport organizations.

As with many areas within the Canadian sport system, economic concerns tend to be of primary concern to Canadian professional sport. Canadian sport franchises competing with U.S. franchises must compete for players (through free agency) and operate with the majority of their revenue being in Canadian dollars and significant expenses (player salaries) being in U.S. dollars. Because the Canadian dollar is often worth less than the U.S. dollar, Canadian franchises are operating at a disadvantage. For that reason, among others, Canadian professional sport teams have asked for public funding support.

The Canadian public has usually been reticent, if not strongly opposed, to the idea of using public money to support professional sport. Although public financing of stadiums and arenas is common in the United States, large-scale public financing of professional sport facilities has rarely occurred in Canada (Church, 2008). Some provincial governments have used lottery revenue to support their professional sport teams, but the federal government was strongly rebuked in their one attempt to offer funding support to professional sport franchise operations. The general view of the public has been that as long as there are unemployed Canadians, public money should not be spent on billionaire sport owners and millionaire athletes (Whitson, Harvey & Lavoie, 2000).

Although Canadian content is not a major concern of professional sport franchises in Canada, it is highly relevant for the CFL and the two Canadian MLS franchises, Toronto FC and the Vancouver FC. The Canadian Football League, which has slight differences in its game versus that of the NFL, mandates that 21 of the 42 players on a team's active roster must be born or trained in Canada (*Canadian Football League*, 2009). Major League Soccer has a similar rule pertaining to rosters. An MLS team roster includes 18 senior roster players and up to 10 youth roster players. A total of 144 international player slots are divided among the 18 teams. Each team began with eight international slots. The slots are tradable, therefore, there is no limit on the number of international slots on each team's roster. Any remaining players must be from the country in which the team is based (all are based in the United States, except for Toronto FC and Vancouver FC). The two teams based in Canada may fill their domestic slots with either Canadian or U.S. domestic players. They are required to have a minimum of three Canadian domestic players on their rosters (Major League Soccer, 2011).

Doping and ethics issues are of significance on the world stage and have received increasing attention in North American professional sport. Most professional leagues, along with their respective players associations, have instituted some form of

Learning Activity

With your understanding of the structure of the Canadian sport system and some of the major issues, assume that you are working for the Toronto FC of Major League Soccer. Decide how your organization could best work with government to address some of their concerns with sport while at the same time benefiting your organization.

testing, doping control, and formal policies and procedures relating to banned substances, but some still have not. In June 2010 the CFL and CFLPA announced the Canadian Football League's first ever drug testing policy. The policy provides for an education program for all players beginning in 2010 with player testing beginning in January 2011 (*CFL Drug Policy at a glance*, 2010). The NHL has chosen not to invoke testing procedures on their athletes. Although the league claims that doping is not prevalent in the NHL and is not a major concern, some have pointed to the league's financial burden as an explanation for why the league has chosen not to institute comprehensive drug testing policies.

Elite Sport

Sport Canada, which is currently housed in the Department of Canadian Heritage, is the federal government body responsible for sport in Canada. Its mission is "to enhance opportunities for Canadians to participate and excel in sport" (Sport Canada, 2009). Sport Canada's responsibilities include executive services, policy and planning, sport support, sport excellence, major games and hosting, business operations, and management strategies. With much of the Canadian sport system relying on federal government support, the survival of most sport organizations depends on the funding programs administered by Sport Canada.

Traditionally, and particularly more recently with the 2010 Olympic Winter Games being hosted in Canada, Sport Canada has been primarily interested in supporting sports that appear in the Olympic Games, giving special attention to sports in which Canadians have the highest likelihood of winning medals. Although this type of treatment of high-performance international sport fits with the political goals of the federal government, some debate has begun concerning the appropriateness of public financing of an elite sport system that supports a small number of Canadian athletes. Critics of the current funding formula include those who believe that sport should not be a sector that government regulates and funds, and those who believe that because of the rising rates of inactivity and obesity in Canadians, particularly in the youth population, any government investment in sport should be at a grassroots level that promotes physical activity for all Canadians.

CASE STUDY

Sport Canada

In 1961, when sport first appeared as a legitimate policy sector for the federal government in Canada, the government body responsible for overseeing sport, the newly created Fitness and Amateur Sport Directorate (FASD), was housed within the Ministry of National Health and Welfare. This configuration made a great deal of sense at the time, because programs that promoted active and healthy living were already being operated through this ministry and the federal government had established the FASD to promote increased participation in sport.

During the campaign for the 1968 federal election, Pierre Trudeau, who was to become prime minister, made sport a part of his platform. He promised to investigate sport after he was elected and to work at improving Canada's performance at the Olympics, particularly in ice hockey. After taking office he appointed a task force that produced a report that made a number of recommendations, including the creation of an organization specifically to oversee elite international sport. This report was seen by many as being highly political in nature because hand-picked appointees came from business and high-performance sport. Although many critics were appalled by the task force's focus on high-performance sport, the report and subsequent government action would come to shape the Canadian sport system for the next four decades.

In 1971 the federal government announced the creation of Sport Canada and Recreation Canada, which became the two divisions within the FASD. In 1973 the FASD was elevated to branch status. Sport Canada became a well-funded division with strong leadership, whereas Recreation Canada floundered somewhat. Recreation Canada was further split into two separate divisions, Recreation Canada and Fitness Canada, and Recreation Canada was eventually dissolved in 1980 when the federal government agreed that recreation was a responsibility of provincial government.

Between 1980 and 1993 the Fitness and Amateur Sport Branch remained intact with roughly the same structure. Sport Canada had its mandate to produce high-performance sport results, and it remained the higher profile and better funded of the two divisions. During this period, however, the branch was shuffled from National Health and Welfare to Secretary of State, to Labor, back to Secretary of State, and finally back to National Health and Welfare. The shuffling of the branch reflected the fact that sport, particularly how the federal government funded it, had a role in labor, health, welfare, foreign affairs, and undoubtedly other government sectors.

In 1993 Prime Minister Kim Campbell decided that a major restructuring of government was necessary. Included in her moves was the decision to move Fitness Canada to the Department of Health and send Sport Canada to the newly created Department of Canadian Heritage. This arrangement remains the current structure of sport and recreation in Canada. Though Sport Canada has expanded its mandate to include promoting participation by all Canadians in sport, high-performance sport remains its priority as far as funding and institutional support is concerned. Fitness Canada remains committed to promoting healthy active living, but the division views sport as being just one component of an active lifestyle. Sport is not its priority.

Amateur Sport in Canada

Besides the high-performance components of the Canadian sport system, sport is also supported and promoted within the education system and through community-based organizations. The following sections describe sport in the school system, provide an overview of postsecondary school sport, and then explain community sport. Each section provides a brief overview of the subject, as well as some trends and concerns for sport managers.

Scholastic Sport

As previously mentioned, the education system in Canada is a provincial responsibility, but a number of similar characteristics and concerns are relevant to sport in schools across the country. Sport, as a component of the curriculum, is typically incorporated into the physical education and health curriculum. Schools also commonly offer extracurricular sport through intramural programs and interscholastic competition.

Although the current trends in Canadian physical education are not typically sport management concerns, they are worth identifying. Physical education is being devalued in the curriculum. Mandatory physical education is being clawed back, qualified physical educators are in short supply, and facilities in many cases are inadequate, whether the problem is crumbling infrastructure or inadequate space to meet the demands of quality daily physical education (Royal Commission on Learning, 1995).

In addition, sport is becoming the new focus of physical education. Instead of the traditional physical education curriculum focused on body movement, fitness, and training, there is an increasing emphasis on sport (Houlihan, 1997). This education problem may be linked to the lack of qualified physical educators, because schools are often using untrained physical educators who may know only about the most popular sports.

Although these trends have been apparent for a number of years, little has been done to contend with them. Because the provinces are responsible for education, these concerns have not been publicized nationally, although the primary advocacy group, **Physical and Health Education Canada**, has been a long-time supporter of quality daily physical education in safe and accessible facilities, offered by qualified physical educators.

Intramural programs, offered in most schools, offer another opportunity for students to participate in sport. Most programs are run by school staff and faculty and, in many cases, by student leaders. The programs typically offer before-school, after-school, or lunchtime opportunities for competitive and recreational sport participation. The program administrators and participants are supported by the national, not-for-profit **Canadian Intramural Recreation Association**. Like physical education, intramural programs often suffer because of poor infrastructure (inadequate facilities and lack of sufficient equipment to meet demand). Some intramural programs have been scaled back or cancelled because of an absence of staff willing to supervise the programs.

The final aspect of sport in schools is interscholastic competition. Interschool competition in Canada has a rich history, beginning with the formal introduction of sport into the physical education curriculum in the 1940s and 1950s (Lally, 2008). City, regional, and even provincial

championships exist, but no national championships are offered for interscholastic sport teams. Each province has a governing body that oversees provincial championships, and local school boards are responsible for overseeing local and regional competitions.

Although these competitive sport programs confront many of the same concerns faced by physical education and intramural programs, notably inadequate infrastructure and lack of qualified staff to supervise, financing is an additional concern. Typically, a school team is composed of a select few students. Because of the high cost of supporting a team—including equipment, uniforms, travel costs, insurance, support staff salary, and facility use costs—some may begin to wonder whether a publicly funded education system in financial crisis should be spending large sums of money on a few students.

Intercollegiate Athletics

Interuniversity competition in Canada is overseen by Canadian Interuniversity Sport (CIS), and competition between colleges is governed by the **Canadian Colleges Athletic Association (CCAA)**. Intercollegiate competition began with ad hoc competitions organized by student leaders at some of Canada's oldest universities—the University of Toronto, McGill University, Queen's University, and the University of Western Ontario (Metcalfe, 1987).

Steps toward a centralized bureaucratic governance structure were taken in 1906 with the advent of the Canadian Intercollegiate Athletic Union (CIAU), which oversaw interuniversity competition in Ontario and Québec. In the years that followed, similar unions were formed to govern competition in the Atlantic provinces and in western Canada. Separate women's athletic unions were established as well. In 1961 the unions merged to form the CIAU, which oversaw national competition. In 2001 the CIAU was renamed CIS (Lally, 2008).

Although the intercollegiate sport system in Canada has become much more centralized, the policies of the various regional governing boards still differ. At present there are four regional governing associations: Atlantic University Sport, Canada West Universities Athletic Association, Ontario University Athletics, and Québec Student Sports Federation. Each of the regional organizations must abide by CIS policies, but slight variations exist in specific policy areas related to university sport.

Currently over 50 major degree-granting institutions take part in CIS competition, and close to 100 colleges compete in the CCAA (Lally, 2008). Although Canadian intercollegiate athletics is nowhere near the size of the collegiate athletics system in the United States, it faces many of the same problems. Issues of equity, doping, hazing, athletic scholarships, and the question of the appropriateness of subsidizing high-performance sport by publicly funded institutions are all current issues facing intercollegiate athletics decision makers.

Although American postsecondary institutions must comply with Title IX legislation that dictates that universities must offer equal opportunities for men and women to participate, Canadian universities and colleges must comply with the Charter of Rights and Freedoms. Recent findings point to the fact that CIS is heading toward gender equity. Although the number of sports offered is close to equal for men and women, inequality still exists in some institutions relating to funding, promotion, opportunities for competition, use of facilities, and other out-of-competition factors (Lally, 2008).

In 1990 the Canadian Centre for Ethics in Sport began submitting CIS student–athletes to tests for banned substances. Although performance-enhancing drugs are not a major problem in Canadian intercollegiate athletics, CIS records indicate that there is a 0.8 percent positive result in tested athletes, estimated to be roughly equivalent to the general postsecondary student population (Lally, 2008).

Sport initiation and hazing of student–athletes have recently received a great deal of mainstream media attention. Although injuries, both physical and psychological, are often associated with hazing, the initiation of new members through sometimes humiliating and physically taxing rites of passage has been commonplace in sport. The recently exposed hazing practices that occurred at several Canadian universities drew outrage from parents, the media, and the general population. As a result many universities have forced athletics departments to monitor the conduct of their athletes better and develop codes of conduct that specifically ban hazing practices (Lally, 2008).

The final two issues in intercollegiate athletics to be discussed are related—athletic awards and the place of interuniversity sport in higher education. Whereas the U.S. collegiate athletics system provides an enormous number of athletic scholarships to students, the Canadian system has traditionally shied away from providing support to students based solely on athletic prowess. The current CIS policy relating to athletic awards is that, although individual regional associations and institutions are able to integrate additional criteria, awards may not exceed the amount equivalent to tuition and other compulsory fees. The university attended must grant and administer the awards; otherwise, the award (which includes scholarships and bursaries) must not have any conditions relating to attendance or participation in sport at a specific academic institution.

Besides the parameters identified earlier, the CIS has also established policies relating to specific eligibility criteria. Incoming first-year students must have a minimum entering grade of 80 percent to be eligible to receive an award, and upper-year students must possess a grade average of 65 percent or higher to be eligible to receive an award (Lally, 2008). In this area significant variation is seen between regional associations and between institutions. Many universities have chosen to have much more stringent academic requirements for student–athletes to be eligible for awards.

Currently a number of athletics departments, coaches, athletes, and supporters of interuniversity sport in Canada are advocating for increased funding to interuniversity sport, which includes arguments for less stringent award-eligibility requirements and additional funds to support student–athletes. At the same time, others question whether competitive sport should even be a part of institutions of higher education. For these people the issue includes both funding, because athletics programs cost a great deal and are funded primarily through taxpayers and fees charged to the student body, and the concern of access and equity. Many argue that providing a small percentage of the student body (student–athletes) with primary access to the campus sport and recreation facilities and draining the student activity budget of the campus sport and recreation department is unfair. Although most athletics budgets and facilities at universities in the United States are dramatically larger than those at Canadian institutions, the philosophical debate continues regarding the place of sport in institutions of higher learning and the associated issues of access and equity.

Learning Activity

Review the policies of the CIS (http://english
.cis-sic.ca) and determine what challenges
an athletics director at a Canadian university faces that an athletics director in
the United States would not have to worry
about.

Community Sport

The most recent numbers regarding active sport participation in Canada are somewhat disconcerting,
yet they could conceivably present opportunities
for prescient sport managers. Recently it has been
determined that only 28 percent of Canadians are
regular active sport and recreation participants
(Ifedi, 2008). This number has been dropping continuously over the last 20 years and may explain
in part the growing rates of obesity and obesity-
related illnesses. Sport managers who make a living
from people engaged in sport and recreation (be it
through event hosting, equipment sales, registra-
tions, memberships, and so on) have significant
cause for concern regarding the continuous decline
in participation numbers.

At the same time as the number of active participants declines, the number of people who watch
sport, officiate, administer, coach, and volunteer in
sport has been increasing (Ifedi, 2008). For sport
managers this trend may offer insight into emerging
markets and opportunities for future business ventures. While Canadians become more sedentary, the
percentage of the Canadian GDP attributed to sport is
increasing and sport is further permeating all aspects
of Canadian life (Bloom, Grant, & Watt, 2005).

Although sport is pervasive in all aspects of
Canadian life, the lack of participation is not a
great concern to the private sector, because there
is relatively little private interest, or benefit, in
sport participation. As described earlier, sport
and recreation is primarily a municipal concern;
the education system and municipally operated
recreation departments are the primary providers
of sport and recreation opportunities in Canada.
Unlike the European sport system that includes
significant active involvement by local sporting clubs in providing opportunities and school

systems that place much less emphasis on competitive sport, the Canadian sport and recreation
system depends heavily on public financing and
support (Macintosh & Whitson, 1990). Therefore,
community sport is often thought of as local not-
for-profit sport leagues that provide opportunities
for children and municipally operated recreation
programs. Although private sport clubs are present in Canada, high membership fees usually limit
access for the public.

Summary

This chapter discussed organizational structures of
sport in North America, specifically addressing the
distinctive features of the sport frameworks of the
United States and Canada in the context of those
countries' historical development and diverse institutions, systems, and practices. Differences between
North American sport and the rest of the world are
explained through the various roles played by the
government, public, economy, competition, and
federal and local laws.

U.S. sport organizational structures differ from
those in other countries in many ways. The sport
industry in the United States is a large, multifaceted
enterprise, but for the purposes of this chapter
it has been divided into two primary segments,
professional sport and amateur sport. Professional sport consists of the big four predominant
sport leagues (MLB, NBA, NFL, NHL), as well as
others such as MLS and various circuits and tours
(NASCAR, PGA and LPGA, and so on). Amateur
sport organizations include the NCAA, USOC,
NIRSA, NFSHS, AAU, Little League, and others.
The structures of these organizations have evolved
over the past one and a half centuries. The United
States has created a unique brand and system of
sport delivery that distinguishes it from most other
countries. The most popular format for U.S. professional and amateur league competition is single
leagues that sponsor round-robin seasonal play
followed by a postseason tournament. The leagues
have relatively few levels of competition. American
college athletics competition is immensely popular
on both regional and national levels, and colleges
serve as the primary feeder system for professional
leagues. In the United States the top four professional leagues have fixed memberships. Professional and amateur sport managers in the United

States need to maintain the knowledge and skills necessary to deal with a range of issues such as finding new ways of financing their organizations and programs, negotiating with the media and labor, developing effective policies, and enforcing competition rules and regulations.

The second section discussed the sport organizational structure in Canada and described the responsibilities of various levels of government in delivering services to the public. The Canadian sport system is unique, although it has many similarities with the systems of other countries where some sports originated and were brought to Canada. The popularity of sport in Canada escalated in the second half of the 19th century. This heightened interest and increased participation created concerns for sport distribution, organizational and policy needs to govern sport, and funding issues. A clear line of separation is evident between professional and other sport segments, related largely to public financial support. Professional sport in Canada is left to seek its own funding sources; amateur sport is largely subsidized by either the federal, provincial, or municipal governments. Because much of the Canadian sport system depends on public financing, perhaps the most significant issues relate to the control of the public sector over sport in Canada and the associated funding concerns.

Professional sport in Canada is reflective of the system in the United States, because many of the leagues are based in the United States and are governed primarily by people living outside Canada. Professional hockey is the most popular Canadian sport. Prominent leagues in Canada include the NHL, CFL, NBA, MLB, and MLS. Because all but the CFL have international stakeholders, the management concerns faced by professional sport in Canada are shared by the franchises in the United States.

This chapter also discussed many of the issues confronting sport managers responsible for sport programs sponsored by the Canadian government at the various levels. Current concerns include the precipitous decline in participation numbers in community-based programs, the need for a more centralized structure in university sport, staffing and financial concerns in interscholastic sport, and funding support at all levels. Sport organizational structures in North America continue to evolve, so managers must continually seek innovative strategies to deliver sport content to the public and ensure that their organizational goals are achieved.

? Review and Discussion Questions

1. In the early 1920s a U.S. Supreme Court ruling played an important role in the development of professional baseball. What was the ruling? Discuss the effect of the ruling on baseball since its passage. Has the ruling influenced the evolution of other professional sport organizations in the United States? How?

2. How does the structure of professional sport organizations in America prevent teams from entering a league if they wish? Contrast this with structures used in other countries around the world.

3. The major professional leagues in the United States all have similar structure and are viable sport organizations. The organizational structure of MLS, however, differs from that of any of the major professional leagues in the United States. In what ways is MLS different? What are the advantages and disadvantages of the structure of MLS? Discuss why (or why not) you think the structure will ensure the survival of the league.

4. Major college sports such as American football, basketball, baseball, and, in some regions of the United States, ice hockey have flourished. Games attract sold-out crowds, and successful teams generate millions of dollars of revenue for their athletics departments. Discuss how American colleges have been able to operate successfully without any competitive overlap with professional sport.

5. Does the level of government involvement in sport in Canada make it easier or harder for a manager of (a) an NSO, (b) a community recreation organization, (c) a university athletics department, and (d) a professional sport team? How? Why?

(continued)

(continued)

6. After reading the section on Canadian sport, what do you think the role of government is in sport in Canada? Do you think that the role is appropriate, or should government take a different approach? Why?

7. In a free-market economy, is it appropriate for professional sport teams to have to meet a quota of domestic or foreign players? What stakeholders would be opposed to, or in favor of, these quotas?

Sport in Latin America

Gonzalo A. Bravo, PhD
West Virginia University, USA

Jaime Orejan, PhD
Winston-Salem State University, North Carolina, USA

Luisa Vélez, PhD
State University of New York College
at Cortland, USA

Rosa López de D'Amico, PhD
Universidad Pedagógica Experimental Libertador,
Venezuela

Chapter Objectives

After studying this chapter, you will be able to do the following:

- Explain the differences and similarities among Latin American countries regarding their sport systems
- Discuss the foundations of how the sport industry has developed in Latin America
- Identify the most popular sports practiced and followed in Latin America
- Discuss the role of government in the development of sport in Latin American countries
- Identify some of the sport governing bodies that rule the sporting scene in Latin America

Key Terms

Key Events

Pan American Games. Hosted every four years since 1951, it is the multisport festival for members of the Pan American Sport Organization (ODEPA).

Central American and Caribbean Games. Hosted since 1926, it is the oldest continuing (never interrupted) multisport games in the world. It involves members of the Central American and Caribbean Sports Organization (ODECABE).

ODESUR Games. Multisport festival for members of the South American Sport Organization (ODESUR), it has been held every four years since 1976. It involves the participation of 15 countries.

South American Club Championship. Better known as Copa Libertadores, it is the prime club championship cup for football club members of CONMEBOL.

South American Championships of Nations. Better known as Copa América, it is the tournament for national team members of CONMEBOL. Hosted since 1916, is the oldest football tournament of its kind in the world.

Caribbean Baseball Series. Hosted since 1946, it is the baseball tournament for club champion members of the Caribbean Baseball Confederation.

Key People

Edson Arantes do Nascimento (Pelé), Brazil. The most influential football player of the 20th century (1956–1977). Appointed as the first sports minister in Brazil (1995–1998). Author of *Pelé Law*, about reforming professional football in Brazil.

Julio Grondona, Argentina. Vice president of the International Federation of Association Football (FIFA), president of the Argentinean Football Association (AFA), and member of FIFA executive committee.

Flor Isava-Fonseca, Venezuela. First woman to be appointed as a member of the International Olympic Committee (IOC). Currently an honorary member of the IOC.

Nicolas Leóz, Paraguay. President of the South American Football Confederation) and president of the Paraguayan Football Association (1971–1986).

Carlos Arthur Nuzman, Brazil. Member of the International Olympic Committee (IOC). President of the Brazilian Olympic Committee (COB), president of the South American Sport Organization (ODESUR), and president of the Brazilian Volleyball Confederation (1975–1995).

Mario Vázquez Raña, Mexico. Member of the International Olympic Committee (IOC) and member of the IOC executive board. Chair of Olympic Solidarity, president of the Pan American Sport Organization (ODEPA), and president of the Association of National Olympic Committees (ANOC).

This chapter examines how sport has evolved and is currently organized in Latin America, and it looks closely at the role of government and nongovernmental organizations in shaping a country's sport structure and system. Although important differences exist among the sport systems across Latin America, many similarities are present as well. For the student to gain a better understanding of these differences and similarities, we have organized this chapter by broad themes that contribute to the understanding of the sport industry in Latin America. In addition, we examine a few issues that are of interest to sport managers. Accordingly, the chapter is organized into five main topics. It begins with a background description that includes a few social and economic indicators for Latin American countries; it continues by examining the cultural foundations that have shaped the adoption and popularity of sport across the region. It follows with an account of how the sport systems are organized; then, five constitutive aspects of the sport industry are presented. The chapter ends with a brief description of the main international sporting events hosted in Latin American countries and a description of the governing bodies that operate in the region.

The information presented in this chapter was chosen based on two criteria: the specific authors' knowledge of the sport system of a given country and the availability of information on how sport is organized in Latin America. Although an extensive strand of literature focuses on the historical and sociological aspects of Latin American sport, studies describing the business aspects of sport and how a sport system is structured, organized, and funded are scarce. According to Miller, "The academic study of sport in Latin America is thus an infant area, lagging behind the growth that has taken place in Europe and North America" (2004, p. 188). The same author also noted, when referring to the state of football in Latin America, that the lack of research in the field is also indicative of the "lack of sophisticated management practices in the industry" (2007, p. 24). Considering these limitations and the space constraints of the chapter, this information cannot be comprehensive or present an exhaustive analysis of the sport industry in Latin America, but it will introduce the reader to the major features of sport in the region.

Geography and Background of Latin America

Latin America encompasses a vast geographical area within the Americas that extends for more than 8 million square miles (21 million sq km). Politically, Latin America is formed by 26 countries (Skidmore & Smith, 2005). For the purpose of this chapter, however, we will refer to Latin America as the area that is culturally bounded by a common language with a strong Hispanic and Portuguese influence. Anglophone-, French-, and Dutch-speaking countries are not included in this analysis. Consequently, in this chapter, 19 countries and the Commonwealth of Puerto Rico represent Latin America. They cover an area from the Rio Grande, the border between the United States and Mexico, all the way to Patagonia. From north to south these countries are

Mexico in North America; Guatemala, Honduras, El Salvador, Nicaragua, Costa Rica, and Panama in Central America; and Colombia, Venezuela, Brazil, Ecuador, Peru, Bolivia, Paraguay, Uruguay, Argentina and Chile in South America. Finally, Cuba, the Dominican Republic, and Puerto Rico are the two Latin American countries and one territory that are located in the Caribbean.

Today, the overall population of Latin America surpasses 550 million people who live in an area that occupies almost two-thirds of the Americas or one-fifth of the world's total land area (Wiarda & Kline, 2007). In a global world, the influence of Latin America cannot be overlooked. For most of the 20th century Latin America was a close strategic, economic, and political ally of the United States as well as many other nations (McPherson, 2006).

Countries in the Latin American region are characterized by their similar cultural and historical roots as well as their adherence to similar approaches to several facets of life. Of these, the most notable is having Spanish as the common language. The exception is Brazil, which has Portuguese as its official language. Furthermore, many countries embrace the Catholic faith as their primary form of religion. Also, many countries share a common base in law, history, and colonial experience. Despite these similarities, the region is also diverse and heterogeneous. In terms of ethnicity, no single group is predominant. Williamson (1997) identified four ethnic groups in Latin America: the mestizo (a term that describes someone whose background is European and Native American Indian); people of European descent; Native Indians; and people of African descent. The predominant group or groups vary by country.

From an economic perspective, Latin American countries are also diverse. Although some countries have extensive natural resources and operate large internal markets that attain high levels of economic growth, the majority still struggle in fighting poverty, have inadequate health standards, and have not reached acceptable levels of education. Nonetheless, and in spite of being referred to as a region of developing countries, Latin America as a region reached an economic growth rate of 4.6 percent during 2008 (ECLAC, 2008). Moreover, the 2009 **Human Development Index (HDI)**, developed by the United Nations Development Programme (UNDP), classified 12 Latin American countries as

high developed and seven as medium developed (UNDP, 2009). The Human Development Index (HDI) is a composite score (0 to 1) that measures a country's achievement in three basic areas: health, education, and standard of living (UNDP, 1990). But for all the trends and signs toward better economic and social conditions, wide economic inequality still exists within many of these countries. Many Latin American nations have among the highest wealth distribution disparities in the world (UNDP, 2009). Table 5.1 shows some demographics and other parameters of development for Latin America.

Cultural Foundations of Sport in Latin America

A basic understanding of the historical, cultural, and socioeconomic conditions of the region is acute to understanding how modern sport has been developed and organized in Latin America. In the section that follows, we examine some of the forces that have influenced the evolution and diffusion of modern sport across the region. Also, we present a description of the popularity of certain sports and how the intensity with which people embrace the sport has been influenced, at times, by their social class, gender, and religion.

Evolution of Modern Sport in Latin America

Although several native and pre-Columbian ritual games (e.g., Mesoamerican ball games in Mexico) existed at the time of the Spanish conquest, none of these activities played a significant role in shaping today's Latin American sporting scene because they were practiced mostly for survival or for celebratory or religious rituals. For example, in Puerto Rico and other Caribbean islands one of the most popular indigenous games practiced before the arrival of the Spaniards was *batu*, which consisted of throwing a ball in the air and passing it from one group to the other without letting it touch the ground. The colonization of Puerto Rico by Spain in 1493 ended this practice and instead brought different sports to the island, among them horseracing and cockfighting (Domenech, 2003).

Most forms of sport that are currently popular in Latin American countries evolved in a similar pattern as they did in other areas of the world. They are

Table 5.1 Selected Parameters of Development in Latin American Countries

Country	Population (millions) 2007	Human Development Index (HDI)	GDP per capita (PPP US$)[a]	Adult literacy[b] (%)	Inequality measure, Gini index[c]	Life expectancy at birth (2007)
Argentina	39.5	0.866	13,238	97.6	50.0	75.2
Bolivia	9.5	0.729	4,206	90.7	58.2	65.4
Brazil	190.1	0.813	9,567	90.0	55.0	72.2
Chile	16.6	0.878	13,880	96.5	52.0	78.5
Colombia	44.4	0.807	8,587	92.7	58.5	72.7
Costa Rica	4.5	0.854	10,842	95.9	47.2	78.7
Cuba	11.2	0.863	6,876	99.8	N/A	78.5
Dominican Rep.	9.8	0.777	6,706	89.1	50.0	72.4
Ecuador	13.3	0.806	7,449	91.0	54.4	75.0
El Salvador	6.1	0.747	5,804	82.0	49.7	71.3
Guatemala	13.4	0.704	4,562	73.2	53.7	70.1
Honduras	7.2	0.732	3,796	83.6	55.3	72.0
Mexico	107.5	0.854	14,104	92.8	48.1	76.0
Nicaragua	5.6	0.699	2,570	78.0	52.3	72.7
Panama	3.3	0.840	11,391	93.4	54.9	75.5
Paraguay	6.1	0.761	4,433	94.6	53.2	71.7
Peru	28.5	0.806	7,836	89.6	49.6	73.0
Puerto Rico	3.9	NA	17,700	94.1	48.4	78.5
Uruguay	3.3	0.865	11,216	97.9	46.2	76.1
Venezuela	27.7	0.844	12,156	95.2	43.4	73.6
United States	308.7	0.956	45,592	99.0	40.8	79.1

[a]Purchasing power parity; [b]Age 15 and older in 2007; [c]A value of 0 represents perfect wealth distribution equality, and a value of 100 represents perfect inequality.

Note: The United States is included for comparison purposes.

Data from UNDP (2009), LAC Databook (2009), and Sotomayor (2004).

mostly a cultural importation that occurred during the end of the 19th century (Arbena & LaFrance, 2002). British immigrants as well as American businessmen, sailors, missionaries, and educators traveled to the major cities in Latin America. Along with their religious missions, educational objectives, and commercial ventures, they carried their favorite pastimes and sports. Thus, football, rugby, cricket, and tennis became the primary sports practiced in areas where British immigrants lived (Chappell, 2002). A similar effect occurred in areas that were influenced by Americans. Hence, baseball became the preferred pastime for those who lived in

cities where American businesses were established (Arbena, 2002).

During this time, the diffusion of modern sport also occurred between Latin American countries. It is thought that Cubans introduced the game of baseball to the Dominican Republic during the latter part of the 19th century, and it quickly became the national pastime and, further, a national passion (Klein, 1989; Cary, 2007). A similar case occurred with baseball in Puerto Rico, which was also introduced by a group of Cubans who were visiting the island while Puerto Rico was still under the rule of the Spanish government. But the main influence for the future adoption of sport in Puerto Rico began after the Treaty of Paris in 1898, when the United States obtained jurisdiction over the island.

The American presence in Puerto Rico not only brought political changes but also heavily influenced the sporting life. Hence, baseball became the national sport, but instead of playing with Cubans as in the early years, Puerto Rican baseball teams had a new rival, American soldiers (Huertas, 2006). Puerto Ricans took such a liking to baseball that as early as 1902 the Puerto Rican Baseball Association was formed. Throughout the 20th century, the American presence on the island continued to influence sport by way of American teachers, who introduced basketball and volleyball. These sports became popular among students. By 1906, high school students and students from the University of Puerto Rico were actively participating in all sorts of interscholastic tournaments. As a result, many athletic facilities were built for the practice of track and field, baseball, basketball, volleyball, tennis, and gymnastics.

Venezuela is another country where the popularity of baseball can be explained by the presence of American business, particularly through the influence of the petroleum plants that were operating there in the early days of the 20th century. Historians have noted that many of these foreign oil companies supported the practice of sporting activities as a way to keep their workers under control, especially after their working hours, thus helping to preclude the formation of workers union movements (Navarro, 2006).

Besides the American and British presence in the region, other European immigrants also exerted a great deal of influence in introducing new sport practices to Latin Americans. Immigrants from Germany, Switzerland, Italy, Spain, and France among many others founded social and sporting clubs in Latin American countries. These clubs had the aim of creating spaces for gathering to help preserve their cultural identity (DaCosta, 1996; Modiano, 1997; Van Bottenburg, 2001). Among these groups, German immigrants who settled in the southern part of Brazil have been credited with the foundation of the modern sport movement in Brazil through the creation of gymnastics clubs (Tesche & Rambo, 2001). Similarly, European immigrants brought cycling and fencing to Venezuela in the late 19th century. These sports were supported by oil companies, gold exploitation enterprises, and, to a lesser degree, by the railroad industry.

Comparable with what occurred in other countries, the ebb and flow of European migration into Argentina are evident by examining its early regional settlements, periods of exploration, and dynamic economic patterns. Much of the country's substantial growth can be traced to a variety of European nations, as can its diverse sporting traditions. The early development of sport in Argentina is linked to the aforementioned flow of European settlers and immigrants to the region. Native Indians also developed their own unique sport practices during the Spanish conquest (Ferrarese, 2008). One of these sports is the game of *pato* (duck), which according to some accounts was played near Buenos Aires as early as the 17th century. Pato is a sport played on horseback that contains elements of polo and basketball. The local Indians who played it became very skillful in equestrian sports (Federación Argentina de Pato, 2008).

Notwithstanding the many ethnic influences in the development of modern sport in Latin America, perhaps the most influential was the late 19th century diffusion of British leisure practices throughout the region (Arbena & LaFrance, 2002; Guttmann, 1994). British merchants near the port of Buenos Aires introduced the game of football in 1840. In their spare time, they played the game in a field near the docks. Numerous tours of British football clubs, beginning in 1904, showcased the game to the masses (Archetti, 2005). By 1913 the population had developed very good players, and the first non-British club (Racing Club) was crowned champion of the Argentine league (Arbena, 1999). Besides football, Argentineans successfully adopted many other sports before the 18th century, like bullfighting and Basque pelota (jai alai). Years later, many other sports, also imported from Europe, were to gain great popularity, such as cricket, rugby, horseracing, boxing, polo, rowing, tennis, cycling, and fencing (Archetti, 2005; Kennedy, 2008; Lupo, 2004).

Sport Culture and Popularity of Sports

The influence of the 19th century Anglo-Saxon immigrants would become a turning point in defining the cultural basis of what would be the preferred sports in the region. During the last two decades of the 20th century, however, another significant wave of sport influences emerged. Technological advances in the form of digital communications, the Internet, and pay-per-view; an overall increase in the standard of living; and the expansion of global corporatism boosted the popularity of other sports across the region. Thus, basketball, volleyball, tennis, motor sports, golf, and a wide array of nature-based sports have become popular in many Latin American countries. Although football is still the most popular sport, its popularity is not felt with the same intensity everywhere. Football is the primary sport in Mexico, Brazil, Argentina, and many others countries, but baseball is the preferred sport in Venezuela, Nicaragua, the Dominican Republic, and Cuba.

A number of sports are followed in Central America, but the number one devotion of its people is a love and passion for football. In the beginning, football struggled against baseball to gain a foothold in the culture. During the 1920s Costa Rica became the first Central American country to establish its own football federation. Subsequent development of the sport across the region was much slower. Today, football is at the center of Central American life and culture. Perhaps an extreme example of this devotion is represented by the link between religion and sport. In Central America, pundits have noted that football can be seen as a second religion that is in constant competition with the Catholic Church. In El Salvador the Catholic Church has even built a chapel within the confines of one of the stadiums that offers services on Sundays and game days, along with prayers for the success of the local team (Sánchez, J., personal communication, September 21, 2007).

Like most Salvadorans, most Costa Ricans (known as *Ticos* in the region) are avid football fans. According to FIFA, one of every four Costa Ricans plays football. That statistic is astonishing considering that in England the ratio does not even reach one player for every 10 people (Big Count, 2006). Fans avidly support their local teams as well as the national team, nicknamed *La Sele*, which has played in the World Cup tournament several times. La Sele has been a big source of pride throughout the years, but it has also brought about great discord among its fans during its not-so-happy moments. These reactions are a result of the immense passion that the Ticos feel for their country, their team, and football. Nonetheless, since the mid-1990s Costa Rica's national team has been the third most successful team in the CONCACAF region after Mexico and the United States, and certainly the most successful in Central America.

Football is as popular in South America as it is in Central America. Many consider South American football players the best in the world. These players are, in fact, one of the reasons that football is so popular there. Perhaps the most popular are the football players from Brazil. Brazilian players are known worldwide, mostly for their natural talent for the sport and for the achievement of Brazil's national team, which has won five FIFA World Cups (1958, 1962, 1970, 1994, and 2002). Therefore, it seems accurate to name Brazil as a football nation. The significance of football in Brazil is exemplified by the number of active participants and followers. Today, more than 13 million people participate at the organized and recreational level. In addition, 87,000 teams play and compete in organized football (Big Count, 2006). Moreover, more than 70 percent of Brazilians follow football on the TV, and 63 percent seriously identify with one of the football teams from the Brazilian League (IPSOS World Monitor, 2002; IBOPE Midia, 2001).

But football is not the only popular sport in Brazil. Brazilians, in fact, have a predilection for many other team sports or ball games such as volleyball, basketball, and team handball (Medeiros et al., 1997). After football, volleyball is the second preferred sport in Brazil (Graca & Kasznar, 2002). In recent years, interest in volleyball showed an increase of 26.3 percent as opposed to 12.8 percent for football. Volleyball is also the preferred sport among women and is considered the most inclusive sport among people from different socioeconomic backgrounds (RPC Pesquisa e Consultoria, 2004).

Despite the popularity of football across Latin American countries, its practice is still culturally bounded as an essentially male activity. In Honduras, for example, many girls still prefer dancing instead of playing football. Dances are held on weekends and holidays in most villages across the country. As a result, girls learn to dance at a young age and often go on to take dance classes in which boys also participate (Ibarra, P., personal communication, December 12, 2007). But in Argentina, a country in which football reigns, the opportunities for women to play the sport are scarce. In 2006 among an estimated 3,300 football clubs, less than 1 percent host women's teams. The situation is no different in Brazil, which has almost 10 times the number of clubs as Argentina but has only 0.8 percent of these hosting women's teams. By way of comparison, in Canada, 43 percent of the estimated 7,000 football clubs host women's teams (Big Count, 2006). Notwithstanding these facts, in many Latin American countries girls and women do actively practice a wide array of other sports.

Although Latin American football has not reached an equal playing field in terms of gender, football fandom reaches across class lines. Social class often plays a role in team identity and team preference among fans. Football clubs across the world are marked by a distinctive class structure (see Miller, 2007; Panfichi & Thieroldt, 2007; Wagg, 2002). Likewise, in Latin America football clubs are associated with both ends of the social spectrum; some attract the wealthy and educated, and others have a fan base mostly made up of the working class. Typical examples of teams associated with the more affluent are Club Deportivo Universitario de Lima (Peru), Flamengo in Rio de Janeiro (Brazil), River Plate in Buenos Aires (Argentina), and Club Deportivo Universidad Católica in Santiago (Chile). Although mostly associated with the working classes, the following popular and successful teams attract fans from every corner of society: Alianza de Lima (Peru); Fluminense in Rio de Janeiro (Brazil); Boca Juniors in Buenos Aires (Argentina), and Colo-Colo in Santiago (Chile). A good example of a "team of the people" is Colo-Colo, considered the most successful club in the history of professional football in Chile. The name Colo-Colo derives from the name of a Mapuche chief and warrior who symbolizes courage, bravery, and wisdom. In part because of this connection with its native and aboriginal roots, Colo-Colo has been referred to as the team of the people. Although the club and its stadium are located in Santiago, Colo-Colo has followers all over the country. During the 1990s, a study indicated that Colo-Colo was the most preferred team among Chileans (49 percent) and the most preferred team among those from the lower socioeconomic strata (53 percent) (Claro, 1999a).

In Argentina, football attracts most of the population's interest. Winners of two World Cups, two Olympic gold medals, and an accumulation of accolades for domestic clubs and players, Argentine football is a source of passion and pride, a passion that at times has been taken to the extreme and thus has become a serious problem for the welfare of football in the country. Members of the barras bravas, which means "fierce supporters" or "fierce gangs," are organized supporters of a football team equivalent to hooligans in the United Kingdom. Typically, they engage in violent acts in and outside the stadium. The persistent operation of the barras bravas from the various clubs routinely disrupts matches and poses a security threat to law enforcement, passive spectators, and the hooligans themselves. Matches are often delayed or postponed, and entire seasons have been suspended because of the serious nature of the problem. The complex social issue includes politics, the justice system, economics, and identity cultures among other factors (Duke & Crolley, 1996). Although disruptive fan behavior occurs in many football countries, the barras bravas from Argentina have become a model for other groups of disruptive fans throughout South America, particularly across the Andes in Chile (Recasens, 1999).

Regardless of the problems of violent fans in football, Argentineans are avid spectators and enthusiastic participants in a variety of sports. They have not only enjoyed the practice of sport but also have effectively succeeded in international competition. Niche sports in which Argentine teams and athletes have achieved global recognition include rugby, polo, tennis, basketball, golf, volleyball, cycling, hockey, yachting, and rowing, among others. Catalyzing and sustaining this popularity are several successful finishes at international sport-specific championships. The year 2007 proved to be a banner year for Argentineans in several of these sports. The Pumas of Argentina finished a surprising third at the Rugby World Cup, Angel Cabrera put golf in the forefront of the Argentine sporting landscape with his U.S. Open victory, and the men's national basketball team finished second at the FIBA Americas Olympic qualifying tournament.

In addition, Argentineans are passionate followers of all motor racing sports, particularly auto racing. Rally racing continues to maintain a significant fan base. The Dakar Rally, one of the most popular international rally races in the world, was successfully cohosted by Argentina and Chile in January 2009. To the pleasure of organizers, the race attracted not only large crowds along the route but also great numbers of viewers following the race online (Dakar, 2009). Overall, the popularity and success of modern sport in Argentina should be neither overstated nor erroneously assumed to be accessible to the populace. With the exception of football and boxing, relevant international results continue to favor sports that are predominantly elite in nature (rugby, tennis, field hockey, and so on), resulting in limited participation.

Structure of Latin American Sport Systems

For the most part, the sport system in Latin American countries has two distinguishing characteristics. First, it has evolved from the club model, and second, it has been supported and funded by a government structure. In many countries, government also provides the legal framework in which the sport system operates. The historical advancement of the sport structures in Brazil, marked by four stages of development, illustrates the relationship between the club model and the role of government.

The rise of sport in Brazil began in the 1870s with the founding of the first sport clubs. The second stage involved the flourishing and structuring of hundreds of clubs, the creation of the first national governing bodies (NGBs), and the founding, in 1914, of the Confederation of Brazilian Sports. During the third stage, the first legal body in sport was enacted—the Sport Law of 1941, which established the National Council of Sports, a structure that set the foundation for the massive spread of sport among the Brazilian people. Finally, the fourth stage is marked by the passage of several laws that affected the current state of sport in the country, among these the Zico law of 1993 and the Pelé law of 1998.

The club model reflects the country's European background, in which sport is mostly organized around a private single-sport or multiple-sport organization. The club model, as it occurs in other parts of the world, became the foundation of the Olympic Movement, which is organized around associations (local level) and federations (national level), commonly known as national governing bodies (NGBs). Although government involvement in sport has increased over time, sport in Latin American countries is not supported exclusively by public funds. The club system, fundamentally a private

structure, has also provided longstanding financial support for the sporting system in many countries. Government funding does exist but rarely reaches its optimum level. Therefore, the standard of sporting facilities and allocation of funding to support high-performance sport are never adequate. Other more urgent and basic needs such as food, housing, and education are more important topics within the governments' agenda (Chappell, 2002).

In terms of the hierarchy of the public sport office within the government structure, there is not a single model. In some countries, sporting activity reaches a ministerial level, a secretary of state, or a department within the ministry of education, youth, or cultural affairs. The emphasis and importance varies from country to country, and to some extent the assigned importance is associated with the political ideology of the current government.

The Club Model

In many Latin American countries the foundation of the sport system resides outside the school system, a trend that resembles what occurs in European countries and in direct opposition to what occurs in the United States. Currently, sport clubs are perhaps the most common way in which sport is organized in Latin America. Clubs may be single-sport clubs or multiple-sport clubs. Some clubs emphasize social benefits through the practice of sport, and others focus more on the development of high-performance athletes. Also, some clubs support professional sport. Despite the fact that many sport clubs in Latin America operate outside the educational system, many successful football clubs started as a part of a major university, such as Club Universidad de Chile and Club Deportivo Universidad Católica in Chile, Club Universitario de Deportes de Lima in Peru, Liga Deportiva Universitaria de Quito in Ecuador, and the team Tigres from Universidad Autónoma de Nuevo León in Mexico. Many of these clubs have kept their names and identities linked to their alma mater but have replaced their collegiate administrative and financial dependence in their business structure.

Although the funding of amateur sport clubs is mostly done through memberships, and in some cases through government subsidies (i.e., infrastructure), the funding of professional sport, particularly football clubs, is still an unresolved issue for many clubs across Latin America (Rachman,

Learning Activity

Explain what the club model is and how this model is different from the North American model of sport development. Look for an example of a multisport club in Latin America and prepare a two-page profile of that club.

2007). Although football enjoys a large following in Argentina, it continues to face challenges because of its unstable forms of revenue and poor management practices. Clubs are organized by laws that restrict them as nonprofit civil organizations. As a result, club members elect a board of directors to manage the club. These individuals are often amateurs who may or may not have experience in the sport business industry; thus, most athletic clubs that support football teams rarely implement strategic plans, organizational missions, or solid business strategies. Additionally, club directors often split time between management responsibilities and their regular paid employment. Nonetheless, these managing directors are charged with all aspects of club operations, including the oversight of multimillion dollar television contracts and the negotiation of player contracts.

The lack of solid management practices is not limited to Argentinean football. Other countries in South America have lived the same culture of amateurism that has prevented the growth and development of professional football. As a way to illustrate the club model, and specifically how the management practices in football clubs have evolved over the years, two Chilean multisport clubs, Club Universidad de Chile and Club Deportivo Universidad Católica, are examined here. The professional football teams for both of these clubs illustrate a pattern of moving from being managed by nonprofit clubs to being separate for-profit entities.

The Club Universidad de Chile was founded in Santiago, the capital of Chile, in 1919 as a multisport club affiliated with the University of Chile, the oldest and the largest public university in the country. Throughout its history, the club hosted many amateur sports, among them track and field, swimming, basketball, volleyball, boxing, skiing, and automobile racing. Although several high-profile Chilean athletes began their careers there, Club Universidad de Chile is internationally recognized because of its professional football team, which it started in 1927. In its first 50 years, up until 1980, the football team was administratively dependent on the University of Chile. During this time, Club Universidad de Chile was part of a larger athletic department of the University of Chile in a fashion similar to the way in which American universities organize their athletics programs. Throughout this time, many fans became loyal because an alumni network was developed. Others simply identified with what this team represents: a nonreligious, nonpartisan, educated, and middle professional class within Chilean society. In 1980 the professional football team, as well as the teams of other amateur sports, ended its administrative link with the university to become a private corporation.

Club Universidad de Chile has traditionally reached large crowds, attracting more than 300,000 fans annually (Claro, 1999b). The club won 12 national titles from 1940 to 2004 and played 14 times in the prestigious continental club championship Copa Libertadores de América, reaching the semifinals on two occasions. Despite this successful football performance, the club suffered from financial instability, particularly since 2000. In 2006 the club declared bankruptcy because of an accumulated debt of US$10.8 million in unpaid taxes. Similar to other football clubs in Chile, Club Universidad de Chile became a **public limited sport company** (**PLSC**) in 2007. A PLSC functions in a similar manner to a public limited company. It is a for-profit organization formed by a group of stockholders who provide the needed funds to operate the organization. The purpose of these companies is to organize, produce, and commercialize professional sporting activities. In 2007 the rights for the administration of the club were granted to a private group of investors named Azul Azul S.A., who took on the task of financially restructuring the club. The agreement included the administration for a minimum of 30 years of all the properties and naming rights. So far, the new formula has shown some positive results. In 2008 Azul Azul S.A. obtained 15 million dollars from the sale of stock in the Chilean stock market and generated a profitable return of 24.9 percent (Azul Azul S.A., 2008).

Learning Activity

Investigate the new trend of transferring Chilean football clubs to ownership through the stock market. What are the benefits and drawbacks (if any) of this type of sport administration?

Club Deportivo Universidad Católica (CDUC) came into existence in 1937 and had the aim of providing an outlet for leisure and recreation to students attending the Pontificia Universidad Católica de Chile in Santiago. Like its rival, Club Universidad de Chile, CDUC was created as a multisport club. Since its early days it hosted a variety of sports including football, boxing, basketball, rugby, tennis, and track and field. Club Deportivo Universidad Católica as a professional football team made its debut in 1937 in the second division of the Chilean league. In the 1980s the club became administratively separated from its alma mater. During those years, CDUC created its own legal and financial structure that provided the institution with a firm and lasting financial structure. Unlike other multisport clubs that host professional football, CDUC became an exemplary model for Chilean sport organizations as well as other clubs across South America. The club directed its efforts to develop not only a world-class football team but also a top place for the practice of other amateur sports.

Club Deportivo Universidad Católica has been traditionally associated with the more affluent segments of the Chilean society. Most of its followers live in Santiago as opposed to other regions of the country. CDUC has won nine national titles and three semifinals (1960, 1966, 1969) in Copa Libertadores de América. In addition, in 1994 it obtained first place in Copa Interamericana, a cup played between the champions of Copa Libertadores de América (South America) and the winner of CONCACAF's Champions Cup (North America, Central America and the Caribbean). Regardless of its many successes, both on and off the field, CDUC followed the same path of Club Universidad de Chile and other football clubs in Chile to become a public limited sport company in September 2009.

Role of Government

The involvement of government in sport is a common practice in most countries around the world. Adequate development of sport plays a central role in governments' political agenda because it can act as a bridge to achieve a number of public policy objectives in areas such as youth issues, health, leisure, education, and national heritage (Gratton & Taylor, 2000; Heinemann, 2005; Houlihan & White, 2002). In Latin America most governments have taken a pivotal role in supporting the development of the sport sector, whether by promoting the value of physical activity among people, by providing opportunities for groups that traditionally have been excluded from the sport practice, by funding the construction of sport facilities, or by supporting the development of elite athletes. Despite these government efforts, keep in mind that nongovernmental structures also play a critical role in the process of sport development.

As previously stated, the entire club model and its Olympic structure of clubs, associations, federations, and confederations are, in fact, a fundamental part of the sport system in any country. For example, in Chile, the entire sport system relies on the network established among regional sport structures and sport clubs that represent the feeding units for the national governing bodies (NGBs) and the basis for the amateur sport system (Bravo, 1996; Bayle & Robinson, 2007). Among these structures is the Chilean Olympic Committee (COCH), a private organization that operates separately from the government but receives most of its funding from the government as part of the national budget. Similar to the framework in Chile, the sport structures in Colombia are organized in levels: clubs, acting at the municipal or city level; leagues, acting at the local and department level (equivalent to state); and national governing bodies (NGBs), acting at the national level. In addition, public structures are represented by the municipal and departmental institutes of sport. All public entities, whose main goal is to support the development of elite and grassroots sporting initiatives, provide technical and financial support to existing and new sporting organizations. These examples illustrate the close relationship that exists between the nongovernment sport organizations, represented by clubs, leagues, and associations,

CASE STUDY

Brazilian Football and the Coritiba Football Club

Fernando Mezzadri, PhD, Universidade Federal do Paraná, Brazil

Brazilian football is known around the world for its players, its national team, and its national championship. In the current structure, the Brazilian championship league is made up of four divisions. Serie League A is the most important because it includes 20 of the strongest clubs in Brazil, among them Coritiba Football Club.

Coritiba FC began its history in the city of Curitiba, the capital of the state of Paraná. The city, located in the southern part of Brazil, has a population of 1.8 million. The ethnically diverse city is well known for its progressive architecture, excellent educational system, efficient system of public transportation, and strong economic development. There are two variations in the spelling of the city's name: *Coritiba*, the European way, and *Curytiba* in the Guarani language; both forms are correct. The city accepted the traditional indigenous name Curitiba, whereas the football club adopted the European name of Coritiba.

Coritiba FC was founded on October 12, 1909, by a group of young men of German descent. The colors of the club are green and white. The history of the club is marked by the achievement of several titles in the Brazilian football competition and the presence of the numerous fans who have followed the club for the past 100 years. The team has won state, national, and international titles. Perhaps the most important title was achieved in 1985, when the team won the national football championship of Brazil.

Coritiba FC is managed by a structure that includes several committees. The administrative committee is made up of a president, vice president, and secretary. The structure of the club also includes seven directorship positions: marketing, financial, football, institutional relations, sponsorships, director of minor divisions, and director of the administrative council. These directors are elected by their club members and do not receive any salary. Their overall responsibility is to oversee the operations of the club. One of the main challenges of the administrative structure is to achieve a balance among the economic interests of the team. In addition, they face the challenge of managing the demands of the media as well as keeping their fans satisfied and attached to the institution. These tasks are not always easy to handle because, as with many sport organizations, the demands and high emotions of the fans often clash with the rationality of certain decisions made by the administration.

The club is organized under a professional structure of management that aims to reach administrative excellence in three defined areas: professional football, minor divisions, and marketing. Each of these three areas is managed by a highly qualified group of paid professionals. To have a competitive professional football team, the club strives to have the best players available to them. To achieve this, the club follows two strategies: It recruits players from other clubs and prepares future talented players within the club as part of the minor division structure. For these players, the club offers quality coaching and education, and constantly assists them throughout their social adjustment. The club has several departments that work in these areas, including physiology, nutrition, psychology, and social assistance.

In its marketing strategies, the club has focused on increasing the visibility and exposure of the club's commercial partners. The involvement of the club and its fans is also fortified with the increase in the number of new partners that perceive the value of being associated with Coritiba FC. Marketing activities include books, posters, magazines, the club's website, and the licensing of the Coritiba brand.

---

and the public sector, represented by a government agency acting at the municipal, provincial (state), or national level. Accordingly, although the entire club model and its Olympic structure occur outside the government's jurisdiction, these structures are heavily influenced by government actions and policies. This section describes the government's involvement in sport in four selected Latin American countries.

Venezuela

The government of Venezuela became involved in sport in 1949 with the creation of the National Institute of Sport (IND). As of 2008 the IND was placed directly below the Ministry of Sport, which represents the highest public office of sport in the country. Government involvement with sport has gone through significant changes since the 1990s. Part of these changes can be attributed to the decentralization process that took place in Venezuela's public administration system. The previous centralized model was criticized because it did not support the development of sport at all (González, 1998). Because of the decentralization process, the Venezuelan sport system was reorganized to operate at three levels: national, state, and municipal (Key, 1998). Besides this reorganization, the biggest effect resulted from the increase in financial resources. Since 2009 the Venezuelan sport system has received more money than it ever did before, and the entire sport structure has benefited. The aforementioned structural changes and the raising of the public office of sport to ministerial rank have put Venezuelan sport into a higher level of discussion within the public sector agenda, thus creating a positive effect for the entire Venezuelan sporting system.

Brazil

Brazilian government involvement in sport dates back to 1937 when the Division of Physical Education was formed as part of the Ministry of Education and Culture. Today Brazil's commitment to sport is manifested in its National Constitution of 1988. Article 217 of this constitution states, "[The] state must promote sport participation, both formal and informal, as a right for everyone" (Política Nacional do Esporte, 2005, p. 9). By raising the status of sport to a "right for everyone," the Brazilian government took a decisive step not only in recognizing the importance of sport but also in setting the legal foundation to achieve the necessary conditions for sport to grow (Medeiros et al., 1997). Because of this, in 1990 President Collor de Melo created the Secretariat of Sport. Five years later, President Fernando Henrique Cardoso created the Ministry of Sport under the leadership of the all-time great football player Edson Arantes do Nascimento, better known as Pelé. In 1998 the Ministry of Sport and Tourism was created. Then, in 2003 sport and tourism were separated to form a sole Ministry of Sport Affairs as mandated by President Luis Ignácio Lula da Silva (Ministério do Esporte, 2007). Today federal policies toward

Learning Activity

Research the structure of the Brazilian Olympic Committee (COB). Find out how NGBs are organized and funded in Brazil. Discuss the role of the government's office (Ministry of Sport Affairs) in charge of sport and its relationship to the work of the COB. In what way do the functions of these two organizations overlap? In what way do they differentiate and complement each other?

sport in Brazil are directed in three main areas: educational sport, mass sport and leisure, and high-performance sport.

The sport system in Brazil is the result of a complex network of many private and public efforts (DaCosta, 1996; Fundamentação Sobre o Sistema, 2006). Because of the intersectional nature of sport, the Ministry of Sport Affairs plays a key role in articulating a national policy by working with a wide array of institutions such as the Ministry of Education, Ministry of Social Development, Ministry of Justice, Brazilian Olympic Committee, and institutions of higher education (Política Nacional do Esporte, 2005).

Chile

The first government initiative related to sport and physical education in Chile took place in 1906 with the creation of the Institute of Physical Education at the University of Chile (Muñoz, 2001). In 1923 the Chilean government created the National Commission for Physical Education to provide policies and funding for sport programs. Although several public agencies existed between the 1920s and 1930s, it was not until the late 1940s that the Chilean government created the Department of Sports, the first office exclusively in charge of matters related to sport, physical education, and recreation. This agency was administratively placed under the Ministry of Defense. Years later this department would become DIGEDER, or the General Directorate of Sports and Recreation. In 2001 DIGEDER became **Chiledeportes** (Sport Chile) with the rank of a subsecretary of state, which falls one level below the Ministry of the Presidency. Chiledeportes has the mandate to promote and develop sport in all

Municipal Sport Policy in Peñalolen, Chile

Loreto Barriga, Chief of the Department of Research and Development, National Institute of Sport, Chile

The development of an effective municipal sport policy has been a major priority for the Municipality of Peñalolén in Santiago, Chile. Peñalolén has a population of 240,000, which puts it among the six largest municipalities in Santiago.

In 2007 the Corporación de Deportes de Peñalolén (Sport Corporation of Peñalolén) became the municipal unit in charge of matters related to sport and recreation. Since then, this corporation has been working on a plan to strengthen the development of sport and recreational services for the people of its community.

The idea to develop a major sport project began in 2004 as a part of the strategic plan implemented by Peñalolén's mayor, Claudio Orrego. Before 2004 a small group of municipal officers managed sport initiatives in-house. At that time, their main responsibilities were to support the development of the few sporting leagues and to allocate a small budget to fund athletic equipment and trophies.

Understanding the whole range of possibilities that sport can provide as a social policy, the municipality of Peñalolén decided to develop a long-term municipal sport strategy. The strategy was built with the input of the community, which included a public consultation held during the Cabildo Comunal del Deporte (communal referendum). During this consultation, a wide array of social organizations provided their input. Through this process of consultation, the needs and priorities of the community were unveiled. The analysis showed that two main areas were in need of urgent attention: training of human resources and improving the sport infrastructure. As a result, a comprehensive plan was designed that included five areas of development: (1) grassroots sports, (2) recreational activities and events, (3) competitive sport, (4) organizations, and (5) sport infrastructure.

The main objectives in the area of grassroots sports were the launching and development of six sports: football, basketball, tennis, track and field, karate, and rock climbing. The goal was to introduce and teach these activities to children who had not been previously participating in these sports. In the area of recreational sport, the goal has been to organize massive sporting events that enhance the community's sport culture. The area of competitive sport organizes tournaments among public and private schools located in Peñalolén. The area of development of organizations focuses on the education of participants and beneficiaries to create a culture of coresponsibility regarding the services that the municipality provides to them. To address these objectives, hundreds of sport instructors, facility managers, and team directors have received training in a variety of themes. Finally, the area of development of infrastructure has focused on a campaign to improve the existing infrastructure by involving the community, by donating either their time (labor) or their resources.

In 2005, because of the need to increase the budget to fulfill the proposed strategies, a not-for-profit sport corporation was established. The creation of a corporation offered several legal and financial benefits and opportunities that the old structure, under the umbrella of the municipal office, could not provide.

The Sport Corporation of Peñalolén began to operate in January 2007 with a budget of US$175,000 given by the municipal office. Shortly afterward, that amount was doubled thanks to several private donations received from a project that looked for partners that would sponsor the Sport Corporation of Peñalolén. These sponsors became part of the overall communication and marketing campaign managed by the Sport Corporation. As a result, their names became associated with the entire project of the Sport Corporation. The strategy was positively received by the private sector. Until that time, companies and other nongovernment organizations rarely received such proposals from a municipal entity.

After only a few years since its creation, the Sport Corporation of Peñalolén has already shown some important achievements. The number of sport programs for children went from none in 2004 to more than 30 in 2009. Similarly, the number of sport workshops for human resources went from zero to 40. Today the total number of beneficiaries is close to 2,500 people, and the amount of resources has tripled. Lessons learned are many, but one of the most significant has been the importance of involving the community. The challenges ahead are many; the goal, however, has been already defined: Peñalolén shall be the most developed sporting community in Chile.

levels of participation. Accordingly, its structure includes several departments that fall under the Division of Sport and Physical Activity, including the Department of Sport Education and Training, the Department of Recreational Sports, the Department of Competitive Sports, the Department of High-Performance Sport, and the Department of Sport Sciences (Chiledeportes, 2006).

The Sport System in Mexico

Mexico's involvement with organized physical culture dates back to 1856 with the inclusion of physical culture courses in the educational curriculum (Comisión Nacional del Deporte, 2001). Sport historians recognized the importance of the reemergence of organized sport immediately after the Mexican Revolution and during the early 1920s and 1930s. For many politicians and educators the value of sport came from the belief that organized sport would contribute to strengthening civil values and teach "team-work, a spirit of sacrifice, loyalty, and appreciation for beauty" (Arbena, 1991, p. 353). Sport and physical education would also contribute to strengthening the national identity among the population, an aspect considered essential in the aftermath of the revolution of the 1920s (Brewster, 2005). Because of many governmental initiatives that took place during the first half of the 20th century, sport would became a much more democratic and inclusive activity among the Mexican population. Because of this, during the 1920s Mexico took a series of decisive steps to organize its sport structures. The Mexican Olympic Committee was founded in 1923, and Mexico participated in its first Olympic Games in 1924 in Paris. In 1926 Mexico led the creation and organization of the first Central American and Caribbean Games. In 1927 the Mexican Soccer Association was founded, and in 1929 Mexico joined FIFA (Arbena, 1991).

Sport in Mexico has been organized no differently than it has been in other Latin American countries, including the amateur movement of clubs, associations, and federations or national governing bodies that fall under the umbrella and jurisdiction of the Mexican Olympic Committee, and the government's intervention to create structures, enact policies, and allocate resources to support sporting activities at all levels of participation (see figures 5.1 and 5.2). Government involvement began officially in December 1932 with the creation of Consejo Nacional de Cultura Física (National Council of Physical Culture). This was the first government office that took responsibility to coordinate efforts among private and public initiatives regarding sport and physical education. Among its objectives was the creation of the Confederación Deportiva Mexicana (Mexican Sport Confederation), a private organization that banded together every structure pertaining to a national governing body. The Consejo Nacional also promoted the creation of local committees for the promotion of sport, particularly among the working class (CONADE, 2007). Several other government structures would be created in the following years: the National Institute of Mexican Youth (1950), the National Institute of Sport (1979), the Sub-Secretary of Sport Affairs (1980), the National Council of Sport (1981), the National Commission for Sport (1988), and in 2003 the Comisión Nacional de Cultura Física y Deporte (CONADE), which is now the government office in charge of sport (CONADE, 2007).

Government involvement in sport in Mexico is now structured following the scheme of the powers of the Union under three separate branches: legislative, executive, and judiciary. The **National Commission for Physical Culture and Sport (CONADE)** represents the public office responsible for the development of sport and physical education. This organization is a public structure that is decentralized from the federal public administration and falls under the scope of the executive branch. It also relates directly to the Secretary of Public Education (SEP) (see figure 5.1). Among the main responsibilities of CONADE are fostering, overseeing, and funding sport programs throughout the country and, most important, proposing and executing a national policy regarding sport and physical activity that contributes to the overall development of sport in Mexico. In addition, it establishes agreements with sport federations, municipalities, and other private organizations to promote the practice of sport. CONADE establishes guidelines for athletes' participation and national teams, at both national and international competitions, in conformity with the policies of the Mexican Olympic Committee (COM). Furthermore, CONADE coordinates with the COM to host international competitions in Mexico. Also, it provides subsidy and financial incentives for both public and private organizations to develop sport initiatives. Finally, CONADE develops projects for building new sporting venues and allocates resources for maintaining existing ones (CONADE, 2007).

(continued)

(continued)

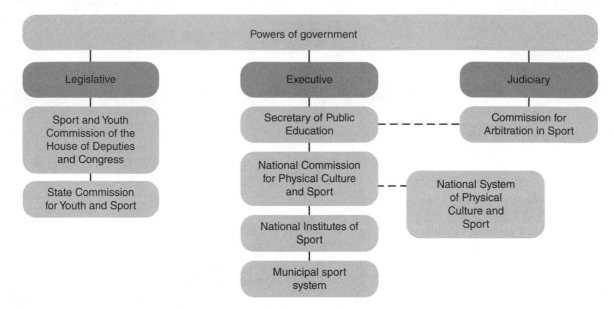

Figure 5.1 Government sport structures in Mexico.

Courtesy of Maria Pilar Rodríguez.

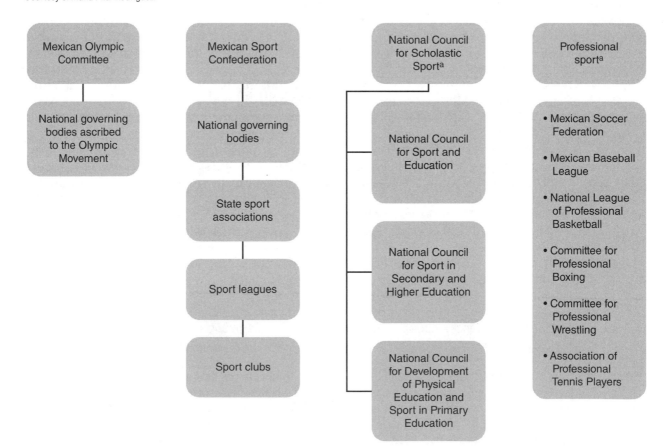

Figure 5.2 Nongovernment sport organizations in Mexico.

[a]Scholastic and professional sport do not have specific governing bodies that rule their plans and actions. Their inclusion in the above model is only for conceptual purposes.

Courtesy of Maria Pilar Rodríguez.

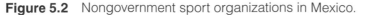

Dominican Republic

In the Dominican Republic the public office for sport is represented by SEDEFIR, or Secretaría de Estado de Deportes, Educación Física y Recreación (State Secretariat of Sport, Physical Education and Recreation). SEDEFIR was established in 1974 to address a variety of sport initiatives in the country. Areas under SEDEFIR are sport management and special projects, sport for all, collegiate and scholastic sport, and programs for elite athletes and prospects (SEDEFIR, 2004a). The Office of Sport Management ensures that the resources allocated to sport are being distributed and used appropriately (SEDEFIR, 2004a), and the Office of Collegiate and Scholastic Sport holds events to promote the practice of sport and assess the talent in the country (SEDEFIR, 2004b). Among the specific actions in place to develop high-performance athletes is the Programa de Atletas de Alto Rendimiento, Nuevos Valores e Inmortales, also known as PARNI (Program for High-Performance Athletes and New Immortal Values). The objectives of PARNI are twofold: first, to improve the quality of life of elite athletes through medical and life insurance, balanced nutrition, educational opportunities, legal guidance, and stipends or pensions; and second, to classify athletes according to their performance. PARNI addresses only those athletes involved in sports recognized by the Dominican Olympic Committee (SEDEFIR, 2004b).

Politicization of Sport

The intersection of politics and sport has been widely addressed in the sport literature, particularly governments' use of sport to justify or promote a political ideology, or simply because sport exalts deep nationalistic beliefs (Barnier, 2001; Gems, 2005; Houlihan, 1994; Smith, 2002). Because governments represent the pivotal force for many sport systems in Latin America, several episodes have occurred over the years that illustrate how sport has been used for political purposes.

The most notorious sport incident in El Salvador's history is known as the **Football War**. In 1969 tensions between El Salvador and Honduras had been heightened by land reform in Honduras that led to the deportation of several thousand Salvadorans. Violence following a World Cup qualifying game then led to a four-day war between the two countries. Although the conflict cannot be attributed solely to that football match, because political tension between El Salvador and Honduras already existed, the effect of the war was tremendous, disrupting trade and economic relationships of the entire Central American region. Before this incident, the Central American Common Market (CACM) was established to improve the overall economic development of the region, but the organization collapsed abruptly because of the Football War (Hill, 2003). Many years later, the five original members of the CACM (Guatemala, El Salvador, Honduras, Nicaragua, and Costa Rica) reestablished the common market, and it has met with relative success ever since (Keegan & Green, 1997).

Cuba is another country in which the development of sport has been influenced by political events. The Cuban sport system can be studied in light of two major eras: before and after the revolution of 1959. Each era is marked by significant changes, both political and economic, that influenced the structure and mission of the sport system in the country. The revolution led by Fidel Castro in 1959 brought to Cuba a centralized, one-party, socialist system of government similar to those of the Eastern Bloc countries after World War II. This new government established a sport structure to develop elite amateur athletes similar to the Soviet model of sport (Foldesi, 1991; Riordan, 1999). The sport structure brought about by the revolution served the purpose of spreading the voice of strength, reinforcing the socialist ideologies of the Marxist-Leninist regime (Slack, 1982). Sport became the platform for the Cuban government to showcase its power and success, thus setting the stage for achieving internal and international goals. Some internal goals to be achieved through sport were to legitimize the revolution, to give Cubans pride in the revolution, to generate a sense of nationalism, and to develop the ideal Cuban citizen—one who is physically, morally, and psychologically strong. International goals were to promote Cuba's leadership to third world countries (Pettavino & Brenner, 1999).

Puerto Rico illustrates the relationship that can exist among sport, national identity, sovereignty, and international politics. Historically, sport participation in the island has been tied to nationalistic pride because of its unique political status (commonwealth form of government) with the United States (Gems, 2005). Hence, sport has served as a way to strengthen the national identity of Puerto Ricans by developing "a sense of pride for everything they are capable of working for and achieving" ("Deporte Como Expresión Cultural de un Pueblo," n.d.).

Puerto Rico's introduction to international sporting events came by way of invitation to the Central American Games of 1930 by the U.S. ambassador to Cuba. The invitation turned more into a problem than an honor because the people in the island had to sort through two major challenges before attending these games. First, they needed to obtain the funds to pay the cost of their participation, and second, they had to face the uneasy situation of competing under the colors and the anthem of the Unites States because of

CASE STUDY

The Sport System in Cuba

The national sport program of Cuba had its beginnings in 1961, two years after Castro's revolution erupted in the island. As such, its goals clearly defined its overt political approach: international sport triumph to highlight the revolution, symbolize its success, and affirm patriotic values and national identity, both nationally and internationally (Bustillo, 1999).

The national sport system in Cuba was developed through a comprehensive research-driven systematic approach. Physical education was the key to the success of the new mass participation approach adopted by the Cuban government. Physical education was implemented in day care centers, schools, communities, the workplace, and homes (Cuban Integrated Model of Sport Development). Physical education and sport became a core subject of all schools and reinforced the core values of teamwork, sacrifice, commitment, and hard work (CARICOM, 2003). A farm system was used to identify talent and funnel athletes to the highest levels of expert training. When a child showed talent for a particular sport, every opportunity was made available for the child to develop his or her performance (Pettavino & Brenner, 1999).

Various organizations were established to address the different aspects or stages of citizen development. INDER related to all aspects of Cuban sport: physical education, recreation, competitive athletics at all levels, use of free time, national athletes, training, national coaches, and specialized sport schools. Cuba's sport program comprises three levels of specialized secondary sport school. The first level, Escuela de Iniciación Deportiva (EIDE), addresses the introduction to the sport. The intermediate level, Escuelas Superior de Perfecciona-

miento Atlético (ESPA), aims to perfect the athlete in the sport. At the highest level is Centros de Alto Rendimiento (CEAR), which prepares athletes for international competition. The two CEARs are both located in Havana, and one offers regular school subjects because of the age of some of the athletes (CARICOM, 2003).

Cuba's sport model seems to have been a successful structure for achieving superior athletic performance. By the early 1990s Cuba's constant strong sport performance in international platforms was one to be feared by other teams. This construct, however, was shaken by several events. The decline of the Cuban economy, the loss of Soviet subsidies after the breakup of the USSR, and the intensification of the U.S. embargo (Pettavino & Brenner, 1999) negatively affected the country's sport programs. Cuba faced a difficult economic situation.

The decline of Cuba's sport performance has been attributed to issues like the large number of Cuban athletes who seek asylum when competing overseas, the cancellation of night baseball games to conserve electricity, and the neglect of facilities and equipment for the masses to fund higher levels of competitive sport. The decreased level of funding led the rapid deterioration of facilities and equipment for athletes. But the Cuban government has made it possible for the sport program to pay for itself through arrangements like charging reporters for interviews with coaches and players. Also, elite baseball players were retired early and were allowed to play for Colombia, Japan, Italy, Nicaragua, and El Salvador. Another technique to increase currency flow was to make tourism available to countries including the United States. These adjustments helped the sport system sustain itself (Pettavino & Pye, 1994).

Puerto Rico's unique colonial status at that time. Puerto Ricans were able to obtain the funds from donations of affluent people and from the galleras, owners of cockfight coliseums (Huertas, 2006). The delegation had to endure much ridicule from other athletes for being a people without a flag. This incident would mobilize efforts among sport leaders in Puerto Rico to create their own National Olympic Committee, which was approved by the International Olympic Committee (IOC) in 1947, the same year that the United States granted Puerto Ricans the right to elect their own governor. As Puerto Rico changed its status from colony to commonwealth and the U.S. government granted more rights to the people of the island, the sporting world also recognized Puerto Rico's sovereignty. In the beginning, the IOC granted Puerto Rico the right to compete independently of the United States but still using the American flag. Not until the Helsinki Olympics in 1952 did the IOC permit Puerto Rican athletes to compete with their own flag and sing their own national anthem (Comité Olímpico de Puerto Rico, n.d.).

In Argentina the relationship between politics and sport was clearly illustrated during the first Perón administration (1946–1955). Argentinean president Juan Domingo Perón is often credited with significantly enhancing the development of sport in Argentina by incorporating elite and traditional games into public policies (Archetti, 2005). While in power, Peron and his wife Eva increased the quality and participation levels for sport by organizing and creating events and organizations such as workers championships, female and male high school students' unions, university Olympiads and school championships, and Evita's Women's Sport Association, among others (Antunez, 2008; Frydenberg & Di Giano, 2000). To date, several athletic venues and achievement awards carry the Perón name, highlighting the importance of this era for Argentine sport development. Decades after the first Perón administration, and not without controversy, sport and politics in Argentina again became a matter of attention. Under the governance of a military regime—a tumultuous period in its history—Argentina hosted the FIFA World Cup in 1978. Accusations of human rights abuses leading up to the tournament and reports of corruption after the event continue to be topics of inquiry (Smith, 2002).

The Sport Industry in Latin America

According to Pitts and Stotlar (2007) the sport industry is defined as "the market in which the business and products offered to its buyers are sport related and may be goods, services, people, places, or ideas" (p. 4). This definition can include almost every aspect that directly or indirectly affects the business of sport. In this section we have limited our description to five aspects that we believe have a direct influence on the sport industry in Latin America. We begin by examining some antecedents of the economics of sport in a few Latin American countries. Then we examine how funding for sport is allocated, and we continue with a description of the development of the main professional sports. Next we examine the role of education and how it has served as a foundational pillar of the amateur sport system. We conclude with a description of how sport management personnel are trained across the region and how the lack of adequate training can restrain the growth of the industry.

Economics of Sport

Although many Latin American countries experience similar challenges in their attempts to develop their sport systems, several important differences across the region add to the complexity of the task for some countries. Larger and more productive economies, like those of Brazil and Mexico, have developed a more advanced and multifaceted sport system because of their greater wealth. In contrast, other countries, particularly those located in Central America and the Caribbean, have not achieved the same level of progress in their sporting systems because their social, economic, and even political systems are not as stable and developed. All of this means that sport, as an economic activity, has not been able to develop at the same pace across the area.

One example can be seen in Honduras, where most of the population lives in mountainous rural areas. Because of the lack of urban population centers, the more traditional spheres of the sport industry such as spectator sport are unable to flourish. But despite these specific realities—the economic and social challenges, complicated by the rough topography and occasional violence of tropical weather patterns—the sport market in Central America still presents tremendous opportunities to develop sport businesses based on what these countries offer: their natural resources and the practice of **nature-based sport**, which involves competitive or recreational activities that take place outdoors in the natural settings of forest, lakes, rivers, fiords, and coastlines (Puchan, 2004). For example, the Honduran coastline offers plenty of opportunities for water sports, such as sailing and sea kayaking, and the Bay Islands are renowned as dive destinations.

Costa Rica is another country that is moving in this direction. The country is recognized not only as a popular tourist destination but also as the perfect place to practice extreme and adventure nature-based sports like whitewater rafting and bungee jumping. Costa Rica is also known worldwide for its outstanding surfing on both the Pacific and Atlantic coasts, along with boogie boarding, windsurfing, water skiing, kayaking, scuba diving, and, of course, sport fishing. Moreover, the country hosts a mountain bike race called La Ruta de los Conquistadores, which in a period of three days covers 249 miles (401 km) of winding roads in a variety of microclimates. This bike race is considered one of the toughest courses in the world. These two examples show that, in spite of the existing challenges, the sport industry market in Central American offers good potential. Sport managers and business entrepreneurs need to find a way to tap into this market.

Across the Caribbean, the economic potential of the sport industry is also underappreciated. But the contribution of baseball to the overall economy of the Dominican Republic is an interesting case to examine. Historically, the Dominican Republic has been a consistent source of talent for Major League Baseball (MLB) in the United States. In 2010 more

Learning Activity

Discuss how the development of nature-based sport could become an important avenue of business in Latin America. What type of sports would you develop there? Find out whether any country has already taken the lead in this direction.

than 10 percent of MLB players came from the Dominican Republic, and 25 percent of the 7,000 who signed in the minor leagues also came from that country, making the Dominicans the largest group of foreign players in both the major and minor baseball leagues (Gregory, 2010).

The overall economic impact of MLB in the Dominican Republic is estimated at US$76 million, yielding 2,000 jobs (Impacto Economía, 2006). The scope of this impact is felt mostly in the areas where baseball academies are located (Spagnuolo, 2003). **Baseball academies** are full-time facilities operated by MLB franchises in the Dominican Republic and Venezuela to produce baseball talent. Because of the large supply of talented baseball players available at relatively low cost, MLB teams began establishing baseball academies to recruit and prepare young players for a future life in the United States. The academies operate similarly to subsidiaries of a foreign company (Klein, 1991). Despite the immediate short-term benefits that the academies create, these enterprises have met some criticism. Some maintain that the economic impact is short lived because it does not provide the needed elements to ignite a significant change in an impoverished economy. The role of MLB in the economy of the Dominican Republic will be discussed in more detail later in the chapter.

If the sport economy is still in its infant stage in Central America and the Caribbean, it has reached a much more advanced standing in some countries of South America, although it still has a ways to go. The case of the economics of football in Argentina is interesting. Amateur managerial practices, lack of competitive balance, and the exodus of talent have severely affected the welfare of the league. In spite of being one of the most attractive leagues in the world, its management is still far behind that of counterpart leagues in Europe. Apart from its lack of a business management approach, several other structural inadequacies have affected the economics of football. For example, an overconcentration of teams in and around the capital city of Buenos Aires limits the potential prosperity for clubs in other parts of the country (Ramallo & Aguiar, 2007). Clubs in this large market are often better positioned and more financially equipped to develop or acquire the best talent (Gilbert, 2007). Although a favorable location is not a guarantee for success, it provides a platform that is more conducive to enduring stability. The lack of competitive balance hits the league as a whole because it suppresses attendance and peripheral revenue streams, both passively and actively. In addition, the exodus of elite talent to other countries prevents the league from reaching its potential. In Argentina the number one source of income for first-division football clubs is the sale of players (Ramallo & Aguiar, 2007). Clubs often face debts that are surmountable only by generating funds from their most profitable resource. The unfortunate effect of this practice is a visible regression in entertainment value from year to year that negatively affects the level of football consumption in both the domestic and global marketplaces.

Brazil may represent an exception in terms of the economic impact of sport, particularly when compared with other countries in the region. According to a 2002 study, the sport industry in Brazil was calculated at R$25 billion (US$8.8 billion), representing 3.3 percent of the country's GDP. Of this amount, R$12.5 billion (US$4.4 billion) is derived from sporting goods such as sporting apparel, shoes, and equipment, and R$8.7 billion (US$3 billion) is derived from services like fees and memberships to sport academies and clubs, facility rental, marketing, and sponsorship. The remaining amount comes from expenses derived from athletes' travel and maintenance of sporting facilities. The economic growth rate for the sport industry between 1996 and 2000 was 12.34 percent compared with a growth rate of 2.25 percent for the nation's GDP (Graca & Kasznar, 2002; Chiarini, 2002). Despite this growth, only a handful of the national governing bodies (NGBs) support their operations completely through private sponsorships. Most are still funded through sponsorship by public companies (Comitê Olímpico Brasileiro, 2008).

Financing Sport

The financing of sport in Latin America is a complex function that in most countries is influenced by the size of the sport industry as well as by the solvency of a government to allocate resources to that area. In Argentina, sport finance is a dual venture. The public and private sectors have influenced sport funding at many levels with varying degrees of success. Social clubs and private educational institutions fund many of their own sporting programs and activities. Governmental influence can be traced to the coordinating efforts of the secretary of sport under the Ministry of Social Development. In 2007 the secretary of sport allocated over US$65 million to help finance a wide array of sport-related initiatives. This number reflects a 145 percent increase from 2003 (Presidencia de la Nación, 2008). Besides direct government support, many other public and private sport finance partnerships exist within Argentina. The most conspicuous examples are the vast stadiums that governments have traditionally helped to build or renovate for athletic clubs (Fabri, 2006). Even so, much of the burden to provide infrastructure for the populace falls on the national governing bodies (NGBs) themselves. Professional athletes often enjoy private sponsorships, but only after they have established themselves (Martinez, 2007). This circumstance yields restricted opportunities for aspiring high-performance athletes who lack the personal financial resources to fund their participation.

In its history of Olympic participation, Colombia has won only 11 Olympic medals, only 1 of them gold. The government, through Coldeportes, has traditionally provided the budget for the Colombian Olympic Committee (COC) to support the preparation of Olympic athletes. In 2007 the government assigned US$21 million for the preparation of Colombian athletes for the 2008 Beijing Olympics (Colombia Presidencia de la República, 2008). In addition to direct government funding, other public initiatives have been instituted to fund high-performance sport. A percentage of the telephone companies' tax is given to support elite athletes. The Colombian government also sponsors a national program called Altius, which supports the preparation of athletes who represent Colombia in international competitions. These athletes, who live and train in the National Training Center in Bogotá, receive a monthly stipend of about US$900. These funding strategies show the critical role of government in the sport system in Colombia, because most NGBs rely heavily on its subsidy.

Recently, a few NGBs have started to market themselves and look for sponsorship and other sources of funding. Football and professional cycling are two NGBs that have successfully worked with the private sector. Football partnered with a beer company that uses the slogan "Live our passion," which become the image of football in Colombia. Cycling is considered the second most popular sport after football, and the biggest televised cycling event is the Tour of Colombia. The national cycling team is sponsored by a coffee brand, so the team is typically referred to as Café de Colombia (Colombian coffee). In terms of funding for amateur sport, special attention needs to be given to the success of the Roller Sports NGB (roller-skating) because those athletes have won several world championships. Because roller sports is not an Olympic sport, this NGB has received minimal subsidy from the government. Nevertheless, the Roller Sports NGB of Colombia has been successful in obtaining resources from the private sector through effective marketing strategies. The success of roller sports in Colombia represents an example to follow by many other amateur NGBs that have traditionally relied on governmental support (Frias, 2006; Patín Colombia, 2007).

In many countries, funding of sport is also influenced by the enactment of laws. In Brazil various sport laws have been passed since the early 1990s. Among the most important is Law 9,615 from 1998, also known as the **Pelé law**. This law is the current legal body for sport activity in Brazil. The Pelé law addressed many issues and aimed to steer the business of football clubs. The law established, among many aspects, free agency, the transformation of clubs into private enterprises, and the end of transfer fees for football players (Política Nacional do Esporte, 2005). Perhaps the most controversial aspects of this law were free agency and the end of transfer fees. Initially, these aspects were perceived to have a negative effect on clubs that had invested in the development of players, because it prevented the stream of income from transfer fees. The Pelé law was intensely debated in the Brazilian Congress; as a result, several amendments were introduced that changed its initial approach. One such amendment governed the contractual relationship of players with their clubs. For example, free agency would be maintained after a player ended his contract, but categories of fees were established for when a player was transferred during or after he ended his first professional contract. These fees, known as *educational compensation* and *promotional compensation*, have to be paid only to the club that first signed a player in the athlete's professional career (Aidar, Bueno de Almeida, & Miralla, 2004).

Two other important laws were passed in Brazil between 2001 and 2004, and these laws made an impact on the funding of amateur sport. These were Law 10,264, or the Agnelo/Piva law, and Law 10,891, also known as the athlete subsidy law. The Agnelo/Piva law assigns 2 percent of the federal lottery to the Brazilian Olympic Committee (COB). Of this amount, 85 percent is assigned to the COB, 10 percent is allocated to sport programs in the school system, and 5 percent is set aside for collegiate sport programs. In 2009 R$75 million (US$43 million) was allocated to the following areas: R$7.5 million (US$4.3 million) to scholastic sport, R$3.75 million (US$2.1 million) to collegiate sport, and R$63.75 million (US$36.6 million) directly to the COB (Comitê Olímpico Brasileiro, 2008). This law has resulted in the largest allocation of money for the Olympic sports in the history of the Brazilian Olympic Committee (Comitê Olímpico Brasileiro, n.d.).

Professional Sport

Professional sport and leagues have also played an important role in the context of Latin American sport. For most countries this means either football or baseball. Other professional sports and leagues that function with relative success are wrestling in Mexico, volleyball in Brazil and Puerto Rico, bull fighting in Venezuela and Mexico, and basketball in Brazil, Argentina, and Puerto Rico.

Professional Football

As previously noted, professional football leagues are by far the most important leagues in Latin America because overall they attract the largest numbers of spectators. In addition, many consider South American football leagues among the toughest leagues in the world. Hence, it is not surprising that FIFA provides CONMEBOL (South American Football Confederation) up to 5 entries, from among 10 countries, to play in the FIFA World Cup finals. Note that professional football is also popular outside South America. According to the Associated Press (2008), football has recently become one of the most popular sports in Puerto Rico. The Puerto Rico Islanders entered the scene in 2004, playing in the United Soccer Leagues First Division (USL-1).

In spite of the popularity and the sporting success of professional football in Latin America, the organizational standards and management of most clubs do not reach the level of development of those in Europe, Japan, or even in Major League Soccer (MLS) in the United States. Because most professional football clubs lack good management practices, the entire Latin American football industry falls behind similar clubs in other parts of the world (Miller & Crolley, 2007). The sections that follow highlight a few aspects of the state of professional football in Mexico, Argentina, and Chile.

Mexico Mexico has been the host of two FIFA World Cups, in 1970 and in 1986. At the end of the 2010 World Cup in South Africa, Mexico's national team was ranked as the 25th best team in the world (FIFA.com, 2010). Professional football officially began in Mexico in 1943, although during the 1930s a major semiprofessional league was established in the Federal District. The league was composed of popular teams such as América, Atlante, and Necaxa. Today's professional football follows a promotion and relegation system across four divisions. There are 18 teams in the First Division, 24 in the Promotion League, 70 in the Second Division, and 180 in the Third Division, comprising overall more than 6,300 players and 1,960 members of coaching staffs (Federación Mexicana de Fútbol Asociación, 2007).

Among the four divisions, the most prestigious is the First Division, which hosts the most popular teams. As in other leagues in Latin America, the most popular teams are located in the largest cities (Gilbert, 2007). These teams are América, Guadalajara, and Cruz Azul, which together account for more than 50 percent of Mexican fans (Zavala, 2001). Over the years, two forces have contributed to the popularity of these teams. The first originated from the natural rivalry that developed between the two major cities of Mexico and its two most representative teams, América from Mexico City, the capital, and Guadalajara, a team from the city of Guadalajara in the state of Jalisco. The second force rose in the 1960s when a television consortium bought the team América (Zavala, 2001) and changed the course of professional Mexican football for years to come. The Mexican media moguls not only made their team América one of the most popular teams in the country but also, and most important, brought business concepts to the management of Mexican football. Over the years, these practices made the Mexican league one of the most successful leagues in the world in terms of attendance and broadcasting rights (Miller, 2007). Since the 1980s the First Division became

Learning Activity

Research the Mexican football league. Describe how the league is organized, structured, and funded. Explain why some say that the league has no competitive balance. What would you do to increase the competitive balance? Think about what American professional leagues do (e.g., NFL and NBA) and decide what type of changes they could implement to achieve such a goal.

a powerful magnet for hundreds of foreign players because of the high-paying contracts it had to offer. Notwithstanding its success and popularity, the First Division lacks competitive balance. Since 1943, four teams have won almost 50 percent of the titles: Guadalajara has won 11 times, América 10 times, and Cruz Azul and Toluca 8 times each (Federación Mexicana de Fútbol Asociación, 2007). To increase the competitiveness of the First Division, in 1996 the league adopted a new format. Two rounds are played within the same year, creating two champions: one for the *Apertura* (Opening) tournament and another for the *Clausura* (Closing) tournament.

Argentina Football is also the most popular professional sport in Argentina. The league structure is made up of eight layers of divisions and hundreds of clubs (Asociación de Fútbol Argentino, 2009). Many of these clubs consistently draw an excess of 40,000 spectators to weekend league matches and weekday international cup fixtures. Argentina's two largest teams, Club Atlético Boca Juniors and Club Atlético River Plate, are routine participants at the various international championship tournaments and are considered among the best teams in South America. Both teams enjoy a fan base of an estimated 13 million people and club membership levels over 45,000 (Ramallo & Aguiar, 2007). By winning the 2008 Recopa, Boca Juniors is now considered the King of Cups for having won the most international titles in the world (Confederación Sudamericana de Fútbol, 2009).

Chile In Chile professional football has endured a long struggle in its more than 120 years since

British merchants first introduced the sport in the 1880s (Guttmann, 1994). In spite of its continuing popularity, the league has faced many challenges, including its lack of competitive balance, the high concentration of clubs within the same vicinities, low attendance, particularly within the past 25 years, and poor financial stability for most clubs (DIGEDER, 1987; Claro, 1999a; Ferreira & Bravo, 2007).

In terms of international success, the national team and Chilean clubs have achieved only a handful of meritorious positions and a few international cups. Among the best performances of all time are third place at the FIFA World Cup in 1962, in which Chile was the host country; a bronze medal at the Olympic Games in Sydney 2000; and Colo-Colo's South American club championship, known as Copa Libertadores de América, in 1991.

The history of Colo-Colo serves to illustrate how professional football clubs have traditionally been run in Chile. Colo-Colo has been the most successful team in the history of Chilean football. Notwithstanding its success, including more than 20 titles in the Chilean league, the club declared bankruptcy in 2002 with a total debt of US$30 million. Many observers noted that the bankruptcy of Colo-Colo was indicative of the old-fashioned way in which Chilean football has been managed—with great passion but with minimal sense of business.

Until the late 1970s gate receipts and resources from the sport lottery represented the two common ways by which most Chilean clubs funded their operations. Sponsorships were minimal, and marketing strategies were rare. As revenue from the sport lottery declined, clubs were forced to innovate in their marketing approaches. By the 1990s some clubs added other sources of revenue like merchandising, naming rights, and TV rights, but the biggest stream of money was the transfer of fees after a local player was sold (or relocated) to an Argentinean, Mexican, or European club. Although Colo-Colo was one of the few clubs that successfully implemented many of these strategies, it failed to keep its finances in the black because year after year its expenditures surpassed its revenues.

In 2000 the emergence of the Football Cable Channel (Canal del Fútbol) provided a new source of funding that benefited all Chilean football (see case study "Chilean Football Television Network"). Although this new stream of resources provided new monies for most teams, it also accentuated the gap between successful and less successful teams because the distribution of resources was based on a criterion of contribution. Thus, popular teams like Colo-Colo and Club Universidad de Chile received more money because their games had the highest viewership and those clubs generated the largest base of subscribers.

Immediately after Colo-Colo's bankruptcy in 2005, the management of the club was taken over by a private group named Blanco y Negro S.A. (BNSA), and Colo-Colo became the first big club in the league to become a public limited sport company (PLSC). As a result, the club was able to trade stocks on the Santiago Stock Exchange. By the end of 2005 the BNSA group obtained US$31.7 million from the sale of stock, and three years later the profitable return of BNSA was 28.1 percent (Economía y Negocios Online, 2006; Iriarte, 2009).

The case of Colo-Colo caused Chilean authorities to rethink the state of football. The transformation of football clubs into PLSCs was not an idea that originated in Chile, nor did this process occur spontaneously. The Chilean experience followed the trend that was initiated by Italian and English clubs during the 1990s. In 2005 Law 20,019 was passed, establishing the creation of public limited sport companies for professional football clubs in Chile. The law required clubs to change their administrative status to become either PLSCs or corporations. The law was enacted with two goals in mind. First, it aimed to end the mismanagement in professional football by requiring owners to be liable in case of bankruptcy. Second, it aimed to improve the business of football in Chile. The law aspired to change the course of Chilean football by instituting new principles that required clubs to be accountable not only for what they do on the field but also for their managerial and financial decisions.

Professional Baseball

Professional baseball also receives significant attention in Latin America. Since the early days of the 20th century, baseball became a recognized export product by countries such as the Dominican Republic, Venezuela, Mexico, Panama, Puerto Rico, and Cuba (Krich, 2002). Today, the imprint of Latino baseball players in Major League Baseball (MLB) is clearly marked by figures such as Alex Rodriguez,

CASE STUDY

Chilean Football Television Network (CDF)

Claudio Echeverria; Executive Director; ELSPORT, Management & Consulting; Chile

During the period 1998 through 2002, the Chilean Football Association (ANFP) received US$54 million (US$10.8 million annually) for the broadcasting rights of the Chilean football championship. For the following period, from 2003 to 2007, the best offer received was lower, a total of US$18 million (US$3.6 million annually). Under that scenario, Chilean businessman Jorge Claro came up with the idea to create a football network with the aim of increasing the profitability of media rights for the ANFP. With that goal in mind, Mr. Claro sought not only to ameliorate a weak business but, more important, to boost the resources to be distributed among the Chilean football clubs through better business practices. At that moment, in 2003, the ANFP decided to accept Claro's proposal and embark on the adventure of creating a television network for Chilean football. If the business succeeds, football clubs will have the opportunity to take ownership of the commercialization and broadcasting of their national tournament and other derivative products (i.e., best plays, goals) to obtain maximum commercial benefits without having to negotiate with intermediaries.

The Football Television Network of Chile, or CDF (Canal del Fútbol), was created as a limited liability company that had the purpose of broadcasting the professional football tournament of Chile. The CDF model was successfully implemented because of the boldness of Mr. Claro, the creator and single investor in this business. Claro not only took over this ambitious yet risky project but also guaranteed an annual payment of US$3.6 million to be shared among the 32 football clubs (an amount equal to the compensation that clubs would have received if they had decided to continue bidding with their former TV networks). Mr. Claro was confident that the football product in Chile could, from the broadcasting point of view, generate a much larger profit. Now, he just had to prove it.

Growth of the total annual income put forth by CDF toward the football clubs (through the ANFP) was US$3.6 million in 2003, US$5.5 in 2005, US$6.2 in 2007, and US$9.6 million in 2009.

As owner of the broadcasting rights of football, CDF had the power to rebroadcast highlights from games, unseen in Chile until that time. In 2005 Channel 13 TV won the bid to show goals scored exclusively during the weekends until midnight on Sundays. The rest of the TV networks, both public (open TV) and cable television, were allowed to show highlights only in news programs. Sport programs had the option of purchasing rights to show their viewers goals scored in matches. Such a situation generated legal action on behalf of the Chilean television networks, who argued the importance of protecting the right to information. Yet the court ruling was in favor of CDF in the matter. Toward the end of 2008, the bid for showing highlights on television rose 57 percent when compared with 2006.

The CDF model has proved successful. As of 2009, subscribers to the CDF premium plan had reached 500,000, and CDF basic had 1,000,000 subscribers. By 2011 the 32 clubs members of the ANFP will likely be sharing a total of US$35 million in that year alone. Despite the larger amount of revenues, the distribution of resources has not come without controversies. In 2009 the ANFP proposed that CDF revenues be distributed equally among first-division and second-division teams. This decision generated objections from the three largest clubs of the first division: Colo Colo, Universidad de Chile, and Universidad Católica. These clubs argued that they should be credited with the success of the business because together they made up 90 percent of the viewer preference of CDF subscribers. As a result, starting in 2011 CDF profits will be distributed as follows: 25 percent for the three largest clubs in the first division, 56 percent for the 15 remaining first-division clubs, and the remaining 19 percent for the 14 clubs of the second division.

David Ortiz, and Manny Ramirez. On opening day of the 2010 MLB season, 164 out of 833 players were from Latin America (Gregory, 2010). The effect of this movement of players has been felt in several ways across the professional leagues in the region. A broad description of the state of professional baseball in the Dominican Republic and Venezuela follows.

Dominican Republic The Dominican League of Professional Baseball (Liga de Beisbol Profesional de la Republica Dominicana) was officially formed in 1955, but organized baseball had existed since the late 19th century. Klein (1989) identified three eras within Dominican professional baseball: romantic, maturation, and post–free agency. An examination of these eras provides us with a picture of how political and economic events influenced the development of professional baseball not only in the Dominican Republic but also in the United States.

The romantic era took place during the first half of the 20th century. In the mid-1920s, and when the United States occupied the Dominican Republic, the popularity of baseball grew significantly because of the matches played between Americans and Dominicans. These games served to enhance the nationalistic feelings of Dominicans, who repeatedly defeated the *Yankis* on the diamonds. During this era, dictator General Rafael Trujillo himself became an avid enthusiast and financially backed the growth of the sport. Trujillo invited to play and paid several renowned baseball stars of the Negro Leagues. Also, private business had an interest in supporting the teams. With the arrival of the maturation era in the mid-1950s, the real influence of professional baseball was felt. During this time, the Dominican professional league was formed and grew from two to six teams, still the number today. During this era the Dominican league established a formal relationship with Major League Baseball. Immediately after the first Dominican player signed for an MLB team in the mid-1950s, American scouts recognized the talent of Dominican players. As a result, more and more MLB teams began looking at the Dominican leagues as a farm system that could supply good-quality, low-cost players. Even though many Dominicans were recruited to play in the major leagues during this time, their exodus did not threaten the survival of the local league. Only after 1980 during the post–free agency era when MLB teams became seriously involved in the Dominican Republic was the direction of the sport seriously affected in both countries (Klein, 1989).

Scholars have noted that dependency occurs when two unequal economies (in size and solvency) enter into a relationship that produces results more detrimental to the smaller economy (Cardoso, 1977; Chase-Dunn, 1982). Although in the short term both sides benefit from this relationship, the long-term effect always hits harder on the smaller economy because the relationship creates a circle of dependency that does not allow for its growth. Spagnuolo (2003) explains this dependency in the Dominican Republic through the relationship established between American baseball interests and the small Caribbean country.

In the early 1980s the end of the reserve clause and the further adoption of free agency brought severe changes to the economy of MLB, particularly skyrocketing players' salaries. MLB teams coped with this reality by aggressively looking for talent overseas that they could obtain at a fraction of the cost of what the same talent would cost at home. As a result, during this time an arms race developed among MLB teams to secure the best Dominican prospects. Teams signed as many players as possible in a sort of "boatload mentality" (Spagnuolo, 2003, p. 271). The impoverished economy of the Dominican Republic offered few alternative opportunities for aspiring ball players, so the prospects had minimum bargaining power.

Baseball academies were set up during the mid-1980s and had the goal of recruiting and preparing aspiring major league players. These academies, also known as camps, offered baseball training and taught the enrollees English, the American work ethic, and social customs (Klein, 1989; Ruck, 1999). In spite of these efforts, some argue that baseball academies have negatively affected not only the quality and development of the local league but also have contributed to some extent to the dependency and its unfavorable effects (Klein, 1989, 1991; Ruck, 1999; Spagnuolo, 2003).

Critics of the role of the baseball academies suggest that what inspires the creation of baseball academies is the economic interest to profit by obtaining cheap labor (Regalado, 2000; Vargas, 2000). As a result, what matter are the results and not how practices are conducted. Instead of young boys developing as ballplayers and making their way through the ranks within the local baseball league, they go directly to the baseball academies with the hope of playing abroad professionally. Consequently, the pool of players for the Dominican professional leagues is made up of those who are not signed by an academy. The academy system has hindered the development and quality of Dominican amateur and professional leagues. Perhaps its most serious effect is that it creates false expectations for the hundreds of young Dominicans who never reach the major leagues; less than 2 percent of those who sign a contract make it to major leagues (Gregory, 2010).

The absence of an international draft rule also contributes to this problem. Although MLB currently applies the international draft rule to some countries (e.g., Canada and Puerto Rico), this rule does not apply to the Dominican Republic, where any prospect can sign as long as he is 17 years old. Critics noted that this measure encourages children and youngsters to drop out of high school or even middle school to focus their time exclusively on baseball. The result for most aspiring ballplayers is failure to break the circle of poverty (Gregory, 2010; Spagnuolo, 2003).

Venezuela In Venezuela the professional league, or Liga Venezolana de Béisbol Profesional (LVBP), drives the interest of most Venezuelan sport fans. Currently, the league includes eight teams that compete from October through the end of January. The winner of the Venezuelan league plays in the Caribbean Series, which includes teams from the Dominican Republic, Puerto Rico, and Mexico (Liga Venezolana de Béisbol Profesional, n.d). The most renowned teams in the Venezuelan league are Leones de Caracas, Magallanes, Tiburones de la Guaira, and Tigres de Aragua. The greatest achievement of Venezuelan baseball was winning the World Series of Amateur Baseball that took place in Cuba in 1941. Even today it is acknowledged as the greatest feat (Ettedgui & Fuenmayor, 2002), and the players are referred to as the 1941 Heroes.

Since the early 1960s, the best and most renowned Venezuelan players have been recruited to play in Major League Baseball (MLB). In 2010, 58 Venezuelan players appeared on the opening-day rosters of MLB teams (Gregory, 2010). Today, Venezuelan-born players represent the second largest foreign group, after Dominican players, within MLB. Similar to their Dominican counterparts, Venezuelan players have developed such a reputation within the world of baseball that MLB franchises have established baseball academies to select and prepare these players for the major leagues in the United States. In 1989 the Houston Astros became the first MLB team to establish a baseball academy in Venezuela. Over the next 20 years many more followed. But when the government of President Hugo Chavez took power in 1999, the relationship

with American interests became more distant and sometimes tense. By 2005 Major League Baseball feared that their interests would be at stake. As a result, many baseball academies decided to end their operations there. By 2007 only 9 baseball academies of the 19 that existed during the mid-1990s were still operating (Grassi, 2008).

In 2007 Venezuelan officials met with MLB executives to discuss the state of baseball in the country. According to Grassi (2008), the Venezuelan government outlined a series of points about how they wanted to conduct business with MLB in the country, including employee and player protection, payment of transaction bonuses for every player signed into MLB, and the assignment of power to the Venezuelan Baseball Governing Body to oversee the relationship with MLB in Venezuela. None of these points have been implemented, and none were accepted by MLB at that time.

Every year the Venezuelan professional league attracts thousands of fans to ballparks around the country. The league is sponsored by private as well as public companies, and it receives significant coverage from the local media. Although the major leagues might still be the ultimate aspiration for most ballplayers in Venezuela, the influence of MLB is not felt there with the same intensity as it is in the Dominican Republic. The passion of Venezuelan fans for their teams, the respect given to their athletes, the financial support from the private and public sector to the league, and perhaps the protective role played by the Venezuelan government help to explain its sustainability and current success.

Amateur Sport and Education

In many Latin American countries, as in other countries around the world, there is and has been a close and historical link between sport, education (particularly physical education), and the development of the amateur sport system. Many pioneering efforts in the area of education from the early days of the 20th century have set the foundation for the many amateur sport structures that exist today in the region.

As previously discussed, the sport system in Latin American countries is organized mostly outside the school domain, but a close relationship still exists between sport and education, as can be seen in many initiatives. Colombia, for example, has a rich tradition in this respect. Physical education was officially included in the school curriculum in 1925 with the approval of Law 80, formally known as Ley de la Piedra Angular de la Educación Física en Colombia (Keystone Law of Physical Education in Colombia) (Gómez & Parra, 1986). Law 80 promoted the practice of physical education at all levels of education as well as helped to create numerous recreational associations. It also influenced the construction of sporting facilities and supported the organization of competitive sport. Because of these efforts, some key institutions of higher education were created to achieve the goals initially established by Law 80. Among these institutions was the National Institute of Physical Education (INEF), founded in 1936, which in 1952 became the National School of Physical Education (ENEF) and then in 1962 became part of the Universidad Nacional Pedagógica de Bogotá (National Teachers' University of Bogotá) (Contecha, 2003). Another important institution was the National Coaching School, which was created in 1984. These institutions played a fundamental role in preparing the workforce who would lead the Colombian sport system. Moreover, in 1995, the Sport Law of Colombia highlighted the importance of physical education in promoting the practice of sport. The Sport Law also established the Ministry of Education as the agency responsible for the organization, promotion, and development of physical education (Contecha, 1999).

Another example that illustrates the relationship between sport and education is seen in El Salvador, where over the past several years the Olympic Committee of El Salvador (COES) has played a vital role in promoting the value of physical education in that country. An assortment of programs and activities has been developed to increase children's participation in physical education and sport. In this manner, physical education, sport, and play are used as vehicles to teach core values of respect, tolerance, equality, and healthy choices—values that represent a fundamental component within the national physical education curriculum in El Salvador.

As in El Salvador, the sport system in Puerto Rico is supported by various educational entities that promote the participation of sport at various levels of performance. Within these entities is the public school system, which offers three levels of physical and sport development. The first level is that of instruction through physical education classes

offered during regular school hours. Every child is required to enroll in three hours of physical education per week according to Law 146, which has been in effect since 2000. The other levels of participation are intramural and interscholastic sport programs, which facilitate sport for the more athletically talented population (Domenech, 2003). In addition, the municipal departments of education and sport and recreation fund after-school programs to continue promoting the participation and involvement in sport activities of children in 7th, 8th, and 9th grades (Departamento de Recreación y Deporte de Puerto Rico, n.d.).

As in the United States, in Mexico the development of collegiate sport has been an important aspect within the extracurricular programs of higher education institutions. Intercollegiate sport in Mexico is organized around the Consejo Nacional del Deporte en la Educación (CONDDE) (National Council for Sport and Education). The organization dates back to 1947 when the first Mexican intercollegiate athletic festival took place. Currently, 294 institutions of higher education are members of CONNDE. In the early 1970s Mexico became part of the International Federation of University Sports (FISU), and in 1979 Mexico hosted the World University Games. The success of that event, which included the participation of 3,000 student–athletes from 94 countries, helped to convince university leaders of the value of promoting and supporting collegiate sport in Mexico. In 1988 the first National University Games took place at Universidad Autónoma de Ciudad Juárez (Consejo Nacional del Deporte de la Educación, 2007). The National University Games, or Universiadas, are a multisport festival that takes place every year over a period of two weeks. Each member school must actively compete year round in prequalification series. Thus, the first round is internal (intramural) in each school. Those who qualify at this level go on to compete at the state level and then move to a regional competition. All participants' schools are organized in eight regional zones in the country. Athletes and teams that reach first and second place in the regional tournaments advance to the national games. In 2008 nearly 800,000 people participated at the intramural level, 67,000 competed at the state level, and 15,000 competed at the regional level. The games have been celebrated every year since 1988 and today involve more than 5,000 participants, including student–athletes and coaches representing more than 150 institutions of higher education from all over Mexico. Student–athletes participate in 17 men's and 16 women's sports (Riojas-Martínez, 2008). Collegiate sport in Mexico is funded by each institution but highly subsidized through the Secretary of Public Education (Stier & Alvarez, 1991). Higher education in Mexico in most cases is free because of the country's 1917 constitution, which guarantees education to every citizen.

Highly influenced by the collegiate system established in the United States, the Commonwealth of Puerto Rico is another example that illustrates the pioneering efforts to develop collegiate sport in Latin America. La Liga Atlética Interuniversitaria de Puerto Rico (LAI) (Intercollegiate Athletic Association of Puerto Rico) was formed in 1929 and continues to operate today. The LAI arose from the need to provide university students with the opportunity to compete in sport and to formalize requirements of student eligibility and such (Sambolín, Ríos de Vásquez, & Stewart, n.d.). The establishment of the LAI marked the beginning of the development of high-performing athletes who would later participate in national and international events representing Puerto Rico (Huertas, 2006).

Sport Management as a Professional Activity

Over the last 30 years, the sport industry around the world has evolved considerably, creating important transformations in the way in which this sector has been organized. As the industry has reached higher levels of sophistication, the management of sport has become a more complex, highly professionalized field. But the growth and development of sport has not occurred in the same way everywhere. In Latin America the sport industry has grown at a more moderate pace. Governments, particularly in their role as welfare states, have taken the lead role in boosting the industry. In spite of the pivotal role of government, the growth of the sport sector has not been exempt from problems, challenges, and controversies. Over the years, recurrent mismanagement cases in sport organizations, both public and private, have been reported in several countries throughout the region ("Carrion Renuncia," 2008; "Chiledeportes: Bachelet Anuncia Estrictas," 2006; "Corrupción Secretaría de Deportes," 2008; "Orde-

nan Captura," 2010; "The Not-So-Beautiful Game," 2002; "Viceministerio de Deportes se Hunde," 2010). Some of these incidents were found to be cases of corruption that not only wasted public resources but also carried a high political price for government officials.

Anecdotal evidence suggests that in Latin America managers and employees working in both the public and private sport sectors do not have much expertise or sufficient professional background to operate these organizations effectively. As a result, poor managerial practices are common in amateur and community sport organizations as well as professional sport organizations. For the most part, these poor practices are characterized by loose approaches to bookkeeping and financial management and minimal transparency in documentation of operations.

A lack of professionalization of the people who work in the sport sector can partially explain the problems described earlier. An additional explanation can be found in the lax hiring practices that some governments use when appointing civil employees in the sport sector. Current studies show that public sector employment in Latin America is still characterized by the practice of patronage, a discretionary allocation of jobs to reward followers and fortify political status and personal relationships (Grindle, 2010). The employment of well-trained employees and managers in an organization is important because mismanagement and abuse of power often lead to corruption of an organization (Doig, 1995). Although monitoring malpractice and corruption in sport is not solely the responsibility of governments, a recent report of Transparency International states, "Part of the work on sport and corruption must focus on how governments behave" ("Corruption and Sport," 2009, p. 6). The intersection between career professionalization and the remodeling of public service administration has been acknowledged to exert a significant influence within the process of modernization of governmental structures (Nef, 2007). This breakthrough suggests that governments in Latin America must focus not only on improving their own public administrative civil services but also on understanding how and where the education and training of sport sector personnel takes place.

The lack of professionalized structure and its effect on sport organizations are reported by

Cornejo (1999). He noted that the sport system in El Salvador has historically been marked by unarticulated efforts and by the absence of cooperation among the various national governing bodies (NGBs) responsible for its development. The lack of professional structure in many of these NGBs as well as with the Olympic Committee of El Salvador (COES) has intensified the sentiments of distrust about how these organizations are run, particularly regarding the lack of a mechanism of accountability for how board members operate. In more severe terms, Sermeño (1993) criticized the leadership of COES of the 1990s for using money to finance tourism instead of to improve El Salvador's international sport performance.

In many Latin American countries, the lack of professionalized structure involves not only administrative personnel but also those in the areas of coaching and athletes' support. A few initiatives have been launched across the region with the aim of curbing this problem. Recently, the Venezuelan government has sponsored two important initiatives: the creation of the Sport School Talent (Unidades Educativas de Talento Deportivo, UETD) in 2004 and the creation of the Ibero-American Sport University in 2006. Although the UETD was created to provide adequate training and education to prospective elite athletes, the Ibero-American Sport University aims to provide education for all kinds of professionals working in the sport industry (Instituto Nacional de Deporte, 2005; López de D'Amico, 2006). Notwithstanding these important efforts, López de D'Amico and Guerrero (2007) noted that in Venezuela the biggest task in this regard is the education of coaches because many of these professionals perceive that these measures do not bring concrete benefits to their careers.

The Colombian government, through Coldeportes, has taken similar steps to prepare and educate sport personnel by implementing a national plan that is coordinated by Coldeportes and the National Service for Learning (SENA). This initiative aims to professionalize and certify all those who work in the sport sector. Yet this initiative has not been exempt from controversy. The main point in question centers on the jurisdiction and legitimacy of the training institutions. Main critics of this initiative are the universities and other institutions of higher education that traditionally have had this responsibility.

International Sporting Events and Regional Governing Bodies

Hosting landmark sporting events represents a long-term aspiration for countries that significantly invest in their sport systems. Countries seek not only to showcase their athletic success but also to increase the overall visibility of the country, enhance their image, stimulate urban development, and even create a psychic boost among the citizens where the event takes place (Howard & Crompton, 2004). In other words, a country or city may achieve many indirect benefits when hosting a landmark event. In many instances, however, hosting these events requires a level of resources, political will, and expertise that many countries do not have.

Latin American governments have used similar approaches to justify the hosting of these events. Despite the economic, social, and political challenges typically found in Latin America, over the past century the region has hosted an array of international sporting events, from those that had a primarily local impact to those that attracted the attention of the entire world. Moreover, many of the regional governing bodies, such as ODEPA, CONMEBOL, and UNCAF, have become instrumental in the creation of international sporting events in the region. The following section describes the evolution of a few sporting events that have been hosted on Latin American soil. It also describes the role played by key sporting governing bodies that oversee sport across Latin America.

International Sporting Events

Over the past 80 years Latin American countries have hosted major world sporting events like the FIFA World Cup and the Summer Olympic Games. Although the frequency of hosting these events still does not match that of other parts of the world (e.g., Europe), in the near future more Latin American countries will likely be bidding to obtain these events and being selected to host them. The FIFA World Cup has been hosted five times in Latin America since it began in 1930. In fact, the first host country for this tournament was Uruguay. The other four countries that have hosted the FIFA World Cup have been Brazil in 1950, Chile in 1962, Mexico in 1970 and 1986, and Argentina in 1978.

The FIFA World Cup will return to Latin America in 2014, this time again in Brazil.

Although the prime world football tournament has been organized several times in Latin America, the same cannot be said for the Summer Olympic Games. In more than 100 years, the Summer Olympic Games have been held only once in Latin America, at Mexico City in 1968. The Summer Olympic Games will return to Latin America in 2016, this time to Rio de Janeiro, Brazil.

As the popularity of these sporting events continues to grow worldwide, the complexity of organizing them increases in almost every aspect (i.e., adequate sport facilities, adequate transportation system, adequate tourism infrastructure, and so on). Aspiring cities and countries need to be prepared to address these needs. One way of paving the path to reach that level of excellence is to host regional games that require significant logistics. Through the years, several major regional tournaments have been organized in Latin America, such as the Central American and Caribbean Games, the Pan American Games, and Copa América (in football).

To organize any major sporting event, countries require not only resources but also a good dose of leadership to persuade others that their bid is the best bet. Mexico has shown leadership in this respect. Mexican sport authorities gained the credibility of the sporting world as early as the 1930s (Brewster, 2005). At that time, Mexican representatives attending an International Olympic Committee (IOC) meeting proposed the creation of the Sport Confederation for the Americas, which years later would become the Olympic regional umbrella for the Americas, now known as the Pan American Sport Organization, or Organización Deportiva Panamericana (ODEPA). Because of this, in 1951 the Pan American Games were born. Since that time, Mexico has hosted the Pan American Games three times, in 1955, 1975, and 2011, twice in Mexico City and once in Guadalajara. Mexico has also hosted the Central American and Caribbean Games on two occasions, in 1954 and 1990. These games, which include participant countries from Central America and the Caribbean, are the oldest continuing regional games in the world. Only the Olympic Games have a longer continuous history. Mexico, Cuba, and Guatemala were the only countries present at the first games in 1926, which at that time were called the Central American Games (McGehee, 1994).

Like Mexico, Brazil has organized some of the most important mega sporting events during the past century, including the 1922 Latin American Olympic Games in Rio de Janeiro, the 1950 World Cup, the 1963 World University Games in Porto Alegre, the 1963 and 2007 Pan American Games in Sao Paulo and Rio de Janeiro respectively, the Formula One Grand Prix in Sao Paulo and Rio de Janeiro since the 1970s, and the 1989 Copa América (Da Costa & Miragaya, 2008). The successful organization of these events has provided Brazil with a solid reputation for organizing and hosting major games. That reputation, along with the attractiveness of the country as a world tourist destination, resulted in the selection of Rio de Janeiro in October 2009 to host the Summer Olympic Games in 2016. Brazil will be the second Latin American and the first South American country to organize the Summer Olympic Games.

Several regional football tournaments are organized in Latin America. Among these, the South American Championships of Nations, or Copa América, is perhaps the most important. This event was the first football tournament in the world organized for national teams. As a result, Copa América is the oldest tournament of its kind. It has been played since 1916, first on a yearly basis and then every two years. This tournament has historically been restricted to the 10 members of CONMEBOL, the South American Football Confederation (the regional arm of FIFA for South America), but since 1993 two teams outside CONMEBOL have been invited. On most occasions it has been played in a host country that now rotates among the 10 members of CONMEBOL. All 10 members of the confederation have hosted the tournament at least once. Argentina hosted it nine times, Uruguay on seven occasions, and Peru and Chile on six occasions (Bravo, 2011).

Sport Governing Bodies in Latin America

Several sport governing bodies oversee sport matters in Latin American countries. In many instances, these governing bodies act as a regional arm of a larger world governing body. Keep in mind, as previously stated in this chapter, that Latin America in a strict sense is not a geographical region but more a cultural grouping of countries that have a common past. As a result, many governing bodies that oversee sport in Latin American countries also include countries that fall beyond this categorization. The following section offers a brief description of the most important governing bodies, including the Organización Deportiva Pan Americana (ODEPA), Organizacion Deportiva Centroamericana y del Caribe (ODECABE), Organizacion Deportiva Suramericana (ODESUR), the Confederación Sudamericana de Fútbol (CONMEBOL), the Confederación de Fútbol de Norte, Centroamérica y el Caribe (CONCACAF), and the Unión Centro-Americana de Fútbol (UNCAF).

◆ The Organización Deportiva Pan Americana (**Pan American Sport Organization [ODEPA]**) is the group of national Olympic committees (NOCs) of the South American continent. As such it involves every country located in the broad region of the Americas. ODEPA was founded in 1948, and since then it has been recognized by the International Olympic Committee (IOC). Acting in accord with each NOC, ODEPA seeks to promote the Olympic sentiment and its social and sporting ideals in the American region (ODEPA.com, n.d.; Thoma & Chalip, 2003). A main objective of ODEPA is the organization of the Pan American Games, which take place every four years (ODEPA.com, n.d.). The first Pan American Games took place in Buenos Aires, Argentina, in 1951, when 21 nations participated in 19 sports. The idea of having the Pan American Games grew from the success of the Central American Games, which were first organized in the 1920s. Although the first Pan American Games were staged to happen in 1943 in Buenos Aires, the event was postponed until 1951 because of World War II (McGehee, 1994). The Pan American Games have been held every four years ever since. Sadly, the Pan American Games have lost their luster in recent years, particularly in the United States, where the games have received little if any airtime from the major U.S. broadcasting stations. Conversely, the Pan American Games receive plenty of attention in Latin America. Table 5.2 shows the performance, expressed in medal count, of 19 Latin American countries participating at the Pan American Games from 1951 to 2007. Over the years, ODEPA has attempted to hold Pan American Winter Games as well, but it has found limited success. Most Latin American countries are in the subtropical region, thus limiting the number

of participating nations and athletes (ODEPA.com, n.d.). In 1990 Las Leñas in Argentina hosted the first and only Pan American Winter Games when eight countries sent 97 athletes, 76 of whom were from the United States, Argentina, and Canada. The United States and Canada won all 18 medals. ODEPA awarded the second Winter Games to Santiago, Chile, in 1993, but the games never took place, and the idea has not been revisited since.

◆ The history of the Organizacion Deportiva Centroamericana y del Caribe (**Central American and Caribbean Sports Organization [ODECABE]**) is tied to the history of the Central American and Caribbean Sport Games (CACSG), which are the oldest continuing regional sporting games in the world. The purpose of ODECABE is to oversee the hosting of these games for countries located in Central America and the Caribbean. Over the years 32 nations have participated in these games, which are held every four years between the Summer Olympic Games and the Pan American Games. Although the Central American and Caribbean Sport Games have been held since 1926, the governing body ODECABE was not founded until 1960 (Montecinos, 2009).

◆ Organizacion Deportiva Suramericana (**South American Sport Organization [ODESUR]**) is the governing body that oversees the South American Games, a multisport festival held every four years. These games have been organized since 1978 and today involve the participation of 15 countries including Argentina, Aruba, Bolivia, Brazil, Chile, Colombia, Ecuador, Guyana, Netherlands Antilles, Panama, Paraguay, Peru, Surinam, Uruguay, and Venezuela. The games include participation in sports that are part of the Olympic programs as well as non-Olympic sports (ODESUR.org, n.d).

◆ Confederación Sudamericana de Fútbol (**South American Football Confederation [CONMEBOL]**) was founded in 1916 and is the regional football confederation of the South American FIFA members. Its objective is to unite the associations of the region to control and develop football in South America. Its member nations include Argentina, Bolivia, Brazil, Chile, Colombia, Ecuador, Paraguay, Peru, Uruguay, and Venezuela. The confederation was founded during the course of a football tournament that took place in Argentina as part of its centennial independence celebration. Retrospectively, this tournament was acknowledged as the first Copa América (Barraza, 2006). Although

Table 5.2 All-Time Medal (1951–2007) Count of the Pan American Games in Selected Latin American Countries

Rank	Country	Gold	Silver	Bronze	Total
1	Cuba	781	531	484	1,796
2	Argentina	258	286	372	916
3	Brazil	239	284	402	925
4	Mexico	155	217	410	782
5	Venezuela	75	157	225	457
6	Colombia	58	109	160	327
7	Chile	36	69	109	214
8	Puerto Rico	21	71	113	205
9	Dominican Republic	19	43	88	150
10	Ecuador	14	13	37	64
11	Uruguay	11	21	41	73
12	Guatemala	7	11	32	50
13	Peru	5	28	54	87
14	Costa Rica	4	6	8	18
15	Panama	3	23	30	56
16	El Salvador	1	6	12	19
17	Nicaragua	0	4	7	11
18	Paraguay	0	1	4	5
19	Honduras	0	1	4	5
20	Bolivia	0	1	2	3
	United States	1,769	1,300	867	3,936

Note: The United States is included for comparison purposes.

Data from Guadalajara 2011 (n.d.).

Guyana, Suriname, and French Guyana are located in South America, for historical, cultural, and sporting reasons, their national associations are members of CONCAFAF instead. Some of the tournaments conducted under the auspices of CONMEBOL are Copa Libertadores de América and Copa Sudamericana, both for club teams, and Copa América for men's national teams, the oldest international football tournament in the world of its kind. From 1930 to 2010, CONMEBOL teams won 9 out of 20 FIFA World Cup tournaments, and as of the end of 2010, 4 of the top 10 national teams in the world were from this association (FIFA.com, 2010).

◆ Confederación de Fútbol de Norte Centroamérica y el Caribe (**Confederation of North, Central America, and Caribbean Association**

Football [**CONCACAF**]) was founded in 1961. CONCACAF is one of the six continental confederations affiliated with FIFA. Its primary administrative functions are to organize competitions for national teams and clubs and to conduct qualifying tournaments for FIFA events including the FIFA World Cup, the FIFA Women's World Cup, FIFA World Championships at youth levels, and beach football and futsal, or indoor football (CONCACAF.com, n.d.). As the administrative body for the region, CONCACAF also organizes training courses in technical and administrative aspects of the game and helps to build football throughout the region.

◆ The Unión Centro-Americana de Fútbol (**Central American Football Union [UNCAF]**) is the regional Central American organization of football that operates under the umbrella of CONCACAF. Its objectives are the promotion and development of football with special interest in youth development through competitions among national teams and clubs. UNCAF runs many tournaments including the UNCAF Nations Cup, which provide four entries for Central American countries to the Gold Cup, CONCACAF's flagship tournament (UNCAF, n.d.).

Summary

Since the mid-1800s, the practice of sport in Latin America has been influenced by people who came to the region to do business, to participate in religious or educational missions, or simply in search of a new homeland. A variety of sports became popular in different countries, but from the very first days football and baseball were extremely popular (depending on the region) and strengthened the national identity of most Latin American nations.

Although sport in Latin America did not evolve the same way in each country, it is possible to identify some common grounds of influence. The inclusion of physical education within the educational curriculum and the role of government, which provides the institutional support to expand the practice of sport to a wider range of society, represent two important sources of influence in sport development. In addition, for most countries, the early establishment of sport clubs, mostly outside the domain of the school system, was a fundamental characteristic of the sport system.

Mexico is the second largest country in Latin America. Its sport system developed from the amateur movement of clubs, associations, and national governing bodies that fall under the jurisdiction of its own National Olympic Committee. Also, through the government's intervention in the creation of structures, enactment of policies, and allocating resources to support sporting activities at all levels of participation, Mexico has become a leading country in hosting international sporting events. In 1968 it became the first developing nation to organize the Summer Olympic Games. Today, Mexico's highest sport governmental office is represented by CONADE, which acts decentralized from the federal public administration and falls under the scope of the executive branch.

In Mexico and Central America, the Central American and Caribbean Games are the most important regional multisport games. These games are the oldest continuing regional games in the world. Although football is the most popular sport in Central America, other sport practices are also popular in the region. Costa Rica is considered by many a perfect destination for the practice and commercial venture of nature-based sport and extreme sports.

Baseball is the most popular sport in the Dominican Republic, and Dominican players are known worldwide for their superb skill and talent. The aspiration for many of these players is to reach Major League Baseball in the United States. The exodus of many talented players, however, has hindered the development and quality of Dominican amateur leagues.

Within South America, the common denominators for the sport systems of many countries are the popularity of football and strong government participation. The exception is Venezuela, in which baseball, not football, is the dominant sport. But government does play a central role in the development of Venezuelan sport. Similarly, the Brazilian sport system has also been supported by its government, although it was not until the 1990s that the government set the legal foundations to improve the overall conditions for sport to grow. Today, the sport system in Brazil is the result of a complex network of many public and private efforts.

Despite of not having the same level of governmental support as Brazil, Venezuela, and Mexico, Argentina has been able to achieve world-class status in several sports, including football, rugby, polo, field hockey, basketball, and tennis. Football, however, represents the true passion of most of the population. Although football is a source of pride within Argentina, the management of professional football has faced serious challenges to its welfare for years. Argentinean clubs are organized by laws that restrict them as nonprofit civil organizations. As a result, many football clubs lack solid management practices, putting both individual clubs and the entire Argentinean league in financial jeopardy.

On the other hand, Chile recently began to change its football structure by requiring its professional football clubs to become either public limited sport companies or corporations with public financial audit. By emulating the trend of some well-known European leagues, Chilean professional football is attempting to transform the old-fashioned structure commonly used in Latin America into a business model that understands both the social importance of sport and its economic value as a part of a larger entertainment industry.

? Review and Discussion Questions

1. Compare and contrast the origin and development of various sports in Latin America.

2. Discuss the role of three governmental agencies related with the development of sport in Latin America. What are the main purposes of these agencies?

3. Discuss the role of three private agencies related with the development of sport in Latin America. What are the main purposes of these agencies?

4. What are some of the problems that have prevented progress in the management of Argentinean professional football?

5. What aspects have influenced the development of professional football in Chile?

6. Discuss some of the shortcomings of the role of baseball academies in the Dominican Republic.

7. Discuss the role of intercollegiate athletics in Latin America. What are the main issues that have prevented its development? Provide an example of a country that has successfully implemented collegiate sports.

8. Reflect about the role of government intervention in sport within the context of a Latin American country. To what extent do you think that the enactment of laws would make a country more or less passionate about sport and eventually allow it to achieve success at the international level?

9. What is the relationship between overall country development and athletic success? (Refer to tables 5.1 and 5.2 in the chapter.)

10. Why have the Pan American Games lost their luster in the United States but not in Latin America? Do you think that competition in this region is not valued by the USOC? Is the reason related to the television networks' disfranchisement of this competition in the United States?

Acknowledgments

The authors express their sincere thanks to the following individuals who provided valuable information for the completion of this chapter (in alphabetical order): Bárbara Schausteck de Almeida, Gladys Bequer, César Federico Macías Cervantes, Luis Correa, Daniel de la Cueva, Vanesa González, Luz María Hoyos, Pablo Ibarra, Samuel Martínez, Fernando Mezzadri, Ignacio Moncada, Ricardo João Sonoda Nunes, Charles T. Parrish, Carlos Rico, Alfonso Rodríguez, María Pilar Rodríguez, and Jorge Sánchez.

Sport in Europe

Elesa Argent, PhD

London Metropolitan University, United Kingdom

Chapter Objectives

After studying this chapter, you will be able to do the following:

- Define Europe as a political and geographical continent
- Define the regions of Western and Eastern Europe
- Understand the European sport model
- Identify the key economic characteristics of the Western European sport market
- Identify key issues and characteristics of European sport law
- Understand the legacy of Communism in post-Communist Eastern European states, with specific reference to sport management
- Identify key economic, financial, and social considerations that affect the management of sport in Western and Eastern European states

Key Terms

1. Switzerland
2. Slovenia
3. Czech Republic
4. Moldova
5. Bosnia and Herzegovenia
6. Montenegro
7. Albania
8. Greece
9. Croatia
10. Macedonia
11. Luxembourg

Key Events

Fall of the Berlin Wall, 1989. Event that paved the way for German reunification and a wave of anti-Communist revolutions across Eastern Europe, which had a significant effect on the landscape of European sport and on understanding of sport doping issues.

Bosman ruling, 1995. European Union legal ruling that allowed freer movement of athletes between teams.

2012 London Olympic and Paralympic Games. Awarded to London in 2005.

European Sport for All Charter, 1975. Adopted by the sport ministers of European member states, had the goal of making sport accessible to all people and supporting high ethical values in sport.

1936 Berlin Olympic Games. Held after the Nazi regime came to power in Germany, a historically significant example of propagandism in sport.

1948 London Games. Hosted just after the end of World War II, relied heavily on volunteers, and initiated volunteering as an important part of European sport.

NFL International Series 2008–2010. Expansion of a North American sport brand into European markets.

Key People

Lord Sebastian Coe, former Olympic athlete, political figure, and chief executive of the London 2012 Olympic bid team.

Vladimir Putin, Russian president, lobbied IOC in support of Russia's successful bid to host the 2012 Winter Games in Sochi.

Tony Blair, formerly prime minister of Great Britain, played a role in the London 2012 Olympic bid and personally intervened on behalf of Formula One to allow an exception to a ban on tobacco advertising in sport.

Andy Burnham, former sport minister for England.

The birthplace of the modern Olympic Games and home to the ancient Olympic Games, Europe possesses a rich sporting heritage arguably unrivalled by any other continent. Critically, the unique geopolitical history of the region has greatly influenced the development of sport in the 20th and early 21st centuries. A look at the fall of the Berlin Wall in 1989, the reunification of Germany, and the subsequent dissolution of the Soviet Union aid in understanding the dynamic and fluid role of the state and the private sector in the management of sport in post-Communist Eastern Europe. Conversely, the highly lucrative domestic sport leagues of wealthy Western European nations offer an example of the complexities of trading across the highly diverse European Union marketplace, as do the mixed fortunes of non-European franchises' (such as the NFL and NHL) aims to establish a presence in the European marketplace.

Consequently, this chapter seeks to examine the key geopolitical factors that affect the management of sport within Europe. We focus first on a geographic and political definition of Europe, further identifying and defining the distinct regions of Western and Eastern Europe, before considering both historical and current events that have shaped the European sporting landscape. The key characteristics of the Western European and Eastern European sport markets are then presented and discussed, focusing on the financial, economic, legal, social, and political factors that influence the management of sport in the region, as well as the legacy of Communism in Eastern Europe. This chapter will provide the reader with a fascinating insight into the operations of sport within the dynamic and culturally rich political and geographical landscape that is the continent of Europe.

Geography and Background of Europe

In geographic terms, Europe is home to 47 countries and two-thirds of a billion people, or 11 percent of the global population. The continent covers an area of 10,600,000 square kilometers (4,140,625 square miles). In exacting geographic definitions, Europe is not a continent, but part of the peninsula of Eurasia, which includes all of Europe and Asia; nevertheless, the region is widely referred to as a continent. Note that the Russian Federation is transcontinental in the sense that it resides geographically across both Europe and Asia. In political terms, 27 of the 47 European nations are members of the **European Union** (**EU**), an economic and political partnership that aims to achieve peace, prosperity, and freedom for the 495 million citizens that reside within its borders. More information about the geographical and political continent of Europe is available at this website: http://travel.nationalgeographic.com/places/continents/continent_europe.html.

In terms of sport, EU members are governed by European sport federations and umbrella organizations for sport, most notably the European Olympic committees, the European Paralympic committees, European nongovernmental sport organizations, national Olympic and Paralympic committees, the Council of Europe's structures for sport, and United Nations bodies such as the United Nations Educational, Scientific, and Cultural Organisation (UNESCO) and the World Health Organization (WHO). The European Association for Sport Management (EASM) is also recognized as an organization that contributes positively to the development of sport in Europe.

The EU requires that member states, in accordance with the Maastricht Treaty, must evidence systems of government that are founded on the principles of democracy. The Eastern European states of the Czech Republic, Estonia, Latvia, Lithuania, Poland, Slovakia, and Slovenia were the first Eastern European countries to join the EU following the collapse of Communism. Romania and Bulgaria became the most recent nations to acquire EU membership in 2007. In 2010 member states constituted Austria, Belgium, Bulgaria, Cyprus, Czech Republic, Denmark, Estonia, Finland, France, Germany, Greece, Hungary, Ireland, Italy, Latvia, Lithuania, Luxembourg, Malta, Netherlands, Poland, Portugal, Romania, Slovakia, Slovenia, Spain, Sweden, and the United Kingdom. Countries under consideration for EU membership included Turkey, Croatia, Iceland, and the Republic of Macedonia.

European countries are subject to both European law (if members of the EU) and national law, although it is acknowledged that national policy takes precedence. National policy can differ significantly between nations and provides the political, economic, financial, and legal framework under which a sport manager must operate. A detailed knowledge of these conditions is therefore critical for the adept sport manager, because they will govern terms of policy and practice in areas as diverse as human resource management, sponsorship, marketing, accounting, sport agency practices, and law.

The European Sport Model

According to the European Commission's 1992 Helsinki Report on Sport, the European sport model can be defined based on several characteristics:

> There are many common features in the ways in which sport is practiced and organised in the Union, in spite of certain differences between the Member States, and it is therefore possible to talk of a European approach to sport based on common concepts and principles.

Essentially, two European models existed between the end of World War II and 1989 (before the fall of Communism)—a Western European model and an Eastern European model. The Western model was based on power sharing and interaction between government organizations and nongovernment organizations (NGOs). Characteristic of all free-market democratic economies, this model was shaped by the growth of the media and the influence of private financing. The Eastern model was markedly different, relying exclusively on centralized state control of all sport systems. **Communism** advocates the creation of a classless society in which private ownership is abolished and within which the means of production and subsistence belong to the community. This ideology became the basis for one-party rule in Eastern Europe. After 1989, the Eastern European model dissolved and the Western model was largely adopted across all European Union member states.

The European model can be contrasted to the American model of sport (Fort, 2000), which is based on a clear separation between closed professional leagues and amateur sport. Whereas the North American professional sport system favors fixed membership leagues and the draft system, the European system favors a promotion–relegation model, whereby the least successful teams (characterized by position within the league at the close of the season) are relegated to the league below and the most successful teams are promoted to a higher league. Position in the league also dictates the proportion of revenue that a club is afforded by the league, based on the income generated by collective bargaining for TV rights for the league. This system provides a potential disadvantage as regard to competitiveness; a poorly performing team will receive a relatively low proportion of media income negotiated by the league, further perpetuating their disadvantage because they may have to sell key players to balance the books and will certainly not be in a position to afford the acquisition of the best players to improve quality of play.

Further difficulties have affected the European model in recent times, most notably because of the 2008 global credit crunch. For example, many Premier League clubs faced financial difficulties because they were heavily in debt. Their overexposed financial position was largely due to the astronomical transfer fees commanded by top athletes. This situation has led some European football leagues, such as the Italian Serie A, to adopt a system of salary capping, and the UEFA has suggested that salary capping be considered for all football leagues. Formula One was also affected by the credit crunch, a situation compounded by the excessive operational costs of Formula One teams. Honda bowed out of the sport in 2008, stating that involvement in Formula One was a luxury that it simply could no longer afford.

The central role of the volunteer in the European sport model should also be noted. The sport management scholar should observe that the inception of widespread sport volunteering occurred at the London 1948 Olympic Games. Volunteers were crucial in a post–World War II society characterized by social and economic troubles, and their role has remained pivotal to the present day. The Olympic and Paralympic Games are scheduled to return to London in 2012, and will, no doubt, contribute further to the continuing redefinition of the European sporting landscape.

The 2007 European Commission *White Paper on Sport* quoted Pierre de Coubertin, father of the modern Olympic Movement, in its opening phrase: "Sport is part of every man and woman's heritage and its absence can never be compensated for" (*White Paper on Sport*, p. 1). So begins the understanding of the founding ideology of sport in Europe: an idealized amateur ethos that stresses the fundamental importance of sport for all European citizens. This ethos exists in parallel with a highly successful professional model of sport.

Western Europe plays host to a multitude of iconic annual amateur and professional events,

Effective Leadership in the London 2012 Bid for the Olympic and Paralympic Games

"To make an Olympic champion, it takes eight Olympic finalists. To make Olympic finalists, it takes 80 Olympians. To make Olympians, it takes 202 national champions. To make national champions, it takes thousands of athletes. To make athletes, it takes millions of children around the world to be inspired to choose sport." So began Sebastian Coe, the chief executive of the London 2012 bid team, in his opening statement to the IOC Commission in Singapore on July 6, 2005. The final presentation was to be remembered as one of the most inspired and emotional moments of a historic and successful campaign that secured Great Britain the rights to host the 2012 Olympic and Paralympic Games.

The Bid Team

The London 2012 bid arguably stands as one of the most exciting examples of sport management, leadership, and teamwork in the history of Olympic bidding.

Besides London, seven other cities—Havana, Leipzig, Rio de Janeiro, Istanbul, New York, Paris, and Madrid—had expressed their intention to bid for the right to host the 2012 Games. Initially, Barbara Cassani, the American executive responsible for the successful creation of the British Airways' Go! low-budget airline, was charged with setting up London's bid. Cassani, a previous Businesswoman of the Year, took the bid successfully through the first round of voting before graciously stepping aside to allow former Olympic champion Sebastian Coe to take the helm. Coe was to carry the bid forward to its successful conclusion. Coe was not only a former Olympic gold medalist but also a close friend of former IOC president Juan Antonio Samaranch, a successful British political figure, and a person who had been suggested at one time as a potential future IOC president.

Coe took over as chairman immediately after the IOC candidate city announcement, which saw Havana, Leipzig, Istanbul, and Rio de Janeiro eliminated from candidature. At that point, Paris, Madrid, London, and New York remained. Coe headed a strong and passionate team, which included celebrated Olympians Steve Redgrave, Kelly Holmes, Daley Thompson, Denise Lewis, Matthew Pinsent, and Paralympian Tanni Grey-Thompson.

The London bid team included heavy hitters from the world of business, politics, the monarchy, and sport. The piece de la resistance of the 2004 IOC visit to London was a gala dinner hosted on the last night of the trip by none other than Her Royal Majesty the Queen, within the sumptuous and spectacular surrounding of Buckingham Palace. Prime Minister Tony Blair was also to prove a central and powerful influence; Dick Pound, former President of the Canadian Olympic Committee, commented to Britons after London's historic victory that "you should get down on your hands and knees and thank your Prime Minister" (Lee, 2006).

Tony Blair had always been in favor of a bid, as were his counterparts who stood in political opposition to him. The presence of opposition leaders Michael Howard (Conservative) and Charles Kennedy (Liberal Democrats) at an IOC meeting (hosted by Tony Blair at 10 Downing Street) proved to the Olympic Federation that the Olympic and Paralympic Games would be valued highly and that plans would be followed through decisively no matter which party happened to be in power by 2012.

Managing Media Coverage

Managing the British and international media proved to be a particularly demanding issue for the London bid team, given the generally intrusive and often negative characterization of the bid by the domestic press. The communications campaign took a strategic move of targeting the international press, because it anticipated negative domestic coverage. IOC correspondents for agencies such as CNN and Reuters were given access to PM Tony Blair through exclusive briefings at his home at 10 Downing Street, but such access was not made available to the domestic press. Similarly, in Singapore in 2004, in the run-up to the announcement of the bid winner, the international press was invited to ask questions but the national British press was not.

On the day of the final presentation, a rousing video speech by PM Tony Blair preceded a heartwarming message of support from Nelson Mandela, who had said that he could not think of a better place than London to unite the world. Sebastian Coe was to conclude the bid with a moving and inspired speech about how he had watched the 1968 Mexico Olympic Games on a small black and white television when he was a child and that this moment had completely changed his life. On July 6, 2005, at 7:46 p.m. Singapore time, Jacques Rogge, president of the IOC, opened the official envelope and announced to the world that London had won the bid—a testament to the excellent bid management that had characterized London's historic campaign.

including the Oxford Cambridge University Boat Race, the Tour de France, and the Wimbledon Tennis Championship. Highly lucrative professional football leagues such the English Premier League and the German **Bundesliga** (a generic term for an intricate framework of German associations, clubs, and members) and powerful Northern American sport brands such as the NFL International Series bring a wealth of rich sporting events to the citizens of Europe. Such a landscape will undoubtedly be strengthened by the arrival of the Summer Olympic and Paralympic Games to London in 2012, the Winter Olympic and Paralympic Games to Sochi in 2014, and the **Commonwealth Games**, a multisport event held every four years involving the elite athletes of the Commonwealth of Nations, to Glasgow in 2014. Although the Russian Federation is not a member of the European Union, it can nevertheless be defined geographically as part of Europe.

European Sport for All Charter

Perhaps the most significant movement in recent years across Europe has been the foundation of the European **Sport for All** Charter, launched in 1975 by sport ministers of European member states. The ideology on which the charter was founded was the concept that sport values could contribute effectively to the fulfillment of Council of Europe ideals. Before 1989 the charter engaged only Western European states, but following the collapse of Communism, decision makers in Eastern European sport enthusiastically adopted these principles.

By 1992 the European Sport Charter had been adopted across the EU. Supported by the Code of Sports Ethics, it states that ethical considerations leading to fair play are integral, not optional, elements of all sport activity, sport policy, and management, and that they apply to all levels of ability and commitment, including recreational as well as competitive sport.

The fundamentals of the charter identify the importance of making sport accessible to everybody, particularly children and young people; that sport is healthy and safe, fair and tolerant, building on high ethical values; that it is capable of fostering personal self-fulfillment at all levels; that it is respectful of the environment and protective of human dignity; and that it stands against any kind of exploitation of those engaged in sport. The charter has established stable parameters within which sport policies can develop, has provided a framework and basic principles for national sport policies, and has provided a necessary balance between governmental and nongovernmental action. The Code of Sports Ethics (1992), passed by the Council of Europe's Committee of Ministers, further sets the boundaries for the principles of fair play (*Qui joue loyalement est toujours gagnant*) among council member nations (note that the Council of Europe is not an EU institution but is instead an intergovernmental organization with 41 member states).

Development of Sport for All in Eastern Europe

As Communism fell in Eastern Europe and the Eastern Bloc became democratized and integrated into the European Union, the radical restructuring of political ideology that favored elite sport as a means of establishing national and ideological superiority has diminished in favor of the Western European sport for all model.

Direct comparison of the development of sport for all in Western Europe and the emergence and likely future development of sport for all in Eastern Europe (Davies, 1996) led to the theorization that conditions in Eastern Europe would necessitate sport management skills at all levels, particularly those at director and senior manager level, to be of high quality. Those managerial skills would prove crucial in the successful development of a coherent government-led sport strategy that would achieve coherence with the ideals of sport for all.

The first seminar for education and training for administration and management volunteers and professionals in sport in Berlin, in 1987, hosted by the Committee for the Development of Sport (CDDS), was an early example of such development. This seminar provided the basis from which various European sport-management-related diplomas and degrees emerged and from which many student exchanges originated. The CDDS went on to organize a number of sport management seminars across Europe in the 1990s under the aegis of the Sprint (1991 Sports Reform, Innovation, and Training) program.

The need for Eastern Europe to develop the volunteering model crucial to Western European sport is also evident. The CDDS (2002) reported that all countries should unite to create a common program for the education and training of sport managers, a lack of which was evidenced by all member states. Organizations such as ENSSEE (European Network of Sport Science in Higher Education, founded in Luxembourg in 1989) exist to meet this need for harmonization. ENSSEE, a member of the European Sport Workforce Development Alliance, operates on a political level and seeks to encourage greater European cooperation in sport-related research, education, and employment. In achieving this goal, ENSSEE also aims to facilitate and increase the

CASE STUDY

Rehabilitation Through Sport—Bosnia and Herzegovina and Croatia

Historically, sport in Europe has occupied an important position as a broker and facilitator of peace. The London 1948 Olympics, for example, characterized the "Blitz" spirit of the time, boosting British national pride and morale in a city torn apart by bombs. Bosnia and Herzegovina and Croatia offer more recent examples of this touching phenomenon.

A first meeting of the CDDS for an Action Plan for Bosnia and Herzegovina Rehabilitation Through Sport took place in Strasbourg in 1996. A task force was set up to identify the role of sport in the rehabilitation of disabled persons in the region. The Second Camp for Children and Young People with Disabilities, hosted by Bosnia and Herzegovina in 1998, played host to 31 children with disabilities, in addition to their parents and caregivers. It is thought that the camp constituted the first moment that people from both Bosnia and Herzegovina had met together within the frontiers of their country for the purposes of taking part in a common activity.

Similarly, since the inception of the post-Yugoslav nation of Croatia, the sporting infrastructure has developed significantly and has played a role in the country's recovery from years of war. By 2002 the existence of 3,427 sport organizations and 52 sport associations had ensured the movement of the nation toward a healthy sport for all ethos that recognized the role of sport in the inclusion of those previously excluded by society. In the case of Croatia, this strategy specifically targeted refugees, using sport as a means of social integration, and provided self-fulfillment opportunities and physical therapy for those with disabilities. One such example was the 2006 first winter workshop for landmine survivors, organized by the Croatian Mine Victims Association (CMVA) and NPA Mine Action Programme Croatia (NPA). The workshop united survivors from both Croatia and Bosnia and Herzegovina in Kranjska Gora, Slovenia, where a team of ski instructors led participants in a weeklong ski program. The ski activities were offered alongside a rich program of other activities that included musical, foreign language, photo, and video workshops. Using sport in this way has proved to be of particular importance in a nation that has a large number of war-wounded citizens. Sport provides a means of integrating refugees into the community and further encourages social cohesion and community building through the provision of volunteer opportunities.

This role of sport, as a means of rehabilitation and development, has been featured in many post-Communist EU member states. For example, the role of physical exercise and sport was identified in the research and treatment of radiation exposure in the wake of the Chernobyl nuclear power station disaster.

Croatia also has a well-developed elite sport system characterized by frequent success in international competition. Rising Croat stars such as Beijing Olympic silver medalists Blanka Vlasic (high jump) and Filip Ude (gymnastics) are examples of prominent Croatian elite sport talents. The men's handball team dominated at the 1992 Barcelona and 2004 Athens Olympic Games, and Janica and Ivica Kostelić continue to be the nation's dominant talents in winter sports. Croatia finished 37th in the 2008 Beijing Olympic Games medal table, ahead of most other former Soviet bloc countries. The number of Croatian Olympic competitors has increased significantly from 39 to 105 since Croatia began competing as an independent nation at the Barcelona Olympic Games of 1992.

Sport has also been used strategically to reinforce and strengthen Croatian identity. In 2006, the Croatian Olympic Committee and the Croatian World Congress organized the first Croatian World Games in a bid to unite the global Croatian diaspora. The first Games were held in 2006 in Zadar. Fourteen countries from North America, South America, Europe, and Australia participated. Croatia finished first in the medal table, the United States finished a close second, and Bosnia and Herzegovina achieved third place.

mobility and transfer of sport-related knowledge and practice of students, teachers, and professionals across the European Union. ENSSEE partners with a number of other EU-funded sport-related projects, such as EQF, EQFOA, EUROSEEN, and VOCASPORT.

The CDDS (2002) identified the need for efficient sport managers who add value to operations and who can lead effectively. They provide the "key to moving forward in terms of the establishment and continual development of sound management practices based on a cycle of planning, monitoring, reviewing and re-planning" (CDDS, 2002, p. 43). The central role of the sport manager is thus evident in the reshaping and restructuring of the sporting landscape across the political union of Europe.

Politicization of European Sport

Sport has often been a site of political protest and involvement in Europe. Key historic events include the 1936 Berlin Olympic Games, the boycott of the 1980 Moscow Olympic Games by Western European nations, and the assassination of Israeli athletes in the 1972 Munich Olympic Games. More recent examples include the central involvement of Vladimir Putin in Sochi's successful bid for the 2014 Olympic Winter Games and the pivotal role of the British government in bringing the 2012 Olympic Summer Games to London and the 2014 Commonwealth Games to Glasgow.

Economics of Sport in Europe

Sport constitutes a considerable economic force in the European landscape. Sport generated an estimated €407billion ($488.4 billion) in 2004, representing 3.7 percent of the EU GDP and 15 million employees, representing a 5.7 percent share of the European labor market (Dimitrov et al., 2006). The influence of media rights and burgeoning sponsorship opportunities in Western Europe has led to the acknowledgement of sport as a lucrative means of generating profit and revenue. Similarly, the ideological and economic post-1989 shift from Communism to a free-market system across Eastern Europe has radically capitalized Eastern European markets and opened up capitalist opportunities (such as the sponsorship of sport) that were previously unavailable within a highly centralized, government-controlled state.

A 2004 VOCASPORT study, commissioned by the European Commission (EC), identified that the sport sector employed around 800,000 professionals in the then 25 member states of the European Union (EU). Although sport is statistically defined through NACE (classification of economic activities in the European Communities), this classification covers only the "operation of sports facilities" and "other sports services" (the core business of sport) but does not include sectors directly affected by sport, such as sporting goods manufacturers, sport media, and sport education. Major professional sport federations and private sport business organizations provide their own statistics. The EU Working Group Sport and Economics has been set up to counter the lack of statistical reporting currently inherent in this European sport market (*White Paper on Sport*, 2007).

Sport as a function of the European common market requires that it conform to the four fundamental freedoms that are enshrined in the 1957 Treaty of Rome: free movement of people, goods, services, and capital (*White Paper on Sport*, 2007). Given the nature of sport, these fundamental freedoms have acquired particular importance in areas such as the sale of media rights, the mobility of athletes, transfer issues, the recognition of Europe-wide sport and business qualifications, sponsorship, and copyright and intellectual property rights and procurement.

A growing concern regarding the economic value of sport relates to intellectual property rights, in which the enforcement of rights relating to copyright, commercial communications, trademarks, and image and media rights is seen to contribute significantly to the economic health of the European sport economy. A notable example of such concerns lies within the example of the collective selling of media rights and equitable distribution of broadcast revenue that has occurred throughout the Barclays **Premier League** (a 20-club league that represents the elite level of English football).

This selling of rights across the Premier League has enabled effective brand awareness and revenue generation for the league as a whole and has provided a notable level of financial stability for Premiership clubs. But the size of clubs is distinctly uneven; the match-day revenue of some clubs dwarfs the entire yearly earnings of others. This financial disparity has been significantly exacerbated by the effect of the Champions League revenue and by the planned disparity in merit payments awarded by the Premiership to clubs based on their end-season position in the league. For example, at the end of the 2007–08 season, champion Manchester United was awarded a merit payment of £14,501,220 (US$23,545,047.66). In contrast, £725,061 (US$ 1,177,279.95) was awarded to Derby County, which occupied the lowest position on the league table (*Premier League Season Review 2007/8*, 2008). At the end of the 2008–09 season (*Premier League Season Review 2008/9*, 2009), United again topped the table as the league champion, earning a merit payment of £15,231,680 (US$24,731,075.87). The lowest-placing club, West Brom, was awarded only £761,584 (US$1,236,564.04). This disparity raises notable questions of competitiveness, particularly when compared with the more equitable funding model of other major leagues such as the NFL.

The league holds lucrative corporate partnership deals with Nike (official ball), Budweiser (official beer), Lucozade Sport (official sports drink), Wrigley (official chewing gum), EA Sports (official interactive games partner), Sporting iD (official letters and numbers), and Topps Merlin (official sticker and trading card collections) (*Premier League Season Review 2007/8*, 2008). The most notable sponsor is Barclays. Robert E. Diamond Jr., president of Barclays PLC and chief executive of Investment Banking and Investment Management, commented, "The Barclays Premier League has been a great success for us. . . . We're able to engage with 600 million potential and existing customers and clients in over 200 countries through the sponsorship" (*Premier League Season Review 2007/8*, 2008).

Expanding Barclays Premier League TV Coverage into the African Market

In 2008 the cumulative global television audience for the Barclays Premier League stood at a reported 4.77 billion. This total marked a significant increase on the 2007 figure, attributable largely to the decision of the league to broadcast selected games to the African terrestrial market by the African television channels Hi-TV and GTV (*Premier League Season Review 2007/8*, 2008).

The Premier League achieved a significant increase in global viewing figures in 2007 by the decision to conduct separate sales of television rights to Nigeria and South Africa (the most populous in terms of Premiership fans) and the rest of the sub-Saharan market. Previously, the Premiership had only been viewable through pay TV, which many Africans were unable to afford, whereas the new deal offered one weekly free-to-air match and highlights. This strategic move increased viewership in one year from 2 million to in excess of 650 million. The integration of the African continent into viewing figures contributed partially to the Premiership's then-unrivalled season turnover of £947.7 million (US$1,895.4 million), a figure that surpassed existing maximum single-season financial records by an incredible 48 percent (*Premier League Season Review 2007/8*, 2008).

The widespread popularity of the Premier League across the African continent can be explained in part by the prominence of African football stars in the Premier League, some of whom command impressive salaries and transfer fees. Notable athletes of the 2008 season included Congolese Christopher Samba (£400,000 [US$800,000], Blackburn Rovers FC); Nigerians Obafemi Martins (£10 million [US$20 million], Newcastle United FC), Yakubu (£11.5 million [US$23 million], Everton FC), and John Obi Mikel (£16 million [US$32 million], Chelsea FC); South African Benni McCarthy; Ghanaians Sulley Muntari (£7 million [US$14 million], Portsmouth FC) and Michael Essien; Togan Emmanuel Adebayor; and Didier Drogba and Kolo Toure (£150,000 [US$300,000], Arsenal) from the Côte d'Ivoire.

Learning Activity

The English Premier League does not currently exercise salary capping of players, although this practice has begun to be adopted in Europe. Compare this system to the salary-capping practices of another league with which you are familiar (you might wish to consider the NFL system; for further information, see www.nfl.com) and identify some potential ramifications of no salary capping for athletes, in terms of the ongoing governance of the English Premier League. Refer to wwww.uefa .com and www.thefa.com for background information.

Sponsorship

Most sponsorship deals in Europe originate within the field of sport. For example, in 2005, 91 percent of sponsorship investment resided in the sport sector. This represented a figure of approximately $7 to $8 billion, compared with an estimated 1 percent of sponsorship investment being located in the culture sector (*White Paper on Sport*, 2007). Sponsorship is viewed as an essential component in the funding of European sport federations, clubs, teams, and in the careers of athletes but is subject to notable conditions relating to the legalities of each member state concerning the use of tobacco, alcohol, and fast food in advertisements. We turn to Formula One for an excellent example of this phenomenon.

Formula One is followed worldwide by 588 million unique viewers, making it the most viewed annual sporting event in the world (Sylt & Reid, 2008). Grand prix are held in major cities around the world, including Melbourne, Kuala Lumpur, Bahrain, Catalunya, Istanbul, Monte Carlo, Montreal, Magny-Cours, Silverstone, Hockenheim, Budapest, Valencia, Spa-Francorchamps, Monza, Singapore, the Fuji Speedway, Shanghai, and Sao Paulo. The locations of the grand prix events render Formula One a truly global event, and as such it maximizes potential for advertising revenue generation across virtually all major markets. Formula One is, as a result, the world's most financially valuable annual sporting event in terms of advertising revenue generation. Deloitte reported 2008 average grand prix revenue figures of $217 million. To contextualize the financial strength of Formula One, observe that its closest competitors in financial terms of per-event revenue are the NFL ($24 million per game), the British Premier League ($8 million per match), and Major League Baseball ($2 million per game).

In the 2007 season Ferrari declared the highest single-sponsor revenue that year by Marlboro ($100 million) (Sylt & Reid, 2008). Note that Tony Blair, formerly prime minister of Great Britain, personally intervened in the decision to exempt Formula One from the nationwide legislative ban on tobacco advertising in sport, a move that potentially maximized Marlboro's sponsorship of Formula One in the absence of other sport-based advertising opportunities. Such intervention is not commonplace, but it provides interesting consideration of the potential role of government interventionism.

Sport Agents

The unique geography of the European continent has further heightened the need for sport agents to adopt a cross-border appreciation of the complexities of the European marketplace. Some international federations such as FIFA have adopted their own rules for agents, and individual member states might enact differing regulations in addition to the overarching European law to which European member states are subject.

Although European players are protected by European law, and collective bargaining has taken place in some instances, there is largely no need for mediators and arbitrators in the way in which, for example, North American sport negotiations are conducted. Thus, the union-based collective bargaining system of North America that has previously led to many lockouts and strikes is not generally considered a major characteristic of European sport. European single-player contract negotiations are also typically less detailed and more quickly resolved than are those in North America (Hoehn & Szymaski, 1999).

Conversely, increased levels of government and private-sector involvement occur in Russia in terms of elite athlete remuneration. Consequently, the requirement for contract negotiators is greater as a result of this focus. Examples of this are the 340 million ruble (approximately US$12 million)

Russia Olympic Fund created by Russia's most successful businessmen as a means of remunerating Russia's top athletes at the 2008 Beijing Games and the awards of €100,000 (US$158,000), €60,000 (US$95,000), and €40,000 (US$63,000) (in addition to an Audi car and Omega watch) that the Russian government gives their athletes for winning Olympic gold, silver, and bronze medals, respectively.

An EC directive specifies the need for recognition of a sport agent's professional qualifications in nation-states where the profession is subject to qualification requirements. The requisite knowledge, experience, and qualifications required of European sport agents differ tremendously from those required of agents in other nations, given the unique geopolitical and legal characteristics of the nations that fall under the jurisdiction of the EU.

European Sport Media

The privatization and deregulation of the European media industry that occurred over the 1980s and 1990s has transformed the economic model of sport in Europe. Before the deregulation of television broadcasting and the growth of multiplatform, multiprovider televisual broadcasting rights, gate receipts had provided the dominant source of revenue for sport clubs. The monopsonistic dominance of one terrestrial TV channel (such as the BBC in the United Kingdom) had heightened the unwillingness of sport clubs to allow extensive coverage of sport events because they feared that it would negatively affect spectator figures and gate receipts.

Sport managers need to acknowledge the bargaining arrangement under which European sport media agreements are currently negotiated. Media rights are typically concentrated within the hands of a small number of sport federations, which typically sell the rights to a large bundle of media products to one bidder under a tenderized bid procedure. This bargaining arrangement requires that individual clubs pass control of bargaining power to the association under which they operate (such as the English Premiership football clubs and FIFA). This strategy, referred to as joint selling, is regarded by European Union law as an effective means of collective selling whereby the redistribution of income can act as a tool for achieving greater solidarity within sport. The negotiated deals guarantee exclusivity to one media provider over a specific and usually significant period.

Learning Activity

Identify whether any non-European media networks broadcast coverage of European sport within their domestic programming. Discuss the economic benefits that might result for (a) the media network and (b) the sport itself, as a direct result of this acquisition.

Strategies such as competitive tendering, limiting the scope and duration of exclusive vertical contracts, and sublicensing are affected within the bargaining procedure to counter anticompetitive practices. For example, in 2003 the EC intervened in the sale of UEFA Champions League media rights to ensure the market availability of deferred highlights and new media rights (Toft, 2006, p. 9). In January 2005 the EC required the Bundesliga to segment media rights into separate packages for TV broadcasting, Internet, and mobile platforms and to dispose of said rights through a process of public tender. The duration of rights agreements were to exist no longer than three years (Toft, 2006, p. 10). Another example is the 2005 sale of Belgian football rights. The Belgian League released a tender for six rights packages for three seasons of coverage. Belgacom, a telecommunications operator, bought all six to strengthen its bid to launch a new IP-based TV service.

Joint selling of media rights creates a single point of sale, thereby reducing transaction costs for the sellers (football clubs) and buyers (media companies). Branding of the media output by a single entity creates efficiencies because the media product gains wider recognition and distribution. This also facilitates creation of a unique league product, which allows viewers to follow the league in its entirety as opposed to the fortunes of only one club—a concept that appears attractive to viewers in this market.

Greater sophistication in marketing of a brand image on a single-club basis (such as the marketing of Manchester United Football Club) has led to the development of a spectator model whereby fans of European teams are no longer limited to the nation-state where the club is based. Consequently, the international fan base of many clubs has grown, which increases the opportunity for bargaining of TV rights, sponsorship opportunities, and the generation of merchandise income.

Some clubs have chosen to increase revenue and return on investment by trading shares on the financial markets, by borrowing funds from banks, or by forging strategic partnerships. An innovative joint marketing agreement between the New York Yankees and Manchester United extended United's global marketing strategy and aided the club in its goal to become the richest club in the Premier League. Under the terms of the deal, both clubs agreed to leverage this new strategic partnership to develop more profitable merchandise and media deals. Crucially, the move could see Manchester United's games broadcast into an additional 12 million North American homes. Current Premiership player information can be found at the official Premier League website: www.premierleague.com.

The media clearly plays a central role in the financing of European sport. This role will continue to grow as new member states join the European Union, bringing with them new generations of online, mobile, press, and television consumers. The sport manager would do well, however, to recognize the fundamental cultural differences that characterize each region if such expansion is to be exploited efficiently. Additionally, the volatility of the euro and other regional currencies (such as the British pound) must be taken into account when operating across a continent that requires business to be conducted across multiple national borders, particularly in times of economic crisis. Such a strategy must take into account all aspects of the management process, including finance, human resource management, marketing, and the collective bargaining of media rights. The manager must also take into account the importance of a solid grounding in European and national sport law.

European Sport Law

As Communism dissolved after 1989 and a democratic free-market economy was established across the continent, a shift toward an EU-based constitutive framework for the sport sector took place. The objective of such a legislative framework was to combine national sporting frameworks across the European Union, while simultaneously entrusting the governance of sport to governing bodies such as FIFA.

Learning Activity

Choose a popular European sport to research. Create a diagram that illustrates the power of government, the sport federation, clubs, and any other stakeholders that you think are relevant (such as athletes, sponsors, shareholders, and spectators).

The European Community Courts recognize the "specificity of sport" in terms of compliance to European Community competition law, based on specific characteristics that set it apart from other economic activities. A landmark ruling in the Meca-Medina case specified that there is no such thing as "purely sporting rules" that allow sport to claim automatic exemption from EC competition law. Rather, organizational sporting rules are considered to carry legal significance within the context of analysis of their conformity to EC competition law on a case-by-case basis. An example of application of the specificity of sport principle is the conditions under which the previously discussed joint selling of media rights by football associations (FIFA, UEFA, Bundesliga) is allowed to occur (under the proviso of specific legal conditions) through the application of an open and transparent tender process.

Athlete Protections and Human Rights

Perhaps the most famous EU ruling applied within the sporting context is the Bosman ruling of 1995. The Bosman ruling concerned the free movement of European athletes across the borders of European nation-states (Jennett & Sloane, 1985). The European Court ruled that the retain-and-transfer scheme enforced by FIFA at that time stood in direct contravention to the Treaty of Rome (1957). As a result, FIFA, in conjunction with UEFA, effected significant changes in its regulations concerning the status and transfers of players. The Bosman ruling irrevocably altered the face of sport management in Europe, most notably in football, but also in sports such as ice hockey, basketball, and rugby. For players under the age of 23, a system of training compensation was passed to encourage and reward small clubs that invested in the development of talent at their clubs.

The Bosman ruling bears significant similarities to the 1975 arbitration ruling in the United States that allowed free agency for baseball players who had played for their clubs for one year without a contract. This ruling was later extended to cover American football, basketball, and hockey. The Bosman ruling irrevocably changed the face of European sport, most notably in the case of football.

The Bosman ruling provides an example of government intervention in the operation of European private-sector sport organizations, primarily to protect competitiveness and to protect the rights of the athlete. Government intervention of this kind can also be observed as a key player in the improvement of international relations between Europe and the rest of the world, in the protection of human rights, and in meeting moral and ethical obligations. The Council of Europe (CoE), whose primary function is to defend human rights, parliamentary democracy, and the rule of law, specifically focuses on the world of sport by supervising the Conventions on Anti-Doping and Spectator Violence and Misbehaviour at Sports Events, and by maintaining the values and integrity of sport through the Sport for All Charter and the Code of Sport Ethics. Although it is generally acknowledged under Euro-pean law that individual federations carry jurisdiction for the leagues, clubs, teams, and athletes that operate under them, it is also acknowledged that governmental intervention may take precedence in exceptional circumstances. A recent example is the intervention of the British government in the proposed bilateral tour of the Zimbabwean cricket team to England in 2009.

European Hooliganism

Spectator violence, frequently referred to as hooliganism, is a negative and enduring characteristic of European sport. Most European countries are affected by this phenomenon, which peaked in the 1980s and early 1990s, but it remains an issue of concern (Council of Europe, 2003). Such violence is generally associated with the professional side of the sport. Violence is generally premeditated by hardcore factions of supporters from within or outside the nation-state from which the club at the focus of the spectator violence originates. Most violent incidents occur away from the club premises, in city centers between or after the sport event has taken place. Attempts to counter hooliganism have been based on the application of national legislation and adherence to the recommendations made in the

CASE STUDY

Government Intervention in Zimbabwe–England Cricket

In 2008 Andy Burnham, sports minister for England, issued a statement on behalf of Her Majesty's Government that the government of Zimbabwe had ceased to observe the principle of the rule of law, that it had terrorized its own citizens and exercised the ruthless and violent suppression of legitimate political opposition, and that the British Government had subsequently sought to isolate Zimbabwe internationally and to bring pressure on other supranational institutions such as the EU to take firmer action against President Mugabe's regime. For this purpose, the government had attempted to persuade the International Cricket Council (the ICC) to reconsider Zimbabwe's tour of England in 2008, expressing its concern that tours should be allowed to be forfeited in cases involving nations where human rights violations were occurring.

The ICC chose not to reconsider its position, and the British government subsequently intervened to cancel Zimbabwe's tour. The British government clearly stated its defense of the autonomy of sport governing bodies but claimed that extraordinary circumstances had occurred and that government intervention had been warranted as a result. Burnham then issued a statement to the chairman of the English Cricket Board (ECB) instructing the ECB not to hold the bilateral tour of Zimbabwe. This action effectively removed the authoritative decision-making power of the English governing body for cricket, an unusual occurrence in British sport. But the ECB welcomed such a move and acted swiftly and decisively to suspend all bilateral arrangements with Zimbabwe Cricket with immediate effect.

For further information about the English Cricket Board, visit the official ECB website at www.ecb.co.uk.

European Convention on Spectator Violence and Misbehaviour at Sports Events (2003).

The particularly tragic Heysel tragedy caused 39 Juventus football fans to lose their lives during rioting at the European Cup Final in Brussels on May 29, 1985. In Croatia one of the earliest signs of ethnic tensions appeared in the late 1980s in the "renewed eruption of interethnic violence at sport events" (Ramet, 1992, p. 245). In Bosnia, after the breakup of the Yugoslav federation, the football league split into three ethnicity-based sections. Efforts by international sport governing bodies such as the Union of European Football Associations (UEFA), the Fédération Internationale de Football Association (FIFA), and the International Olympic Committee (IOC) were not powerful enough to reunite them. Interethnic violence unfortunately remains a common feature of sport in former Communist states, particularly in the Balkans. In 2002 violent exchanges sparked by the 2–0 Yugoslav victory over Bosnia in a "friendly" football match led to the injury of 26 fans and 2 police officers. In a particularly unusual incident, 30 delegates were detained by police in the Republic of Macedonia after a brawl broke out at the end of a conference that had been aimed at preventing football violence (Crampton, 2004)!

The Czech Republic might offer a positive way forward with regard to early preventative measures by creating a culture antithetic to that of spectator violence. Government programs help clubs set up junior fan clubs that target 8- to 12-year-olds (Council of Europe, 2003). The clubs provide social and educational activities for children and access to social workers within a "clubhouse" environment. The aim is to generate a positive mentality and new culture of sport spectatorship amongst the next generation of sport fans. Fan coaching schemes also exist in Belgium, Germany, and the Netherlands. Such schemes exist within the wider framework of the prevention of hooliganism at the municipal level.

Overall, the Council of Europe has exerted a significant effect on the fight against sport hooliganism. In August 1985 the European Convention on Spectator Violence and Misbehaviour at Sports Events and in Particular Football Matches (OJ C 22, 24/1/2002; OJ C 322, 29/12/2006) was adopted.

Although examples of sport hooliganism have often betrayed ethnic tensions across the continent, positive examples of the role of sport in the uniting of cultures and ethnicities also persist. The **Maccabi Games**, created to unite the Jewish diaspora, provides an excellent example of this positive sentiment. Organized by the international Jewish Sports Organization, the games are managed by the Maccabi World Union (MWU). The first ever European Maccabi Games were held in Prague in 1929 and most recently were held in Rome in 2007. The philosophy behind the games is to promote sport as a lifestyle, as an essential instrument in youth education, and as a way to promote wholesome social values.

European Sport in the Global Marketplace

European sport plays a crucial role in projecting a positive image to the rest of the world, in commercial as well as social and cultural terms. Although the social and educational roles of European sport are characterized by developmental projects such as the development of football in African, Caribbean, and Pacific countries, facilitated as part of the 2008 Sport for Development and Peace International Working Group, Europe is also regarded as a lucrative commercial market for global brands such as the NHL, NBA, and NHL. An excellent example of attempted global expansion is the NFL extension into Europe and the wider international market. The case study investigates this attempted expansion.

Learning Activity

Identify two Super Bowl stars that started their playing careers in the NFL European league. Discuss how the NFL has achieved greater success in the European market through a change in strategic direction, and consider player development in your answer.

Sport in Eastern Europe

After World War II, sport became subsumed under the totalitarian ideology of Eastern bloc nations. Before 1989, sport under Communism was viewed as a political institution that provided an ideological battleground in the fight against capitalism. A 1949

CASE STUDY

NFL Expansion Into European Markets

The NFL Europe league played its inaugural season in 1991, operating under the auspicious title of the NFL World League. Despite achieving record attendance figures of an average of 20,000 spectators per game by 2007, a strategic decision was taken to close the NFL European developmental league that same year, following 15 years of operation. The closure was attributed to notable financial losses that had been exacerbated by a significant drop in the number of operating teams; by 2007, only six sides existed, five of which were based in Germany. Even the London Monarchs, whose hometown had played host to the highly successful International Series games in 2007 and 2008, had ceased operation years earlier in 2004.

The failure of NFL Europe to expand significantly within its target market was attributed largely to the lack of focus on grassroots development. The NFL has now adopted an international strategy to concentrate on the NFL International Series events and an engagement with grassroots amateur American football organizations, most notably with the International Federation of American Football (IFAF), a worldwide umbrella organization that governs the 59 member nations that together make up European, Oceanic, Asian, and North American regional American football federations.

NFL International was formed in October 1996 in response to growing worldwide interest in American Football. That same year, NFL owners approved a plan to stage a limited number of regular season games outside the United States, billed as the **NFL International Series**. On October 28, 2007, the Miami Dolphins played the New York Giants at Wembley Stadium, London, in what was to be the historic first regular season game held outside North America. A sellout crowd of 81,176 watched the Giants drive home a 13–10 victory and contributed to an overall economic generation of £20 million (US$41 million) for the London economy. Mark

Waller, NFL senior vice president, acknowledged that Sky Sports viewership of NFL football rose 45 percent following the game.

British demand for NFL football did not dissipate by the time the following year's fixture between the Oakland Raiders and the San Diego Chargers was announced. The first 40,000 tickets released for the October 26, 2008, game sold out in 90 minutes. The popularity of the NFL International Series no doubt exacerbated the decision by the British BBC to air the Super Bowl for the first time ever in February 2008 and contributed to the NFL's ambition for American football to achieve status as a top five sport in the United Kingdom, worth up to £100 million (US$196 million) per year (*Commissioner Goodell*, 2010).

Mark Waller, the head of NFL International Development, commented, "We will see increasingly more games internationally. . . . We will work hard to structure our season to allow every team to play once a season outside the United Sates" (*Commissioner Goodell*, 2010, p. 1). The NFL may have been enticed into developing an ambitious international growth strategy following the successful global expansion of football (soccer), most notably the English Premier League, in foreign markets.

The league aims to play up to two regular season games annually beyond the borders of the United States. Initial plans extend until 2012 and target Canada, the United Kingdom, and Germany. At the time of the first International Series game held in London, almost 300 countries and territories broadcast NFL programming. The United Kingdom, Canada, China, Japan, and Mexico were afforded the status of the NFL's five priority foreign markets. For more information see the following news reports: Blitz, R., October 26, 2007, "Dolphins face Giants; Devils on ice in Newark," FT.com; and Blitz, R., October 26, 2007, "US Sports Make London the Goal," FT.com, p. 2, *Financial Times*.

Soviet government resolution claimed, "The increasing number of successes achieved by Soviet athletes . . . is a victory for the Soviet form of society and the socialist sports system; it provides irrefutable proof of the superiority of socialist culture over the moribund culture of capitalist states" (Riordan, 1994).

Many Communist nations achieved great sporting success. During the 1980s the success of Eastern German athletes was so exceptional that they were 16 times more likely to win an Olympic or world gold medal than their Soviet or U.S. counterparts (Riordan, 1994). Such success did not go unnoticed.

Western sport organizations now employ a significant number of ex-Communist coaches and medical experts from nations such as Poland and the former East Germany to improve their elite performance systems and to attain greater success at the Olympic and world championship level. Democratic Western European nations can probably learn much from former Communist states in the quest for Olympic and world sporting dominance.

Armed forces and security forces typically provided strong support of sport under Communist rule in countries where military sinecures were provided for athletes. Armed forces clubs such as the Central Sports Club of the Army (USSR and Bulgaria) and security forces sport clubs such as Dinamo (USSR, East Germany, Yugoslavia, Romania, Czechoslovakia, and Albania) provided funding and sponsorship. Under Communism, elite athletes were unable to trade their skills on the free market and to engage in professional sport or sponsorship deals.

The fall of the Berlin Wall and the subsequent anti-Communist revolution that swept Eastern Europe after 1989 dramatically altered the role of the state in the governance of sport, opening up the possibilities for athletes to engage in international professional competition and disengaging the state from its centralized role and focus on elite sport. The 1991 Sports Reform, Innovation and Training (Sprint) program was one of the earliest EU interventions implemented in the aftermath of the sweeping political reform of Central and Eastern Europe. Virtually all aspects of the sport systems across these geopolitical regions required significant reform and democratization, and the Sprint program offered a means of enabling this transition. The first countries to join the Sprint program (between 1989 and 1997) were Hungary, Poland, the Czech Republic, and Slovakia (CDDS, 2002).

Twenty years later, the sporting landscape of Eastern Europe has changed considerably. One might consider the example of Slovakia, described in the case study, as an illustration of some of the changes that have taken place across this geopolitical region.

The issues facing Eastern European sport systems after the fall of Communism have highlighted the need for new training of sport managers in the region. The Workshop on Sports Management Training held in Berlin, Germany, in 1991, was one of the first educational events to target Central and

Learning Activity

Write a description of two key aspects of sport management theory and practice that might be significantly influenced by the transition from Communist to democratic governance in European nation-states. Identify how these influences would affect sport management.

Eastern European countries, supplying Western European sport management models that could be applied to the redesign of their sporting systems. The concept of voluntary workers was a particular focus of the workshop, given their importance to the Western sport model. Lectures addressed the concepts of democratic processes in sport organizations, basic principles of voluntary management, sport law in Portugal, sport in the community, and marketing and sponsorship. The workshop included a visit by a former GDR Army sport club that had been successfully converted to a Western European–styled sport club.

The workshop enabled Eastern European sport managers to identify specific concerns such as the challenges presented by the social, economic, and political instability of the region; the need for real change as opposed to simply the redesign of organizations; the need for agents of change within sport organizations; the important role of Western European experts; and the need to differentiate information to the needs of each transitioning member state.

Eastern European nations are also emerging as strong sites for international sport megaevents. For example, the successful joint Poland–Ukraine bid to host Euro 2012 shocked rival bidders Italy and Croatia and Hungary, and it underlined the fluidity of the Eastern and Western European sporting landscape. The East has not hosted a major football tournament since the former Yugoslavia hosted the 1976 European Championships; speculation abounded that the move to host the championship event in Kiev was partly a political move to place the Ukraine closer to European sentiments and further from the significant influence of the Russian Federation. Euro 2012 is expected to create powerful incentives for economic growth of the country.

Sport Systems Before and After the Fall of Communism in Slovakia

Igor Kováč

The beginning of the Communist period in Slovakia dates back to February 1948, when a Soviet-supported coup by the Communist Party of Czechoslovakia resulted in Slovakia becoming part of the new Czechoslovak Republic. The totalitarianism and dictatorship of the Communist regime resulted in a situation whereby the government exercised centralized control of sport, enforced with the assistance of the armed forces.

The State Office for Physical Education and Sport constituted the first step toward establishment of state control over the sport system. During this era, sport was funded through a state budget, a state-run lottery funding system, and a separate budget for elite sport. There was no professional sport, and the absence of free-market mechanisms meant that no Czechoslovak sports were sponsored, marketed, or open to lucrative business opportunities. This situation was to change rapidly and significantly with the dramatic political changes in 1989.

Sport in Slovakia After the Fall of Communism

The "Velvet Revolution" of November 1989 resulted in the democratization of Czechoslovakia, and the face of sport was again transformed. By 1993 the country regained its independence and became the Slovak Republic.

The central body of state administration for sport in Slovakia is now the Ministry of Education of the Slovak Republic, which governs all sport, sometimes in cooperation with the Ministry of Education. Notable NGOs include national sport organizations, national sport federations, the Slovak Olympic Committee, the Slovak Sport for All Association, the Association of Sports Clubs of the Slovak Republic, the Slovak Sport Union, the Association of Technical and Sporting Activities of the Slovak Republic, and the Slovak Union of Physical Culture. Approximately 4,000 sport clubs and associations are now in existence in Slovakia.

Financing of Slovakian Sport

The three main sources of funding for Slovakian sport are state funding, lottery funding, and private-sector investment.

The Slovakian sporting landscape has changed dramatically from its pre–Velvet Revolution days.

Private financing now offers NGOs the only route to gaining financial independence from public funding, and the marketplace has effectively opened up to private sponsorship and funding opportunities in a manner not seen before. Such an ideological shift is characterized, of course, by sport management issues inherent to any free-market economy. These days, sport managers are aware of significant financial opportunities such as sponsorship and a commercial sport market far from saturation. The Olympic Marketing Company, owned by the Slovak Olympic Committee, is one of the most successful sport brands in the country. Football and ice hockey have notable commercial success in Slovakia, when compared with other sports. Minor sports are generally able to gain coverage only through international competitive success, as is the case in water slalom (the most successful Olympic sport in Slovak history), flat-water canoeing, shooting, and athletics. The new Slovakian sports TV channel, STV3, is expected to extend Slovakian national sport coverage.

Issues in Slovakian Sport Management

Slovakian sport has experienced significant opportunities since the fall of Communism, but problems have inevitably arisen. This issue is largely related to sport management. Formerly, the government took central control of all aspects of the sport system, but the sport market is now governed by a multitude of private and public stakeholders. This shift has resulted in a decline in both the number and the quality of sport facilities in the country. A more adequate and efficient model of governmental management and financing appears to be needed within the Slovak sport system to counter such problems. Charges of political influence, corruption, bureaucracy, and incompetence have been leveled at decision makers in modern-day Eastern European sport, a possible hangover from the Communist days when central government agencies were never made accountable for financial decisions. The implications for the sport manager are clearly challenging, particularly to those who have not yet operated within an Eastern European context.

Further information about Slovakian sport can be found at www.sportslovakia.sk/sportslovakia_en/index.htm.

Summary

The geopolitical region of Europe remains steadfast as a global hub of sporting excellence, innovation, and entertainment. Many of the most lucrative sport franchises in the world either reside in, or are attracted to, the affluent and prosperous shores of Europe (Formula One, the Premier League, the NFL). The wealthy nations of Western Europe offer a well-established free-market economy where commercial sport opportunities and large-scale sport events (the Olympic and Paralympic Games, Wimbledon, the Commonwealth Games) proliferate, and the post-Communist nations of Eastern Europe offer a veritable smorgasbord of unexploited commercial opportunities to foreign and domestic investors in the field of sport. In terms of national diversity, European leagues appear to offer the richest ethnic sporting environment in the world, where domestic, European, Mediterranean, and international competitions regularly take place. Many of the world's greatest sport stars are of European descent, and the sport systems of many European nations continue to dominate the international stage in athletic competition (most recently, Great Britain finished fourth in the 2008 Beijing Olympic Games). A true joy of European sport can be seen in the specific use of European sport events to unite global diasporas (in the case of the Croatia World Games and the European Maccabi Games) and in their use both to assuage ethnic tensions and to rebuild nations following wars and other violent ethnic clashes (as in the case of Croatia and Bosnia and Herzegovina).

But political tensions have persisted into the 21st century—a situation that will undoubtedly continue to exert a detrimental effect on the world of sport. Regional and international tensions and terrorist activity have raised concerns over security at European sport megaevents (such as the London 2012 Olympic and Paralympic Games), and the recent violence between the Russian Federation and Georgia threatens to cast a shadow across preparations for the Sochi 2014 Winter Olympic Games. The global financial crisis sparked by the subprime mortgage fiasco that originated in the United States in 2007 has further added to difficulties in the financial and economic management of sport-related activities (Honda's withdrawal from Formula One, the sale of Newcastle United FC, the reduction of the London 2012 Olympic funding budget, the reduction in salaries and employment across the region leading to a fall in disposable income and spending, the fall in the value of the British pound, and overall reduced sales of sport retailers as a result of the crisis). Claims of corruption in post-Communist nations have further complicated the potential for investors to capitalize on the promise of these emerging markets. In this sense, the European territory might well constitute the most complex single market for the sport manager in terms of the social, economic, financial, and political knowledge required to succeed.

In conclusion, note that Europe appears at once overcommercialized (Western Europe) but undercapitalized (Eastern Europe), that it stands proud as the original creator and purveyor of the amateur ethos in sport (the playing fields of Eton and the Modern Olympic Games), and that it currently boasts a profile that is as seductive as it is challenging to a host of powerful international brands (Formula One, NFL International Series, 2012 London Olympic and Paralympic Games). The winds of ideological change that have swept through the continent since 1989 have fundamentally redefined the character of European sport economics, financing, law, media, marketing, and management practices, culminating in a region that is once economically and politically united, and ethnically and ideologically diverse.

? Review and Discussion Questions

1. What are the main characteristics and shared principles of the European sport model?

2. How did Western and Eastern European sport models differ before the fall of Communism in the late 1980s?

3. What are the key economic trends affecting professional sport in Europe?

4. What effect have actions and rules of the European Union had on sport in the region?

5. What are the major issues facing the sport event manager who is hosting an event in Europe? Consider social, cultural, political, and economic factors in your answer.

6. How might knowledge of modern European history aid the sport manager in understanding the various strengths and opportunities of marketing a sport brand in (a) England, (b) Germany, and (c) Bulgaria?

7. Some major European sport leagues, teams, and brands were negatively affected by the credit crunch of 2008. Most notably, Honda had to pull out of Formula One. What lessons might be learned about the financing of European sport in the wake of such difficulties? What aspects of the European sport model might change because of this?

8. What are the key considerations that you would take into account when launching a non-European brand (such as the NFL) in Western and Eastern Europe?

Sport in Africa and the Middle East

Adel Elnashar, PhD

Mosaad Ewies, PhD
University of Helwan, Egypt

Gerard Akindes, PhD
Ohio University, USA

Chapter Objectives

After studying this chapter, you will be able to do the following:

- Describe the geographical and demographic makeup of Africa and the Middle East
- Describe the historical background of formalized sport with a focus on the influence of colonization on the development of sport and physical education
- Identify some of the chief geographical, sociological, and political factors that influence sport in Africa and the Middle East
- Explain how sport in Africa and the Middle East is generally governed
- Identify future trends in sport development in Africa and the Middle East
- Describe the influence that apartheid had on the evolution of sport in South Africa and international participation

1. Congo
2. Central African Republic
3. Equatorial Guinea
4. Benin
5. Togo
6. Lebanon
7. Jordan
8. Kuwait
9. Qatar
10. Eritrea
11. Uganda
12. Rwanda
13. Burundi
14. Malawi
15. Swaziland
16. Lesotho

Key Events

2007 All-Africa Games. Held in Algiers, Algeria, these games included 24 sports and competitors from 36 countries. The 2007 games were the third All-Africa Games in which competitions for athletes with disabilities were included.

2001 Mediterranean Games. The most recent Mediterranean Games hosted in Africa, held in Tunis, Tunisia.

2010 FIFA World Cup finals. The first World Cup finals to be hosted in Africa, these matches were held in 10 stadiums in nine host cities in the country of South Africa.

South Africa is readmitted to the Olympic Movement in 1991, marking the end of apartheid in sport.

Libya gains independence in 1951 to start a wave of decolonization that continued throughout the 1950s, 1960s, and 1970s, during which most countries on the continent gained independence from colonial rule.

Key People

Sheikh Ahmad Al-Fahad Al-Sabah, IOC member, president of the Olympic Council of Asia, and vice president of the Islamic Solidarity Sports Federation. He has served as the president, vice president, or founder of many regional sport organizations and is currently minister of national security in Kuwait.

Issa Hayatou, from Cameroon, is vice president of FIFA, chairs several FIFA event organizing committees, and is a member of the Organizing Committee for the World Cup. He is also president of the African Football Confederation (CAF) and an IOC member.

Mustapha Larfaoui, from Algeria, is president of the Union of Confederations of Sport in Africa (UCSA) and a member of the Executive Committee of the Supreme Council for Sport in Africa (SCSA). He has also been president of FINA and of Algeria's National Olympic Committee and is an IOC member.

Nawal El Moutawakel-Bennis, from Morocco, is an IOC member and serves as Moroccan minister of youth and sport. As an athlete, she was the first African woman to win an Olympic gold medal. She has also held leadership roles in IAAF, FIFA, and numerous national and regional sport organizations.

Dr. Rania Elwani, from Egypt, is an IOC member, founder of the Egyptian Olympians Association, member of the Egyptian Olympic Committee, and member of the World Anti-Doping Agency (WADA) Foundation Board and Executive Committee.

Lamine Diack, from Senegal, is president of the International Amateur Athletics Federation (IAAF) and an IOC member. He has also served as a member of the Executive Committee of the Supreme Council for Sport in Africa (SCSA) and as president of the Senegal NOC.

HRH Prince Nawaf Faisal Fahd Abdulaziz, from Saudi Arabia, is vice president of the Saudi NOC as well as vice president of the Union of Arab Football Associations and Arab Sports Confederation. He has served in a number of roles in the Saudi Arabian Football Federation and is an IOC member.

This chapter provides an African and Middle Eastern perspective on the field of sport management. To contextualize the management of sport, this chapter gives a brief background to the origins of formalized sport and the major influences of European colonization, explains the effects that apartheid has had on sport development and participation, and describes the demographics that influence sport. In addition, the chapter examines the role of sport in the region, the political and legal landscape within which sport functions, and the governance of sport on the African continent and in the Middle East.

Geography and Background of Africa and the Middle East

The African continent is surrounded by the Indian Ocean on the east, the Atlantic Ocean on the west, the Mediterranean Sea on the north, and the Red Sea on the northeast. Africa is made up of 54 independent countries. Because of its vast area, from both east to west and north to south, several unique geographical features and conditions characterize what was once called the Dark Continent. The equator divides northern and southern Africa into almost equal portions. In central north Africa is the Sahara Desert, and in the south are the Kalahari and Namib deserts. Several mountain ranges span some of the countries. The main ranges include the Atlas Mountains in Morocco, the Ethiopian

Highlands, Mt. Kenya, and the Drakensberg in South Africa. The largest rivers in Africa are the Nile flowing across Egypt, the Zaire across Congo, the Niger across Nigeria and Mali, the Zambezi across Zimbabwe and Mozambique, and the Limpopo across South Africa. The most well-known lakes in Africa are Lake Victoria in Kenya, Lake Kariba in Zimbabwe, Lake Malawi in Malawi, and Lake Chad in Chad.

Africa generally is characterized by hot, sunny weather throughout the year. Winters are mild. Snow is found on mountain peaks only in winter, except for a couple of the highest peaks. Most of the continent receives low rainfall. Although agriculture was the major contributor to the GDP of most countries in earlier days, it was overtaken by mining and manufacturing in several countries in the 1990s. In some countries, sport and tourism flourish because of ideal year-round weather that favors outdoor sport and leisure.

The Middle East consists of an area of more than 5 million square miles (13 million sq km) when parts of southwestern Asia and Egypt are included. Opinions vary regarding the definition of the Middle East. For our purposes, the states of the Middle East include Egypt, Bahrain, United Arab Emirates (UAE), Saudi Arabia, Oman, Kuwait, Lebanon, Turkey, Iraq, Syria, Qatar, Yemen, Iran, Jordan, Tunisia, Morocco, Algeria, and Israel. There is some overlap here with Africa—several countries on this list are located in North Africa but have cultural and linguistic ties to the Middle East region.

Deserts are common in parts of the Middle East. Well-known deserts include the Sahara Desert and the Arabian Peninsula Desert. Rainfall is not common in the desert regions. Only about 4 inches (10 cm) of rain fall each year on average. But many regions of the Middle East are developed and wealthy. Furthermore, other regions are known for having adequate rainfall and substantial rivers. Examples include the Jordan River, the Tigris–Euphrates river system, and the Mediterranean coast. Strong agricultural systems are found in such regions. Note that water passageways control much of the sea travel in the region. Examples include the Suez Canal, a passageway between the Mediterranean Sea and the Red Sea; the Bosporus and the Dardanelles, a passageway between the Black Sea and the Mediterranean Sea; the Gibraltar, a passageway between the Mediterranean Sea and the Atlantic Ocean; the Strait of Hormuz, a passageway between the Indian Ocean and the Persian Gulf; and Bab el Manded, a passageway between the Indian Ocean and the Red Sea.

Some parts of the Middle East have mountains as high as 19,000 feet (5,800 m). Many areas have a hot climate similar to that of south Florida, whereas locations along the Mediterranean Sea, Caspian Sea, and Black Sea have cooler climates.

All African countries consist of several ethnic groups unique to their region, and most countries have more than one linguistic group. Whereas native languages are common in the more rural areas, colonial languages including English and French are commonly used in many countries. The influence of colonization has resulted in French being the first language in Algeria, Congo, and Guinea, and Portuguese being the leading language in Mozambique. In several countries females slightly outnumber males. African people have traditionally been active and mobile, but modernization, globalization, and technology have caused many youth and children to become sedentary. Because of famine, drought, economic recessions, and poor governance, poverty, malnutrition, and diseases such as malaria and TB are common in Africa.

The Middle East consists of many ethnic groups, such as Arabs, Kurds, Jews, Turks, Armenians, Persians, Aramean Syriacs, Greeks, Georgians, and Circassians. This diversity gives rise to many religions, such as Islam, Christianity, and Judaism. The most dominant religion in the region is Islam. Many other

Learning Activity

What demographic conditions affect the practice of sport in Africa and the Middle East? Do some research on ethnic groups, languages, or religions in Africa and the Middle East, and discuss what effect they might have on sport in the region.

religions exist at a lesser extent, such as Yazdanism, Baha'I, and Zoroastrianism. The main languages spoken are Arabic, Persian, and Turkish. English is the main second language spoken. Another second language spoken in some countries of the Middle East, such as Egypt, Lebanon, Algeria, Morocco, Tunisia, and Syria, is French. Arabic is commonly spoken throughout the Arab countries in the Middle East. Persian is usually spoken in Iran, and Turkish is used in Turkey. Other languages include modern South Arabian languages, Berber, Armenian, Azerbaijani, Kurdish, Greek, and Hebrew.

The Colonial Experience and Sport in Africa

Sport in Africa and the Middle East traditionally had a spiritual component to it. Naturally, the environment shaped the practice of sport; people who lived near water played water sports. Then European colonialism took over parts of Africa and influenced the kinds of sports and physical activity that people participated in. By contrast, people in the Middle East generally had the freedom to come up with their own sports, and sport participation was not formalized in many countries until governments and schools were established after independence. Today, sport in Africa and the Middle East is heavily funded and controlled by governmental entities.

The history of Africa, particularly in the 19th and 20th centuries, has been shaped by **colonialism** and **acculturation**. Colonialism refers to the establishment of control by certain nations over other foreign nations or territories for the sake of political and economic domination. Acculturation, on the other hand, is concerned with minority groups' adaptation of and assimilation to the dominant culture in a nation. These processes had effects on culture, economics, and sport, including football, cricket,

African Triple Heritage in Sport

Jepkorir Rose Chepyator-Thomson, PhD, Janet Musimbi M'mbaha, MEd, and Kipchumba Chelimo Byron, BEd; University of Georgia, USA

According to Ali Mazrui (1986), a triple heritage of cultures characterizes the African continent during the postcolonial era: indigenous, Islam, and Western. The sport culture also follows this triple heritage. Before the coinage of the term *triple culture,* however, the African people took part in a variety of games and sporting activities during the precolonial era. Hence, indigenous heritage characterizes precolonial Africa. The African people's engagement in indigenous cultural games and sports was widespread during the precolonial period. Children and youth took part in games and sports that modeled adults' involvement (Chepyator-Thomson, 1986); the engagement was thought to "develop physical development and acquire health and bodily exercise" (Kenyatta, 1938, p. 104) and to "enhance social interactions among children of different ages and same age-groups, as well as to develop cognitive, affective and psychomotor skills in children and youth" (Chepyatyor-Thomson, 1990; Chepyator-Thomson, 1999, p. 37).

Games of physical skill were popular across the continent during the precolonial period; young men in Africa practiced wrestling and used the sport to bring honor to their ethnic groups and communities. Running and wrestling were very common, and "the best performer in these activities is marked out for leadership" (Kenyatta, 1938, p. 101). Among the Keiyo people in Kenya during the precolonial period, boys took part in running and wrestling games extensively (Chepyator-Thomson, 1986).

Along with diverse indigenous cultures is the presence of Islamic culture in Africa. The arrival of Arabs in Africa, particularly East Africa, dates to the 8th century, making Islamic cultural force felt in the area of recreational activities and sports. Contemporary Africa, considered a postcolonial era, represents the full spectrum of triple heritage in sport activities and involvement. A devout Muslim is expected to avoid wearing indecent sport clothing in both practice and competition venues. For example, schoolchildren wear clothes that conform to the national moral code of attire in school physical education classes—that is, no leg and body exposure (Ndee, 2010). According to Mazrui (1986), women's sport participation is curtailed in Islamic countries because law practices and customs disallow such involvement based on the sport attire used. But, despite the fact that Islamic cultures limited the development of sports in Northern Africa, the most secularized and westernized part of the continent, sports like soccer and distance running received considerable success.

The early outside people to trek the African continent were European explorers and missionaries, and through them, Africans were socialized into European ways of life; missionary schooling acted as the primary agent of change. Sport was introduced to Africans through mission schools as far back as the 17th century. The establishment of boarding schools ensured successful adaptation of a variety of sports in the colonies. Sport was a significant instrument of moral training. It inculcated the spirit of fair play in the context of athletic competition. Missionaries considered sport and games to be useful in the establishment of positive contact with the African people (Hokkanen, 2005). European governments used administrators and missionaries to institute European sports in the form of leisure in missionary- and government-sponsored schools. Scottish missionaries, in their work with African people and in their mission schools, introduced European sports such as cricket, which helped foster the games' ethic during late 19th- and early 20th-century central Africa. Preparation of African children for adulthood was best completed through mission schools' focus on moral, mental, and physical training and education. Sport served the purpose of a "civilizing" mission of the British Empire; football was made "a part of the imperial civilizing process" (Hokkanen & Mangan, 2006, p. 1267).

In contemporary Africa, indigenous cultures are more responsive to sport participation than both Islamic and formerly European-ruled African nations. However, British and Islamic policies respected indigenous cultures much more than the French or other European powers, and the British people were more responsive to sport development in the continent than other European nations. As Mazrui (1986) explained, the British "assisted Anglophone Africans to succeed in international sports more than Francophone Africans south of the Sahara" (p. 124) and helped to institutionalize sport activities through mission and government schools. Contemporary sports are featured mostly as extracurricular activities in schools in postcolonial Africa.

rugby, netball, tennis, boxing, and gymnastics. Colonial domination took over all aspects of African life, and the Europeans showed scant regard for the traditional values of Africans.

The Traditional Period

Before the arrival of Europeans in Africa, there were no formal schools. Locals in all countries participated in indigenous cultural practices that included games, hunting, spear throwing, archery, wrestling, stick fighting, and dance. Up to about the age of six, boys and girls played together. Many of the traditional physical activities had a spiritual dimension to them. In regions such as Uganda and central Africa, board games were also played. Survival activities such as running, jumping, and climbing were common in most regions. The Watutsis of Rwanda were tall and famous for their high jump ability.

The nature of activities was naturally influenced by the physical environment. For instance, people living near rivers or lakes tended to prefer water sports. Certain class distinctions affected participation in activities. The boys' games were competitive and aimed at preparing them for adult lives; the girls' games were more social and group oriented. Women generally did not participate in competitive games.

The common denominator for most African countries is that European colonial powers had a powerful influence over their early history. Sport historians and sport sociologists have amply discussed how colonialists practiced and spread their culture, leisure, and sport globally. On several levels of society, European customs and norms were imposed on Africans, although not in a uniform fashion. Colonial administrators and missionaries, especially the British, French, and Portuguese, introduced Western forms of sport to Africa (Van der Merwe, 2007). But people across the globe, even sport practitioners, academics, and students, know little about sport and the management of sport on the African continent (Krotee, 2003). It is thus essential to give a brief historical sketch of the origins of Western sport forms in Africa.

The Colonial Period

From the 17th to the 19th century external powers competed for colonies in Africa, motivated primarily by the presence of abundant natural resources and the economic benefits that could be derived from them. It was inevitable that through acculturation,

sports such as football, cricket, rugby, netball, tennis, boxing, gymnastics, and athletics developed a foothold among African nations.

In contrast to traditional sports and games, the Western sports emphasized the individual participant. Participation was an end goal. Because of colonial domination in all aspects of African life, the Europeans showed scant regard for the traditional values and rich culture of the Africans. Further, black participation in "white" sport gradually acquired status, leading to the demise of traditional sport activities (Van der Merwe, 2007).

As more blacks were absorbed into the armed forces of the various African colonies, they were also trained in Western sports according to the idea of **muscular Christianity**, a Victoria-era philosophy that advocated physical strength and health in conjunction with Christian ideals. This emphasis on the preparedness for war and the subsequent involvement of the armed forces in World War II led to Western sports becoming established among Africans. The growth of Western sport in Africa occurred in parallel with the growth of modern sport throughout the world. But the achievements of most black sportsmen were downplayed by colonialists, and in some countries teams were made up mainly of whites, owing to their self-imposed notions of racial dominance.

The Postcolonial Period

From the 1950s onward, African nations began gaining their independence. This process was not always peaceful. Initially, sport was not given high priority because other social imperatives prevailed in the impoverished states left behind by the colonialists. As athletes from Africa began winning medals in the Olympic Games and Commonwealth Games, governments and politicians began recognizing the potential of sport in gaining international

Learning Activity

Briefly describe the early origins of sport and physical education in Africa. Compare and contrast the traditional, colonial, and postcolonial periods and discuss which time frames you believe were the most influential on sport in Africa today.

recognition and promoting national pride and unity. Increasingly, leaders manipulated sport as a social tool to achieve their broader social ends (Amusa & Toriola, 2003).

In South Africa, forced racial segregation and disenfranchisement of nonwhites persisted through the late 1980s as part of the policy known as **apartheid**. The history of apartheid and sport is explored in the case study. The background provided in this case study is important for any student of sport management. Against this backdrop several developments occurred in the sport industry as well as in academic institutions offering professional preparation programs. These changes guided the evolution of further new national structures that are engaged in the coordination of sport.

CASE STUDY

Apartheid and Sport in South Africa

In no other country was sport manipulated more to achieve government ideology than South Africa. Under British rule, blacks (an inclusive term for Africans, Coloureds, and South Africans of Indian origin) were treated as second-class people and did not have political franchise. Subordination was common in all forms of social life, and sport was no exception. By the time of Union in 1910, sport was totally under the control of the British. Consequently, all clubs and sport bodies at all levels were structured along racial lines (Alegi, 2006).

Several talented black sportsmen had no option but to leave their country to engage in top-level sport abroad. Boycotts against South African sport intensified. The ruling Nationalist Party was at a quandary. White politicians exploited every loophole they could find to re-enter the international sport arena by altering international perceptions of South African sport, even adjusting their policy to make sport "multinational" and later "multiracial," but without eliminating apartheid. The black sport movement stood firm in its demand for nonracial sport. The maxim of the nonracial sport movement was "No normal sport in an abnormal society." South Africa was expelled from the International Olympic Committee in 1970.

After 1970 the South Africa government made several concessions regarding sport. Nevertheless, the Special Branch of the South Africa police kept a close eye on proceedings to ensure that the terms of permits were complied with. For the first time, Maoris were allowed to play on the All Blacks New Zealand rugby team in South Africa in 1970. The first multiracial athletics meeting was held in Green Point, Cape Town, in 1973. The Aurora Cricket Club became the first mixed club to be admitted by a white league, the Maritzburg Cricket Union, in 1973 (Merrett, 2006). Multiracial sport began being played at club level, and blacks were allowed to play on national teams and became eligible for Springbok colors. The majority of blacks, however, refused to participate in or support multiracial sport until the "playing fields were leveled."

The political landscape was undergoing a major change in the early 1990s. A new political dispensation was being negotiated for South Africa to become a democracy. With the unbanning of black political organizations such as the African National Congress and the South African Communist Party, the release of imprisoned black leaders such as Nelson Mandela, and the return of several black leaders from exile abroad, expectations grew that South Africa would quickly be readmitted into international sport participation.

The National Olympic Sports Congress (NOSC), launched in July 1989, linked sport to the broader freedom struggle and set the eradication of apartheid as a prerequisite for the normalization of sport in South Africa. In 1991 South Africa was readmitted by the Olympic Movement and successfully participated in the 1992 Barcelona Olympic Games, for the first time without the old Nationalist government flag, anthem, and Springbok emblem.

The first democratically elected government took office in 1994. For the first time in history, a black (Nelson Mandela) was appointed president. The National Ministry of Sport with a Department of Sport and Recreation was established. By 1995 it produced a draft *White Paper on Sport and Recreation*. This document provided the national policy framework for sport and recreation. In 1996 the *White Paper* was published, and attention began to be focused on implementing the new strategies to address the discrepancies and injustices in sport provision and participation that had existed in the past.

Current Role of Sport in Africa and the Middle East

Researchers of the current state of sport in Africa should refer to the history of sport in ancient Egypt. In his great book *Dawn of Conscience*, the historian James Breasted (1976) stated that the ancient Egyptian civilization in Africa and the Middle East is the origin of all civilization. In fact, the ruins of ancient Egypt in Bani Hassan in Alminia province support the fact that the "dawn of conscience" originated there. When the Greeks thought of holding the first Olympic Games in 776 BC to spread peace all over the world, they consulted ancient Egyptians about how to approach those games. The ancient Egyptians recommended that the Greeks follow the instructions of Maeth, god of justice, to achieve fair games between the participating teams. It is therefore believed that the African and Middle Eastern people started the initiative to organize sport games and activities and to spread them to other civilizations around the Mediterranean Sea. Thus, it should not be surprising that sport is highly valued in these societies.

African and Middle Eastern countries are constantly attempting to clarify the diverse values and symbols in sport, particularly those relevant to sport culture, physical education, sport education, sport for all, and recreational sport. They also tend to determine the aims of sport in different perspectives, such as physical, mental, psychological, and social. Egypt, among other Middle Eastern countries, has caught on to the idea that sport can be a source of national pride (Wagner, 1989).

In the international arena of sport, traditional or indigenous games developed in Africa and the Middle East are instrumental in resisting **cultural imperialism** (the promotion by the dominant nation of its culture over the cultures of other countries), developing a national identity, and promoting national unity (Burnett, 2006). Additionally, sport activities have been represented in all public organizations, including institutions of higher education, sport clubs and federations, civic organizations, the business sector, the police, and the army.

The modern period has witnessed incredible development in several aspects that have influenced the concept of sport as an effective way of achieving political, economic, educational, religious, and social development. Sport is also seen as an efficient way to prepare individuals for life. Sport, in this sense, is considered a fundamental part of public culture through both its tangible and intangible components.

CASE STUDY

Sport in Kenya

Jepkorir Rose Chepyator-Thomson, PhD, Kipchumba Chelimo Byron, BEd, and Janet Musimbi M'mbaha, MEd; University of Georgia, USA

Kenya is a sub-Saharan nation that is located on the eastern region of Africa. The country received its independence from Great Britain in 1963, and Jomo Kenyatta served as the first president. A diversely populated country, with over 42 ethnic groups, Kenya is best known not only for wildlife and tourism but also for its great distance runners.

In precolonial times, the area known as modern-day Kenya was home to multiple African ethnic groups that have resided there over the past 4,000 years. Foreign presence began with Arabs and Persians who established settlements between the 1st and 8th centuries AD. Europeans arrived in the area during the 17th century, and Britain established itself as a colonial power in the 19th century. In precolonial times, as Kenyatta (1938) said in his anthropological book *Facing Mount Kenya*, the Kenyan Africans had a variety of games and sports aimed at promoting cultural identity and enhancing children's acquisition of cognitive, social, and physical skills.

Following the arrival of Europeans in Kenya, the indigenous sports were severely restricted; sports derived from European cultures took center stage primarily in high-cost schools such as Nairobi High, which had a predominantly European student population, and to a lesser extent Asian- and African-populated schools. The year 1951 marked the beginning of organized sports in Kenya, leading to the formation of the Kenya Amateur Athletics Association (KAAA), which was entrusted to prepare athletes for local and international competition through a variety of clinics that trained coaches.

After independence was established in 1963, sport became an important social institution. It played a key role in putting Kenya on the world map through track and field, particularly the Olympics, World Championships, and World Cross Country Championships. Kenyan athletes excelled in sports such as distance running, boxing, cricket, rugby, and women's volleyball. Runners emerged out of this system with their stellar performances, putting Kenya at the forefront of international athletics starting with the 1960 Olympic Games and continuing to the present day.

The management and administration of sport in Kenya have been, for the most part, run by federations in individual sports driven by their own governing constitutions and policies, but government resources play a key role in supporting sport. The Ministry of Education and the Ministry of Youth and Sport have a relationship in organizing and funding sport activities at two levels: school and social service programs. Kenya's president explained that the government put forth great efforts to promote development of up-to-date training grounds, facilities, and equipment; he also acknowledged that qualified personnel were required to impart technical knowledge and nurture the country's young athletes to lead Kenya on the world stage (Guanqun, 2010). The Ministry of Education works closely with the Youth and Sports Division to identify excellent athletes from schools (Ayieko, 2010) because they are responsible for organizing primary and secondary schools sport programs from the district to the national levels. Sport is used in meeting the national goals of education, and an emphasis is placed on physical education to meet the needs of schoolchildren. The culmination of these sporting activities is international junior championships such as those seen in track and field's World Junior Championships, where Athletics Kenya and the Ministry of Youth and Sport organize the national trials to select Kenya's team for the IAAF World Junior Championships, World Youth Championships, and World Cross Country Championships.

The government's role is to finance sport teams participating at national and international events, where athletes represent their nation (Ministry of Youth and Sport, 2011). The Ministry of Youth and Sport oversees the management and liaises with international sport organizations such as FIFA and IOC to promote the development of sport in Kenya without exerting political influence on the governance of the sport or the affairs of the federations. The Kenya National Sports Council's role is to mediate the direction of sport policy and act as the link between the federations and the government for the interest of sport development (Nyanjom, 2008). Each of the sport federations is affiliated with its international sport organization and has branches at the provincial as well as district level to coordinate the sports at their own jurisdiction, and schools are the base of sport development.

Sport in Kenya follows a two-pronged system: The government promotes development of basic movement skills through physical education in schools via the Ministry of Education, hence helping to meet the basic needs of children; they also promote advancement of sport for competitive purposes through various federations in order to put Kenya on the world map, particularly in track and field, cross country, road racing, and volleyball.

Because of the cultural importance of sport in Africa and the Middle East, sport-focused schools, institutes, colleges, and academic organizations have been established, including the Middle East Sports Academy in Riyadh, Saudi Arabia; the Active Sports Academy in Dubai, UAE; and the Sport Science Institute of South Africa. These educational organizations have made it part of their role to assist in preparing and orienting sport leaders who can carry the responsibility of publicizing the culture of peace and sharing through sport. These efforts began in communities of the first world, but now in the Middle East and Africa, governments and nongovernmental organizations, universities, and schools have conducted peace programs. These programs promote sport development (e.g., Olympic Solidarity), humanitarian relief (e.g., Right to Play), postwar reconciliation (e.g., Playing for Peace), and broad social development (e.g., Kicking AIDS Out). A major focus of the programs' direction and development has been the United Nations Sport for Development and Peace International Working Group (SDP IWG) and the Commonwealth Advisory Body on Sport (Kidd, 2008).

At the level of government, many countries have established higher councils and ministries to govern and supervise the huge process of managing and organizing sport activities. Substantial sums have been budgeted to support these activities. The private sector has not been participating actively in funding and sponsoring sport activities in Africa and the Middle East as compared with the West, where large corporations sponsor sporting events and even build sporting venues.

The observer of the sport movement in this region can recognize how the sport movement has been cultivated by nationalist impulses. Many counties in the region aim to institute a sport as their national game, such as football in Egypt. Another goal of some governments, such as Yemen, Oman, and the United Arab Emirates, has been to present physical education as a compulsory subject in the national curriculum. Countries with the requisite financial resources have built stadiums, established clubs, and specified the fields and pitches on which to practice the various sports.

Governments in Africa and the Middle East typically play a significant role in sport organization in their countries, which often includes the following activities:

1. Establishing rules and regulations for the various sports

2. Establishing clubs and federal sport unions

3. Joining international sport organizations and federations

4. Developing and organizing physical education in educational institutions

5. Developing the reality of sport in educational organizations

6. Establishing modern mandates to cope with the new development movement in the world

7. Organizing Olympic and federal sport committees for the various sports

8. Arranging participation in sport on national and international levels

Sport in the region is continually changing and developing. Some of the other recent patterns and developments in sport in Africa and the Middle East include the following:

- *Sport publications:* Several publications that concern sport activities and issues are published regularly. Some professional publications aimed at students of physical education in colleges and schools investigate ways through which sport can be developed in the region. *SA Sports Illustrated* is an example of a magazine devoted specifically to covering sport news and events in South Africa.

- *Sport media:* Notable development has occurred in audiovisual media; the number of sport media channels and journals has doubled in recent years. For example, Non-Stop Sports is an Israel television network that covers sport news and competitions.

- *Professional sport:* Professional sport appeared in the region 20 years ago, but it has not stabilized or fully developed yet.

Sport in Africa and the Middle East is considered an essential element of civilization. It represents a model of the social values and customs of people. Thus, sport can respond to people's needs and interest and aid their personal, competitive, and creative development.

Economics of Sport in Africa and Middle East

Africa and the Middle East face many problems when it comes to sport funding. To begin, few sources of funding are available in Africa besides governments. Thus, other supplies of funding must be sought, such as international cooperation or international aid. Also, the Middle East and Africa lack corporate sponsorship of sport. The media needs to play its part in attracting sponsors. Furthermore, the IOC, Olympic Solidarity, and IFs should work with the NOCs to aid in setting up ventures to manufacture sport equipment. Another main issue is the lack of a sport development plan. Other problems with funding in Africa and the Middle East arise because governments are inconsistent in their funding of sport and sport education. This unpredictability occurs both within and across nations, making it challenging for the region to come together to play competitive sports.

Given the relative economic opportunities available to elite athletes in Africa versus European and

Western nations, many African football players have migrated to play on foreign teams. The sidebar explores this pattern in more detail.

The situation in South Africa is one of the exceptions to the lack of private sponsorship for sport in the region. A recent study of sport sponsorship in South Africa shows that the industry is vibrant and growing, although it is becoming an expensive business. A study of the top 100 sponsors in South Africa done by BMI SportInfo found that the industry is worth R2.6 billion (US$330 million) and spends an additional R2.2 billion (US$280

Migration of African Footballers

Statistics compiled by Gerard Dreyfus (2007) show that more than 502 African players have a contract with European first-division teams. Ricci (2000) identified 894 African players employed by first- and second-division Europeans teams. Although Europe is historically the privileged and more attractive destination of footballers from Africa, African footballers also have global presence because Europe is not the only place where these footballers are found. At the 2002 African Cup of Nations (CAN), there were players from 26 non-African championships, among them China, the United States, Australia, India, and Saudi Arabia (Boniface, 2002; Bale, 2004). Every edition of the CAN shows that the African football elite in most countries has migrated. This phenomenon, especially remarkable in Europe, started during the colonial era.

Colonial Migration

The tradition of migration of African footballers appeared early during colonization and evolved throughout history. The creation of the first leagues in Algeria in the 1920s was followed later by the North African Club Championship, and the North African Cup contributed to the development of the football game and the training of the first generation of migrant football (Darby, 2002; Murray, 1994). By 1938 there were already 147 African footballers playing in first- and second-division French leagues. The Moroccan Larbi Ben Barek ("the black bead") built a career in Europe, playing in France and Spain as a North African migrant. Similarly, Portugal and Belgium encouraged the integration of athletes from their colonies into their competitions and national teams. In 1954, Marion Coluna arrived in Portugal from Mozambique. Eusebio Ferreira da Silva followed in 1961. Mario and Eusebio are still ranked among the greatest players Portugal has ever had. Eusebio was the top scorer (9 goals) at the 1966 World Cup held in England and was the top scorer in the Portuguese and European leagues for several years: Portuguese top scorer in 1964, 1965, 1966, 1967, 1968, 1970, and 1973 and European top scorer in both 1968 (42

goals) and 1973 (40 goals). Contrary to Portugal and France, Great Britain as a colonial power had fewer integrating policies, because it did not integrate footballers from its colonies to its leagues. Under British authority, the Gold Coast (Ghana) had already put in place football clubs such as Ashanti United and Heart of Oak since 1911 (Alegi, 2010). They established the Gold Coast Football Association in 1922 (Murray, 1994). In spite of this development of local football, none of these players migrated to Great Britain.

Postindependence

Until the 1980s, postindependence football in Africa had a limited global presence beyond a few world-class players such as Eusebio da Silva and Salif Keita. After Egypt's first participation in the World Cup in 1934, there was no African team presence until 1970. Except for a few individuals playing mostly in France, Portugal, and Belgium, African football teams had a restricted world value and recognition. From the mid-1980s, a transformation occurred. Darby, Akindes, and Kirwin (2007) justify the transformation by the growing profile and status of African national teams from the mid-1980s. Indeed, the introduction by the FIFA of the Under-20 (1977) and Under-17 (1987) World Cups and the performance of African teams put young African footballers in the spotlight of the media and recruiters. Very early, young African players found themselves in the world youth football elite. The rising profile of African football led to what Darby described as the "new scramble for Africa." The flow of African footballer migrants drastically increased and continues to rise. During the 2008-2009 season, Radio France International, a French international online radio station, listed 670 African players in 10 European countries' first- and second-division leagues. These lists also show that West African countries—principally Nigeria, Ghana, Cameroon, Senegal, and Côte d'Ivoire—are the main suppliers of footballers to European leagues. According to Poli (2010), these five countries account for 54 percent of the African football diaspora in Europe. France, England, and Belgium are their privileged destinations.

million) on leveraging sponsorships. The year-on-year growth rate of the local industry is almost 14 percent, which is well ahead of the international growth rate of just below 11 percent. Sponsors continue to view football, rugby, and cricket as the sports that offer the best exposure. Basketball, golf, and tennis are identified as sports that offer the best sponsorship growth opportunities. Sponsors believe that the FIFA 2010 World Cup, huge consumer interest, and unexploited sport potential provide good sponsorship opportunities. On the downside, they identified political intervention in sport, bad management, and poor performance as factors negatively affecting sport sponsorship

(Thornton, 2003). Another interesting example of a sport gaining sponsorship and becoming a thriving business is the sport of wrestling in Senegal, which is explored in more detail in the case study.

Governance of Sport in Africa and the Middle East

The governance of sport in almost all African countries is still not decentralized. Most countries do not have a dedicated ministry of sport. The sport portfolio is generally incorporated in ministries of education, arts, culture, social welfare, or even agriculture. But several national government

CASE STUDY

Senegalese Wrestling: An Original Example of Sport Management in Africa

Wrestling has a long tradition in most African societies and communities. In precolonial Africa, wrestling was generally practiced during the dry season and among sedentary societies (Baker & Mangan, 1987). Wrestling was a very popular sport in many African societies and has been characterized by a diversity of rules, prematch rituals, and dress codes (Melik-Chakhnazarov, 1970).

In contemporary Senegal, despite the diffusion and practice of other sports such as football and basketball, wrestling has retained its originality and gained an increasing national popularity. The exceptionality of wrestling in Senegal is its management, where traditional forms of wrestling rings and rules, entertainment, and practices coexist with contemporary marketing techniques, broadcasting rights, and sponsorship.

The most prominent wrestling matches, or galas, are often organized in the capital city of Dakar and are staged in football (soccer) stadiums. Senegalese mabalax drumming bands and dancers are vital components of the entertainment. Mystic practices are also part of the entertainment package. Individual vendors of peanuts, coffee, and homemade drinks or snacks circulate around and in the arena. They represent what is commonly described as concession in American sport arenas. Beside these original aspects of Senegalese wrestling, contemporary sport management techniques are applied.

Indeed, Nicholson's (2007) three main components of the nexus that bind media and sport are visible in Senegalese wrestling. The history and popularity of wrestling in Senegal provide for a wide audience of viewers and supporters, which attract sponsors and television broadcasters. Gaston Mbengue, one of the most prominent sport and wrestling promoters speaking of sponsorship, says, "It wasn't hard to sell them sponsorship rights, because they go where there is an audience. Since wrestling attracts a lot of people, they are necessarily interested by it too" (Skelton, 2010).

In fact, the broadcasting rights, after bidding, are controlled by the national public media entity (Radiodiffusion Télévision Sénégalaise, or RTS) and a private television broadcaster (RDV). Advertisements on all media, including television, newspapers, and radio, announce the major wrestling matches. Sponsors such as mobile phone companies complete the nexus of media and wrestling in Senegal.

The popularity of wrestling and its management have transformed the sport into a business worth millions of CFA francs (the local currency). Serigne Sarr, head of marketing at the RTS station, estimates that wrestling generates 500 million to 1 billion CFA francs ($1 to $2 million) in sponsorship a year (Skelton, 2010). Built on old traditions and contemporary sport management strategies, Senegal wrestling is a vibrant and original case study of African sport management.

departments of sport have now taken on a strategic approach to developing their nations through sport and recreation. Their focus is on social development through the development of communities. They find sport and recreation to be ideal vehicles to achieve their goals. These departments are thus responsible for national policy development as well as monitoring, public funding, and advocacy functions.

Generally, most government departments in Africa experience severe constraints in terms of appropriate human resource capacity, because personnel do not have adequate or appropriate sport management qualifications. In many countries, departments of sport and related sport organizations have functions that overlap, creating a duplication that depletes scarce resources and leads to confusion of roles. Accountability for results is lacking. Governments create unnecessary bureaucratic channels of communication, particularly for athletes and their sport federations. Governments

have the view that anybody can manage sport and that no specific qualification in sport management is required. Indeed, the sooner such a view can be reversed by the new breed of qualified sport management graduates, the better the chances that sport governance in Africa will transcend this state of affairs now evident across the continent.

In the Middle East, governments are also the primary financial supporter and administrator of sport activities. Few other agencies are involved in sport in the Middle East. In some countries, Egypt,

CASE STUDY

Government Support of Sport in Egypt

Before the 1952 Revolution in Egypt, there was no central body that could plan, coordinate, and supervise the activities of sport and youth in general. Many organizations, ministries, schools, and clubs were actively involved with sport and youth, but they lacked coordination. The activities of the many agencies were neither planned nor directed toward specified objectives, and accordingly could overlap or contradict each other. The need for a central body to give direction and leadership to Egypt's national and international sport interest could hardly be underestimated.

The first attempt to organize sport and youth activities occurred in 1953 when a committee was formed to study the possibility of establishing a Supreme Council for Youth and Sports. A year later the council was established as an affiliated body within the permanent Council for Services. Later it was discovered that the affiliated position did not give the council sufficient flexibility to carry out its responsibilities. Accordingly, Act 197 was issued in 1956, giving the council an autonomous identity, a separate budget, and more power to

implement its decisions. These powers were further reinforced between 1964 and 1979 (Supreme Council for Youth and Sport Printing Office, 1981). In 1999 the responsibilities of the Supreme Council for Youth and Sports were absorbed by the Ministry of Youth. In 2005 the Ministry of Youth was divided into two structures: the National Council for Youth and the National Council for Sports. The National Council for Sports is responsible for promoting sport, developing sport establishments and talent, and developing various sport-related legislations.

Throughout history, many cultures have influenced sport in Egypt. Furthermore, Egypt continues to implement modern sport in schools, universities, and clubs. Even so, much remains to be done. For example, although there are many sport stadiums and clubs, sport facilities in schools are inadequate, thus limiting the number of students who can participate in sport. After the 2011 popular uprising in Egypt, the government of the country is in transition, and the effects, if any, on government sport programs remain to be seen.

for example, governments have spent lavishly to support sport.

In Yemen the government and the Supreme Council have been successful in using sport as a means for increasing the connection between the capital and isolated rural areas. Because sport has a large influence on the younger population, participation in the sport movement means that the next generation of Yemeni will have a stronger involvement with and recognition of the government. The effects of the 2011 Yemeni uprising on governmental support of sport are not yet known.

Sport Organizations in Africa and the Middle East

The sections that follow introduce several sport organizations in Africa and the Middle East and explain how the history of these organizations affected the related sport. The organizations are directly related to governments because many are created, maintained, and even manipulated by the government.

Supreme Council for Sport in Africa

The **Supreme Council for Sport in Africa** (SCSA) is the sport arm of the African Union, which succeeded the Organization of African Unity (OAU). The OAU was formed in 1965 by André Hambessa, the interior minister of Congo–Brazzaville. Apart from using the name for the initial purpose of organizing the first All-Africa Games in his own country, Hambessa did not define the structure of the council as a continental organization. The official founding conference of the SCSA in Bamako, Mali, in 1966 was equally vague on the issue of the organizational structure of the council. Because of this ambiguity from the outset, the SCSA never had the legal mandate to represent or lead African sport, nor was it responsible to any defined continental constituency. Its obscure power base emanated from a tricky recognition of the All-Africa Games by the summit of the OAU, held in Kinshasa, in what is now the Democratic Republic of the Congo, in 1967.

The situation was manipulated by the second president, Chief Abraham Ordia, and the secretary general, Jean Claude Ganga, to avoid elections so that they could hold on to their positions for the greatest part of the council's early years. Encouraged by the continued support of ill-informed African politicians and the grand name attached to this shallow organization, the two men claimed undue authority over the continent's autonomous national Olympic committees and sport confederations. The first victim of this intrusion was the better-organized Confederation of African Football (CAF), which was constitutionally founded eight years before the council itself.

During the congress of the CAF in Addis Ababa, Ethiopia, in 1968, Ganga suggested that the SCSA coordinate the activities of all sport bodies in Africa. Members of the CAF pointed out that it was an autonomous body responsible to its member associations on the continent and to FIFA on the international level. It could therefore agree only to cooperation with the SCSA. Hence, the first attempt to control the confederation under the guise of coordination was successfully resisted.

Unfortunately, the SCSA's strategy changed to creating dissent within CAF. It encouraged football clubs and players to report to it with their grievances, indirectly posing as the superior authority on the continent's football matters. The SCSA also became the self-appointed fault-finder on the CAF. These interferences in the affairs of the confederation caused endless controversy. Sadly, the SCSA had full-time paid officials who were idle because they had no mission of their own. Ganga also failed to understand that the SCSA was not the mandated association of the national Olympic committees of Africa.

The SCSA failed to restructure itself into an effective participatory council of the African sports ministers, the national Olympic committees, and the confederation of African sports. Thus, the SCSA's influence and power dwindled. Its flagship event, the All-Africa Games, was beyond the hosting capacity of most African countries. Hence, the early years of the SCSA were uneventful.

When the round table of African sport leaders met in Tunis in 1980, they had had enough of the ineffectiveness of the SCSA and decided to remove Ganga from office. They restructured the SCSA in line with the requirements of the IOC and the international federations. They established an autonomous Association of National Olympic Committees of Africa (ANOCA) and an autonomous Union of Continental Confederations. These bodies, together with a ministerial general assembly, constituted the

SCSA. This new African sport structure was adopted by the congress of member countries in Lomé, Togo, in 1981. This action heralded the establishment of the present day ANOCA and Union of Confederations of Sport in Africa (UCSA), and this structure has governed sport on the continent ever since. The SCSA now consists of representative ministers of sport of member countries and is responsible for the political governance of African sport.

Confederation of African Football

The Confederation of African Football (CAF) was established in Khartoum, Sudan, in 1957. Its membership currently includes 55 national associations. The founding countries were Egypt, Ethiopia, Sudan, and South Africa. The permanent residence of the CAF is in Egypt. According to its statute (Confederation of African Footabll, 2007), the objectives of the CAF include the following:

◆ Improve the game of football in Africa and promote its unifying, educational, cultural, ethical, and humanitarian values, particularly by implementing youth and development programs

◆ Organize its own continental and international competitions

◆ Draw up regulations and provisions related to its activities and ensure their implementation

◆ Control all forms of football and, by taking any necessary or appropriate measures, prevent infringements of FIFA and CAF statutes, regulations, and decisions, as well as the Laws of the Game

◆ Prevent practices that may jeopardize the integrity of the game or its competitions, or give rise to the abuse of football

◆ Maintain relations with FIFA, the other continental football confederations, and zonal unions

◆ Promote football free of discrimination against any country, person, or group of persons for ethnic, gender, language, religious, political, or any other reasons

◆ Encourage all national associations and public authorities to do their utmost to secure the professional and social future of footballers

◆ Fight against doping and take measures to combat the use of prohibited substances in order to protect the health of footballers

◆ Promote friendly relations between national associations, zonal unions, clubs, officials, and players

◆ Adhere to the fundamental principles of the Olympic Movement and engage itself in the promotion of peace, solidarity, and unity in African sport; support the actions of the African Union and nongovernmental organizations related to youth, sport, and culture; and support the United Nations system in its fight against the scourges which ravage the continent and threaten humanity

The current president of the CAF is Mr. Issa Hayatou from Cameron. He was elected to the position in 1988.

Association of National Olympic Committees of Africa (ANOCA)

Created in Lomé, Togo, on June 28, 1981, the **Association of National Olympic Committees of Africa (ANOCA)** is an association constituted among the national Olympic committees (NOCs) of Africa. ANOCA abides by the fundamental principles of the Olympic Charter and therefore has the following duties:

◆ Promote understanding, cooperation, and mutual assistance among NOCs of Africa

◆ Help African NOCs propagate, develop, and protect Olympic ethics throughout the African continent

◆ Plan and coordinate the action of African NOCs to rationalize the intervention of Olympic Solidarity

◆ Organize and coordinate the preparation and participation of Africa in the Olympic Games

◆ Harmonize cooperative relations between African NOCs, the International Olympic Committee, and the Association of National Olympic Committees of Africa

◆ Celebrate, in close cooperation with the NOCs concerned, African sport confederations, the

SCSA, and the All-Africa Games in pursuit of the ideals of the Olympic Charter

◆ Cooperate in general with governmental and nongovernmental sport bodies to facilitate the elaboration and implementation in Africa of a coherent strategy for sport development that translates in terms of operational programs the right for all to participate in sport and physical activities

◆ Foster, through the introduction and support of training programs and planned action, a more rational and higher quality preparation of African athletes for the Olympic Games

◆ Encourage the participation of women in the Olympic Movement

◆ Secure, in accordance with the fundamental principles that govern the Olympic Movement, funding sources likely to support the action of African NOCs

SCSA Zone VI

The SCSA divided Africa into seven competition zones. Hence, the zonal structure of SCSA was established to govern sport in the regions. Zone VI was established to represent the southern African countries, approximately those located south of the equator. This zone is the most active one in Africa. **SCSA Zone VI** is responsible for all sport development programs in southern Africa and is the official arm for all SADC sport programs. Zone VI has an active sport strategic plan that has the following priorities:

◆ Capacity building
◆ Building the case for sport
◆ Equity and inclusion
◆ HIV–AIDS campaign
◆ Zone VI Games
◆ Complementary and regional integration

The objectives of SCSA Zone VI include, among other things, the following:

◆ To support the organization, promotion, and development of sport in member states and Africa at large

◆ To encourage and assist in the formation of zonal sport confederations in all sport disciplines

◆ To solicit sponsorships and raise funds from sources and means as the council may approve to enable Zone VI to achieve its aims and objectives

◆ To encourage and promote the teaching of the physical education and sport in all schools, colleges, and universities in member states

◆ To prevent any undesirable practices in sport and any form of racial, political, religious, or any other form of discrimination against any member state, team, or group of individuals

Sport and Recreation South Africa (SRSA)

Sport and Recreation South Africa (SRSA) is the national department responsible for sport and recreation. See www.srsa.gov.za for additional information. The primary objective of SRSA is to grow participation in sport at the grassroots level, including school sport. In addition, SRSA is responsible for

◆ interprovincial and national activities and competitions, in collaboration with the Department of Education and the South African Sports Confederation and Olympic Committee (SASCOC), and

◆ international competitions, in collaboration with SASCOC.

Although the main purpose of SRSA a few years ago was the funding of federations, that function has diminished dramatically in importance; only about 5 percent of its budget is now allocated to this function. The change to a project-driven organization has been accompanied by a dramatic rise in the organization's budget, which was still in the double-digit millions only a few years ago. Now it stands at more than R400 million (US$50 million), and that excludes the billions of rands that SRSA is paying out in 2010 FIFA World Cup funds. The move to a project-based organization accelerated after the merging of the South African Sports Commission into SRSA, which brought a wealth of experience and skills into SRSA.

The main projects of SRSA focus on mass participation and school sport. School sport is a relatively new project area, whereas mass participation is well established through projects such as Siyadlala, which reaches millions of people of all ages in disadvantaged communities, as well as the highly successful Indigenous Games program, implemented in conjunction with provincial sport departments.

The focus on "getting the nation to play"—a nation in which far less than half of its citizens participate in organized physical activity—means that its focus on projects is expected to remain and even expand. As the broader value of sport in terms of the nation's social, mental, and physical health becomes apparent, SRSA will be on hand to implement additional sport projects that will spread sport to those who are still excluded.

SRSA's Strategic, Monitoring, and Evaluation Directorate has assessed and audited the strategies that guide the work of SRSA as a national government department responsible for sport and recreation. The five-year strategic plan of SRSA was updated and submitted to Parliament. Thereafter, the task of revising the *White Paper* and creating a national plan for sport was tackled.

As the governmental representative of sport in South Africa, SRSA is responsible for all sport-related relationships with other countries. The main functions of the international relations section of SRSA are to promote and oversee bilateral agreements with foreign governments and to provide support for sportspeople from South Africa travelling abroad, as well as those from other countries who are visiting South Africa to take part in sporting activities.

Mass participation projects were developed after investigation of various local and international models suggested an approach that could be effective in sport and recreation development. The programs encourage mass participation while removing access barriers such as cost, elitism, race, gender, and intricacy of both activity and equipment specifications.

SRSA began working on school sport in 2005 when a Framework of Collaboration, subtitled Co-ordination and Management of School Sport in Public Ordinary Schools, was signed by the minister of sport and recreation and the minister of education. The framework document describes the common understanding that SRSA and the Department of Education (DoE) have about the important role of physical activity and sport in schools. Beside emphasizing the importance of providing all children with access to physical activity at school,

it touches on educator capacity building, sport facilities, and the importance of linking issues of national importance such as HIV–AIDS and crime prevention to school sport.

The National Coordination Committee (NACOC), made up of representatives from SRSA and the DoE, is responsible for the coordination, management, and setting of policy. It is also responsible for coming up with working plans on how to implement the framework's vision. It consists of five subcommittees that deal with tournaments, policy, international affairs, funding, codes, and talent identification.

SRSA has established a Directorate for School Sport within the Chief Directorate of Mass Participation. It consists of two sections: Competitive School Sport and Mass Participation in Schools. The difference between the two is that the first focuses on supporting competitive events, whereas the other supports festivals that are about maximizing participation rather than winning.

South African Sports Confederation and Olympic Committee (SASCOC)

The South African Sports Confederation and Olympic Committee (SASCOC) is the controlling body for all high-performance sport in South Africa. It was formed as a Section 21 company by representatives of all the sport bodies at a general meeting held on November 27, 2004. According to the Memorandum of Association, its main objectives are to promote and develop high-performance sport in the Republic of South Africa and to act as the controlling body for the preparation and delivery of Team South Africa at all multisport international games including the Olympic Games, Paralympic Games, Commonwealth Games, World Games, and All-Africa Games.

Figure 7.1 shows the structure of sport governance in South Africa, including the roles played by SRSA and SASCOC.

The executives of SASCOC comprise a president; a first and a second vice president; five elected members; any IOC member resident in South Africa; one member appointed by each of Disability Sport SA, SA Student Sports Union, and the School Sport Association of SA; and one member representing the Athletes' Commission.

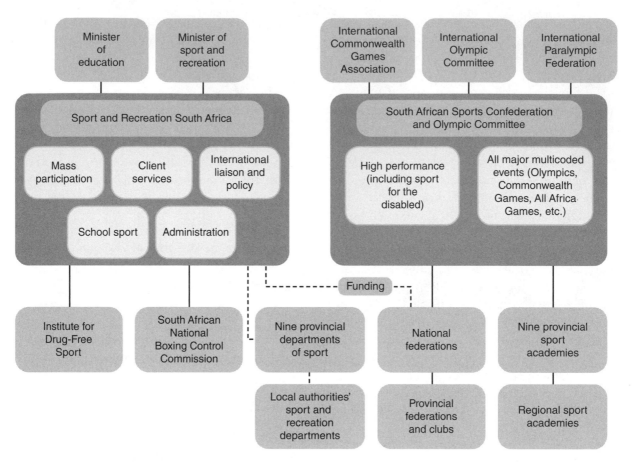

Figure 7.1 Structure of sport in South Africa.

Arab Sports Federation

The **Arab Sports Federation** (**ASF**) was established in Riyadh, Saudi Arabia, in 1976 as a response to the Olympic Saudi-Egyptian Committee. Thirteen Arabic Olympic committees participated. The federation now consists of 21 members and 48 sport federations. The ASF has the following aims:

◆ Uniting the Arab world in international and Olympic celebrations
◆ Developing the Olympic Arabic movement
◆ Fostering Olympic values and principles
◆ Encouraging participation in the Games

The ASF sponsors the Pan-Arab Games. The first president of the ASF was Prince Faisal bin Fahad. The current president of this federation is Prince Sultan bin Fahd bin Abdul-Aziz Al Saud.

Arabic Federation for Sport for All

The **Arabic Federation for Sport for All** was established in 1992 in response to the Sport and Youth Ministers' Council No. 9 in a meeting in which 15 counties participated: Jordan, UAE, Bahrain, Tunisia, Algeria, Saudi Arabia, Sudan, Oman, Palestine, Qatar, Kuwait, Lebanon, Libya, Yemen, and Egypt. The first president was Mr. Abdul Munem Wahba of Egypt.

ASEC Mimosa Football Club of Côte d'Ivoire

ASEC (Amicale Sportive des Employés de Commerce) from Abidjan, Côte d'Ivoire, is a multisport institution; their football section is the oldest and the driving component of the group. ASEC football was created in 1947-1948 by Beninese businessmen from the Côte d'Ivoire: Alfred Seho, Louis Boah, and Francois Ouegnin (Poli, 2002). ASEC has won 14 Côte d'Ivoire championships from 1993 to 2010. ASEC also holds the unofficial world record of 108 consecutive victories, a feat they achieved between 1989 and 1994 (Copnall, 2004). ASEC is characterized by an exceptional local, regional, and international popularity and an integration of the supporters into the club management. ASEC is a popular club in the whole of West Africa with supporting clubs in Burkina-Faso and in places such as Paris, Naples, and New York (Poli, 2002). The club website estimates the number of supporters in the Côte d'Ivoire to be 8 million, and 15 million supporters are in the subregion of West Africa (ASEC Mimosa Equipe, 2008).

Structure and Organization

The top of the organization of ASEC has a president and five vice presidents. Four of the vice presidents serve more traditional roles in the sport organization structure, while the third vice president and the Committees for Action and Coordination represent the management of ASEC. The third president is president-coordinator of the CNACO.

National Committee for Action and Coordination (CNACO)

The third vice president presides over the National Committee for Action and Coordination, which is the central structure of ASEC's fans organized in committees. In fact, the CNACO has the responsibility of coordinating all the committees. The committees are registered by the club and operate under the vice president of coordination. ASEC has 350 committees organized on a geographic, socioprofessional, or gender base. Villages, communes, schools and universities, enterprises, professions, and women are some of the categories of committees. The members pay dues that entitle them to the status of *actionnaires* (shareholders). They attend the annual general body meeting and vote for the board of directors. Estimated at 40,000, the shareholders

pay dues of 3.00 F CFA (US$6.00) for a member card; students pay 2.500 F CFA (US$5.00). The third vice president suggests that the desire to remain a popular club for all social classes encourages ASEC to keep their membership dues affordable for all. He estimates that shareholders' dues represent only 1 to 2 percent of the club budget. ASEC shareholders own their headquarters in the Abidjan with a merchandising store. Although contributing to only 1 to 2 percent of the club budget, they have a significant role in fund-raising for games and special events. ASEC merchandising is managed by the CNACO and can represent substantial contributions mostly when the club performs well in the continental competitions. The third vice president of the club generally resorts to the fund-raising capacity and organization of the CNACO.

The size of the fan base and the CNACO mobilizing capacities are among the best reasons for sponsorship of the club. The first vice president highlighted a significant example of their influence on the club sponsorship:

> Nissan was one of our sponsors giving us a percentage of the car sales. Knowing the deal with Nissan, supporters decided to only take Nissan taxi to encourage taxi owners to buy Nissan and consequently to increase Nissan sponsorship. As board of directors we did not give any instruction, but the CNACO decided that was a way to help their club.

The CNACO also provides logistical support by covering the team's hotel and food expenses on road games. The first vice president acknowledges the importance of ASEC shareholders for their exceptional human support and indirect economic contribution. In terms of the media, ASEC has a newspaper focusing solely on the club; 30,000 copies sell out every Friday with the support of the CNACO.

Despite their limited financial contribution, ASEC's shareholders are an important component of the club management. Having a dedicated vice president is an original model that formalizes the role of fans in the management of one of the most successful professional football organizations in sub-Saharan Africa.

The mission of this organization is to promote sport for all in the Arab world. The organization aims to achieve the following objectives:

◆ Promote the importance for all people in Arab nations to be engaged in the practice of sport

◆ Train and prepare leaders for the sport for all movement in Arab nations

◆ Develop policies to facilitate the achievement of the objectives of sport for all

◆ Encourage cooperation and partnership between various public and private constituents

◆ Promote and utilize the scientific research and theories to plan and develop programs for sport for all

◆ Raise funds to support the activities of the sport for all program

Regional Sport Events in Africa and the Middle East

In addition to international events such as the 2010 FIFA World Cup held in South Africa, there are many established regional international sport competitions in Africa and the Middle East. This section introduces a few of these events.

◆ *All-Africa Games.* These games were originally planned to be held in Algeria in 1925 but were delayed because of the British and French occupation of the region. Games were also planned for Alexandria, Egypt, in 1928 and two cycles were to be held, one for English-speaking countries and another for French-speaking countries. The first games held for all African countries was in Congo–Brazzaville in 1965 and included 10 sports. Subsequent games were held in Lagos, Nigeria, in 1973; in Algiers, Algeria, in 1978; in Nairobi, Kenya, in 1987; and in Cairo, Egypt, in 1991. The All-Africa Games have been held every four years since. The 2011 Games were held in Maputo, Mozambique.

◆ *Confederation of African Football Champions League.* The Champions League, sponsored by the Confederation of African Football (CAF), is open to all CAF-affiliated national league champions and the Cup holder from the previous season. The Champions League started in 1997, replacing the African Cup of Champions. A total of 64 teams compete.

◆ *African Cup of Nations.* The African Cup of Nations, also sponsored by CAF, is one of the oldest competitions in Africa. It is held every four years. When it was established in 1957, only three nations, Egypt, Sudan, and South Africa, participated in the competition. In 2008, 16 teams qualified for and competed in the tournament.

◆ *Arab Sports Tournament.* This tournament was first held in Alexandria, Egypt, in 1953. The aim was to educate Arab youth physically, create legal competition and cooperation among them, and increase national spirit among Arab youth. The celebration included various sports such as basketball, volleyball, boxing, football, and running.

◆ *Mediterranean Games.* After the 14th Olympic Games in London 1948, the Egyptian Olympic Committee originated the idea for these games and presented a proposal in Rome in 1949. The celebration was held in 1951 in Alexandria, Egypt. Its aim was to promote peace and create familiarization among people in the region. The Mediterranean Games have been held every four years since 1951. Recent games were held in Tunisia (2001), Spain (2005), and Italy (2009). Greece will host the 2013 games. The charter of the Mediterranean Games includes these goals:

• Participating in developing Olympic principles

• Fostering relations among Olympic youths

• Encouraging cooperation and coordination to develop sport in the region

• Cooperating with other international and national authorities and organizations

• Fostering sport ethics

• Continuing celebration of the Mediterranean Games

• Participating in achieving fair games

• Participating in fighting sport-active drugs

Summary

The development of sport in Africa took a different route from that of the Middle East. While European colonization impacted greatly the sports that Africans play, governments and schools have played a crucial role in the development and promotion of sport in the Middle East. The development of sport in Africa has gone through three periods: the traditional period, the colonial period, and the postcolonial period.

Sport today has been seen and used by governments in Africa and the Middle East as an effective means to achieve goals in political, economic, educational, religious, and social development. As such, governments in this region are heavily involved in sport development and are the major source of funding to support sport operations.

? Review and Discussion Questions

1. Discuss how sociological factors affect sport in the Middle East and Africa.
2. Discuss how geographical and demographic conditions affect sport in the Middle East and Africa.
3. Discuss how political factors affect sport in the Middle East and Africa.
4. Discuss how key events of sport in the Middle East and Africa have added to the field.
5. Discuss the key people who affected sport in Africa and the Middle East.
6. Discuss how governmental funding affects sport in Africa and the Middle East.

Acknowledgments

The editors express their sincere thanks to Dr. Lateef Amusa from the University of Venda in South Africa for his valuable comments and feedback on this chapter.

Sport in South Asia, Southeast Asia, and Oceania

Megat A. Kamaluddin, MSC
University of Malaya, Malaysia

Wirdati M. Radzi, MSA
University of Malaya, Malaysia

Chapter Objectives

After studying this chapter, you will be able to do the following:

- Appreciate the heterogeneous characteristics of the region and their effect on regional sport governance
- Understand the role of sport in the region
- Identify the types of sports being played at the mass and competitive levels
- Identify the influence of tradition and culture in sport activities regionally
- Recognize the role of the public sector in governing regional sport structures
- Consider and compare the changing roles of regional and local sport managers to their counterparts in other jurisdictions
- Identify key economic, political, and social considerations that shaped the management of sport in the region

Key Terms

Key Events

Establishment of Sport Management Association of Australia and New Zealand (SMAANZ) in 1995, a scholarly organization for the study of sport management.

2000 Sydney Summer Olympics. These Games marked the second time that the Olympics were held in the Southern Hemisphere; the first was in Melbourne, Australia, in 1956.

Establishment of Asian Association for Sport Management (AASM) in 2002, a professional organization for sport managers in Asia.

2010 Commonwealth Games in New Delhi, India. This quadrennial multisport event, a solidarity games that brought together the former colonies of the British Empire, is the second biggest in the world after the Olympics.

2010 Hockey World Cup in New Delhi, India. Officially known as the Hero Honda FIH World Cup Delhi 2010, the event was held February 28 through March 13, 2010. The Hockey World Cup is a quadrennial event, comparable to the FIFA World Cup series.

Key People

Mohamed Hamam, president of the Asian Football Confederation (based in Kuala Lumpur, Malaysia).

HRH Sultan Azlan Shah, president of the Asian Hockey Federation.

Jonah Lomu, International Rugby Hall of Famer, the first true global superstar of rugby union.

Nicol David, reigning world number 1 in women's squash.

The fact that the discussion of sport in Asia is spread over three chapters in this book can be seen as an indication of the vastness and complexity of the continent in terms of its geography, its people, and its cultures. Oceania is a point of great interest as well. As the smallest continent on the planet, it has experienced strong influences of culture and tradition that are juxtaposed against the challenges of modernity and development, a social situation that can be demanding at times. In terms of development status of the nations in these three regions, we see a mixture of developed, developing, less-developed, and least developed countries (categorization proposed by the International Monetary Fund), which is a unique feature of the regions. For instance, the South Asian region is made up almost entirely of countries categorized as developing (India, Pakistan), less developed (Bangladesh), and least developed (the Maldives). The Southeast Asian region consists of a developed country (Singapore) and developing countries (such as Thailand and Malaysia), whereas Oceania consists of two developed countries (Australia and New Zealand) and a combination of less-developed and least developed countries (such as the Cook Islands, Dominica, Papua New Guinea, Samoa, and Tuvalu). Developed countries have advanced industrial economies, high incomes, and democratic governments. The gross domestic product (GDP) of these countries is in excess of US$10,000 per capita. Developing countries are the bottom group of the IMF's hierarchy of advanced economies. Less-developed countries have low levels of output, low living standards, and limited technology. They have a GDP per capita of US$5,000 or less, often much less. The least developed country classification includes countries with no significant economic growth, low literacy rates, and per capita GDP of US$1,000 or less.

This divergent socioeconomic, political, cultural, and religious background of the regions is the starting point of our discussion on managing sport in the region. This chapter seeks to understand the role that sport plays in South Asia, Southeast Asia, and Oceania and outline some of the sport management structures and issues within the regions. Because the chapter is introductory in nature, we will look at some of the complexities and the resulting social dynamics that were put in motion to manage sport in the regions.

Geography and Background of South Asia, Southeast Asia, and Oceania

To promote clarity, the geographical description and demographic makeup of the respective regions are briefly discussed here, starting with South Asia and followed by Southeast Asia and Oceania. The description is intended to provide a general idea of the sociocultural diversity that uniquely distinguishes and characterizes the regions. This background is important to framing the discussion of sport in the region.

South Asia

South Asia is geographically defined as the region located at the southern end of the Asian continent. Also sometimes known as the Indian subcontinent, South Asia is made up of India, Pakistan, Nepal, Bhutan, Sri Lanka, Bangladesh, and the Maldives. It is one of the world's most densely inhabited regions, having a population of more than 1.5 billion people. The region has a rich combination of ethnic backgrounds and religious affiliations; Buddhists, Hindus, Muslims, and Christians call South Asia home. The region also boasts an illustrious political history. Archaeological evidence of past ancient civilization points to the region's ancient political and economic prosperity. These civilizations included the Mohenjodaro-Harappa in the Indus River valley and subsequent political empires such as the Mauryan, the Kushan, and the Mughals, which form the historical foundations of modern India. The population of India is made up of two major ethnic groups: the Indo-Aryan and the Dravidian. Combined, the groups share more than 1,000 languages, 18 of which are recognized as India's official languages (2002). The European intrusion in the region started in the 15th century when Portuguese merchant vessels sailed into the waters and ended in the late 1940s when many nations in the region gained independence from their colonial masters.

South Asia today is an emerging economic force. India and Pakistan have surged ahead with advances in space and nuclear technology and innovation that have placed South Asia on the global map. India, for instance, is the fourth largest economy after the United States, China, and Japan. It has a GDP of US$3 trillion in terms of **purchasing power parity** (**PPP**) (*India at a Glance*, 2005). Purchasing power parity, a way of understanding the long-term exchange rates of money based on relative price levels in two countries, is used throughout this chapter. The concept of PPP is based on the fact that goods are priced differently in different markets. For example, a U.S. dollar exchanged and spent in India will buy more goods than the same dollar spent in the United States.

The nations of South Asia have formed the **South Asian Association for Regional Cooperation** (**SAARC**) to enhance regional cooperation and development. Established on December 8, 1985, SAARC has a specific aim to promote economic, social, and cultural cooperation among member states. The member states comprise, in alphabetical order, Afghanistan, Bangladesh, Bhutan, India, the Maldives, Nepal, Pakistan, and Sri Lanka. Other members of the SAARC with observer status are Australia, China, the European Union, Iran, Japan, Mauritius, Myanmar, and the United States (*Central Intelligence Agency: The World Factbook*, 2009). An observer country has direct or indirect interests or stakes (be it economy, political, military, or other types of interests) in any of the SAARC member countries.

Southeast Asia

Southeast Asia covers a vast area that borders the Indian subcontinent in the west, China in the north, and Australia in the south. Measuring 4,523,000 square kilometers, the region is divided into two smaller regions: the mainland nations of Cambodia, Laos, Myanmar, Thailand, and Vietnam and the maritime nations of Indonesia, Malaysia, the Philippines, Singapore, and Brunei (also known historically as the Malay world, because of similar anthropological characteristics of the Austronesian people, the Malay). The South China Sea divides Malaysia into the Peninsular on the mainland and East Malaysia on the island of Borneo. Chong (2005), when commenting on the regional diversity, stated that with "over five hundred million population, one thousand languages, a religious smorgasbord of Animism, Buddhism, Taoism, Hinduism, Islam and Christianity, the sheer diversity of Southeast Asia defies simple categorization" (p. 1).

The geographical composition of the region also plays an important role, especially in shaping the historical and political past and current conditions. For example, the coastal and island character of the region helped people create extensive international maritime trading networks. Originally, Indian and Chinese traders came to Southeast Asia in search of spices and other produce to be exchanged in a barter trade system at various ports of call. Eventually the merchants, especially the Indians, began to settle down and influence local ways of living. Archaeological evidence traced the Indian (or the Hindu faith) influence throughout Southeast Asia by the beginning of the 1st century BC. Ancient megastructures such as the Angkor Wat in Cambodia and the Borobudur in Indonesia, both magnificent testaments of the architectural genius and engineering technology possessed by the people of Southeast Asia, were temples dedicated to Hindu gods (Abdul Wahid, 1970).

In terms of political history, the region saw the rise and fall of empires such as the Majapahit, the Srivijayan, and the Malaccan Sultanate of maritime Southeast Asia, as well as the Khmers and the Cholas of the mainland Southeast Asia. Western powers gradually came in to replace the old kingdoms, ironically through the same trade route that had brought prosperity to the region. Beginning with the Portuguese, the British, the Dutch, and the Spaniards, almost the entire territory, with the exception of Thailand, was colonized by the West from the 16th to the 18th centuries. Colonialism replaced the native economic, legal, and education systems besides altering the geopolitical boundaries of the region, both literally and physically. For example, the Malay world that made up the maritime region was divided into modern-day Indonesia and Malaysia when the British and the Dutch exchanged their economic interests over the territories in the 17th century (Hashim, 1992).

The 19th and 20th centuries saw the gradual withdrawal of the Western powers and the beginning of newly independent modern states. Southeast Asia maintained its regional cooperation through the formation of the **Association of the Southeast Asian Nations** (**ASEAN**) in August 1967. ASEAN maintains that the main purpose of the association is to accelerate economic growth, social progress, and cultural development of the region as well as to promote regional peace and stability (*Overview— Association of Southeast Asian Nations*, 2005). ASEAN membership consists of 10 states, listed here in alphabetical order: Brunei, Cambodia, Indonesia, Laos, Malaysia, Myanmar, Philippines, Singapore, Thailand, and Vietnam. The association has 11 dialogue partners: Australia, Canada, China, the European Union, India, Japan, South Korea, New Zealand, Russia, the United States, and the United Nations Development Plan (UNDP) (*Central Intelligence Agency: The World Factbook*, 2009). ASEAN also promotes cooperation with Pakistan in areas of mutual interests, and Papua New Guinea is a member state with observer status.

Southeast Asia is an emerging economic power, emulating the economic success of South Asia, specifically India. The region has a GDP of approximately US$900 billion and purchasing power parity (PPP) of US$2.8 trillion (*Southeast Asia*, 2007). As a whole the region's economy is as diverse as its geography. Countries like Singapore have already attained developed status through significant economic development following independence, whereas countries like Laos and Vietnam are lagging at a much slower economic growth rate. Most countries in this region became involved in the industrialization process when regional governments put into place policies that encouraged the development of manufacturing plants, which increased individual nations' GDP. The strategic location of Southeast Asia has proved to be an advantage for trade, which has traditionally been the region's strong point given the maritime trade history of the Straits of Malacca. Malaysia and Brunei export large quantities of commodities such as palm oil (Malaysia) and petroleum (Malaysia and Brunei). Indonesia, as a petroleum-producing country, diversified its export trade commodities to include rubber, coffee, and textiles. The region's economy depends not just on trade exports within the region but also on exports to countries outside the region. The United States, Japan, China, and Korea are major trade partners with the region.

Oceania

Many interpretations have been offered about what constitutes Oceania, a name that has gradually replaced the term *South Pacific*. Some have argued that the islands of Oceania are divided into Melanesia, Micronesia, and Polynesia. Common use, however, defines Oceania as the region that includes Australia, New Zealand, Papua New Guinea, New Guinea, and various islands of the Malay Archipelago (*Oceania*, 2007). Although the geopolitical boundaries of the region are predetermined, they do not conclusively represent what the region stands for in sociocultural and historical terms. For example, the island of Hawaii is considered the northern corner of the Polynesian Triangle (and New Zealand is the western corner), although politically it is part of the United States. Anthropologically, the Hawaiian language is a Polynesian member of the Oceanic language family (*Oceania*, 2007). Western powers claim a number of islands in Oceania as their territories, such as French Polynesia, American Samoa, and the British Pitcairn Islands. Approximately 28 nations constitute the region, which includes the islands of Micronesia, Melanesia, and Polynesia such as Cook Islands, Christmas Islands, Norfolk Island, Chatham Island, and Tokelau.

Compared with the rest of the archipelago, Australia and New Zealand have more structured sport management organizations (their developed economic status has certainly helped in this area). Little information and research are available on organized sport and sport management on the smaller island nations. For those reasons, this chapter focuses on Australia and New Zealand.

Before the arrival of Europeans in Australia and New Zealand, archaeological findings suggest that the earlier inhabitants of Oceania were involved in agricultural practices circa 7000 BC. The maritime nature of the region combined with the seafaring skills of the natives aided the transmigration of the Austronesian inhabitants to neighboring and sometimes distant islands, including the Indonesian archipelago and as far away as Hawaii (*Oceania, 8000–2000 BC*, 2000).

The first known sighting of the Australian continent by Europeans was in 1606, and the first European explorer arrived in New Zealand in 1642 (*Oceania*, 2007). The British established settlements in both territories by placing formal claims of the territories in the name of the Crown, putting in place the English economic and penal system. This "progressive" development effectively marginalized the native inhabitants of Oceania. An example is the imposition of the English economic and legal system that led to most of New Zealand's land passing from the indigenous Maori to Pakeha (European) ownership, subsequently leaving the Maori impoverished (*History of New Zealand*, 2007).

The Commonwealth of Australia was proclaimed in 1901 as a Dominion of the British Empire, and autonomy to govern the country was vested in the Australian Parliament. Similarly, New Zealand ceased to be a colony of the Empire and achieved Dominion status in 1907. Today, in contrast with their South Asian and Southeast Asian counterparts that are categorized as developing countries (Singapore excluded), Australia and New Zealand are considered developed countries. They have a combined GDP of US$902 billion in 2006 and US$589 billion in terms of purchasing power parity (PPP) (*List of Countries by GDP [PPP] per Capita*, 2007).

The nations within the Oceanic region also arranged themselves in a group styled as the **Pacific Islands Forum** (**PIF**) in 1971. The forum aimed to strengthen cooperation between the independent countries of the Pacific Ocean and to represent their interests. Because Australia and New Zealand are two of the more developed countries of the region, they are significant aid donors as well as major market exporters (*Pacific Islands Forum*, 2009). In 2005 the forum also laid out the Pacific Plan, a regional integration blueprint that focuses on the four objectives of enhancing and stimulating economic growth, sustainable development, good governance, and security for Pacific countries through regionalism (*Pacific Islands Forum Secretariat*, 2009).

Role of Sport in South Asia, Southeast Asia, and Oceania

Sport, especially in South Asia, Southeast Asia, and Oceania, has always been viewed as an important tool in social integration (Megat Daud, 2000) as well as a means to develop national identities. People generally equate their national team with their country in international sport competition. Outstanding performances by a national team lead to an increase in the nation's international eminence, such as the celebrity status of the internationally successful Indian national cricket team among the Indian populace (Nalapat & Parker, 2005). South Asia, Southeast Asia, and Oceania provide an interesting backdrop for the inquiry into the sport management movement because they are part of the largest continent in the world and are exceptionally diverse in experiences—ethnically, culturally, religiously, sociologically, economically,

and politically (Mangan, 2003). To simplify the experience of sport in South Asia, Southeast Asia, and Oceania from a single perspective would be futile and counterproductive, and should the need arise, the exercise should be done with extreme caution (Mangan, 2003).

Traditional Sports

In a multicultural, multiethnic, and multireligious South Asian, Southeast Asian, and Oceanic society, the interest in sport transcends the differences and shared objectives, such as the public health benefits of sport for all. The history and development of regional sport have a firm link with the political past. Europeans left a lasting impression politically on what was to become modern South Asia, Southeast Asia, and Oceania. For instance, the English legal system formed the backbone of the modern Malaysian legal system that in turn had a trickle effect into other aspects of the Malaysian life (Brownfoot, 2003). Sports introduced to the region by the colonizers are popular today. But before the introduction of the Western concept of team sports in the region around the turn of the 20th century, the natives indulged in activities that are physical and sportlike in nature. The Malays, for instance, worked the land and were master practitioners of vital local living skills. The sport-related emphasis at that time was on individual sporting talents, as Brownfoot (2003, p. 130) further elaborated:

> Malays admired the sporting talent of individuals such as hunters, elephant tamers. Malay sports requiring crafts skills and manual dexterity were also popular, including kite-flying, top-spinning, finger and arm-wrestling and races on bamboo stilts. Boat racing, fishing and diving was also greatly enjoyed since the Malay kampungs (villages) were usually located near rivers or by the sea.

Similar conditions were probably observable in other parts of the region. Sriboon (2007) related that traditionally, the majority of the Thais were involved with agriculture, so folk and craft games were more popular. One such game that gained reputation in the region is *sepak takraw*. Originally thought to be a game introduced by Chinese traders to Southeast Asia, sepak takraw is considered by many countries in the region as their own traditional game. Sepak takraw was already popular in Malaysia and Thailand by the early 1400s (*Sepak Takraw*, 2007).

Learning Activity

Look up sepak takraw on the Internet. Find out how it is played. With a ball fashioned out of crumpled papers, try playing a game of circular sepak takraw with a few of your friends.

The word *sepak* is a Malay word meaning "kick," and the word *takraw* is Thai for "rattan," because the ball is made of rattan. The game was known in Thailand only as takraw. Sepak takraw is the formal name of the game, a name that paid homage to the two Southeast Asian countries that claimed to have originated at least the modern, structured version of the game. Not surprisingly, Malaysia and Thailand were considered traditional rivals at this game. Today, sepak takraw is played competitively at the biannual regional games, the Southeast Asian, or SEA, Games, which will be explained in detail later in the chapter.

Other types of traditional sport are played across the region. Martial arts are also categorized as sport, such as *kabaddi* in India and *pencak silat* in Southeast Asia. Kabaddi is a team contact sport that originated in the state of Tamil Nadu in India. A war strategy game in orientation, kabaddi reached international status with the establishment of the International Kabaddi Federation as the international governing body for this sport. Pencak silat is a combative art of fighting not unlike taekwondo of South Korea and karate of Japan in principle. The difference is

Sepak Takraw

From Peasant Game to International Sport

Sepak takraw is a game of speed, agility, and dexterity. The origin is said to be Chinese. In Thailand at Wat Phra Kaew, murals of the game being played by the monkey god Hanuman can be found. Sepak takraw was also mentioned in the Malay Annals, an epic chronicling the life and times of the Malaccan sultanates that was said to have been written in the 14th century. In 1829 the Siam Sports Association drafted the first rules for sepak takraw competition, retaining its original circular form of play. In 1833 the badminton-styled netting was introduced. Today, sepak takraw requires an area measuring 13.4 by 6.1 meters with a center line dividing the court. The ball is spherical and can be made of either rattan or synthetic fiber. The three-man team in sepak takraw is called regu, and two regus play against each other. The formation of the players' position is quite similar to volleyball. Two players flank the net placed in the middle of the court at either side, and the server, or tekong, is at the center of the court. The net measures about 1.5 meters. The tekong serves the ball, which has a circumference of 0.42 meters and weighs 170 grams, to the other court using the feet. The ball is pitched to him or her by one of the players at his or her side who flanked the net. The regu on the other side then attempts to receive the ball using either the feet or the head. The objective of the game is to maintain the ball airborne as long as possible. The team that allows the ball to drop or fall outside the court lines loses a point. The game is played in two sets, separated by a two-minute rest. The scoring system is similar to that of other court and net games such as badminton and volleyball. When either the serving side or receiving side commits a fault, a point is awarded to the opponent's side, including making the next service. The winning point total for a set is 21 points, unless the set is tied at 20–20. In that case, the set shall be decided on a difference of 2 points, up to a ceiling of 25 points (extracted from www.sepaktakraw.org/pdf/lawofthegame.pdf).

Sepak takraw has evolved into a full-fledged, international sport having its own international sport governing body, the International Sepak Takraw Federation (ISTAF). Currently, the international federation includes 21 member countries: Thailand, Indonesia, Singapore, Brunei, Malaysia, Korea, Laos, China, Myanmar, Philippines, Japan, Sri Lanka, India, Pakistan, Bangladesh, Vietnam, United States, Canada, Puerto Rico, Iran, and Brazil. The federation also lists 8 playing countries that have been granted observer status: Germany, Switzerland, Sudan, Nepal, Denmark, Colombia, Mongolia, and Hong Kong. The current headquarters of ISTAF is Singapore. Sepak takraw is included in international multisport events such as the Southeast Asia (SEA) Games, the Asian Games, and the World Games as well as having its own regional and international single-sport events. For more information on ISTAF, visit the official website at www.sepaktakraw.org/.

the technical moves and the meaning assigned to the movements by the respective society. Pencak silat today is a competition sport at the regional level. *Pesilat*, or martial artists, participate from all across the region.

The roots of pencak silat (or Malay martial arts) can be traced back to the concept of the Malay world, which was based on the idea of a Malay race in terms of a cultural and sociolinguistic sphere of influence. Geographically, this area covers modern-day Indonesia, Malaysia, Brunei, Singapore, southern Thailand, and southern Philippines. As such, early accounts of pencak silat vary across the region. One common theme, however, appears to emerge— that pencak silat was created out of necessity of the time. In Asia the 14th century was an interesting period. The ancient Malay kingdoms were at their height. These city-states were constantly at war with one another for a multitude of reasons. Kingdoms such as Srivijaya, Sailendra, Majapahit, and Mataram of ancient Indonesia were constantly in need of massive, well-organized, and highly mobile armies to maintain and expand their empires. In these conditions pencak silat began to flourish. Those who were strong and skilled in pencak silat gained prominence in society. The teaching and learning of pencak silat were originally reserved exclusively for the royal family because the skills were greatly honored as part of leadership capability. Later, however, as the old Malay kingdoms disintegrated, the teaching and learning of pencak silat spread to other levels of society and were disseminated throughout the Malay world. In the wake of revolutions arising from the collapse of empires, pencak silat became not just a specialized skill but also a survival skill. According to Wilson (2002), an example of the best known groups of professional pesilat was the Bhayangkari during the Majapahit realm (circa AD 1334–1359) led by Pateh Gadjah Mada, who eventually rose to prominence as the kingdom's prime minister.

Today, pencak silat has become a full-fledged sport. Having a strong historical root in Indonesia, it is natural that the International Pencak Silat Federation (PERSILAT) was established in Jakarta, Indonesia, on March 11, 1980. In terms of governance, the membership of the PERSILAT is divided into four groups. The founding members consist of the national pencak silat governing bodies of Indonesia, Malaysia, Singapore, and Brunei; affiliated members are countries that have national-level pencak silat organizations that have been recognized by the relevant public authority of the country; associated members are countries in which the national-level pencak silat organization has not received government recognition; and junior members are countries in which links have been established between PERSILAT and clubs or an individual but that do not qualify for a higher level of membership. PERSILAT has six regions (Asia, Europe, Middle East, Africa, America, and Oceania) and 39 member countries.

Besides pencak silat, other traditional games reflect the societal life of the region and often involve everyday activities such as plowing the fields. At the end of the harvest season, farmers organize themselves to celebrate, both as a symbol of seasonal change and as an opportunity to enjoy recreation. Events that highlight their skills are common. These sometimes involve a beast of burden (usually bulls or water buffaloes but sometimes Asian elephants in Thailand). Lutan (2005) described a type of traditional sport played in Indonesia:

> One of the best known of the traditional activities is *kerapan sapi*, the colourful bull racing of Madura. Plough-teams of two bulls race over a length of a rice paddy. This event has spread from the island of Madura to East Java and the district and regency heats in August lead to the finals in September. Today's bulls are specially bred for racing and are never used for ploughing; the ploughs pulled will not survive a day in the paddies. However, the winning team achieves great status and an early defeat in the district rounds is accompanied by a severe loss of "face" for the owner. (Lutan, 2005, p. 306)

Folk and traditional games are still very much alive in many parts of South Asia, Southeast Asia, and Oceania. Boomerang-throwing festivals have a large following among the locals in Australia, as do traditional kite-flying games on the east coast of Malaysia. These activities provide farmers respite from the hard work of toiling in the fields. The simple games evolved to become community events and a good excuse for people to celebrate the end of the harvest. We have seen so far the influence of tradition and culture on the people in the region, including the types of sports that they play. The next section looks at the development of modern, Western-styled sport in the region. It begins with the introduction of structured and formatted

Western-styled sport and games to the regions and subsequent assimilation as well the local peoples' reaction and adaptation to such introduction.

Modern Sport in South Asia, Southeast Asia, and Oceania

As mentioned earlier, the region was formerly colonized by the West, notably the British, Dutch, Portuguese, and Spanish. Along with the Western law and other systems, the British brought with them Western sports to the whole empire "from football and cricket to tennis and swimming, indoor and outdoor, played on field, track, court and in water, in teams and by individuals" (Brownfoot, 2003, p. 129).

As a result, sport as the modern, organized, and structured activity of today is a legacy of European (particularly British) colonial rule. For instance, football was introduced to Asia by British army officers, as were other Western sports such as cricket, rugby, and tennis. Similarly, when the British settled in Australia and New Zealand, they introduced the game of rugby. The locals now embrace it as their own. Almost all known Western-styled sports are being played across the region. Currently, the Western sport of football is unrivalled as the favorite pastime in many Southeast Asian countries such as Indonesia, Malaysia, Vietnam, and Thailand. The possibility of tapping into the huge Southeast Asian market is what prompted Manchester United of England to launch its Asia tour in the summer of 2009 to position its products to cater to that clientele (www.tinyurl.com/asiatour2009). Similarly, in Oceania, modern Western sports such as football and rugby are preeminent. The popularity of football in Australia and New Zealand received a boost when the two teams qualified for the FIFA (International Federation of Association Football)

World Cup 2010 in South Africa. Australia and New Zealand are founding members of the Oceania Football Confederation (OFC), a continental affiliate of FIFA. Compared with other members of the OFC, Australia has been making great strides in international football, qualifying in three World Cup campaigns. Looking for more challenges, Australia left the OFC to join the Asian Football Confederation (AFC) in 2006. Although Oceanic in origin, Australia represented the Asian continent in the 2010 FIFA World Cup and became one of the first countries to reach the finals without losing a match (http://en.wikipedia.org/wiki/Australia_national_association_football_team).

In the Indian subcontinent, another modern, Western-styled sport, cricket, is considered the national sport. Cricket players are revered by the populace. Legendary names such as Imran Khan of Pakistan and Sachin Tendulkar of India reverberate along the corridors of cricketing fame. In countries like Indonesia and Malaysia, yet another modern, Western sport, badminton, is popular among the masses. Like football in Australia, badminton has gained further popularity through the success of individual and team players of the countries at international competitions.

Clearly, among the people in these regions, modern, Western-styled sports are more popular than "traditional" modern sports such as sepak takraw and martial arts. The role of the media is crucial in elevating the status of Western-styled sports over traditional sports. Despite the popularity of modern, Western-styled sports, traditional sports still occupy a place in the hearts of the locals and continue to spread in terms of popularity to nonlocals. One example is the spread of martial arts such as Muay Thai (traditional Thai-style kickboxing) among Thais as well as tourists in Thailand.

In general, participation of sport in the region can be divided into two sections: elite sport and mass, or grassroots-level, sport in both Western-styled and "traditional" modern, organized sport. In terms of elite sport participation, football is big in South Asia, Southeast Asia, and Oceania, except probably in India, where cricket and hockey (also known as field hockey in contrast to North American ice hockey) are the most popular sports. Badminton and squash are examples of sports that are dominated by South Asian and Southeast Asian countries, which have produced world champions such as Pakistani squash champions Jansher and Jahangir Khans, Indonesian badminton champion Taufek Hidayat, and Malaysia's reigning world number one squash queen, Nicol David. The Kiwis (a colloquial reference to a New Zealander), with sport legends like Jonah Lomu of the New Zealand All Blacks, dominate rugby in the region. New Zealand's All Whites and the Australian Socceroos proudly represented their respective countries in the FIFA 2010 World Cup campaign. The celebrity status that these sport stars enjoy results from a combination of their extreme talent as well as the massive endorsements and extensive advertising campaigns waged on their behalf. At the elite level, the globalization and commercialization of sport are affecting the situation of elite internationals in South Asia, Southeast Asia, and Oceania. These sport stars obviously benefit from the sport development policies and programs of their countries of origin, and they now become the source of inspiration for sport development at the grassroots level.

In terms of hosting sport events, various mega-events of international stature have been held in the region. The Sydney 2000 Summer Olympiad, the 2010 World Cup Hockey Delhi, the 2010 Commonwealth Games Delhi, and the annual Melbourne and Sepang Formula One Grand Prix were but a few of international sport megaevents that have recently taken place in the region. In 2008 another international sporting event was unveiled in Singapore that further promoted the region as a major player in organizing mega sport events. Dubbed the Singapore Night Race, it was the first nighttime race in Formula One history (www.formula1.com/news/headlines/2007/10/7040.html).

Sport Development and Governance in South Asia, Southeast Asia, and Oceania

Throughout South Asia, Southeast Asia, and Oceania, the role of the government appears to be important in the development of mass sport as well as sport at the elite level. Regardless of the economic status of the nations in the regions (developed, developing, less developed, or least developed), the role of the public sector in sport is instrumental within local sport development structures. The active involvement of the public sector

in local sport only points to the emphasis given to sport by governments as part of the nation-building agenda. Nations are reconstructing their own image and identity as independent nations, and sport has always been regarded as contributing to the participation of the masses in rebuilding the national identity. In this sense, Booth (2002) maintained that Australian nationalism was for the most part, founded on international sporting achievements that provided a yardstick by which to measure the strength of the nation and contributed "more to the formation of Australian national identity than either the bush or the goldfield" (Booth, 2002, p. 153).

In India, the National Sports Policy was proclaimed in 1984 but was later replaced in 2001 on claims that it was not implemented properly and that its goals were not realized (Chelladurai et al., 2002). The objectives of the 2001 National Sport Policy are twofold: to promote sport at a broad level and to achieve excellence at the elite international level. The policy also stated the responsibility of state governments to push for the development of mass sport. In Malaysia, sport is also regarded as an important part in the nation-building process. The National Sport Policy (National Sport Policy, 1989, p. 3) acknowledges the contribution of sport to Malaysian society:

> It is the hope and aspiration of the Government to foster the growth of a united, healthy, active, disciplined and productive society and at the same time to create a generation of capable athletes to enhance national pride and prestige in the international sporting arena.

Similarly, in Singapore, although the initial emphasis of the government was to promote the policy of sport for all Singaporeans, the pursuit of excellence in sport became the focal point of the government with the initiation of Sports Excellence 2000 (SPEX 2000) in 1993 (Horton, 2002). A further policy on sport participation was announced by the Singaporean government in May 2008 through the Singapore Sport Council with the Let's Play Campaign. Singapore aspires to be the leading city for sport in Asia, heralding the evolution of Singapore sport from the grassroots level to international sport participation.

What Singapore is experiencing as a country is occurring in other nations in the region. The evolutionary process of mass participation in sport turning into mega sport events is occurring across the nations. Table 8.1 presents some of the regional competitions and the frequency of such events.

A review of some of the national sport policies in the region reveals the increasing effort made by governments to regulate local sport. Sport has now become important enough for governments

Table 8.1 Frequency of Regional Games

Competition	Frequency
SEA Games	Biennial
Asia Games	Every four years
AFC Football Championship	Biennial
South Asia Games	Biennial
Commonwealth Games	Every four years
SEA Universities Games	Biennial
Pacific Games	Every four years

to invest in its development and utilize it as part of national developmental programs. The governments of Singapore and Australia in particular have also considered sport policy as a "particularly malleable and high profile policy instrument" (Green, 2007, p. 925). In Australia, sport policy was linked to the planning agenda as far back as the 1970s (Green, 2007), although it initially aimed at developing local sport and recreation facilities. Green (2007) further observed that a clear demarcation of the aim of the policy came in 1981 with the establishment of the Australian Institute of Sport (AIS) that "signaled the government's determination to improve international sporting performance following the disappointing results of the 1976 Montreal Olympics, where just five medals were won" (Green, 2007, p. 926). The case study looks in detail at how sport policy has aided and responded to the growth of elite and commercial sport in Australia.

CASE STUDY

The Australian Sports Commission and the Growth of Elite and Professional Sport

Sport is so popular in Australia that some believe it rivals religion in importance to society. Australia achieved its first great Olympic success at the Melbourne Games in 1956, when the country's athletes won 13 gold medals and placed fourth in the medal tally. A performance that surpassed even the Melbourne Games was again achieved on Australian soil, in the 2000 Sydney Games, when Australians won 16 gold medals and again placed fourth in the final medal tally. Although many attributed the renewed interest by the government to develop Australian sport to the dismal performance of the national athletes at the 1976 Montreal Olympic Games, efforts were already underway in 1973 when the government commissioned a report on the sport development plan for the country.

The successes in sport by Australians at international events in the years following the Melbourne Games were achieved with minimal government funding or involvement. The 1976 Montreal Games served as a turning point in which the involvement of government became more apparent as a response to the national outcry about the marginal performance of the national athletes. As one of the efforts

to modernize and develop human performance in local sport, the Australian Institute of Sport, a division under the Australian Sports Commission, was established in 1981. According to Dickson (2000), "This high-technology training centre was located in Canberra, based on the East German and Chinese models and focused on Olympic sports in particular" (p. 5). The philosophy that underpinned the establishment of AIS was the assumption that grassroots participation would be stimulated by elite sport successes and the creation of national sport heroes, role models, and champions.

In 1977 a breakthrough concept in managing modern Australian sport was led by Kerry Packer. A media mogul and avid cricket fan, Packer was convinced that Australian sport (in his instance, cricket) should embrace the commercialization of sport and benefit from it. Throughout the 1980s and 1990s significant growth occurred in professional leagues as well as sponsorship values and television rights fees in Australian sport. The growing importance of the area was not missed by the government, which markedly increased funding and support to the sector. With massive allocations to sport from all sectors,

(continued)

(continued)

contemporary sport managers were tasked with greater accountability to improve the management of sport at all levels of participation. As the Australian population gained access to a greater quantity of sporting opportunities, a change in the spending pattern occurred. With higher disposable income, consumers spent more in the pursuit of healthy lifestyles. Investment in sport is now expected to yield returns in terms of delivery of services for the private sector as well as excellence in sport participation for the public sector.

The commercialization of sport in Australia also brought to surface the need to reevaluate the national governance structure of sport in the face of increasing corporatization of sport and complex issues surrounding ownership. Foreman (2001), for example, stated that although "the AFL (Australian Football League) clubs were defined as small businesses individually on the basis of turnover or profitability, collectively with the AFL Commission they contribute approximately A\$350 million to GDP." What this meant was that the AFL was already a major revenue-generating business that defied the categorization as a small business. The AFL is one of the richest sport leagues in the country, and the administration of the league, especially in financial matters, is dictated by corporate governance principles more than the ordinary sport governance

structure. Organized sport structures follow the federated model, whereby local sport clubs elect representatives to make up the state associations and subsequently the national governing bodies. At the same time, both the state-level and national-level sport associations are highly dependent on volunteer support and have a small number of full-time employees. Sport management academic programs offered locally were also on the rise in the 1990s, which contributed to creating awareness of the need for professionally qualified sport managers with special knowledge of the industry.

The call to review the governance structure nationwide became an important agenda for the Australian Sports Commission (*About the ASC*, 2009). Through one of their five divisions, the ASC as a public delivery agency of funding programs to national sport organizations created an annual funding review process based on the reports of full governance review of each organization.

The ASC continues to be at the forefront of sport development programs in Australia, working closely with national sporting organizations, athletes, and other key stakeholders of national sport to fulfill their mission of enriching Australian lives through sport and realize their vision "to continue to be recognized as the world leader in developing high-performance and community sport" (*About the ASC*, 2009).

The Australian sport policy showed a gradual shift from developing local sport and recreation infrastructure in the earlier part of the 1980s and 1990s to aiding the country in producing a steady supply of medal hopefuls from the 1990s well into the new millennium. Now, however, a movement seeks to achieve a balance between elite sport development and mass sport development, as evidenced by the functions of the ASC that recognize the interrelation between mass and elite sport development. In this instance, Green (2007) asked that

> in principle, the ASC/AIS (Australia Institute of Sport) amalgamation in 1989 was established with the aim of neutralizing perennial, but somewhat "passive," arguments surrounding the balancing of the twin objectives relating to mass participations and elite sport. Whether such balance is ever achieved is open to question. (p. 927)

The shift in emphasis can also be found in the governance of sport in Malaysia. The Ninth Malaysian

Plan (*Ninth Malaysian Plan*, 2006), a five-year national development blueprint, allocated close to US\$200 million for sport development programs directly under the Ministry of Youth and Sport. In addition, other relevant ministries such as the Ministry of Education, the Ministry of Higher Education, and the Ministry of Tourism allocate substantial funding for sport programs. Although the financial allocation covers all levels of sport development programs, the most visible recipient of funding has always been the elite sport programs. The extensive media coverage of high-profile sports contributed to this imbalance.

The commercialization and globalization of sport have prompted many regional governments to consider including elite sport programs in their sport policy. Success in sport has been viewed as having positive outcomes to both citizens and the government where nation building is concerned. The emphasis is no longer about just promoting sport at the broader base; achieving excellence in sport along the way is crucial. Obviously, the

Establishing Sport Governance in Malaysia

In the later part of the 1940s and leading into the 1950s, mass participation in local Western-styled sport grew in Malaysia. Before independence, Malaysians were also competing at international levels in some competitive sports such as football, badminton, hockey, and athletics. The period after the independence leading up to the formation of Malaysia in 1965 saw renewed interests in both mass and competitive sport (Brownfoot, 2003). The newly formed Malaysian government was enthusiastic about using sport as a foundation to develop healthy and strong Malaysian youth, who would in turn achieve "the task of building a harmonious unified nation" (Kim, 1985).

Nonetheless, starting in the late 1960s the interest in and standards of sport, especially competitive sport, were declining. Khoo Kay Kim (1985) suggested that the reason behind this decline was that in British Malaya, sport was regarded with high esteem by the Western social elite. Therefore, a cultural backlash against sport followed independence. The Malaysian government was keen to address the declining position of sport in the national agenda by drawing up several measures directly related to sport. The Ministry of Youth and Sport was created in 1972. In 1967 the National Sport Foundation was established with an objective to further public participation in sport, and in 1972 the National Sport Council, which was aimed at managing elite sport participation, was established. Later, as the government continued to seek a solution to the dismal sport conditions locally, the national sport policy was drawn up in 1988 to emphasize the importance of sport in achieving national development, unity, and continued stability (Brownfoot, 2003).

In 1998 the Sports Development Act came into force. This act was the first legal provision ever promulgated that related specifically to sport. The rationale behind the promulgation of the act was the need to streamline the governance of sport associations. All sport associations were required to register with the Office of the Sport Commissioners, a public agency created under the act. Failure to register with the office would result in discontinuance of funding or future removal from the list of recipients of funding. This development was viewed as both the recognition of the importance of the role that sport has played in Malaysia and the beginning of a new era in sport management whereby sport was taken more seriously as a significant industrial sector (Radzi, 2000).

The national sport policy highlights the role that sport plays in the nation-building and development agenda. The Malaysian government continued to affirm the role of sport as a social integration tool in many sport-based projects to highlight the success of the agenda. The biggest sport event ever hosted by the country was the 16th Commonwealth Games in Kuala Lumpur in 1998. The experience, confidence, and success of hosting that event had a major influence on the development of local sport management. It reminded Malaysians and proved to the world that Malaysia has carved a niche for itself in the area of organizing and hosting major international sport spectaculars. With this experience under their belt, Malaysians went on to organize other regional and international sport events.

The main providers of sporting opportunities in Malaysia are the public sector, voluntary sport clubs, local authorities, schools, higher education, and the private sector. The organization of sport in Malaysia is highly fragmented, reflecting its haphazard development over a long period and its roots almost entirely in voluntary organizations. The professional administration of sport is a relatively recent phenomenon, and many sports remain largely untouched by it. The Malaysian sport scene is a relatively small community of public, private, and nongovernmental organizations directly or indirectly involved in sport and working primarily to achieve the core purpose of leading Malaysia to sporting excellence. Some sport governing bodies lack the basic administrative knowledge and professional support that are essential for any organization.

National governing bodies (NGBs) also play an important role in sport in Malaysia. Generally, these organizations are affiliated with the relevant international federation for the sport in question. The activities of an NGB relate to the regulation and development of a sport from the grassroots up to the national or executive level. These activities themselves are unlikely to generate income; instead, they require funding. All NGBs have to fund their running costs and activities out of their income. Although some established NGBs like FAM (Football Association of Malaysia) and BAM (Badminton Association

(continued)

(continued)

of Malaysia) can count on their own commercial activities to generate substantial income (through sponsorship of events and teams, merchandising, ticket sales, and hospitality), many newly established and inactive NGBs rely on other sources of funding to survive. As a result, most NGBs are overdependent on government funding and would find themselves in significant difficulties if that funding were reduced. The government, on the other hand, has a direct interest in ensuring that governing bodies in receipt of public funding have the system and structures necessary to make effective and efficient use of that funding. NGBs are the key to the delivery of sport in the country. For many years, the NGBs have survived despite their weakness rather succeeded because of their strength. Systematic and interrelated structures do not exist in the sport industry in Malaysia. It is vital to develop a modern sport parent body to associate the individual sport bodies and establish a network in partnership with NGBs. This will be a key component of change in the management of modern sport in Malaysia.

---

national sport policies in countries such as Australia, Singapore, India, and Malaysia would have repercussions in terms of financial allocations to either category of sport participation. Tensions will arise, especially when a small number of elite athletes compete for funds with a community sport program for the elderly that is aimed at a larger segment of the population. Countries in the region face this continuing dilemma, and absolute solutions are absent. What might be important for sport managers to think about is how to improve the mechanisms in place and how to balance priorities when deciding between the needs of the population and the aspirations of the country.

Managing Sport in South Asia, Southeast Asia, and Oceania

The concept of sport being a professional endeavor in South Asia, Southeast Asia, and Oceania follows a natural course in the global phenomenon and trend of managing sport professionally. The development of the regional sport industry has unquestionably progressed in recent years. Hong commented that 2002 was the Year of Asian Sport, during which the whole world was watching Asia (Hong, 2002). She was referring to the 2002 World Cup, which was jointly hosted by Japan and South Korea, as well as the Asian Games, which were held the same year in Busan, South Korea. The growth of Asian sport is more prominently evident in the sport primary industry structure that spilled over into a secondary industrial structure such as the management of sport facilities and arenas. An underlying assumption is that with the progress that South Asia, Southeast Asia, and Oceania are making in hosting sport events, sport management is developing on a parallel course in terms of human capital.

Economics of Sport in South Asia, Southeast Asia, and Oceania

That sport is big business in these regions is undisputed. In Australia the sport industry contributes A\$7.9 billion to the Australian economy and consequently generates employment for more than 90,000 people (Foreman, 2001). Foreman further stated that "including an imputed value for the volunteer contribution to sport of A\$1.6 billion, the industry ranks with the financial services, transport and defense in importance to Australian Gross Domestic Product (GDP)."

According to Manzenreiter (2007), although sport has been associated with the business sector for a long time, a straightforward equation of sport with profit making and commercialization is a recent phenomenon. This view is exemplified by the complexity of estimating the global market size of sport-related goods and services. The market value of the global sport industry was roughly made up of gate revenues for live sport events, television broadcasting rights fees, merchandising, sport sponsorships, and other related business activities. Although data on sport GDP in South Asia and Southeast Asia have not been comprehensively compiled to date (largely because sport is not considered or categorized as a revenue-generating sector in many developing countries), the annual budgetary allocations for sport from governments remain high or on the increase. An exception is Singapore, which recently announced that its sport GDP has crossed the S\$1 billion mark.

CASE STUDY

Singapore Sport Industry

In 2005 Oon Jin Teik, the chief executive of the Singapore Sports Council (SSC), envisioned the city-state's sporting future and the role of sport in the continuing economic development agenda of Singapore (Roberts, 2005). Singapore is a small, developed-status nation-state located in the Southeast Asia region. The mainstay of Singapore's economy is the financial and business industry. According to Roberts (2005),

> Since independence from Britain in the mid-1960s, Singapore has grown exponentially to become the financial and commercial hotspot of its region. Many of the world's leading corporations have regional headquarters in Singapore. They have been attracted by its stability, the quality of the communications infrastructure and the built environment, its proximity to the tremendously exciting growth markets of China and India. (p. 4)

Although Singapore does not possess world-renowned athletes and record breakers, it aspires to capitalize on the sport services sector as a major income generator for its economy and as an international operational hub for international sport organizations (ISOs).

According to Dr. Vivian Balakrishnan, the minister of Community Development, Youth and Sport,

> Singapore is a natural draw for sports spending, thanks to our friendly business environment, existing events assets and infrastructure, and sound strategies in cultivating a strong sports culture. Our sports industry value had crossed the $1 billion mark in 2007, placing us on course for our target of reaching a $2 billion GDP contribution by 2015 (Roberts, 2005)

Singapore has been campaigning in earnest to attract multinational sport companies to establish their business in the city-state, which resulted in the success of major international and regional sport events being held in Singapore in 2009 and 2010. Some examples of these international multisport megaevents are the Youth Olympics, Asian Youth Games, and the Men's Hockey Junior World Cup. With the Singapore government committed to growing its sport industry, SSC believes that more companies will realize its untapped potential. Mr. Oon also announced that the SSC would be issuing a request for proposals (RFP) for the Changi Motorsports Hub. "The SSC has spent the last few months refining the project specifications to make it a more compelling and attractive product for potential investors. Despite the current economic climate, potential investors have expressed positive interest in bidding for the project," he said (*Sports Investment*, 2009).

On the new media front, SSC's www.singapore sports.sg website recorded more than 3 million hits in just 10 months. The Asian Youth Games capitalized on the new media platform as its main broadcast medium. Speaking at the event, Mr. Kelven Tan, chief of sports marketing, emphasized that youths between the ages of 14 and 17 are the first generation in Asia to grow up with new technology and that they will be the next generation of direct consumers, alongside volunteer coaches, officials, and event organizers. "The Asian Youth Games offer consumer-driven companies the opportunity to reach out to youth across Asia in various media platforms that they understand. The Games can connect the unique identity of brands with the different characters and personalities of the events," he added (*Sports Investment*, 2009).

From Roberts (2005) and *Sports investment* (2009).

The globalization of sport meant that new sport market opportunities are constantly being discovered. With the proliferation of sport products and services in Western (European and North American) markets, Asian markets are now drawing the attention of major global sport players. An example is the marketing campaign of major European football clubs (such as Manchester United) that go on promotional tours through the region. Manzenreiter (2007) observed, "Generating systematic income from buying East Asian players to raise new opportunities for club merchandise sales, television deals and sponsorship is nowadays a widespread business plan" (p. 8) among European football clubs.

The field of sport management in Asia and Oceania is gradually changing in line with the rest of the world. Australia and New Zealand are already on the map, and South Asian and Southeast Asian countries are slowly making their presence felt. The progress that they are making now mirrors that of their Western counterparts. The process of sport globalization works two ways; apart from the fact that lifestyle changes are occurring, people must have the desire to accept the change. According to Hong,

> The desire of international organizations to conquer new markets has brought a new version of internationalization of sport to the Asian world. U.S. Major League Baseball, NBA basketball, NFL football and Europe's Championship League football are being watched by millions of Asian people through their domestic media networks. (Hong, 2002, p. 403)

The new markets appear to be tempting for marketers, especially when there is a demand for the product in the South Asia, Southeast Asia, and Oceania market. Asia as a whole is now riding on the prospect of China's burgeoning economy. Megaevents such as the Formula One Grand Prix are good revenue generators for local regional economies. For example, following the success of Sepang and Melbourne, Singapore wanted a piece of the action in hosting the event. Table 8.2 presents the number of attendees at the Grand Prix in Sepang and Melbourne.

Table 8.2 Formula One Grand Prix Attendance in Malaysia and Australia

Year	Malaysia	Australia
2007	115,000	105,000
2006	107,634	103,000
2005	106,442	118,200

Culture and Approaches to Management

Managing sport in a multiethnic, multicultural, and multireligious society, especially in Asia, requires special knowledge and skill. At the outset, it would be unwise to disregard the cultural differences that exist and the deeply embedded ways of life of the various societies (Abraham, 1988). Abraham argued further that, although cultural differences must be taken into account when making management decisions, they are not the main impediment that

necessarily affects the institutional structure of work in a systematic and consistent way over a prolonged period (Abraham, 1988, p. 59).

Abraham suggested that the management perspective (including for sport) must be directed toward creating an economic climate that enhances local initiative and entrepreneurship and that

> the value orientations must necessarily identify and develop within the context of the culture where development is to take place. The culture itself is to be seen not as a residual concept in isolation from the totality of economic, political and social concerns, but as integral to such concerns. The ideological basis for management, therefore, will be self-reliance rooted in the cultural dimension of development as a whole. (Abraham, 1988, p. 62)

Therefore, developing a managerial culture in South Asia, Southeast Asia, and Oceania is a unique effort, as suggested by Abraham (1988), whereby the sensitivity and integration of divergent sociocultural aspects are the essential element for success. Local values and good practices aside, Mendoza (1992) remarked that Asian managers were still not adept in scanning their own environments and lacked literacy in technology. In addition, Asian managers seemed to think in vague terms, did not seem to be aware of and appreciative of their own country's potential and untapped heritage, and did not look beyond the confines of their geographical shores. Mendoza's study focused on Southeast Asian managers more than 15 years ago, when advancement in information technology management was a major breakthrough in the region. But things have changed significantly from that time. Lately, a shift has occurred in the study of Asian managers that focuses less on the differences between Asian and Western sport managers and more on the unique aspects of the region that influence and shape how managers think and act. Hofstede (2007) believed that because management is about people, the values that people have determine the type of management styles that they adopt. In his extensive study, Hofstede found that the priorities of Indian managers differ from those of their American counterparts.

Hofstede divided the findings of his study into the five most important and least important perceived goals ascribed to successful business leaders and compared the perspectives of Indian and American managers. According to Hofstede, the first priority of Indian managers is securing "family interests," whereas their American counterparts most value the "growth of the business." The goal of "personal wealth" is important to both managers, although Indian managers place it as their third priority while the American managers rank it second (after "growth of the business").

Hofstede further found that American managers consider "staying within the law" as one of the five most important goals for a successful business leader. Indian managers, on the other hand, ascribe it as one of the least important. Interestingly, both agree that "responsibility toward employees" and "creating something new" are among the five least important priorities for a manager.

There are a number of implications that can be drawn from Hofstede's work. First, despite sociocultural and geographical differences, successful business leaders of the world ascribed to a certain, standard formula of success (such as diligence and hard work). Second, the motives that drive the leaders are as divergent as their backgrounds. A good example is the "family interests" focus favored by Indian managers. This cultural trait may be able

to shed some understanding on the sustainability of dynastic family-based companies over a long period of time, such as the Mittal Steel Company of India that rose to become one of the biggest steel manufacturers in the world. Conversely, American business leaders, who are more focused on "growth of business," are constantly looking at possibilities of expanding their business into new markets, which has resulted in the creation of multinational companies such as Exxon Mobil and McDonald's.

Similarly, Mendoza (1992) advised that local managers need to look objectively at their own cultural values, use them to filter practices that were based on Western or foreign values, and critically select practices from both local and Western or foreign values that support positive management practices. Mendoza further suggested an appropriate model of hybrid Asian managerial practice, as illustrated in table 8.3.

Asian managers were also thought to be able to contribute more to the organization if they were made to feel like part of a family, as Hofstede (2007) noted in his study of Indian managers. Mendoza also appeared to encourage the preservation of the

Table 8.3 Model of Hybrid Managerial Practice

Elements	Western	Eastern	Hybrid Eastern managerial practice
Management practice	Counseling	Counseling and advising	Group counseling and problem solving
Basic assumptions	The role of supervisor is to enable subordinate to set own directions for improvement.	The role of supervisor is that of a facilitator who can give advice and point to correct ways.	Supervisor should develop a caring, nurturing, and supportive role.
Values underlying practice	• Information • Direct and to the point • Task focus • Specificity	• Feelings • Indirect • Generality • Face • Nurturing	• Face • Specificity • Future orientation • Group orientation
Style	• One to one • Hard facts • Time orientation	• Autocratic • Avoidance	• Brotherly • Specificity • Caring • Effect on team's productivity
Techniques	• A formal step-by-step process • Can be confrontational	• Not known • Not specific	• Generate a familial climate • Put group pressure on individual to improve • Use informal leader to provide guidance • Foster group unity • Use input from customer

Compiled from Mendoza (1992).

paternalistic nature of Asian management because he believed that the value system had been shown to work in making an organization successful in the Asian context. Asian managers can benefit from ideas and theories developed from the West, but they still have to develop their own styles and techniques based on local values. By developing their own managerial practices based on local cultures and blending them with positive Western or foreign values, Asian managers can pioneer a new range of hybrid management theories and managerial practices suited to the local scenario. According to Chatterjee and Pearson (2003),

> As Asian management emerges as an area of intellectual and practical attention, no other managerial concern attains more significance than ethical dimension in ethically divergent contexts. This is particularly relevant as the challenges they present are rooted in the cultural, social, religious, political and managerial traditions of Asian countries. Responses to these challenges cannot come from development of Asian ethical codes of behaviour. Western approaches are based on individual freedom, democratic nuances, universalism of rules and a key focus on strategy. In contrast, attachment to extended family, deference to social interest, thrift, respect for authority and fulfilling traditional obligations are key Asian characteristics. Universalistic principles and practices of the mainstream management ideas need to be explicitly accommodative and responsive to Asian context-relevant imperatives.

For example, in Thailand, Chareanpunsirikul and Wood (2002) observed that when relating the Western theory of managerial roles (they used Mintzberg's) to an Asian hospitality industry setting, it appeared that the theory was applicable to Thailand managers (both Thai nationality and expatriates) in terms of the roles. The only differences appeared to be the work culture. Thai managers observed local cultural norms and procedures, where the work culture was highly dependent on negotiation, discussion, and bilateral interaction, whereas the expatriate managers appeared to be more directive in their role and task approach, as well as more unilateral in their interaction.

Hofstede (2007) stated that management problems remain the same over time but that their solutions differ from country to country. Although global business requires global management solutions, Hofstede was convinced that not all global solutions would be the best antidote to specific managerial problems and further stated that because "businesses have home countries, . . . these play an essential role in their effectiveness and their corporate identity" (p. 419). What Hofstede (2007) was suggesting was that for an international business to be successful in a particular Asian country, it must be sensitive to the core values that define a home country. Similarly, because countries in the region are defined by their philosophical, cultural, and religious roots (Chatterjee & Pearson, 2003), sport managers must be sensitive to these values when making decisions. For instance, religious holidays must be observed and locals must be consulted on the aspects. For example, planning a water-based sport event during the fasting month of Ramadan in Indonesia is completely out of the question, because fasting athletes must avoid swallowing water, whether accidentally or intentionally. Indonesia is the largest Muslim-majority country in the region. In observance of Ramadan, Muslims fast from dusk to dawn for a whole month and so must refrain from rigorous physical activity to conserve energy. Because Muslims use the lunar (not Gregorian) calendar to determine when Ramadan begins and ends, sport managers are advised to determine the matter before making any decision.

Training Sport Managers

Operating and managing today's sport industry efficiently requires extensive knowledge and skill. The industry demands that human resources be professionally prepared for the job and academically educated to function effectively in a variety of sport settings. Sport management is generally defined as "any combination of skills related to planning, organizing, directing, controlling, budgeting, leading, and evaluating within the context of an organization or department whose primary product or service is related to sports" (DeSensi et al., 1988). This definition had been applied extensively to the field in North America. A comparable situation can be observed in South Asia, Southeast Asia, and Oceania, where the sport industry has grown steadily over the years. This occurrence heightens the need for professionally qualified sport managers in every sector of the local sport industry.

Sport needs qualified, competent managers to manage it. Parks and Quarterman (2003) believed that career paths associated with sport management are not as well defined as they are in other vocational areas. Initially, sport managers are usually employed from visible groups such as professional sport or college athletics. Especially in Asia, this situation is typically exemplified by hiring a former professional footballer or a physical education teacher to become a sport director for a university's sport program. Although this formula might work to a certain extent, it is questionable whether their real expertise or training (as in the PE teacher's case) would be relevant to the unique aspects of sport management. The objective of physical education academic programs is to train and turn out physical education teachers (an example of curriculum content would be a course in human anatomy or sport physiology); the physical education curriculum was never designed to train sport managers (Lizandra, 1993). Parks commented that sport management exists in two forms (Parks & Quarterman, 2003):

a. Professional endeavor—a multitude of professional career paths that are available in the current job market
b. Professional academic preparation—academic pursuits in higher education institutions in the form of major courses as preparation for professional career paths

These two forms exist interdependently in South Asia, Southeast Asia, and Oceania. The academic preparatory programs are being given serious attention as the demand for skilled and competent managers in sport rises alongside the phenomenal growth of the industry. One clear example of the attention is a legal provision in the Malaysian Sports Development Act of 1997:

> The Minister (of Youth and Sports) could, towards the development of sports, take all the necessary actions towards encouraging the development of sports science in the institutions of higher learning in Malaysia and for that purpose shall extend all the assistance as he renders necessary.

This healthy and conducive environment boosted many institutions of higher learning, both public and privately funded, to begin offering sport science and sport-related academic programs (Radzi, 2000). The University of Malaya, the first university in Malaysia, started the initial baccalaureate program in sport

science in 1995 with three areas of specialization: sport management, sport psychology, and exercise physiology. So sport management as an academic program did not reach the Malaysian shores until 1995, although sport management activities had been in existence much earlier. More than two decades after Ohio University started its sport administration programs, the University of Malaya followed suit by becoming the first university in Malaysia to offer sport science as a degree program (Radzi, 2000) and one of the earliest in the region to do so.

In Australia the need for qualified sport managers also emerged as sport organizations and sport clubs began modernizing and evolving from adhocracy to organized, structured, and professional management practices, particularly in the wake of the globalization of the sport industry in the 1990s. Increasing commercialization and the pursuit of commoditization of local sport put pressure on local managers to equip themselves to gain an edge over their competitors. This condition triggered the movement of sport management academic programs in Australia. Smith and Westerbeek (2004) placed the beginning of academic sport management programs in Australia in 1991. The program is relatively young, and according to Smith and Westerbeek (2004),

> Presently, in a market comprising 37 public and two private universities, 10 institutions offer three-year, full-time bachelor degrees in sport management or administration, with a further six sport management majors in the area offered by other universities under the umbrella of more generic sport studies. Of the 10 bachelor degrees, five are embedded in commerce or business, three in arts, and two in applied science. Similarly, of the six sport management majors available, four are within applied science degrees and two are within arts degrees. Most of the institutions offering sport management degrees or majors in the context of applied science also offer similar qualifications in leisure or recreation management. A total of around 1,500 students are accepted into some form of sport, leisure or recreation management bachelor degree or major each year. This now exceeds exercise science (human movement and physical education) as the most populated sport-related topic studied in Australia. In fact, demand for sport management programmes continues to grow steadily while exercise science is diminishing in terms of student interest.

Staging Sport Megaevents in South Asia, Southeast Asia, and Oceania

The regions have hosted many international sport megaevents including the Olympic Games (Sydney 2002), the Commonwealth Games (Kuala Lumpur 1998), and the Asia Games (India and Thailand). Apart from international sport megaevents, regional multisport events (such as the South Asian Games and the Southeast Asian Games) and single-sport events (such as the Formula One Grand Prix, the Hockey World Cup, and the Badminton Thomas Cup) have also been organized. Malaysia became the first developing nation to host the Commonwealth Games in 1998, the second biggest multisport mega event in the world. The Commonwealth Games marked a major turning point for Malaysian sport. The Ministry of Youth and Sport of Malaysia made massive investment in infrastructure and economic activities to drive the development of local sport.

Regional sports play an important part in fostering stronger cooperation among the nations in the region. Regional sports have deeply embedded historical backgrounds that are often a result of the sociopolitical and economic dynamics among regional nation-states. As mentioned earlier in the chapter, all the regions organized themselves into regional cooperation entities such as the SAARC, ASEAN, and PIC. Later, interest developed to strengthen multilateral ties through sport and other social initiatives. For example, the first **South Asian Games (SAG)** was held in Kathmandu, Nepal, in 1984. The motivation for the event was to strengthen cooperation and relationships among South Asian countries through sport. Note that although Afghanistan is a member of the regional economic cooperative, the nation was barred from participating in the event because of allegations of human rights violations. The event was initially held annually, but from 1985 onward it was held every other year.

The **Southeast Asian (SEA) Games** were initially styled as the Southeast Asian Peninsular Games (SEAP). The first SEAP Games were held in Bangkok in 1959, and it too had an objective of promoting regional cooperation through sport. The 9th SEAP Games held in Kuala Lumpur saw the unveiling of a new name for the event—the SEA Games. The SEA Games are a biennial event. The 2009 Games were hosted by Laos, and the 2011 games will be hosted by Indonesia.

The **Pacific Games**, which began in 1963, were formerly known as the South Pacific Games. First hosted by Fiji, the event was held every four years. According to the Pacific Games Council, the objective of the Games was, among other things, to create "bonds of kindred friendship and brotherhood amongst people of the countries of the Pacific Region through sporting exchange without any distinction as to race, religion or politics." The 2007 Pacific Games were hosted by Samoa, and the 2011 Games will be hosted by New Caledonia. Papua New Guinea has won the bid to host the 2015 Pacific Games.

We have so far seen that South Asia, Southeast Asia, and Oceania have been hosting major megaevents, including the 2000 Sydney Olympics and the 2010 Commonwealth Games in New Delhi. The regions are also unique in that countries that are dissimilar in various aspects can still be considered neighbors. Ironically, the disparities have brought countries in these regions together. One of the challenges of staging mega sport events in these regions is negotiating these disparities. Achieving this goal requires a thorough understanding of the various issues that surround and shape a particular region. Sport marketers must understand the various political, philosophical, cultural, and religious norms that affect the value system of the country. Sport marketers in northern Thailand may be able to list an alcoholic beverage manufacturer as a major event sponsor, but having the same event sponsorship in southern Thailand would draw protests from the district's majority Muslim population. Issues of sustainability and social and environmental impacts are also raised when countries host sport megaevents. The 2010 Commonwealth Games in New Delhi faced these issues, as described in the case study.

Summary

The evolution of sport in South Asia, Southeast Asia, and Oceania saw the development of individual life skills and talents, the assimilation of Western-based sport, and participation at the international level in a number of Western sports. Another important point is that hitherto, sport has always been a public concern. The involvement of the private sector, especially in terms of funding and sponsorship, was not as prevalent then as it is now because of the social context of sport participation. Lately, sport in South Asia, Southeast Asia, and Oceania has developed into a commercial endeavor. Multinational corporations have invested millions of dollars in sport programs. The local sport management circumstances were largely influenced by the development of this field in other, developed countries in North

CASE STUDY

Staging the 2010 Commonwealth Games in Delhi, India

The Delhi 2010 Commonwealth Games, the 19th installment of the Games, were held in October 2010. This was the first time that the Commonwealth Games were staged in India, and only the second time that an Asian country hosted the world's second largest multisport event, following the hosting of the 16th Games by Kuala Lumpur in 1998. Delhi won the rights to host in 2003 at the Commonwealth Games Federation General Assembly in Jamaica, eliminating Hamilton, Canada, for the rights. The Indian government and the Delhi Commonwealth Games Organizing Committee began work in earnest immediately following the conferment of rights to ensure that the Games would be a success, thereby solidifying the status of India as a key player in organizing international sport events in the region and the world.

Although the preparations were not all smooth sailing (with issues such as corruption and delayed constructions that threatened to stall delivery of the venues in time for the Games), problems did not slow the rapid pace of development work undertaken by the government of India. Billed as the most expensive Commonwealth Games in history (the cost reportedly escalated to US$1.6 billion), major infrastructure was designed and mobilized to ensure that the Games would be able to showcase the technological advancement of the new India. The 2010 Games also attempted to portray India as an environmentally friendly player that is concerned with the sustainability issues surrounding the hosting of the event through the concept of the Green Games, a program jointly undertaken by the government of India and the United Nations Environment Program.

This effort, however, did not fully address, let alone eradicate, environmental issues, such as the demolition of the national forest (Siri Forest) in favor of a Games facility and the construction of the Games village that was in breach of ecological principles. In both cases, the government was awarded the rights by the Supreme Court of India on the premise that the development would benefit the country in the long run. These are some of the issues that must be addressed by the Indian government in its pursuit of organizing major international mega sport events. The immediate challenge for India as a country is striking a balance between modernizing the Indian sport landscape (both the infrastructure and the people) and preserving the values that define what it means to be an Indian in India. Other sport managers in the region also face this predicament—deciding what to hold on to and what to let go, all in the name of sport.

America, Europe, and Asia. The region unsurprisingly follows similar assimilation processes and has always displayed readiness to adopt and accept modern sports. Issues that plagued regional sports, especially in South Asia, Southeast Asia, and Oceania, have also affected the management of modern sport, such as overreliance on government funding, sport governance, modernization needs, moral and ethical issues in sport, and the dilemma between the priorities for mass sport participation and the aspiration for sporting excellence.

From observation, the management of sport and sport organizations in South Asia, Southeast Asia, and Oceania is in need of development and modernization. Many reasons could be behind this matter, but one thing remains for certain—sport has never failed to receive support, particularly from governments and sponsors.

Clearly, the role of the government is central to the development of sport in Asia. This is evident mainly through the financial allocations and expenditures on sport made by governments as well as the promulgation of sport-related legislation that some may see as controlling mechanisms. Some factions deem this control appropriate on the premise that governments are merely accounting for public expenditures in sport as opposed to dictating the direction of local sport. A danger is that future expenditures and development of public sport programs will be for only a selected few elitist sports. For example, funding may be concentrated on sport events that have the potential to bring fame and fortune to the country, and spending would be limited for grassroots mass sport.

As with any discipline, sport management goes through the professionalization process (Koehler & Lupcho, 1990). Essentially, this process covers three phases (Parks & Quarterman, 1998):

◆ Phase 1—building of theoretical foundations and body of knowledge
◆ Phase 2—creation of a distinctive subculture and finally
◆ Phase 3—sanction and acceptance by the community

This region appears to have gone through the first phase and be well into the second phase, although Oceania may have completed the process. For instance, the Sport Association of Australia and New Zealand (SMAANZ), which aimed at "facilitating ongoing professional conduct of sport management," was established in 1995 as the governing body for sport management professionals. Local scholars in Asian sport management are being trained locally and abroad for that same purpose. The establishment of the Asian Association for Sport Management (AASM) in 2002 signified the start of the second phase, which would speed up the progress into the final phase, when the community would be aware of the need to have professionals managing sport in Asia.

? Review and Discussion Questions

1. What traditional and adopted sports are the most popular in countries in this region?
2. What are the roles of the public sector in sport organizational structures in the region?
3. Discuss how colonial rule influenced and shaped sport development in the region.
4. How has the global sport industry affected sport in this region? Do you think that the effects have been good or bad?
5. Assess the difference between managing sport in the West and in South Asia, Southeast Asia, and Oceania.
6. Discuss the economic trends that are important to sport in the region and what opportunities these might bring for sport organizations, sponsors, or other businesses.

Sport in Northeast Asia

Yong Jae Ko, PhD
University of Florida, USA

Di Xie, PhD
Active Sport International Co., Ltd., China

Kazuhiko Kimura, MS
Waseda University, Japan

Chapter Objectives

After studying this chapter, you will be able to do the following:

- Define Northeast Asia as an economic and geophysical continent
- Be familiar with the sport governance systems in China, Japan, and South Korea
- Compare and contrast the approaches taken by China, Japan, and South Korea in governing their respected sport systems
- Identify the major legislations enacted by nations, particularly China, Japan, and South Korea, for sport development
- Understand the arms race among China, Japan, and South Korea in Olympic sports
- Identify major international and continental sport events held in Northeast Asia

Key Terms

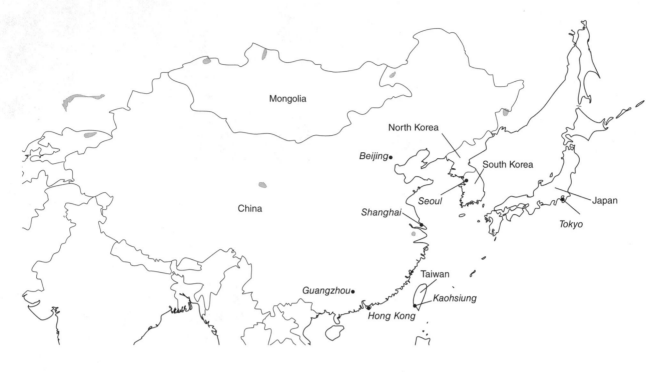

Key Events

FIFA 2002 World Cup Korea and Japan, first FIFA World Cup event held in Asia.

1988 Seoul Olympic Games led to a substantial increase in sport interest among South Koreans, which helped the implementation of the first Five-Year National Sports Promotion Plan.

2008 Beijing Olympic Games saw China, Japan, and South Korea win a combined 71 percent of the total medals awarded. More than 11,000 athletes from over 200 countries participated in 28 sports and 302 events.

2009 East Asian Games, Hong Kong, fifth East Asian Games, hosted more than 2,300 athletes who competed in 22 sports.

2010 Asian Games in Guangzhou, China, hosted athletes from countries throughout East Asia, Southeast Asia, and the Middle East who competed in 42 sports, 28 of which were Olympic sports and 14 were not.

Key People

Zhengliang He, currently the honorary president of the Chinese Olympic Committee, chairman of the International Olympic Committee's Culture and Olympic Education Commission.

Chiharu Igaya, president of the Japan Triathlon Union (JTU) and Japan Olympic Academy, joined the International Olympic Committee in 1982.

Kun-Hee Lee, honorary president of the Korean Olympic Committee since 1996 and a member of the International Olympic Committee since 1996.

Peng Liu, director of the State General Administration of Sport in China and president of the Chinese Olympic Committee.

Yong Sung Park, member of the International Olympic Committee since 2002, where he serves on the highly influential Marketing Commission.

Un Yong Kim, vice president of the IOC for many years and president of the World Taekwondo Federation until mid-2000, a major figure in the sport industry of Korea and the Olympic Movement.

Apowerful sport boom has been under way in Asia, particularly in Northeast Asia, over the last three decades, evidenced by the successful staging of the Seoul Summer Olympic Games in 1988, the Nagano Winter Olympic Games in 1998, the 2002 World Cup co-hosted by Japan and South Korea, and the 2008 Beijing Olympics. The boom is also evidenced by the success of athletes from nations in Northeast Asia in various international competitions. This chapter introduces the sport industry in various nations in Northeast Asia, specifically examining the structure of the sport industry and the policies and issues concerning its development in three core nations—China, Japan, and South Korea. Also, the influence of geopolitical and cultural factors on sport governance in these three countries will be reviewed.

Geography and Background of Northeast Asia

There is no commonly accepted version of the geographical makeup of Northeast Asia (NEA). According to Kim (2004), NEA is a region that encompasses Greater China (including Hong Kong, Macau, and Taiwan), Japan, Mongolia, North Korea, South Korea, and the Russian Far East. The United Nations Environment Programme (2004) defines NEA as a subregion of Asia comprising five countries: China (including Hong Kong, Macau, and Taiwan), Japan, Mongolia, North Korea, and South Korea. This area "has the highest population of all the subregions with a total of 1.48 billion people" (United Nations Environment Programme, 2004, p. 9). While discussing sport in this region, this chapter focuses on the three biggest sport nations in the region in Asia—China, Japan, and South Korea.

The countries in this region are rising in economic power in the world. China (including Hong Kong, Macau, and Taiwan), Japan, and South Korea collectively accounted for about one-fourth of world GDP in 2000 (Kim, 2004). As of September 2002, NEA was home to the world's five largest holders of foreign-exchange reserves: Japan (US$443,09 billion, or 19.3 percent of the global total), China (US$259.43 billion, or 11.3 percent of the global total), Taiwan (US$156.12 billion, or 6.8 percent of the global total), South Korea (US$117.09 billion, or 5.1 percent of the global total), and Hong Kong (US$108.20 billion, or 4.8 percent of the global total) (Kim, 2004, p. 8).

Besides those amazing economic strengths, NEA consists of people of racial, linguistic, and cultural complexity. Although NEA nations have their own distinct linguistic forms of expression, many have their roots in the Chinese language.

The cultures of the NEA countries can be labeled as neo-Confucian because the ideology of Confucianism is their shared common cultural root (Hu, 2006). As a set of ethical and philosophical beliefs, Confucianism developed from the teachings of an ancient Chinese scholar called Confucius, who lived in the 6th century BC (Yao, 2000).

China, the world's largest country by population, is home to more than 1.33 billion people (www.cpirc.org.cn/en/eindex.htm). The world's population is now nearly 6.7 billion, so about one in every five people on earth is Chinese. Physically, China is the third largest country in the world after Russia and Canada, and the largest nation in Asia, encompassing an area of 9,596,960 square kilometers (U.S. Department of State, 2009). China has 34 province-level administrative units, including 4 municipalities, 23 provinces (including Taiwan), 5 autonomous regions, and 2 special districts. China's economy has experienced a more than 10-fold increase in GDP since 1978 after changing from a centrally planned system to a market-oriented economy. Reforms by China's Communist government started in the late 1970s with the phasing out of collectivized agriculture. Restructuring expanded to include the gradual liberalization of prices, fiscal decentralization, increased autonomy for state enterprises, the foundation of a diversified banking system, the development of stock markets, the rapid growth of the nonstate sector, and the opening to foreign trade and investment (Central Intelligence Agency, 2010). Measured on a purchasing power parity basis that adjusts for price differences, China in 2008 stood as the second largest economy in the world after the United States, although its large population means that per-capita income is still in the lower-middle range (Central Intelligence Agency, 2010). Today, China plays an important role in the global economy.

The development of the sport industry in China has gone through four stages: the formation stage (1985–1990), the market-oriented development stage (1991–2001), the sport industry revitalization stage (2002–2008), and the post–Beijing Olympic stage (2008–present). The mid- and late-1980s was an important period in the development of the sport industry in China. Before 1990 China never had the opportunity to host a high-profile international sporting event. With steady economic growth, Beijing hosted the country's first large-scale international sport event, the 11th Asian Games, in 1990. China invested ¥2.5 billion (US$525 million) to build or renovate facilities to stage the event. The Beijing Asian Games served as a precursor to China's sport facilities construction boom, because the country went on to bid for the 2000 Summer Olympics.

After the successful hosting of the Beijing Asian Games in 1990, China became an attractive place for a variety of international events because of its rapid economic growth. A professional football league was formed in 1994, and a professional basketball league followed in 1995. During this period, sport media became a strong player in the promotion of the sport industry in the country. In 1993 China hosted its first Sporting Goods Fair. More than 200 manufacturers displayed their products. During the sport industry revitalization stage, the entire nation had one focus: to make the 2008 Olympics the most successful ever in the history of the Olympic Movement. Marketing through sport for nonsport products and marketing of sport products became the main themes of this stage. How to use and maintain the sport facilities built and used in the Olympic Games, how to maintain the level of sport consumption, and how to strengthen the sporting goods market and develop the sport service industry are some of the main issues of the post–Beijing Olympic stage.

Japan has the 11th largest population in the world with a little more than 127 million people (U.S. Department of State, 2009). Its national gross income is the highest in the subregion (United Nations Environment Programme, 2004). Administratively, Japan is subdivided into 47 prefectures (or subnational jurisdictions). After experiencing tremendous growth in the years from 1960 to 1990, the Japanese economy suffered a severe recession in early 1990s. Slow recovery has occurred since the economic downturn. Japan's GDP in 2008 was US$4.844 trillion.

According to Cheng (2006), the development of the sport industry in Japan can be divided into six eras. The six eras include the beginning era (1880–1940), the expanding era (1950–1960), the highly developing era (1960–1970), the maturing era (1970–1980), the transiting era (1980–1990), and the second growing era (1990–2000). During the beginning era, modern sport was introduced to Japan from the West. The Mizuno Corporation, the world's oldest sporting goods company, was established in the early 20th century during this era (Harada, 2010).

Many sport facilities were built in the expanding era. Leisure sport took shape during the highly developing era. The period from 1980 to 1990 saw the booming of health clubs as Japanese participation in various recreational or health-related sports such as golf increased tremendously. The government recognized the sport sector as an industry during this era (Harada, 2010). Professionalism and commercialization in sport were the two key traits of the second growth era in the sport industry in Japan. For example, the Japanese Soccer League, or J League, was formed in 1991. The sport industry in Japan has experienced another growth period in first decade of the 21st century.

Compared with China and Japan, South Korea has a relatively small population (48,379,392 people in 2008) (U.S. Department of State, 2009). Geographically, its land area covers 98,480 square kilometers. Because of the rapid growth of its economy, South Korea was labeled one of the "four dragons" in Asia (alongside Hong Kong, Singapore, and Taiwan) in the 1980s. It has since become one of the most economically dominant nations of Asia. In 2008 its GDP was US$1.278 trillion (U.S. Department of State, 2009).

The sport industry experienced a great leap in the 1980s after the nation successfully hosted the Seoul Asian Games in 1986 and the Seoul Olympic Games in 1988. The Japan–Korea World Cup in 2002 was another stimulus to the sport industry in Korea. Professional sport, amateur sport, and sport events play an important role in the 21st century in Korea. Collectively, they were valued at approximately $348 million (Cheng, 2006). Specifically, the professional sport market alone is about US$246 million. According to Kim (2004), the total number of spectators for professional sport games was more than 20 million in 2001.

Learning Activity

Research and write a brief report to describe the implications of Northeast Asia's strategic significance in the world economy for sport industry managers.

Sport in Northeast Asia

To depict the status and development of the sport industry in NEA, it is necessary to conduct a detailed appraisal of the major sport nations in the region—China, Japan, and South Korea—because they have become so dominant on the world's sport stage. Figure 9.1 is an illustration of the total medal count of China, Japan, and South Korea in each of the Olympic Games from 1976 through 2008. The combined medal count of these three countries as a percentage of the overall medals won by all Asian nations in the past eight Olympic Games, including the 2008 Beijing Olympic Games, is revealed in figure 9.2. As figure 9.2 shows, the medals won by athletes from China, Japan, and South Korea collectively made up a large percentage of all Olympic medals won by Asian competitors. In the Beijing 2008 Olympic Games, the three nations collectively fetched nearly one-fourth of the gold medals.

The following section provides an overview of sport development in Northeast Asia. Also included is an examination of the issues related to

sport governance, such as government agencies, sport-related government legislation and policies, and nongovernmental agencies and organizations in sport in Northeast Asia, particularly in each of China, Japan, and South Korea. The last part of the section examines the organized sport system in each of the nations.

Sport in China

Although China is known for its martial arts and table tennis, many other sports are popular, such as football, basketball, badminton, and Chinese chess.

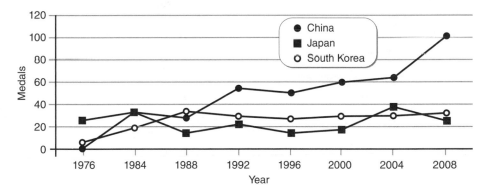

Figure 9.1 Total medal count of China, Japan, and South Korea in the Olympic Games from 1976 through 2008.

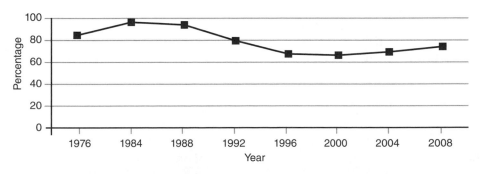

Figure 9.2 The combined medal count of China, Japan and South Korea as a percentage of the medal count of all Asian nations from 1976 through 2008.

CASE STUDY

Arms Race in Olympic Competition Among Nations in Northeast Asia

Japan and South Korea collectively received 31 medals, accounting for 82 percent of all medals awarded to Asian nations in the 1976 Montreal Olympic Games. The return of China to Olympic competition in 1984 not only drastically increased the number of medals won by the Asian nations but also started an arms race among these three Northeast Asian countries. At the Los Angeles Olympic Games, Chinese and Japanese athletes won the same number of medals (32) for their respective countries, and South Korean Olympians won 19 medals. The combined medal count of these three countries accounted for 92 percent of the overall number of medals conferred to Asian Olympic competitors. At the Athens Olympic Games, Asian Olympians took home 181 medals, of which 130 were contributed by China, Japan, and South Korea combined, accounting for 66 percent of the total medals won by Asian countries. Among the 220 medals awarded to Beijing Olympic participants from various Asian nations, 156, or 71 percent, were won by these three nations (100 by China, 25 by Japan, and 31 by South Korea). The medal-winning trends over the years have several interesting characteristics.

1. Since the 1988 Seoul Olympic Games, South Korea has become a noteworthy Olympic medal producer, outmatching Japan in the next three Olympic Games. Its medal count has been consistent between 27 and 33.

2. Japan dropped out of the second-place position as an Olympic medal-producing powerhouse in Asia after the 1984 Los Angeles Olympic Games. Its Olympic medal count decreased substantially from 32 at the Los Angeles Games to 14 at the 1988 Seoul Games, 22 at the 1992 Barcelona Games, 14 at the 1996 Atlanta Games, and 18 at the 2000 Sydney Games. In the 2004 Athens Games, however, Japan regained second-place position over South Korea. Its medal count surpassed the nation's best performance in history at the 1984 Los Angeles Games, reaching 37. In the recently finished Beijing Olympic Games, its medal count fell again to 25.

3. The domination by China, Japan, and South Korea in Asia is gradually slipping. The medals won by these three nations together accounted for 92 percent of the total medals awarded to the Asian Olympians at the Los Angeles Olympic Games. But the percentage was down to around 66 percent at the 2004 Athens Olympic Games. It went up slightly to 71 percent at the 2008 Beijing Olympic Games (because of the unprecedented performance of the Chinese athletes). This trend implies that a greater number of Asian nations are becoming stronger Olympic medal contestants. In 1984 the national anthems of only six Asian nations were sung at that Olympic Games. Two decades later, athletes from 16 Asian nations had the opportunity to stand on the medal award podiums at the 2004 Athens Olympic Games. Seventeen Asian Countries were represented in the medal chart of the 2008 Beijing Olympic Games.

4. The return of China to Olympic competition in 1984 brought a new sense of competition among nations in Asia.

Besides the just mentioned characteristics, the medal-winning trends are a microcosm of the political and economic competition among these three nations. Historically, animosity existed for a long time between Japan and its two close neighbors. Japan invaded China and Korea multiple times over the last two centuries. This animosity has found its way into various geopolitical and economic competitions and rivalries among the three nations.

These sports have high participation rates, consumer following, and spectatorship (Xiong, 2007). Currently, the portion of the Chinese population that participates in sport is less than 30 percent. According to Chou and Gao (1999), the sport population in China was defined as those who take part in sport activities two or three times a week, for more than a half hour each time, and at proper exercise intensity. In large metropolitan areas, the number may be higher. According to a report released recently by the Center for Monitoring the Chinese Economy that describes the patterns of sport participation of Chinese in metropolitan areas (D2PD.com, 2006), 67.9 percent of those surveyed said that they had a desire to participate in sport and physical activities. About 71.4 percent of them indicated that they watched sport programming on television regularly. Close to one-third (32.9 percent) of the respondents mentioned that they spent money for sporting clothes. Among the surveyed participants, 30.2 percent had purchased sport-related books, magazines, and newspapers.

According to buyusainfo.net (*Sporting goods*, 2006), the Chinese sporting goods market was worth over US$2 billion in 2004 and had an annual growth rate of 12 to 15 percent. Currently, there are more than 3,200 sporting goods manufacturers, wholesalers, and retailers in China (Chinese Sporting Goods Federation, 2005). According to the International Sporting Goods Manufacturers Association, approximately 65 percent of sporting goods and 70 percent of athletic shoes sold in the world were manufactured in China by Chinese sporting goods manufacturers. Nevertheless, many of these companies are in their infancy stage. Less than a handful of them have a strong international presence and brand recognition, such as LI-NING. Household sporting equipment is the main line of production of many Chinese sporting goods manufacturer. Foreign countries such as the United States, Japan, and Germany are still the source of the equipment and gear used in important domestic and international games. For example, the statistics from China's Swimming Equipment Commission indicate that 80 percent of specialized swimming products in China are imported. Elite Chinese swimmers often prefer imported brands, such as Speedo or Arena, to inexpensive, low-end products provided by domestic companies.

The gross domestic sport product (GDSP) of the Chinese sport industry was around US$13 billion in 2004 ("The Tremendous Potential of the Sport Industry in China," 2006). The figure accounts for approximately 0.7 percent of China's GDP. In its sport reform and development strategic plan published in 2000, the Chinese government set a goal for the Chinese sport industry to increase its GDSP so that it would account for 1.5 percent of the nation's GDP in 2010 (State General Administration of Sport, 2000).

With the growth of the sport industry in China, many foreign sport agencies have started operations in China. IMG, Octagon, Infront, Frontier, and Detsu are a few names on the list. The NFL, NBA, and MLB all have branch offices in China. Take IMG as an example. Asia has been a huge part of IMG's international expansion. IMG China was founded in 1979. Since then, IMG China has been responsible for founding and shaping many of the professional leagues in China, including those for badminton, football, and basketball.

Sport in Japan

As for traditional sport, Japan is known for judo, karate, and sumo. These sports existed long before the introduction of Western sports such as baseball, basketball, football, and so on. "Sumo is said to be Japan's national sport. It has a nearly 2,000 year history and could boast of professionals as far back as several hundred years ago" (Web Japan, 2009, p. 1). Baseball was introduced to Japan in 1872. Track and field, rugby, football, and ice skating were introduced to the country during the 1870s. Among nontraditional sports, baseball is one of the most popular spectator sports in Japan. Since the inception of the J League in 1993, football (soccer) is gaining popularity. "Soccer has now become the second most widely practiced sport among boys in elementary school after baseball" (Web Japan, 2009, p. 2).

The National Sports Festivals (winter, summer, and autumn) are held each year. Athletes compete in skiing and ice skating at the winter festival. The summer events include swimming, boating, and sailing. Track and field, gymnastics, and various ball games are among the athletic events included at the autumn festival. The first National Sports Festival was held in 1946 for the purpose of reviving sport and raising the morale of Japanese citizens (Web Japan, 2009).

The Emperor's Trophy is awarded to the prefecture that earns the most points in the competition. The Japanese government has designated the second Monday of October as Sports Day, declaring it a national holiday to promote the importance of sport and commemorate the Tokyo Olympics.

According to the results of a national survey conducted by the Sasakawa Sports Foundation (2008),

Beijing International Marathon

Since 2002 the Beijing International Marathon (BIM) has represented a successful cooperation between the Chinese Athletic Association (CAA), a government organization, and Octagon, a foreign sport marketing agency. The BIM is an annual race that has been held every October in Beijing since 1981. It is one of the International Association of Athletics Federation's (IAAF) Gold Label Road Races. Besides the main marathon, several other races are held, including a half marathon, 10K, minimarathon (6.8 km), and a kids' run. The organizer of the event is the CAA. The American sport agency Octagon has been the event promoter since 2002.

Octagon is a well-known sport marketing firm. In 2008 *SportsBusiness Journal* named Octagon the Sports Agency of the Year. Octagon, a unit of Interpublic Group, represents such athletes as Chris Paul, Michael Phelps, John Elway, Jelena Jankovic, and famous marathoner Paula Radcliffe. Octagon also represents corporate clients who want to become involved with sporting events. Its services include athlete representation, event management, TV rights sales and distribution, licensing and merchandising, TV production, sponsorship consulting, and new media. Octagon manages more than 3,200 events each year (9 events per day) worldwide.

Octagon began working in China in 2001. Today it influences the sport industry in China in the following areas:

- Sales and sport events, including sponsorship sales, event management, and representation. The main events promoted by Octagon are the BIM, the Hangzhou International Marathon, the Beijing Golf Open, and World Cup Gymnastics.
- Sponsorship consulting, including bid development, strategic planning, concept creation, implementation, and measurement. The main clients are Manulife, Samsung, Yanjing Beer, Heng Yuan Xiang Group, and COC.

Cooperation History

To try to ensure the long-term commercial promotion and marketing of its national teams and events, the CAA signed an eight-year contract with Octagon in March 2002. The CAA and Octagon work together to build up national awareness of athletics. Octagon pays a guaranteed fee to the CAA each year for the commercial rights to all promotional, advertising, marketing, media, and broadcasting related to CAA events and national teams.

Based on that agreement, Octagon has owned the BIM event in association with the CAA since 2002. Its main responsibilities include

- executing all event operations, marketing, promotion, and athlete recruitment;
- selling and servicing sponsorships; and
- controlling TV relationship and rights sales.

Results

Between 2002 and 2008 BIM experienced great changes, transforming itself from an unknown event to an IAAF Gold Label event (top eight) and from no sponsorship to US$2.5 million in sponsorship revenues from such global brands as Nike, Swatch, and Honda and local brands such as Heng Yuan Xiang Group (one of China's leading knitwear producers) and China Life Insurance. BIM attracted about 30,000 runners in 2008 and 1.5 million TV viewers, and a media equivalent value of over US$10 million. The event is broadcast live on CCTV5 in China and TBS in Japan every year.

Lessons

A sport agency that wants to develop its core businesses in China should have strong connections with government organizations, either at the national level (such as the CAA under the GASC) or at the prefecture level (Hangzhou City Sports Bureau) for local events. Without getting approval or permission from the appropriate government organization, running an event and selling related sponsorship services are difficult. Another challenge is that if the government does not officially approve an event, the company may have difficulty promoting the event to mainstream media channels, leading to poor exposure and no event sponsorship.

The sport industry in China is a people business. Just as networking is important in the United States, so is *guanxi* in China. With cities such as Beijing, Shanghai, and Guangzhou hosting more international and national events each year, sport agencies like Octagon should have a great opportunity for growth in the near future. But because of the economic downturn that began at the end of 2008 and the changes in sport culture that occurred after the 2008 Olympic Games, the speed of that growth may vary in coming years.

the most popular physical activities in Japan were leisurely walking (30.8 percent), fitness walking (22.4 percent), calisthenics and light exercises (17.5 percent), bowling (15.1 percent), weight training (11.1 percent), swimming (9.0 percent), bathing in the sea (8.9 percent), and golfing (8.7 percent). "The number of sports enthusiasts who exercise regularly more than once a week was estimated to be 58.31 million or 71.9 percent of the people ages 20 and older in Japan" (p. 3). Although baseball is the most popular nontraditional spectator sport in Japan, it ranked only 18th in terms of the participation rate of Japanese adults.

In terms of the level of engagement in exercise or sport, 20.3 percent of the respondents showed satisfaction, 23.2 percent wished to do more, and 43.6 percent "wished to do exercise/sports but cannot." Because of the continual promotion of the importance of exercise and sport, the population that is "not particularly interest in exercise/sports" has decreased drastically from 19.1 percent in 2006 to 12.8 percent in 2008 (p. 19).

According to Web Japan (2009), total spending by individuals and businesses in Japan for sport equipment, training and instruction, stadiums, arenas and other facilities, admission to events, and so on were about US$52.74 billion in 1996 data. Specifically, Japanese spent US$5.14 billion on golf equipment and US$3.63 billion in skiing, skating, and snowboard-related equipment. The Waseda University Research Institute for Sport Business has estimated that Japanese GDSP was about US$100 billion in 2001, accounting for approximately 2 percent of Japan's GDP. About 73 percent of it was contributed by sport services, including professional leagues and teams, sport facilities, sport-related travel, and educational expenses. The GDSP estimation included sport media and gambling. Sponsorship sales, however, were excluded (Kimura, 2007). Although the Japanese GDSP is about half that of the United States, its contribution to the nation's GDP (about 2 percent) is truly impressive. According to Wolfers (n.d.), the GDSP of the United States is also around 2 percent of the country's GDP. These expenditure

Structure of the Sport Industry in Japan

As in other nations in Northeast Asia, the sport industry in Japan has grown tremendously over the last decade. This case provides a brief illustration of the sport industry in Japan.

Harada (2010) maintained that the sport industry in Japan has three key sectors: the sporting goods industry, the sport facility industry, and the sport service and information industry. As shown in the model depicted in figure 9.3, interactions among these three sport industry sectors have created several composite sectors, such as the sport facility management industry, the sport-related distribution industry (i.e., the industry created to move products from manufacturers to retail stores to consumers), and the hybrid sport industry. The interactions of the sport industry with other industries have also created some other industry segments such as sport medicine, food sold in sport facilities and events, and sport facilities and events as tourism destinations. E-sport, a new phenomenon, is a joint product of the information technology industry and the sport industry.

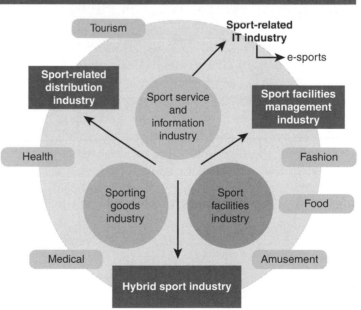

Figure 9.3 The Japanese sport industry model. The interactions among the three main sport industry sectors in Japan have created additional sectors.

Adapted, by permission, from M. Harada, 2010, "Development of the sport industry: Japan's experience." Paper presented at the 2010 Annual Conference of the Asian Association for Sport Management, Kuala Lumpur, Malaysia.

figures collectively suggest that the sport industry in Japan is healthy and promising.

The 2011 Tohoku earthquake and tsunami devastated not only the Japanese economy but also the nation's sport industry. Such devastation has cast some uncertainty on the future of the Japanese sport industry. After the disaster, various Japanese professional sport leagues canceled their 2011 seasons. A number of international sport organizations also rescheduled events or moved them elsewhere.

Sport in South Korea

As for traditional sports, Korea is known for tae-kwondo and ssireum. These sports existed long before the introduction of Western sports, such as baseball, basketball, and football. Taekwondo is Korea's national sport. Since 1973 when the World Taekwondo Federation (WTF) was formed as the legitimate governing body, the traditional martial art of taekwondo has spread to 191 countries and WTF has become one of the largest sport organizations. Taekwondo became an official event at the 2000 Sydney Olympics (WTF, 2010).

The modern history of sport in Korea began in the late 19th and early 20th centuries when Western countries, notably England and the United States, introduced their modern sports such as football (1882), baseball (1905), basketball (1903), and volleyball (1917) to Korea through missionary work and business (Ok, 2007). Today, sport is closely linked with Korean national identity. Sport plays a role in continuing to change Korean society with emphasis on cultural diffusion and national assimilation (Ok, 2007). Historically, sport has been used as a venue for political, ideological, and symbolic competition between nations (Chehabi, 2001). International sporting events such as the Olympic Games have been used as a political tool to generate national identity and prestige (Stevenson & Nixon, 1987). Athletic success in megaevents (the Olympic Games and FIFA World Cup) is considered an achievement that represents the power of a country. This is the case in South Korea, where the increased patriotism inspired by international sport has been used as political means of creating national identity and assimilating various groups.

The international sporting community recognized the Korean success over the last two decades in hosting the 1988 Seoul Olympics and the 2002 Korea–Japan World Cup. Considering the size and population of Korea, its success in the international sport arena has been impressive. Golf, marathon, taekwondo, judo, wrestling, archery, shooting, badminton, field hockey, and short-track speed skating are among the sports in which Koreans have excelled. The Korean national football team has qualified for the FIFA World Cup finals six times, five of them continuously since 1986, an achievement unparalleled in Asia. Many professional football and baseball players have been recruited by major professional clubs in Japan, the United States, and Europe. In the past decade, Korean golfers have won LPGA and PGA tournaments, which has facilitated phenomenal growth of the sport in Korea (Korean Overseas Information Service, 2008).

This fast-growing sport industry needs highly talented and educated professionals to manage organizations and people. Currently, sport management and marketing is the most popular area of study within the field of sport and physical education. Interest in and awareness of this field continues to increase.

Sport as an industry segment in South Korea was born with production of sport apparel and shoes to export in the 1970s (Ministry of Culture, Sport and Tourism, 2006). Today, the sport industry has become one of the fastest growing industries. Measured by annual revenue generated by sport organizations and consumer expenditure, the sport industry increased in size from US$17.9 billion in 2003 to US$19.7 billion in 2005 and US$20.7 billion in 2006 ($1 = 1,000 won). The industry makes up 2.24 percent of GDP in Korea, larger than the proportion in the United States (1.71 percent) or Japan (2.02 percent). The Korean sport industry has been classified into three general segments: (1) facility and management (US$2.7 billion), (2) sport products and merchandising (US$7.9 billion), and (3) sport services (sport events, marketing, information, and other sport services) (US$8.9 billion) (Ministry of Culture, Sport and Tourism, 2006).

The most popular sports and physical activities in South Korea are mountain climbing, football, jogging, walking, badminton, bodybuilding, and gymnastics. South Koreans hope to participate in swimming (16 percent), golf (12 percent), yoga (7.2 percent), tennis (5.1 percent), mountain climbing (3.9 percent), squash (3.6 percent), and football (3.3 percent). Mountain climbing is popular because about 70 percent of the country is mountainous. The common reasons not to participate in exercise are lack of time (44.1 percent), laziness (21.5 percent), body weakness (13.8 percent), lack of interest (11.7 percent), lack of facilities (2.8 percent), and lack of money (2.4 percent) (Ministry of Culture, Sport and Tourism, 2006). Understanding such constraints will help managers and marketers develop successful segmentation and targeting strategies.

Sport Governance in Northeast Asia

Most nations in Northeast Asia have an administrative unit in the central government that oversees sport-related affairs and operation. The State General Administration of Sport, or SGAS, in China (formerly, the State Sports Commission); the Ministry of Education, Culture, Sports, Science and Technology in Japan; and the Ministry of Culture, Sports and Tourism in South Korea are the administrative units in the national governments responsible for sport development in the three major countries. Nevertheless, the **sport governance system** used in China differs substantially from those adopted by other nations in the region. The term **centralized sport governance system** can be used to label the sport governance system in China. A centralized sport governance system refers to "the sport managing system in a nation in which a specific government unit at every level of government is responsible for overseeing sport-related affairs and operations" (Eschenfelder & Li, 2006) and for the promotion and development of sport. On the other hand, the sport governance system adopted by other Northeast Asian countries approximates the one referred to by sport economists as a **mixed sport governance system**. The governments in nations that adopt the mixed sport governance system have a great deal of involvement in developing sport policies for the public sector, but they exercise limited supervision over the sport operations controlled by the private sector.

Role of Government in Sport in China

Before the 1980s the Chinese sport governance system was a huge state-run enterprise. The Chinese government was responsible for funding and overseeing sport-related affairs and operations under a centrally planned, hierarchical economic system (Jones, 1999). The country's adoption of the open-door policy in the 1980s led to the transformation of the sport system in China. The sport governance system then gradually evolved under the free-market system to become more self-sufficient (Hong, 2003). The State Sports Commission was restructured to become the State General Administration of Sport in 1998. Although the sport governance system has been reformed considerably in the last two decades, the governments at all levels still has extensive control of sport operations in China.

The **State General Administration of Sports (SGAS)** is an administrative unit under the State Department. As shown in figure 9.4, it has three branches, administrative departments, sport competition management centers, and other support and services institutions. The SGAS is closely tied to the All-China Sports Federation and the Chinese Olympic Committee. Besides forming strategies for sport development, overseeing their implementation, and developing mid- and long-range sport development plans, the SGAS is responsible for a number of functions:

◆ Creating a national sport framework

◆ Promoting physical activity and exercise participation in schools and local and regional communities

◆ Organizing national sporting events

Figure 9.4　Administrative structure of the SGAS.

◆ Organizing international sport events in China

◆ Enforcing antidrug and anticompetitive measures

◆ Liaising and cooperating with Hong Kong, Macau, and Taiwan

◆ Supporting research into the development of sport

◆ Implementing regulations governing the sport industry, sport market, and sport-related business activities

◆ Implementing national physical training standards and supervising public health in coordination with the Ministry of Health

◆ Overseeing sport activities with foreign associations and teams, and sport-related cooperation and communication with countries and regions outside the mainland

To fulfill the nation's Olympic strategies and ambition, the SGAS and sport authorities at the provincial level have played a key role in promoting sport development in China. One of the strategies is sponsorship of the **Chinese National Games (CNG)**. Modeled after the modern Olympic Games, the CNG are the largest and most important sport extravaganza in China. Each province-level administrative unit sends a team to compete in the CNG. The preparation for and competition at the CNG allow the government to cultivate elite Chinese athletes for major world competitions.

The essence of Chinese Olympic strategies and ambition is a unique system of selecting and training elite athletes (figure 9.5). China is one of the few countries in the world that dedicate and use spare-time sport schools extensively to train and prepare future elite athletes. A spare-time sport school is a boarding school specialized in sport and established to train Olympic hopefuls. Students are selected for their athletic talent. They take academic classes in the morning and engage in rigorous sport training sessions in the afternoon. These sport schools serve as a reserve pool for elite sport teams at the provincial and national levels. Currently, 360,000 students attend about 3,000 sport schools at all levels in the country. Many issues are associated with this centralized athlete development system, including early entry (e.g., diving starts at age four or five), arbitrary selection methods, poor training facilities and conditions,

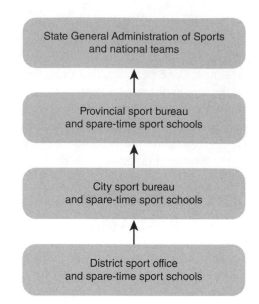

Figure 9.5 Chinese elite athlete preparation and delivery pipeline.

inhumane training methods, and inadequate education. On the other hand, this system provides China with an advantageous position for winning medals in the Olympic Games and other world sport competitions, leading to tremendous national pride among its citizens.

The Sports Law of the People's Republic of China became effective on October 1, 1995, becoming the first fundamental legal document for sport since the current regime was established in 1949. The Sports Law establishes the main tasks and key principles in managing the sport industry, confirms the importance of mass sport, and identifies the duties and responsibilities of sport-related organizations. Essentially, the law sets the framework for the development of sport in China (Jones, 1999). The enactment of the law signified that the sport industry in China has entered a new era under the protection of the country's legal system. Based on the Sports Law, local governments at provincial and city levels have the right and authority to make their own rules for managing sport within their jurisdictions.

The Plan for Olympic Glories was released by the SGAS in 1995. The plan outlined three goals: (a) restructuring the system in elite sport training and management, (b) enhancing the elite athlete delivery pipeline and system (including sport schools), and (c) maintaining the nation's leading position in world sport competition, particularly the Summer Olympic Games (Chinese Olympic Committee, 2009).

In 1995 the State Council promulgated the guidelines for a national fitness program. The guidelines were drafted with the aim of improving the health and the overall physical condition of the general population. The guidelines encouraged everyone, especially children and adolescence, to engage in at least one sporting activity every day, learn at least two ways of keeping fit, and have a health examination every year. The hope was that by 2010 about 40 percent of China's population would be regularly participating in physical activity and that clear improvement would take place in the physical fitness level of Chinese citizens (Chinese Olympic Committee, 2009).

Role of Government in Sport in Japan

As mentioned previously, the governmental unit in charge of the promotion and development of sport in Japan is the **Ministry of Education, Culture, Sports, Science and Technology (MEXT)**. The MEXT has three administrative divisions dealing with sport: the Policy Planning Division, the Sports-for-All (Lifelong Sports) Division, and the Competitive Sports Division.

Two major governmental policies and laws serve as basic blueprints for sport development in Japan: the Sports Promotion Law and the Basic Plan for the Promotion of Sports. The Sports Promotion Law, enacted in 1961, was intended to encourage and increase sport participation. This law not only provides a legal basis for promoting sport in the country but also clearly outlines the duty of both national and local government in the promotion and development of sport. In addition, this law has facilitated the promotion of sport by creating a system for maintaining and improving sport facilities, establishing the position of physical education advisor at municipal boards of education, and providing guidelines for organizing and funding the National Athletic Festival (MEXT, 1991).

The Basic Plan for the Promotion of Sports is another important legislation. The Japanese government, particularly the MEXT, launched the Basic Plan for the Promotion of Sports in 2000. Under the same premises outlined in the Sports Promotion Law of 1961, this policy serves as a comprehensive guideline for governments at various levels to promote sport development and achieve a number of long-term goals, such as (1) improving regional sport environments with a view to achieving lifelong participation in sport, (2) improving Japan's international competitiveness, and (3) enhancing the link between lifelong and competitive sport and school education and school sport (MEXT, 2000).

The policy target set for the implementation of this plan envisaged a period of roughly 10 years starting from fiscal year 2001 and set forth the policy measures required to achieve this target.

In the course of implementing the policy, assessments were to be made to measure the level of progress reached, and a total plan review was due to take place after 5 years. This plan was partly revised in 2006. The Japanese government is deliberating on a new plan for the next decade (MEXT, 2001).

Sport Governance in South Korea

The Ministry of Culture, Sport, and Tourism in South Korea is the administrative unit in the national government responsible for developing and implementing policies to promote culture, arts, sport, and religion in the country. The Sports Bureau is one of the offices in the ministry. A number of sport-related government legislations in South Korea have profoundly affected the development of sport in the nation.

The National Sport Promotion Act was government legislation enacted in 1962 (and revised in 1982) to increase people's physical fitness and mental health by promoting sport participation. This legislation influenced all aspects of the sport industry in South Korea, including intercollegiate athletics, amateur and professional sport, and leisure sport activities in schools, job settings, and local communities. The SaengHwalCheYuk movement (sport for all) began with the Hodori plan in 1989. The sport for all movement in Korea grew rapidly because of increased health awareness accompanied by economic growth and proactive implementation of welfare policies by the government after the 1988 Olympic Games in Seoul (Korean Overseas Information Service, 2007). To generate revenues and support the various segments of the sport industry, the Seoul

Olympic Sports Promotion Foundation (SOSFO) was established in 1989 after the 1988 Seoul Olympics (Ministry of Culture, Sport and Tourism, 2006).

A few years later, the Korean government developed its first Five-Year National Sports Promotion Plan (1993–1997) to increase sport participation and leadership in the world sport business. The plan focused on five major tasks: (a) to improve the quality of life of citizens through sport, (b) to provide continued support for elite sport, (c) to increase international corporative efforts, (d) to advance sport science and its application, and (e) to solidify the sport administration system. The plan was quite successful because public interest in sport grew after the 1988 Seoul Olympics (Ministry of Culture, Sport and Tourism, 2006). A major sport facility construction boom occurred during this period, during which 49 stadiums, 74 arenas, 17 swimming pools, and 1,728 neighborhood sport facilities were built (Korean Overseas Information Service, 2007).

The second Five-Year National Sports Promotion Plan (1998–2002) modified and incorporated several major tasks (e.g., to make the 2002 Korea–Japan World Cup successful and to improve the efficiency of sport administration). In particular, the government developed a strategic plan to foster the sport industry in Korea during this time by focusing on (a) support to develop high-quality sport products and branding efforts, (b) improvement of sport facility management, (c) fostering the sport service sector (develop sport information systems and produce highly qualified sport marketers), and (d) a long-term sport development plan (Ministry of Culture, Sport and Tourism, 2006).

The third Five-Year National Sports Promotion Plan (2003–2008) focused on (a) a drastic increase in sport participation, (b) improvement of elite sport to be among the top 10 in the world, (c) national development and balanced development of regions through the development of the sport industry, (d) improvement of the national image through increased international sport relationships, and (e) development of a positive political and cultural environment between North and South Korea by promoting sport exchanges (Ministry of Culture, Sport and Tourism, 2006). As a result of the systematic planning and implementation of sport policies, sport participation (at least once a month) among Koreans increased from 48.3 percent in 1989 to 62.2 percent in 1997 and 71.4 percent in 2006 (Ministry of Culture, Sport and Tourism, 2006). Table 9.1 shows government expenditures on sport in South Korea in the period from 2000 through 2006, which shows government financial investments correlated with the increased number of sport participants during the same period.

Noting the increased public interest and greater participation in sport, the Korean government considered sport a major industry segment. The Sports Industry Promotion Act was enacted by the Ministry of Culture and Tourism in October 2007 to provide systematic support for further development of the sport industry in Korea. Specific tasks were (1) to establish a basic developmental plan for the sport industry, (2) to train market-oriented industry professionals, (3) to provide sport facilities and funds, (4) to establish business organization in the sport industry, (5) to appoint the sport industry support centers, (6) to strengthen the

Table 9.1   Annual Budget for Sport Segments in South Korea

Segments	2000	2001	2002	2003	2004	2005	2006
Elite sport	47.1	51.2	54.1	53.1	68.4	79.6	98.3
Sport for all	9.0	21.0	29.7	32.7	31.1	23.5	25.8
International sport participation and relations	123.0	90.0	73.7	54.2	7.3	8.0	13.9
Other sport industry	0.3	0.8	1.4	2.6	2.5	2.7	11.0
Total	**180**	**164**	**159**	**143**	**109**	**114**	**149**
(% of government budget)	**(.19%)**	**(.16%)**	**(.15%)**	**(.13%)**	**(.09%)**	**(.08%)**	**(.10%)**

Amounts are in millions of U.S. dollars. One dollar is roughly equivalent to 1,000 South Korean won.

Adapted from Ministry of Culture, Sport and Tourism (2006).

competitiveness of the national sport industry including improvement of sport product quality and marketability, and (7) to promote professional sport. The Taekwondo Promotion Act was passed in July 2005 to improve and develop the global position of taekwondo by building and managing a taekwondo park and promoting taekwondo to contribute to national development.

Nongovernmental Sport Agencies

The nongovernmental sport agencies in Northeast Asian countries have played a critical role in promoting sport development in the region. The All-China Sports Federation (ACSF), the Japanese Sport Association (JASA), and the Korea Sports Council are examples of such nongovernmental sport agencies.

Nongovernmental Sport Agencies in China

The Chinese Olympic Committee (COC) is a nongovernmental, nonprofit national sport organization whose major objective is to develop sport and promote the Olympic Movement in China. The COC represents China in handling international affairs related to the Olympic Movement. The **All-China Sports Federation** (**ACSF**) is also a national nongovernmental, nonprofit sport organization that oversees an array of sport associations in China. The ACSF is an important linkage between the government and those involved in sport. The aim of the ACSF is (a) to strengthen ties between athletes and others who engage in sport to promote the development of elite sporting excellence, (b) to increase public participation in sport activities and

improve health outcomes for all Chinese, and (c) to improve sporting achievements in the world arena. Although both the COC and ACSF are supposed to be nongovernmental in nature, they are under the supervision and guidance of the SGAS. In fact, the director of the SGAS, Mr. Peng Liu, is also the president of the COC. The profound involvement of government in sport is a characteristic of the sport governance system in China.

Nongovernmental Sport Agencies in Japan

The **Japanese Sport Association** (**JASA**) and the Japanese Olympic Council (JOC) are the two major nongovernmental agencies that provide leadership in sport development in Japan at the national level. Although the JASA is mainly responsible for promoting lifelong sport, or sport for all, in the country, the role of the JOC is to improve Japan's international sport competitiveness. Before the Seoul 1988 Olympic Games, the JASA was the sole entity and governing body in sport in Japan and had the dual responsibility of promoting competitive sport and sport for the public. The unsatisfactory performance of Japanese Olympic athletes in the Seoul 1988 Olympics led to the creation of a separate entity to oversee competitive sport and raise the level of Japan's competitiveness in the world of sport. The JOC was then created out of a former committee within the JASA as a single legal corporation in 1989 (Ministry of Education, Culture, Sports, Sciences and Technology, 1991). Figure 9.6 depicts the nongovernmental sport governance structure in Japan.

As figure 9.6 shows, the JASA fulfills its duties in sport development in coordination and collaboration with other nongovernmental agencies, such as the Japan Sports Association for the Disabled, the Nippon Junior High School Physical Culture Association, some national sport federations, and the prefectural amateur sport associations or the local chapters of the JASA.

Nongovernmental Sport Agencies in South Korea

In South Korea, besides the leadership provided by the Ministry of Culture, Sport and Tourism, many nongovernmental sport organizations assume the responsibility to advance sport. One of those organizations

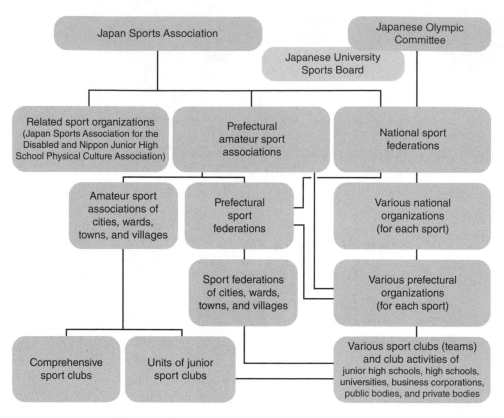

Figure 9.6 Nongovernmental sport governance structure in Japan.

is the **National Council of Sport for All (NCSA)**, authorized by the Ministry of Culture, Sport and Tourism in 1991. Three main objectives of NCSA are (a) to enhance people's health and fitness through promotion of sport for all, (b) to lead people to effective sport and recreation systems, and (c) to build a basis for unification of the Koreas (North and South Korea) by developing identity and patriotism among Koreans worldwide. The main business of the organization includes (a) promoting sport clubs and amateur sport participants by supporting federations and hosting various club leagues and festivals; (b) promoting sport for all by offering public sport services to citizens, extracurricular activities for youth, and exchange programs between Korea and other nations (e.g., China and Japan); and (c) developing sport-for-all welfare programs by supporting disabled amateur sport participants and hosting such events as Mother's Festival and Senior's Festival (NCSA, 2007, internal source). Currently, 16 city and province councils of sport participate in this movement as members of NCSA, and national federations for 52 sports have been organized. NCSA's activities benefit more than 12 million

people per year (Ministry of Culture, Sport and Tourism, 2006).

The **Korea Sports Council (KSC)** was established in 1920 to train national athletes, help improve the physical fitness of all Koreans, and create a wholesome social atmosphere through the promotion of sport. The council also helps develop Korean culture and international friendship through participation in various international sport events and hosting national and international sport events. The KSC has hosted numerous international sport events (e.g., the 1988 Seoul Olympics and the 1986 and 2002 Asian Games) and major international conferences (e.g., the 6th Sports-for-All Congress in 1996 and the IOC Executive Board Meeting in 1998). The Korean Olympic Committee (KOC) was established in 1947. In 1968 the KSC adopted the Korean Olympic Committee as a suborganization. Currently, the KSC has 47 member associations (Ministry of Culture, Sport and Tourism, 2006, internal source).

The **Seoul Olympic Sports Promotion Foundation (SOSFO)** was established in 1989 as a public corporation to promote public interest in accordance with the National Sports Promotion Act. Its goal is to preserve and promote the outstanding achievements of the 1988 Seoul Olympic Games and to raise and manage the Sports Promotion Fund to support various sport agencies and organizations (SOSFO, 2007, internal source). Specifically, the foundation focuses on the following specific objectives and business areas: (*a*) managing the Seoul Olympics commemorative businesses, (*b*) managing the Olympic facilities and construction of sport infrastructure, (*c*) providing various sport organizations (e.g., the Korean Olympic Committee, the National Council of Sport for All, the Korea Sports Association for the Disabled) with financial support through creative fund-raising efforts (e.g., cycle and motorboat racing, and Sports Toto), (*d*) supporting research in sport science, and (*e*) fostering the sport industry (SOSFO, 2007).

For example, the SOSFO has been supporting the KOC and KSC (US$43.2 million) and Korea Sports Association for the Disabled (US$68 million) annually. In addition, the foundation has been supporting the Korea Sport Science Institute (KSSI), which has established and maintained an extensive sport-related information database. The KSSI has published sport science journals including the *Korean Journal of Sports Science* and the *International Journal of Applied Sports Science* in English and has hosted international conferences such as the Asian Sports Science Conference. In addition, the SOSFO developed national sport centers (90 sites), grass and urethane sport facilities (547 sites), football centers and parks (3 centers and 16 parks), and village sport facilities (3,186 sites) and helped develop the stadiums for the 2002 Korea–Japan FIFA World Cup (6 sites). In 2007 the SOSFO contributed US$230.1 million overall to the promotion of national sport. To raise funds for its sport promotion activities, the SOSFO runs several businesses such as cycle racing, motorboat racing, and a lottery called Sports Toto (SOSFO, 2007).

The Taekwondo Promotion Foundation was established in July 2005 to help develop and manage

Learning Activity

In a small group, compare and contrast the functions and roles of nongovernmental sport agencies in China, Japan, and Korea in promoting sport development.

Taekwondo Park and to promote the sport. The goal of the foundation is to raise the status of taekwondo, a national sport in Korea, to a world martial art and a sport in the global community.

Professional Sport in Northeast Asia

Although sumo wrestling, the oldest professional sport in the region, if not the world, has been in existence in Japan for more than 1,000 years, professional sport as a whole in Northeast Asia is relatively a new phenomenon. The first professional baseball league was established in 1936 (Daly & Kawaguchi, 2003).

China had no professional sport league until 1994 when football became the first sport to take that road. Since then, professional competition has started in other sports, including basketball, volleyball, badminton, table tennis, and go (encirclement chess). China Basketball Association (CBA) events attract an average 80 percent box-office rating. Professional volleyball, table tennis, and badminton also have high fan appeal. The following details briefly describe some professional sport leagues in China:

◆ China Basketball Association (CBA)—established in 1995

◆ Chinese Football Association Super League (CSL) (formally the Football A League)—established in 2004, http://csl.sport.org.cn/da/

◆ China Table Tennis Super League (CTTSL)—established in 2003, http://cttsl.sports.cn/

◆ Chinese Volleyball Association (CVA)—established in 1996

Professional sport in China is still in the developmental stage. In 1998 the Football A League had an average of 21,300 on-site spectators per game and a total of 5,800,000 spectators over the year. Many scandals and charges of match fixing and corruption have hit the sport in the past few years, causing a loss of spectators and sponsors. Most clubs are losing money and having a hard time surviving. For the 2005 season the league had no title sponsor. In March 2009 Italian tire manufacturer Pirelli signed a three-year, multimillion-euro agreement with the Chinese Football Association (CFA) to become the title sponsor of China's Super League. With new leaders named at the CFA in early 2009 and new sponsorship deals, the league is expected to improve over the next couple of years.

More Chinese athletes are joining professional leagues in other countries and are playing overseas. For instance, basketball stars Yao Ming and Yi Jianlian are now playing in the National Basketball Association in the United States. Many football players have been enlisted to play in other countries. One of the latest examples is Li Weifeng of the Korean Football League. This go-global phenomenon has a number of significant implications to sport management education and the sport industry in China. First, to produce effective client representatives, the Chinese sport education system must be able to prepare sport agents who are not only proficient in English but also familiar with the operations of professional sport leagues in other parts of the world. Second, the phenomenon helps increase the public's interests in a particular sport, in both watching and participating. For example, many Chinese people love basketball because Yao Ming is playing in the NBA.

Many high-profile sporting events have been held or will be held in China, including the HSBC Championships in Shanghai (golf); the ATP World Tour Masters 1000 in Shanghai and the China Open in Beijing (tennis); the World Games of 2009 in Kaohsiung, Taiwan; the Formula One World Championship; the Chinese Grand Prix in Shanghai; the 5th East Asian Games in Hong Kong; and the 2011 Summer Universiade in Shenzhen.

The major professional sports in Japan are baseball, football, and sumo wrestling. Professional athletes also participate in horseracing, bike racing, boat racing, golf, boxing, tennis, and many other sports. The Nippon Professional Baseball (NPB) was formed in 1950. The NPB has two divisions, the Central League and the Pacific League, each made up of 12 teams. All teams except one are named after their corporate owners or sponsors rather than the cities or regions in which they play. For example, the Tokyo Yakult Swallows are owned by Yakult Honsha Co., Ltd., a corporation that sells probiotic milklike products. The following is a list of professional sport leagues in Japan:

- Nippon Professional Baseball (NPB)—established in 1950
- J League—established in 1991, www.j-league.or.jp/club/tokushima/
- Japanese Professional Sumo League—established in the Edo period (1603–1867)

Professional sport in Korea was born with professional boxing and wrestling. But it was not until 1982 when the Korea Baseball Organization (KBO) was formed that professional sport became a significant industry segment in Korea (Ministry of Culture, Sport and Tourism White Book, 2006). Currently, Korea has 11 professional leagues in nine sports:

- Korea Baseball Organization (KBO)—established in 1982, www.koreabaseball.or.kr
- The Korean Professional Football League (KPFL or K-League)—1983, www.kleaguei.com
- Korean Basketball League (KBL)—1996, www.kbl.or.kr/
- Women's Korean Basketball League (WKBL)—1997, www.wkbl.or.kr/
- Korea Volleyball Federation (KOVO)—2004, www.kovo.co.kr/
- Korea Professional Golfers' Association (KPGA)—1968, www.koreapga.com/
- Korea Ladies Professional Golf Association (KLPGA)—1978, www.klpga.com/
- Korea Professional Bowling Association (KPBA)—1995, www.koreapba.com/
- Korea Boxing Commission (KBC)—1947, www.koreaboxing.co.kr/
- Korea Ssireum Organization (KSO)—1981, www.ssirum.or.kr/
- Korea Professional Wrestling Association (KWA)—1967, www.wwakorea.com/buindex.htm

In 2006 football (49 percent respondents attended football events) was the most popular spectator sport among Korean people followed by baseball (27.1 percent), basketball (12.3 percent), tennis (1.5 percent), and golf (1.4 percent). Factors that negatively influenced spectatorship included lack of interest (33.2 percent), lack of time (27.7 percent), lack of event and facility available (13.8 percent), watching on TV (13.3 percent), and lack of money (5.2 percent) (Ministry of Culture, Sport and Tourism, 2006). Understanding such constraints will help sport managers and marketers develop successful segmentation and targeting strategies for professional sport organizations.

Major Sport Events in Northeast Asia

Because the nations in Northeast Asia are becoming politically, economically, and culturally important to the world, many international sport organizations are bringing their events to countries in this region. The three Olympic Games held in Asia so far were all hosted by nations in Northeast Asia (Japan in 1964, Korea in 1988, and China in 2008). In addition, this region is the favorite option for many international sport federations to organize their competitions. For example, the World Championship of the International Table Tennis Federation (ITTF) took place in Korea. The **Asian Games**, held every four years, are a major international sporting event in the region. This competition includes athletes from the entire continent of Asia, except Russia, as well as athletes from island nations in Southeast Asia.

To strengthen the ties among nations in East Asia, the national Olympic committees in the region discussed the idea of having an East Asian Games and endorsed the plan in 1991. In the following year, the Coordination Committee of the East Asian National Olympic Committees (EANOC) was officially formed and its charter was passed. Shanghai, China, was selected to hold the inaugural **East Asian Games** in 1993. The EANOC was renamed the East Asian Games Association (EAGA) that year. The East Asian Games is a smaller multisport event held every four years. Only members of EAGA (China, including Hong Kong, Macau, and Taiwan; Japan; Mongolia; North Korea; and South Korea) take part in the Games.

Summary

This chapter provided a brief introduction to sport in Northeast Asia, a region encompassing a number of nations that are culturally, economically, and politically important to the world, such as China, Japan, and South Korea. This region has experienced tremendous growth and development in sport in the late 1990s and early 2000s. In addition, the region has also demonstrated its dominance on the world sport stage, which is reflected particularly in the success of the Northeast Asian nations in the Olympic Games.

It is a common phenomenon among most Asian nations that an administrative unit is established in the central government to administer sport; however, the systems each country adopted in managing sport are different. In addition, the nongovernmental sport agencies also play a critical role in promoting sport development in the region.

? Review and Discussion Questions

1. Can you justify why Northeast Asia is considered a strategic region in the world, both politically and economically?

2. What are the differences between the sport governance systems adopted by China, Japan, and South Korea?

3. What are the key laws or major legislations enacted by China, Japan, and South Korea for sport development?

4. What are the interesting characteristics of the arms race in Olympic sports among China, Japan, and South Korea?

5. What major international and continental sport events have been held in Northeast Asia?

Part III
Governance in International Sport

Fireworks explode over the Olympic Stadium and the National Aquatics Center during the opening ceremonies of the 2008 Summer Olympic Games in Beijing, China.

Olympic and Paralympic Sport

Ted Fay, PhD
State University of New York at Cortland, USA

David Legg, PhD
Mount Royal University, Canada

Nikki Dryden, JD
Fragomen, Del Rey, Bernsen and Loewy, LLP, New York, USA

Chapter Objectives

After studying this chapter, you will be able to do the following:

- Describe the structure and governance of the Olympic and Paralympic Movements
- Understand the role of commercialism in the Olympic Games as it has grown over the past several decades
- Identify the major issues at stake for a city hosting the Olympic and Paralympic Games
- Discuss the history and status of women's sports in the Olympics and Paralympics
- Understand the arguments surrounding inclusion of athletes with disabilities in the Olympics
- Describe the structure and recent history of antidoping and techno-doping efforts surrounding Olympic athletes
- Discuss the difficulties introduced by new assistive technology in regulating athlete behaviors and categorizing athletes as disabled or nondisabled

Key Terms

Arguably, the new millennium has borne witness to the fact that the International Olympic Committee (IOC) has adroitly positioned itself, its Olympic Games, and its corresponding interlocking five-ring logo as one of the most recognizable and dominant international brands in the world. Founded in 1894, the IOC has strategically positioned itself over a full century later as the preeminent sport brand, usurping even the International Football Federation (FIFA) and its World Cup of men's football. The IOC has set its sights on new global priorities by virtue of its being granted official observer status by the United Nations. With this seat at the table at the world's largest political forum, the IOC is now able to solidify and expand its role as one of the world's most influential nonstate actors. The IOC, as a sport and cultural movement, has power and influence well beyond the normal reach of governments, beyond the scope and power of international trading unions, defense alliances, and international financial institutions (Burton & O'Reilly, 2010a).

This chapter, while providing a brief historical context of the International Olympic Committee (IOC) and International Paralympic Committee (IPC) along with an overview of their respective organizational structures, focuses primarily on the current and future organizational, sociocultural, financial, and legal issues facing the IOC, the IPC, the respective national Olympic and Paralympic committees (NOCs and NPCs), the designated organizing committees of the Olympic Games (OCOGs) and Paralympic Games, and the related international sport federations (IFs) responsible for conduct, including rules and officials, of each Olympic and Paralympic sport. Space limits the ability to go into depth regarding any of the domains of these key stakeholders of the Olympic and Paralympic Movements. Therefore, we will create a set of frameworks and contexts to touch on the core issues that jointly challenge both the IOC and the IPC by intertwining their relationship from a leadership and management perspective.

Based in Lausanne, Switzerland, the **International Olympic Committee** (**IOC**) has a charter, or constitution, a flag, an organizational anthem, and

Resources for More Information on the Olympic Movement

For more on the IOC, its history, its mission, its core strategic goals and objectives, and its dimensions beyond the business of its quadrennial Summer and Winter Games, visit these websites:

- International Olympic Committee at www.olympic.org and its companion site at www.olympic.uk
- Past and future hosts of Olympic and Paralympic Games (e.g., www.vancouver2010.com, www.london2012.com, and www.sochi2014.com)
- A select array of national Olympic committees (NOCs) (e.g., www.usolympic.org, www.olympic.ca, www.olympics.org.uk)

A similar scan of websites related to the International Paralympic Movement would be a good starting point in understanding the background and evolving relationship between the Olympic and Paralympic Games and the Olympic and Paralympic Movements. See these websites:

- The International Paralympic Committee (NPCs) at www.paralympic.org

- Select companion national Paralympic committees (NPCs) (e.g., www.USParalympics.org, www.paralympic.ca/, www.paralympics.org.uk/)

A number of other websites will give you a more critical view of the Olympic Games and Olympic Movement and the corresponding Paralympic Games and Paralympic Movement. Some of these nonofficial Olympic- and Paralympic-related sites are the following

- www.tas-cas.org/
- http://ioa.org.gr/
- www.wada-ama.org
- www.sportaccord.com
- www.gamesbids.com
- www.playthegame.org
- www.transparencyinsport.org
- www.infoplease.com/spot/olympicstimeline.html
- http://olympics.india-server.com/olympicshistory.html
- www.games-encyclo.org/?id=11837&L=1

some of the other typical symbols of nations, but it exists without an army, a significant land mass, or other traditional trappings of a nation-state. The United Nations has 192 member nations, but the IOC recognizes 205 national Olympic committees (Burton & O'Reilly, 2010a). The Summer Olympic Games currently attract over 11,000 athletes competing in 28 sports from more than 200 national Olympic committees (NOCs). At the Vancouver 2010 Olympic Games, its winter counterpart attracted nearly 6,500 athletes competing in 15 sports from 82 NOCs (*Paralympic Games Vancouver 2010*, 2010).

The **International Paralympic Committee (IPC)**, based in Bonn, Germany, was founded in 1989 and took over its first games management with the 1992 Summer Paralympic Games in Barcelona. It has been historically dependent on the IOC for much of its financial, logistical, and political support. The Paralympic Games, which involve elite athletes with physical and sensory disabilities, are one of the world's largest quadrennial mega sporting events. At the 2008 Summer Games nearly 4,000 athletes from close to 150 national Paralympic committees (NPCs) competed in 20 sport disciplines in the Paralympic Summer Games. Meanwhile in Vancouver in 2010, over 500 athletes from over 40 NPCs competed in 5 sports in the Paralympic Winter Games (Burton & O'Reilly, 2010c).

The Paralympic Winter and Summer Games occur approximately two weeks after the Olympic Games at the same location, in the same facilities, and under the same management structure of the host organizing committee for the Olympic Games,

or have since 1988. The first Paralympic Games were held in 1960. The organizing committees of the Olympic Games (OCOGs) are now mandated by the IOC to organize and conduct the Paralympic Games as well. The present agreement is set to expire in 2018. Thus, the management of the Olympic bidding process and the subsequent awarding of the Olympic Games to a particular host city include a corresponding responsibility to organize the Paralympic Games (Brittain, 2010).

Olympic and Paralympic Organization Structure and Governance

Governing, policy, and decision-making structures differ substantially within the International Olympic and Paralympic Committees. Table 10.1 gives a brief overview of the governance of each organization. The IOC describes itself as the "supreme authority" of the **Olympic Movement**, which supports a philosophy of life, in which the blending of sport and culture with art and education aims to combine in a balanced whole the human qualities of body, will, and mind. It currently consists of 115 individual members who are elected to initial eight-year terms and then an unlimited set of multiple terms thereafter. An executive committee consisting of 15 members, including a president, 4 vice presidents, and 10 members at large, is then elected and assumes overall responsibility for the administration, management, and overall policy decisions of the IOC. The president is elected to an initial eight-year term with an option for an additional four-year term if supported by the members (Hums & MacLean, 2009).

The IOC is further organized, structured, and managed by its 25 IOC commissions, its relations with all organizing committees of Olympic Games (OGOGs), its relations with 203 national Olympic committees (NOCs), and its collaboration with a number of other recognized and affiliated organizations representing a wide range of international sport-related entities.

The governance of each of the 33 Olympic sports is actually controlled independently by international sport federations (IFs) and their related national sport governing federations or bodies (NSFs or NGBs). Thus, the IOC cooperates and collaborates directly and individually with each of these international federations as well as through the auspices

Table 10.1 Snapshot of Olympic and Paralympic Governance

Quick facts	Olympic	Paralympic
Current headquarters	Lausanne, SUI	Bonn, Germany
Current website	www.olympic.org	www.paralympic.org
Founder	Baron Pierre de Coubertin	Sir Ludwig Guttman
First president	Demetrios Vikelas (1896)	Dr. Robert Steadward (1992-2001)
Current president	Dr. Jacques Rogge	Sir Philip Craven
Total number of presidents	8	2
Governance and voting members	119 individuals	146 nations
Year of founding Games	1896 Athens, Greece	1960 Rome, Italy
Year of founding Winter Games	1924 Chamonix, France	1976 Örnsköldsvik, Sweden
Number of NOCs and NPCs	205	146
Number of sports (IFs)	33	26

of an umbrella coordinating organization, SportAccord, formerly known as the General Association of International Sport Federations (GAISF). SportAccord consists of 104 member organizations, including 87 international sport federations and 17 associate members representing organizing committees of international games and sport-related international associations (www.sportaccord.com, n.d.).

The IPC operates arguably with more transparency and democracy through the aegis of its biennial general assembly and consists of representatives of all member groups that make up the IPC, including 161 national Paralympic committees (NPCs), 4 international organizations for sport for the disabled (IOSDs), the representatives of 27 Paralympic sports that include 9 IPC-managed sports, 7 IOSD sports, 11 independent Paralympic sport federation (IPSFs), and representatives from 5 IPC regional organizations (Brittain, 2010, pp. 38–44). Correspondingly, each of the 26 Paralympic sports is governed by one of three entities: (a) the IPC as it serves in the capacity of an international federation for 9 sports (this model will be phased out by 2016), (b) an international organization for sport for the disabled for 7 sports, or (c) the relevant international sport federation for an Olympic sport in 7 sports (*Paralympic Games Vancouver 2010*, 2010).

With the birth of a new International Paralympic Committee in 1992, many nations created a corresponding national Paralympic committee. In the early 1990s, the **national Olympic committee (NOC)** and **national Paralympic committee (NPC)**

within a given nation were often separate organizations with separate boards of directors, financing, and organizational structures. An analysis of national Olympic committees reveals a more recent trend wherein the NOC of a given nation has assumed the duties and responsibilities of the NPC for its country. Although not universal and still controversial in some sectors, this growing organizational integration of NOCs becomes a critical foundation from which greater integration of Olympic and Paralympic athletes can occur (Fay & Wolff, 2009).

Relationships With Outside Stakeholders

As illustrated in figure 10.1, the past 25 years have witnessed a number of new entities becoming more directly involved in international sport governance as it relates to Olympic and Paralympic Games management. A number of factors have contributed to this development, including the relaxing of the eligibility rules and criteria to allow openly professional athletes to compete in the Olympic Games, the emergence of the Paralympic Games as a major multisport quadrennial world event, and the inclusion of new Olympic and Paralympic sports on the Games program. The principal additions to this interlinking international sport governance model relevant to the Olympic and Paralympic Games include (1) professional sport organizations (PSOs) such as sport franchises, leagues, tours, and circuits beginning in 1992; (2) professional athlete unions and professional athlete representatives (PPUs and PARs) beginning in 1992; (3) the **Court of Arbitration for Sport (CAS)**, created in 1993, to adjudicate international athlete eligibility issues, breaches of fair play issues, and so on; (4) the World Anti-Doping Agency (WADA), created in 1999, which acts as an independent testing and research organization established to eliminate the use of banned performance-enhancing substances and techniques from international sport competition; and (5) sport organization and event

sponsors (SOs and ESs) that provide critical support and funding to athletes, organizations, and events.

A perfect example of why these additional groups are included can be drawn from the multiple stakeholders and governing bodies involved in negotiating the availability of professional ice hockey players for the Olympic men's ice hockey tournament. Some speculate that the National Hockey League and its club owners will withdraw their support for suspending their regular season

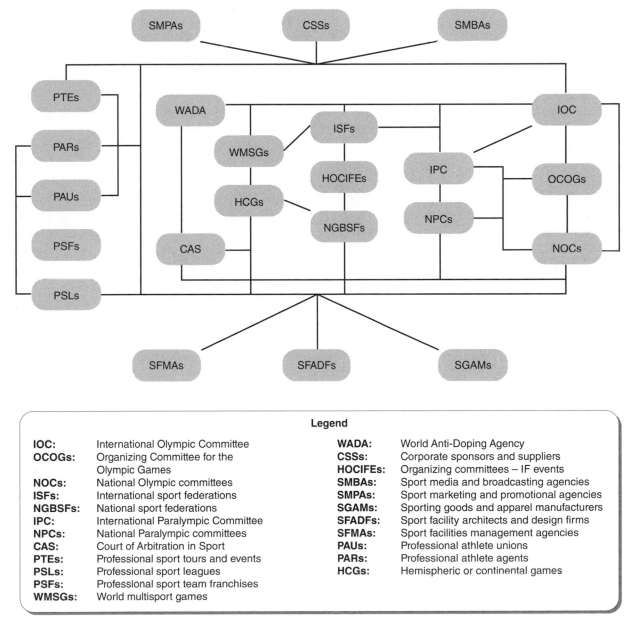

Figure 10.1 Universe of key international sport governance and industry relationships.

Reprinted, by permission, from T. Fay, L. Velez, and J.B. Parks, 2011, A North American perspective on international sport. In *Contemporary sport management*, 4th ed., edited by P.M. Pedersen, J.B. Parks, J. Quarterman, and L. Thibault (Champaign, IL: Human Kinetics), 404. Created by Ted Fay, 2006.

Learning Activity

Select a sport, other than ice hockey, where professional players compete in the Olympics. Discuss what some of the pros and cons of Olympic competition are for the professional tour or association (e.g., ATP or WTA for tennis, PGA for golf, FIS for ski racing) or for a professional league (e.g., NBA or WNBA for basketball, MLS or Premiership for soccer) as well as for the players, their agents, and unions.

for two weeks in February for the Winter Olympic Games in Sochi, Russia, in 2014, an accommodation that was made for Salt Lake City in 2002, Torino in 2006, and Vancouver in 2010. Owners may drop their support for the Olympic hiatus because they are concerned about injuries and fatigue to players as well as the financial repercussions of extending the regular season and playoffs for an extra month. Despite the best-ever television ratings achieved at the 2010 Vancouver Games, clear agreement on the value of Olympic ice hockey competition is lacking among its primary stakeholders, which include the International Olympic Committee (IOC), the International Ice Hockey Federation (IIHF), the National Hockey League (NHL), the National Hockey League Players Association (NHLPA), as well as other entities such as the Kontinental Hockey League (KHL), the new Russian professional hockey league (Burton & O'Reilly, 2010b).

Olympic Movement

The first Olympic truce, or *ekecheiria*, was held during the ancient Olympics in 776 BC. The idea was to suspend fighting between warring sides temporarily so that athletes could travel to the Games in safety. In 1992 the IOC resurrected this ancient tradition, calling on nations of the world to observe the Olympic truce and cease all hostilities during the Olympic Games. By 1993 the United Nations (UN) General Assembly did the same, and the Olympic flame relay in 1996 was the part of this movement of promoting the ideals of peace before and during the Olympic Games.

The IOC offers idealistic statements about the power of the truce "to encourage searching for peaceful and diplomatic solutions to the conflicts around the world," with an aim of using "sport to establish contacts between communities in conflict, offer humanitarian support in countries at war, and more generally to create a window of opportunities for dialog and reconciliation" (*Olympic Truce*, 2009).

The movement stalled in 2008 despite another UN General Assembly resolution calling for a truce around the Beijing Olympic Games. Repeated calls by human rights organizations for the Chinese government to end violence in Tibet and other parts of China, and to use its relationship with Sudan to promote peace in Darfur went unheeded, despite previous promises to the contrary (Amnesty International, 2008; Team Darfur, 2008).

When pressed about peace in China, IOC president Rogge said in March 2008, "I have no message to give to China for what the sovereignty of China is concerned. But the Games cannot be held in an atmosphere of violence. We are concerned about what is happening in Tibet" (Reuters, 2008a). Just months later in July 2008 on the eve of the Olympic Games, he so much as admitted defeat about the power of the Olympic truce, noting that when it came to China he had to be careful about his comments and actions. "I am at the head of an organization. . . . In view of my responsibilities, I have lost some of my freedom of speech" (Reuters, 2008b).

At the 1994 Winter Games in Lillehammer, Norway, Norwegian Olympic speed-skating champion Johann Olav Koss donated his prize money to support Olympic Aid, an organization whose goal was to raise funds to support people in war-torn areas. Koss urged fellow athletes to follow him, and $18 million was raised to support refugees in Afghanistan, help children with disabilities in Lebanon, and build schools in Eritrea and a hospital in Sarajevo.

By 2000 Olympic Aid had become Right-to-Play and transformed from a funding agency to one that implemented sport and play programs to improve health, develop life skills, and foster peace around the world. Right-to-Play, the leading sport-for-development agency, delivers programs in 23 countries affected by war, poverty, and disease. Over one million children participate in regular programs and special sporting events, and more than 700,000 children participate in Right-to-Play sport and play programs every week. Of those, almost half are girls, and over half of all coaches, teachers, and community leaders are women (Right to Play, 2010).

Right-to-Play is supported by a team of elite athletes from 40 countries who raise funds and awareness about the organization's programs. In 2006, following in the footsteps of his fellow speed skater, Joey Cheek donated $25,000 in prize money from his Olympic gold medal to Right-to-Play. The American leveraged his pledge with core sponsors and other athletes, which led to a flurry of donations that amounted to $300,000 in one week (Dryden, 2009). At the 2008 Games in Beijing, a unique campaign with TOP sponsor Johnson & Johnson was created, and Right-to-Play athlete ambassadors raised $450,000 through Johnson & Johnson, including $80,000 by American swimmer Natalie Coughlin (Dryden, 2009).

Right-to-Play was also the policy leader on sport for development. As the Secretariat to the International Working Group on Sport for Development and Peace, Right-to-Play brought together governments, UN agencies, and civil society. They created recommendations for governments about how to use the power of sport as a tool for development and peace, thereby solidifying the ideals of sport for development around the world.

History and Commercial Development of the Olympic and Paralympic Games

The modern Olympic Games were not always the colossal mega sporting and cultural event that they have become in the past quarter century (1984–present). During the founding period from 1896 to 1928, the form and organization of the Games was not standardized or consistent. The events instead resembled a "Culture or Identity Games" for nations and amateur athletes who could afford it (Brittain, 2010). For example, athletes competed in events over a period of 79 days for the 1904 St. Louis Olympic Games, which were little more than a sideshow attached to the St. Louis World's Fair of 1904. With the exception of nominal participation in a few sports practiced only by the elite social classes of the times (e.g., golf and tennis in 1900 and 1904), women were excluded from the Games until 1924 (Johnson, 1993, 1996).

Other historical tidbits of the Olympic Games reveal that the evolution of games management occurred in fits and starts. For example, the awarding of gold, silver, and bronze medals for first, second, and third places started at the 3rd Olympic Games in St. Louis in1904. The Olympic Games in Antwerp, Belgium, in 1912 marked the first occasion when the Olympic flag was raised at the Opening Ceremony and the Olympic Oath was recited by and for competitors. The first Olympic village, first Closing Ceremony, and first official inclusion of women into the Olympic Games did not occur until Paris in 1924. Often, the host country included indigenous sports ranging from lacrosse to rugby as medal events.

Attendance by nations in the founding period often depended on the cost of travel, thus giving an advantage to the richer nations of Europe and North America. Participation by Asian, African, Caribbean, and South American nations remained low until the 1960s and 1970s (*Olympics History*, n.d.; *NOCs & Athletes*, n.d.).

As decolonization was birthing new and independent nations around the world, the IOC stepped forward to assist those countries in creating sport programs. During the 1960s the IOC created the precursor to the Olympic Solidarity program, which now funds NOCs to develop and manage these programs themselves. As the money from television rights grew in 1984, so did aid to NOCs. Today three main programs receive assistance: the World Program, the Continental Program, and Olympic Games Subsidies. For the period 2009 through 2012, $311 million is budgeted for these programs, which include everything from athlete grants to coaching clinics, NOC management programs, and the promotion of Olympic values. Olympic scholarships for athletes training for Vancouver 2010 amounted to US$9 million, and the budget for 2012 Games scholarships is US$19 million.

Globally, many identify 1948, when Sir Ludwig Guttmann introduced the first Stoke Mandeville Games for World War II veterans with spinal-cord-related injuries, as the founding year of the Paralympic Movement. The first Paralympic Games, however, did not take place until 1960, when they were held in Rome two weeks following the Olympic Summer Games. This came about because of Guttmann's proposal to then IOC president Avery Brundage that the Paralympic Games occur in parallel to the Olympic Games in the Olympic city (Brittain, 2010). Between 1964 and 1992, before the formal ascendancy of the new International Paralympic Committee, efforts persisted to conduct parallel Games in Olympic cities or, if not within the actual Olympic city, at an alternate site within the same country. During this time, the Paralympic Games became more diverse concerning an athlete's type of disability. The 1972, 1976, and 1980 Games saw the increasing inclusion of athletes with visual impairments, amputations, and cerebral palsy. Up until that time, the Games and Movement had been managed by four different independent disability sport groups (Brittain, 2010).

During this period, fallout from the massacre of Israeli athletes and coaches at the Olympic Games in Munich in 1972; the successive boycotts of 1976 (Montreal), 1980 (Moscow), and 1984 (Los Angeles); and the excessive public debt incurred by the citizens of Quebec and Montreal in 1976 of over $2 billion dollars led to the near collapse of the Olympic Games by 1984. Following the Summer Games in Moscow in 1980, the IOC, under the leadership of its new president, Juan Antonio Samaranch (1980–2001), began to institute dramatic changes to the IOC Charter that led to a revaluing of the Olympic Games as a global brand.

Beginning with the launching of a new marketing and corporate sponsorship strategy built from the unexpected financial success of the Los Angeles Olympic Games in 1984, Samaranch was able to convince his fellow IOC members to purge any reference in the Olympic Charter to the term *amateur*, thus redefining athlete eligibility and opening the door to participation of openly professional athletes into the Games after 1988 (Mickle, 2010d). The **Olympic Charter** is a set of rules and guidelines established by the IOC to organize the Olympic Games and govern the Olympic Movement.

During this period, the Paralympics were held for the first time in the same venues as the Olympics in Seoul, Korea, in 1988. For this reason, some have considered those Games to be the start of the modern Paralympic era. The IOC's request to correspond and collaborate with one umbrella organization was the genesis of the International Paralympic Committee. Dr. Robert Steadward met with IOC president Juan Antonio Samaranch in Calgary, Canada, during IOC meetings leading up to the 1988 Olympic Winter Games. Steadward stressed to Samaranch the importance of leaders from Paralympic sport continuing to meet with the IOC leadership in the hopes of developing a formal working relationship by creating a memorandum of understanding as well as moving forward on the IPC's integration policy (Legg & Steadward, 2011).

Changes in IOC eligibility criteria, coupled with the aftershocks of the fall of the Berlin Wall in 1989, then had a profound effect on the scope, structure, and conduct of the Olympic Games. The collapse of the Soviet Union and East Germany eliminated two of the most powerful nations in Olympic history. At the same time, the independence of the former Soviet republics resulted in the addition of 15 new nations to the Olympic family.

Commercialization

The encroachment of commercialism into the Games began in the late 1960s with the first athletic shoe war between the German sport shoe companies Adidas and Puma. The companies gave free shoes to track and field athletes in Mexico City in 1968 and expanded their feud to swimmers such as Mark Spitz at the Munich Olympics in 1972 (Guttman, 2002). Many had suspicions that athletes were receiving payments under the table, thus violating the code of amateurism outlined by the eligibility requirements to compete in the Olympics at that time. IOC president Avery Brundage and others in the IOC fought hard to preserve the notion of amateurism but struggled to reconcile the presence of quasi-professional athletes from the Soviet bloc, who began to dominate certain Olympic sports. But these were not new issues for the Olympic Games. The first commercial sponsor of the Olympics was a Greek shipping magnate who was willing to underwrite the first Olympic Games in Athens in 1896. U.S. track athlete Jim Thorpe was the first athlete to be ruled ineligible for allegedly being a professional and thus was stripped of his gold medals in the pentathlon and the decathlon in Antwerp in 1912.

Karl Schranz, reigning World Cup and World Champion alpine skier from Austria, was ruled ineligible for the 1972 Winter Olympics in Sapporo because he admitted that he was not a "pure" amateur athlete, having allowed his photo and name to be used in an advertisement and TV commercial in his native Austria. During the period from 1948 to 1972, international sport governance was managed by a small group of wealthy men who controlled the key international sport federations that were focused on maintaining their own brand of hegemony over international amateur sport and the Olympic Games (Guttman, 2002).

Despite the protests and best efforts by IOC president Brundage (1952–1972) to rebuff the incursions of commercialism into the Olympic Games, the dominance of athletes from the USSR, East Germany, Cuba, and other countries from the Soviet bloc, who were decried as professionals, supported Samaranch's request noted earlier and accelerated eventual changes in the Olympic Charter in 1983 to allow each international sport federation to define its own eligibility rules. This landmark decision opened the door to professional athletes and teams in both the Summer and Winter Olympic Games and served to help level the playing field between the state-supported athletes of the Soviet bloc and their Western counterparts. One result was the dominance by the first Dream Team at the 1992 Barcelona Olympic Games (Pound, 2004).

The foundation on which the Olympics have evolved from a quadrennial event organized by volunteers for some of the world's best amateur athletes into an extravaganza staged by host organizing committees and staffed by highly trained professionals for some of the world's best professional athletes was built on an ever-expanding and technologically enhanced media and broadcasting platform. Some of the world's largest multinational corporations have chosen to showcase their global marketing and promotional strategies on this platform. The media and marketing numbers are so staggering that it is not hard to understand why the IOC so fiercely protects its brand and trademarks.

Broadcast Rights

The era of Olympic broadcast television began with the sale of the first-ever broadcast television rights to U.S.-based ABC-TV for the Winter Olympic Games in Squaw Valley in 1960 for US$50,000. Since then spending on broadcast rights has steadily climbed, as shown in table 10.2. The first Olympics to be broadcast in color followed at the Winter Olympic Games in Grenoble in 1968. These developments occurred nearly 30 years after the introduction of television to a localized audience in Berlin for the 1936 Summer Olympic Games. The decision to split the Winter and Summer Games into an offset two-year cycle has been attributed to the needs of the U.S. Olympic broadcast rights holder to be able to leverage its investment with respect to selling

advertising space on its broadcasts. These early events and technical advancements culminated in NBC's astounding US$2.201 billion bid in 2003 for the rights to the 2010 (Vancouver) and 2012 (London) Olympic and Paralympic Games (Mickle, 2010c, 2010h, 2010i; Mickle & Durand, 2010b).

One of the issues facing the IOC after the 2012 London Games is whether to forego its practice of hiring a media consultant such as Neil Pilson to help manage the bidding process for the U.S. media rights or try to sell them on their own. With the conclusion of the 2008 Beijing Olympic Games, the IOC began to shift its strategy away from its dependence on predominantly U.S.-centric media rights to a more global and diversified platform of broadcast and digital rights, including Internet and mobile rights sold to other broadcasters (e.g., Eurosport, China Central Television). This move also affected its strategies to sign non-U.S.-based companies as TOP sponsors (Mickle & Durand, 2010a; Mickle, 2010e, 2010f). Another change is the inclusion of the Paralympic Games as part of this package beginning with NBC in 2010. This arrangement was made possible by the signing of a mutual agreement in 2001 between the IOC and the IPC that committed these two governing bodies to a joint bidding process, joint games management, joint media and broadcast relationships, and joint marketing and sponsorship relationships under the auspices of the IOC (Legg & Steadward, 2010).

Corporate Sponsors

Given the high stakes involved, the IOC, its host Olympic organizing committees, and various national Olympic committees have been able to extract many millions of dollars from companies seeking to cobrand themselves in exchange for exclusivity in a given product or service category. Traditionally, sponsorship in the **Olympic Partner Programme (TOP)** has been limited to about 10 companies based on constantly escalating rights fees over the past 40 years (Mickle, 2010e, 2010f, Rosner & Shropshire, 2011). These fees do not include the costs of activation and fulfillment, which effectively double the cost of Olympic sponsorship over a typical quadrennial period. Some companies like Coca-Cola and Panasonic have been Olympic sponsors since the inception of the TOP program in 1984, whereas others such as UPS, Fed Ex, John Hancock, and IBM decided to drop out of the global Olympic marketing game after 2004

Table 10.2   History of Olympic Broadcast Rights

Year	Olympics	Location	Network	Broadcast fee paid[1]
1960	Summer	Rome, Italy	CBS	$394,000
1960	Winter	Squaw Valley, California	CBS	$50,000
1964	Summer	Tokyo, Japan	NBC	$1,500,000
1964	Winter	Innsbruck, Austria	ABC	$597,000
1968	Summer	Mexico City, Mexico	ABC	$4,500,000
1968	Winter	Grenoble, France	ABC	$2,500,000
1972	Summer	Munich, Germany	ABC	$7,500,000
1972	Winter	Sapporo, Japan	NBC	$6,400,000
1976	Summer	Montreal, Canada	ABC	$25,000,000
1976	Winter	Innsbruck, Austria	ABC	$10,000,000
1980	Summer	Moscow, Russia	NBC	$87,000,000
1980	Winter	Lake Placid, New York	ABC	$15,500,000
1984	Summer	Los Angeles, California	ABC	$225,000,000
1984	Winter	Sarajevo, Yugoslavia	ABC	$91,500,000
1988	Summer	Seoul, South Korea	NBC	$300,000,000
1988	Winter	Calgary, Canada	ABC	$309,000,000
1992	Summer	Barcelona, Spain	NBC	$401,000,000
1992	Winter	Albertville, France	CBS	$243,000,000
1994	Winter	Lillehammer, Norway	CBS	$300,000,000
1996	Summer	Atlanta, Georgia	NBC	$456,000,000
1998	Winter	Nagano, Japan	CBS	$375,000,000
2000	Summer	Sydney, Australia	NBC	$705,000,000
2002	Winter	Salt Lake City, Utah	NBC	$545,000,000
2004	Summer	Athens, Greece	NBC	$793,000,000
2006	Winter	Torino, Italy	NBC	$613,000,000
2008	Summer	Beijing, China	NBC	$894,000,000
2010	Winter	Vancouver, Canada	NBC	$820,000,000
2012	Summer	London, England	NBC	$1,181,000,000

[1]All amounts are in U.S. dollars.

Reprinted, by permission, from Z. Anderson, 2008, London Olympics broadcast rights top $1 billion. [Online]. Available: http://branddunk.com/2008/08/22/london-olympics-broadcast-rights-top-1-billion [February 14, 2011].

and 2008. They decided that they were not receiving adequate value and return on investment (ROI) to their core businesses by their sponsorship investment, estimated at US$100 million for rights fees alone for one Winter and one Summer Games (Rosner & Shropshire, 2011). Table 10.3 shows sponsor totals and revenues from the TOP program since 1984.

Ambush Marketing and Sponsor Conflicts

Other companies have decided to play a different game by developing and executing ambush marketing strategies to position themselves as being related to the Olympic Games at a fraction of the

Table 10.3 TOP Olympic Sponsor Totals Since 1984

Quadrennium	Games	Partners	NOCs	Revenue[1]
1985-1988	Calgary and Seoul	9	159	$96,000,000
1989-1992	Albertville and Barcelona	12	169	$172,000,000
1993-1996	Lillehammer and Atlanta	10	197	$279,000,000
1997-2000	Nagano and Sydney	11	199	$579,000,000
2001-2004	Salt Lake City and Athens	11	202	$663,000,000
2005-2008	Torino and Beijing	12	205	$866,000,000

[1]All amounts are in U.S. dollars.

Reprinted, by permission, from International Olympic Committee, 2009, *Olympic marketing fact file*. [Online]. Available: www.olympic.org/Documents/IOC_Marketing/IOC_Marketing_Fact_File_2010%20r.pdf [February 14, 2011].

cost of an IOC or NOC sponsorship. One way that companies have engaged in successful ambush marketing campaigns since 1984 has been to link images of Olympic sports or athletes to the host city (e.g., "Good luck to our athletes in London"), being careful not to use terms such as *Olympic* or *Olympic Games* in their advertising. Campaigns have included print and television advertisements as well as billboards in the months leading up to and through the Games. Consumers often infer a relationship between the product being advertised and a particular Olympic Games or Olympic team (Rosner & Shropshire, 2011). Some of the more notorious ambush campaigns between TOP sponsors and their chief rivals were Kodak versus Fuji Film (1984), Visa versus American Express (1988–), Coca-Cola versus Pepsi (1984–), and Nike versus Reebok (1992–).

A classic case that illustrates the complexities of authority and control in Olympic sport, including the role of official Olympic sponsors, NOC sponsors, and pretenders, involved the 1992 U.S. men's Olympic basketball team (a.k.a. the Dream Team) in Barcelona. Some members of the U.S. team, made up almost exclusively of NBA players, had endorsement contracts with sponsors that directly conflicted with official U.S. Olympic Team sponsors. Reebok, the official U.S. Olympic outerwear sponsor, provided warm-up jackets and pants to all Olympic athletes in all sports. Some members of the U.S. basketball team, such as Michael Jordan and Magic Johnson, chose to cover the Reebok name with American flags as they stood on the victory podium to accept their gold medals. Jordan initiated this action. As a Nike-sponsored athlete, he refused

to be seen implicitly endorsing his company's competitor. This incident thrust the U.S. Olympic Committee (USOC), Nike, Reebok, USA Basketball, the National Basketball Association (NBA), the NBA Players Association, and Jordan into a high-stakes public relations battle (Fay & Snyder; 2006; Katz, 1994). After 1992 the USOC amended its code of conduct to include language that requires all U.S. Olympic athletes to wear the official apparel provided by official U.S. Olympic sponsors of a given Olympics on the podium without exception (Fay, Velez, & Parks, 2011). Technical wear (team uniforms, swimsuits, jumping suits, ski suits, and so on) are exempted from this rule, and supplying such items continues to be a legal way for companies to ambush each other with respect to trademarks and logos on competitive uniforms.

The IOC and its NOC members have become forceful in limiting and counteracting ambush marketing campaigns by corporations and organizations intent on circumventing the costs of sponsorship. The IOC, NOCs, and local Olympic organizing committee (OCOG) must be diligent in protecting and supporting their corporate partners who have been granted exclusive advertising rights in exchange for millions of dollars in sponsorships. A direct result of this effort was evidenced by the city by-laws passed by the Vancouver City Council curtailing free speech in order to conform to the Olympic host city contract for the 2010 Olympic and Paralympic Games (Shaw, 2009). The years between 1980 and 1984 represented a crossroads for the Olympic Movement between its idealist philosophy as espoused by IOC presidents from de Coubertin to Killanin from 1896 through 1980 to a more pragmatic approach to power, control, and money as advanced by IOC presidents Samaranch and Rogge from 1981 to the present. With the advent of new financial power and marketing windfalls in the 1980s, the IOC and its host country organizing committees for the Olympic Games (OCOGs) fell prey to new scandals and challenges to the sanctity of the Olympic Games philosophy of fair play (Pound, 2004).

Corruption and Reform

Bribery, scandal, and abuse of power within the IOC were first seriously investigated in 1992 by journalists Vyv Simpson and Andrew Jennings, when their book *The Lords of the Rings* first revealed the darker sides of the IOC. Jennings wrote two more books detailing bribery and cover-ups in the IOC, including events that led to the biggest corruption trial in sport history. Held in Switzerland, home to the IOC, the 2008 trial concerned the sport marketing company International Sports Licensing (ISL). It was found that from 1989 to 2001 ISL had paid $128 million in "commissions" to members of the IOC in exchange for television and marketing contracts. Despite this finding, under Swiss law at the time, it was not illegal to pay these so-called commissions (Jørgenson, 2009; Kaerup, 2009b, 2009c). Jennings was also the first to identify bribery surrounding host city selection, and the biggest shakeup happened to the IOC on U.S. soil. The scandals surrounding the Salt Lake City bid for the Winter Olympic Games led to a demand by U.S. lawmakers for major IOC reforms (Longman, 1999).

In December 1998 IOC member Marc Hodler announced that certain IOC members had taken bribes. U.S. Department of Justice and Congressional investigations followed, revealing that IOC members and their families had taken bribes from Olympic bid city organizing committees to secure members' votes for future hosting duties. In the bidding process for the 2002 Winter Games in Salt Lake City, everything from expensive gifts to fake jobs (and a green card for the son of one IOC member), cash, scholarships, medical treatment, and shopping sprees were given in exchange for votes (Longman, 1999). Ten IOC members (including those from Sudan, Congo, Mali, Chile, Kenya, and Ecuador) either resigned or were kicked out for their involvement (Longman, 1999; Siddons, 1999).

With the U.S. Congress threatening to withdraw the IOC's tax-exempt status along with lucrative television contracts (Longman, 1999; CNN/Sports Illustrated, 1999a), the IOC adopted a set of 10 reforms in 1999. From the addition of more athletes to the creation of an Ethics Commission, the IOC tried to change its image. Commentators, however, noted that reforms were unlikely to transform the IOC (Longman, 1999; Deford, 1999). During U.S. Congressional hearings, Congressman Fred Upton, Republican of Michigan, foretold the future when he said, "The conduct by IOC members and the bidding cities did not spring up yesterday and it will not go away simply because there are new rules written on a piece of paper" (CNN/Sports Illustrated, 1999b).

Ten years later after its creation, the Ethics Commission released its findings of an investigation into IOC member Kun-Hee Lee. Mr. Lee, who is worth US$7.3 billion and heads Samsung, an IOC TOP sponsor through 2016 (BBC News, 2010; *Samsung Concludes Contract*, 2007), was convicted in 2009 in Korea for tax evasion to the tune of US$100 million. Mr. Lee found reprieve not just from the president of Korea, who pardoned him halfway through his three-year suspended jail sentence (Lewis, 2010; BBC News, 2010) but also from the IOC, which "reprimanded him" and handed out the penalty of not allowing him to sit on any IOC commission for the next five years (Zappelli, 2010).

Staging the Olympic and Paralympic Games

There are a number of issues that must be addressed in order to successfully stage an Olympic and Paralympic Games. Such issues include, but are not limited to, (a) the costs in bidding for the hosting right; (b) the challenges facing the host cities; (c) the additional costs resulting from the expansion in the Olympic family; (d) the continuous growth of media in size, price, and scope; and (e) environmental impacts.

Bidding Costs

Despite IOC reform efforts, the costs of bidding for the privilege of hosting an Olympic–Paralympic Games continue to increase. Preuss (2008), in his work *Economics of Olympic Bidding*, provided a detailed history of the Olympic bidding process from Munich in 1972 through Beijing in 2008.

Preuss, who has served as consultant to a number of Olympic candidate cities, illustrated the cost–benefit relationship of being part of the bidding process and theorized that a city and nation could maximize their cost–benefit ratio by being a finalist in the Olympic bidding process, but not the ultimate winner.

Estimates are that the three finalists for the 2018 Winter Olympic–Paralympic Games (PyeongChang, South Korea; Munich, Germany; and Annecy, France) will have spent an amount ranging from US$21 million to US$42.5 million during the bidding cycle by the time the winner is announced on July 1, 2011. This sum does not take into account the total costs of bidding by a city such as PyeongChang, which narrowly missed being selected for the 2006, 2010, and 2014 Winter Games ("2018 Olympic Candidates," 2010). PyeongChang is the odds-on favorite because its facility infrastructure is essentially in place and it has a revenue/cost projection of US$651 million. Munich, on the other hand, estimates a revenue/cost projection of nearly US$1.074 billion, and most of its sport facility infrastructure is in place and used frequently as World Championship and annual World Cup venues for a variety of sliding and ski sports ("Bringing Show Business," 2010).

Host Cities

Whatever the actual costs of bidding, the costs of hosting can be much more challenging to pin down. The difficulty lies in trying to forecast seven years in advance the state of the global, regional, and national economies to produce estimates of revenue from broadcast, sponsorship, and ticket sales and projections of the demand for public spending (Preuss, 2004). The volatility of global economic and security issues and the unpredictability of currency markets (e.g., U.S. dollar versus the euro versus the yen or yuan) can wreck havoc with the best-laid plans of any Olympic–Paralympic Organizing Committee ("London 2010 Budget," 2010). National politics can also dramatically affect support for public spending, as occurred with the change in government that took place in the United Kingdom just two years before the 2012 Olympic–Paralympic Games ("London 2010 Budget," 2010).

Growing the Olympic Family

The desire and possibility for cities to be in "the game" as an Olympic candidate city received a boost from the IOC in 2007 when the members swiftly and unexpectedly voted to create a new Olympic property—the Youth Olympic Games (YOG) for aspiring Olympic athletes between the ages of 14 and 18. These games debuted in Singapore in August 2010. The YOG is set to unveil the winter version in Innsbruck, Austria, in February 2012. In the first case, the Youth Olympic Games were hosted by a nation-state that likely would never be able to host an Olympic–Paralympic Games, while in the instance of Innsbruck, the IOC will return to a former Olympic city (1964 and 1976), thus allowing the IOC to extend itself to more cities itching to be directly connected to the Olympic brand (Mickle, 2010g). In a report circulated in August 2010, apparently 17 cities indicated an interest in hosting a future YOG, including many in the United States.

Billed as one of the key legacies of Jacques Rogge's tenure as IOC president (2001–2012), the Youth Olympic Games has generated skepticism about whether it is a strategic extension or a dilution of the Olympic brand. Some international federations and national Olympic committees have expressed concern over the new costs of YOG events and their interference with well-established existing competitions. Some skeptics believe that the Youth Olympic Games is a way for the IOC to maintain its brand presence in its battle for global sport brand supremacy with FIFA and its men's World Cup of football. The IOC hopes that the YOG will help it connect to a younger audience, foster youth participation in sport, and increase the interest of youth in the Olympic Games. What it has done is build a ready platform to provide new extension and activation opportunities for its current family of official broadcasting networks and TOP sponsors (Mickle, 2010g).

Observers speculate that the cost burden to cities of hosting this event will steadily increase because of increasing competition among cities interested in hosting. Singapore, for example, reportedly spent nearly US$400 million to host nearly 3,600 athletes from 202 countries in 26 Olympic sports. This amount is more than 3 times the estimated original cost of nearly US$120 million and well over 10 times the US$30 million cost originally estimated by Rogge himself when the Games were approved in 2007 (Mickle, 2010g). Note that no parallel Youth Paralympic Games has yet to be created under the behest of the International Paralympic Committee.

Media Coverage

The Youth Olympic Games also provides the IOC the opportunity to expand its digital media offerings, ranging from on-demand highlights on YouTube prepared for distribution by its Olympic Broadcasting Services division to its new social networking strategies. All TOP sponsors and the IOC's major broadcast partners such as NBC Universal signed on to be involved in the inaugural event in Singapore because of their desire to extend their market reach into the lucrative and largely untapped Southeast Asian region (Mickle, 2010f).

As the IOC makes a strategic effort to move into new regions of the world with new events such as the Youth Olympic Games and to build on its sizable reserves, estimated at nearly US$500 million, garnered through the sale of its international broadcast rights and corporate sponsorships, it is unclear how and to what extent it will be able to maximize and protect its digital rights in the universe of decentralized social media and social networking sites. Questions have arisen over who will control the rights of social media and networking sites used by Olympic and Paralympic athletes before, during, and after Olympic–Paralympic Games. These developments will likely create new complexities surrounding intellectual property rights that need to be negotiated by and between NOCs and NPCs with their respective athletes, coaches, and officials as well as with the IOC, IFs, and OCOGs. This situation is further complicated by the efforts of the IOC and IPC to capitalize on the popularity of their star athletes by building greater fan interest with the Olympic and Paralympic Games (Lombardo, 2010; Mickle, 2010b, 2010i).

As Olympic-related media continue to increase in size, price, and scope, concern is growing over controls and suppression of a free press that can effectively shut out solo journalists who are often openly critical of the IOC or a host city's conduct in organizing the Games. This action is similar to the leverage that the IOC has been able to impose on various host cities and host governments in its attempts to control ambush marketing efforts by companies, organizations, and corporations not officially related to NOCs or the IOC (Rosner & Shropshire, 2011). For example, the host city contract between the Vancouver 2010 Organizing Committee and the IOC stated that no propaganda or advertising material could be within view of spec-

tators at the venues or television cameras covering the sports or "in the airspace over the city and other cities and venues hosting Olympic events during the period of the Games." In response, before the Games, Vancouver's city council passed an omnibus by-law amending dozens of existing laws, including the creation of so-called free-speech zones and blocks of the city where no political pamphlets, leaflets, graffiti, or "noncelebratory posters" would be allowed (Burton & O'Reilly, 2010d, Mickle, 2010a).

Environmental Impact and Games Legacies

Because of its efforts to institute reforms regarding the processes of bidding, awarding, and hosting of the Games (Olympic, Paralympic, and Youth), the International Olympic Committee became increasingly concerned over the legacies of a given Games, including the lasting impacts on the local and regional environments of the physical infrastructure requirements for facilities, transportation, communication, public health, and security. Unique among the factors considered by the IOC Review Commission in its progress reports on Olympic candidate cities was a new focus on universal design that would provide adequate and appropriate accessibility and accommodation for people with disabilities, including the ability to host the Paralympic Games. The results of these efforts also allowed greater accessibility for people with disabilities attending either the Olympic or Paralympic Games as working professionals (e.g., members of the media, OCOG personnel) or as spectators. Given previous criticism over the cost and lack of use of Olympic venues after the Games had ended (known as White Elephants), the IOC has also encouraged greater use of temporary structures for spectator seating, media and broadcast facilities, and the large structures necessary to accommodate a given Olympic and Paralympic village (Burton & O'Reilly, 2010d; Crary, 2010; Mickle, 2010a).

Regardless of the advances in environmental awareness and the practices by OCOGs, often working in cooperation with national, regional, and local governments, to use the requirements of hosting of an Olympic Games as a means to regenerate blighted sections of their cities, a healthy skepticism remains over whether these efforts really help the people targeted by displacement from their neighborhoods. Typically, displaced people lack the political and economic power to resist these changes. Such public debates over housing rights and neighborhood regeneration efforts have occurred consistently since Seoul in 1988, where 720,000 people were forcibly evicted (10 percent received replacement housing). In 1992 in Barcelona 600 families were displaced and house prices rose 240 percent between the time the city won the right to host the Games and their actual start, which led to secondary displacement (many of whom were Romas). The building of the Olympic Stadium (now Turner Field) in Atlanta for the 1996 Games coincided with the arrests of 9,000 homeless people between 1995 and 1996 and the evictions of tens of thousands of low-income residents. In 2000 in Sydney no forced evictions occurred, but the acceleration of gentrification in the city caused house prices to double between 1996 and 2003. As had occurred in Barcelona, the Athens Games in 2004 had a disproportionately negative effect on the Roma, but the Olympic Village now provides 10,000 people with subsidized housing. Beijing in 2008 was a disaster for housing. Approximately 1.5 million people were evicted to make way for Games construction. In Vancouver in 2010 a report by the United Nations Special Rapporteur on adequate housing found that Canada was not doing enough to protect people from Olympic construction (UN General Assembly A/HRC/10/7/Add.3, 2009). In particular, the construction of the Vancouver Olympic Village displaced over 3,000

homeless people. In London the redevelopment of a number East London neighborhoods notorious for poverty and crime has already forced 1,000 people from their homes (Center on Housing Rights and Evictions Report: Fair Play for Housing Rights, 2007). Accurately projecting the future legacies of any Olympic–Paralympic Games and its overall impact on the people left behind is difficult. One thing for certain is that staging an Olympic–Paralympic Games requires an astounding amount of human and fiscal capital.

Social and Ethical Issues in Olympic and Paralympic Sport

Social and ethical issues in Olympic and Paralympic sport often emerge from the disparities between the stated mission and principles of the Olympic and Paralympic movements and the actual realities of what happens at the Games themselves. It is often noted that women do not share equally in the number of participants, the number of sports, and power and voice in the decision-making of these two bodies (Carr, 2009). Athletes with a disability also seek a similar desire for inclusion and equity (Steadward, 1994; Fay & Wolff, 2009). The desire for a greater equity paradigm also challenges the IOC and IPC with respect to transgendered and sexual ambiguous athletes (e.g., Semenya). The following section explores some of the more pressing social and ethical issues found in both the Olympic and Paralympic movements.

Gender Equity

Despite the IOC's charter goal of promoting equal rights of men and women athletes, when the Games first began women athletes were not invited to compete. Pierre de Coubertin, the founder of the modern Olympics, thought that the inclusion of women would be "impractical, uninteresting, unaesthetic, and incorrect" (Johnson, 1996). He also believed that the Olympics should "be reserved for the solemn and periodic exaltation of male athleticism with internationalism as a base, loyalty as a means, arts for its setting, and female applause as its reward" (Johnson, 1996).

At the 1900 Olympic Games, 23 women competed in six sports: tennis, sailing, croquet, golf, ballooning, and equestrian. Boxing, the only sport not available to women at the 2008 Olympic Games in Beijing, was actually held as a demonstration event for women at the 1904 Olympics in St. Louis. The local organizing committees of the host cities of the early Olympic Games were often responsible for organizing separate women's events until 1912, when the IOC took charge of setting the event schedule (Wamsley, 2008). Women were officially included in the Olympic Games starting with Paris in 1924. Not until Tokyo in 1964 was a women's team event, volleyball, added to the Olympic event schedule. Women's basketball and team handball followed in Montreal in 1976 (Johnson, 1996; Pfister, 2000).

Although women's participation increased over the next few decades, in 1954 the IOC voted to limit events for women to those "particularly appropriate to the female sex" (Olympic Women, 2008; British Columbia Supreme Court, 2009). Not until 1981 did the IOC invite women into its membership, and 30 years later just 19 out of 114 IOC members are women, of whom 3 are princesses. In 1995 the IOC created a Women and Sport Working Group, which did not become an actual commission until 2004. The powerful IOC Executive Board includes among its 15 members just 1 woman (The Women and Sport Commission, 2009).

At the 2006 Winter Olympics in Torino and the 2008 Summer Olympics in Beijing, just 38 percent and 42 percent of the athletes competing were women. At those same Summer Games four countries, Brunei, Saudi Arabia, Qatar, and Kuwait, did not send women to compete at all. Brunei and Saudi Arabia said that "cultural and religious reasons" do not allow women to participate in the Olympics, although they sent teams of men (Al-Ahmed, 2008; Reuters, 2008c; Terman, 2008). At the Torino Games 22 countries sent only men's teams to compete.

Many scholars argue that apartheid in South Africa ended in part because of international sporting sanctions against the country (Booth, 2003). With a record of penalizing nations that discriminate based on race and the power to disqualify nations that systemically dope, why does the IOC not penalize countries that systemically discriminate against women? In 2010 IOC Women's Commission head Anita DeFrantz said that the IOC pressed Saudi Arabia, Qatar, and Brunei to send women to the 2012 Games in London. Qatar has since stated that it will send women's teams in 2012, thus showing the power of the IOC to directly influence the actions of given countries.

In 2007 the Olympic Charter was modernized to include antidiscrimination and gender equality clauses. The mission of the IOC now includes acting "against any form of discrimination affecting the Olympic Movement . . . and to encourage and support the promotion of women in sport at all levels and in all structures with a view to implementing the principle of equality of men and women" (Olympic Charter, 2010). These revisions now put the IOC in line with international law and provide a framework for real change. But without affirmative action and real enforcement mechanisms, these changes will be meaningless. The IOC could easily use a modified version of the U.S. Title IX program to make gender equity in the Olympic Movement a reality (Carr, 2009). The IOC needs women in leadership positions, especially the IOC Executive Committee, and it must increase the number of women IOC members from 17 percent up to 50 percent.

The IOC must also find a way to ensure that the number of female athletes competing at both Winter and Summer Olympics is equal to the number of men. These efforts can start by equalizing the number of events and sports offered to women and men, and forcing countries to send teams of both men and women. The effort could also include creative approaches such as offering more events or teams in sports that have large numbers of women athletes. Finally, the IOC must create an enforcement mechanism to ensure gender equity throughout the Olympic Movement. Discrimination against women's participation at the Olympic Games forces nations to fund women's sport at lower levels because countries often prioritize money for Olympic sports. An enforcement mechanism would create a forum for athletes to assert their rights not only to equal participation but also to equal funding and opportunity.

These positive changes could reverse a decade of systematic discrimination against women. Wamsley (2008) explored the rise of women's participation in sport, ensuing questions about their femininity, and the rise of gender testing. He noted that sport for women was originally structured to guarantee "ladylike" behaviors. In the early 20th century, sport leaders, particularly in the IOC, sought to ensure that men's and women's roles were clearly defined. Problems emerged, however, when women showed feats of athleticism in sports that formerly were the domain of men. Wamsley (2008, p. 9) noted, "The common view of male physical supremacy diminished when the public watched women performing in similar contexts. All men were not faster and stronger than all women."

Early IOC leaders including de Coubertin and Count Henri Baillet-Latour did not want women competing at the Olympic Games, nor did the fourth president, Sigfrid Edstrom. But Edstrom realized that if the IOC was to maintain control over world sport, they could not let continue the Women's Olympics of the 1920s and 1930s, which had emerged as an alternative forum for women athletes (Wamsley, 2008). American Avery Brundage's time at the helm of the IOC focused on women's participation in "feminized sports" like swimming, tennis, figure skating, and gymnastics, in which women's "natural" attributes like grace, rhythm, and artistry were important. According to Wamsley (2008, p. 11), "Female athletes who did not meet these standards of beauty or feminine grace were accused of being mannish, lesbians, or of being unnatural."

Despite the rise of women's participation in the postwar era, two lawsuits filed before the 1984 and 2010 Olympic Games showed that the IOC program and structure for selecting sports continued to perpetuate discrimination against women at the Olympic Games. In 1984 female runners including Norwegian Grete Waitz and American Mary Decker filed suit in Los Angeles stating that the offering of certain men's track events without the corresponding women's races was discriminatory (*Women Runners*, 1984).

In 2009 a coalition of international female ski jumpers filed a lawsuit in Vancouver on similar grounds because ski jumping was offered only for male competitors. The court in Vancouver ruled that the women were being discriminated against under the Canadian Charter of Human Rights and Freedoms but that they had brought the wrong violators into court (British Columbia Supreme Court, 2009). Despite finding that the Vancouver Organizing Committee for the 2010 Winter Olympics (VANOC) was discriminatory, an adverse decision was entered against the women because it was determined that VANOC had no power to set the Olympic program. The judge stated, "The IOC made a decision that discriminates against the plaintiffs. Only the IOC can alleviate that discrimination by

Learning Activity

Break into small discussion groups and brainstorm all the different forms of prejudice and discrimination that might be experienced by members of different identity groups seeking to participate in the Olympic Games or in the IOC organization and governance. Women have taken a very pro-active role in seeking greater gender equality with both the Olympic and Paralympic movements. What are some other groups that might feel marginalized, and why? If given the opportunity to provide suggestions to the IOC and IPC, what would you recommend? What are some of the complexities and challenges in achieving equity in sport, particularly at the international level?

including an Olympic ski jumping event for women in the 2010 Games" (British Columbia Supreme Court, 2009, p. 42).

Although the criteria for adding new events to the Olympic program is not discriminatory against women per se, past discrimination seems to have played a factor. The judge in Canada further found that the IOC's actions stem from historical discrimination against women in ski jumping because in 1949 men's ski jumping was "grandfathered" into the Olympic Games "for the sake of the Olympic Tradition" (British Columbia Supreme Court, 2009, p. 29).

A second issue related to female participation is gender testing. When drug testing was introduced to the Olympics in 1968, so was gender verification testing. The first gender tests conducted at international track events were visual exams, but the IOC used chromosome testing (obtained from a mouth swab) at the 1968 Games in Mexico City. Testing was mandatory only for female athletes. If the test was negative, the female had to undergo further testing. Unlike drug testing, which focused on ensuring an equal playing field for all athletes, the reasoning behind gender testing involved deeper concerns about the femininity, or lack thereof, of certain female athletes (Wamsley, 2008).

CASE STUDY

Caster Semenya

One of the most sensational sport stories of 2009 and 2010 was the Caster Semenya case, which involved a 19-year-old female track and field athlete from South Africa who won the 800-meter event at the 2009 IAAF World Championship race in Berlin in a time more similar to a top men's result than a top women's result. Because of Semenya's muscular build, masculine appearance, and accelerated improvement, the IAAF suspended Semenya from further competition, pending the results of a series of gender verification tests. Fully a year later on July 6, 2010, official results from the IAAF medical examiners cleared Semenya to resume international track competition as a woman, positioning her as the favorite for Olympic gold in London in 2012 (Goldman, 2010). The results of those tests were not made public.

Semenya issued a public statement in 2010 declaring that the circumstances before and after her win in Berlin in 2009 had violated her human rights, including her rights to privacy and dignity. Semenya was just 18 years old when she won the world title, and questions about her gender placed her into the international spotlight. "Since my victory in the female 800 m event at the Berlin world championships in August last year, I have been subjected to unwarranted and invasive scrutiny of the most intimate and private details of my being," said Semenya (Longman, 2010). Some of those details include Australian press reports stating that she did not have either a womb or ovaries and was going through hormone treatment similar to the type that other "gender ambiguous" athletes have received in the past (Goldman, 2010). Ironically, the introduction of hormone therapy in this case, which purportedly was intended to "womanize" an athlete such as Semenya to help make her less dominant as an athlete, begins to blur the line with the antidoping efforts that focus on identifying those who seek to gain an advantage by increasing strength and speed through the use of anabolic steroids and human growth hormone (HGH).

Was Semenya cheating? Should she and other gender ambiguous athletes be banned from competition based on the traditions and norms of fair play? To understand the rationale in support of gender testing and the complexities of trying to develop a reliable and valid testing procedure, one needs to look back at some of the more sensational stories about athletes who were suspected of or caught gender cheating in the Olympic Games.

Suspicion reigned in sports such as track and field between 1932 and 1968 over whether a given athlete was a male posing as a woman. Some of the more interesting Olympic-related cases during this period involved Stella Walsh, Hermann "Dora" Ratjen, who competed as a high jumper for "her or his" native Germany in 1936, and the Press sisters, Tamara and Irina, who won five gold and one silver medals for the Soviet Union in track and field in 1960 and 1964. With the introduction of gender tests at the 1966 European Track and Field Championships in Budapest, Hungary, in 1966, the Press sisters vanished from sport competition.

Ironically, Ewa Klobubowski of Poland, who was a bronze medalist, became famous as the first female to fail a chromosome test in 1964, yet she gave birth to a son in 1965, bringing into question the reliability of the newly introduced chromosome test at that time. World alpine ski champion Erika Schingger of Austria, on the other hand, failed a chromosome test given by her national ski federation and did not compete in the 1968 Olympics in Grenoble even though she was the strong favorite to win the downhill event. In Erika's case, the test results proved accurate as confirmed by the fact "she or he" fathered two sons. (Johnson, 1996; Guttman, 2002).

The Caster Semenya case is a perfect example of what initiated gender testing in the 1960s—"a culture of hyper competition and suspicion" (Olympic Women, 2008).

By 1992 the IOC had replaced chromosome testing with DNA-based testing, and in 1996 before the Summer Games in Atlanta seven women were found to have partial or complete androgen insensitivity. People with androgen insensitivity are identical to females with XX chromosomes at birth but in fact have XY chromosomes. All the athletes were allowed to compete, and because of concerns about widespread testing, the IOC ended gender verification tests before the 2000 Sydney Olympic Games.

New rules give the IOC the power to carry out gender testing of females on a case-by-case basis when gender is "ambiguous," including the involvement of female athletes in "pre-participation examinations" and the creation of medical centers to "diagnose and treat athletes with disorders of sex development" (Wilson, 2010a). The assumption that only females' gender should be tested violates international laws against gender discrimination and the IOC's own gender equality policy. The Caster Semenya case, described in the sidebar, is a recent highly publicized case of an athlete being required to undergo testing. Transgender athletes who have fully completed sex reassignment surgery and completed two years of hormone therapy are eligible to compete in their chosen gender at the Olympic Games.

Inclusion of Athletes With a Disability in the Olympic Games

Disability sport began with a desire to reintegrate persons with disabilities into mainstream society, which has been further described in an article published by Legg, Fay, Hums, and Wolff (2009). These authors noted that for over 50 years this issue has held a significant place within the growth and development of disability sport. Inclusion is a topic that inspires tremendous emotional undertones based on philosophical debate and practical issues related to autonomy, economies of scale, and equity. Not surprisingly then, inclusion is one of the most "discussed, debated, and contentious issues facing disability sport and the Paralympic Movement" (Steadward, 1996, p. 26). For the purposes of this chapter inclusion will be defined as the "final stage in which a particular identity group has been vertically integrated throughout all levels of a given organizational structure, as well as accorded acceptance and respect for its cultural identity at each of these levels" (Fay, 1999; Fay & Wolff, 2009).

Beginning in the early 1990s, the IPC under the direction of its first president, Dr. Robert Steadward, created the Commission for the Inclusion of Athletes with a Disability (CIAD). CIAD played a central and successful strategic role in lobbying the 1994 Commonwealth Games held in Victoria, Canada, to grant events for athletes with a disability with full medal status (Christie, 1997). This meant that athletes with disabilities were not only allowed to compete in what was previously an able bodied competition but their medals were respected as any other and contributed to the overall medal tally.

Four years later when the Commonwealth Games were held in Malaysia the inclusion of athletes with a disability was not followed but it did return in 2002 when the Games were held in Manchester, England. In 2006, the International Commonwealth Games Federation (ICGF) declared that all games starting in 2006 must have full medal status events for athletes with a disability. This model was then hoped to be followed in the Olympic context although this was not to be the case.

Dick Pound, who was then a senior IOC member from Canada, noted that within the Olympic Games there were

> lots of choices to be made, and whenever there are choices to include or exclude [the idea that] you're talking about "discrimination" is a moot point, or a debatable point. Any exercise of distinctions requires discriminating. We [the Olympic Games] cannot be all things to all people. (Clark, 1992, p. 4)

Negotiations between the IOC and IPC, under the auspices of CIAD continued for years and came to a head just prior to the 2004 Olympic Games in Athens.

In July 2004, just weeks before the opening ceremonies, athletes competing in the two wheelchair events were informed that their events would remain in exhibition status. In response, two athletes from the United States who were scheduled to compete in their respective events, Cheri Blauwet and Scot Hollenbeck, wrote to the United States Olympic Committee (USOC) requesting support to contest this decision. In addition, a personal letter dated July 20 to IOC president Jacques Rogge and the president of the Canadian Paralympic Committee (CPC) Patrick Jarvis suggested that a terrible injustice was about to unfold at the birthplace of the modern Olympic Games (Legg, Fay, Hums, & Wolff, 2009).

The situation appeared to be inequitable to the point of outright discrimination. With the indignation that existed within their member organizations and this perceived inequity, the CPC was compelled to take a position and inform both the IPC and the IOC that the situation as it existed was unacceptable and that the treatment of the athletes competing in the wheelchair events contradicted some of the principles that both the Paralympic and Olympic Movements were founded on, namely fair play and sport for all. Jarvis further questioned whether the events still served a purpose, or whether the time had come to discontinue exhibition events. As it related to the

> situation in Athens where the athletes competing in the wheelchair demonstration events are being excluded from the Opening Ceremony and being denied privileges afforded to all others who are members of their country's contingents. It appears to be discriminatory and I appeal to the IOC that they act in accordance with the underlying values of the Olympic Movement such as the sense of fair play, respect and sport for all. . . . We are of the opinion that they should be treated the same as other athletes in Athens or not participate in any fashion: please do it the right way or don't do it all. (Legg, Fay, Hums, & Wolff, 2009)

IOC officials responded by stating in a series of press releases and press interviews that the wheelchair athletes in Athens were being treated exactly the same way as any athlete who had ever competed within an Olympic demonstration event. But were they? To be treated equally manifests the essence of equity. Although they were not being granted full medal status, the athletes with a disability were to receive the same treatment as their Olympic counterparts and the same as countless others who had competed in demonstration events throughout the history of the Olympic Games. But the athletes with a disability did not receive the recognition accorded past demonstration or exhibition athletes in other sports at other Olympic Games (e.g., taekwondo, curling, freestyle skiing, short-track speed skating, softball) (Fay & Wolff, 2009).

In fact, athletes with a disability did not receive the same recognition they had in prior Olympic programs. At the 1988 Olympic Games, athletes with a disability participating in alpine and Nordic ski events were housed, clothed, and credentialed in the same manner as other demonstration sport athletes at a level nearly equal with Olympic athletes from their respective nations. In Beijing at the Olympic Games in 2008, more than 20 years after the events were first included, the inclusion of wheelchair exhibition events ended (Beijing, 2008; International Association of Athletics Federations, 2008; Legg, Fay, Hums, & Wolff, 2009).

Given his past advocacy for inclusion into the Olympic Games, it was not surprising when Dr. Robert Steadward, the initial IPC president, suggested that putting the Olympic and Paralympic Games together would create efficiencies and allow the Paralympics to take advantage of public support for the Olympics. Steadward suggested that the natural evolution of the Paralympic Movement would call for it to be included more in the Olympics. "I wouldn't mind seeing the 100-metre men's final, the 100-metre women's final, the 100-metre wheelchair final and the 100-metre final for blind runners," he said. Pointing to the intense national pride that emerged in Vancouver during the Olympics in 2010, he said that it was a shame for the Paralympics to have to "re-energize" the city 10 days later (Battistoni, 2010).

Phil Craven, the second president for the IPC, rejected the idea of combining the Olympic and Paralympic Winter Games into one megaevent, saying that the Paralympic Movement was doing just fine as it was. Craven, who became president in 2001, said that the Paralympics had become a force of their own over the last decade (2000–2010) and would be diminished if they were melded into the Olympic Games:

> Any coming together would, I think, by its very nature, be restrictive from a logistics point of view. We have it as we like it at the moment, and we don't see any need to change. We believe by having the Paralympics and the Olympics separate, we're able to have our own identity while coming together in a festival of sport that gives a wonderful face to the world of what sport can do.

Gilbert Felli, then executive director of Olympic Games for the IOC, stated in 2010 that the two groups had worked out an agreement that allowed the IOC to assist the IPC. Putting the two events together, Felli reiterated, would only hamstring the events, resulting in fewer Paralympic athletes participating in any given Games. Craven also dismissed the idea that consideration be given for the Paralympics to be held in advance of the Olympics to take advantage of the more than 10,000 media and broadcasters who typically descend on an Olympic host city. Historically, far fewer journalists stick around for the Paralympics. Craven, however, was adamant and said that Paralympics want to stand on their own merit. "I believe the Paralympic Games have to attract the media in their own right," he said (Battistoni, 2010).

A final issue that has been at the root of the Paralympic Movement since its inception has been one of the valuing and recognition of Paralympic versus Olympic athletes by given nations. A prime example of this was evident in Canada in 2004 after the Athens Olympic and Paralympic Games when Chantal Petitclerc shared the honor of Athletics Canada's Female Athlete of the Year (Jack Davies Trophy) with Perdita Felicien, winner of the hurdles competition in the 2003 IAAF World Championships. Despite being the heavy favorite, Felicien did not finish in the finals of the 110-meter track event at the Olympics in Athens in 2004 because of a fall. Petitclerc, on the other hand, won the Olympic 800-meter wheelchair track exhibition event at the Olympic Games as well as four Paralympic gold medals at various distances just two weeks later.

The question was whether the accomplishments of Petitclerc and Felicien should be valued equally. In a *Globe and Mail* article following the 2004 Games that profiled Petitclerc as one of Canada's Nation Builders, she noted her disdain with the perception that it is easier to win a Paralympic medal than an Olympic medal. "That may have been true 15 years ago. That's not the case now" (Wong, 2004, p. F1). Two weeks after Athletics Canada announced its Jack Davies Trophy cowinners, *Maclean's Magazine*, Canada's national weekly news magazine, named Petitclerc the 2004 Canadian of the Year (Gillis, 2004).

Even with outstanding performances by athletes such as Petitclerc and others, Paralympic sport is not always seen as being elite. As noted by Bell (2002), "The issue is really quality of competition." The reality according to Bell (2002) was that only a few events mirrored the competitiveness found in the Olympic Games. Bell (2002) determined that from 1960 until 2000 Olympic athletes had a 1 in 10 chance of receiving a medal, whereas Paralympic athletes had a 6 in 10 chance. Bell (2002) also clarified, however, that he was not suggesting that Paralympic performances equated to poor performances; instead, they were fraught with poor quality of competition that could not be considered equal to that found in Olympic competitions. He recognized that the men's 1,500-meter and women's 800-meter wheelchair races that had been showcased as Olympic exhibition events from 1984 through Athens in 2004 were exceptions. The results from the exhibition events in Athens in 2004 support this proposition; the difference between the gold medal and sixth place was .84

second in the men's contest and 1.02 seconds for the women's event.

Returning now to how athletes with a disability have competed against able-bodied athletes, Brian McKeever, a visually impaired cross-country ski racer and decorated Paralympic champion, narrowly missed becoming the first winter athlete to compete in both the Paralympic and Olympic Games in Vancouver 2010. Other athletes such as Natalie du Toit and Natalie Partyka had also competed in both Olympic and Paralympic Games two years earlier in Beijing, and athletes with a disability have competed in the Olympic Games going back as far as 1904 (Legg, Burchell, Jarvis, & Sainsbury, 2009; *Paralympian*, 2009). Although named to the Canadian Olympic team, McKeever did not get to realize his dream because his national team coach decided not to start him in the 50K race on the final day of the Games. Given that a number of athletes have already demonstrated the ability to qualify and compete in both the Paralympic and Olympic Games despite the competitive disadvantage (or advantage) of their disability, what will the future bring?

Athlete Human Rights

Another issue within the Olympic and Paralympic Movements that has garnered considerable attention can be captured under the general heading of human rights. Outside of sport, the last 25 years have seen an explosion of human rights discourse. From the passage of new international treaties and declarations to the creation of regional and human rights courts across the world, human rights encompass a wide range of political, civil, economic, and cultural protections. Sport and athletes are an important part of this framework. Most international and national sporting charters state that sport should promote human rights (Dryden, 2006). The Olympic Charter itself states, "The practice of sport is a human right" (*Olympic Charter*, 2010).

Furthermore, the goal of the Olympic Movement is "to contribute to building a peaceful and better world by educating youth through sport practised without discrimination of any kind, in a spirit of friendship, solidarity, and fair play" (*Olympic Charter*, 2010). Lacking a global police force, international organizations have traditionally aided international human rights regimes by developing creative enforcement mechanisms to promote and protect human rights (Alvarez, 2005). The role of international sporting organizations in the antiapartheid movement reflects this function. But decades of nationalistic pursuits and the systematic doping of young athletes, claims that particular women's sports are not significantly developed to be viable, and statements that sport and politics should be separate have led to conflict between international human rights law and the IOC. As noted by Human Rights Watch before the Beijing Olympics, "The question isn't whether the IOC is a human rights organization. It's whether the Olympic Movement respects human rights" (Human Rights Watch, 2008).

Under international law, children have special rights, and athletes under age 18 are no exception. From the right to health and play to protection against forced labor, the Convention on the Rights of the Child mandates that nations uphold these rights for all children. Yet in countries like China (and in the former East Germany and USSR), children are taken away from their families as preteens and sent to sport schools to train full time, where they are provided with negligible education and few outside activities (Gabriel, 1998; Harvey, 1988; Ungerleider, 2001; Hong, 2006). When a child's performance produces financial rewards for parents or provides coaches and agents with salaries and prize money, the child's sport can be seen as a form of child labor (Donnelly & Petherick, 2006).

But when does a paternalistic approach to protecting child athletes rise to a violation of their right to choose? The sports of gymnastics, figure skating, and tennis have all ruled that children under the age of 16 cannot compete internationally or, as in the case of tennis, turn professional. Protecting a child from exploitation and abuse must be balanced with a child's right to pursue his or her athletic dreams. National and international sport federations seemed best poised to protect the health of child athletes and promote athlete education as well (Donnelly & Petherick, 2006).

The trafficking of children and other young athletes in sports like football, hockey, and basketball has also begun to receive attention. In 1999 Belgium was revealed as one of the worst offenders when it came to importing football players from Africa to "sell on the European market" (Donnelly & Petherick, 2006). This "new slave trade" led to laws restricting the importing of athletes under age 18, but the practice continues for young athletes over this age (Donnelly & Petherick, 2006).

The right to health is found in the International Covenant on Economic, Social, and Political Rights and in the Olympic Charter. In the wake of the era of state-sponsored doping in East Germany, former athletes who were doped as children and young adults took their cases to the German courts, asking for compensation for the myriad of health problems that they suffer decades after the fall of the Berlin Wall (Ungerleider, 2001; Longman, 2004). The German government set up a $2.18 million fund to help pay the medical bills of doped athletes (10 Drug Scandals, 2003), and the rise of the World Anti-Doping Agency has helped.

Although it is an idealist document, the Olympic Charter comes in direct conflict with international law in one particular area: freedom of expression. This human right is outlined in the Universal Declaration of Human Rights as well as the International Covenant on Civil and Political Rights, yet the Olympic Charter expressly prohibits athletes and spectators from expressing themselves freely in all Olympic venues (Olympic Charter, 2010). In 1968, IOC president Avery Brundage ordered American Olympic gold and bronze medalists Tommie Smith and John Carlos expelled from the Olympics after they raised black-gloved fists on the podium at the Mexico City Olympics in support of civil rights in the United States (Hartmann, 2003; Smith & Steele, 2007). But the same Avery Brundage was president of the USOC during the 1936 Olympic Games where, without objection, every German athlete made the Nazi salute on the medal podium (Berkes, 2008). This Olympic Charter rule curtailing freedom of expression, along with guidelines published by the Chinese government, in 2008 prevented athletes and spectators from speaking out about human rights violations in China and Sudan leading up to and at the Olympic Games in Beijing (Amnesty International, 2008; Team Darfur, 2008).

The Olympic Games has the power to promote human rights, and many believe that the sporting boycotts against South Africa during apartheid were key to its eventual demise (Booth, 2003). Yet the IOC and host Olympic organizing committees continue to violate the rights of athletes in spite of their own rules supporting human rights and in violation of both national and international law. Athlete rights in professional sport have been protected not by their governing bodies but by athlete unions. The first attempt at an Olympic athlete union was created to oppose the Olympic bribery scandals in 1999. OATH (Olympic Athletes Together Honorably) lasted only a few years, but the creation of an athlete union focused on athlete rights and supported by international law might possibly begin to challenge a century of violations.

An athlete's commission was created in 1981 at the IOC. Today the commission is made up of 12 athletes who are elected for eight-year terms by the athletes who participate in the Olympic Games. Seven more athletes are appointed by the IOC president, and there are two ex-officio members—one from the World Olympians Association and one from the International Paralympic Committee. The power and influence of this and other athlete commissions is debatable (Houlihan, 2006).

Fair Play On and Off the Playing Field

Similar to social and ethical issues, Olympic and Paralympic sport also face serious challenges to fair play both inside and outside the sport venue. Athletes and officials take an oath before every game to play clean and play fair and yet we know that cheating of many different kinds occur (Hill, 2008; Fisman, 2010). The business and commercialization of the Games has created additional pressures on National Olympic and Paralympic Committees to field successful teams to satisfy corporate sponsors and national pride. Antidoping, illegal performance enhancements, techno-doping, and match fixing all conspire to denigrate the sense of fair play. The following section will address some of the more egregious issues facing the IOC and IPC with respect to fair play by athletes, officials, and organizers.

Official and Athlete Fixing

The issue of match fixing by athletes or game officials is not a new phenomenon. With the rapid increase in sports betting over the past several decades in soccer, basketball, and other professional sports, as well as the increase in spending by national Olympic committees to insure better podium results by offering bonuses to medal winners, it is no wonder that this issue has become an Olympic and Paralympic issue of high concern (Hill, 2008; Kaerup, 2009a). In 2007 the IOC began to consult IFs on the issue of match fixing and sport betting (Wilson, 2010b). By 2008 they had established a disciplinary commission to investigate the issue at the Beijing Olympic Games (Kelso, 2008). By 2010 the IOC had agreements with major legal betting companies and Interpol to monitor "irregular gambling patterns" because of links between match fixing, organized crime, and professional referees and athletes (Wilson, 2010b). Play-the-Game conference organizers called for an independent anticorruption body (Anderson, 2009). In 2009 at the IOC Congress later that year, IOC president Rogge heeded the call, stating, "We will establish a new independent monitoring body to combat irregular betting and match fixing" (IOC Re-Elects President Jacques Rogge, 2009).

No sooner had the IOC recovered from the host city bribery scandal in 1999 than the shady underside of Olympic figure skating reared its ugly head. At the Salt Lake City Games in 2002, Russian skaters Yelena Berezhnaya and Anton Sikharulidze were awarded the gold over Canadians Jamie Salé and David Pelletier. Marie-Reine Le Gougne, the French judge, allegedly confessed (but later denied) to the chair of the International Skating Union (ISU) that she had been forced to vote for the Russians by the French federation so that the Russians would assist the French ice dancers later in the Games program (Macdonald, 2010).

Eric Zitzewitz, an economist at Dartmouth College, researched the 2002 Salt Lake City figure-skating competition and was able to calculate that the problem went much deeper. He studied the data on 3,000 performances from 2000 through 2002 and found that judges from an athlete's country scored their countrymen and women 0.2 points higher, which often was sufficient to move them up one position in the rankings (Fisman, 2010). In the aftermath of the scandal the ISU overhauled the judging system, but Zitzewitz discovered that it was worse than originally thought. In a subsequent study he found that fellow judges from a skater's country now provided a 20 percent advantage (Fisman, 2010).

Doping

From ancient Greek athletes who used potions to cyclists in the 19th century who used everything from strychnine to cocaine, the use of performance enhancing substances is as old as the Olympic Games themselves (World Anti-Doping Agency, 2009a). Despite the constant testing of athletes, laws criminalizing it, and rules banning it, doping is still widespread throughout the world of sport (Longman, 2004).

Drug testing was first conducted at the 1968 Olympic Winter Games in Grenoble and the Summer Games in Mexico City. By the 1970s most international federations (IFs) were drug testing, but the tests were doing little to catch the dopers, who were always one step ahead of the testers. In 1996 investigative reporter Andrew Jennings revealed cover-up stories of widespread doping at the 1984 Olympic Games in Los Angeles (Jennings, 1996). But catching cheaters was especially difficult when an entire state was orchestrating the doping program.

The former East Germany codified a systematic, state-sponsored doping program into State Planning Theme 14.25 in 1974. For almost 30 years from 1969 to 1988 the Communist regime systematically doped over 10,000 young athletes to promote its international political agenda (Ungerleider, 2001). Somewhere between 500 and 2,000 of those athletes are thought to be victims of the long-term health risks of prolonged steroid abuse (Ungerleider, 2001; Longman, 2004), evidence of which was known by those in power as early as the 1960s (Ungerleider, 2001).

But it was not the East Germans who were busted at the 1988 Olympic Games, but a runner from Canada. Just before the fall of the Berlin Wall, one of the most famous doping scandals occurred at the Olympic Games in Seoul when Ben Johnson won the 100-meter running event only to test positive for an anabolic steroid. Despite rumors that Johnson was not the only dirty athlete on the track, the IOC did not ramp up efforts to fight doping (Jennings, 1996).

By the mid-1990s East Germany was a memory, but those in charge had relocated to China (Gabriel, 1998; Ungerleider, 2001). In 1994 alone, 31 Chinese athletes tested positive (Goodbody, 1995). At the Chinese National Games in September 1993 and the World Swimming Championships in August 1994, Chinese female swimmers and runners exploded into the international spotlight. The runners smashed world records in three events in 1993, and the swimmers won 12 of 16 women's events at the 1994 World Championships and set five world records. Within a matter of weeks, 11 swimmers, including 2 of the women who had dominated in

the pool, tested positive for steroids in an out-of-competition drug test (Whitten, 1995). In 1998 Australian customs agents found a team's supply of HGH in the suitcase of Yuan Yuan, a Chinese swimmer headed to the World Swimming Championships in Perth (Montville, 1998).

With outside law enforcement beginning to reveal the extent of the problem, the IOC took action. In February 1999 the first ever World Conference on Doping in Sport was held. By November, after 30 years of state-sponsored doping in East Germany and a decade of doping scandals in running, swimming, and cycling, the World Anti-Doping Agency was created. The World Anti-Doping Code (World Anti-Doping Agency, 2009b) went into force in 2004, and in 2005 UNESCO's General Conference adopted the International Convention Against Doping in Sport, which took effect on February 1, 2007.

The creation of WADA, which is funded partially by the IOC and governments, and the adoption of the code helped to regain the trust of the world sporting community (Houlihan, 2006). By 2010 an antidoping violation could be leveled against an athlete, coach, or anyone in the chain from production to distribution to injection or ingestion. The code requires several pages to define doping, including everything from providing a dirty sample to trafficking and possession, and use of a long list of performance-enhancing substances and methods.

WADA's tasks include scientific research, education, development, and harmonization of antidoping rules and procedures in all sports and all countries, as well as monitoring and ensuring compliance to the code. Adding further strength to its mission, WADA began to cooperate with law enforcement, UN agencies, and individual governments to combat manufacturing and trafficking of doping substances.

Today, law enforcement agencies play a huge role in antidoping activities because of its links to international crime syndicates and drug trafficking (Donati, 2007; Kelso, 2009). In 2002 the Internal Revenue Service began initial investigations into the U.S.-based Bay Area Laboratory Co-Operative (BALCO), which resulted in years of federal probes and prosecutions of trainers, suppliers, and athletes in sports as diverse as baseball, judo, football, and track and field ("Bay Area Laboratory Co-Operative," 2009). In Australia, national legislation allows the Australian Sports Anti-Doping Agency the legal authority to deter and detect doping, and enforce antidoping laws.

In 2008 the International Cycling Union (ICU) created the first athlete biological passport, and by 2009 WADA's Athlete Biological Passport Operating Guideline took effect. The guideline lays out the science behind the Athlete Biological Passport, which instead of comparing an athlete's sample with those of other athletes, allows scientists to measure the sample against the athlete's own history (World Anti-Doping Agency, 2009c). A passport contains results of urine and blood tests as well as blood and steroid profiles. Many believe that biological passports are the key to catching dopers because they create individual benchmarks for each athlete that can be measured over time (Cribb, 2010).

According to Munthe, human genome mapping may affect sport in four ways. Athletes may use knowledge of their genes to "optimize" training and nutrition or "fine-tune the chemical composition of a drug to suit their genetic makeup," modify red blood cells or make genes and then insert hormones such as insulin-like growth factor 1 (IGF-1), genetically modify the fertilized egg or embryo, or use genetic markers for talent identification (Houlihan, 2006).

The first three of these forms of genetic engineering remain cutting-edge technology, but such tactics could be a reality in the near future. Professor H. Lee Sweeney and assistant professor Elisabeth Barton of the University of Pennsylvania's Department of Physiology used gene therapy to increase the muscle strength of mice by 35 percent by producing increased levels of IGF-1 (Sokolove, 2004). When performed on athletes, such therapies could override healthy normal genes with gene transfers to improve strength or endurance; these therapies are considered gene doping and would be caught only by tissue biopsies (Ruibal, 2004; Houlihan, 2006).

Sweeney said in 2004 that he gets "dozens of calls every week" from athletes who want to volunteer for IGF-1 human trials (Ruibal, 2004). "For safety reasons, those trials are at least five years away, but that knowledge hasn't deterred those eager for transformation now. . . . There are a number of scientists who have the wherewithal to do this to a human," he said, adding, "There are plenty of athletes willing to spend $100,000 for a new set of muscles" (Ruibal, 2004).

Questioning the Fair Play Framework

After a decade in existence an unintended consequence of the increased vigilance was the perceived intrusion on athletes' rights. Serious backlash against WADA and the code emerged from certain professional athletes fed up with onerous reporting requirements and the 2009 updates to the "whereabouts rule." The whereabouts rule is part of the code and requires certain elite athletes to provide their exact whereabouts for one hour of each day between 6 a.m. and 11 p.m. to their international sport federation (IF) or national antidoping agency. Before, the rule required athletes to keep officials aware of their whereabouts daily, but without the specific one-hour requirement. If an athlete missed three tests in an 18-month period, he or she would be banned for at least one year (FIFA, 2009; World Anti-Doping Agency, 2010).

Lawsuits have been filed by athletes in the Court of Arbitration for Sport and in Belgium, the latter based on privacy protections set out in the European Convention on Human Rights. FIFA lashed out immediately, as did the top stars of tennis and even rowers, who said that the system was a "constant hassle and panic" (Macur, 2009). FIFA and UEFA issued a statement about the new rule stating that they "formally reject" the whereabouts rule and "want to see it replaced by collective location rules" (FIFA, 2009). WADA executives responded that there would be no concessions for football.

The provision and management of samples had serious implications for athletes' rights, including the right to a fair hearing, right to privacy, right to work, and even the rights of child athletes (Schneider, 2006; Houlihan, 2006). Antidoping rules follow strict liability, meaning that the athlete is held strictly liable for the presence of a banned substance in her or his body (Schneider, 2006). Furthermore, there is no distinction in the code for children, who are held to the same strict liability standard (Houlihan, 2006).

The world of antidoping involves a host of duties and rights, and the process is not nearly as simple as it was in 1990 when Justice Dubin said these words during his inquiry into drugs in Canadian sport: "It is to be observed that an individual's participation in sport is not a right, but a privilege,

CASE STUDY

Oscar Pistorius

Elite athletes are constantly seeking ways to gain a competitive advantage over their competitors through a variety of means ranging from altering their bodies through doping to embracing new equipment technologies to enhance both training and performance. Thus, advances in science and technologies adapted and adopted for sport purposes can challenge social norms and values of what is "normal" and blur the perceptions of what is fair and what is not.

2004 and 2008 Paralympic champion Oscar Pistorius is a 400-meter runner who worked hard to meet the IAAF individual qualifying standards required to compete in the 2008 Beijing Olympic Games for his native South Africa. Pistorius was born without a fibula in both legs and had his legs amputated just below the knees as a child. What makes Pistorius's case noteworthy was a decision rendered by the IAAF stating that he was ineligible to compete in the 2008 Olympic Games because his prosthetics provided him an unfair or competitive advantage. This perceived advantage was based solely on the results of a specifically designed study contracted by the IAAF to test Pistorius against the results of four national-level athletes (Hoy, 2009; Legg, Burchell, Jarvis, & Sainsbury, 2009; Wolbring, Legg, & Stahnisch, 2010).

Pistorius challenged this decision by taking legal action. He argued before the Court of Arbitration in Sport (CAS) that the tests employed by the IAAF were neither conclusive nor reliable (Klein, 2008). CAS overturned the IAAF decision, giving Pistorius new hope for qualifying for the individual 400-meter race in Beijing. Although he just missed the qualification standard, he remained among the top four fastest standing athletes in South Africa with or without a disability, thus qualifying for selection to the South African 4 by 400-meter relay team, which participated in the Games (Pistorious, 2008). Despite overwhelming proof that his times warranted selection, the South African Olympic Committee and the South African Athletics Federation chose to leave Pistorius off the 2008 Olympic team for what appeared to be political rather than performance reasons (Wolbring, Legg, & Stahnisch, 2010). The action, or rather the inaction, of the SAOC and SAAF relative to Pistorius indicates the concern within the international sport governance community over the meaning and consequences of the ruling by the Court for Arbitration in Sport with respect to fair play issues.

The CAS ruling reinforces the view that the Olympics are not about "normative biological" bodies (Wolbring, Legg, & Stahnisch, 2010) and in fact create a precedent for a person with a disability to compete in the Olympic Games. If the "artificial" prosthetic does not lead to a competitive advantage, athletes with disabilities should be able to compete against able bodied athletes. If the prosthetic is deemed to create a competitive advantage, then perhaps there is a place where these individuals could compete against each other treating the artificial body part similar to an external tool such as a hockey stick (Wolbring 2008a; Wolbring 2008b; Wolbring, Legg, & Stahnisch, 2010). Pistorius is presently training with the hopes of competing in both the 2012 Olympic and Paralympic Games.

---

and as such it is subject to the rules governing the sport in which the athlete wishes to participate" (Dubin, 1990).

Rising expectations of athletes and the pressure to win have triggered research and development in new products and processes that can be used to move the bodily functioning of athletes and their external equipment to ever-higher levels of performance. These advances are used by so-called impaired and nonimpaired athletes. This issue raises a variety of questions:

1. Should there be a limit to the enhancements allowed?

2. Where should the line be drawn between legal and illegal human enhancement technologies?

3. Will there be a difference in the future between impaired and nonimpaired athletes?

4. Who will be the impaired and nonimpaired athletes of the future?

5. Will the Olympics become the Paralympics and vice versa?

Learning Activity

On a piece of paper, write down what the phrase "athlete with a disability" means to you. Then, in a group, share your definitions and discuss possible situations in Olympic sports that would make having a disability more difficult to define. In what situations would it be likely for athletes identified as having a disability and athletes who are not identified as having a disability to compete against each other? What changes to competition rules, eligibility rules, and classification rules might need to be considered? What questions would this raise?

Olympics (Paralympics) Games of 2036—The Inclusive Games

Based on the various issues that have been presented, an interesting process would be to look inside the mythical crystal ball and envision what the Summer Olympic and Paralympic Games of 2036 organized on the 140th anniversary of the modern Olympic Games will look like. What is fascinating about such a process is that one often finds more similarities than differences in similar organizations such as the IOC and IPC, particularly when studying evolutionary patterns of organizational change.

So, what might the 2036 Olympic Games look like? One might conjecture their being staged for the first time in a primarily Islamic nation. After narrowly losing out to the winning bid of Delhi and Mumbai, India, for the 2032 Games, Turkey was finally rewarded by the IOC for its years of persistence and commitment to the Olympic ideals as evidenced by decades of unsuccessful bids to stage the Summer Olympic Games. The controversial selection of Istanbul to host the 140th anniversary Games was ironic given the centuries of war and animus between Greece, the ancient land of the Olympic Games, and neighboring Turkey, which were exacerbated by the centuries-long dispute over control of the island of Cyprus. Perceived as a statement of the power and ability of the Olympic Movement to bring peace to historically war-torn places, this achievement positioned the IOC and

its new president, Dmitry Chernyshenko, president and CEO of the hugely successful 2014 Olympic and Paralympic Winter Games in Sochi, Russia, to be strongly considered for a 2036 Nobel Peace Prize.

Beginning with the 2008 Olympic and Paralympic Summer Games in Beijing, China, and followed by the successful staging of the 2014 Winter Games in Sochi, the 2016 Summer Games in Rio de Janiero, Brazil, the 2024 Summer Games in South Africa, and the 2032 Summer Games in India, the IOC successfully shifted the locus of its financial, marketing, and media strategies from its traditional European and North American base deep into the heart of the largest of the world's new economies (Rosner & Shropshire, 2011). Following the lead of several international federations involved in some of the larger Olympic sports (e.g., FIFA, FIS, and FIBA) and their bold strategies of placing their respective single-sport world championships in the new economies of Brazil, Russia, India, and China together with South Africa and Turkey (a.k.a. BRICSAT), the IOC was able to take a low-risk approach by piggybacking on the logistics and infrastructure already in place from past single-sport megaevents (e.g., track and field, basketball, and skiing) to ensure a successful multisport extravaganza that the Olympic (Paralympic) Games had become (*Brazil's decade of sport*, 2010).

The decision to invite wheelchair basketball, wheelchair rugby, and a select number of previously Paralympic-only track, swimming, and cycling events to become official Olympic sports in time for the 2024 Olympic Summer Games in South Africa forced the IPC to reconsider its separate but equal position with respect to the IOC. Faced with losing its top athletes and most marketable sports to the Olympic Games, the IPC capitulated and agreed to be absorbed as a new division of the IOC in 2025 with full inclusion occurring for the first time at the 2028 Olympic Winter Games held in Harbin, China (*China embraces*, 2009). This groundbreaking inclusive arrangement between the IOC and IPC was achieved as the result of years of international advocacy and pressure by the United Nations and the European Parliament along with individual governments, labor unions, corporations, and volunteer groups that have been working to remove barriers to full participation in many sectors of civilized society in partial fulfillment of the UN Millennium Goals

(United Nations, 2006) and the Convention on the Rights of Persons with Disabilities (UN, 2007).

The acceptance by the IOC in 2020 that all Paralympians would henceforth be referred to as Olympians was a testament to the resolve, persistence, and dedication of a number of former Paralympic and Olympic athletes with a disability, beginning with the track and skiing athletes who competed in the first Olympic exhibition events in Sarajevo and Los Angeles in 1984 through Athens in 2004 to a number of individual athletes who qualified and competed in the Olympics despite their respective disabilities for many decades to follow (Legg, Fay, Hums, & Wolff, 2009; Legg, Burchill, Jarvis, & Sainsbury, 2009). But it was Oscar Pistorius's highly publicized quest to qualify for the 400-meter sprint at the 2008 Olympic Games, along with the bid of Canadian Paralympic champion Brian McKeever to become the first Paralympian to qualify as a Winter Olympian at the 2010 Vancouver Olympic Games, that provided the tipping point for sport governing bodies and sporting officials to begin to question the future of the Paralympic Games in relation to the Olympic Games (Legg, Burchill, Jarvis, & Sainsbury, 2009).

Some sport historians cited the debate that occurred after the 2010 Winter Paralympic Games in Vancouver between the first and second presidents of the IPC, Dr. Robert Steadward and Sir Philip Craven, over the purported right place for the Paralympic Games to be governed and staged by the IOC as a critical turning point in the eventual full integration of Paralympic athletes as Olympians beginning with the 2028 Olympic Winter Games in China (Battistoni, 2010). A separate agreement was negotiated in 2025 by the IOC with Special Olympics International (SOI) regarding its continued use of the term *Olympic* in its name and its ongoing oversight of the major international multisport Winter and Summer Games in odd-numbered years for athletes with an intellectual disability. A similar agreement was reached between the IOC regarding the Deaflympics for athletes who are deaf or have a significant hearing impairment.

The 2036 Istanbul Summer Olympic (Paralympic) Games were also noteworthy regarding fair play and doping issues, as well as gender equity issues, that had long plagued the Olympic Movement. A new, relatively simple genetic test developed by an international consortium of sport scientists virtually brought to an end over a half century of drug and blood doping. Critics hailed this achievement as the start of a new era of fair play. Arguments over whether athletes who undergo genetic regeneration, hormonal therapy, smart limb replacement, or augmentation therapies are able to compete against athletes with more "normalized" bodies was decided by the Court of Arbitration for Sport (CAS) in favor of a more inclusive, open, transhumanist approach (Wolbring, 2008b).

The 2036 Summer Olympic Games followed the precedent-setting 2034 Winter Games, where for the first time in Olympic history more women than men competed. This feat was the result of an extensive audit by the IOC Olympic Program Commission, chaired by Angela Ruggiero, IOC vice president and four-time U.S. Olympic ice hockey medalist (1998–2010), that created a new set of equity principles forcing international federations of Olympic sports to balance their event schedules, funding, and leadership and coaching figures with respect to gender. The audit also resulted in the addition of women's ski jumping in the Winter Games and a return of softball for women in the Summer Games. Ruggiero's leadership, based on the principle of universal access and equity in sport for all, helped bring the IOC full circle from its founding in 1896 as an exclusive bastion of white, male privilege to being a farsighted organization that truly lives its principle of valuing diversity, equity, and fair play. Many journalists speculate that Ruggiero will become the first female IOC president, succeeding Chernyshenko's when his term of office ends in 2042.

Summary

The Olympic and Paralympic Games have linked and somewhat parallel histories. Each has had to deal with issues pertaining to governance, equity, management, and enabling fair competition at the highest levels. The future of the two movements is now more intertwined than ever before and it will be interesting for future scholars in sport management to track how they have grown, evolved, and contributed to our sporting systems worldwide.

? Review and Discussion Questions

1. What are the differences in structure and governance between the International Olympic Committee and the International Paralympic Committee?

2. Name five key stakeholders that the IOC and IPC must engage when organizing the Olympic and Paralympic Games.

3. In what ways have the Olympic Games become more commercialized over the past several decades? What are the benefits and drawbacks of this trend?

4. Describe the history of women's sports in the Olympic Games.

5. What forms of gender testing have been used at the Olympics? For which athletes have tests been required?

6. Discuss whether sport events for athletes with a disability should be included in the Olympic Games as opposed to the Paralympic Games. What is meant by an exhibition event, and what issues has that status raised for some athletes with disabilities?

CHAPTER 11

International Sport Federations

Li Chen, PhD
Delaware State University, USA

Chia-Chen Yu, EdD
University of Wisconsin-La Crosse, USA

Chapter Objectives

After studying this chapter, you will be able to do the following:

- Define international sport federations
- Describe the major managerial functions of international sport federations
- Outline the common organizational structure and governance model of international sport federations
- Describe the relationship between international sport federations and other international sport governing bodies, such as the IOC
- Explain how international sport federations are financed
- Identify the stakeholders of international sport federations
- Identify the key managerial issues facing international sport federations

Key Terms

International sport federations, also simply referred to as IFs in the Olympic vocabulary, are governing bodies in various sports at the international level. They play a significant role in promotion of global sport development and the Olympic Movement. Although the International Olympic Committee (IOC) is the highest governing body for the Olympic Movement, the IFs are mainly responsible for administering each of the sports at the international level. In this chapter, we discuss how the IFs, IOC, and other Olympic organizations cooperate with each other to set up rules and policies for Olympic competitions, and develop and promote international sport in the world. Also described are the mission, purpose, and operations of a typical IF and its relationship with other Olympic sport organizations, ranging from the IOC to the **organizing committees of the Olympic Games** (**OCOG**), which are authorized by the IOC to organize the Olympic Games, and the national Olympic committee (NOC), which is the national sport governing body in each country. Furthermore, issues related to management of an IF are discussed.

What Are International Federations?

An **international (sport) federation** (**IF**) is a nongovernmental organization established to govern one or more sports at the international level. Although most IFs represent only one sport, a number of them oversee several sports, such as the Fédération Internationale de Natation, which sanctions swimming, diving, water polo, synchronized swimming, and open-water swimming.

Although each IF maintains independence and autonomy in governing its own sport or sports to be continuously recognized by the IOC, the IF must cooperate with the IOC to make sure that its statutes, practices, and activities conform to the Olympic Charter. According to the Olympic Charter (Olympic Charter, 2007b), the common missions and roles of the IFs within the Olympic Movement include the following:

a. to establish and enforce, in accordance with the Olympic spirit, the rules concerning the practice of their respective sports and to ensure their application;

b. to ensure the development of their sports throughout the world;

c. to contribute to the achievement of the goals set out in the Olympic Charter, in particular by way of the spread of Olympism and Olympic education;

d. to express their opinions on the candidatures for organizing the Olympic Games, in particular as far as the technical aspects of venues for their respective sports are concerned;

e. to establish their criteria of eligibility for the competitions of the Olympic Games in conformity with the Olympic Charter, and to submit these to the IOC for approval;

f. to assume the responsibility for the technical control and direction of their sports at the Olympic Games and at the Games held under the patronage of the IOC; and

g. to provide technical assistance in the practical implementation of the Olympic Solidarity program (p. 58).

Besides its role in the Olympic Movement, a key purpose of an IF is to govern and promote a particular sport or sports internationally. As indicated by Theodoraki (2007), other purposes of IFs include (a) to administer and monitor operations and competitions of the sport worldwide, (b) to engage in the development of the sport and related regulations and policies, and (c) to organize international championships and other competitions. For example, the types of competitions and events organized by the International Biathlon Union (IBU) consist of the World Championships, Biathlon World Cup, Continental Championships, Biathlon Continental Cups, and Summer Biathlon World Championships (IBU, 2009).

The major functions of the IFs are consistent with their common missions in promoting their sports, organizing competitions, and developing new programs (FINA, 2009a). The following are the major functions of an IF:

a. Cooperating with the IOC for recognitions and participation of the Olympic Games

b. Functioning as a legislative body of rules, regulation, and policies for its sport

c. Determining competition levels

d. Playing a role in defining eligibilities and statuses of competitions

e. Determining affiliations with business organizations

f. Developing rules, policies, and measures against illegal or unethical practice in the sport

g. Making a decision on the equipment and site requirements for competitions

h. Determining qualifications of judges or referees and appointing the officers

i. Collecting, analyzing, examining, and maintaining all data and records of the sport federation (FINA, 2009a; ITTF, 2009)

The IFs also collaborate with the OCOG for all the technical functions during the Olympic Games. Each IF is responsible for technical control and elements of the competitions of its sport, including the schedule, field of play, and training sites. All equipment must comply with the rules of the IF. According to the Olympic Charter (2007c), the major responsibilities of IFs concerning technical functions at the Olympic Games include the following:

a. Establishing the technical rules of their own sports, disciplines, and events

b. Establishing the results and ranking of Olympic competitions

c. Selecting judges, referees, and other technical officials from the host country or from abroad

d. Enforcing, under the authority of the IOC and the NOCs, the rules of the IOC concerning the eligibility of the participants before the Olympic Games (preliminaries) and during the Olympic Games

e. Requiring technical provisions such as training facilities, technical equipment at the venues, technical installations, and so on (p. 92)

International Federations and the Olympic Movement

Although all IFs are autonomous and independent, the IOC does not recognize all IFs. The IFs can be classified into four categories based on whether their sports are part of the official programming of the Olympic Games and the degree to which they are recognized by the IOC. Each of these categories

has an international federation associated with it. These associations may act as spokespersons to discuss common issues or interests of the members and decide on their calendars of competitions with the IOC. Those IFs recognized by the IOC become one of the four main constituents of the Olympic Movement. Only IOC-recognized IFs are eligible to have their sports included in the Olympic Games, but many sports with IOC-recognized IFs do not compete in the Olympic Games (Gladden & Lisandra, 2004) because of the restrictive rules of the IOC and the scope of the Olympic Games.

Learning Activity

Select one of the sport federations (e.g., basketball, volleyball, track and field, swimming, tennis) in your country and set up and conduct a 20- to 30-minute phone interview with one of its executives. Ask these questions:

- What are the key missions of the organization?
- What are the major competitions that the federation sponsors and sanctions?
- What are the main sources of funding for the federation?
- What is the scope of its membership?
- What is its relationship with the national Olympic committee (NOC)?
- What is its procedure used in the selection of athletes for the world championship in the sport?
- What new rules have been developed by the federation in the past five years?
- Who are the major sponsors and donors for the federation?
- What are the challenges facing the federation?
- What are the job opportunities for sport management graduates?

The associations of IFs for sports included in the Summer and Winter Olympic Games are the Association of the Summer Olympic International Federations (ASOIF) and the Association of the International Olympic Winter Sports Federations (AIOWF). The associations of IFs recognized by the IOC but whose sports are not included in the Olympic Games are the Association of the IOC Recognized International Sports Federations (ARISF) and the General Association of International Sports Federations (GAISF), or SportAccord. All these associations are formed to ensure that member IFs have a close relationship with the IOC but still maintain their authority, independence, and autonomy (IOC, 2009). The following are the four categories and their federations recognized by the IOC. These categories indicate whether the sports could be included in Olympic competitions or compete internationally only outside the Olympic Games.

◆ *Association of Summer Olympic International Federations.* Currently 26 IFs are affiliated with the **Association of Summer Olympic International Federations (ASOIF)** (two others have recently been added) and recognized and permitted to participate in the Summer Olympic Games. ASOIF represents the common interests of all affiliated IFs in the Summer Olympic Games and governs all related professional issues of the Summer Olympic Games (IOC, 2009).

◆ *Association of International Olympic Winter Sports Federations.* Similar to ASOIF, the **Association of International Olympic Winter Sport Federation (AIOWSF)** is recognized by the IOC and is responsible for organizing the Winter Olympic Games. There are currently seven IFs whose sports are included in the competition programs of the Winter Olympic Games (see table 11.1).

◆ *Association of IOC Recognized International Sports Federations.* The **Association of IOC Recognized International Sports Federations (ARISF)** consists of 32 member IFs that compete internationally but not as part of the Olympic program. Such IFs include baseball, softball, bowling, and motorcycle sport.

◆ *General Association of International Sports Federations, or SportAccord.* The **General Association of International Sports Federations (GAISF)**, renamed SportAccord in 2009, is made up of 90 international sport federations (IFs) and 17 associated members (organizations of international games and sport-related international associations). The IFs in this category could be either members or nonmembers of the IOC. Examples of associated members are the Commonwealth Games, school sport, military sport, and sport press (SportAccord, 2009). The mission of SportAccord is "to unite, support and promote its Member International Sports Federations and Organizations for the coordination and protection of their common aims and interests, communication and cooperation, while at the same time conserving and respecting their autonomy" (SportAccord, 2009).

The primary mission of the IFs recognized by the IOC is to cooperate with the IOC and administer the designated sports at the global level. The IFs work closely not only with the IOC but also with the national governing bodies (NGBs) or national sport federations in each country. Each affiliated national sport federation must also be recognized by the national Olympic committee (NOC) in its country. At present, the number of member nations affiliated with an IF that is represented in the Summer Olympic Games ranges from 35 to 213. The International Association of Athletics Federations (IAAF) is the largest IF, involving 213 countries and territory affiliations (International Association of Athletics Federations [IAAF], 2009a), whereas the Union Internationale de Pentathlon Moderne (UIPM) has only 35 member nations (IOC, 2009).

Currently, 33 official sports with their respective IFs appear with the status of official sports on the program of the Olympic Games. The program of the Olympic Games (hereafter, "the Olympic program") refers to all competitions of the Olympic Games established from each edition of the Olympic Games by the IOC. The Olympic program consists of the sports, disciplines, and events (Olympic Charter, 2007a) and encompasses core sports and additional sports for both the Summer and Winter Olympic Games. Currently, the Winter Olympic Games consist of eight core sports. The Summer Olympic Games, on the other hand, contain at least 26 core sports approved by the executive board of the IOC, and more sports may be added to its programming. For the sports to remain in the Olympic program, the IFs of the sports must adopt and implement the World Anti-Doping Code.

For inclusion in the Summer or Winter Olympic Games program, a sport and its IF must first be recognized by the IOC. According to the Olympic Charter, the IF of an unrecognized sport can make a formal petition to the IOC, but it must ensure that all activities of the sport adhere to the fundamental principles and rules of the Olympic Movement and the by-laws adopted by the IOC. The IOC takes approximately two years to observe the federation and its sport to determine whether the sport should officially become a recognized sport (Gladden & Lizandra, 2004). Nowadays, the IOC has approved 26 IFs as recognized sports for the Summer Olympic Games and 7 for the Winter Olympic Games. The list of sports recognized by the IOC is presented in table 11.1.

Table 11.1 International Sport Federations Recognized by the IOC for the Summer and Winter Olympic Games

Sport	Name of federation	Founding year
For Summer Olympic Games (26)		
Aquatics	Fédération Internationale de Natation (FINA)	1902
Archery	International Archery Federation (FITA)	1931
Athletics	International Association of Athletics Federation (IAAF)	1912
Badminton	Badminton World Federation (BWF)	1934
Basketball	Fédération Internationale de Basketball (FIBA)	1932
Boxing	Association Internationale de Boxe (AIBA)	1946
Canoeing	International Canoe Federation (ICF)	1924
Cycling	Union Cycliste Internationale (UCI)	1900
Equestrian	Fédération Equestre Internationale (FEI)	1921
Fencing	Fédération Internationale d'Escrime (FIE)	1913
Football	Fédération Internationale de Football Association (FIFA)	1904
Gymnastics	Fédération Internationale de Gymnastique (FIG)	1881
Handball	International Handball Federation (IHF)	1946
Hockey	Fédération Internationale de Hockey (FIH)	1924
Judo	International Judo Federation (IJF)	1951
Pentathlon	Union Internationale de Pentathlon Moderne (UIPM)	1948
Rowing	Fédération Internationale de Sociétés d'Aviron (FISA)	1892
Sailing	International Sailing Federation (ISAF)	1907
Shooting sport	International Shooting Sport Federation (ISSF)	1907
Table tennis	International Table Tennis Federation (ITTF)	1926
Taekwondo	World Taekwondo Federation (WTF)	1973
Tennis	International Tennis Federation (ITF)	1913
Triathlon	International Triathlon Union (ITU)	1989
Volleyball	Fédération Internationale de Volleyball (FIVB)	1947
Weightlifting	International Weightlifting Federation (IWF)	1905
Wrestling	Fédération Internationale des Luttes Association (FILA)	1912
For Winter Olympic Games (7)		
Biathlon	International Biathlon Union (IBU)	1993
Bobsleigh and skeleton	International Bobsleigh and Tobogganing Federation (FIBT)	1923
Curling	World Curling Federation (WCF)	1965
Ice Hockey	International Ice Hockey Federation (IIHF)	1908
Luge	International Luge Federation (FIL)	1923
Skating	International Skating Union (ISU)	1892
Skiing	International Ski Federation (FIS)	1924

Data from websites of the IOC and international federations (October, 2009).

After each of the Olympic Games, the Olympic Programme Commission reviews the composition of the sport program, including sports, disciplines, events, and the number of athletes in each sport for the Olympic Games. The commission ensures that the Olympic program continues to meet the expectations of future sporting generations. To control the growth of the Olympic program, the IOC has decided to cap the number of sports at 28 and the number of athletes at 10,500 for the Summer Olympic Games (Olympic Programme Commission, 2009). The Olympic Programme Commission developed 33 criteria in seven categories to define the procedure of evaluating sports for the Olympic program. The seven categories include (*a*) history and tradition, (*b*) universality, (*c*) popularity of the sport, (*d*) image, (*e*) athletes' health, (*f*) development of the IF, and (*g*) costs (Olympic Programme Commission, 2009). After the review and analysis, the Olympic Programme Commission then reports on the review of the composition of the sport program and makes recommendations to the IOC Executive Board. Softball was dropped from the Olympic program after the 2008 Olympic Games.

For the recognized sports that are not included in the Olympic program, the IFs of the recognized sports can present their proposals to the Olympic Programme Commission of the IOC to request consideration. Their requests may be approved if the sports are widely practiced around the world with restricted criteria. The sports for men need to be played in at least 75 countries across four continents, and the sports for women must be played in at least 40 countries over three continents to be qualified in the Summer Olympics program. The Winter Olympics program requires a sport to be practiced in at least 25 countries across three continents (Gladden & Lizandra, 2004). Golf, for example, has been approved by the members of the IOC to be part of the 2016 Olympic Games because of its popularity. According to Malcolm and Crabtree (2008), golf is played in every continent by over 58 million people.

International Federations and Other International Sports Governing Bodies

To achieve its mission, an IF has to maintain a close relationship with other international sport governing bodies, such as the IOC. In terms of its relationship with the IOC, the IF is involved in the preparation for the Olympic Congresses and serves on various IOC commissions. In addition, the IF also provides suggestions and opinions to the IOC about candidate cities' technical capabilities to host and organize the Olympic Games.

Moreover, the IFs also maintain professional relationships with associated international federations or continental associations that help the IFs promote their sports at the international level. Such associated international federations include the Commonwealth Games Federation, International Paralympics Committee, International School Sport Federation, and International University Sports Federation. For example, the International Archery Federation (FITA) has been supported by the archery federations at the continent level and the associated international federations mentioned earlier for achieving its missions internationally.

International Federations and National Federations

Besides maintaining a close relationship with other international sport governing bodies, an IF also cooperates with **national sport federations (NFs)**. An NF is a sport governing body responsible for promoting the development of the sport in an individual country. For instance, the International Basketball Federation (FIBA) has built a stable relationship with the Chinese Basketball Association (CBA) and provides assistance in its daily operation and administration in the aspects of strategic plans, financial and event management, promotion

Learning Activity

Identify a sport (either summer or winter sport) that has been added or dropped from the Olympic program in recent years. Discuss the reasons why it was included or excluded from the Olympic program. Do you agree or disagree with the rationale and decision to add or drop this particular sport? Why or why not?

Sports Petitioning to Be Included in the 2016 Olympic Games

The process for a sport to be included in the Olympic program for either the Summer or Winter Olympic Games requires the IF of the sport to become recognized by the IOC. After the IF has become recognized, it may then petition to add the sport to the Olympic program if the sport is perceived to be widely practiced and meets certain criteria. For the 2016 Summer Olympic Games, the 15-member IOC Executive Board recommended adding two sports to the Olympic Games. As a result, roller sports (e.g., inline speed skating), golf, rugby, and several other sports competed for two seats of sports that would join the 26 sports of the 2016 Summer Olympic Games in Brazil.

According to Michaelis (2009), the IOC Executive Board reviewed and evaluated seven petitions for adding sports to the 2016 Summer Olympic Games; each sport had strengths and weaknesses. The seven sports that petitioned for inclusion were baseball, softball, golf, karate, roller sports, rugby, and squash. While baseball could attract the world's top players to the Olympic Games, its doping problem was one of the reasons it was excluded from the London 2012 Olympic Games. In comparison, softball has been promoted by its officials internationally after the IOC dropped it from the 2012 Summer Olympic Games. Nevertheless, its similarity with baseball was still an issue. For golf, the sport's popularity and the support for its inclusion by many of the top players in the world, including Tiger Woods, were the key rationales given by the petitioners. The strength of karate was from being practiced in 180 countries with 10 million competitors. Its similarity with judo and taekwondo, which were already Olympic sports, became a main concern. Given skateboarding's popularity, its exclusion from the roller sports petition was seen as a weakness. Rugby's greatest negative concerned its impact on the size of the Olympic Games even through it was very popular among European countries. The inclusion of squash was not supported as it was only popular in Asia and a few countries in other regions.

IOC President Jacques Rogge indicated that committee members were looking for the two sports that would be universal, fit well with the Olympic program, and add value to the Olympic Games by having wide appeal, especially among young people (BBC, 2009a).

Inline speed skating, the most practiced of the four roller sports disciplines, has been included in the Pan American Games, Asian Games, and World Games. Due to its increasing number of participants, the International Federation of Roller Sports (FIRS) has petitioned for inline speed skating to be included in the 2012 and 2016 Summer Olympic Games. Concerns about the petition for the 2012 Olympic Games include the limited numbers of participants and limited media interest and sponsorship opportunities. After the failure of its bid for the 2012 Olympic Games, the FIRS has recruited 32 additional member nations to reach a total of 117 national federations, display streaming events on its website, and launch and execute a global advertising campaign (Gomez, 2009). However, FIRS was unsuccessful in its attempt for inclusion in the 2016 Olympic Games.

For golf and rugby union, one of the biggest challenges was whether the Olympics could be the pinnacle of those sports (Bandini, 2009). To address the concern, the International Rugby Board (IRB) proposed the seven-a-side version for both men and women and ensured that the Olympics would be the sport's top event for that version of the game (BBC, 2009b). The International Golf Federation presented a format that included a 72-hole stroke-play tournament for men and women and 60 players in each field. The best 15 players in the world would qualify automatically for each draw, and no major championships would be staged on the Olympics dates (Bandini, 2009). Besides modifying the format of their sports and making a commitment to the IOC, both international sport federations showed strengths that they could add to the 2016 Olympic Games. The IRB stressed the commercial appeal of the abbreviated form of golf and its ability to attract world viewers and traveling spectators (Kelso, 2009). The International Golf Federation highlighted the commercial popularity of golf, its ability to draw from a truly global field, and the rise of the women's game (Kelso, 2009).

The 107 IOC committee members decided in October 2009 to add both golf and rugby to the 2016 Summer Olympic Games because of their increased popularity and global appearance. In addition, because the IOC is still keen to remain an attractive broadcast product, adding golf and rugby would provide existing and emerging markets with content that adds a premium to rights fees (Kelso, 2009).

Questions of Age Eligibility at the 2008 Olympic Games

During the 2008 Olympic Summer Games in Beijing, National Broadcast Corporation (NBC) News in the United States reported on August 22, 2008, that several Chinese female gymnasts were allegedly underage. Two international governing bodies, the International Olympic Committee (IOC) and the Fédération Internationale de Gymnastique (FIG), launched an investigation of the allegation. China was asked to provide documentation of age for those female gymnasts.

As reported by NBC News (MSNBC, 2008), IOC spokeswoman Giselle Davies stated that the IOC had referred the case to the FIG and asked it to work with the Chinese national federation to collect evidence of age. According to the spokeswoman, the IOC had received copies of those female gymnasts' passports, ID cards, and family residence permits and would analyze them. But it would not make a ruling until it had received a report of the FIG. Depending on the outcome of the investigation, four Chinese medals could be stripped away if evidence was found that the gymnasts were underage.

The allegation has caused much concern. A Chinese coach responded to the allegation by saying, "Asian gymnasts are naturally smaller than their American and European rivals. It is a question of race. European and American athletes are all powerful and very robust, but Chinese athletes cannot be like that but [by] nature [are] small." The FIG executive committee met to discuss the issue. The investigation conducted by the FIG yielded no evidence of cheating based on the verification of government-issued documents (MSNBC, 2008). Accordingly, the IOC dismissed the allegation based on the report of the findings submitted to the IOC by the FIG.

---

of basketball, media relations and communications, sponsorship, and marketing. Another example is that the Fédération Internationale de Football Association (FIFA) keeps a close relationship with the Spain Soccer Association regarding rule changes and qualifications of players who participate in World Cup competition.

Although the national sport federation of a particular sport (i.e., the national governing body, or NGB) provides opportunities for people to participate in that sport, it also has to implement the rules and regulations set up by the IFs, which sometimes change to adapt to new issues surrounding the sport. For example, the Fédération Internationale de Natation (FINA) released decisions in July 2009 regarding the use of high-tech swimsuits in FINA-sanctioned competitions. Before 2009 FINA did not have specific rules prohibiting materials and design of swimwear that may aid swimmers' speed, flow, and endurance. When a swimwear manufacturer launched the high-tech LZR Racer swimsuits in early 2008, more than 130 world records were broken, including seven (in eight events) by Michael Phelps during the Beijing Olympics (Crouse, 2009). The high-tech materials assist swimmers by repelling water, aiding flow, and enhancing buoyancy, which are critical elements in competitive swimming (Fermoso, 2008;

Roberts, Kamel, Hedrick, McLean, & Sharp, 2003). The major controversies and concerns came from whether the new world records were set as a result of the swimmers' performance or the new swimwear technology. Thus, FINA established new rules and regulations to respond to the concerns about the use of high-technology swimwear fabric during swimming competitions. The NGB affiliated with FINA for swimming in each country has to implement and comply with the new rules and regulations on swimwear. The new rules were enforced beginning on January 1, 2010. Some of FINA's major requirements for swimsuits are as follows (Fédération Internationale de Natation, [FINA], 2009a):

a. Type of material: The material used for swimsuits can be only "textile fabric(s)" defined for the purpose of these rules as material consisting of natural and/or synthetic, individual, and non-consolidated yarns used to constitute a fabric by weaving, knitting, and/or braiding. The definition of "textile" will be made by a group of scientific experts chosen by FINA.

b. Surface covered: Men's swimsuits shall not extend above the navel nor below the knee, and for women, shall not cover the neck, extend past the shoulder, nor extend below the knee.

c. Thickness: The material used shall have a maximum thickness of 0.8 mm.

d. Buoyancy: The swimsuit shall not have a buoyancy effect above 0.5 Newton measured after application of vacuum.

e. Use: In the regulation approved by the Congress, the swimmer can only wear one swimsuit and no taping is allowed.

f. Construction: No zippers or other fastening system is allowed. Seams shall be limited to functional systems and shall not create outside shapes.

As a result, in July 2010 FINA published a list of FINA-approved swimsuits for open-water competition (FINA, 2010a) that swimmers can choose from for approved competitions of FINA and national governing bodies. If competitors want to wear swimsuits with a new design, construction, or materials that are not on the FINA-approved swimsuits list, manufacturers of such swimwear need approval of FINA for swimwear to be worn in competition (FINA, 2010b). To implement FINA's new rules for swimsuits, national governing bodies thus enforce new regulations and require their swimmers to wear approved swimwear during competitions. For example, the United States Swimming Association amended that "only swimsuits complying with FINA Open Water swimsuit specifications may be worn in any USA Swimming sanctioned or approved open water competition" (USSA, 2010). Thus swimmers competing in competitions sanctioned or approved by USA Swimming must wear suits approved by FINA.

Management of International Federations

As mentioned previously, each IF is responsible for only one sport or a group of similar sports. Management of the IFs is based on a set of comprehensive missions and an extensive system that permits them to function well at various competition levels, such as worldwide or continental competitions. The managerial authority of an IF is given by its general assembly, which is made up of the national sport federations or associations. As the governing body of the sport, the IFs are primarily independent governing bodies that manage the

sport (International Basketball Federation [FIBA], 2009). Their officers are elected democratically and carry ambassador responsibility for the sport, but they must be recognized by the IOC (Hums & MacLean, 2004).

The sports of many federations are currently not included in the Olympic Games. The mission, structure, and routine operation of these federations are largely similar to those of the federations affiliated with the IOC. The following two federations demonstrate the similarities and differences:

◆ The International Baseball Federation (IBAF) is a member of the Association of IOC Recognized International Sports Federations (ARISF) but is not in the Association of Summer Olympic International Federations (ASOIF). The IBAF serves as the worldwide governing body for the sport of baseball. It sanctions play between teams sponsored by the national baseball federations of member countries through tournaments such as the Baseball World Cup, the World Baseball Classic (in conjunction with Major League Baseball), and the Intercontinental Cup (IBAF, 2010a). Its organizational mission includes promoting the sport of baseball, organizing world competitions, and ensuring the cooperation of national federations to improve the sport. Its organizational structure is similar to that of other federations in the Olympic program. IBAF is operated by an executive committee that includes a president, vice presidents, secretary general, treasurer, and members at large. All decisions of the federation are made by the committee and approved by the president (IBAF, 2010b). IBAF, not the IOC, is the highest authority for organizing international competition in baseball.

◆ The International Life Saving Federation (ILS), a member of the General Association of International Sports Federations (GAISF), is an international, not-for-profit, nongovernmental, and non-Olympic organization that is composed of national lifesaving organizations. The ILS works to support and coordinate lifesaving development activities of member federations and regions. Its general assembly has the highest authority for external audit and contains the Departments of Drowning Prevention, Lifesaving, and Sport, as well as board committees such as commissioners, equity and diversity, and finance. As with Olympic federations, these committees provide effective functions for the federation.

Confederations

Confederations are zoned or regional governing bodies of national sport federations located in the same continent. They are the umbrella governing bodies of the IFs in each continent. For example, the Fédération Internationale de Football Association (FIFA) has six confederations:

a. Asian Football Confederation (AFC) in Asia

b. Confederation of Africa Football (CAF) in Africa

c. Confederation of North, Central American and Caribbean Association Football (CONCACAF)

d. South American Football Confederation (CONMEBOL) in South America

e. Union of European Football Associations (UEFA) in Europe

f. Oceania Football Confederation (OFC) in Oceania (Fédération Internationale de Football Association [FIFA], 2009a)

The missions of the continental sport confederations are consistent with their IFs. They have to adhere to the rules and regulations of the IFs, cooperate with the IOC, and assist their member national sport federations. The continental sport confederations are responsible for organizing continental competitions and championships among member nations located in the continent. Examples of such continental competitions and championships are the Asian Games and the European Football Championship.

Learning Activity

Visit the website of the Union of European Football Associations and describe the major functions of the confederation.

Membership

The national sport federations make up the primary membership of the IFs. Each IF has its established constitution that clearly states the membership eligibilities and qualifications. The general membership rules of the IFs maintain that the national sport federation should (a) be recognized by the IFs with eligibility and qualifications, (b) agree to pay subscriptions or dues, and adhere to the rules and eligibilities of the IFs, (c) be responsible for the sport in its country and organize teams to participate in international competitions, and (d) be subject to suspension and termination if a member association has any violation (International Basketball Federation [FIBA], 2009a; FIFA, 2009a).

Although some IFs, such as the International Table Tennis Federation, allow personnel honorary membership (International Table Tennis Federation [ITTF], 2009), other IFs divide the membership into different categories. For instance, the International Tennis Federation (ITF) categorizes its member associations as Class A, B, or C memberships. Each membership category has a set of particular requirements and benefits (International Tennis Federation [ITF], 2009). A national sport federation must be successful in the procedures of application, election, review, and approval by the executive board or board of directors of a particular IF before it would be granted membership in that IF. After a national sport federation is granted membership with an IF, it assumes all membership rights, obligations, and responsibilities (ITF, 2009).

Governance Models

The governance models used by the IFs are similar in terms of organizational authorities, functions, and relationships with other governing bodies. Figure 11.1 depicts a common governance model of the IFs and their relationships with confederations, national federations, the IOC, and the national Olympic committees.

Most of the IFs use a congress or assembly formed by member nations as a legislative body to develop rules and policies and to approve changes recommended by the executive committee. Consisting of the president, vice presidents, secretary, and other officers, the executive committee (or board of directors, bureau, or central board) has the responsibility of managing the IF. With a fixed term to assume the

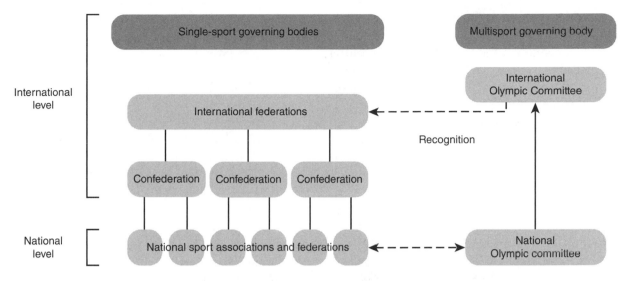

Figure 11.1 A common governance model of IFs and relationship with the IOC.

leadership roles in the organization, the president and executive committee are usually granted power to handle federation affairs. Numerous standing committees or commissions, ranging from 4 to more than 20, are functional groups responsible for a variety of tasks delegated by the executive committee or the president. For example, here is a list of some of the standing committees of FIFA (Fédération Internationale de Football Association [FIFA], 2009a).

◆ Executive Committee

◆ Finance Committee

◆ Organizing Committee for the FIFA World Cup (TM)

◆ Organizing Committee for the FIFA Confederations Cup

◆ Futsal and Beach Soccer Committee

◆ Referees Committee

◆ Medical Committee

◆ Legal Committee

◆ Ethics Committee

◆ Technical and Development Committee

All decisions made by the standing committees must be ratified by the executive committee or the president according to the FIFA statutes or constitution. Figure 11.2 shows another example of the management structure of an IF, the Fédération Internationale de Natation (FINA), the governing body in international aquatics (FINA, 2009a).

The management structure of some large and popular IFs consists of functional departments to execute routine operations. For instance, the Federation of International Basketball (FIBA) has six

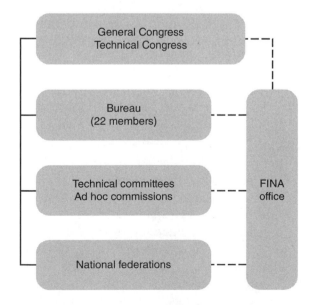

Figure 11.2 Organizational flow chart for the International Aquatics Association.

functional departments, including the Administration Department, which handles general operation of routines such as membership and planning competition events; the Financial and Human Resources Department, which manages the affairs of employment and financial operation for the federation; the Sport and Eligibility Department, which focuses on verifying eligibilities of players and other participants such as referees in the competitions or world events organized by the federation or the IOC; the Sport and Development Department, which seeks and provides opportunities for continuous growth and expansion of the sport; the Commercial Department, which executes all related areas of marketing, sponsorship, and advertising to generate more revenue for the federation; and the Informational Technology Department, which provides technical support for the organization and events and ensures effective communication with all related international governing bodies and the national federations (FIBA, 2009b).

Finance

All IFs are primarily considered not-for-profit membership organizations based on their stated philosophies and missions. The revenue generated may be used mainly to support functions of the federations, the operations of the organizations, and further development of the sport (Chen, 2004). Although some IFs have experienced a shortage of funds in operations, many IFs have been successful in revenue generation through fund-raising, broadcast rights, naming rights, and sponsorships for worldwide events.

Most IFs charge annual membership dues or subscriptions from their member nations. The amount of income from this source, however, is insufficient to offset the expenses incurred from operations. To cover the costs, many IFs actively pursue and develop partnerships, create sponsorship opportunities, and solicit donations. Other commercial activities often engaged in by IFs to generate needed revenues include licensing, advertising, and selling broadcasting and naming rights (Chen, 2004; FINA, 2009b). The revenue generated from these business activities improves the financial bottom line of the IFs and allows them to focus on their core activities, such as holding competitions and events, promoting global development of their sport, and providing monetary support to their member nations as needed (FINA, 2009b).

The revenues and expenses of the International Federation of Association Football (FIFA) for fiscal year 2008 provide us an opportunity to examine the financial operation of an IF. FIFA generated a total of US$957 million in 2008. Of the total revenue, 94 percent was from FIFA-sanctioned events (e.g., the World Cup), including sales of television rights (US$556 million), marketing rights (US$253 million), brand licensing and FIFA Quality Concept (US$32 million), and investment and interest (US$22 million). The expenditures of FIFA in the same year included promotion of FIFA-sanctioned events, organization, and labor cost (US$441 million); development of projects (US$133 million); governance spending (US$46 million); exploration rights (US$8 million); and other financial expenses (US$6 million). The total expenditure was US$773 million. The net income was US$184 million, despite the worldwide financial crisis. Tables 11.2, 11.3, and 11.4 illustrate FIFA's revenues, expenses,

Table 11.2　FIFA Detailed Revenue 2008 (in US$ million)

Financial income	
Foreign exchange effects	2
Interest income	20
Subtotal	22
Other operation income	
Brand licensing	4
Quality concept	9
Penalties, appeals, levies	5
Other (e.g., rental income, film sales, gain from sale of fixed assets)	14
Subtotal	32
Event-related revenue	
TV broadcasting rights 　2010 FIFA World Cup 　Other FIFA events	 550 6
Marketing rights	253
Licensing rights	15
Hospitality rights	40
Others	39
Subtotal	903
Total	**957**

Data from *FIFA Financial Report 2008*, FIFA 59th Congress (FIFA, 2009b).

Table 11.3 FIFA Detailed Expenses 2008 (in US$ million)

Event-related expenses	
2010 FIFA World Cup	345
Contributions to IOC	130
Teams and officials	17
Marketing rights and TV production	48
Other (e.g., IT solutions, ticketing)	150
Other FIFA events	96
Subtotal	441
Development-related expenses	
Financial assistance program	52
Confederations	15
Goal program	30
Win in Africa with Africa	14
Other (e.g., course)	22
Subtotal	133
Football governance	
Committees & Congress	30
Legal matters	13
Other (e.g., CIES)	3
Subtotal	46
Exploitation of rights	
Marketing	6
Broadcasting and media rights	10
Licensing	2
Subtotal	18
Other operating expenses	
Personnel expenses	52
Depreciation	16
Acquisition and production costs	14
Rent, maintenance, office equipment	9
Other (e.g., IT, travel, PR)	38
Subtotal	129
Financial expenses	6
Total	**773**

Data from *FIFA Financial Report 2008*, FIFA 59th Congress (FIFA, 2009b).

Table 11.4 FIFA 2008 Income Statement (in US$ million)

Revenue	
Event-related revenue	903
Other operating income	32
Financial income	22
Total	957
Expenses	
Event-related expenses	(441)
Development-related expenses	(133)
Football governance	(46)
Exploitation of rights	(18)
Other operating expenses*	(129)
Financial expenses	(6)
Total	**(773)**
Result	**184**

*Including personnel expenses, depreciation, and amortization.

Data from *FIFA Financial Report 2008*, FIFA 59th Congress (FIFA, 2009b).

and an abridged income statement for fiscal year 2008 (FIFA, 2009b).

Table 11.5 is the balance sheet of FIFA for its 2008 operation. As of December 31, 2008, it had total assets of US$1,631 million, including current assets of US$1,130 million and noncurrent assets of US$501 million, against current liabilities of US$717 million and noncurrent liabilities of US$12 million. FIFA thus had equity of US$902 million in 2008. The strong performance was achieved by implementing the foreign currency hedging strategy of the financial management team of FIFA.

These published sources of financial information provide a brief picture of how IFs generate revenues from various resources and what areas an IF could spend its money on. In the case of FIFA in 2008, the major source of both income and costs was sanctioned events. The balance sheet of FIFA in 2008 also shows equity of US$902 million, which provides a strong foundation to support the functions of the federation and demonstrates the effectiveness of the financial management team. Because IFs have no ownership, the revenue generated from activities is used either to cover expenditures of the federation itself or to support the organization of international competitions such as the World Cup. The more popular a sport is globally, the more financial support its international federation needs to support the sport, and the more effective the IF must be in obtaining the resources or developing sound programs to generate revenues. Financial management is always a

Table 11.5 FIFA Balance Sheet at December 31, 2008 (in US$ million)

Assets		Liabilities and equity	
Current assets	1,130	Current liabilities	717
Cash and cash equivalents	706	Payables	43
Receivables	276	Income tax liabilities	1
Derivative financial assets	55	Derivative financial liabilities	8
Prepaid expenses and accrued income	93	Accrued expenses and deferred income	665
Noncurrent assets	501	Noncurrent liabilities	12
Property and equipment	214		
Intangible assets	2		
Financial assets	285	Equity	902
Total	**1,631**	**Total**	**1,631**

Data from *FIFA Financial Report 2008*, FIFA 59th Congress (FIFA, 2009b).

challenge to IFs and other sport governing bodies. Sound leadership and an effective financial management system ensure the survivability of the federation and continuous promotion of the sport in the world.

Learning Activity

After studying the 2008 report of revenue and expenses of FIFA, what are your predictions for each category (increase or decrease) in the income statement for 2010, given that the World Cup was held during June and July of 2010 in South Africa? Do you expect revenue to be greater than expenses or vice versa? Conduct a search to find the results. How accurate were your predictions?

Summary

International sport federations (IFs) are governing bodies in various sports at the international level. IFs are mainly responsible for administering particular sports internationally. They maintain their independence in governing a specific sport or sports. IFs work closely with the IOC and national governing bodies (NGBs) or national sport federations in each country. The major functions of IFs are consistent with their mission of promoting their sports, organizing competitions, and developing new programs. Each IF has its established constitution that clearly states membership eligibilities and qualifications. Confederations are regional governing bodies of national sport federations located in one continent. They are the umbrella governing bodies of IFs in each continent.

This chapter should have given you a clear picture of what international sport federations are and how they function to promote and govern sport in the international environment. You should be able to define each type of international sport federation, describe the major organizational structure and governance system, understand the relationship between international sport federations and other international sport governing bodies, and comprehend the major financial resources that IFs use to support their operations and satisfy their stakeholders.

? Review and Discussion Questions

1. What are the relationships among international sport federations, the IOC, and national sport governing bodies? Can you draw an organizational chart to show the relationships between international sport federations and the other Olympic sport organizations?

2. What are the major purposes and missions of international sport federations?

3. If a sport is not currently part of the Olympic program, what is the process for the IF of that sport to petition for inclusion?

4. What are the seven major categories of criteria that the Olympic Programme Commission uses to evaluate sports for future Olympic programs after each Olympic Games?

5. What is the relationship between the international federation in a particular sport and the governing body of the sport in a nation?

6. Is the United States a member of all international sport federations? Check the websites of four categories of IOC-recognized IFs grouped in the four related associations to find out which international sport federations do not include the United States as a member nation.

7. What are the major financial resources supporting the operation of an international sport federation? You may list all possible categories.

Professional Sport Leagues and Tours

James Skinner, PhD
Griffith University, Australia

Wayne Usher, PhD
Griffith University, Australia

Chapter Objectives

After studying this chapter, you will be able to do the following:

- Explain the structure and common features that underpin the governance of international professional sport leagues

- Describe specific professional sport leagues in North America, Australia, Europe, and Asia

- Explain the economic nature of professional sport leagues including the differences between the operation of leagues in North America, Australia, Europe, and Asia

- Identify how professional tours have established themselves in the international sport management landscape

Key Terms

At one level, professional sport leagues and organizations are no different from any other type of business organization. They have investors, mainly the franchise owners, who desire an adequate return on their investments. They use suppliers of sport equipment, food, league merchandise, and subcontractors, such as security firms, merchants, facility cleaners, and so on that provide vital services directly to the franchises. The franchises also have employees (namely, the players but also backroom staff, administration, maintenance workers, and others) who seek financial remuneration, job security, good working conditions, and an opportunity to grow. Finally, franchises have customers, the spectators who demand to see their team win championships (Oebbecke, 1998). When we scratch beneath the surface, however, we begin to see that although the professional sport industry has an economic rationale anchored in the principle of profit maximization, its business practices are unique and distinctive. This chapter explores these unique differences by examining the nature of professional sport leagues and tours and the models that shape their governance structures and operational practices.

Structure and Governance of International Professional Sport Leagues

This section outlines the structure and common features of international professional sport leagues in team sports throughout the world. The governance of sport leagues operates at different levels, depending on the league. Leagues may be governed at the international, regional, national, or local levels, as highlighted in figure 12.1.

Although sport may be governed globally, regionally, or only nationally, professional sport leagues tend to follow one of a few models of ownership and management. Not all professional sport leagues operate at an international level, but those that do are generally governed by regulatory bodies that monitor and control all aspects of international competition by establishing game rules and codes of conduct that must be enforced at the regional, national, and local levels. The International Cricket Council (ICC) is an example of a league that operates at an international level. The ICC's governance

Figure 12.1 Governance of sport at different levels. ICC = International Cricket Council, WTA = Women's Tennis Association, UEFA = Union of European Football Associations, SANZAR = collective which operates the international rugby competitions between South Africa, New Zealand, and Australia.

structure is clearly defined on its website (International Cricket Council, 2008). The council operates on behalf of the 105 member countries, and there are three levels of membership. Ten countries are full members; they are most represented at the international level. Also, 35 countries are associate members and 60 nations are affiliate members (for a total of 95 other member countries). Voting rights of each membership type reflects its importance within the organization (Hoye & Cuskelly, 2007). Nine committees fulfill specific governance functions. This structure is depicted in table 12.1.

The **Fédération Internationale de Football Association (FIFA)**, one of the largest international sport governing bodies, has overseen the phenomenal growth of world football and the increasing profile of the World Cup. Tomlinson (2005) described how the world governing body

of the game has established partnerships that have changed the financial base of the game and established the FIFA World Cup as a "major global spectacle and . . . a marketing opportunity for the world's most powerful corporate investors" (p.39). FIFA is one of the world's oldest and largest nongovernment organizations. Founded in 1904, it has since expanded to include 204 member associations. Tennis is another sport that has its governance at an international level. Starting out as an amateur sport, tennis became professional many years ago, much to the advantage of players. Women players compete on the WTA Tour, and men on the ATP

Table 12.1 ICC Subcommittee Structure and Membership

ICC subcommittee	Membership	Main responsibilities
ICC Annual Conference	Delegates from all full, associate, and affiliate member governing bodies	Ratifies major decisions, considers applications from potential new member countries, and appoints the ICC president
ICC Executive Board and IDI Board of Directors	Presidents or chairs of the 10 full-member countries and three representatives of the associate members	The key policy body for international cricket, responsible for major financial and commercial policies
ICC Chief Executives' Committee	CEOs of the 10 full members and three representatives from the associate members	Key forum for making recommendations on the business of cricket, refers policy to the executive board for approval
ICC Cricket Committee	Five people nominated by the players of full-member teams, five nominated by boards of full-member teams, one nominated by the players of associate member teams, one nominated by boards of associate member teams, and the president and CEO of the ICC	Makes recommendations to the CEC on matters of the game of cricket
Audit Committee	Representatives from two full members, an independent appointment, an alternate appointment, and the president and CEO of the ICC	Reviews the ICC's financial reporting process, internal controls, risk management, audit process, and compliance issues
Code of Conduct Commission	Nominated representative from each of the full-member countries	Oversees formal enquiries into conduct that may be prejudicial to the interests of the game and makes recommendations to the executive board
ICC Development Committee	One nominated representative from each of the five ICC regions, an MCC delegate, an associate member delegate, the chair of the ICC Women's Committee, and the CEO of the ICC	Reviews and monitors all policy matters relating to the structure and delivery of the ICC Global Development Program
HR, Remuneration and Appointments Committee	Representatives from two full members, a representative from one associate member, and the president and CEO of the ICC	Reviews and monitors all policy matters relating to the ICC's human resources
Governance Review Committee	Representatives from two full-member teams, representative from one associate member team, and the president and CEO of the ICC	Reviews the ICC governance structures and makes recommendations to the executive board on the effectiveness of organizational decision-making processes

Adapted from ICC (2008).

Tour, which is now divided into ATP Tour events and Grand Slam events. Golf also has major international tours operated by the Professional Golfers' Association (PGA), which conducts matches in the United States, Europe, and Australasia with significant prize money attached.

Regional sport leagues operate across international boundaries but tend to be isolated to a particular regional location. For example, UEFA is the administrative and controlling body for European football. SANZAR (South Africa, New Zealand, and Australian Rugby Unions) emerged because of occurrences in rugby union in Australia, South Africa, and New Zealand. In early 1995 Rupert Murdoch's News Limited introduced its Super League competition in Australia as an attempt to control the administration of rugby league worldwide and in turn provide product for cable and pay television (Fitzsimons, 1996). In Australia this resulted in a bitter struggle between Super League and the Australian Rugby League (ARL), the traditional governing authority of the code. The ugly struggle created ongoing hostility between both clubs and players (Masters, 1997). One of the most significant outcomes was a massive increase in player salaries, which resulted from the restricted market of player talent, the potential presence of two elite competitions, and the financial support provided to Super League by News Corporation and to the ARL by the Optus telecommunication company. With salaries of rugby league players seemingly out of control, rugby union officials in Australia, New Zealand, and South Africa became concerned that they were going to lose most of their leading players to rugby league. This unease led to the formation of a Southern Hemisphere consortium, collectively known as SANZAR. The consortium announced on June 23, 1995, before the commencement of the Rugby World Cup, that it had signed a 10-year joint venture agreement with Rupert Murdoch's News Corporation worth US$550 million over 10 years, with a 5-year option (Skinner et al., 2003). In return for News Limited's heavy investment in rugby union, the Southern Hemisphere consortium was required to provide two products. The first was a Super 12 competition of five regional teams from New Zealand, four from South Africa, and three from Australia (this has now developed into a Super 14 competition that includes two more teams in Australia). The second was a Tri-Nations series among the three countries.

At the national level the structure and features of professional sport leagues vary depending on the sport. Some leagues modify their "rules of play, eligibility, and behaviour of governing bodies" (Noll, 2003, p. 543). The National Basketball Association (NBA) in North America, for example, has rules that are slightly different from those of the International Federation of Basketball Associations (FIBA). In international matches, however, NBA players must abide by FIBA's rules (Noll, 2003). By contrast, FIFA exerts much greater control over national leagues. FIFA has established a "pyramid of authorities" to control the increasing international complexity of football. As a result, "FIFA has invested its 204 member associations authority at national level" supported by "the formation of continental football confederations as middle tiers of control between the national and the international levels" (p. 27). Each national league however, can have its own structural variations. For example, the emergence of the Premier League in England in 1992 resulted in premiership clubs becoming independent members of a consortium whose control extends to the marketing of the league independent of the lower leagues. The national governing body (NGB), the Football Association (FA), has responsibility for overseeing the running of the England teams (Morgan, 2002).

At the lower levels, clubs, players, and coaches abide by the rules and regulations established by the international governing body (IGB) when competing in international competitions, but they may play under different rules and regulations when participating in regional or national leagues. Clubs competing in national league competitions are affiliated with the NGB, which in turn is affiliated with the IGB. Players are registered with their NGB, and to play in international events they need to be registered with their IGB. In some leagues, coaches are required not only to be properly licensed, as in Japan, but also to hold appropriate coaching qualifications as stipulated by the relevant governing body.

Economic Nature of Professional Sport Leagues

Professional sport is a business operation capable of generating billions of dollars in revenue every year, but how does an organization make a business out of sport? In a business the aim is to destroy the opposition, but in sport a team needs to have someone to battle against or there is no point. Sport is an industry in which teams need competitors to make a product. Sport leagues use rules and regulations to encourage **competitive balance** to maintain fan enthusiasm by keeping them in suspense. Competitive balance is a concept often used by governing bodies to justify exemptions and interventions made to ensure that the outcome of competitions remains uncertain. Smith and Stewart (2010) drew on the work of Morgan (2002) when they suggested that there are "four major trans-national models for the **league governance** of sport at the highest level" (p.10). League governance refers to the system by which professional sport leagues and organizations are directed and controlled. The following sections discuss these models.

Pyramidal Hierarchical Model

The first model that Morgan (2002) identified was the traditional pyramidal hierarchical model that can be seen in "traditional European sports such as swimming and badminton and collegiate sport in the United States" (Smith and Stewart, 2010, p. 10). Morgan suggested that in such a model the national governing body (NGB) is the key decision maker of the "structure, conduct and marketing of the sport" (p. 49). The NGB has control of "the key assets such as the national team brand and the ability to reward members through the distribution of revenue" (p. 49). He went on to suggest that when the sport has significant commercial value at the highest international level, the model would succeed. Before rugby union became a professional sport in 1995, it operated under this model. To some extent Morgan suggested that this model can still be seen in the SANZAR rugby union discussed earlier. This Southern Hemisphere consortium of national rugby unions maintains "a hierarchical governance system within their respective countries" (p. 50).

In general, this model is becoming obsolete with the continued **commercialization** of professional sport. Commercialization refers to the application of business principles to professional sport to run it as a business, generally to profit from it.

Amara et al. (2005), however, argued that it is possible to conceptualize the control of international football (soccer) as a hierarchical model. In this model "FIFA was the ultimate authority in world soccer with responsibility for the premier competition, the World Cup, and with UEFA and national FAs occupying lower tiers in the authority structure" (p. 191). Although this description is simplified, "In this model of power clubs and then players lay at the bottom of the decision-making hierarchy" (p. 190). In the contemporary setting, Amara et al. (2005) suggested that it has become "impossible to think in terms of a national or international governing body as being the sole author of its own sport's destiny" (p. 191). They suggested that the rise of the G14 clubs (the 14 most powerful and influential clubs in European football), the strategic ownership alliances established between satellite broadcasters and powerful clubs that has provided enhanced broadcasting opportunities for both parties, and the pressure that can be applied by other groups such as **players associations**, who are a collective and representative voice of professional players involved in a particular sport and established to safeguard the interests of their members, player agents, and sponsors, mean that the traditional hierarchical model is no longer relevant. This "top-down system, has given way to a complex network of interrelationships between stakeholders in which different groups exert power in different ways and in different contexts by drawing on alliances with other stakeholders" (p. 191).

North American and Australian Model

The second model that Morgan (2002) referred to is what he suggested is a distinctive North American cartel structure, although the model can also be seen in countries like Australia. Unlike more traditional industries, the sport industry in North America and Australia is often allowed by government to pursue what are effectively anticompetitive practices (Szymanski, 2003). This system arises from tacit agreement that a variety of restrictive practices are essential for sport leagues to sustain public interest and long-term viability. It has been argued that a completely unregulated sport league would be unsustainable because a few clubs would use their superior fan and revenue bases to capture the best players and dominate the competition. This argument claims that although the resulting conduct may be anticompetitive (or a restraint of trade), it is not unreasonable, nor is it against the public interest (Ross, 2003). Consequently, in North America and Australia, free-market capitalism is limited. In North America and Australia it is argued that sport leagues perform poorly under competitive or free-market conditions, so some form of self-regulation is essential to produce the outcome uncertainty that attracts fans, sponsors, and media interest (Szymanski & Kuypers, 1999).

In North America and Australia professional sport leagues operate as joint ventures or **cartels**. A cartel can be defined as a collective of individual clubs, firms, or organizations that by agreement work collectively to maximize benefits to each. A cartel has a complex set of rules and practices designed to restrict business competition among its members and divide markets among firms in the industry. The agreement on joint policies allows cartels to minimize competition, restrict the entry of new firms, control the supply and cost of their products, coordinate advertising and promotion, set prices, and, most fundamentally, protect the interests of member organizations (Stewart, Nicholson, & Dickson, 2005).

Continued domination by one team in a league would theoretically lessen the dramatic value of the contests and inevitably lead to a lack of interest in games, thereby reducing the league's ability to command high prices in exchange for its events. A league therefore operates to disperse playing talent and instill public confidence in the honesty of the game. The three major types of restrictions that are imposed relate to competition among teams for player services, sale of broadcasting rights, and the location and licensing of teams. Stewart et al. (2005) suggested that the success and effectiveness of a cartel hinges on its ability to restrict the conduct of its members and secure member compliance to the rules and regulations of the cartel. Violations of these rules and regulations will ultimately lead to sanctions and penalties against the offending team. Moreover, they suggest that to be successful and effective, sport cartels adopt particular structures, policies, and strategies. These include (1) establishing a centralized decision-making organization that regulates member teams and clubs, and disciplines members who breach the leagues rules and regulations; (2) aiming to expand profits by implementing various cost minimization regulations that restrict competitive bidding for players and set ceilings on total player wage payments; and (3) aiming to increase revenue by extending the market for their sporting product, improving its overall attractiveness, and enhancing the community standing and status of the league.

Sport cartels can also work collectively to improve the attractiveness of their sport and hence the marketable product. Cartels can be instrumental in developing player skills, improving sporting facilities, and ensuring that the outcomes of games are uncertain, which, it is argued, is a key component to success for sport. Cartels employ two strategies—**drafts** and **salary caps**—to ensure this. A draft is a process generally used in North America and Australia in which players are allocated to teams within the professional sport league. A draft allows teams to select players in turn from a pool and then receive exclusive signing rights to that player for a specified period. Salary caps place a limit on the amount of money that a professional sport team within a league can spend on player salaries, as either a per-player limit or a total limit for the team. The drafting process and salary cap restrictions help create uncertain outcomes and consequently raise spectator and television interest. This system, coupled with the collusive market power that sport cartels possess by negotiating as a single entity, maximizes broadcast rights fees for the league. These broadcast revenues are subsequently subject to an **equalization policy** and redistributed to the clubs within the league. Equalization policies aim to ensure that fiscal inequities between professional sport teams do not allow some teams to become so dominant within a league that they eliminate competition. Less successful clubs are thus able to maintain a level of financial security and remain viable entities (Stewart et al., 2005).

The popularity and status of a sport league can also be heightened by centralized advertising and promotion campaigns that aim to improve the integrity, public image, and overall reputation of the sport. Rules are put in place to regulate the conduct and behavior of team administrators, coaches, and players. This high degree of discretionary decision making and monopoly power, which is used to regulate members and reduce competition among teams for resources, aims to control costs and increase revenue for all members of the cartel (Stewart et al., 2005). **Monopoly power** refers to the exclusive control by a professional sport league or organization over the means of producing or selling that sport. Some of the actions that professional sport leagues employ to operate as a cartel are identified in table 12.2.

Table 12.2 Does a Sport Operate As a Cartel?

Policy aim	Action by the league
Manage structure, composition, and team location	Control the admittance of new teams, set policies that require the merger of teams, and set the fixture and playing schedule
Increase game quality and improve competitive balance	Create player drafts and establish salary caps
Ensure the reputation of the game	Implement codes of conduct for players and officials and control public behavior at games
Expand the market and increase profits	Centralize marketing and coordinate advertising and promotional activities
Maximize broadcasting rights	As sole supplier of broadcasting rights, negotiate the best result
Redistribute revenue back to the league	Funnel income back to members as well as supplement the income of less financially viable members
Increase revenue streams	Maximize opportunities to benefit from advertising and promotional activities of sponsors
Regulate league costs	Regulate wages, set salary caps, and set the prices for publications and merchandise

Adapted from *Sport Management Review* 8(2), B. Stewart, M. Nicholson, and G. Dickson, "The Australian Football League's recent progress: A study in cartel conduct and monopoly power," 95-117, copyright 2005, with permission from Elsevier.

European Model

The third model that Morgan (2002) outlined is the oligarchy model, which can be highlighted through reference to the Premier League in England. To understand this model, it is important recognize that almost no intervention occurs in Europe. Ensuring competitive balance is difficult because European Union antitrust legislation is applied to sport as it is to any other industry. European law requires sporting competitors to be economic competitors; each team is treated as an economic unit (Edwards & Skinner, 2006). For example, English Premier League clubs are not constrained by salary caps, and they can offer players whatever money it would take to lure them away from another team. Premier League clubs do not have to abide by a draft system or share their broadcast revenues equally among themselves, as do NBA and NFL teams in North America, whose least successful clubs receive as much cash as the most successful ones. The big Premier League teams such as Manchester United, Arsenal, and Chelsea earn more money from broadcast rights because they appear more often. Those teams can spend their larger broadcasting revenue returns and merchandising income on expensive players, which in turn widens the gap between themselves and other clubs in the league.

In the broader European context, attempts to redistribute television revenues equally among all league teams have resulted in conflict. For example, the top four clubs in Holland (PSV, Ajax, Feyenoord, and Vitesse Arnhem) broke away in 1997 from their national league association and signed a separate television deal with Canal Plus. The European commissioner Karel van Miert supported the strategy on the grounds of free market competition (Giulianotti, 1999). In North America and Australia it is argued that sport leagues perform poorly under competitive or free-market conditions and that some form of self-regulation is essential to produce the outcome uncertainty that attracts fans, sponsors, and media interest (Szymanski & Kuypers, 1999). Ultimately, however, the primary beneficiaries of this regulation are the leagues themselves (Sage, 1998).

Smith and Stewart (2010) indicated that league structures can also highlight the differences between the North American and European governance models. North American leagues are characterized as closed systems. The makeup of the league is predetermined; the same teams participate regardless of their league standing in the previous year. By contrast, the European governance model employs a promotion and relegation system. This system, it is argued,

> can bolster interest in championship standings at the top and bottom of the competitive ladder, provide the opportunity for numerous teams from a single city to compete for a place in the

NHL as Cartel

Since the formation of the National Hockey League (NHL) in 1917, the business of hockey has grown spectacularly. The NHL began with franchises in Toronto, Ottawa, Montreal, and Quebec. In its growth since 1917 the NHL has acquired a corporate orientation that emphasizes the necessity of achieving cooperation among the owners to maintain league control over both the game and its players to maximize profits (Mills, 1991).

Beamish (1991) identified three types of ownership patterns among NHL teams: (1) individual (or small group), (2) family, and (3) conglomerate. According to Beamish, this difference in ownership pattern is one of the factors that affect the level of corporate control within the NHL. At all levels, however, ownership of an NHL franchise is generally only part of the portfolio of the owner (Mills, 1991).

One of the largest ongoing expenses incurred by professional sporting leagues is player salaries. Because leagues operate as cartels, players associations have developed in many professional sporting leagues to protect the rights of players. But as Beamish (1991) pointed out, the National Hockey League Players Association (NHLPA) has not enjoyed the increase in negotiating power generally associated with unionization because of the nature of the corporate ownership that represents NHL teams. Even when a team owner can be identified as an "individual," ownership is still in the hands of a "corporate entity with a diverse economic portfolio" (p. 216), the huge financial resources of which, in concert with all other members of the NHL, represent a financial behemoth that players cannot hope to contend with in negotiations. Players unions also negotiate with team owners "within the context of strongly market-oriented liberal ideology" (p. 216). Thus, Beamish suggested, the players unions are confronting not only a massive financial fortress but also a conservative social construct that tends to look unfavorably on collective action in general. Against this background the NHL locked out players for the 2004–2005 season, effectively causing the first entire cancellation of a hockey season since the NHL's inception in 1917.

The 30 teams in the NHL had been set to start opening training camps the day after the expiration of the existing labor contract, first agreed to in 1995 and extended two years later through September 15, 2004. Initial meetings between NHL management and the players union failed to bring any resolution to the main issues. Management demanded cost certainty, which players said would be tantamount to a salary cap. Even before the announcement, teams had given Commissioner Gary Bettman authority to cancel the season.

The financial power of team owners and their ability to withstand collective action by players were evidenced by the fact that they had already contributed, before the commencement of negotiations, US$300 million to a league work-stoppage fund to help get them through a lockout. NHL management claimed that it needed changes in the labor contract because teams were losing money—US$273 million in 2002–03 and US$224 million in the 2003–04 season. The average salary of an NHL player had risen from US$733,000 at the time of the last lockout in 1994–95 to $1,830,126 in 2003–04, according to the NHL Players Association. Although NHL revenue rose from US$732 million in 1993–94 to US$1.996 billion in 2002–03, the league said that player costs had increased from 57 percent of revenue to 75 percent over that period. The union disputed those figures (RedOrbit, 2004). Finally, after continuous negotiations, a tentative deal was brokered in July 2005, which, against the wishes of players and the union Executive Director Bob Goodenow, included a salary cap.

Although the NHL appeared to have got what it wanted, commissioner Bettman had promised "cost certainty" in the form of a hard salary cap to the owners, and he had delivered it. Players still under contract had their salaries reduced by 24 percent. Some high-priced players also found themselves on the market as teams pared payrolls to get down to the cap. But there was no way to measure the damage done to the sport, which already was the least popular of the four major leagues in the United States. Reselling the sport to disgruntled fans would be the next major hurdle confronting the NHL.

Several years after the lockout, the future of the NHL looks promising. Baranko noted in 2008 that fans had returned to the game, and the league had adopted new marketing strategies, including the addition of the Winter Classic. An overall improvement in attendance at games was matched by an increase in revenue. The NHL worked hard after the resolution of the lockout to maintain its high-profile sponsors such as Pepsi and AMP Energy. Anheuser-Busch also renewed its sponsorship as the NHL's official beer sponsor for three years in a deal reportedly worth US$75 million (Baranko, 2008). The fallout from the lockout reinforced to the NHL the importance of growing its fan base and ensuring its financial stability so that it would be in a position to ride out any damage occasioned by events similar to the 2004–05 lockout.

Learning Activity

Investigate the clubs that made up the G14 group of teams in Europe between 2000 and 2008. How did these teams exert influence on the governance of football in Europe? Why was the organization disbanded?

highest league, and remove incentives for team relocation given that it is less expensive to buy more talent in order to win promotion. (p. 8)

Promotion-Led Model

The fourth and final major transnational model for the governance of sport, as described by Morgan (2002), is the promotion-led structure. This structure can be seen in sports such as boxing. This form of governance is market led and fragmented. Contests are arranged as one-off events in which a promoter brings together the participants, organizes the venue, and arranges broadcasting rights and sponsorship opportunities.

The promotion-led model remains a threat when the established hierarchy no longer meets the needs of the stakeholders. The threat of a breakaway rugby union competition in the Southern Hemisphere was one of the factors that precipitated the International Rugby Board's support of the introduction of professionalism. Morgan, however, suggested that "such breakaways are usually followed by a renegotiated rapprochement with the traditional authorities, as the appeal of the sport depends on offering a legitimate and therefore significant championship rather than a travelling circus" (p. 50).

Emerging Models of Sport Governance

Although the models presented by Morgan (2002) are the most commonly referred to in the literature, as sport becomes increasingly globalized new models of economic governance are emerging. These new models are shaped by "local histories, local political and sporting cultures and local economic conditions" of a country and "reflect the local adaptation to global pressures in sport business" (Amara et al., 2005, p. 189). Examples from three countries follow.

China

In 1992 China adopted proposals for a "new socialist market economy." This reform process would bring about significant change in China across numerous industry sectors including sport. In 1992 the Chinese Football League was established, and the governing body of the league, the Chinese Football Association (CFA), was redefined as a nongovernmental body, although strong links to the state remained (Amara et al., 2005). Hence, the form of sport governance in this system has been termed "state sponsored restricted capitalism" (p. 194).

Some of the governance practices employed by the league have similarities with the cartel system that exists in North America and Australia. For example, under this system clubs are franchised controlled, and the CFA has taken responsibility for negotiating and controlling the sale of television rights at the national level, although at the local level broadcasting rights are owned by the clubs, which have the power to negotiate locally. Salary levels for the league ranged between 80 and 100 times the average salary, and the CFA set transfer values. Therefore, to a large degree the transfer market is a controlled environment. Despite this, the number of foreign players, most of whom are from Brazil, is growing (Amara et al, 2005).

With this rapid rise of professionalism, problems have emerged. Allegations of corruption and match fixing have arisen, and the ability of some clubs to retain their financial viability has been called into question (Amara et al., 2005). The system of governance in Chinese football is still evolving and perhaps can be best described as "a hybrid between traditional centralized control of vertical government of the game and the network system of governance evident in the European context" (p. 195) discussed earlier.

Japan

Two professional sport leagues in Japan that have established high public profiles are baseball and football. Professional baseball in Japan has a longer history than football. The first professional baseball league began in 1936. By contrast, the professional football league, known as the J League, consisted of 10 teams and was formed in 1991 (Daly & Kawaguchi, 2003) and will be the league focused on here.

The J League was launched on the back of a £20 billion injection of funds and the imposition of conditions on clubs who wished to be part of the league. According to Amara et al., (2005, p. 199), these conditions included the following:

◆ Clubs had to be registered corporations that had football as their core business function rather than the club being a subsidiary of another business.

◆ Teams were not allowed to be based in Tokyo initially because the league wished to decentralize the distribution of teams.

◆ Stadiums had to have a minimum of 15,000 seats, and floodlighting was required.

◆ Clubs were required to field a reserve team.

◆ All coaches were required to be licensed, and teams had to have a minimum of 18 players under contract.

Two conditions were clear departures from the Nippon Professional Baseball League in Japan. First, the requirement that clubs be named not after their owner or sponsor but on their location removed the possibility that team ownership was undertaken mainly as a means of corporate advertising. Second, the decision to share broadcast rights equally between the clubs established a relatively even distribution of major revenue sources, similar to what is done under the cartel system. It was soon realized that if the J League were to survive, it would require strong local government support as well as corporate backing because only a small number of the clubs have been able to operate with a profit. The remainder relied on other sources of funding (Amara et al., 2005). As a result, in Japan the professional baseball system is "built on coalitions of public-private interests serving local markets" (p. 200).

Learning Activity

Compare and contrast the Nippon Baseball League of Japan with Major League Baseball in the United States. In doing this identify the similarities and differences in how the leagues are structured and governed.

Algeria

The model of professional sport under development in Algeria is similar to that of China in that it is state designed and is experiencing implementation problems (Amara et al., 2005). In the 1990s Algeria began to experience economic problems, so the government started to encourage a shift from amateur to professional sport structures to reduce its public financial commitment. This change resulted in a "partial government disengagement from football (soccer) in 1999 with the intention of total disengagement to occur within a three- to five-year period" (p. 197).

The status of football in Algeria was beginning to change. Government disengagement was identified as the first stage in a shift toward the professionalization of a number of sports within Algeria. If this shift was successful it was envisaged that the practice would be extended to sports such as "handball, volleyball and basketball" (p. 197). It was hoped that this reorientation of sport structures in Algeria might also present other commercial opportunities and lead to the presence of players' agents, the formation of players associations, greater television revenue, and growth in employment both directly and indirectly associated with professional sport (Amara et al., 2005).

The first season of professional football in Algeria was in 1999. The structure adopted was based on the Swiss football system, which was a fusion of amateurism and professionalism. The Swiss league was similar to the system adopted in Tunisia, and it involved two divisions using a promotion and relegation system (Amara et al., 2005). This model did not succeed, and key stakeholders including government representatives, the presidents of the professional clubs, and representatives from the governing body and both divisions of the league decided that reorganization of the system was necessary. A new professional league was formed. The league was composed of 12 clubs who "would be managed by an autonomous structure known as 'le groupement professionel' (GPF)" (p. 197). The GPF was to take responsibility for organizing the planning and management of the professional league now named the Super-Division, and on behalf of the club presidents, it negotiated television broadcasting rights. The relegation system would not be used for the first two years to allow clubs a period of transition to the new environment (Amara et al., 2005). This change required relinquishing some of the governance practices that characterize the oligarchy model, in particular promotion and relegation, for the cartel practices of collective negotiation of broadcasting rights.

Accompanying the shift to Super-Division were several financial problems:

> The steady growth of players' wages; budgeting problems; poor performance; the absence of clear judicial procedures regarding transfer of players; and the lack of a taxation system for professional players; all of which, together with the internal lobbying and conflicts inside the AFF and GPF and the lack of external financial investors, rendered the survival of the new professional system problematic. (Amara et al., 2005, p. 198)

These factors were confounded by the fact that the major sponsor,

> the Khalifa Group (which had interests in airways, banks, medicines, TV, radio), who sponsored a large percentage of the Super-Division clubs as well as Olympic Marseille in France, and the Algerian Football Federation terminated its sponsorship arrangements due to financial concerns. (p. 198)

This occurrence left the league and the clubs in a precarious financial position. As such, by 2003 the experience of professional football in Algeria has yet to assume "a clear final form" (p. 198) of governance.

Learning Activity

Research a professional sport league in Korea. First, discuss the unique economic, political, and cultural characteristics of Korea. Second, identify key governance features of the league. Finally, determine whether there is a link between these unique characteristics and the model of governance that is being applied to the league.

Revenue Sources for Professional Sport Leagues

The most significant factors in revenue generation for professional sport leagues include ticket sales attributable to spectator attendance (Burton &

Cornilles, 1998), broadcasting rights, merchandising sales, and sponsorship (Zhang, Pease, & Smith, 1998). Sponsorship involves an organization or corporate identity financing part or all of a league, team, or athlete as a business enterprise to obtain access to the exploitable commercial potential associated with that league, team, or athlete. The objectives for making such an investment for the organization or corporate identity are quite clear—potentially huge financial gains. For the professional league, team, or athlete the reasons (apart from financial) may vary, but the two most widely cited are increasing public awareness of the league, team or athlete, and changing or enhancing the image of the league, team, or athlete (Meenaghan, 1991). Other reasons for entering into a sponsorship agreement may include the forging of links with business and political communities and the entertaining of corporate customers (Shaw & Amis, 2001). Irrespective of the rationale for entering into a sponsorship agreement, measuring its effectiveness is extremely difficult because separating the effects of a particular sponsorship investment from the effects of other marketing strategies is complicated.

Perhaps the greatest potential for achieving some of these objectives exists in China. Amara et al. (2005) pointed out that in 2003 the league was sponsored for one year by Siemens for €10 million (US$11.6 million). This amount was €2 million (US$2.3 million) less than it was paying for the sponsorship of the Spanish football giant Real Madrid in the same year. Furthermore, Amara et al. suggested that "the potential value of the league, in sponsorship terms, is reflected in the fact that its television audience is estimated at just less than 4 billion per year, and that Siemens as a mobile phone producer is attacking the Chinese market, which is estimated as the world's biggest market with 200 million subscribers" (p. 195). Clearly, tremendous opportunities are available to generate commercial incomes.

Broadcasting rights and ticketing also provide revenue-generating commercial opportunities, but these elements vary depending on the location of the club and the market in which it operates. For example, in North America and the United Kingdom, News Corporation and other media giants have not ignored the dominant role that the acquisition of broadcast rights continues to play. Law, Harvey, and Kemp (2002) pointed to the increase for the rights to broadcast American football (NFL) to US$395 million and to the right of the National Football League to renegotiate its contract after just five years than after eight years. Moreover, they pointed out that

> News Corporation's worldwide coverage continues to expand as they add the exclusive broadcasting rights for the Super Bowl, NHL games, and the MLB World Series, as well as the World Cup of Cricket and English Premiership football to their broadcast rights stable. (p. 284)

Contrast this to the broadcasting amounts paid in Algeria.

> Algeria's sole terrestrial channel paid €2.5 million (US$2.6 million) for the broadcasting rights for the first year of operation in 1999. Similarly, in Japan, although the major source of revenue shifted from merchandising rights (€26.3 million [US$30.2 million], or 40 percent) in 1993 to broadcasting rights (€36 million [US$30.5 million], or 46 percent of income) in 2001, (Amara et al., 2005, pp. 198–199)

The amounts are relatively small compared with the amounts in the more developed sport media economies of North America and the United Kingdom.

This variation in price and demand is also evident in ticket prices. Amara et al. (2005) noted that ticket prices in China are set by clubs and have been subject to agreement by the local Price Management Department of the state. Clubs are required to pay either 5 percent (Jia A League) or 2.5 percent (Jia B League) of their ticket income to the CFA. In France, live spectating demand for football can vary noticeably

> from 88 percent and 85 percent for Marseille and PSG (the biggest football clubs in the French League), but only 48 percent for Strasbourg, also competing in the top flight, with ticket prices at one-third the average level for the English Premiership reflecting the variable nature of this demand. (p. 200)

This discussion indicates that in some instances the very rules and regulations that seek to protect the members of a league can work against the maximization of financial benefits and perceived growth of popularity of the sport itself. Jane-Anne Lee (2001) reported that the Association of Surfing Professionals (ASP) had turned down a lucrative

broadcasting deal worth an estimated US$50 million over five years because of industry fears that control of the sport would be lost. This occurred at a time when sponsorship of surfing in the 1990s had begun to wane. Arthur (2003) believed that a lack of a television profile was part of the reason for this.

Competition Among Leagues

Although rival leagues have arisen from time to time to challenge established and official leagues, the history of rival leagues suggests that they often either fail or eventually merge with the established leagues. For example, four teams in the World Hockey Association (WHA) joined the National Hockey League (NHL). Similarly, as previously discussed, in Australia in early 1995 Rupert Murdoch's News Limited introduced its Super League competition in an attempt to control the administration of rugby league worldwide, and in turn provide a product for cable and pay television (Fitzsimons, 1996). Two separate national rugby league competitions were played in 1997, but because of mitigating factors the two rival leagues established a joint venture and formed one professional league known as the National Rugby League. World Series Cricket in Australia lasted only two years before an agreement was reached with the traditional governing body, now known as Cricket Australia, for the rebel players who joined World Series Cricket to return to Cricket Australia. Players from both leagues received increased pay and benefits. The traditional governing body also achieved greater financial gain because of a restructuring of broadcasting rights.

Competition among leagues has emerged recently in India. The battle of the Indian Cricket League (ICL) against the Board of Control for Cricket in India (BCCI) and the International Cricket Council (ICC)

Professional Surfing

The two major organizations responsible for the governance of world surfing are the International Surfing Association (ISA) and the Association of Surfing Professionals (ASP). The ISA was first established in 1964 as the International Surfing Federation (ISF), and it became the ISA in 1976. Today the organization represents over 50 national surfing federations. To be a member of the ISA, national member associations must be recognized by their governments as the major organizing body for surfing in their respective countries. The ASP eventually emerged in the 1970s as isolated pockets of structured competition surfing began to emerge. Surfers in the 1960s and early 1970s received little in the way of financial compensation or reward from endorsements, and prize money was virtually nonexistent.

By the mid-1970s, events had popped up from Sydney to Rio, from Florida to Durban. This loose-knit belt of tournaments was strung together in 1976 in what would prove to be the embryonic stage of ASP. By 1984 the professional surfing tour had expanded to over 20 internationally rated events (ASP, 2009). The ASP consolidated its position as chief governing body, organizer, and policy maker in relation to all major international surfing events during the 1980s and 1990s, which by then had become known as the World Championship Tour (WCT).

The commercialization of surfing through sponsorship, endorsements, and media coverage has mirrored to some extent the commercialism of other sports that developed during the 20th century. In 2003 the global surf industry was reportedly worth in the region of A$7.4 billion (US$5.0 billion) (Arthur, 2003). The concept of surfing sponsorship has its origins in the 1960s when Ampol Petroleum was among the first corporate supporters of the sport. Sponsors during the 1970s included Smirnoff, Coke, Stubbies, Rip Curl, Quiksilver, and Qantas—all looking to tap into the potential of the "rapidly expanding and lucrative youth market" (Booth, 1994, cited in Lanagan, 2003, p. 171). As the popularity of surfing increased, so did the willingness of corporations to invest capital. Corporate sponsorship of surfing, which had peaked during 1970s and 1980s, began to wane in the early 1990s. Multinational conglomerates such as Coca-Cola began to pare back on the millions of dollars they had previously poured into surfing events as surfing became marginal-ized from mainstream sport. Arthur (2003) cited a lack of a television profile as part of the reason for this. Additionally, he said that the growth of surfing sponsorship in the 1970s and 1980s came at a time when commercial interest in sport was growing generally, and surfing had benefitted from this development. Surfing, however, was ill equipped to weather changes in the global corporate sponsorship battle, and the sport's governing bodies may have made decisions based more on issues of control than on shoring up commercial possibilities and securing the financial viability of the sport. Other sports realized the potential for commercial linkages and seemed better equipped through their mainstream, traditional, mass-market appeal to connect with corporate sponsors. Jane-Anne Lee (2001) reported that the ASP had turned down a lucrative broadcasting deal worth an estimated US$50 million over five years because of fears within the sport's governing body that they would lose their control of the sport.

The ASP could not, however, insulate the sport forever from advances in media technology and the potential benefits that mass media exposure and corporate sponsorship could bring in promotion of the sport to the public. The 10-year US$50 million deal that the ASP entered into with International Management Group (IMG) in the early 2000s was a step into uncharted waters, which would lead the surfing community to reassess its cultural values (Arthur, 2003). This realization is perhaps reflected in the ASP's being at the forefront of live web streaming of major WCT events. Live web streaming brings WCT events to the computer screen of anyone with an Internet connection. The surfing fan therefore does not have to rely on the broadcasting schedules of television producers.

With the increased sponsorship profile of surfing, surfing professionals are now acutely aware of their profiles and are trained to deal with the media in a manner that avoids controversy. Arthur (2003) suggested that this change brings into question some of the characteristics traditionally associated with surfing and surfers themselves, such as individualistic, unconventional, and antiestablishment. In the regimented corporate world of athletes as endorsers, the traditional core values of surfing could be seen as being sacrificed in pursuit of the corporate dollar.

Learning Activity

Find a case of an individual sport (as opposed to a team sport) in which an attempt was made to establish a rebel, or rival, tour. Research who was behind this proposal and their motivation for doing this.

backed Indian Premier League (IPL) is currently being played out in the courts. The rebel ICL is seeking recognition as unofficial cricket, and the BCCI and ICC support the continuing sanction of players who are participating in the rebel league. With the popularity of the sanctioned IPL growing, and sponsors such as Coca-Cola, Honda, and Vodaphone on board, the ICL looks set to follow the route of its rebel-league predecessors.

CASE STUDY

Rebel Leagues and International Cricket

The international governing body for cricket is the International Cricket Council (ICC). The Dubai-based body is responsible for promoting, developing, and regulating the way that cricket is played around the world. Initially constituted in 1909 as the Imperial Cricket Conference, it assumed its current name in 1989. Over the next seven years the ICC expects to raise about US$1.5 billion from broadcast rights and key global sponsorships, and will use about US$300 million of this as seed money for emerging cricket markets (Hiscock, 2009).

In 2007, in a much more optimistic financial climate, ESPN Star Sports had agreed to pay a record US$1.1 billion for exclusive global broadcasting and marketing rights for all ICC events from 2007 through 2015. The importance of cricket as an international market with huge potential returns for sponsors is evidenced by the range of sponsors, which include ESPN Star Sports, Pepsi, Yahoo!, Reebok, and Emirates. Each of the member nations of the ICC has its own domestic governing body. In Australia, this is Cricket Australia, initially formed in 1892 as the Australasian Cricket Council. In India the governing cricket body is the Board of Control for Cricket in India (BCCI). In incidents that occurred more than 30 years apart, both Cricket Australia (then the Australian Cricket Board) and the BCCI faced serious attacks on their authority and financial control of the game by the establishment of rival leagues. Coincidentally, both situations arose over disputes about broadcasting rights.

In the late 1970s media mogul Kerry Packer established World Series Cricket in Australia after failing to secure the lucrative broadcasting rights to Australian and international cricket for his television network. World Series Cricket attracted the biggest names in international cricket, all willing to sign on for lucrative pay packets despite the threat of sanctions from both the ACB and ICC (then called the International Cricket Conference). When the dust settled in 1979, Packer had won the television broadcasting rights he had wanted from the beginning, previously sanctioned players returned to their national teams, day–night cricket and protective headgear were almost accepted factors of the game, and the fast-paced one-day cricket was more popular than the traditional five-day test match.

Over time, however, it was deemed that the original one-day format was becoming tired. Changes to the rules were implemented in an attempt to revitalize the product, yet it was thought that a new cricket product was required to appeal to a new generation of potential cricket followers. The loss of public interest in cricket was particularly evident in the United Kingdom in the 1990s. The England and Wales Cricket Board sought to introduce a relatively new form of limited over cricket, the Twenty-20 competition, in an attempt to attract new fans and reattract lost fans by virtue of this fast-paced, action-packed variant of the game. The Twenty-20 product was launched in the United Kingdom in 2003 and was predominately aimed at new market segments that may not have seen much appeal in attending the game of cricket. The results of the inaugural competition in 2003 were extremely successful and continued to improve over successive years. Attendances at the ground were not the only success story; television viewing figures were up by 62 percent (Kitchin, 2008). The international cricketing community recognized that the new product had the potential to reinvigorate current fans and attract a new generation of cricket fans.

In what could perhaps be seen as an echo of Kerry Packer's establishment of World Series Cricket to obtain domestic broadcasting rights in Australia, Subhash Chandra, promoter of Zee Telefilms, created the Indian Cricket League (ICL) following failed bids for telecast rights to the Cricket World Cup in 2003 and 2004 and the ICC Champions Trophy in 2006. Chandra hoped to capitalize on the recent popularity of Twenty-20 cricket, an even faster-paced version of one-day cricket that is played over a three-hour format and had been gaining a higher international profile.

The six-team, 17-day ICL included stars like West Indian Brian Lara, South African Lance Klusener, and Pakistan's Inzamam-ul-Haq. The first season of the league was in November 2007. The governing body of cricket, the ICC, refused to recognize the competition, as did the BCCI, which also threatened players with lengthy bans. The £12.5 million (US$26 million) competition was led by legendary Indian cricketer and former captain Kapil Dev (BBC News, 2007). The concept again proved successful, prompting the development of an officially sanctioned rival, the Indian Premier League (IPL), which began in April 2008 and boasted its own star names including Ricky Ponting of Australia and Muttiah Muralitharan of Sri Lanka (BBC News, 2007).

The success of the ICL sent a clear message to the ICC and the BCCI that professional sport leagues need to evaluate the product that they are providing to the public. All professional sport leagues need to be aware that media and sport entrepreneurs will look for commercial opportunities within the international sport management landscape. Governing bodies that fail to respect the needs of their fans and embrace innovative sport management practices could find that commercial opportunities will pass them by and be taken up by competitors. This case has clearly demonstrated this possibility.

Learning Activity

The Indian Cricket League and the Indian Premier League currently have separate Twenty-20 cricket professional leagues. Determine which league you believe will be the most successful and justify your decision.

Summary

Professional sport leagues in North America and Australia use their rules and regulations to encourage competitive balance so as to maintain fan enthusiasm by keeping fans in suspense. In the European Union, which applies antitrust legislation to football just as it would to any other industry, that tactic would constitute illegal collusion among members of a cartel. In Europe the best run and most financially viable leagues and teams are successful. This scenario is desirable in free-market economies but not necessarily in sport. In countries such as China, Japan, and Algeria the governance of professional sport leagues is being shaped by local factors such as history, political and sporting cultures, and the prevailing economic conditions. Although sport management academics argue that sport is a business, some would accept the fundamental principle that equality of outcomes (at the expense of overall standards) is a desirable way to maintain spectator support, league financial viability, and the infusion of sponsorship.

The examples of ice hockey, surfing, and cricket used in this chapter indicate that in the international arena the ongoing viability of professional sport leagues and tours is subject to specific and unique circumstances. The infusion of sponsorship into professional sport leagues and tours continues to be the key to ongoing financial stability, but their long-term viability depends on the ability of their administrators to formulate business strategies that appeal to current and future fans while enhancing the public perception and image of their sport product. Success within a professional sport industry underpinned by this relationship depends on management's ability to respond to the needs of sport consumers—the media, sponsors, and spectators—and to provide a platform for promoting continued interest.

? Review and Discussion Questions

1. Identify and provide examples of how sport is governed at the international, regional, national, and local levels.

2. List and discuss the key features of the four major transnational models for the governance of sport leagues.

3. Identify the key characteristics of a country that can influence the governance models used in its professional sport leagues. Provide an example of how these characteristics could influence the application of the model.

4. Outline the major revenue sources available to professional sport leagues and how these revenues are managed.

International Youth, School, and Collegiate Sport

Joanne MacLean, PhD
Brock University, Canada

Chapter Objectives

After studying this chapter, you will be able to do the following:

- Define and provide examples of youth, school, and club sport
- Discuss organizations for governing international youth sport
- Outline the organization structure, leadership, and governance of international sport for youth within school-based and club-based sport organizations
- Identify key international competitions for youth sport
- Identify stakeholders in school-based and club-based sport

Key Terms

Thinking about international sport conjures images of top athletes competing in huge multisport events like the Olympic Games. The athletes are the best in the world at their respective sports, and their physical maturity enables them to be the fastest, strongest, most accurate, or most aesthetically pleasing. These athletes are obviously experienced in their sports, and this image of international sport therefore involves mostly mature, adult athletes. Logically, then, elite international sport excludes participation by younger, school-aged athletes. But many high-profile international sporting events and multisport competitions are organized for younger athletes. The International Children's Games and World Youth Games have been in existence for many years, and thousands participate in as many as 15 individual and team sports. International competition for youth is also organized regionally, in such events as the Alps–Adriatic Winter Youth Games, European Youth Olympic Festival, New Zealand Colgate School Games, and the Canada Games. In addition to regional events, world youth championships are also organized in individual sports such as baseball, athletics (track and field), football, boxing, basketball, and swimming, to name a few.

This chapter examines international sport opportunities for athletes in youth, school, and club-level organizations. The organizational structure, leadership, corporate culture, and decision-making processes will be described for organizations that deliver international opportunities for youth athletes. The sheer volume and complexity of international athletic events for younger athletes should foster a better understanding of the evolution and intricacy of international sport and the role played by sport organizations for youth participation on the world stage. The world of sport is truly global, and many international competitions exist for younger athletes. The next section looks at the organizations that are propelling younger athletes into international competition.

Defining Youth, School, and Club Sport

The term *youth* is usually defined as the time of life between childhood and adulthood. Organized sport during childhood involves huge numbers of participants in clubs and leagues that organize modified games of football, baseball, basketball, hockey, tennis, golf, and virtually all other sporting activities. But youth sport includes the period when children's games evolve into more organized teams and events. Although children's sport is popular in countries around the world, it mostly involves local participation and a "sport for all" philosophy in which everyone plays an equal amount of time and a variety of goals beyond winning and losing is emphasized, such as teamwork, skill development, and physical activity. Pinpointing the precise time at which children's sport becomes youth sport is difficult. For the purposes of this book we broadly define **youth sport** as organized activities involving youngsters between the ages of about 6 to 18 years old and college age. The breadth of this definition makes sense because world youth sport incorporates international sport events for a wide variety of ages: from youngsters to teenagers (World Little League Championships for each of four male and female divisions, ages 5 to 18), early teenagers (International Children's Games for 12- to 15-year-olds), high school students (Scholar Athlete Games for high school students having completed grades 9 through 12), and college and university students (the World University Games).

Although youth sport is organized through various means in countries around the world, the education system and clubs typically play a lead role. Virtually all colleges, universities, and high schools and over half of all elementary schools in the United States and Canada sponsor competitive sport teams. In fact, **school sport** is popular throughout the world at the college level. Many countries, such as the United Kingdom, India, Japan, and Australia, also operate school sport systems. **Sport clubs**, developed and made popular in Europe, are another common avenue for youth sport participation virtually worldwide. Clubs are usually specific to a particular sport, and they sponsor teams and opportunities for participation through either public or private groups within a municipal area. Some clubs are private, for-profit ventures in sports such as tennis, golf, skiing, and curling. Other clubs are public, nonprofit ventures organized by people interested in specific individual and team sports in which the goal is opportunity for participation. Such clubs might be supported by municipal recreation departments that organize events and leagues and may provide facilities.

Learning Activity

Take an hour in your library or online to discover and list a minimum of three international sporting events being held next year for youth in each of the following continents: Africa, America, Asia, Europe, and Oceania. Identify three distinguishing factors for the events.

The types of activities in school and club sport programs vary. Traditional team and individual sports maintain varied popularity on a regional basis. But newer activities, sometimes referred to as alternative sports, are gaining widespread popularity, and clubs that encourage youth to participate are popping up around the world. Boarding sports, such as skate, snow, mountain, and wake boarding, along with surfing, adventure, and extreme adventure activities such as rock climbing and mountain bike jumping have exploded in popularity. Snowboard-cross involves four racers competing on a downhill course over rolling terrain and jumps. It debuted as an Olympic sport at the 2006 Winter Games in Turin, Italy, and was continued at the 2010 Vancouver Winter Olympics, pointing to the increased popularity of this emerging sport. It is a distinct possibility that the Olympic snowboard-cross competitors will be athletes in the youth age group. In any case, a variety of international opportunities are available for younger athletes, and they will emerge from the school and club sport systems around the world. Which organizations are working to provide opportunities for younger athletes internationally, and how are they governed? The following sections examine both the destination (governance and organizational structure of youth sport international events) and the origin (governance and organizational structure of school, club, and youth sport activities) for young athletes who compete internationally.

Governance and Organization of International Youth Sport Events

Competing in a chosen sport or sports is a significant thrill during one's youth, but imagine the excitement of competing internationally. Perhaps the joy comes from the idea of competing against and beating those from another part of the world, or from the opportunity to travel and to experience the culture of another country, or from just being away from home. Whatever the reasons, most athletes are thrilled at the prospect of competing in an international sporting event, and the anticipation of such competition is only heightened for younger athletes. Many opportunities are available for international youth competition in multisport and individual sport formats, for teams that represent cities or entire countries, in events that may be small or tremendously large in scale. The next sections examine the governance of three international youth sport competitions: world youth championships (individual sporting events), International Children's Games (multisport games), and the Little League Baseball World Series (large, age-group specific international youth sport championships). The organizational structure, leadership, corporate culture, and decision-making processes for each of these events are presented.

World Youth Championships

World youth championships are age-group specific international championships hosted under the auspices of the international federation for a particular sport. For example, FIFA, which is French for Fédération Internationale de Football Association, is the international governing body for football. FIBA (originally, Fédération Internationale de Basketball Amateur, now just Fédération Internationale de Basketball but maintaining the acronym) oversees and regulates the sport of basketball, and the IAAF (Internationale Amateur Athletics Fédération) governs track and field, and so on. International Federations were discussed in detail in chapter 11. A World Youth or Young Men's or Women's Championship is hosted by each of these federations. Let's investigate the **FIFA U-20 World Cup**, known before 2005 as the World Youth Football Championship, in further detail. The U-20 designation identifies the age group of the athletes eligible to compete in the event. In this case all the athletes were under 20 years of age on January 1 in the year of competition.

Held every two years since 1979, the FIFA U-20 World Cup involves national youth teams representing countries who qualify to attend by winning a berth allotted to their region of competition. The host country's team automatically qualifies to compete, and the host site is allocated by FIFA on a bid process. The FIFA U-20 World Cup is governed with a structure similar to that used for the Olympic Games and is comparable to other youth championships in sports like basketball, athletics, and swimming. FIFA is the international federation responsible for the event. It awards the hosting privileges to a country through its national federation (NF), the organization responsible for managing the sport within a particular country. This NF works with a specific city or area to form a hosting committee that manages the championships. National federations, such as the U.S. Soccer Federation, the Canadian Soccer Association, and Federación de Fútbol de Chile (Chilean National Federation), already exist in 208 countries around the world (FIFA, 2008a). The hosting committee then manages the championship event for all participating national teams.

The location of the FIFA U-20 World Cup has moved from continent to continent since its inception in 1977. Host countries have included Tunisia, Japan, Australia (twice), Mexico, Russia, Chile, Saudi Arabia, Portugal, Qatar, Malaysia, Nigeria, Argentina, the United Arab Emirates, Netherlands, Canada, and Egypt. Originally involving 16 participating countries, the championship became a 24-team event in 1997 (FIFA, 2008b). Typically, a FIFA vice president chairs the FIFA Youth Championships Committee.

The organizing committees for each of the U-17 and U-20 Men's World Cups and the U-17/U-20 Women's World Cup are standing committees of FIFA. Each is normally led by a FIFA vice president, who presides as the tournament chairman. The committees are made up of a deputy chairman, 10 committee members elected from association representatives to FIFA, and a representative of the host country. The national federation (NF) of the host country develops a local organizing committee at the site of the championships to complete the hosting, marketing, and fund-raising details. In each case, members and leaders of committees are elected by FIFA or the national federation respectively. The goal of these groups is to work cooperatively to deliver an exceptional youth championship that is well organized, entertaining, and a developmental step for younger athletes to move on to the World

Learning Activity

Suppose that you have just been awarded the bid to host the U-17 World Cup of Football for men and women. Draw the organizational structure of the host committee for the World Cup. Be sure to include all important operating components that must be organized to deliver a successful World Cup.

Cup of football. FIFA holds final authority and decision-making power regarding the event as outlined in the FISU (Fédération Internationale du Sport Universitaire) statutes and agreement with the NF of the hosting country. Of course, the stakeholders of all decision making for the championships include a diverse group of football administrators at FIFA, the host NF, and participating NFs. Organizers and sponsors at the local level are also major stakeholders in decision-making intent on hosting a successful experience for athletes, coaches, fans, media, and local citizens. Showcasing local talents and putting a spotlight on the social, cultural, and economic way of life are tremendously important in the rare hosting opportunities that invite the world's focus.

The description provided for hosting the FIFA U-20 World Cup is a common approach to delivering world youth championships. In sports like cycling, rowing, and climbing, the NF of the host country bids to the IF to secure the rights to the event. After securing the winning bid the NF forms a host committee to organize the event. Similar to the World Cups hosted by FIFA for football, the International Children's Games is another interesting example of competitive athletic opportunities for youth internationally.

International Children's Games

The **International Children's Games (ICG)** is a multisport event in which thousands of participants compete in sport, educational, international trade and commerce, and cultural and arts events. The Games originated in Yugoslavia in 1968 to promote peace and friendship through sport and are now held in communities around the world. The 2010 International Children's Games were held in Manama, Kingdom of Bahrain, in the Persian Gulf. More than 1,200 athletes 12 to 15 years old from 71 towns around the world competed in several sports including handball, sailing, soccer, swimming, table tennis, taekwondo, track and field, and volleyball (International Children's Games, 2011). But the Games are much more than just athletic competition. According to former ICG organizers,

> The International Children's Games are extraordinary because the fostering of cooperation is as crucial as the competition. It's about boys and girls breaking through cultural barriers, stretching and redefining what the term "personal best" means. The Games are a proving ground where young athletes discover that winning is not about keeping score. A high jumper realizing that a handshake can be just as powerful as strong legs in overcoming hurdles. (International Children's Games, 2004a)

Organizing an event of the magnitude of the ICG involves years of planning. The event is sanctioned by the International Olympic Committee (IOC) because the ICG is a recognized member of the IOC, but the organization and funding of the Games is largely the responsibility of the host city. A full-time and part-time staff and a considerable number of volunteers spend several years preparing competition schedules, accommodations, public

relations, travel, security, marketing and fundraising, and special events. The staff is led by an executive director who might report to a member of the host communities' commission or council for sport, youth, or tourism. An example of the organizational structure of the host committee for an ICG is presented in figure 13.1.

The individuals holding the positions illustrated in the organizational chart (figure. 13.2) are hired to fulfill the mandate of the position and presumably will step down at the end of the Games. The mission of the organizing committee is to have

Figure 13.1 Governance of FIFA World Youth Football Championship.

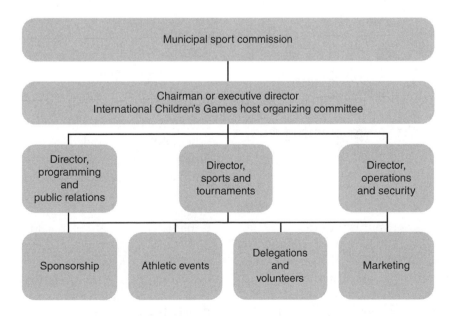

Figure 13.2 Example organizing committee of the International Children's Games.

the host community "open its arms and hearts to welcome athletes, coaches, spectators, dignitaries, and business leaders from around the world, promising a unique and unforgettable experience for all" (International Children's Games, 2004b). The chairman of the organizing committee holds significant decision-making responsibility and reports key financial, security, and operational concerns to the chief executive and board of trustees of the municipal sports commission (MSC). The MSC is a nonprofit organization mandated to enhance the economy, image, and quality of life within a geographical area by attracting sport events, encouraging youth participation in sport, and maximizing community resources to assist with such hosting.

A host of stakeholders are interested in the events of the ICG. Community members benefit by promoting their city and gaining economic benefit through hosting thousands of participants and spectators from around the world. Athletes, coaches, and parents are other major stakeholders. They are concerned with safe and effective delivery of truly unforgettable experiences. Governments, communities, and educators from around the world are intent on bringing youth together to teach principles of peace, tolerance, fairness, and integrity. "[It] is the only global, youth athletic event that combines sports, educational programs and peace-motivated cultural exchange" (International Children's Games, 2008).

Learning Activity

Read the case study on hosting the ICG. Identify the issues that Mayor Frances is facing in the case. If you were his chief advisor, how might you recommend that he deal with these issues?

Youth sport championships like the World Cup in football and the multisport International Children's Games are important opportunities for international competition for younger athletes. They are examples of the most common types of events staged for international competition at the youth level. Multisport championships like the International Children's Games are larger and more complex to manage given the number of sports delivered. Regardless of size and complexity, events with a long history like the World Little League Baseball Championships (formally referred to as the Little Baseball League World Series) are often the best known and most popular with media.

Little League Baseball World Series

Little League Baseball was founded in 1939. Little League International is a nonprofit organization that promotes and assists youth participation in baseball and softball (Little League Online, 2008a). Four levels of organization contribute to Little League play:

1. The local Little League
2. The district
3. The region
4. International headquarters

The stakeholders interested in competitive youth baseball include approximately 7,400 local Little League organizations in communities in more than 100 countries worldwide offering opportunities for youngsters to compete in Little League baseball and softball (Little League Online, 2008b). Example stakeholder groups are athletes, coaches, parents, volunteers, organizers, and sponsors. Geographical boundaries are established, and volunteers organize the leagues and coach and umpire the games. Everyone is encouraged to play regardless of ability to pay for uniform fees, and every child plays in every game. Roughly 10 to 20 leagues make up a district (Little League Online, 2008c). A district administrator, an experienced volunteer, organizes the district tournament and attends the International Congress where rules and other policy are decided. Nearly 500 Little League Baseball districts exist in the world (Little League Online, 2008c). District administrators report to a regional director. There are five regional directors in the United States, and one each in Puerto Rico, Canada, Japan, and Poland (Little League Online, 2008b). Regional directors are involved in organizing regional tournaments, which are made up of district winners. Each of the 16 worldwide regional tournaments sends its winner to the **Little League Baseball World Series**, held annually in August at the Little League Baseball International Headquar-

CASE STUDY

Hosting the International Children's Games

The International Children's Games (ICG) seek to "enable, develop and advance the meeting, understanding and friendship of students [aged 12–15] from different countries around the world and promote the Olympic Ideal" (International Children's Games, 2008). On June 29, 2010, the ICG Committee president, Mr. Torsten Rasch, announced that the city of Windsor, Ontario, Canada, would host the International Children's Games in June 2013. Windsor is located directly across the river from Detroit, Michigan, on the United States–Canada border.

The mayor of the City of Windsor is Mr. Eddie Francis. He is ecstatic to have won the bid to host the Games after travelling to the Persian Gulf nation of the Kingdom of Bahrain to formally bid for the ICG hosting rights. He believes strongly in the mission of the Games and is intent on generating economic benefits from the tourism and promotion that the Games will bring to the City of Windsor. Although approximately 2,000 coaches, athletes, and delegates will attend the Games to compete, significant economic impact will occur in the region from spectators who will visit to support their teams. In addition, the city will benefit from promotion through media coverage and resultant tourism.

The mission of the City of Windsor is stated on its website: "Our City is built on relationships—between citizens and their government, businesses and public institutions, city and region—all interconnected, mutually supportive and focused on the brightest future we can create together." The population of the city is approximately 200,000, and it has a diversity of people and cultures. The region is a manufacturing center in Canada and therefore was heavily affected by the world economic downturn of 2008–2009 and resultant negative effect on the automobile sector.

Recently, ICGs have featured participation in sports like athletics, basketball, futsal, gymnastics, handball, sailing, football, swimming, table tennis, taekwondo, and volleyball. Windsor is home to both a university and college that have a host of excellent athletic facilities, including indoor and outdoor tracks for athletics, indoor court facilities, outdoor grass and artificial fields, and the adjacent Lake St. Claire and sailing marina. In addition, municipal facilities and high schools also contribute adequate to good indoor and outdoor sporting amenities. One problem, however, is that Windsor does not have an Olympic-sized pool, which is required for hosting the ICGs.

Another problem exists for Mayor Frances and his team. Not all the citizens of Windsor believe that hosting sporting events is a good idea, and in fact, many are opposed to the idea. The opposition believes that the sole focus of the current municipal government should be job creation. Hosting an event such as the ICGs will not, in their opinion, create any enduring jobs and not enough economic impact. One angry citizen remarked: "This is bogus. We'll be playing games, but we'll also be on welfare!"

Further compounding the issues for Mayor Frances, the city's facility inventory and plan does not call for the development of a new pool facility. But in favor of the building of a pool has been a call within the community strategic plan to enhance society by providing facilities to promote healthy living through physical activity. Local community sport coaches and administrators believe that the hosting of the ICGs will promote the development of programming and facility development and that a proper aquatics facility will boost swimming in the area. The wish list for an aquatics center includes a 50-meter pool, warm-up pool, ample seating along one wall, an exercise facility, and possibly a diving structure that includes a 10-meter platform. The estimated cost is C$40 million dollars.

---

ters in South Williamsport, Pennsylvania. At the event about 110 full-time staff liaise with volunteers from every other level of Little League, providing a full range of support services, promotion, and opportunities for research pertinent to Little League activities. The headquarters is located on 66 acres (27 hectares) of land and includes practice facilities, living facilities, and the Howard J. Lamade Stadium, home of the annual Little League World Series. The various levels of play in Little League Baseball are defined in figure 13.3.

The operations of Little League Baseball are led by the president and chief executive officer. This person reports to the Little League Baseball Board of Directors and leads a professional staff of 110 people who work at the World Headquarters. The

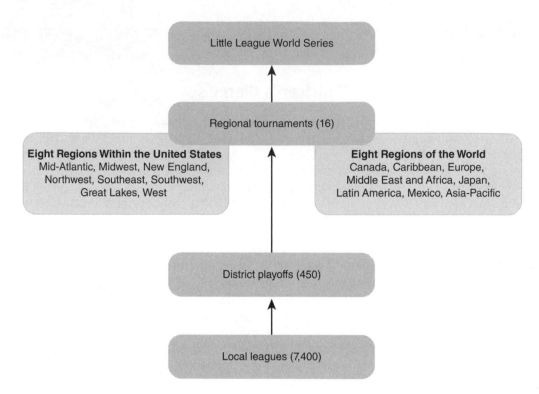

Figure 13.3   Levels of play in Little League Baseball.

ultimate authority for the management of Little League Baseball, Inc. is vested in its 24-person board of directors. The officers of Little League Baseball, Inc. include volunteers in the positions of chairman and treasurer and staff members in the positions of president and CEO, chief financial officer, and vice president of operations and corporate secretary. The board comprises volunteers elected to their positions for three-year terms. Nine members of the board of directors are elected from delegates attending the Little League International Congress, and other members are assigned by geographical region and stakeholder. The International Congress is held every three years and functions to set policy and future direction for all levels of Little League Baseball. The organizational structure of Little League Baseball, Inc. is summarized in figure 13.4.

Youth sport activities like the Little League Baseball World Series, the International Children's Games, and world youth championships in selected sports involve an extensive array of opportunities organized by sport managers for international competition by young athletes. The Little League Baseball World Series is an example of an event managed by an enduring organiza-

tion set up to run the event at the same location each year. This differentiates it from the two other events, for which specific organizing committees are formed to stage the event and after which dissolve. Another competitive avenue for international youth competition is school sport. The following sections describe the governance of school sport and the opportunities for international competition resulting from various levels of the school sport system.

Learning Activity

Find the website of the most recent International Children's Games. Search the website to learn how the Games were organized, how the governance structure was set up for decision making, and who was responsible. Compare your findings with the setup for the most recent Little League Baseball World Series baseball championships. Contrast your findings regarding the organization and delivery of the two events.

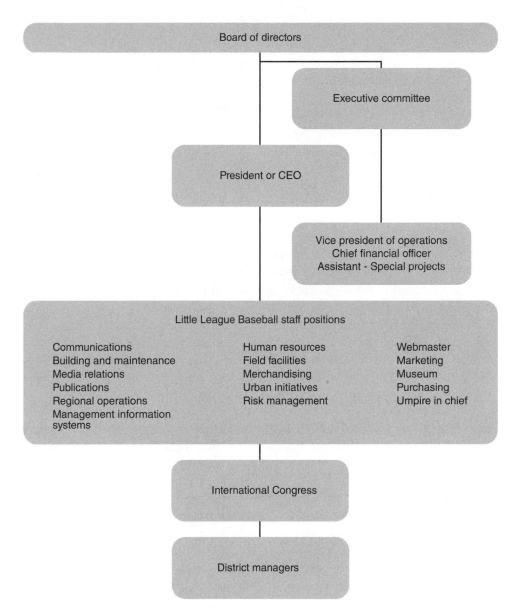

Figure 13.4 Organizational structure of Little League Baseball, Inc.

Governance and Organization of School Sport

For our purposes, school sport refers to competitive athletics in which athletes represent an educational institution by virtue of their enrollment in that particular institution. The spectrum of school sport is broad, involving elementary and middle school sport teams, along with high school and college or university athletics. The majority of school sport international competition involves high school and college-level athletes. Collegiate athletics is prevalent in countries around the world. School sport at other levels is dominant in North America. In contrast, younger athletes in other parts of the world might compete for an age-division team of their local sport club. The following sections identify the dominant organizations that govern international school sport and provide examples of opportunities for international competition.

International School Sport

Three main levels of organizations govern high school sport: (*a*) individual schools and school districts, (*b*) regional (state and provincial) high school athletic associations, and (*c*) national federations of regional high school associations. Much of the decision-making authority rests at the school district and regional level where rules and regulations are defined. National organizations such as the National Federation of State High School Associations (NFHS) in the United States and its Canadian counterpart, the Canadian School Sport Federation (CSF), act primarily as service, administrative, and advocacy groups for school sport. Over 60 such organizations in countries like Germany, Australia, Italy, Russia, Slovenia, and Chinese Taipei act as liaisons to the International School Sport Federation located in Brussels, Belgium.

The mission of the **International School Sport Federation (ISF)** is to coordinate and organize international school sport contests involving students 13 through 18 years of age: "It organizes international competition in different sporting disciplines and encourages contests between school students with a view to promoting better mutual understandings" (International School Sport Federation, 2008a). Competitions are hosted every two years in the following sports: athletics (track and field), badminton, basketball, beach volleyball, cross country running, floorball, football, futsal, gymnastics, handball, judo, orienteering, skiing, swimming, table tennis, tennis, and volleyball. Founded in 1972 with 13 countries, the ISF has grown to include around 70 countries in five continents.

The ISF is organized using a combination of full-time staff members hired to conduct the business of the organization throughout the year and volunteers elected to various positions. The policy and decision-making body is the **ISF General Assembly (GA)**. It is composed of one representative from each country's authorized school sport national organization. Membership is made by an application procedure in which other members of the GA vote to accept the new member based on the credentials of the application. Besides deciding membership, the GA reviews the general administration, financial reports, calendar of events, budgets, membership fees, statutes, and appointment of honorary members (International School Sport Federation, 2008b). The other important task of the GA involves the election of auditors. Two auditors (and one substitute) are elected for terms of four years to examine and verify the financial accounting of the organization. The GA meets once every two years at a minimum.

Learning Activity

Search online for the website of the International School Sports Federation. Identify the role of the general assembly of the organization. Who are its members? Who are the auditors? What is the role of the auditor within this context? Identify a technical commission (TC). What is its role, and who makes up the TC?

Reporting to the GA is the ISF Executive Committee (EC). The EC is composed of positions elected for four-year terms. It is led by the ISF president and includes the vice president, secretary general, treasurer, five continental vice presidents (Africa, America, Asia, Europe, and Oceania), and 12 assessors. The EC must meet at least once per year to carry out decisions of the GA, confirm motions of the technical commissions and rules of competition, oversee hosting plans and liaison to events, and deal with emergency or time-sensitive matters for the organization (International School Sport Federation, 2008b).

Each sport delivered by the ISF is managed by a technical commission (TC). TCs debate and decide matters pertaining to their specific sport and competition. The TC president attends EC meetings to propose and provide support to the executive committee on matters related to the sport. The organizational structure of the ISF is presented in figure 13.5. It represents another stakeholder group in international youth sport.

ISF-sponsored events are usually organized for single sports, such as the 2010 badminton championships held in Sofia, Bulgaria, and the volleyball championships in Baotou, China. But the ISF also delivered the first Pan American School Games in Brazil, for North, Central, and South American school sport organizations in the summer of 2010 for competition in athletics, swimming, basketball, volleyball, handball, and football. The ISF is an important organization for international youth sport because it organizes international events in school sport competitions in a variety of sports and encourages friendly competition that promotes mutual understanding between the youth of countries around the world. As well, the ISF is

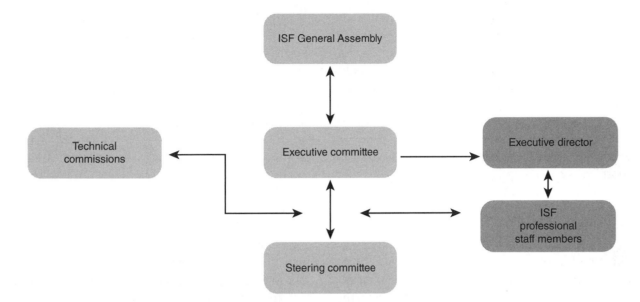

Figure 13.5 Organizational structure of the International School Sport Federation.

an acknowledged international sport federation involved in school sport in five continents and is recognized by the International Olympic Committee.

The ISF estimates a worldwide reach of millions of 13- through 18-year-old youngsters through school sport competitions. The next section examines international opportunities for university-level student–athletes.

International University Sports Federation

University or collegiate sport is pervasive around the world. The policy and rules-making power within college sport is similar in structure to that in high school sport. Individual college athletics departments hold the most basic level of authority. Usually they belong to a league or conference with like-minded institutions that develop competitive schedules and structures, rules, and policy for managing the athletics enterprise. The individual institution also belongs to a national association that provides another level of governance, specifically related to events and policy for national and international issues. The National Collegiate Athletic Association (NCAA) in the United States is the largest, wealthiest, and best-known national association in intercollegiate sport. Other organizations seek to manage the national agenda for college sport within their jurisdictions in countries around

the world. Table 13.1 provides examples of national collegiate athletics organizations.

The goal for virtually all collegiate athletes is to win the national championship in their sport. Another highly coveted goal is to represent one's country in international competition. The International University Sports Federation is known as FISU, which is French for Fédération Internationale

Table 13.1 National Collegiate Athletics Organizations

Country	National organization
Australia	Australian University Sport
Canada	Canadian Interuniversity Sport Canadian Colleges Athletic Association
China	Federation of University Sports of China
Hong Kong	Hong Kong Post Secondary Colleges Athletic Association
India	Inter-University Sports Board
Great Britain	British Universities Sports Association
Ireland	Council of University Sports Administrators in Ireland
Switzerland	Swiss University Sports Federation
United States of America	National Collegiate Athletic Association National Association of Intercollegiate Athletics National Junior College Athletic Association

du Sport Universitaire. FISU is the governing body that supervises the operations and hosting of World University Championships in individual sports, and the World University Games, or Universiade, a multisport competition. The **World University Games** provide the opportunity for college athletes aged 17 through 28 to compete at a large, multisport festival held every two years in winter and summer. The Summer Universiade involves 12 compulsory sports and up to 5 optional sports, and the Winter FISU Games schedules 7 compulsory sports and offers the opportunity for additional optional sports. The Summer Universiade involves thousands of competitors from over 150 countries (the largest number of countries competing in the FISU Games was 174 in Daegu, Korea, in 2003) and is the largest multisport games in existence other than the Olympics Games.

The World University Games are conducted in a fashion similar to the Olympics. The events occur over a 10-day period that commences after an elaborate opening ceremony and torch-lighting procedure. Athletes live in a village, and the Games promote elite competition, friendship, and cultural exchange. Gold, silver, and bronze medals are awarded, and the Games are completed with a parade of nations at the closing ceremonies. FISU is the organization responsible for supervising the World University Games.

FISU was founded in 1949. The mission of FISU is to provide international sport opportunities for university students who will one day be the leaders of society, holding positions of responsibility throughout the world. The leaders of FISU express the importance of promoting sporting values that include friendship, fair play, perseverance, and integrity. To accomplish this mission, FISU articulates a set of objectives that illustrate the core culture of the organization. An example set of FISU objectives is presented in the sidebar.

Membership in FISU is granted to a country's national university sport federation, the governing body with jurisdiction over university sport (see table 13.1 for examples). In 2010 FISU had 153 members (FISU, 2010). Because several organizations manage university sport in the United States, the United States Collegiate Sports Council, composed of membership from both the NCAA and NAIA, was formed. In Canada the organization

Learning Activity

Visit your college athletics department and ask whether any of the coaches, administrators, trainers, or athletes have participated in the FISU Games. If so, ask your instructor to invite the person (as an individual or as one of a panel of speakers) to come to class to speak about her or his experiences at the FISU Games.

Objectives of FISU

- To ensure the quality of their sports events by entrusting the members of its commissions to guarantee the right execution of the specifications and the regulations sent to the organizers, and through a tight collaboration with the technical directors of the International Sports Federations.

- To develop its reputation and assert itself in University and Sporting circles, to enhance its credibility, and that of the Movement.

- To develop existing National Federations in the various countries and to support them in their dealings with Government.

- To contribute through Study Commissions to strengthen the links between universities, the Sports Movement, and students.

- To approach political and economic authorities and the media to obtain new means of financing for developing University Sport in all countries.

- To identify a sports development programme through education, and establish a set of moral standards in line with the evolution of contemporary sport and education issues throughout the world.

Reprinted from FISU (2008b).

known as Canadian Interuniversity Sport (CIS) has the right to FISU membership. Each organization must pay memberships fees and provide proof of their status as the governing body of collegiate sport to gain membership in FISU. Such membership provides the opportunity for that country's eligible athletes to compete at University World Championships and World University Games, and gives voice in the governance of FISU through one vote per member nation at the general assembly. The athletes, coaches, administrators, and personnel at their respective national university sport federations are the stakeholders of FISU, along with a significantly larger group of sponsors, government personnel, media, facility managers, and volunteers who represent the stakeholder groups of a FISU Games.

FISU is governed through a general assembly (GA) that meets every two years. Each national university sport organization member is accorded one vote in managing the affairs of the overall organization. The GA sets policy and direction for FISU, supervises the financial practices of the organization, and sets the program of FISU activities. It also elects an executive committee (EC), made up of 27 members who meet twice yearly to supervise the operations of FISU. The responsibility for enacting the operational plans and day-to-day activities of FISU rests with the full-and part-time employees who work at FISU headquarters in Brussels, Belgium, under the leadership of the secretary general.

CASE STUDY

Growth of the World University Games

The World University Games (Universiade) and single-sport World University Championships have significant numbers of participants. Records in the documented history of FISU indicate the following:

• The World University Games (held every two years during odd years) went from a total of 1,407 participants in Turin, Italy, in 1959 to a total of 6,675 in Beijing, China, in 2001. In China, more than 165 countries were represented. In Daegu, Korea, in 2003, 6,643 athletes from 174 countries participated. In 2005 at the Summer Games in Izmir, Turkey, 7,805 athletes competed. The highest number of participants was registered at the 2007 Summer Universiade of Bangkok, Thailand, where 9,006 athletes participated.

• The Winter Universiades experienced similar success. Statistics show that 98 athletes participated in 1958 at the Universiade in Zell-Am-See, Austria. A record of 2,511 participants competed in Torino, Italy, in 2007, and a record 50 countries came to the Winter Universiade in Innsbruck, Austria, in 2005.

• World University Championships are also important FISU events. For 38 years, 148 World University Championships have been organized, covering a large range of events and gathering nearly 25,500 participants from 135 different countries. These championships, which take place on even years and which have had increasing success as the years go on, guarantee continuity in the competitions program. They also allow a large number of students and university sport leaders to unite on occasions other than at Universiades. In 2000, 20 World University Championships, with 3,623 participants, were held, each in a different place for a different sport. In 2002, 24 World University Championships were held, attracting 4,228 participants from 83 countries. In 2004, 26 championships were staged, bringing together 4,845 participants. In 2008, growth continued with 29 World University Championships staged, involving 6,652 participants from 229 countries worldwide. Already 31 are attributed for 2010, and several years before staging, 18 are committed for 2012 (FISU, 2008c).

• These participation numbers suggest that FISU is engaged in organizing a substantial international sport enterprise and that over time the number of events and participating athletes has grown significantly. The World University Games for summer have been organized 25 times between 1959 and 2009. The host sites for these Games have included 14 cities in Europe, 7 in Asia, 3 in North America, and 1 in South America. For 24 Winter Games delivered between 1960 and 2009, European cities have hosted 20 times. The Games have gone to Asia 3 times and to North America once. The Summer and Winter Games have been held in Italy 9 times (4 times in summer, 5 times in winter).

Core members of the EC make up the steering committee: president, senior vice president, four vice-presidents, secretary general, treasurer, and senior assessor. The steering committee is charged with managing the business affairs of FISU between meetings of the EC. The other business of FISU is conducted by committees called commissions (FISU, 2008b).

The national sport organizations of many countries consider the World University Games an excellent high-performance competitive opportunity. The competition is outstanding, and the entire atmosphere is similar to and considered good preparation for the multisport atmosphere of the Olympic Games. These Games, along with World University Championships, International Children's Games, world youth championships, and individual sport events like the Little League World Series are all tremendous opportunities for young athletes to compete internationally. Another component of international competition exists in the club sport system, described in the next section.

Governance of Club Sport

Sport clubs exist all over the world. They are a primary source for sport participation in Europe and provide a wide range of sporting opportunities in Russia, North America, New Zealand and Australia, and Asia. Clubs offer opportunities for a variety of participating age groups, ranging from youth to senior categories. Although club participation often includes leagues local to a particular community, teams might host or travel to compete in international competitions. The Boys & Girls Clubs of America and YMCA are two prominent examples of organizations that promote and support teams to compete internationally. Other sport-specific clubs also have an interest in sending teams to international competition. How are these organizations structured and governed?

YMCA

The YMCA plays a role in international sport because it is truly an international service organization. Ys exist all over the world, providing a diverse range of programming for more than 30 million children and adults in over 120 countries. The YMCA was founded by Sir George Williams (1821–1905), an extraordinary English businessman with a social conscience. Williams gave both his time and money to improve the working conditions of the masses and began YMCA gatherings to meet the spiritual, physical, and mental needs of people from all walks of life. The concept of the YMCA grew quickly into a worldwide movement endeavoring to help develop people through building a healthy spirit, mind, and body. The organization's motto remains, "We build strong kids, strong families, strong communities" (YMCA, 2008). A significant component of the YMCA purpose involves amateur sport opportunities, mentoring, and exchange programs. The YMCA also strives to advocate for human rights, nurture health, provide instruction, empower youth, foster dialogue between people of different faiths, promote cultural diversity, and work in solidarity with the poor and oppressed (YMCA, 2008).

The organizational structure and decision-making processes of the Y are similar to those of the Boys & Girls Club. Local YMCAs have volunteers and professional staff to set policy that enables activities and programming to run efficiently. The local Y (e.g., YMCA of Greater Kansas City) is affiliated with the national YMCA office (e.g., YMCA of the USA) within its respective country. National YMCAs are similarly members of the world YMCA organization (World Alliance of YMCA). Each of these levels of organization ensures that all YMCAs refrain from practices that discriminate against any individual or group and help to promote the mission of the Y worldwide. Decision making and policy setting for programming, staffing, and operations remain the responsibility of personnel at the local Y level.

The professional staff of the local Y typically includes programmers and administrators. The leader of the professional staff is usually called an executive director or chief executive officer. These employees report to the board of directors of the Y through the executive director. The board of directors is led by a chairperson and includes a variety of positions such as vice-chair, treasurer, secretary, immediate past chair, and as many as two dozen directors. YMCAs offer many opportunities for participation in sport and other activities for youth participants. In this way they function similarly to sport clubs that are popular worldwide and serve to govern sport participation in virtually all categories of sporting activities.

Club Sport Organizations

A vast number of sport clubs exist in countries all around the world. In most communities, it is likely that a club exists to offer age-group sport competition in one or more sports. Many clubs are nonprofit organizations managed by volunteers that exist to organize instruction and competition in one or more sports. Some clubs focus on local, recreational-level participation, whereas others are highly competitive and may regularly send teams to international competitions. Other clubs are both recreational and competitive, depending on the age group and interests of members. For example, the St. Catharines Rowing Club in Ontario, Canada, sent junior rowers (under 18 years of age) to the 2010 World Rowing Junior Championships in Racice, Czech Republic, an event organized by the World Rowing Association. Clubs also organize international events. The St. Catharines Rowing Club hosts the Henley Regatta late each summer. Categories of competition include rowers under 17 years old and junior (under age 19) rowers. The Canadian Henley has been in existence for over 100 years and draws more than 150 teams from around North America and Europe each year.

In North America sport clubs exist parallel to school sport for youth and expand into a greater variety of sports for adults. In Europe the club system is the dominant method of delivering sport, and clubs exist with many age groups and categories of competitive play based on skill level. In this setting clubs are often oriented to family membership, and joining the club may involve the entire family over each of its member's lifespan. Sport clubs are also popular in Russia, Asia, and Australia.

Depending on the size of the club, its structure might be loosely configured or highly structured. Smaller clubs often operate with a president and a few other elected volunteers who divide up the tasks of facility bookings, scheduling, special events, and financial management. Smaller organizations can run efficiently after policies are developed to cover the management of finances, risk, and rules and regulations. Such operations normally focus on running a set number of special events or a sport league. Conversely, a larger organization that operates programming for large numbers of participants in many different age groups might have an elaborate organizational structure. Examples of sport clubs focusing on a single sport include the Liver-pool Football Club (United Kingdom), Clovercrest Swimming Club (Australia), Guangdong Southern Tigers Basketball Club (China), and the Golf and Sport Club Fontana (Austria). Multisport clubs existing worldwide include the National Sports Club (India), Società Sportiva Lazio (Italy), Jugoslovensko Sportsko Društvo Partizan (Serbia), Cardiff Athletic Club (Wales), and Energy Academy (France).

As an example of the club sport system popular throughout the world, especially in Europe, the Energy Academy is a sport club for children located in Paris, France. The Energy Academy is a for-profit business that offers sport instruction in tennis, golf, basketball, football, swimming, gymnastics, table tennis, and other activities. The coaches and instructional staff are full-time, paid employees of the business. The emphasis is on enjoyment, learning, security, and sport development.

Another sport club example that involves competition of teams from the club is the Liverpool Football Club (United Kingdom), formed in 1892 (Liverpool Football Club, 2008). Memberships exist in both junior and adult categories, providing opportunities for instructional academies in football, age-group teams for boys and girls, youth teams, professional football for spectators of all ages, club facilities for special events and conference hosting, and other benefits. The club is governed by a 13-member board of directors, led by a chief executive and comprising two cochairmen, four directors, a secretary, and a manager. In addition, one honorary life president and four honorary life vice-presidents are board members. This club is also a profit-making business that operates its merchandising, ticket sales, public relations, and event management in ways similar to those used by professional sport organizations in North America and elsewhere in the world. The defining characteristic of this club involves its delivery of youth sport and sport-specific training and memberships to the general public. International competition for each of the competitive teams housed with the Liverpool Football Club is embedded in the club's league membership, which may involve competition locally, nationally, and sometimes internationally.

Summary

Sport clubs and sport organized through schools play a central role in international sport competition experienced by younger athletes. Team and individual sport tournaments, championships, and multisport festivals for youth and young adults are organized and governed by a variety of national and international organizations. World youth championships such as the U-17 and U-20 World Cups in football are examples of youth sport events organized by international sport federations like FIFA. The Little League World Series involves teams in baseball and softball from regions around the world. The International Children's Games are a multisport festival held every second year that involves competition of children from cities around the world. The organizations delivering these events set policy to govern the activities in an optimal competitive environment. Similarly, school sport organizations bring together age groups of athletes for single-sport and multisport competitions. The International School Sport Federation hosts multisport competitions, and FISU organizes both single-sport championships and the World University Games in both winter and summer for collegiate-level athletes. At a local level, sport clubs are popular in Europe and other regions of the world, and organizations like Boys & Girls Clubs and YMCAs function to provide international sport opportunities for young athletes through events, festivals, and leagues. Although set up for younger athletes, these competitions are an important sector of the business and governance of international sport.

? Review and Discussion Questions

1. Identify three international sport events organized for youth competition. Compare and contrast the governance of these events.

2. What human resources are involved in organizing the International Children's Games? Draw the organizational chart for this event. How might the chart need to change based on recent world events involving (*a*) terrorism, (*b*) natural disasters, and (*c*) an economic downturn?

3. How do club sport and school sport differ in terms of governing structures and international opportunities for participation? How might the age of the participants affect your answer to the preceding question?

4. What factors have contributed to the growth in number and size of FISU events? In which regions of the world are FISU events hosted most often and least often, and what factors might contribute to this circumstance?

5. What factors may limit international competition in youth sport in the coming years?

6. Consider why some sport organizations are profit driven whereas others are not-for-profit. What are the pros and cons of each type of organization?

7. What factors are involved in selecting hosts for international sport championships and events? Consider the importance of leadership from within the bidding groups and from the organizations selecting the host committees. How do the groups differ?

Part IV

Management Essentials in International Sport

Michael Clarke bats during a semifinal match
between South Africa and Australia at the 2007
Cricket World Cup, held in St. Lucia, West Indies.
Over the following seven years, the International
Cricket Council expects revenue of about US$1.5
billion from broadcast rights and global sponsorships.

Macroeconomics of International Sport

Holger Preuss, PhD
Johannes Gutenberg-University Mainz, Germany

Kevin Heisey, PhD
Liberty University, Virginia, USA

Chapter Objectives

After studying this chapter, you will be able to do the following:

- Explain the general importance of sport in the economy
- Identify the fundamental ways sport influences the macroeconomy
- Distinguish between tangible and intangible benefits
- Determine the primary economic impact of sport on an economy
- Explain the induced impact, or multiplier, effect
- Discuss short-term, long-term, and legacy effects of international sport events

Key Terms

In the science of economics, the macroeconomic perspective is the broad perspective, considering the economy of a nation (or other defined political or geographic area) as a whole. This viewpoint is distinct from microeconomics, which considers the economic situations and decisions of a firm or a household to allocate limited resources. Macroeconomists study aggregate indicators such as the national production and income measure gross domestic product (GDP), import and export, unemployment rates, and price indices to understand how the whole economy functions and develops over time (that is, business cycles in the short run and economic growth in the long run). For this purpose, a focus of macroeconomic investigation is the interplay of aggregate supply (production) and demand (consumption) of the whole economy and on its submarkets (on the one hand, collective sectors of similar production and single industries, on the other hand, final demand of private consumers and corporate demand of primary and intermediary products). The relevant data that macroeconomists need for their work are collected in detail by the national accounting in terms of the monetary values composing the GDP calculation. The key message of macroeconomics is that (developed) economies are huge, complex, and highly interconnected structures of a multitude of individual decisions that, in addition, are closely linked with the rest of the world by international trade. The ultimate aim and result of macroeconomic analysis is therefore to provide knowledge, data, and advice for political and corporate decision makers to cope effectively with this complexity.

This chapter focuses on the role of sport in a country's economy. The economic importance of sport relative to the rest of a country's economy is discussed first. Next comes an account of the fundamental ways in which sport influences an economy through the creation of sport-related goods and services. Important distinctions are made between tangible and intangible economic benefits associated with sport and the ways in which both types of benefits affect an economy. A focus on mega sport events such as the Olympics and the FIFA World Cup is used to illustrate the process of how primary economic impacts of sport can work through an economy, leading to potentially greater total impacts. Shown as well are the characteristics of an economy that make induced economic impacts

more likely. These megaevents can be economically significant and provide comprehensive examples of the effects of sport on the economy because they are temporary. Using megaevents as examples, one can see how an initial intervention of spending on sport builds up and works its way through the economy. Finally, long- and short-term economic benefits from sport and the legacy effect that remains after a sport event has concluded are discussed.

Role of Sport in a National Economy

From the macroeconomic perspective on sport an important question arises: Does sport contribute to increases in economic well-being in the overall economy, and if it does, how significant are the increases or how many jobs does sport create? In absolute terms, the revenues associated with sport appear quite large, but relative to the economy as a whole the economic significance of sport is rather low. Global spending on sport events (including tickets, media rights, and sponsorship), for instance, was over US$85 billion in 2005 (Milner, 2006), a number that represented less than 0.2 percent of the global GDP that year in US$ terms for the US-economy. Similarly, global spending on sport equipment, apparel, and footwear in 2007 was US$278.4 billion (Korkki, 2008) which represented 0.54 percent of the GDP that year. Developed countries typically spend from 1 to 4 percent of their GDP for sport. In the European Union the average spending for sport was 3.7 percent of the GDP (of the 25 member states) in 2005 (Dimitrov et al., 2006). Indeed, such minor relative figures are found for most economic sectors and industries, but they may not necessarily be insignificant for the functioning and growth of the economy as a whole, given the interconnectedness within the economy. Keep in mind that large national economies account for trillions of dollars. Thus, even big multibillion-dollar businesses tend to be a financial drop in the economic ocean.

When considering the role of sport in the economy, it is therefore important to differentiate between benefits that accrue to a particular interest group of the economy and benefits that accrue to the economy as a whole. Economists use the term **Pareto optimal**, which is defined as an outcome in which no member of the economy can be made better off without making another member worse off

(Frank, 2006, p. 591), as a desirable characteristic of an economic equilibrium or outcome. Reflect on what that definition means. A Pareto optimal outcome means that for a given amount of resources (natural resources, knowledge, talent, number of people, or any other productive resource) the economy is producing as much benefit as possible. No unexploited opportunities remain that could make somebody better off. When the economy is at a Pareto optimal outcome, the only way a person can improve his or her situation occurs at the expense of somebody else.

Applied to sport, consider an economy that hosts a sport event and assume that the people who spend money to attend the event would have otherwise spent the same amount of money on dinner and a movie if the sport event had not occurred. The organizers of the sport event are better off, but only at the expense of the restaurant and movie theatre owners. In this case, overall well-being in the economy has not improved; the reallocation of money has simply caused a shift of economic activity between sectors. An enhancement of overall well-being in an economy is called a **Pareto improvement**, an improvement in economic well-being that does not come at the expense of others (Varian, 1990, p. 17). When considering the economic impact of sport on an economy, one has to be able to distinguish an increase in well-being in the overall economy (Pareto improvement) from a shift of well-being between sectors or individuals within an economy.

The benefits of sport to an economy can be categorized as either quantifiable (**tangible benefits**) or nonquantifiable (**intangible benefits**). It is possible to measure the amount of tangible economic activity related to a sport event, team, or facility in monetary terms. As noted earlier, the tangible impact of sport is relatively low compared with that of other sectors of the economy. Sport, however, brings many nonquantifiable monetary (intangible) benefits to the economy that often lead to indirect economic benefits. For example, if a sport event motivates children to increase participation in sport, overall health costs may decrease. If people reduce stress by watching sports, productivity at work may increase and the illness rate may decrease. Communities rally around and take pride in their sport teams, facilities, and the events that they host. Many residents of Phoenix, Arizona, are likely to have fond recollections of the Arizona Diamondbacks' Major League Baseball World Series Championship in 2001, whereas they probably have no recollection of how the local Wal-Mart stores fare from year to year.

It is often said that hosting a mega sporting event like the FIFA World Cup or the Olympic Games puts a city or country "on the map." In the United States, having a major professional sport franchise is often seen as making a community a "big-league city." Measuring the monetary value of the benefits of being on the map or being a big-league city is difficult, but the benefits clearly exist, are likely to be significant, and could very well far outweigh any tangible benefits that can be much more easily measured.

But sport should never be seen as an economic panacea or as a major component of an economic development policy. Although hosting an international mega sport event can bring tangible economic benefits, they are small relative to the economy as a whole and their impact is short lived. The FIFA World Cup 2006 in Germany increased the German GDP by only 0.13 percent that year (Kurscheidt et al., 2008). The intangible benefits of hosting such an event are likely more significant. Increased happiness, improved image of the city or country as a place to visit or do business, and emotional investment are among the intangible benefits that seem to make up the major effect of hosting a megaevent. The unique quality of sport and competition is its universal nature. Little else in society has an appeal as broad as that of a major sport event such as the great marathons in the cities of Berlin and New York, international football, or Olympic competition. People across cultures and ages can enjoy, appreciate, and celebrate the excitement of athletic competition. This effect is the major benefit of a sport event.

Macroeconomic Effects of Sport

A useful practice is to examine and categorize the ways that sport influences the macroeconomy. What are the goods and services provided by sport? (See table 14.1.) Goods are physical items that are sold. The goods that make up sport's influence on the economy are consumption goods and investment goods. Examples of services related to sport are entertainment; instruction, coaching, and officiating; and sport travel and tourism.

Table 14.1 Examples of Goods and Services in Sport

Type	Examples
Goods	
Consumption, direct	Equipment, apparel, nutrition, sports drinks
Consumption, indirect	Transportation, lodging, concessions
Investment, direct	Facilities: golf course, tennis court, stadium, arena
Investment, indirect	Parking, club house, ski lodge
Services	
Professional sport	Coaches, personal trainers, referees
Tourism	Travel and tour agencies, skiing instructors
Entertainment	Spectator sport, media broadcasts, sport shows

Consumption Goods

A consumption good is something that an individual consumer purchases for use, such as a sports drink, which he or she physically consumes, or sportswear and equipment that is consumed over time. If the good is directly related to the sport, we call it a direct consumption good. Table 14.2 presents global sales of major categories of direct consumption goods. Sport also contributes to indirect consumption spending, which is spending on consumption goods that are not directly sport related but would not have been made without the sport event. Transportation to and from sport events is an example of indirect consumption spending that is generated by sport. Other examples of indirect consumption expenditures that are significant to sport are spending on food, beer, soft drinks, and lodging that occurs

Table 14.2 Global Sales of Sport Direct Consumption Goods

Direct consumption good	Global sales
Sporting goods—apparel, footwear, equipment, and bicycles	$278.4 billion (US$, 2007)
Licensed sport products	$19.3 billion (US$, 2006)
Sports drinks	9,700,000,000 liters (2005)

Data from Korkki, 2008; Browne, 2007; and Zenith International Ltd., 2006.

because of sport events and tournaments. Sport-related spending on consumption goods is often linked to the heavy sport sponsorship and advertising spending by the companies in industries, such as beer and sport apparel companies.

Investment Goods

Investment goods are to be used by many consumers over a long period. Their key feature is that they are designed to result in increased future productive economic activity. All the for-profit-facilities or parks where sport is played are considered direct investment goods. Prominent examples are stadiums such as Emirates Stadium in North London, which cost £430 million (US$790 million) (Arsenal Holdings plc, 2007), and the O_2 World Arena in Berlin, which cost €165 million (US$260 million) (Nolan, 2008). About €1.5 billion (US$1.9 billion) was spent on new stadiums and upgrades to existing stadiums before the 2006 FIFA World Cup in Germany (Kurscheidt, 2009). One can often see what kind of sports are popular in an area when flying in an airplane by looking down at the golf courses, baseball fields, tennis courts, football pitches, and swimming pools. All of these would be considered small-scale, direct sport investment goods instead of consumption goods but only if these contribute to an increase in productive economic activity (e.g., generate income by giving swimming lessons, charging rent for tennis courts). Sport equipment may also be considered investment goods in the case where it is used to earn money. For example a tennis trainer's racket or a professional golf player's equipment are investment goods while the same equipment used for leisure sports are considered consumption goods.

Examples of indirect investment goods that can be attributed to sport are parking areas, transportation hubs, lodging at ski resorts, and clubhouses that are built as part of or next to the sport facilities in many parts of the world. Other indirect investment goods are all the machines that produce sport equipment and apparel. Although none of these expenditures are directly caused by sport, they would not exist without sport.

Services

Sport-related services that are sold can be directly related to a sport, such as tennis instruction, coaching, umpiring or refereeing, personal training, and setting up and managing a recreational sport league. Tourist agencies that focus on sport-related tours are another example of a sport-related service. Backroads, an outfitter based in Berkeley, California, that specializes in active holidays, led approximately 16,000 people on biking, hiking, and multisport tours in 40 countries on six continents. The company generated over US$50 million in revenue in 2006 (Stahlberg, 2007). Other tour operators such as Discoverfrance.com offer tour packages related to specific events. Discoverfrance.com offered three versions of its 2007 France Grand Tour, which they bill on their website as "Cycling tours to watch the professional cyclists race for yellow."

The final service is entertainment, which is the raison d'être for spectator sport. People pay to attend and follow sport events so that they can be entertained, and entertainment is the product that sport leagues sell. The media, whether it presents events, reports results, presents highlights, recaps and dis-cusses past events, or predicts the outcome of future events, is also selling entertainment. Modern events are packaged and presented through various media so that millions of people worldwide can often enjoy them simultaneously. Television, radio, live Internet video streaming, and other new media allow major sport events to entertain people around the globe. The next several sections focus on international sport megaevents. Study of these short-term interventions in an economy can increase our understanding of the macroeconomic effects of sport.

Tangible and Intangible Effects

An additional characteristic that is a key to understanding the macroeconomic effects of sport activities is the distinction between tangible and intangible effects. Tangible economic effects are often

CASE STUDY

Manchester United: Superstar Effect and the Global Sport Economy

In recent years technology has redefined the potential export market for sport. American baseball games can be watched live on the Internet by streaming video for a relatively modest fee on MLB.com. Likewise, American soccer fans have affordable access through cable or satellite television to the Spanish La Liga de Futbol Profesional, the German Bundesliga, and UEFA Cup qualifying matches through Gol TV. The NBA attracts a television viewing audience in China that may soon rival its audience in the United States.

The access and affordability that arise from technology contribute to what economists call the superstar effect. The logic behind the superstar effect is that, all things being equal, consumers want to consume the very best of a product if they have the option. It follows, then, that because sport is mostly consumed by live video, consumers who have affordable access to many viewing options will likely choose the highest quality sport. If sport fans at home, with a click of the remote, can watch the best leagues, teams, and athletes in the world, those leagues, teams, and athletes will become increasingly popular globally. Therefore, the potential target market and audience for the most successful entities in sport are enormous.

The popular English Premier League powerhouse Manchester United is a great example of how large a sport club's export market can be. According to Anheuser-Busch and Manchester United (2008), the club has 333 million fans around the globe, and more than 80 million fans in 200 countries watch each match on television. U.S.-based businesses like Anheuser-Busch and insurance giant AIG do not enter sponsor partnerships with Manchester United to reach the relatively minor United Kingdom market or the 76,000 fans who pack Old Trafford for each home match. They do it to reach a global audience. The Budweiser–United agreement that ran through the 2009–10 season gave the brewer rights to use Manchester United marks and player images in advertising, point of sale displays, and packaging in Europe, Asia, Africa, North America, and South America. Manchester United, one of the top sport properties in the world, through the superstar effect, is using technology to export its product to the entire global market, while bringing additional autonomous spending to the United Kingdom economy.

defined as those that can be measured in monetary terms, but it is more accurate to define them as those that can be easily measured in units. Clearly, if an event drew 50,000 nonregional visitors to the region and those visitors spent on average $200 each attending the event, then a measurable $10,000,000 of spending was brought into the regional economy by the visitors who came to the event. And we can also measure air quality, noise levels, and traffic counts that are affected by the existence of a sport event. All those elements contribute to the overall well-being of the economy, so a more inclusive definition that includes a greater number of effects that can be measured in units is a more accurate definition of tangible economic benefits.

Intangible economic effects are those that cannot be measured in units, but they are important because they often make up the most significant economic impact of a sport event. Examples of intangible effects are local pride (either in the success of a local site or the ability of the city to host a major event or both), happiness, motivation and other psychological effects, local image, cultural identity, increased know-how, reduction of crime, changes in pollution levels and environmental quality, or option value (the benefit of knowing that you, your family, friends, or offspring have the option to use and benefit from a resource, even if you currently choose not to) (Asafu-Adjaye, 2005, p. 111). Intangible benefits can be enormous for individuals and for societies as a whole. As an example, when the French national team won the 1998 FIFA World Cup in France with a multiethnic roster, its success helped heal racial divisions. Evaluating the extent of the intangible benefit derived from France's win is difficult, but it was clearly significant (Dauncey & Hare, 1999).

Because intangible effects are difficult to measure and, as stated earlier, often the most significant benefits that an economy derives from sport, devising ways to measure intangible benefits is a growing area of research in the field of sport economics. This is all the more the case when considering that substantial intangible benefits may even arise in economic market transactions by exchanging dollars between sellers and buyers of a sport commodity or service. An example of such an intangible effect is the change in a consumer's surplus associated with sport. Simply defined, **consumer surplus** is the extra benefit that a consumer enjoys when he

or she purchases a good or service (Frank 2006, p. 160). For example if a cricket fan is willing to pay $100 to attend a test but is able to purchase a ticket for $75, economists say that she enjoys $25 of consumer surplus, because attending the match is worth $100 to her but she paid only $75. If a person freely makes a purchase, then it can be assumed that she is enjoying consumer surplus greater than or equal to 0. Except when a person is paying exactly the maximum that she is willing to pay, consumer surplus will be positive. In another example, suppose that a person pays $100 for a ticket with a $20 face value to attend a sold-out event. The person was not forced to pay an exorbitant price to attend the event, because he could have chosen not to purchase the ticket. Attending the event is clearly worth at least $100 to him. If he buys a ticket for $20, he would enjoy at least $80 worth of consumer surplus.

Why is consumer surplus significant in examining the macroeconomic effect of sport? When measuring tangible benefits, economists normally do not consider expenditures on sport made by people who ordinarily spend their money in the economy as additions to tangible economic benefit. Logically, those people normally spend their money in the economy anyway, so the existence of a sport option only causes their economic activity to shift within the economy, not add expenditure to the economy. But when considering overall economic well-being or welfare through the framework of consumer surplus, if people are choosing to spend their time and money on sport, we can assume that they are enjoying greater consumer surplus than they otherwise would have. For simplicity's sake, if we assume that all entertainment options cost the same, although we cannot readily measure consumer surplus (unless consumers are willing to tell us their maximum willingness to pay to attend each event), we can infer from their choices which event gives consumers the most surplus—it is the event that they choose to attend. So if members of the local economy are choosing to attend sport events rather than other entertainment options available to them, although their actions do not represent a net increase in spending in the economy, they do represent an increase in consumer surplus and therefore an increase in economic well-being.

Therefore, a macroeconomic income measure like the GDP does not really reflect the welfare of a nation, although in the public debate it is often

Estimating the Intangible Economic Benefits of Sport

The intangible benefits associated with sport are clearly significant and may overshadow any tangible economic benefits. Residents of a city that hosts a major event do not have to spend money on the actual event or even consume it to enjoy its benefits, whether it is through the excitement generated by the event or civic pride in the successful hosting effort. A movement has developed among economists to estimate the magnitude of the intangible benefits.

An increasingly common method of evaluating indirectly intangible benefits associated with sport is the contingent valuation method (CVM). The CVM was originally developed as a way for environmental economists to estimate the value of the benefits of environmental goods, like water quality or air quality, not normally bought and sold in a market. The essence of the CVM is for researchers to create a hypothetical market scenario that describes varying levels of the intangible good being studied and provides a payment method used to attain more of the good. A statistically significant number of people are chosen by a random sample in the appropriate geographic area and are asked how much they would be willing to pay for increased levels of the good. For example, respondents could be asked how much additional sales tax they would be willing to pay for an increased level of air quality.

Some examples of recent studies that used the CVM to estimate the intangible benefit enjoyed by host citizens as the result of an international megaevent are Atkinson, Mourato, Szymanski, and Ozdemiroglu (2008) and Heyne, Maennig, and Suessmuth (2007). Atkinson et al. interviewed 602 residents of London, 152 residents of Glasgow, and 151 residents of Manchester to estimate the intangible benefit experienced by United Kingdom residents of London's hosting of the 2012 Olympic Games. They estimated that the willingness to pay in increased taxes (among Londoners) and donations (for the rest of the country) is just short of £2 billion (US$3.98 billion), which roughly approximates the planned public expenditure of £2.375 billion (US$4.726 billion) at the time of their study.

Heyne et al. surveyed German residents before and after the FIFA World Cup 2006. Their hypothesis was that any increase in willingness to pay after experiencing the event could be described as the money value of the intangible experience. They found that the difference between residents' willingness to pay before and after the event amounted to €495 million (US$634 million) for the entire country. The result is interpreted as additional intangible benefit on top of the €351 million (US$449 million) that people were willing to pay before they experienced the event.

Countries and cities that are considering hosting events should consider all the relevant benefits and costs associated with the events so that they can make sound policy decisions. The intangible benefits are clearly significant for major international events; therefore, efforts to measure and quantify those benefits can play a key role in providing criteria to key decision makers.

---

seen and used as an indicator of well-being. But this notion refers to the microeconomic concept of utility like the consumer surplus, which is difficult to measure and is not an explicit object of macroeconomic analysis. In contrast, the GDP may rise while the social utility falls and vice versa. For instance, sport injuries can be clearly qualified as undesirable and as causing diminished welfare. Yet, an injury enhances the sport-related GDP by expenditures for doctors, medicine, surgeries, and so forth. Such unpleasant incidents that increase total income are called "bads" in macroeconomic national accounting. The opposite effect can also occur if, for example, prices tend to fall because of enhanced competition from foreign companies in the sports shoe industry. The buyers benefit

from a rise in their consumer surplus, whereas the increase in imports reduces the GDP. Thus, the GDP is simply the aggregated reflection of all money flows in the economy at current prices that are observable in the market place and recorded in the national accounting. The GDP does not incorporate any judgment or (normative) evaluation of the underlying occurrences as being positive or negative for society. Likewise, the national income could be extremely unevenly distributed among individuals, which may be perceived as unjust. Ultimately, the GDP can only tell us whether a country is rich or poor in terms of money circulating in the economy (that is the part of social utility that actually materializes in monetary values) or whether an economy is growing or shrinking during a certain period.

Primary Impact of a Sport Event

Is it useful to think of the economic impact of sport in terms of a simplified version of Keynes' circular flow model of an economy (Mankiw, 2007, p. 208). For simplicity's sake, we assume that government is neutral in this example.

$$Y = C + I + (X - M)$$

Where:

Y = the size of the economy measured as total income.

C = total consumption spending in the economy.

I = total investment spending in the economy.

X = total export spending in the economy, or the sale of goods produced in the economy to people outside the economy.

M = total import spending in the economy, or the purchases by people in the economy of goods produced outside the economy.

(X − M) = net exports.

Using this model we can think of changes to total consumption spending (C), investment spending (I), or net exports (X − M) resulting in changes to the overall size of the economy. As mentioned before, changes in the patterns of consumption or investment spending that amount to a shift in spending among sectors in the economy would not result in a change in the size of the economy. Changes in net exports, however, would directly result in changes to total income level for the economy.

For a closer look at net exports, consider the Olympic Games, which trigger economic impacts all around the world but cause the strongest impact in the host nation and the host city. The **primary impact** is the change in consumption, investment, and export spending that can be attributed directly to the sport event. Obviously, the calculation of the impact of the Beijing 2008 Olympics on China or the city of Beijing does not include the payments of national sponsors in Australia or expenditures to dress and equip the South African Olympic team. But the calculation becomes complex when indirect effects, such as the change of infrastructure in Beijing itself, have to be considered. To isolate the primary regional economic impact from the total primary impact, each flow of money has to be analyzed.

A matrix of four variables can be used to calculate the regional primary impact and Olympic expenditures for a sector in the economy or category of expenditure. The origin of spending can be autonomous (coming in from outside the area) or regional (from people already living in the area), and the money can be spent regionally (stays in the area as income) or on imports (leaves the region). For example, an Australian Olympic tourist spends money in a local restaurant during the Olympics in London 2012. The tourist's expenditure is considered autonomous spending (a) and therefore creates a regional benefit, because "fresh" money enters the city (R). The origin, (a)utonomous or (r)egional, and destination, (R)egion or (I)mport, of each expenditure determines whether a regional economic impact occurs. Each expenditure can create one of the four following effects:

1. Benefits: Autonomous spending means that "fresh money" from outside the region is spent and stays in the region (a × R).

2. Costs: Regional spending used for imports and that leaves the region (r × I).

3. Reallocations: Regional funds that are spent in the region (r × R). To be precise, reallocations also can create costs and benefits. If regional funds are spent in another industrial sector than they would have been without the sport event and if that sector has stronger (weaker) "creation of value," benefits (costs) will occur. For example, spending on a product that was produced in the region creates more value in the economy when compared with spending on a product that was imported. The economy will always have winners and losers even though the size of the total economy may remain unchanged. Recall from earlier that although the reallocation of money is neutral to the mac-

roeconomy in monetary terms, it may result in a higher consumer surplus.

4. Neutrals: Autonomous funds that are used for imports (a × I). To be precise, neutrals can indirectly create costs and benefits. The streams of money are neutral because the autonomous money is directly spent for imports and does not remain in the region as income. Something was imported, however, and that can create follow-up costs or benefits. For example, a sport arena financed by the state government and constructed by a foreign company for the Olympics is a neutral stream of money for the host city. After the Games the arena hosts other events that entertain citizens, but it has to be maintained. So those effects are considered postevent costs and benefits.

Each sport-related stream of money therefore will be split into four parts: (1) direct benefits or (2) direct costs or (3) reallocations within the economy to value-increasing sectors or value-decreasing sectors or (4) neutrals. The sum of these effects forms the primary regional impact for the period considered.

Note that the primary regional impact can be negative. If net exports to the region are negative, which means that the region imported more than it exported for the event, and spending is reallocated from value-increasing sectors within the region to sectors outside of the region, then the event will lead to a negative economic impact, even if gross spending is significant. If a self-sustaining extreme sport festival comes to town—that is, the promoters provide their own set-up, tear-down, ticket and refreshment sales, and so forth—the economic impact of the festival would be to generate spending that is removed from the local economy and taken with the promoters, performers, and staff. In other words, despite generating a great deal of economic activity, the festival would take money from the economy and the direct economic impact would be negative. This effect is often a concern for cities that host professional sport teams that generate a lot of the money from regional spectators. The money goes to the team owner and the players, who may not spend the money in the region.

Export of Services

Tourism spending as a result of hosting a sport event is considered an export of service and a benefit to the regional economy. The service being exported is the entertainment of the event or other tourist attractions associated with the event. The nonlocal or foreign visitors literally take the service back home, that is, they import it to their region or country of origin, in the form of consumed food, memories, good feelings, and photos. This service is considered an export because it is created within the region and is paid for and enjoyed by people from outside the regional economy. The result is autonomous money entering the region from outside and an increase in economic benefit to the host region. But it is important to consider whether the tourist would have visited the region if the event had not taken place (Preuss, 2005). The proper calculation of the primary impact of tourist spending has to be done with great care to avoid double counting of visitor spending as well as to avoid erroneously counting the spending of those who do not bring "fresh" money into the region.

Import Spending

Costs paid to outside construction firms hired to build sport facilities and event infrastructure are considered import spending. To the extent that South Africa used foreign construction companies in its build-up to hosting the 2010 FIFA World Cup, it was importing services from outside its economy (the manpower and know-how of architects, civil engineers, skilled construction workers, and others coming into the country). That spending can be a cost to the host economy if South African spending is leaving the country, or it can represent money passing through the economy because of the event. If sponsorship money originating from outside the country was used on construction provided by firms from outside of the country, then the direct monetary effect passed through the host economy. Recall, however, that the existence of the new facilities and infrastructure will result in future benefits and costs for the host economy. Moreover, wages for local construction workers or expenses for local subcontractors paid by the foreign company will stay in the economy and will thereby create an inflow of money.

Import Substitution

The final example explains the case of import substitution (Cobb & Weinberg, 1993). Coca-Cola, which has its headquarters in Atlanta, Georgia, host

CASE STUDY

Economic Impact of Public Viewing Areas at the 2006 FIFA World Cup

Ex-post calculations of the primary economic impact of extra visitor spending in Germany brought about by the 2006 FIFA World Cup are €3.2 billion (US$4.1 billion) (Preuss, Kurscheidt, & Schütte, 2009). The study estimated that the primary impact of non-German visitors to the World Cup stadiums brought in €1.47 billion (US$1.88 billion) and that non-German visitors to the free public viewing areas

Concession Items Consumed by Fans at the Berlin Fan Mile, FIFA World Cup 2006

Item	Quantity	Units
Beer	809,000	liters
Cola	718,880	liters
Water	86,826	liters
Sprite	39,116	liters
Berliner Weisse	31,780	liters
Coffee	26,000	liters
Fanta	21,290	liters
Apple juice and water	23,790	liters
Ice tea	11,068	liters
Powerade	8,250	liters
Total	1,776,000	liters
Sausages	2,000,000	portions
Hamburgers	1,100,000	portions
Ice cream	138,000	portions
Total	3,238,000	portions

Data from organizers in Berlin.

brought in €1.09 billion (US$1.40 billion) of autonomous spending.

Modern video technology has led to a variety of new ways to consume sport media, and the public viewing phenomenon is one of them. During the 2006 World Cup, cities across Germany and their individual sponsors provided public viewing areas that allowed millions of football fans to enjoy the matches in an atmosphere of crowds and excitement. The Berlin Fan Mile consisted of 20 massive video screens. As many as one million fans gathered there to cheer on their teams in World Cup matches.

During the World Cup (from the opening match on June 9, 2006, until July 7, 2006) the consumption at the Berlin Fan Mile was enormous. Berlin revived the Fan Mile for German national team matches during the UEFA Euro 2008 tournament.

For the World Cup, the exciting atmosphere of public viewing areas provided a reason for people unable to obtain tickets to the matches to visit the host country for the event anyway. As noted earlier, visitors who came to Germany because of the World Cup but did not attend any matches brought a significant amount of autonomous spending into the country. The public viewing areas also increased the intangible well-being of German residents by providing an enhanced atmosphere for viewing matches and an additional way for fans to have a more intense and enjoyable World Cup experience. Hosts and organizers of future events can look to this example for ways to increase the economic benefits of hosting an event. In the case of Germany 2006, the public viewing areas were shown to attract visitors and their spending to the country, and they likely caused a significant increase in the intangible benefit of the experience for local residents as well.

---

of the 1996 Olympics, is one of the major sponsors of international sport events. Because Coca-Cola is an Atlanta company, we might think that any of its sponsorship dollars that ended up with the Atlanta Olympic Organizing Committee could not be considered a net gain in spending for the Atlanta regional economy. But this special case of import substitution represents additional spending in the local economy. As a primary Olympic sponsor,

Coca-Cola spends dollars sponsoring the Olympics no matter where they are held. If the 1996 Games had been awarded to Athens, Greece, the runner-up in the selection process, Coca-Cola sponsorship dollars would have been spent in Athens rather than Atlanta. In effect, for the typical Olympic Games, Coca-Cola is importing an association with the Olympics from the host city. When the Games were held in Atlanta, the sponsorship money stayed in the region instead of being spent elsewhere. Coca-Cola's typical import spending on the association with the Olympics stayed at home in 1996 and resulted in a gain in spending to the local economy because had the Games not been held in Atlanta, Coca-Cola's dollars would have gone to the alternate host city.

Multiplier Effect

Besides the primary regional impact of an event on an economy, we must also consider the **induced impact**, which is the additional change in consumption, investment, and export spending that results from the initial change in spending working its way through the economy. To understand induced impact, we must recognize the concept of the **multiplier effect**. The multiplier effect can be described as an increase in spending that leads to an increase in the size of the overall economy that is a multiple of the original increase (Mankiw 2007, p. 483). The basic reason that the eventual change in the size of the economy is a multiple of the initial increase in spending is that one person's spending is another person's income. When visitors spend their money in the local economy, the spending results in increased income for members of the local economy, who in turn increase their spending, which further increases other peoples' incomes, and so on. In its most basic form, the multiplier is determined by the propensity of people to spend the additional money they receive on consumption. If they are more likely to save their extra money or spend it outside their region, the multiplier effect will be smaller. If they are more likely to spend it, the multiplier effect will be larger.

The total economic impact of a sport event on a region consists of the primary regional impact (the direct effect) times the multiplier (the induced effect). In the usual case of a positive total effect, the value of the multiplier is at least larger than one.

Learning Activity

Investigate the general economies of the Republic of South Africa and Germany to determine how the economic impact of the 2010 FIFA World Cup differed from the economic impact of the 2006 FIFA World Cup on the respective host nations.

A neutral effect would give a multiplier that equals or is close to unity because the initial economic injection to the region would remain (nearly) the same, even after the circular process described earlier. Note that the multiplier is influenced by many factors, particularly the characteristics of the local economy. UK Sport, which conducts economic impact studies of sport events hosted in the United Kingdom, does not consider the multiplier effect when reporting results. Because the purpose of their studies is to compare the economic impact of many hosted events and because the multiplier is a characteristic of the regional economy and not the event, UK Sport focuses only on the primary regional impact.

The main factors influencing the magnitude of the multiplier effect are the diversity and size of the economy. A mature, diverse economy will have a greater multiplier effect than a developing economy because more of the spending can be captured in a diverse economy and therefore the leakage is smaller. Such economies provide more productive opportunities to spend money that is earned from the initial injection or from induced income in the following rounds of spending. So the medium- and long-term productivity of economic activities where the funds go is an important determinant of the multiplier.

The multiplier effect is similarly influenced by the breadth of the definition of the regional economy. The extra spending that makes up the primary regional impact is much more likely to stay in the region if the defined region is large. In other words, the mentioned leakages are smaller. Only diversified national economies have the potential to create multiplier effects as large as 2.5 to 3.0.

The economic situation affects the multiplier as well. If the economy is close to full employment, the multiplier will be lower than it would be if many resources were underemployed (unemployed labor, idle equipment, unused building materials). For an economy close to full employment, additional economic activity is more likely to result in **crowding out** of existing economic activity (Mankiw, 2007, p. 486), resulting in less induced impact and a lower multiplier. In contrast, if many resources are underemployed and crowding out does not occur, the multiplier will be much higher. So the multiplier depends on the macroeconomic business cycle (how close the regional economy is to full employment) at

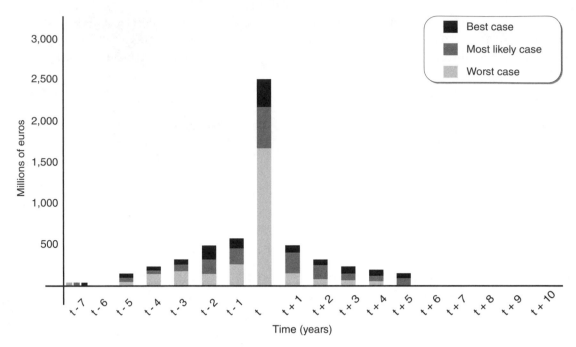

Figure 14.1   Discounted net benefit of Olympic Games for host city.

the time of the highest event expenditures as well as the overall maturity, diversity, and productivity of the economy and the productivity of the activities on which the money is spent.

The total economic impact (primary regional impact times the multiplier) for all one-off projects, such as mega sport events, is short lived. Figure 14.1 shows the annual net benefits simulated for an Olympic host city in 2012.

The yearly net benefits peak during the event and lose power after the event. Depending on the legacy created through the event, a city can experience annual positive net benefits following the event (e.g., through stimulated postevent tourism) but also net costs (e.g., through high cost for maintaining the event facilities). To understand how the event-driven economic impact fades away, we go back to the Keynes model and add government to the model. Injections to the circular flow of money in the economy are investment, government spending on goods and services, and exports (tourist consumption). Leakages are savings, taxes, and imports. The primary regional impact occurs through the injections; the host city may have spent money on facilities construction (investment) assisted by government subsidies (government spending on goods and services), and tourists came and spent money while they enjoyed the event (exports). Most of the injections occur before and during the event. The sidebar lists examples

Injections and Leakages Associated With a Major Sport Event

Injections

Autonomous investments

Government spending on goods and services (if local region)

Exports (e.g., tourism)

Consumption of the organizing committee (funded by autonomous money)

Import substitution

Leakages

Savings

Taxes

Imports

of injections and leakages associated with a major sport event.

Although leakages also occur before and during the event, after the event they dominate. The amount that made up the primary regional impact and its induced effect quickly dwindles away because of people saving (rather than spending), paying federal taxes that leave the region, and importing goods and services from outside the economy. The impact created through the event necessarily returns to its preevent state, and the direct, total economic impact has run its course. Only if the new infrastructure permanently attracts new money to the economy will the regional economy reach a higher level (Spilling, 1999). This result may occur because of a permanent increase in tourism to the former host city or the staging of future events in existing facilities. This effect is called a positive event **legacy effect**.

Learning Activity

In a small group, identify three specific examples of ways in which the initial amount of increased money brought into an economy by a sport event leaks from the economy over time. What strategies can slow these leakages and extend the benefit of the event?

Long- and Short-Term Benefits From Sport and the Legacy Effect

Few past megaevent impact analyses have recognized the clear limitations of the multiplier, namely that the effect of a nonrecurring expenditure weakens over the course of time and then vanishes completely. The increase in income declines with every new period, and in the long run falling demand leads back to the equilibrium income that existed before the event if there is no positive legacy effect. Typically, the multiplier impact over time for a nonrecurring autonomous expenditure can be calculated using this equation:

$$c^n \times \Delta A$$

where ΔA is the initial direct and indirect impact and where c (where $0 < c < 1$) represents the level of induced impact. As n (the number of time periods) increases to infinity, the value of the induced impact tends toward zero. But the Olympic Games are a special case. The increased demand lasts for many years. During this period, autonomous expenditures are made so that the equilibrium income will not immediately return to the starting point following the event. Caused by varying autonomous injections (ΔA), permanently changing demand functions will exist during the remaining time. Long after the Games, increased demand will persist, depending on the type of long-term infrastructural changes. For example, the operation and maintenance of sport facilities will continue and the number of visitors will remain high because of improved attractions and the Olympic image. The sport facilities and the changed structure of the city can enhance the attractiveness of the city, as seen in the example of the Munich Olympic Park, and lasting income increases can be the consequence.

Because the direct economic impact dwindles quickly because of leakages that cause the primary impact to lose power over time, a one-time event cannot directly improve the economic welfare of a region in the long run.

But the event can create intangible effects, in particular changes of location factors such as infrastructure or knowledge, and leave a so-called positive legacy. If the event improves the normal economic structure, which is called event legacy, then it can indirectly increase economic activity in the region in the long term.

Overall, six types of event structures are usually preserved after a megaevent. Four of these—infrastructure, know-how, networks, and culture—develop almost as a matter of course through the preparation of the event, whereas a further two—emotions and image—depend on the momentum that the event develops (Preuss, 2007, pp. 92–97). Each of these six event structures transforms the location factors of the host city.

Figure 14.2 shows six event structures that affect a city by a change of location factors. When hosting a megaevent, decision makers are wise to plan with the legacy in mind by investing not only in the event but also in additional infrastructure needed to change location factors. For example, the tourism product at a destination is affected by the following event structures: new physical tourist attractions, upgraded and new hotels, better public transportation, a better and more interesting image, more knowledge in the tourism service industry, a more interesting cultural presentation, and cultural identity (see Solberg & Preuss, 2007). Another example is a better business destination developed through event infrastructures such as an upgrade of the general infrastructure (particularly traffic systems), knowledge (e.g., organizational and service skills, security), skilled labor, image as a business location, and political and business networks.

Increased tourism activity in the city may lead to long-term economic growth and additional jobs. But such economic growth based on event-related improved location factors does not obviously appear in many evaluations as being event related.

For example, new and improved infrastructure and facilities could result in the hosting of future events that attract visitors and again bring autonomous money into the economy. Museums and parks built for the Olympic Games could become a per-

manent tourist attraction that leads to a long-term increase in the number of visitors to the region. This result certainly occurred after the Barcelona 1992 Olympic Games (Preuss, 2004). Additionally, the knowledge gained by local organizers in hosting the event could become a future export good as they become consultants for future hosts. Although the direct economic impact of an event on a region is short lived, the indirect, long-term impact can potentially be quite large if the legacy effect of the event results in useful permanent

Learning Activity

Compare the long-term legacy benefits of the 2008 Beijing Summer Olympics and the 1994 Lillehammer Winter Olympics to the respective host cities. Consider the size, location, and economic characteristics of the host cities.

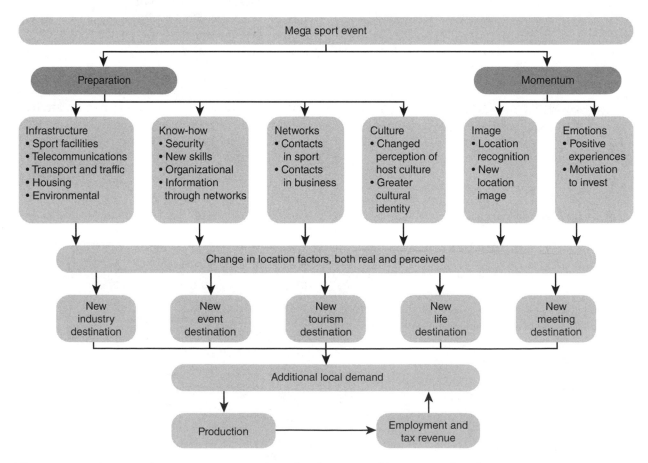

Figure 14.2 Impact of event structure on location factors and its economic relevance.

changes in the region, such as an enhancement of its image, an increase in the skills and knowledge base its workforce, or its ability to attract and host future large-scale events.

Summary

This chapter explained the macroeconomics of sport by using the economic impact of mega sporting events on a host region or country as an example. The same mechanisms hold for the economic impact of other sport-related activities in a region, even small local events. Consider a new sport equipment manufacturing plant, a newly constructed arena, or an increase in participation in active sport and health clubs. The economic effects of all these actions must be seen as attracting autonomous money to the region and creating jobs, taxes, and income in the same way as was explained in the example of hosting a mega sport event. The macroeconomic effect, however, will be long term as long as the manufacturing plant or arena are operating and as long as people maintain their increase in athletic activity. Unlike the mega sport event, the macroeconomic effects in these examples will probably not create any legacy that induces economic activity after they end.

From a macroeconomic perspective the key welfare issue is whether a sport event achieves efficient outcomes given the potentially incompatible aims of various stakeholders. Invariably, these differences lead to some debatable investments of scarce public resources. An enormous intervention such as Olympic Games always affects the location where it takes place. Any structural change of a location means that in the long term other industries are stimulated that would not have been without the event. For example, a larger number of tourists increases demand in the tourism industry, or new transport infrastructure increases the number of corporations that settle in the region. Note that the smaller the event or sport intervention is, the smaller the macroeconomic impact is.

Whatever sport intervention takes place, some stakeholders will not be interested or will not want the event or sport activity. Each decision for a major sport activity will satisfy demand for some, which can be seen as beneficial, but others will claim that the resources would have been better used for other activities. These people can be seen as losing economic benefit because of the sport event.

? Review and Discussion Questions

1. How does the economic significance of sport in an economy compare with that of a retail center or a university?

2. What are some of the intangible economic benefits associated with sport? Are the intangible economic benefits more significant than the tangible benefits?

3. Does spending on a sport event by residents of a host city normally increase the overall spending in the host city?

4. What are the differences between direct and indirect investment goods in sport?

5. How does public spending on direct and indirect investment goods affect the larger economy?

6. What are the macroeconomic impacts of the relocation of a major sport franchise on both the city that is losing the franchise and the city that is gaining it? What is the overall significance of the team to the economy, and what tangible and intangible benefits are generated by the franchise?

7. How will the proposed expansion of the UEFA European football championship field from 16 to 24 nations affect the economic impact on nations that host the tournament in the future?

CHAPTER 15

Business and Finance of International Sport Leagues

Brad R. Humphreys, PhD
University of Alberta, Canada

Nicholas M. Watanabe, PhD
University of Missouri, USA

Chapter Objectives

After studying this chapter, you will be able to do the following:

- Understand the North American and European models of sport league organization
- Understand differences in team ownership in these two models
- Understand differences in player movements in these two models
- Understand how these competing models lead to different on-field and financial outcomes
- Understand how hybrids of these two models have been adapted for other leagues and sports around the world

This chapter focuses on business and finance of international sport at the professional level. The chapter discusses differences in league design, team ownership, and financing in international sport, highlighting the important distinctions that exist between North American, European, and Asian professional sport. Major differences include methods of determining league membership (static leagues versus promotion and relegation), ownership of teams (private ownership versus stock, as well as corporate holding companies), financing of teams, including differences in revenues and costs, and differences in player movements (free agency and player trades versus transfers). The differences in the organization of teams and leagues across countries are striking, and these differences generate radically different on-field and financial outcomes. As Rosen and Sanderson (2001) point out, the North American model punishes success, whereas the European model punishes failure.

The organization of professional sport leagues is an important business decision made by all professional team sport organizations. At the professional level, most team sports are organized into leagues, although there are exceptions. The primary alternative to leagues in a team sport setting is an unorganized collection of "barnstorming" teams that operate much like the Negro Leagues did in the first half of the 20th century in the United States. A current example of a professional team sport operating outside a league structure is professional cricket at the international level, which does not have a league structure. At the national level, only one cricket league is organized along traditional lines, the recently formed Indian Premier League.

Sport leagues perform important business functions. In general, these functions can be divided into two types: single-entity cooperative functions and joint-venture cooperative functions. **Single-entity cooperative activity** includes all cooperative actions that must occur for play to take place. These actions include the determination of the teams in the league, setting of the league schedule and season length, agreements on a set of rules governing play, and the determination of the structure of the league championship. Without these actions, teams would have to schedule their own games, which would make business activities like selling tickets and signage, arranging sponsorships, and scheduling travel difficult. **Joint-venture cooperative activity** includes all cooperative actions undertaken by a league that raise the profits of all teams in the league. Team owners who engage in joint-venture cooperative activities give up some autonomy to earn higher profits. These actions include the creation of exclusive territories, collective selling of broadcast rights, and labor relations, including rules governing player mobility. The primary goal of joint-venture cooperative activities is to generate market power for teams in a league. In addition, league rules specifying permissible team ownership forms and other business-related factors like debt limits also fall under joint-venture cooperative activities.

The key features of the organization of professional team sport leagues are schedule and championship format, league composition, team ownership form, and player movement rules (Noll, 2003).

The nature of particular sports dictates many important factors in schedule format. For example, baseball position players can perform at a high level on a daily basis, basketball players can perform at a high level three to four days per week, but football players in both North America and Europe can perform at a high level only once per week. This fact has an important effect on both the frequency of play and the length of the season. The format of the league championship is at the discretion of the league. One key feature of a league championship format is postseason play. A league can award the championship to the team that performs the best over the course of the season, or it can award the championship to the winner of a postseason tournament participated in by a subset of the teams that perform the best over the course of the regular season. The format of the championship has an important effect on the revenues and costs of the teams in the league. League composition can be either static or dynamic. In **static leagues**, the composition of teams is the same from season to season. In dynamic leagues, the composition of the league varies from season to season. In addition, leagues may periodically expand by adding new teams or contract by eliminating teams. Note that this possibility is different from dynamic membership, because expansion and contraction are permanent whereas dynamic changes are temporary.

Team ownership can take many forms. Teams can be owned by private individuals, private for-profit corporations, public for-profit corporations, or nonprofit organizations. Team ownership has important effects on team goals and policies, as well as having important tax implications. Player movement rules include rules about the nature of contracts between teams and players and the type of trades that are allowed in the league.

A surprising amount of variation in league and team organization exists in the sport business. No two professional sport leagues have identical organization, and leagues often use quite different methods for dealing with similar problems. For more on the organization and role of sport leagues, see chapter 12. Differences in league and team organization can lead to important differences in team revenues and costs, which will be explored in this chapter. In general, two broad forms of league organization have emerged: the European league model and the North American league model. These two models are the dominant league organizational forms in professional team sport. The next sections describe these two competing models of league organization in detail and discuss the effects of these organizational forms on teams' business operations.

North American League Model

The North American league model refers to the common features of the high-profile team sport leagues in the United States and Canada: the National Football League (NFL), the Canadian Football League (CFL), the National Basketball Association (NBA), the Women's National Basketball Association (WNBA), Major League Baseball (MLB), the National Hockey League (NHL), and Major League Soccer (MLS). This organization is used as well in other North American leagues, such as minor league baseball, the National Lacrosse League (NLL), and others. The key features of the North American league model are static league composition; ownership by private individuals, for-profit corporations, or nonprofit organizations; and player movement in the form of trades or free agency. Note that although the North American league model is based most strongly within that region, it has been emulated to some extent by leagues in other regions, such as the Nippon Professional Baseball (NPB) league of Japan and the Indian Premier League.

Organization of North American Sport Leagues

The key organizational features of the North American league model are static composition with periodic expansion, free agency after a specified period of service, relatively large numbers of teams qualifying for postseason play, and player-for-player or player-for-draft-pick trades. Static composition means that the same teams participate in league play every season, and they have no chance of being moved to another division or level of play based on performance. In the North American static model, the only method of entry into professional sport leagues is through expansion, which requires a variety of things, including the consent of a majority of owners in the league as well as payment of a large expansion fee that can run to hundreds of millions of dollars (Eckard, 2004). Additionally, the North American model is unique in that the regular season of play does not crown a league champion but rather is employed to decide the seeding for teams for a postseason playoff series. In this setup, the champion of a North American sport league is the franchise that wins its way through the playoff series, not necessarily the one that performed consistently the best over a long regular season (Noll, 2003). Probably the biggest exception to this in North America is Major League Soccer (MLS), whose teams compete in regional North American competitions, the MLS Cup, and the Lamar Hunt U.S. Open Cup.

Another hallmark of the North American model is the use of the **reverse-order draft** to allow the teams that performed the worst to have the first pick of new players coming into a league. In this manner, the team that finishes last is rewarded with potentially getting the best new talent. North American leagues rely heavily on secondary and collegiate systems to identify, develop, and train the young athletes who will be drafted. In this sense, North American teams benefit by having other organizations and systems pay much of the training costs. This system is markedly different from the European one, in which players are often brought up through youth academies from a young age. Another important point about the reverse-order draft system is that in essence it rewards teams for doing poorly, whereas in the European model teams are often punished for poor performance by being relegated to lower leagues.

Player movement in North America from one team to another is done through trades, in which one or several players from a franchise are exchanged for one or several players from another franchise, or in some cases future considerations such as draft picks or players to be named later. Players in North America are also contracted to a team until they become free agents. Free agency has existed in North America for about three decades, whereas before its existence the reserve clause system was employed. Under the reserve clause, players were not allowed to move freely from one team to another, even after their contract expired. With the creation of **free agency**, players in North America were given the right to move to any team they wished after their contract with their original team expired. A further discussion and comparison of the differences between the North American and European models of league organization can be found in the European model section of this chapter.

Ownership of North American Sport Teams

The primary form of ownership in North American sport leagues is private ownership of teams by individuals or small groups of people. Although there are some notable exceptions, such as the Chicago Cubs, who were owned by the Tribune Corporation for many years, and the Atlanta Braves, who are owned by Liberty Media, most North American professional sport teams are owned by individuals, as privately held corporations. Teams owned by individuals are often incorporated under subchapter S of chapter 1 of the Internal Revenue Code, and thus are called S corporations. The primary feature of S corporations is that they do not pay corporate income taxes. The earnings or losses of an S corporation are passed through to the owner or owners and paid as individual income taxes. This arrangement provides an important tax advantage to many team owners, because they are not subject to the corporate tax code.

Also, because S corporations do not have publicly traded shares, they are not obligated to file audited financial statements, making their finances difficult to assess. When professional sport team owners claim to be losing money, these claims must be regarded with considerable skepticism because of the lack of audited financial data to back up the assertions. Team owners using the S corporation model differ from corporations with publicly traded stock like Liberty Media in that a publicly traded corporation must by law release financial data compiled and certified by outside auditors. Although private ownership is not as common outside North America, in other countries some teams are controlled by a single owner, such as Manchester United of the English Premier League (EPL) or the Seibu Lions of the Nippon Professional Baseball (NPB) league. The Seibu Lions are controlled by a parent organization that is owned by a single individual, in effect making him the sole owner of the team. Manchester United, on the other hand, was once publicly traded, but the stock was entirely bought out by American businessman Malcolm Glazer, effectively making him the sole owner of the club. The S corporation model is unique to North America, but as these examples indicate a single person can also entirely own or control teams in other countries.

In addition, some teams in the Canadian Football League (CFL) are owned and operated by community-based nonprofit organizations. This relatively rare ownership form came about because of fears that CFL teams would move to relatively more profitable U.S. markets. The Edmonton Oilers, Winnipeg Blue Bombers, and Saskatchewan Roughriders are community-owned CFL franchises.

In a few rare instances, North American professional sport teams have been operated as for-profit corporations with shares publicly traded on a stock exchange. The primary example of this ownership form is the Boston Celtics, who were operated in this way throughout much of the 1990s. The Cleveland Indians and the Vancouver Canucks, discussed in the case study, also briefly operated this way during the past 20 years.

Learning Activity

Consider the numbers presented in the case study of the Vancouver Canucks. Discuss the implications of the figures presented in this case study. Do you think that leagues have to implement salary caps because of spending on player salaries? What does the current state of finances in the NHL tell you?

CASE STUDY

A Publicly Traded North American Sport Team

From 1971 until 2000 the Vancouver Canucks of the National Hockey League were owned and operated by Northwest Sports Enterprises, Ltd., ticker symbol NSE, a corporation with publicly traded shares on the Toronto and Vancouver stock exchanges. Shares in NSE traded at a high of $100 per share on November 29, 1996, and at a low of $23.50 per share on August 17, 1993. The table shows Northwest Sports Enterprises' audited income statement for 1998 and 1999, in Canadian dollars. Indeed, the Vancouver Canucks were one of the few North American sport teams that were publicly traded instead of being owned

by private owners or ownership groups. In this time, the public ownership of the Canucks provided the financial numbers that were released to the public, something almost unheard of for privately owned professional sport franchises. This rare case allowed researchers and the public to view and investigate these numbers and thus gain a better overall picture of the financial operations of a professional sport team in the North American model.

The Canucks lost quite a bit of money in these two years, as indicated by these audited financials. The largest expense, hockey operations, is player salary and travel, which exceeded total revenues in both years. Clearly, the team did not bring in enough revenue over these years to cover player salaries and travel, let alone the other costs of business. The currency assistance revenue came from the Canadian government, which subsidized Canadian NHL teams because they have to pay players in U.S. dollars but earn revenues in Canadian dollars. Many lessons can be learned from having the open books of the Canucks. Note that during this period the NHL operated without a salary cap, much as teams in Europe did. The lack of a salary cap coupled with high player salaries eventually forced the owners to have a lockout, during which they refused to let games be played because of the large losses that they were taking. After the end of the lockout in 2004–05, the NHL finally came to a collective bargaining agreement that included a salary cap, which helped to improve the financial well-being of many of the franchises within the league.

Northwest Sports Enterprises' Audited Income Statement for 1998 and 1999

Revenue	1999	1998
Ticket sales	$27,131,799	$32,632,393
TV and radio broadcast	$17,101,062	$10,366,201
Merchandise	$2,137,846	$3,925,717
Advertising	$4,139,545	$3,660,075
Currency assistance	$3,804,032	$814,342
Expenses	$54,368,254	$51,398,728
Hockey operations	$75,623,519	$77,395,111
Merchandise	$1,707,339	$3,547,606
Administrative	$6,075,683	$7,471,108
Broadcasting and games	$1,130,525	$594,366
Operating loss	($30,168,802)	($33,028,539)

Financing of North American Sport Teams

Because nearly all North American professional sport teams are privately held, getting reliable data on their revenues and expenses is difficult. *Forbes* magazine, however, estimates teams' revenues and expenses each year. These estimates are based on public information like attendance and **broadcast revenue** contracts and estimates of items like merchandise sales. Broadcast revenue is payments from media outlets for the rights to broadcast some or all of a team's games.

Figure 15.1 shows the average revenues and source of revenues for teams in the four major North American Leagues in 2008. The height of each bar on this graph represents total revenues. Teams in the NFL earn the highest revenues on average, and teams in the NHL earn the lowest. In all four leagues, the revenues from ticket sales, luxury boxes, and other gate-related revenues average about $50 million per team per season. The difference in revenues across leagues comes from the other sources of revenue, primarily media rights. Here, teams in the NFL, with its huge network television contracts, earn far more

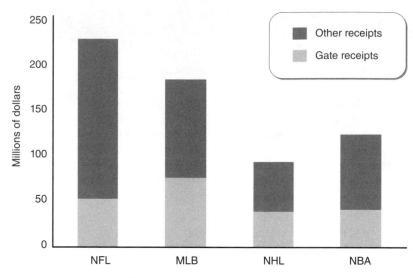

Figure 15.1 Average revenues, and their sources, of the four major North American sport leagues in 2008. The light gray shows revenues from gate receipts (e.g., ticket sales, luxury boxes). The dark gray shows revenues from other receipts (e.g., media rights, merchandise sales, food sales).

than teams in the other three leagues (Van Riper, 2009).

Figure 15.2 shows average expenses for teams in the four major North American sport leagues in 2008. Other expenses, primarily travel, coaching and scouting, front office salaries, and the costs of staging games, advertising games, and producing licensed merchandise, are roughly equivalent across the leagues. The player salary costs, including signing bonuses, differ significantly across leagues. The NFL and MLB have the highest player expenses,

followed by the NBA and then the NHL. Part of these differences in player expenses comes from the larger roster size in the NFL and MLB. Considering this graph with the previous one, note that the leagues that have higher **revenue sources** outside of gate receipts, such as broadcast revenue and sponsorships, tend to pay more total salary to players. This relationship can be explained by the provisions in the collective bargaining agreements (CBAs) of many of these leagues. These CBAs often stipulate that a certain percentage of television

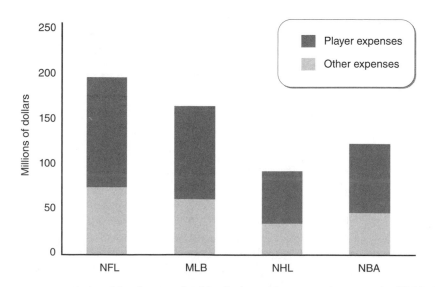

Figure 15.2 Average expenses of the four major North American sport leagues in 2008. Other expenses, in light gray, include such things as travel, advertising, and coaching. Player expenses, in dark gray, are the largest for each league.

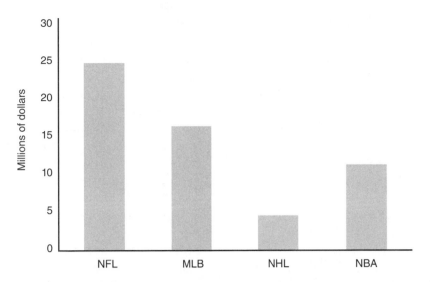

Figure 15.3 Average operating income of the four major North American sport leagues in 2008.

revenue determines the salary cap for the entire league. In this sense, the expenses of North American leagues are directly related to the revenue that these leagues bring in.

Finally, figure 15.3 shows average total operating income, defined as total revenues less total costs, for each league. Teams in all four leagues are profitable, on average, but NFL teams earn a much larger operating income than teams in the other three leagues each season. Placing these three graphs together, note that the leagues with the highest revenue also offer more money for player salaries and in turn also have the highest total operating income. This relationship is not a coincidence, because there is a link between revenue, salary, operating income, and profitability of teams in these leagues.

European League Model

The European model of professional sport, along with the North American model, influences the organization and financing of professional sport leagues and franchises worldwide. The European model of professional sport has proved to be quite popular in other countries, especially in the formulation of professional football leagues such as those found in Brazil, Japan, and many other countries. Note that other countries and sports borrow from the European model to create variations. The North American and European league models display important distinctions and divisions. The following sections examine the organization and structure of European professional sport leagues. Much of the

attention is focused on professional football teams, because these teams are the largest in terms of their fan following and revenues. Besides examining league structures and organization, the following sections discuss and compare differences in ownership methods and financing between European and North American professional sport leagues.

Organization of European Sport Leagues

In examining the structure of sport leagues around the world, one of the primary distinctions is whether the league is static (closed) or uses the open (promotion and relegation) system. As discussed in the previous section on the organization of North American sport leagues, static leagues are more common in the United States and Canada. In Europe, however, **promotion and relegation** is a much more commonly used league format, one that rewards stronger teams and punishes weaker ones. Promotion and relegation works by having a multitiered system of connected sport leagues in which teams are exchanged from one league to the next based on performance. That is, teams finishing at the bottom of a higher league will be relegated to a league one tier down, and teams finishing at the top of a lower league will be promoted to the league in the next tier up. Thus, at the end of each season teams move between leagues; typically three are promoted and three are relegated each season. In some cases four teams are promoted and four are relegated each season. Leagues in the middle of the tier system will have between six and eight new teams each season.

Although promotion and relegation is quite simple, the form that it takes differs from league to league in the number of teams that are promoted and relegated as well as the presence or absence of a promotion and relegation playoff. This playoff system is usually a series of games played between teams with a chance of being promoted to the next higher league, as well as the teams that are being relegated from the league that the promoted teams are trying to enter. In this system the playoffs are used to determine which of the promotion and relegation teams should be allowed to play in the higher league and which should be placed in the lower one (Noll, 2003).

A primary example of the use of promotion and relegation can be seen in English professional football. At the top of the tier structure is the English Premier League (EPL), which consists of 20 teams. The bottom three of these teams are demoted to the league below the Premier League, the Npower Football League Championship (formerly Division 1) after every season. Within the Npower Football League Championship, the top two teams are directly promoted to the Premier League each season, and the third- through sixth-place teams compete in a playoff, the winner of which is awarded the third promotional spot to the Premier League. Additionally, the Npower Football League Championship demotes the bottom three teams to the next lower league in the tier system, the Football League One. This process continues, with slight variations, across the six tiers of professional football in England. The promotion and relegation system has been successfully re-created across the world in a number of leagues, most commonly in football leagues such as the J League of Japan and the Brazilian Campeonato Brasileiro Serie A. In this way, promotion and relegation has become a standard in football, although Major League Soccer, the premier professional football league in North America, does not use it.

Promotion and relegation presents a different landscape for professional sport than static (closed) leagues do. Whereas static leagues see almost no change of member teams in a league, promotion and relegation forces a yearly turnover in teams. Furthermore, by including promotion and relegation, even the weaker teams in a league have an incentive to continue to compete and win games at the end of a season. At the end of the season in static leagues in North America, teams often have more incentive to lose matches and not put forth as much effort, because the bottom teams in a league are rewarded in a reverse-order draft, in which they will be given first choice of drafting the best new talent for the next season. European leagues do not use reverse-order drafts. Moreover, promotion and relegation gives the weaker teams in a league incentive to win as many matches as possible. In this sense, promotion and relegation could be said not only to generate more interest in matches among weak teams in a league but also to produce better competitive balance within a league.

Another major effect of the promotion and relegation system on professional sport leagues is that it presents a different method of entry into leagues for franchises. In North American leagues, entry to a league is often bought for a large sum after approval by other owners. In a promotion and relegation system, however, teams are not allowed simply to pay a fee to enter the top league. Instead, a new franchise must work its way through from the bottom of the tier system all the way to the top. Achieving this goal takes a serious investment, and it may require several years to a lifetime, that is, if a franchise can even accomplish such a feat.

Although promotion and relegation is often seen as the main factor distinguishing the North American and European models, another issue is the number of competitions that teams participate in. As mentioned before, teams in the four major professional sport leagues in North America are involved in only a single championship competition each season. Under the European model, teams play in multiple competitions at the same time, including the league championship, league cups, international competition, and so forth. The English Premier League provides a good example of multiple competitions. Every team in the league competes in league matches for the league championship, which has no playoffs. The EPL championship is determined solely by the final league standings. Additionally, all teams in the Premier League compete in the League Cup, as well as the FA Cup, both of which are domestic knockout tournaments. Additionally, higher-ranking teams within the Premier League compete in intercontinental competitions, such as the UEFA Champions League or the UEFA Europa

League. The UEFA Champions League and UEFA Europa League are annual pan-European football tournaments that include the top teams in each European national professional football league. Participants in the Champions League earn huge revenues relative to teams that do not compete in this league, because of the large television rights contracts. In this manner, some teams in Europe are likely to be involved in three or more competitions at the same time, and the schedules of these competitions are intermixed with one another. Although these competitions give teams more chances to win championships and trophies, they also overload the schedules of some teams, forcing them to choose which competitions are more important to them. This pattern of multiple competitions can be found around the world, mostly in football competitions that offer a variety of prizes. For example, a team in Japan may compete for the J League title, the Emperor's Cup, the Nabisco Cup, as well as in the Asian Champions League. Although the richer and stronger football nations are more likely to have a higher number of competitions, a large number of teams in every country typically compete in a number of football competitions.

The Premier League resembles a North American league more than other football leagues in Europe do in that the EPL operates as a corporation. All 20 teams in the league have an equal vote to decide important issues. This organizational structure is also new; the Premier League was formed in 1992 to organize the top flight of football in England better and to increase television revenues earned by top-tier teams. Through this structure, the Premier League not only placed itself at the forefront of European football in terms of television revenue generation but also gradually made itself into the dominant professional sport league in Europe. With access to new revenue streams, the EPL clubs were slowly able to improve their quality by buying top-quality talent from around the world. The EPL domination has grown to the point that Sepp Blatter, the head of FIFA, the governing body for international football, has proposed what is called the 6+5 rule, under which all teams across the world would be limited in the number of international players that they could field at a single time (Ennis, 2008). Critics have claimed that this move was specifically targeted at EPL teams that have become melting pots of international talent. In this way, the EPL

altered the European model of professional sport to suit its needs and gain more revenue. Through these changes, the EPL has become dominant to the point where governing bodies of football seek to reduce its dominance; meanwhile, fans around the world are becoming more interested in the league.

Finally, consider the differences in player movement between North American and European professional sport leagues. It was not until the Bosman transfer ruling in the mid-1990s that players were able to move from one European team to another freely after the expiration of their contracts (Szymanski, 1999). Additionally, whereas new players are obtained through drafts, trades, and free agency in the North American model, European teams use youth systems, transfers, and loans to obtain new players for their teams. Due in great part to the Bosman ruling, many leagues around the world have adapted a free transfer system, especially to accommodate the movement of players between football clubs in different regions of the world. The ability to transfer freely is something that most professional footballers are able to enjoy in most countries around the world.

European leagues do not use an entry draft to allocate young players to teams. Instead, teams operate youth academies that identify star players at a young age, sign them to contracts, and bring them into the club for training. Under this system, European clubs cover much of the cost of developing and training young athletes. European clubs bear all scouting, training, and development costs, which produce only a handful of very good young players from each cohort. This system is still probably best performed in Europe, although countries such as South Africa, South Korea, and Brazil use it profitably as well. The system is most often related to professional football in countries outside of Europe.

After young players have signed with a team, important differences are also seen in player movement from one team to another. In North American leagues, teams often make trades by exchanging individual players, groups of players, and in some cases draft picks. European leagues do not use trades. Instead, they use transfers, in which one club pays another club a sum of money, known as a **transfer fee**, to purchase rights to a player. These fees are paid mostly to the player's former club, but players get a percentage of the fees. In addition, in European leagues teams often loan players to another team. Under this arrangement, players are sent from one team to another for a set period, and the loaning team is compensated with a fee for the player's services.

Through promotion and relegation, multiple competitions, and player allocation and movement, the European model of professional sport leagues differs significantly from the North American model. These differences have consequences for on-field and financial outcomes. As we will see, these differences may lead to radically different distributions of revenues, costs, and wins in leagues.

Learning Activity

1. Research a professional sport league that uses promotion and relegation.

2. Create a chart showing the rules of team movement and how teams move from one division of a tiered league system to the next.

3. After completing the chart, consider the implications that this vast number of teams and team movements will have on the financing of professional sport teams in that system.

Ownership of European Sport Teams

Ownership of European professional sport teams differs from the typical arrangement in North America. North American franchises are often owned by individuals or small groups, whereas European franchises are commonly owned by corporations that have shares trading on stock exchanges. In Europe fans and other members of the public are able to buy a stake in their favorite team. Note that in many areas of the world there are teams that are publicly traded or are owned by corporations that are publicly traded. Most notably, the Nippon Professional Baseball (NPB) league of Japan has an interesting mixture of teams that are owned by either private or publicly traded corporations. In this manner, it is possible to have either of these types of ownership not only in a single country but also within the same league. Despite this difference

in ownership structure, the trend of ownership has slowly been changing in Europe toward individual private ownership of teams. In this sense, the Premier League has led the way, because the majority of the teams in the EPL are currently owned either privately by an individual, by a group of individuals, or by a company that places ownership in the hands of a few people.

While the model in England drifts toward individual private ownership, the rest of Europe still uses a corporate model, in which clubs have shares that are publicly traded on a stock exchange. Many of these clubs hold annual shareholder meetings when elections are conducted to decide who will become the president or leader of the club. Real Madrid of Spain's top professional football league, La Liga, is an example of this method of ownership. Shareholders of Real Madrid elect a president to run the club through majority voting. This style has been extremely successful for Real Madrid, which stands at or near the top of the yearly revenue rankings of professional football clubs in Europe.

Manchester United, another one of the world's most recognized sport franchises and one of the perennial top teams in the Premier League, exemplifies the effect of an individual buyout. Up until 2005 Manchester United was a publicly traded corporation. Shares in the team were slowly bought by American businessman Malcolm Glazer over a period of three years until he controlled enough shares to delist the team from the stock exchange. Although Glazer's delisting was met with anger by fans of the club, Manchester United has continued to be one of the top teams in Europe in performance on both the field and the income statement. Many other top clubs in England have been bought out in a similar manner, so now there is a mixture of individual and corporate ownership within the EPL.

One notable feature of the rise in individual ownership of European clubs, especially those in the Premier League, is that owners who have taken over clubs in recent years have been foreigners. The wave of foreign investment has left 10 of the 20 current EPL clubs either solely or partially owned by a non-U.K. citizen. The more notorious owners of this group include the aforementioned Malcolm Glazer (and family), Mohamed Al-Fayed (Harrods), Roman Abramovich (oil and armaments tycoon), and Stanley Kroenke (American real estate mogul and husband to a Wal-Mart heiress). These owners are all relatively new to investing in European professional sport, and their investment shows that the Premier League is now viewed as a lucrative league to be involved in.

An issue that arises from the changes in ownership concerns the motivations of those who have purchased Premier League clubs. In cases such as Abramovich, it may be that the owner truly cares for the sport, wishes to win titles, and is not afraid to spend his own money to do so, even if it gets his club, Chelsea, dubbed "Chelski" by the media and has fans talking about him in a negative manner. But others like Shinawatra may be using the league solely as a means to gain positive publicity (and some financial gain). Malcolm Glazer may have purchased Manchester United entirely for financial gain, helping to pay off some of the debt that he had incurred in other business ventures. In each instance, a Premier League club has served as a different vehicle for its owner. Although it is not a negative for owners of sport franchises to make a profit from their clubs, the very nature of their takeover of these clubs should be considered. In cases where the takeovers are politically motivated, the influx of foreign investment into the league could be quite negative. But the attraction of the Premier League will remain high, and foreign investment into the top professional sport leagues around the world is sure to continue as long as a good payoff is still possible.

CASE STUDY

International Ownership in the English Premier League

The English Premier League has become the standout among European professional sport leagues for a variety of reasons. The league has become dominant in European competitions of late and has come to be one of the top leagues in terms of revenue, viewership, and popularity worldwide. It could be said that the Premier League is fast becoming a juggernaut among professional sport leagues, and it is poised to continue seeing large profits in the coming years. But with all these changes has come an outcry that the league is fast becoming a foreign one, not just in the sense that teams are buying the best talent from all over the world but also in that more teams are in the hands of foreigners than ever before. Although FIFA has considered enacting the 6+5 rule to try to combat this trend, other issues within the Premier League must be examined, especially the increasing trend of foreign ownership.

In the middle of 2007, foreigners owned 8 of the 20 Premiership clubs. That number has now increased to its current number of 10 overseas owners, so half the teams in the league are partly or entirely owned by foreign individuals, groups, or consortiums. Although the owners who are getting into the Premier League are from a variety of backgrounds, it is intriguing to note that many of them have previous experience in sport, mostly through ownership or some stake in North American professional sport franchises. Furthermore, as this influx of foreign owners continues to take over more of the clubs in the Premier League, the league's style of ownership moves more toward that of a North American style, although the lack of salary caps and other such spending controls is notable.

Three Premier League teams are particularly high-profile cases of teams acquired by foreign owners:

Manchester United

- Acquired by Malcolm Glazer, American investor and owner of the Tampa Bay Buccaneers NFL franchise.
- Purchased by a slow takeover between 2003 and 2005. The final price that Glazer is reported to have paid is somewhere around US$1.45 billion.
- Fans strongly opposed the takeover because it placed the club in a debt of around US$850 million and caused a sharp increase in ticket prices.
- Despite these issues, the club has continued to perform well, winning the UEFA Champions League in 2008. The value of the club has increased to US$1.8 billion, and its following and popularity have continued to expand worldwide.

Chelsea

- Purchased in 2003 by Roman Abramovich, Russian oil tycoon, for £140 million (US$232 million).

(continued)

(continued)

- Abramovich loaned hundreds of millions of pounds to the club so that they would be able to purchase top talent and compete for the Premier League and UEFA Champions League titles.
- The press and opposing fans were unhappy with Abramovich's strategy of spending at all costs to win. But it led to on-field success, and Chelsea won the Premier League title twice, as well as the FA Cup.
- Chelsea is now on its fifth manager in six seasons; Abramovich has been quick to fire those who do not perform well.

Manchester City

- Purchased in 2007 for £81 million (US$164 million) by Thaksin Shinawatra, the deposed former prime minister of Thailand.
- Shinawatra was found guilty of corruption in Thai courts. He has applied for asylum in the United Kingdom.
- Many believed that he was bringing too much negative publicity to the club, despite large investments in it that led to on-field success.
- In September 2008 Shinawatra sold the club for £200 million (US$364 million) to Abu Dhabi United Group Investment and Development Limited (Sky Sports Online, 2008), mainly owned by Sheikh Mansour Bin Zayed Al Nahyan, one of the members of the ruling family of Abu Dhabi in the United Arab Emirates (UAE).

In recognizing the Premier League as the most powerful and dominant professional sport league in Europe, consider the trends that come about in this league. As the trendsetter in professional sport in Europe, it could be that the Premier League will serve as a springboard for foreign investors to move into other leagues in Europe. Furthermore, the Premier League could help bring about administrative and organizational changes within European professional sport leagues, including items such as caps on salaries or transfer fees, which are currently a large burden in European sport. In this, the Premier League could possibly be a beacon of change and innovation for European sport leagues, and because of the high rate of foreign ownership, it may help to set the tone for more financial stability and fiscal responsibility for the other professional sport leagues in Europe.

Financing of European Sport Teams

The model of European sport finance is still evolving. This model was first dubbed SSSL, or spectators, subsidies, sponsors, and local (Andreff & Staudohar, 2000). But many clubs have abandoned the traditional SSSL model because television revenue has come to supplant traditional revenues streams (Baade, 2003). Research now indicates that the European revenue model should be revised to the MCMMG model, or media, corporations, merchandising, markets, and globalized (Andreff & Staudohar, 2000). That is, media rights fees, corporate sponsorships, and sale of merchandise in markets around the globe are now the main sources of revenue for professional sport teams in Europe. Although these sources of revenue are important for all professional sport leagues in countries around the world, the total amount and breakdown of the revenue sources is unique to Europe. One example of this uniqueness would be corporate sponsorship, whereby jersey sponsorship generates a significant percentage of club revenue. This section discusses each of the three main sources of revenue for the financing of professional sport franchises in Europe.

Even with the mix of individual and corporate ownership of European professional sport teams, some broad similarities in the methods of financing are found, because most of the revenue earned by clubs comes from television broadcast deals, commercial sponsorships, and match attendance (Parkes, Houlihan, Ingles, & Hawkins, 2007). These three sources of revenue have become the drivers of revenues worldwide. The relative proportions of these three types of revenues vary from club to club, because leagues have a number of factors such as television deals and stadium sizes that affect the proportions. For example, Italian clubs generally rely on revenue from broadcast more than clubs in other countries do, because the Italians have lucrative television contracts, especially for the larger clubs.

Based on revenue estimates produced by the Deloitte Group for the 2005–06 season, Italian club Juventus had total revenues of about €250 million (US$295 million), 68 percent of which came directly from broadcast revenue (about €172 million, or US$203 million). Recognizing the team's strength and performance is important when examining its revenues because clubs in competitions such as the UEFA Champions League receive large media payouts for advancing to the later stages of the competition. AC Milan, another Italian club, earned around €20 million (US$24 million) in the 2005–2006 season for reaching the semifinals of the Champions League. Furthermore, other revenues are often associated with performance in league competition and domestic cups for professional football teams in Europe.

Because of these additional revenue streams, inequality appears to be growing among the top football clubs and between the top leagues and the rest of the pack in Europe. As the stronger teams advance further in European competitions, they realize larger payouts, whereas weaker teams have a harder time accessing the European competitions that generate these payouts.

Although television and other broadcast deals form the financial backbone of most clubs, corporate sponsorship and **match-day revenues**, such as those from ticket sales, concessions, and other sales at the venue, still play a key role. Real Madrid, the richest club in terms of revenue according to the 2005–06 Deloitte Football Money League (Parkes, Houlihan, Ingles, & Hawkins, 2007) report, relied on corporate sponsorship more than any other item. Much of this money came from merchandising and licensing of products as the club began to expand its global brand, especially in Asia, which is an emerging hotbed of football fans. A unique part of corporate sponsorship in Europe is the jersey sponsorship concept. In North America most franchises do not put the name of corporate sponsors on jerseys, or do so discreetly. Some North American leagues ban this type of sponsorship. European teams have no qualms about prominently placing the names and logos of sponsors on the front of their jerseys. In fact, this practice is standard in European professional sport leagues.

Shirt sponsorship deals are important revenue sources. Large clubs gain better deals because of their status, popularity, and strong performance on the field. In the 2005–06 season Real Madrid signed a deal with BenQ Mobile Phone, which was said to be worth between €20 and €25 million (US$24

and US$30 million) per year in 2005, but has hence switched sponsors to online betting company BWin for about the same amount. Other clubs such as Manchester United have signed large deals as well; Manchester United's deal with AIG is reportedly worth a little over €20 million (US$24 million) per year. Manchester United's shirt sponsorship deal is further enhanced by its partnership with Nike, which agreed to pay Manchester United €438 million (US$517 million) over 13 years, or about €33.7 million (US$40 million) per season (Parkes, Houlihan, Ingles, & Hawkins, 2007). In total, about 70 percent of Manchester United's corporate sponsorship revenue comes from these two deals, and the AIG and Nike sponsorship earnings represent about one-fifth of the club's annual revenues. Shirt sponsorship deals are quite important in the financing of European professional sport clubs; some teams bring in almost 10 percent of their annual revenue from shirt sponsorship alone. Uniform sponsorship generates significant revenue for European teams, but teams in North America continue to be reluctant to sign such deals. This source of revenue has some potential for professional sport teams in North America, especially those in need of new and innovative ways of generating revenue. The practice of shirt sponsorship has found its way to many countries around the world, including those in Asia, South America, and Africa, and the practice is accepted in a variety of sports. Major League Soccer (MLS) in North America has recently started adopting shirt sponsorships, so it may only be a matter of time before the practice becomes more widespread in the region.

The final component of revenue in Europe is gate, or match-day, revenue. Teams possessing larger stadiums and fan bases, and fielding higher quality teams will have higher demand for tickets and will realize more revenue from match-day sources. An additional determinant of match-day revenue is a team's performance in cup and European tournaments, because teams progressing further into these competitions will play more matches, leading to an increase in match-day revenues. Therefore, teams strive to perform well in multiple competitions.

Although revenue sources in European professional sport leagues resemble those in North America, some key differences occur in the European model, such as shirt sponsorships. Additionally, because more European clubs are being bought by wealthy individuals, many teams have begun to look to their owners as a source of financing. For example, Chelsea, another top-tier EPL team, recently received loans totaling around £578 million (US$1.4 billion) from their new owner, Roman Abramovich. The team will use the money to help buy more talent to compete with the other top teams in their league as well as in European competitions.

The largest difference between European and North American methods of financing comes through the use of initial public offerings (IPOs) of stock. This practice is common in Europe. Many famous teams have used IPOs to generate funds, although the price of stocks of many clubs have fallen in recent years. Furthermore, with the changes in ownership occurring in European sport leagues, especially in the Premier League, the use of IPOs to raise funds seems to be on the decline. The MCMMG model of finance has come to represent the current sources of revenue that drive the operation and performance of European professional sport teams (Andreff & Staudohar, 2000).

East Asian League Models

Although Western countries use the two dominant models of professional sport league organization in the world, the rapid growth of professional sport is not limited to these two areas. Because of population growth and economic development in many countries in Asia, especially those that have seen booms of modernization such as Japan, China, and South Korea, the supply and demand of professional sport has increased. The model of professional sport found in Asia includes a tendency to mix and match elements of the North American and European models. Consider the case of Japan and the way in which it followed both North America and Europe models in the development of its professional sport leagues.

The sport of baseball, or *Yakyu* (field-ball), as it is known in Japan, has roots that date back to the late 19th century. Although it is not a traditional sport such as the martial-arts sports of sumo, judo, or kendo, baseball has fast become one of the national pastimes in the Land of the Rising Sun. Baseball was brought to Japan by Americans, of course, and after starting at Tokyo University, it quickly spread to the rest of the country. As a professional sport, baseball dates back to 1934 in Japan, with the creation of the Greater Japan Tokyo Baseball Club. But it was not until 1950 that the current professional league, the Nippon Professional Baseball (NPB) league was formed (Whiting, 1990). The league copied the design of the MLB, creating a Pacific League and a Central League that emulated the rules (whether or not to use a designated hitter) of the two North American leagues respectively. The NPB also emulates the MLB by using a reverse-order draft, as well as playoffs and a closed league system, thus making the NPB in many aspects a Japanese version of the MLB. In this way, Japanese baseball has sought to copy MLB, the oldest and most high-profile baseball league in the world.

A similar approach was used by founders of the other professional sport leagues in Japan, such as the professional football league, the J League. With its formation in 1993, the J League sought to reproduce professional football in Japan using a league design similar to the Apertura and Clausura design used in South America, where the season is divided into two parts. The winners of each section then meet each other at the end of the season to determine the overall champion. This format was used for over a decade until the J League decided to change to a European format, in which the winner of a single season would be crowned the league champion. This setup avoided confusion and helped the J League emulate the European professional sport model by allowing multiple competitions and creating less confusion among fans about which contest teams were competing in. These changes also came about because of the growing popularity of European football in Japan, as well as diminished interest in South American leagues. The J League catered to the wishes of fans by molding its league structure into one that emulated leagues that had higher popularity in Japan. Additionally, the J League has recently created several tiers of football leagues, so that the league is open and has promotion and relegation like leagues in Europe.

Although the structure of leagues is one element that the Japanese professional sport model has copied from North America and Europe, the case of ownership is quite different. Whereas in North America ownership comes in the form of a mix of individuals and some corporations, and European ownership is through a mix of private and corporate ownership, Japan uses an entirely different model. The Japanese model of ownership in professional sport is entirely based on corporate ownership of teams, often as a part or subsidiary of a larger parent company. Even more notable is the manner in which corporate ownership involves itself with sport teams in Japan. In other countries, corporations run a sport team as part of their business, seeking to maximize profits either for the team or for the organization as a whole. In the Japanese model, the parent company uses the sport team as a form of advertising and public outreach; the primary function of the team is to heighten the public image of the parent corporation. To do this, Japanese corporations subsidize the sport teams that they own, often dumping tens of millions of dollars per year into the teams with no expectation of positive financial return.

A primary example of this is the Yomiuri Corporation, Japan's largest nongovernmental media organization. The Yomiuri Corporation has invested heavily in sport teams, owning both the Yomiuri Giants (Tokyo Giants) as well as Tokyo 1969 (formerly Kawasaki Verdy) of the J League. The Yomiuri newspaper and television outlets reach a large number of households throughout Japan, and through these media channels, the organization managed to promote the Tokyo Giants and Kawasaki Verdy as "Japan's team." Because of the wide media reach of the corporation, they positioned their own baseball product ahead of all competing baseball teams. This practice extends to the point that only in the last decade or two have fans been able to watch more of their own local games on television than those of the Yomiuri teams. Although the Yomiuri Corporation has managed to capitalize on this system, others have not been so successful.

The Daiei Corporation was the former owner of the Fukuoka Softbank Hawks, a team on one of Japan's smaller islands. Although the corporation had a stable business in the form of department stores across the country, they tried to expand too much around their sport team, believing that they could bring in more business to the retail outlets in this way. Daiei took on a massive building project that included a domed stadium with a three-piece rotating roof, a luxury 40-story hotel connected to the stadium, and a huge shopping-mall complex that sprawled around the stadium. Although this type of project was common in other countries, Daiei did this on prime real estate in one of the most expensive countries in the world at the time.

Massive losses soon followed. The department store business was able to maintain the corporation for a time, but when the department stores experienced financial hardship, the corporation began to sink and was forced to sell off assets. The Softbank Internet company bought the baseball franchise and took over its operation. Within Japan, other corporations that own professional sport teams include Nippon Ham (ham and meat products), Yakult (yogurt and dairy), Seibu (department stores and railways), Mazda (automobiles), and Lotte (various food products and a fast-food chain) (Whiting, 1990).

This hybrid model of league structure, which matches that found in the country in which each sport is most popular, coupled with ownership by large corporations engaged in other businesses, is found not only in Japan but also in other countries throughout East Asia. The Korean professional baseball and football leagues both use a similar approach. The Korean Baseball Organization uses a closed model like North American leagues but places all teams into a single league, mostly because of the lack of enough teams in the country to fill out two leagues. Similarly, the K League (Korea's professional football league) follows the European model by using a single league season and having teams play in multiple competitions. The league is closed because of the lack of any lower-tier league big enough and strong enough to have a reliable rotation of teams for promotion and relegation in each season. The K League is similar to the J League in that many of the K League franchises are owned by corporations who consider the team to be part of a promotional tool for their other businesses and do not necessarily focus on running the team as efficiently as possible. Although the formats slightly differ from country to country, most leagues in Asia follow this method of copying the dominant league model in that sport, as well as having corporate ownership of teams to heighten the visibility and reputation of that corporation. In the case of football they follow the European professional sport league structure, and for baseball and basketball they tend to follow the North American model. Professional sport in Asia is thus a hybrid model that emulates the best leagues in each sport rather than uses a standard across all sport leagues in a country or the region.

Chinese professional sport provides one of the more confusing yet interesting prospects in considering the structure, ownership, and modes of financing professional sport teams. The three leagues that stand out in China are the China Baseball League, China Super League (football), and the Chinese Basketball Association. The China Baseball League and Chinese Basketball Association, both related to the North American model, follow the North America structure of league organization to some extent. The ownership of these leagues, however, is rather mixed. Some teams are owned by individual owners, and others are owned by corporations. Besides being owned by corporations, some teams have corporate sponsorship agreements that bring in revenue, but these arrangements are somewhat volatile and have been known to change even during the season.

Like most Asian football leagues, the Chinese Super League, the top professional football league in China, follows the European model. Although the promotion and relegation system was not included in the league's early years, it has now been put in place because of the newly formed second division. Additionally, the teams in the league can compete in multiple competitions and use transfers to obtain and sell players. The ownership structure of the Chinese Super League is much more convoluted, partly because of the political situation in China. Although China has risen as an economic power in the last several decades, the government still controls many industries, so team ownership in the Chinese Super League takes several forms. Private or publicly traded corporations own some clubs, but in other cases clubs are controlled and owned by state-owned corporations.

The nature of the Chinese economic boom coupled with the current political climate and desire for professional sport within the country has contributed to the formulation of a hybrid model of ownership that is probably unique to China. Although the connection between politics and sport is often frowned upon, the existence of state-run teams in Chinese professional football has yet to cause any major issues or prevent teams from competing in domestic or international competitions. The Asian hybrid model of professional sport has truly come to life in China, allowing a variety of structures and ownership groups to coexist within the Chinese sport environment and produce leagues that, while still relatively small, could potentially grow into one of the best environments for hosting top-flight professional sport leagues.

Asia is proving to be a hotbed of professional sport, which is growing in popularity among both local and regional fans. This popularity has come from a combination of participating in international competitions and using the structural models from leagues that have proved to be the most popular. At the same time these structures are combined most often with corporate ownership, which subsidizes the sport teams. Although this arrangement has led to the folding of many teams and fiscal irresponsibility, a trend toward better responsibility and teams being able to survive as stand-alone entities is developing. Thus, the hybrid model of professional sport in Asia that combines their own ownership style with the league structures of the powerful leagues from Europe and North America is proving to be successful.

Learning Activity

1. Investigate a professional sport league not described in this chapter, from a country other than your own.
2. How does the league operate?
3. What aspects of the models of professional sport presented in this chapter describe the league?

Consequences of League Design and Team Ownership

The design and ownership methods of North American and European leagues lead to a variety of interrelated outcomes for each region. In Europe the multiple competitions that are an essential part of European sport require teams that wish to have good performances in all these competitions to buy more talent than they would need if they were to compete only in a single league competition. Competing in multiple contests often requires teams to play more matches in a week than a single squad of players can realistically handle. Teams in Europe thus must spend more money on player salaries and transfer fees. Combined with the lack of any kind of cap on player salaries or transfer fees, this system drives up salary costs for many teams but increases revenues for only a few successful teams.

This circumstance is exactly why Abramovich made his massive loan to Chelsea after purchasing the club—so that they could pay the transfer fees for players needed to compete for titles in multiple competitions. This action has been effective in this particular case. Chelsea won their first Premier League title since the 1950s, repeated as league champion, and even won the FA Cup after the loan was made. Again, the important point is that teams must spend a lot to perform well in multiple competitions and reap the benefits of playing in them. In this case a team needed to spend money to make more money, which is not a big problem for the rich larger clubs, but the smaller clubs are usually unable to access these competitions and the profits that come along with them. This situation differs from that in North America because most leagues, with the exception of Major League Baseball, have caps on the amount of money that teams can spend on talent. Therefore, teams are forced to limit their spending on talent, so even smaller teams still have some access to star players in the league. In this sense, the North American model could be considered more efficient because it not only reduces costs and improves competitive balance but also prevents bidding wars and the arms races of trying to stockpile the top talent among the richest teams.

Although the structure of European leagues plays a role in these outcomes, some blame needs to be put on ownership, especially the ever-evolving nature of ownership of English clubs. Teams owned by shareholders must be more responsible with their finances, whereas teams owned by wealthy people can spend large sums on salaries and transfer fees to compete with other top teams. An arms race among top teams has developed, especially in the Premier League, whereby increased spending by a few teams leads other teams to respond in kind, creating a feedback loop. This type of loop cannot occur in most North American leagues, because of institutional controls placed on spending. Even in Major League Baseball, which lacks a true cap, a luxury tax is in place that taxes teams' spending on player talent over a certain level. Because teams in most North American leagues play in only one championship, even the luxury tax is significant enough to deter most teams from spending too

much money on player talent. Additionally, the combination of the organizational structure of European leagues and ownership has led to disastrous situations for some clubs. Leeds United, a former EPL club, is one such case. In the 1990s Leeds United began to acquire talent that helped the team finish high enough in the Premiership standings to qualify for the UEFA Champions League. Over the next several years, the club continued its strong performance and gained millions of euros from Champions League play. The club took out loans to acquire more playing talent, assuming that the team would qualify for Champions League again. The club failed to qualify the following season and found itself with excessive debt, which led to a fire sale of the club's top talent to other top-tier teams in Europe. The club ownership had gambled, looking to profit from the structure of European professional sport leagues, and failed. The club was subsequently forced to sell its training grounds and stadium (BBC Sport Online, 2004), was placed in administration (bankruptcy), and has still not recovered from the financial difficulties. This example shows that the ownership model, combined with the league structure within Europe, drives up costs, which in turn leaves many teams in immense debt and increases the disparity between the top and bottom of the leagues in terms of on-field and financial outcomes.

The consequences of promotion and relegation are also intriguing, especially in terms of the financial incentives attached to teams that are seeking promotion. Research shows that promotion increases fan interest, which translates to a large increase in attendance and revenue for the club after promotion to a higher league (Noll, 2002). Furthermore, the promotion and relegation system produces an incentive for mediocre teams to bounce back and forth between leagues, because the increase in revenue and fan attendance lasts several years after promotion, in some cases even after teams are demoted back to a lower league. Sport franchises operating in a promotion and relegation system may have an incentive to be dropped to a lower league, so that they can fight their way back up and continue cycling back and forth to reap the rewards of promotion repeatedly (Noll, 2002). In comparison, the North America closed leagues would seem to be inefficient because of the static nature of the teams in a league. The lack of incentive to perform better, and in some cases, enhanced incentive for teams at the bottom of a league to perform worse in North America, would seem to lead to a potential loss of attendance and viewership, and thus lower revenue.

Although the promotion and relegation and ownership systems of Europe are beneficial to many clubs, in some instances teams may not put forth full effort in these leagues to maximize their potential profits. In other cases, teams that wish to compete at a higher level must make heavy investments in their squads, leading to increased costs and the possibility of falling into deeper debt. Thus, the ownership and league design of professional sport leagues in Europe causes teams to put forth different levels of effort in leagues. A certain level of disparity results, caused by teams being forced to decide whether they want to spend large sums to compete with the top of a league or to field marginal teams that are able to be promoted repeatedly and gain the rewards of doing so.

The North American and European models of sport leagues and ownership are quite different, and both have positives and negatives. Where one league is more efficient in one aspect, it is often hampered in another area. Both systems have some inefficiencies. This conclusion would seem to point toward the use of a hybrid of these two models to create a league structure combined with certain ownership types to create a more efficient professional sporting league. Yet to date, most of the hybrid models have not chosen to innovate. Most have just copied these two models and made small adjustments to fit the needs of the league, fans, and owners in that region. Thus, it is difficult to say which of these models is best for organizing a professional sport league.

Learning Activity

1. Look online for various sources of sport finance data (such as *Forbes*). The data can take the form of financial reports, databases of income, expenses, player salaries, and so forth.

2. Examine the data and write a report that critically examines the financial well-being of the league or team that you investigated.

Outcomes With the North American League Model

After the explosion of media broadcast rights in the 1970s, professional sport in North America quickly become a multibillion-dollar industry. With this increased media attention came increased scrutiny of team performance on and off the field. As we will see, performance on the field, and on the balance sheet, is influenced by league design.

On-Field Performance

Within the major professional sport leagues in North America, some teams have been dominant. Their names are traditionally synonymous with winning and championships in their leagues. Teams in this group include the New York Yankees in MLB, the Boston Celtics and Los Angeles Lakers in the NBA, and the Pittsburgh Steelers and Dallas Cowboys in the NFL. Although this group of teams remains strong, parity within North American leagues has increased in recent years, especially in the distribution of championships. As mentioned earlier, the North American model uses a playoff system that allows a certain number of teams to compete for the championship through a single-elimination tournament. A champion eventually emerges from this system. This postseason system generates a more equal distribution of championships in North American leagues than does the system in Europe, where champions are decided purely on the final standings.

Consider the case of the NFL, arguably the most popular league in North America. Eleven different champions have emerged in the last 16 seasons, which represents a much more even distribution compared with European professional sport leagues. The distribution of championships among MLB and NHL teams also includes 11 different teams winning championships in the last 16 seasons of play. The NBA has been the most concentrated of the North American leagues in terms of championship distribution; only seven different teams have won a championship over the last 16 years, although the NBA championship distribution is less concentrated than that of many European leagues. Overall, North American professional sport leagues appear to have greater parity than European professional leagues do, based on championship distribution. So far this argument has proved to be somewhat legitimate in considering the Indian Premier League, one of the few other leagues in the world that has an elimination playoff system to decide its league champion. Although the league has existed for only three years and has a relatively small number of teams, it has had a different champion every year, and every one of the eight teams has made it to within a game of the championship match. But the small sample size does not offer conclusive evidence that the North American system provides a better distribution of championships.

Although some of the parity in North American leagues can be attributed to the playoff system, other factors come into effect. Indeed, balance is a point of emphasis in North American sport leagues. Managers, the media, and fans constantly discuss the subject. Key factors that improve competitive balance in North American leagues include the reverse-order entry draft, which rewards the weaker teams in a league with the first pick of new talent in each season, salary caps, and revenue sharing that provides teams with a minimum level of funds to spend on playing talent. These institutional differences drive much of the parity in North American leagues and constitute a vital part of how this model creates more uncertainty of outcome about league champions in each season (Maxcy & Mondello, 2006). Note that the reverse-order draft was instituted by the aforementioned NPB of Japan in their attempt to emulate the North American model of professional baseball. Curiously, the NPB has in recent years continued using the reverse-order draft but has experimented with a variety of manipulations of the usual draft system, including the *gyaku-shimei* system, which allowed a consensus top pick to choose which team he would play for.

Financial Performance

The financial performance of North American teams varies across leagues. Two leagues (the MLB and NHL) have suffered numerous work stoppages because of disagreements between owners and the players unions. Although the most recent MLB work stoppage dampened fan interest in the sport for a few years, the league eventually recovered. The weaker NHL, on the other hand, which recently had a season-long lockout, was probably the least popular of the major North American professional sport leagues. Some thought that the strike would

lead to the demise of the league. In addition, in recent years MLB has raised the threat of contraction, while the NFL and NBA have continued to try to expand their leagues into new markets. In this environment, the financial health of clubs in North America seems to be quite variable. To illustrate this variability, consider the recent experience of the NHL and NFL.

In the 2003–04 season, the NHL was in a period of financial difficulty, and the teams reported an aggregate operating loss of about US$96 million. The owners claimed that salary expenses were too high and that there was need for a salary cap, which the players rejected because they were unwilling to take a pay cut. After a lockout canceled the 2004–05 season, the players union and the owners finally negotiated a collective bargaining agreement (CBA) that placed both a cap and a minimum on salaries that teams could pay in a season. Resuming play in the 2005–06 season, the league saw attendance grow, and the teams as a whole earned an aggregate operating income of around US$125 million, a reversal of fortunes from where they had been just two years earlier. In the seasons after the lockout, the NHL as a whole has continued to have financial success. The salary range has allowed teams to cut expenses, and the league has seen a boom in revenues. Although the league as a whole remains in good financial shape, several teams are losing millions of dollars every season. Yet in comparison with leagues from the European model, the NHL seems to be headed toward better stability as a whole because the new CBA helps to keep salaries low. In contrast, European football clubs and organizations are still dealing with the lack of controls on player salaries and transfer fees. Although the top European clubs continue to see great success, the rest of the teams are forced into mediocre roles or crushing financial debt. North American teams enjoy both better stability for all and greater profit potential across the board.

Turning from one of the weaker leagues in North America to the strongest, we now examine the NFL, which has become probably the most powerful league in the world in terms of financial performance. The NFL as a whole has seen its profits jump from an aggregate operating income of US$589 million in 2006 to US$1.033 billion in 2008. Five teams reported operating losses during the 2006 season, but only two, the Seattle Seahawks and the Oakland Raiders, reported operating losses in 2008. In its 2009 financial rankings, *Forbes* magazine listed 19 NFL franchises with values of over US$1 billion; 6 of the 10 most valuable franchises in North America were in the NFL. Although Manchester United was considered the world's most valuable team, only one other team in England made the top ten (Arsenal), and Real Madrid was the only other European team to make the rankings. The NFL has the most billion-dollar teams, and Van Riper (2009) estimated that the league has a collective worth of about US$33.3 billion. The NFL's dominance of the team valuation rankings results not only from its loyal fan base and TV contracts but also because of its existence within the North American model, which differs from the European model that places fewer restrictions on team spending.

The numbers clearly indicate the sheer size and power of North American franchises; only 4 of 24 clubs valued at US$1 billion or more play in Europe. Although the NFL makes up the majority of the billion-dollar club, note that the other leagues in North America are valuable as well. MLB franchises are worth an estimated US$14.1 billion in aggregate, the NBA is worth about US$11.4 billion, and the NHL is worth an estimated US$6.6 billion. Van Riper (2009) is quick to point out that North American sport franchises may have peaked in value, especially given the recent drop in foreign investment in the big four major sport leagues in North America. This trend is quite the opposite of that seen in Europe, where more foreign investors are becoming interested in investing in professional sport teams, especially those within the Premier League. Thus, although North America may hold

CASE STUDY

The Indian Premier League: The New Power in Professional Sport

Often overlooked by much of the world, the Indian Premier League (IPL), the top professional cricket league in India, is fastly growing into one of the most valuable and powerful sport leagues in the world. Formed in 2008, the IPL is composed of eight teams owned by a mixture of private owners, private corporations, and publicly traded corporations. Thus, the IPL is truly a hybrid ownership model, whereby the franchises in the league are owned by three different types of owners. The formation of the league was also unique in that the owners were chosen by being the eight highest bidders in an auction, which generated over US$700 million for the league to help begin operations. Although the ownership style and methods of generating revenue have been unique, the structure of the league has mostly followed along the lines of the North America model. The league is a closed one, with no chance of teams being promoted or relegated from the league; additionally the league champion is decided by a series of playoff games after the regular season. One structural element that was not copied from North America is a reverse-order draft that would give the worst teams in the league the first chance to sign the top players coming in to the league. But a call has arisen from many in the league, media, and the public for a draft system to

be implemented in upcoming years. Thus, the IPL will probably soon evolve to emulate more closely the structure of leagues found in North America.

Another curious element to the IPL has been its quick growth in both the value of the league and the salaries of players. As of 2010 the IPL as a league was valued at over US$4 billion, but the eight individual franchises have been valued at only around US$100 million each. In this case the whole is truly worth more than the sum of the parts, because the brand image and marketing done by the league has helped to increase the value of the IPL. With the growth in the value of the league, the growth in salaries has also been spectacular. The IPL offers the second highest average salary of any sporting league in the world, trailing only the National Basketball Association (NBA). Two new franchises are set to join the league in the 2011 season, and the profitability of the league seems to be growing because most of the franchises in the league turned a profit in the 2009 season. Although most of the Western world focuses on football, baseball, American football, and basketball, cricket, which is played in a large number of booming countries, could prove to be a new and exciting professional sport from both a financial and spectator perspective.

its place as being stronger in terms of team values and profitability in professional sport, this circumstance could change with the current trends in the professional sporting landscape.

Outcomes With the European League Model

Some concern has arisen in European leagues that the financing model produces increasing disparity between the top teams in leagues versus the others. Nowhere is this issue more evident than in football, where the gap between the top and bottom teams in top leagues seems to be growing constantly. Much of this disparity is a product of the organization of these leagues, as well as the financing that teams receive.

On-Field Performance

Generalizing about the on-field performance of European professional sport teams is difficult, partly because of the multiple competitions that clubs are involved in throughout the season. But in the domestic leagues in Europe, especially football, a few clubs continually dominate the leagues from one year to the next. Take the example of the Premier League, which in its first 16 seasons of play has had only four clubs win the championship and has seen Manchester United win the championship 10 times. Similarly, the German Bundesliga has been dominated by Bayern Munich, who has won 9 of the last 16 league titles. The Spanish La Liga has been dominated by two teams, Barcelona and Real Madrid, who in the last 25 years have won 9 and 11 league titles respectively. Although the overall competitive balance of these leagues may be quite good compared with leagues in North America in terms of distribution of wins during the regular season, or even win shares, a great deal of disparity is apparent in terms of championships. And with multiple competitions, the more prestigious and higher the payout is, the greater the chance is that one of the top-tier teams will win it. Consider the situation in the United Kingdom, where only four teams have won the EPL title in the last 16 years. Six different teams have won the FA Cup, and nine teams have won the League Cup (Carling Cup) championship over this period. Teams usually focus more on winning in the league and winning the FA Cup than they do the League Cup, which is often a competition in which teams field squads composed of substitutes who would not get much playing time in other competitions. Although leagues in other countries have copied the European model to some extent, other factors in these countries must be considered in looking at championship distribution. In the J League in Japan, which has copied the European model, only seven different teams have won the 17 J League championships. Thus the J League displays a pattern similar to that seen in the United Kingdom in that a few select teams win most of the championships. This circumstance lends credence to the belief that the structure of the European model creates some imbalance when it comes to the distribution of championships.

The better balance, in terms of distribution of wins in European sport leagues, can be directly connected to the incentives generated by the promotion and relegation system. Although it is fairly certain which group of teams will be competing for the championship in each season, the teams at the bottom of the **league table** (the standings in the league in terms of wins, ties, and losses) will always be trying to win as many games as possible to avoid relegation. This situation is opposite that in North America, where teams often have an incentive not to win games at the end of a season so that they can obtain a high draft pick in the next reverse-order entry draft. The European and North American models generate different performance incentives within leagues. In North America, teams in the middle of the table will often be close to a position in the playoffs, especially in leagues in which a large number of teams qualify for the postseason. In this case, teams in the middle of the standings will have an incentive to try hard, whereas teams at the top and bottom will not because they either will have already sealed a playoff berth or will be out of the playoff picture and will shirk to gain a better draft pick.

Europe presents the opposite case. Teams at the top of a league will play hard through a season to fight for the championship based on the final standings of the league, as well as battle for the top few spots in the league to gain entry into international competitions such as the UEFA Champions League and the UEFA Europa League. The teams at the bottom will play hard to avoid relegation. But teams in the middle of the table will have no incentive to put forth maximum effort. Those teams who know that they are secure from being relegated but are not able to compete for the championship or a place in European competitions will have no reason to try as hard to win matches.

Research into differences between the closed leagues of North America versus the open (promotion and relegation) leagues of Europe has found that the use of open leagues tends to produce incentives for teams to put forth maximum effort toward winning each match (Ross & Szymanski, 2002; Szymanski & Valletti, 2005). Furthermore, the improved match effort and competitive balance in open leagues should create increased fan interest, leading to higher team revenues. But Fort (2000), in his examination of the differences between European and North American professional sport leagues, noted that differences in revenue could cause differences in competitive balance. The growing revenue disparity in European professional sport leagues, as well as the incentives generated by the long-lasting effect of promotion for teams to shirk strategically and field weaker squads and then put forth maximum effort to jump back and forth between leagues (Noll, 2002), creates additional on-field imbalances. Thus, the European league model should lead to more balance in leagues and ownership forms (e.g., mixture of both public and private ownership), as well as differences in revenue and popularity of teams that cause some of the imbalances that exist in European professional sport leagues.

The difference between having playoffs, salary caps, and a reverse-order draft versus multiple competitions and promotion and relegation creates different outcomes in terms of on-field performance (Fort, 2000). For example, the North American model uses a single competition, which allows a large number of teams to compete for a single championship through a playoff system based on regular season standings. The European model, on the other hand, uses multiple competitions, awards the league title solely on team performance during the season, and creates other championship possibilities through knockout cup competitions and European super leagues. These markedly different championship structures in North America and Europe present very different methods of organization, which in turn create these differences in on-field performance between leagues that follow these two models of

professional sport. North American and European leagues generate different incentives for teams to perform at different levels, making it impossible to say which system is truly better.

Financial Performance

An analysis of the financial performance of European teams further highlights the growing disparity that exists within leagues and illustrates how the professional sport business has become less profitable because of the growing expenses that all teams are facing. In an environment in which a few clubs are earning records profits, the disparity among organizations suggests that the expenses in terms of player transfer fees and salaries may be excessive. Also, many teams have been saddled with large debt from building new state-of-the-art facilities with larger capacity and improved amenities to try to increase attendance and match-day revenues. Even with the increased revenues earned by European professional teams, the 2010 Deloitte Football Money League report showed that only about 20 or so clubs in all of Europe brought in annual revenue of more than €100 million (US$144 million). Most of the clubs on this list are from England, Italy, Germany, France, and Spain, which illustrates the growing disparity in European professional leagues.

Further evidence of disparity can be seen in the financial performance across specific European leagues. Table 15.1 shows the financial estimates for the Premier League, including revenue, profits, and debts for many of the clubs. First, note that only three EPL clubs in 2006 turned a profit: Arsenal, Tottenham Hotspur, and West Bromwich Albion. Furthermore, the two most profitable teams, Arsenal and Tottenham, are both based in London. Although Arsenal earned among the highest profits and revenue, and had among the highest estimated values, the team also had one of the largest outstanding debts of teams in the EPL. At least five teams in the EPL had outstanding debts of more than £100 million (US$187 million), and all but one of these clubs could be considered to be among the top teams in the league. This number could possibly be higher, because Malcolm Glazer's takeover of Manchester United reportedly put them several million pounds in debt.

Table 15.1 paints quite a dismal picture of the financing of the Premier League, because only four

Table 15.1 EPL Club Financial Information Entering the 2008–09 Season

Club	Value	Revenue	TV revenue	Expenses	Profit	Debt
Arsenal	£598	£164	£47.0	£127	£37	£416
Aston Villa	£95	£53	£42.3	£56	−£3	£64
Blackburn Rovers			£40.2		−£3	£17
Bolton Wanderers			£32.0		−£2	£40
Chelsea	£381	£190	£45.6	£266	−£76	£578*
Everton	£98	£51	£42.1	£60	−£9	£59
Fulham			£31.3		−£16	£182
Hull City					−£2	£1
Liverpool	£523	£134	£45.4	£112	£22	£350
Manchester City	£95	£57	£39.7	£68	−£11	£154**
Manchester United	£897	£196	£49.3			***
Middlesbrough			£34.2		−£13	£84
Newcastle United	£150	£87	£39.2	£120	−£33	
Portsmouth			£40.4		−£23	£32
Stoke City					−£3	£3
Sunderland			£33.6		−£15	£45
Tottenham Hotspur	£207	£103	£36.0	£75	£28	£45
West Bromwich Albion					£5	£4
West Ham United	£97	£57	£36.8	£79	−£22	£36
Wigan Athletic			£33.4		−£1	£54
Total			**£668.5**		**−£140.5**	**£1,431.8**

Notes: Numbers are in millions of pounds (£1 = about US$1.97). The totals presented in the last line are estimates; the actual number may be higher or lower.

*Chelsea's debt is entirely owed to its owner, Roman Abramovich.

**Manchester City's debt is its value before the current takeover.

***Manchester United's debt is unknown but is estimated to be the largest in the Premier League.

Data from www.footballeconomy.com/reports.htm.

teams turned a profit and two of those were saddled with high debt. Although EPL membership guarantees high television revenues as well as corporate sponsorship and match-day revenue, the expenses associated with fielding an EPL-caliber team seem to weigh heavy on the pocketbooks of most of these clubs. The majority of EPL clubs have yearly losses of several million pounds, which, combined with the limited access to European competitions by weaker clubs, leads to a league in which only a few teams have the financial ability to challenge for a title and gain access to additional revenues with-

out running the risk of failing and going broke, as Leeds United did. Although a number of clubs in Europe are in financial trouble, the same cannot usually be said about football clubs following the European model in other regions of the world. Some clubs in South America and Asia have lived beyond their means, but in these cases much of the failure of the team was not because of the sport franchise but because of the failure of parent corporations and organizations.

Another disturbing feature of EPL finances is that some teams have debts that exceed the estimated value of the club, and a few more that have debts that are a large percentage of their estimated value. Notable among these are Chelsea and Manchester City, the former of which is considered one of the top teams in Europe and ranks very high in the Deloitte Football Money League Rankings. Chelsea is probably one of the strangest cases in football in that the team has debt that exceeds the club value, although this debt is actually owed to the owner. This debt has come about because of Abramovich's constant quest for high-quality football at Chelsea, no matter what the cost. In this sense, Chelsea's financial position is not as bad as the numbers indicate because the personal wealth of the oil tycoon keeps them afloat. But if Abramovich tires of his quest for on-field success and sells the team, the financial consequences could be disastrous.

The case of Manchester City is more dubious in that the club was not backed by their current owners at the time that these numbers were released. Rather, Manchester City has always been among the clubs consistently stuck in the middle of the table in the EPL, usually safe from relegation by the end of the season but too far from qualifying for European competitions to care much about winning. These high debts may have kept the club mired in mediocrity and led to the purchase of Manchester City by the former prime minister of Thailand, Thaksin Shinawatra, who was kicked out of office by a military coup, possibly brought on by his own corrupt dealings (Fetini, 2008).

Overall, the evidence indicates that few European teams turn profits. At the same time, the revenues earned are constantly increasing and top clubs can definitely earn large profits. One major theme that emerges repeatedly in this chapter is the disparity in European professional sport. In the case of football, significant disparity is clearly seen in terms of on-field and financial performance. The European model of financing and organization of professional sport leagues may be due for a change if current trends continue. As more teams face financial difficulties, teams across Europe will need to slash costs to turn any kind of profit. One method that might improve this situation is the installation of some type of salary cap or transfer fee cap that would reduce payroll costs enough that teams in the middle or bottom of a league could afford to field more competitive teams.

In conclusion, the European professional sport environment features rich and poor clubs existing and competing in the same leagues. The positions of teams within the leagues and the talent and revenues that each receive are polar opposites. Windfalls generated from the popular teams at the top of the tables prop up the leagues, but many teams face difficult choices between being fiscally responsible and risking relegation because they do not buy enough talent or gambling on the team's continued success and spending a fortune on talent, as Leeds United did, with the hope of ensuring long-term success. Although it may be wrong to state that the North American model of professional sport is better, it can be argued that the franchises in the top leagues in North America have much more stability than their counterparts in Europe.

Summary

This chapter focused on the financing and business of professional sport leagues around the world. Specifically the structure and organization of sporting leagues in North America, Europe, and Asia were considered and discussed in depth. It is clear that there are many differences in how sport leagues are organized within each of these regions and that these factors have financial implications. One of the primary differences is the concept of open and closed sporting leagues, as well as the use of promotion and relegation to move teams from one league to another in those leagues which are open. Additionally, leagues in different regions vary in regards to methods of ownership, financing and costs, and player movement.

Not only do North American sport leagues follow the closed model and European leagues the open model, but these leagues also are different from one another in terms of ownership, player movement, and many other organizational and financial areas. In examining Asian leagues, we find that leagues within this region tend to use a more hybrid model, where leagues copy the financial and organizational methods most suited to their sport. In all, it is clear that there are a large number of factors which change from one region to the next when considering the finances and organization of sport leagues. These differences impact the management, organization, and operation of sport leagues around the world.

? Review and Discussion Questions

1. Explain promotion and relegation in your own words. How does this system of league structure differ from that used in North American professional sport leagues?

2. Discuss the feasibility of implementing a promotion and relegation system in North America. Do you think that it would be successful? Why or why not?

3. From a financial perspective, what differences are brought forth by having different ownership styles for North American and European professional sport leagues?

4. Discuss the roles of different types of revenue streams in financing professional sport franchises. Consider how the current revenue streams differ from previous ones.

5. Compare and contrast the North American and European models of sport finance. Which do you believe is more feasible, and why?

6. Considering the material presented in this chapter, what future trends do you think will take root in the financing of professional sport? Will this be a global phenomenon, or will it be one that is more localized (i.e., North America, Europe, Asia)?

7. Consider the various league models employed in Asia. Can something be learned about how the various models have been changed and hybridized to meet local needs? Do you think that this approach could prove to be a new model of considering sport ownership and finance around the world? Why or why not?

Corporate Social Responsibility, Sport, and Development

Lyndsay M.C. Hayhurst, MA
University of Toronto, Canada

Bruce Kidd, PhD
University of Toronto, Canada

Chapter Objectives

After studying this chapter, you will be able to do the following:

- Define corporate social responsibility
- Describe the emergence and evolution of corporate social responsibility
- Describe and interpret corporate social responsibility using both managerial theory and critical theory
- Understand the efforts of workers and NGOs to win fair labor conditions and responses of corporations
- Examine how corporations are responding to the call to conform to basic human rights
- Describe and critically analyze the role of corporations in international development

Key Terms

Many corporations today proclaim their commitment to social responsibility. The cell phone giant Vodafone promises to conduct its business in line with the highest standards of environmental sustainability, fair labor practices, and accountability. Its website publicizes the United Nations' Universal Declaration of Human Rights and the International Labour Organization's (ILO) core conventions; spells out the company's obligations to employees, customers, and the public at large; and gives annual reports on its suppliers. Vodafone also sponsors the Homeless World Cup and a number of other "sport and music projects to benefit some of the most disadvantaged young people and their communities" (Vodafone, 2009). Under the slogan "Acting with a global mind," the Canadian retailer Hudson's Bay Company has committed to "foster and enhance sustainable business practices throughout our organization, particularly in the areas of the environment, associate wellness, community investment and ethical sourcing" (HBC, 2007). HBC currently supplies the uniforms for Canadian teams in the Summer and Winter Olympic Games. Companies that are heavily involved in the global sport marketplace are prominent in their commitment to corporate social responsibility (CSR). The sporting goods leaders Adidas, Puma, Nike, and Reebok all boast such policies and practices, and contribute to the development of sport in the two-thirds world. The World Federation of the Sporting Good Industry tracks CSR among its members and publicizes best practices (WFSGI, 2009). CSR has become an indispensable part of international sport management today.

What are the origins of corporate social responsibility, and why has it become so important? How is CSR regarded by the companies themselves, their workers and consumers, and social scientists who study the modern corporation? What are the links between CSR and human rights? How has it shaped international sport development? The purpose of this chapter is to answer these questions.

Throughout this chapter, we will use the terms *one-third world* (to refer to the advanced economies of Europe, North America, Japan, and Australia) and *two-thirds world* (to refer to the rest of the world) as discussed by Gustavo Esteva and Madhu Prakash (1998). We do so for three reasons: to encourage critical thinking about how income and opportunity is distributed between regions of the globe, to

indicate that the majority of the world's population lives outside the advanced economies, and to avoid judgments about people's quality of life. We fear that the terms *developed world* or *first world* and *developing world* or *third world* are misleading; these terms suggest that all people living in developed societies live unproblematic lives and that those living in developing or third-world countries are always plagued by inadequacies. Neither circumstance is true.

Defining Corporate Social Responsibility

Corporate social responsibility (CSR) has been defined in many ways. The term overlaps with similar concepts such as corporate sustainability, corporate sustainable development, corporate responsibility, and corporate citizenship. At its most basic level, CSR connotes a commitment to behave ethically and harm no one. In more elaborate definitions, it means that corporations will act in accordance with approved labor codes and environmental policies and become advocates for human rights. Four ideas are contained in the most ambitious use of the concept:

1. that the company will abide by internationally accepted labor practices and ensure that its suppliers and sellers do the same;

2. that its production and business practices, from the initial extraction of raw materials through the manufacture, advertising, and distribution of products to the ultimate disposal of its used products, will be environmentally sustainable;

3. that it will be transparent and accountable, that is, it will provide regular reports on its business practices to its shareholders, employees, governments, and members of the public; and

4. that it will be supportive of **human rights**, or rights that one has because one is a human being. These rights aim to preserve and protect human dignity and ensure civil, economic, and social well-being.

Those who support CSR believe that it makes companies more competitive by supporting operational efficiency gains, improved risk management, favorable relations with the investment community and improved access to capital, enhanced employee relations, stronger relationships with communities and an enhanced license to operate, and improved reputation and branding (Canada, 2009).

In this definition, CSR is distinct from **philanthropy**, the act of donating money or goods, resulting in no financial or material reward to the donor, to a religious, charitable, or educational organization or social cause. An increasing number of sport corporations and even professional athletes have established foundations for philanthropic purposes (Babiak, Tainsky, & Juravich, 2008). CSR is also distinct from celebrity- or cause-related marketing, the practice of sponsoring individual athletes, teams, or social campaigns to increase a firm's legitimacy, brand, or market share, although such marketing may blend with the support of human rights. For example, in 2007 Puma launched its Peace One Day football collection, linking the sale of a special line of gear and accessories to the United Nations International Day of Peace and the 2008 African Cup of Nations (Peace One Day, 2009). Although philanthropy and cause-related marketing stem from the same impulses and pressures as CSR, keeping these distinctions in mind is important, as table 16.1 sets out.

Emergence of Corporate Social Responsibility in Sport

Although *corporate social responsibility* (CSR) is a recent term, it stems from ambitions and concerns as old as capitalism itself about the social impacts

Table 16.1 Taxonomy of Global Corporate Social Engagement Activities and Examples in Sport and International Development (Hayhurst, 2009b)[1]

Type of GCSE activity	Example
Corporate social responsibility (CSR)	Adidas partnered with the SOS Children's Villages and FIFA (International Federation of Association Football) campaign to raise funds for "20 villages across Africa for 2010" (SOS Children's Villages, 2009).[2]
Professional sport league philanthropy	The NFL uses community outreach activities to enhance their public image and strengthen relationships with local communities (see Babiak & Wolfe, 2006).
Cause-related marketing	Nike's partnership with the Lance Armstrong Live Strong campaign (see McGlone & Martin, 2005).
Private foundation philanthropy	Nike Foundation's activities for adolescent girls in the two-thirds world (see Nike Foundation, 2008).
Sport celebrity diplomacy	Right to Play's athlete ambassadors (see Cooper, 2007, for more about celebrity diplomacy in international development more broadly).
Consumer-based philanthropy	Right to Play joined forces with Adidas through a limited edition of the signature Right to Play red ball that as of June 2007 was sold in Adidas stores worldwide and on adidas.com (Right to Play, 2007). All proceeds from the sale of the mini red ball go to support Right to Play's projects around the world.
Social entrepreneurship	Nike's changemakers competition, a partnership with Ashoka, the largest social entrepreneurial NGO in the world (see Changemakers, 2007).
Corporate-NGO partnership	Nike's partnership with the Homeless World Cup (see Homeless World Cup, 2008).
Market multilateralism	Nike Inc.'s partnership with UNHCR (see UNHCR, 2006).

[1]This table was outlined in Hayhurst (2009b) and builds on research conducted by Zahra Bhanji (2008) on GCSE interventions in the education sector.

[2]In 2004 Adidas joined the SOS Children's Villages and FIFA (International Federation of Association Football) campaign to raise monies for "6 Villages for 2006." The mission of the campaign was to build six SOS Villages (including a football pitch, classrooms, and medical facilities) in two-thirds world countries around the globe by the final match of the 2006 World Cup (Adidas Group, 2007).

and responsibilities of business. In fact, since the beginnings of the industrial revolution in the 18th century, the responsibility of the corporation to its investors, workers, consumers, the environment, and the public has been the subject of ongoing, intense politics. Entrepreneurs who took an active interest in the welfare of their workers and practiced public-spirited philanthropy have tended to enjoy a high measure of regard, but every generation has known legislative and journalistic inquiries, labor organizing, and consumer boycotts against companies that engaged in abusive, unhealthy practices. In the 19th century, for example, consumers organized boycotts against firms that engaged slave and child labor (Blowfield & Frynas, 2005). Many of these campaigns succeeded in pressuring companies and the state to end harmful practices and make reforms. The very structure of the modern corporation today and the most important social institutions and legislative benefits and protections in most countries stem from these initiatives, conflicts, and responses. In 1948 after the United Nations approved the **Universal Declaration of Human Rights**, a statement of the political, legal, economic, and social rights that every person in the world should enjoy, multinational corporations increasingly came under scrutiny for their practices in the two-thirds world (Watts, 2005).

The development of CSR in the last two decades follows the centuries-old dynamic of public criticism, labor organizing, consumer boycotts, and government and corporate response. An important instructional battleground in the 1970s was the Swiss-based corporation Nestlé. Health activists and journalists in Britain and the United States became concerned that the company's marketing of infant formula as a replacement for breast milk in the two-thirds world contributed unnecessarily to the malnutrition of children and impoverishment of families. They began a boycott, which quickly spread around the world. The issue was then taken up by the United States Senate, the United Nations Educational Scientific and Cultural Organization (UNESCO), and the World Health Organization (WHO). In 1981 the World Health Assembly (WHA) adopted an international code of conduct for the marketing of breast-milk substitutes. The code bans the promotion of breast-milk substitutes and sets out labeling requirements. In 1984 Nestlé agreed to implement the code, and the boycott was lifted, although debate continues about compliance. Nestlé Canada proclaims its CSR under the slogan "Creating shared value" (Nestlé Canada, 2009). The International Baby Food Action Network (2011) remains critical of Nestlé and the entire industry.

CSR among sporting goods companies emerged during the 1990s, in response to activism about child labor and exploitative practices in the production of athletic shoes, uniforms, insignia gear, and equipment like footballs in the two-thirds world. As leading companies like Nike moved more production into the two-thirds world, it became evident that children and women carried much of it out for paltry wages in unsafe conditions. In North America, a coalition of U.S. and Canadian university students, Students Against Sweatshops, brought these abuses and the moral contradictions involved to the attention of consumers and university buyers of branded apparel through boycotts and sit-ins (Sage, 1999; Pearson, 2007). At the University of Toronto, for example, a weeklong sit-in in the president's office in the spring of 2000 persuaded the university to adopt a code of conduct for the production of all clothing and merchandise, including athletic uniforms, bearing its name. The university was the first Canadian university to do so. Today, 18 other Canadian universities, five major municipalities, and a growing number of school boards have such policies. U of T's code requires suppliers to agree to a set of fair labor conditions and accept independent monitoring (University of Toronto, 2001). Industry leaders like Nike and Adidas followed with their own undertakings. Activists, universities, and even the companies themselves have established

Learning Activity

Discuss to what extent the global economic crisis that began in 2008 and governments' and corporations' responses to it changed the ways that people think about capitalism. Have the responses varied in different countries and among different classes, genders, ethnic groups, and people in different regions? How has the sporting goods industry been affected by the global economic crisis? Has it affected their use of CSR?

monitoring organizations such as the Fair Labor Association, the Workers' Rights Consortium, and the Maquila Solidarity Network (MSN).

What is new about CSR is the extent to which global companies have committed themselves to the realization of human rights. They have created their own codes of conduct, complete with self-monitoring and reporting. Many corporate leaders and their supporters accept that **capitalism** should be socially responsible. Capitalism, the economic

CASE STUDY

Maquila Solidarity Network (MSN)

The Maquila Solidarity Network (MSN) is a Toronto-based labor- and women's rights organization that "supports the efforts of workers in global supply chains to win improved wages and working conditions and a better quality of life." MSN conducts research into the conditions of employment in the two-thirds world, evaluates the CSR undertakings of global companies, particularly in the apparel and sporting goods industries, and publishes annual reports on conditions and report cards on the major companies. For example, its 2006 report, *Revealing Clothing Transparency Report,* graded 30 global companies and retailers selling clothes in the Canadian market, including Levi Strauss, Nike, Adidas, H&M, Mountain Equipment Co-Op, Roots, La Senza, and Reitmans, on their labor practices and the transparency and accountability of their policies and programs. The scores ranged from 76 for Reebok, 74 for Mountain Equipment Coop, and 72 for Adidas to zero for eight retailers and suppliers, including Forzanis and Harry Rosen. MSN has also contributed to and coordinated many campaigns to force change in both the two-thirds world (helping workers organize) and the one-third world (by pressuring large purchasers to adopt codes for suppliers). In Canada, it inspired and assisted the successful Students Against Sweatshop campaign to persuade the University of Toronto to impose a code of conduct on suppliers, and it coordinated the Clean Clothes and Fair Play at the Olympics campaigns to win the same from the Canadian Olympic Committee, the City of Vancouver, and the Vancouver Winter Olympic and Paralympic Games. It has created the Ethical Trading Action Group, a coalition of religious, labor, and nongovernmental organizations that has significantly broadened the campaigns to induce public institutions to adopt ethical purchasing policies and companies to disclose their factory locations in the interests of transparent monitoring. Its website provides a history of the antisweatshop movement, clear statements of what activists expect from companies practicing CSR, and a compendium of relevant resources (Maquila Solidarity Network, 2009).

Most recently, MSN has begun to enter into discussions directly with the companies involved to bring about acceptable conditions of employment. As cofounder Bob Jeffcott wrote recently,

Our focus has always been on supporting the efforts of the women and men who make our clothes to organize to improve their wages and working conditions, not on shutting down factories with bad conditions or giving shoppers ethical choices. From the beginning, the labor rights/anti-sweatshop movement has criticized retailers and brands whenever they cut and run from factories where worker rights violations had been reported, rather than staying to fix the problem.

And while we often work with other organizations that describe themselves as corporate social responsibility (CSR) groups, we've always been more interested in and committed to finding new ways to make corporations more accountable rather than in helping them to better regulate themselves.

Organizations like MSN have been leading advocates of purchasing policies that require internationally accepted standards of production. The adoption of such policies by governments, universities, and major games organizing committees—an important achievement of the last 20 years—would simply not have occurred without them. They also provide an indispensible source of independent analysis of CSR for consumers, policy makers, researchers, and the corporations themselves, and advice and other resources to those directly affected, such as the workers and communities where the production of sporting goods takes place.

system characterized by private property and wage labor, in which some people own the means of production, hire others to carry out the work, and sell the resulting goods and services to make a profit, has been the dominant economic system in much of the world for many years, but it is constantly changing in response to changing conditions and technology. In countries like the United States where neoliberal governments have watered down or eliminated state regulation of the economy and the environment, corporations had to show that self-regulation can work. Employees in the companies involved contributed to the articulation, elaboration, and monitoring of codes of conduct and other practices of CSR. But in virtually every case, the impetus for them came from outside pressure and the fear that if they did not self-regulate, then fair trade campaigners might persuade governments to impose regulation.

Approaches to Understanding Corporate Social Responsibility in Sport

The next sections outline two approaches to explain the development of CSR in the area of international sport development and human rights. The first, managerially based approaches, generally tends to examine how CSR may be profitable for business. The second uses a critical theory perspective. This viewpoint challenges those with power to consider how CSR affects the lives of those who are marginalized and disadvantaged within society.

Managerial Theory

Managerial theory, the dominant body of knowledge in sport management studies, is used to explain how a given business operates in society. In keeping with **neoliberalism**, it assumes that the corporation and the free market can solve social problems. In considering CSR, managerial perspectives focus on the win–win aspects of being socially responsible, emphasizing the business case for corporations involved, and the effect of CSR on shareholders, managers, and taxpayers (Newell & Frynas, 2007). Managerial approaches discuss how CSR is a useful strategy for corporations to act responsibly, enhance their public images, increase profits, and reach

untapped markets. For example, in 2007 Reebok introduced its Global Corporate Citizenship platform, involving "a series of programs designed to support underserved communities and groups. They provide underprivileged youth with the tools they need to fulfill their potential and lead healthy, happy and active lives" (Adidas Group, 2007, p. 4). From a managerial perspective, this CSR platform should be evaluated primarily in terms of its effectiveness in enabling Reebok to penetrate new consumer markets and enhance its image.

Benefits to Companies

A great deal of research in CSR focuses on producing practical findings and recommendations that corporations could use to strengthen their accountability to shareholders, enhance customer relations, and enhance their bottom lines. Examples include shareholder studies, marketing research, feasibility studies, economic impact studies, and evaluation research (Frisby, 2006). A recent example of such research is an evaluative report by the International Business Leaders Forum (IBLF), titled *Shared Goals Through Sport: Getting Sustainable Return for Companies and Communities* (Prescott & Phelan, 2008). The research was funded by Standard Chartered, Nike, and UK Sport. The report considered the economic and social benefits for corporations that engage in sport for development and peace (SDP) activities, a strategy of intervention linked to the promotion of human rights. It noted that by engaging in SDP activities, companies benefit by "achieving social investment objectives, engaging with employees, improving government relations, and reaching new target markets" (Prescott & Phelan, 2008, p. 2). Other profitable aspects of CSR to firms include

1. supporting projects to invest in the communities in which a given corporation operates;
2. supporting activities that focus on global problems, but not in specific communities where the company, its suppliers, or stakeholders work;
3. enhancing employee engagement;
4. achieving social objectives;
5. meeting sustainability commitments;
6. reaching and accessing two-thirds world markets;
7. sponsorship and support of major tournaments, teams, and players;

8. producing sport-related goods and services in the two-thirds world; and

9. strengthening relations with two-thirds world governments to grow business in emerging markets (e.g., Standard Chartered in India) (Prescott & Phelan, 2008).

The IBLF report details four examples of CSR in SDP, including Standard Chartered's recent initiative in South Delhi, India, that aims to empower 60 underprivileged women through the power of netball. Other corporations engaged in SDP in the two-thirds world and detailed in the study are Nike, British Airways, and Vodafone.

Other research investigates how sport managers gain a competitive advantage by viewing CSR as an opportunity-driven concept that can assist in accomplishing an enhanced strategic direction (Breitbarth & Harris, 2008). Still other research examines the ethical and discretionary components of CSR to understand how corporations can improve their reputations and build brand image and customer loyalty through community-based outreach programs. Instructive examples can be drawn from professional sport, where both teams and entire leagues use community outreach activities to enhance their public image and strengthen relationships with local communities (e.g., Babiak & Wolfe, 2006). The NBA Basketball Without Borders initiative, which operates basketball camps around the globe for 50 to 100 of the most talented teenage boys in a given community, is a two-thirds world example (Millington, 2009). NBA players, coaches, and scouts are involved in these camps, actively providing lessons ranging from skill development to education on HIV and AIDS (Basketball Without Borders, 2008).

Primary and Secondary Stakeholders

CSR may also be explored using stakeholder theory to uncover how corporations seek to improve relations with communities, suppliers, consumers, investors, and the environment when implementing profit-driven activities (Misener, 2008). Such research is primarily concerned with identifying and analyzing how corporations are accountable to the various stakeholders who are affected by and involved in CSR interventions. For example, Chauhan (2008) employed a stakeholder perspective to investigate the socially responsible practices of the Vancouver Organizing Committee for the 2010 Olympic and Paralympic Games (VANOC). His study demonstrated that the needs and decisions of primary stakeholders (i.e., those groups whose involvement was central to the achievement of organizational goals, such as corporate sponsors, international sport organizations, and government) often conflicted with or were incompatible with the needs of secondary stakeholders, or those who were affected by the organization (Chauhan, 2008). Secondary stakeholders might include local community members, volunteers, and municipal sport organizations. For example, Vancouver's downtown eastside is a local community that was plagued by unemployment, HIV and AIDS, high crime rates, and drug abuse, and its residents would be categorized as secondary stakeholders in the 2010 Games (Chauhan, 2008). In his study, Chauhan argued that public funds should have been used to improve this area, as opposed to satisfying the economic priorities of Vancouver's elites, who may have been more interested in putting public monies toward building new athletic facilities. Although the Games organizers attempted to reach out to multiple stakeholders, the jury is out on whether the secondary stakeholders, especially the disadvantaged residents of the downtown eastside, benefitted significantly.

Other research has considered the socially responsible practices in the other mega sporting events (e.g., Hums et al., 2008), the role of professional athletes as philanthropists (e.g., Babiak, Tainsky & Juravich, 2008), and the intersections among CSR, corporate citizenship, and sport management studies (e.g., Mallen & Bradish, 2008). Smith and Westerbeek (2007) asserted that there is a distinct connection between sport and CSR, because sport builds community and fosters powerful connections between individuals, facilitating trust and strengthening ties between neighbors and nations. It has also been suggested that sport corporate social responsibility can be "pervasive, youth-friendly, health-oriented, socially interactive, environmentally aware, culturally liberating and fun" (Smith & Westerbeek, 2007, p. 52). For example, the IBLF report argued that "sport attracts companies in a way that other social issues don't—it's a subject matter that business people can empathize with. This makes it an unusually effective means of engaging companies in development issues." (Prescott & Phelan, 2008, p. 6).

Despite the benefits that it may bring, sport corporate social responsibility is not always fun. At times it is controversial, messy, unpredictable, and therefore worthy of critical investigation. Although it may benefit some, it may not benefit all, and it may unwittingly set back the communities directly affected. One of the goals of this chapter is to encourage sport managers, especially those working in the areas of sport, CSR, and international development, to broaden their focus and ask how they can contribute to the enhancement of the entire society, not just their own corporations (Frisby, 2005). Many standpoints outside managerial theory have enormous potential for critically investigating the intersections between sport, international development, human rights, and CSR. In the next section, we argue that critical theory is the most useful standpoint in terms of uncovering the relationship between global capital and power, and for understanding domination and resistance in terms of CSR, development, and human rights.

Critical Theory

If those who use managerial perspectives tend to focus on how and whether corporations benefit from CSR, those who study it from a critical perspective tend to apply a more comprehensive lens and investigate the effects of CSR on entire societies, emphasizing a human-centered approach, one that aims to include the views of those who are ignored in managerial approaches (Sharp, 2006; Prieto-Carron et al., 2006). Prieto-Carron et al. (2006) refer to this as the people case on CSR, as opposed to the business case.

Critical theory focuses on social relations, including the struggles over social power, representation, and ideology. It does not assume that either the corporation or the state acts in beneficial ways. Instead, it attempts to understand their roles and effects in our complex, dynamic, globalizing world. Critical thinking also involves reflecting on one's social position in the world (in terms of class, gender, ethnicity and race, sexuality, ability, and age) and holding up one's own beliefs to scrutiny, recognizing that there is significant inequality in the world and that people from different backgrounds may experience a particular intervention quite differently. In the realm of sport management, a key consideration may also be to examine which voices

are represented or unaccounted for in sporting practices, policies, and organizations.

From this perspective, it is important to recognize the complexity of CSR as an intricate system that involves not only corporations, other stakeholders, and partnerships but also the recipients of programs and the societies in which they live. In particular, critical approaches focus on how CSR activities influence and affect those targeted by these programs. It is also important to recognize that CSR may have unintended consequences (Sharp, 2006).

For example, Vodafone recently sponsored the Homeless World Cup, a football tournament that delivers programs around the world for marginalized people using football to foster leadership skills and promote healthy living and social entrepreneurship (Homeless World Cup, 2008). Although research using a managerial perspective may investigate this tournament using a cost–benefit analysis for Vodafone (i.e., by considering how Vodafone was able to increase its branding, public image, and revenue by sponsoring the Homeless World Cup), a critical perspective would focus on the ways in which Vodafone's sponsorship of the Homeless World Cup affects the recipients or participants and the underlying power relations involved in this program. For example, what is the long-term effect on the participants after the tournament ends? Does the experience give them skills that can be transferable beyond football to enable them to improve their life chances? How are decisions made? Who holds the power in this CSR initiative? If the same amount of money were invested in a political campaign to end homelessness through housing and other social initiatives supported by a more progressive tax structure, would that help more people?

Nike Inc. and Nike Foundation

Nike is one of the top 50 brands in the world. It sells products in more than 160 countries and employs over 800,000 workers worldwide in contracted factories (Nike Inc., 2006). It has been a leader in the development of safer, performance-enhancing footwear and other equipment in a number of sports and has helped transform sports gear into worldwide fashion. Long before CSR became a popular term, the company and its foundation contributed significantly to the popularization of adult fitness, girls' and women's sport, and other progressive campaigns, and Nike has been an industry leader in the development and elaboration of CSR.

Nevertheless, a history of antisweatshop activism has plagued the corporation for many years, creating an "image problem by setting the company's self-identity at odds with a growing public reputation for sweatshop practices" (Knight & Greenberg, 2002, p. 565). In the 1990s critics maintained that, alongside its advocacy of sport as a tool to empower women through the use of female sport celebrities (in the one-third world), Nike ignored the degradation and violations of the women in two-thirds world countries who "stitch and glue the swoosh to shoes" and who "are more likely to see and feel the effects of an aggressive marketing strategy aimed at women in Nike's continued attempts to expand what has already become the largest segment of the athletic shoe market" (Cole & Hribar, 1995, p. 366).

The central issue for activists has been the working conditions of Nike factories located in Asia, where the corporation produces most of its products. Activists want Nike to improve the conditions for these workers, the majority of whom are women, pay them a living wage, enable them to organize on their own behalf, recognize their rights, and treat them with respect (Sage, 1999). Although considerable evidence shows that Nike has cleaned up its act and improved the working conditions in its factories (e.g., Spain, 2007; Nike Inc., 2006), there is still concern that a gap remains between its socially responsible rebranding and the reality of its local labor practices (Knight & Greenberg, 2002). The combination of this history

with Nike's presence in the UN Global Compact and ongoing criticism of its marketing to girls and women have maintained the pressure on the company to demonstrate socially responsible practices on the global stage.

Nike has always been interested in penetrating untapped markets, particularly the women's sport market. Its ads use feminist rhetoric, suggesting to girls and women that Nike products will help them overcome their historic marginalization in sport (Cole & Hribar, 1995; Lucas, 2000). More recently, Nike designed the Air Native N7 shoe specifically for "American Indians," which was perceived by many as a racist and patronizing product, to "help [them] overcome a propensity for diabetes and other health problems related to a lack of fitness" (Cole, 2008, p. 3). These campaigns are problematic and reveal a history of sexist, racist, and classist tendencies that contextualize Nike's recent activities related to girls' empowerment.

As an attempt to revamp their image as the solution to the oppression of girls in sport, and the marginalization of girls more generally, Nike launched the Nike Foundation in 2005 to help overcome "poverty alleviation through girls' empowerment" (Nike Foundation, 2005, p. 3) and "foster innovative models of corporate philanthropy" (p. 9). The foundation actually started as an initiative in 1994 called the Nike PLAY (Participate in the Lives of American Youth) Foundation, focused on supporting community-based entities in the United States, Australia, Canada, and Europe with programs based on youth, sport, culture, and social services (Nike Foundation, 2005, p. 4). Currently, the foundation invests explicitly in activities related to girls' empowerment and poverty relation, principally in two-thirds world countries that already have a Nike presence. Another key component of the foundation's work is facilitating partnerships with NGOs, UN agencies, and partners with experience in addressing "developing-country poverty" (Nike Foundation, 2005, p. 8). The three cornerstones of the work of Nike Foundation include driving resources, changing the system, showing impact, and spreading the word (Nike Foundation, 2008).

This case was originally presented at the Bodies of Knowledge Conference, University of Toronto, Ontario (Hayhurst, 2009a).

Would Vodaphone support that kind of initiative? Whose perspectives are being represented, and how are taken-for-granted beliefs about homelessness and poverty being produced, strengthened, or resisted through this CSR initiative? A study investigating the ways that homeless people take up and challenge this CSR initiative would be beneficial for highlighting the ways that the recipients or targets are influenced by Vodafone's seemingly benevolent activities regarding homelessness and poverty. In this way, using critical theory to understand the CSR activities of corporations allows us to uncover not only the norms embedded within acts that are claimed to be socially responsible but also the power, authority, and influence interwoven within such actions. This type of analysis is applied to Nike's advocacy for women and girls in the case study.

One important strand of critical theory is critical feminist theory, which assumes that social order and social life are highly gendered, that is, organized around gender, and that within contemporary societies, the interests of men with power tend to predominate. A key question from this standpoint pertains to "how gender relations privilege men over women, and some men over other men" (Coakley & Donnelly, 2004, p. 47). In contemporary one-third world societies, researchers in sport, health, and management have documented the upsurge in cause-related marketing campaigns that focus on women (King, 2004; Polonsky & Wood, 2001).

Samantha King's research program on sport, health, gender, and corporate philanthropy serves as a good illustration of a critical feminist approach to understanding CSR. Through her research, King (2001, 2006) effectively showed how women have increasingly become both targets and purveyors of CSR initiatives and cause-related marketing campaigns. She also showed how the pink ribbon campaign for breast cancer, known mostly through the Run for the Cure activities, has evolved into a market-driven industry of survivorship, in which mostly white, middle-class women from the one-third world participate. The Run for the Cure is one form of CSR that King (2001) defined as "international public relations programs that mesh community involvement . . . with philanthropic activity" (p. 268). Her investigation showed how corporate sponsors such as Avon Products Inc., BMW, and Ford Motor Company eagerly support breast cancer philanthropy as a "profitable strategy through which to market their products" (King, 2006, p. 2), illustrating that companies use the managerial perspective to plan and evaluate their activities.

Undoubtedly, campaigns such as Run for the Cure make an important contribution by generating research monies for a form of cancer that hitherto had been neglected. Fund-raising runs, walkathons, skiing events, bicycle excursions, and so on reinforce the links between physical activity and health, another benefit. Both authors have participated and financially contributed to such campaigns for these very reasons. But at the same time, such campaigns narrow and therefore distort the debate about the cause of cancers, the priorities of cancer research, and the appropriate public response by glossing over the environmental and social causes of cancer, and simplifying the solutions. A more comprehensive approach would be to examine the entire spectrum of health issues affecting women across class, ethnicity and race, and the one-third world and two-thirds world, not just women in the sponsors' markets, and examine how they are addressed within public health care (King, 2006). King's research is extremely useful in this regard, showing us how women take up CSR programs, who is excluded from them, and why. She also reminds us about whose interests are being served by such philanthropic endeavors. In keeping critical theory and its various strands in mind, we now turn to consider CSR activities in the two-thirds world as they intersect with sport and international development.

Corporate Social Responsibility in Sport and Economic Development

Research investigating CSR in the two-thirds world context in general is scant (Newell & Frynas, 2007). To our knowledge, most of the studies on sport and CSR in the two-thirds world pertain to critiques of Nike's labor practices in Asia (e.g., Sage, 1999; Knight & Greenberg, 2002). Moreover, most studies use the managerial approach, focusing on the contribution of CSR to a corporation's bottom line and its appeal to shareholders. We argue that researchers must study CSR critically as a development tool, focusing on the most marginalized and disadvantaged groups in a collaborative, accessible, and participatory way (Newell & Frynas, 2007). This approach may mean providing the tools for poorer groups to protest against "badly conceived investments in which their interests may have been overlooked" (Newell & Frynas, 2007, p. 676).

Although most of the world's greatest social and economic inequalities are located in the two-thirds world, these nations also represent the most rapidly expanding and untapped growth markets for business. Many refer to this as the bottom of the pyramid model, suggesting that those residing in extreme poverty (three billion low-income consumers outside mainstream markets at the bottom of the pyramid) can be a market in themselves that can be served with low-cost goods and services (Prahalad, 2005). For a company such as Nike, the bottom of the pyramid is an innovative form of CSR that drives new forms of business and contributes to their bottom line. In fact, the bottom of the pyramid model is advocated by the IBLF as a useful strategy for reaching markets in the two-thirds world: "Sport is a significant social force in developing countries, and therefore it represents—for companies who are thinking laterally—a means to meet the needs of markets 'at the bottom of the pyramid'" (Prescott & Phelan, 2008, p. 11). Besides this example, Visser (2008) suggests that CSR in the two-thirds world has many specific characteristics, such as the following:

1. CSR is more informal in the two-thirds world, because labor and environmental legislation and regulations are less likely to be enforced.

2. Formal CSR practices are usually exercised by transnational corporations (as opposed to local or national-based businesses).

3. Formalized CSR codes, standards, and guidelines that pertain to the two-thirds world are most often "issue specific" and "sector led" (p. 492). For example, they may pertain to HIV and AIDS, or be focused on mining or the agricultural sector.

4. Economic investments are the most pertinent ways that corporations may foster a social impact (e.g., through job creation).

5. CSR is more tied to charity in the two-thirds world, particularly through corporate social investment in terms of private foundation philanthropy (e.g., Nike Foundation) or, for instance, by investing in sport development.

Some scholars accuse governments, UN agencies, and **nongovernmental organizations** (**NGOs**, such as Oxfam or Save the Children) of failing to "rid the planet of underdevelopment and poverty," and argue that the time has come for large corporations to step in by taking responsibility for promoting economic development and filling the governance gap (Hopkins, 2006, p. 2). But is development really only about economics? In fact, development is a complex term, with multiple definitions and understandings, particularly depending on the context in which it is used. Here we briefly historicize **development** to help explain how it connects to CSR and sport.

Following World War II, the "development era" was initiated in U.S. president Harry Truman's 1949 inaugural address, in which he proposed to launch a worldwide "program of development" (under the leadership of the United States) to enable impoverished countries to "industrialize" (Rapley, 2007). Truman's understanding of development was inherently modernist, equating economic growth with notions of progress and liberation (Roy, 2007). Put differently, his conception of development sought to advance a country characterized as backward and primitive, and industrialize nonindustrialized economies. Since then, the concept of development has been further elaborated and revised, in large part in response to shifting ideological and political power. In the 1970s it focused on "satisfying basic human needs." In the 1980s the brief rise of two-thirds world alliances added the ambition that development ensures a broad distribution of economic growth and the spread of liberal democracy. In its Declaration on the Right of Development (1986), the United Nations defined development as a "comprehensive economic, social, cultural and political process, which aims at the constant improvement of the well-being of the entire population and of all individuals on the basis of their active, free and meaningful participation and the fair distribution of benefits." But, with the end of the cold war and the fall of the Soviet Union, neoliberal, market-based solutions to poverty became dominant. The current campaign concentrates on the achievement of the **United Nations Millennium Development Goals** (**MDGs**) by 2015. In 2000, 189 world leaders committed to realizing the MDGs, the eight goals that aim to fight poverty and support a framework for designing and implementing development programs in nations throughout the two-thirds world:

1. Eradicate extreme poverty and hunger
2. Achieve universal primary education
3. Promote gender equality and empower women
4. Reduce child mortality
5. Improve maternal health
6. Combat HIV and AIDS, malaria, and other diseases
7. Ensure environmental sustainability
8. Develop a global partnership for development

Importantly, the MDGs uphold human rights by aiming to preserve and protect human dignity.

Similarly, the **sport for development and peace** (**SDP**) movement seeks to promote and protect human rights. SDP has both old and new characteristics. It is an expression of the old idea of "sport for good" (as opposed to "sport for sport's sake") that has motivated school, municipal, religious, political, and community-based organizations in the one-third world for more than a century. But it is new in its focus on the two-thirds world; in its attempt to bridge sport and other forms of intervention in health, education, foreign policy, and social development; and in its youth leadership (Hayhurst, 2009b). The movement reflects the 1990s that gave it birth; the optimism generated by the end of apartheid and the cold war; the determination to end genocidal civil wars, famine, and disease; and the new wave of youth-led social justice organizations. Not surprisingly, SDP tries to mobilize

its cause using other human rights campaigns as catalysts for furthering its policy objectives. As Kidd and Donnelly (2000) contended, "Some of the most important advances in extending sporting opportunity have been made in step with human rights campaigns" (p. 137). In many countries, SDP organizations grew directly out of the antiapartheid movement (Guelke & Sugden, 1999) and the fight for workers' rights in campaigns against the sporting goods industry (Sage, 1999).

The SDP movement has received a great deal of attention from academics, UN agencies, NGOs, and other stakeholders seeking to demonstrate the potential of sport to contribute to the MDGs and other pressing international development issues and to advance human rights. SDP positions sport as a tool to fight HIV and AIDS, build social cohesion, foster peace among conflicted groups, and address gender inequities (SDP IWG, 2006; Kidd, 2008). Table 16.2 outlines three approaches to understanding the relationship between sport and development. SDP and high-performance sport development may be distinguished in terms of their diverging agendas and histories (Houlihan & White, 2002). Although the aim of SDP is to contribute to development objectives mostly in partnerships with governments in the areas of health, education, and sport, the goal of high-performance sport development is to prepare athletes to participate in sport at an elite level through organized training and major competitions (Kidd, 2008).

An example of a SDP NGO is the Mathare Youth Sports Association (MYSA), an organization based in Kenya that uses the power of football to encour-

Table 16.2 Approaches to Understanding the Relationship Between Sport and Development (Kidd, 2008)

Concept	Definition	Example
Sport humanitarian assistance	Focuses on supporting humanitarian interventions in the two-thirds world (e.g., vaccinations, emergency food, and clothing to children in war).	Right to Play, in cooperation with UNICEF, contributes to smallpox and TB vaccinations in Afghanistan.
Sport for development (SDP)	Uses sport to contribute to international development issues encompassed by UN MDGs (e.g., using sport as a tool to fight HIV and AIDS, build social cohesion, foster peace among conflicted groups, and address gender inequities).	Mathare Youth Sports Association (MYSA), an organization based in Kenya that uses the power of football to encourage youth to challenge gender stereotypes, contribute to environmental sustainability, and empower young people (Willis, 2000).
Sport development	Uses sport to develop and prepare athletes to participate in elite sporting competitions through organized training and major competitions.	Olympic Solidarity.

age youth to challenge gender stereotypes, contribute to environmental sustainability, and empower young people (Willis, 2000). Another example is Right to Play, an international humanitarian NGO that uses sport and play programs to enhance the health and life skills of marginalized children in the two-thirds world. The organization also administers programs to promote conflict resolution through "the power of sport" and is now one of the largest SDP NGOs in the world, reaching 600,000 children in 23 countries (Right to Play, 2009).

Significantly, Right to Play recently joined forces with Adidas through a limited edition of the signature Right to Play mini red ball that as of June 2007 was sold in Adidas stores worldwide and on adidas.com (Right to Play, 2007). All proceeds from the sale of the mini red ball (US$10) go to support Right to Play's projects around the world. Furthermore, Adidas employees are assigned with the task of being Right to Play ambassadors, and each Adidas store serves as a venue to publicize Right to Play's projects in Africa, Asia, and the Middle East (Right to Play, 2007). The day of the announced partnership between Adidas and Right to Play, Right to Play president and CEO Johann Koss proclaimed "by buying this special mini ball, children in this country [the United States] can give the gift of laughter, hope and health to children in need around the world" (Right to Play, 2007).

This example serves as an important entry point for using critical theory to uncover the norms embedded within acts that are considered socially responsible, as well as the power, authority, and influence enmeshed in such actions. For instance, what interest does Adidas have in pursuing a partnership with Right to Play? When consumers in North America purchase a mini red ball, how does this form of consumer-based philanthropy, linked to CSR, build the Adidas brand, help the corporation sell its products, and enable them to "portray themselves as both 'caring' and 'cool'" (Ponte, Richey, & Baab, 2009, p. 302)? Other critical questions to ask are how this form of CSR actually helps children in the two-thirds world and whether more direct strategies would be more effective. If the only way that social problems can be addressed is through the sale of products produced by global corporations, the range of political options narrows significantly. We worry, too, about the rights and responsibilities of citizenship if the only way in which people can comment on the issues of development, international trade, and foreign aid is through purchase and consumption.

The United Nations Global Compact

Since its launch in July 2000, the **United Nations Global Compact** has grown to be the world's largest global corporate citizenship initiative, and it is focused on building the social legitimacy of business and markets. The 10 principles of the compact ask companies to "embrace, support, and enact" human rights; labor rights, including the rights to freely formed trade unions, collective bargaining, and the abolition of child labor; environmental responsibility; and anticorruption. The compact has now grown to over 3,800 participants, including over 2,900 businesses in 100 countries worldwide (UNGC, 2007).

Not surprisingly, the socially responsible behavior of companies reflects patterns of corporate interests (Himmelstein, 1997). Despite the tensions of CSR, its normative values continue to shape the behavior of transnational corporations such as Adidas and influence these corporate interests. Therefore, examining the relationships between the UN Global Compact, corporations, and SDP NGOs is useful for understanding how CSR norms permeate the landscape of sport for development.

For example, Nike has been a member of the UN Global Compact since its official creation. By enlisting in the compact, Nike was legitimized by the UN by agreeing to follow nine principles drawn from the Universal Declaration of Human Rights, the International Labour Organization's (ILO) Fundamental Principles and Rights at Work, and the Rio Declaration on Environment and Development. These principles are meant to influence and direct Nike's behavior by building a shared meaning of good corporate practices as defined by the wider global community (Ruggie, 2003).

It must be recognized that the UN Global Compact and the commitments it has engendered from global corporations constitute a progressive step forward for the corporate world. On the other hand, critics contend that the compact is merely an innovative way for corporations to enter into new spheres of influence and to penetrate new markets, particularly in the two-thirds world (Zadek, 2007). Others worry about compliance, suggesting that the compact enables companies to be branded as socially responsible entities while they may be acting in opposition to the principles of the compact behind closed doors. The compact is voluntary and cannot be legally enforced; therefore, the social and environmental aspects of businesses cannot be strictly regulated (Capdevila, 2007). Given these issues, is the UN Global Compact then just a "brand-aid solution" to addressing the negative effects of the increasingly globalized world economy, as corporations continue to prioritize short-term profits and promotion over social and environmental considerations? What are the implications of the compact in terms of CSR? Does it present a hope for a new democratic world order or simply circumvent the challenge to existing institutions? These are all important questions to consider in terms of the future of CSR, sport, human rights, and international development.

Learning Activity

Go to the UN Global Compact's (UNGC) website at www.unglobalcompact.org/aboutthegc/thetenprinciples. Examine the UNGC's 10 principles. Under what theoretical framework (as discussed in the chapter) do these principles fall? What, in your perspective, are some positive and negative aspects of these principles?

Summary

Most who enter the field of sport management do so because they love sport and want to encourage others to participate, play, and engage in sporting opportunities. But those who work in the field need to think critically about the current sporting landscape and understand how multiple actors such as NGOs, UN agencies, elite sport organizations, and, of course, corporations influence sporting experiences. Undoubtedly, throughout the last 20 years, the global expansion of the sport industry has both extended opportunities to many people and touched off a critical response. In response, many transnational sport corporations have taken up CSR practices, policies, and programs. Everyone working in sport management today will be acutely shaped by this development and will have the opportunity to contribute to its improvement. The definition, forms, and problems of CSR in sport and development are constantly evolving, and the issues arising from its influence cannot be neglected. Sport managers need to think critically about how sport can contribute to the improvement of society, foster social change, and improve the lives of disadvantaged groups, particularly those in the two-thirds world. We are not suggesting here that sport will cure all the world's ills, but we hope that this chapter has encouraged students to think more about the possibilities of its reach.

? Review and Discussion Questions

1. What were the origins of CSR?

2. What are the strengths and weaknesses of the two theoretical frameworks outlined in this chapter: (a) managerial theory and (b) critical theory?

3. The authors have argued that CSR is not a form of philanthropy, but others suggest that it is. What do you think and why? To what extent is CSR altruistic? To what extent is it not?

4. What were the origins of sport for development?

5. Do corporations necessarily need to be involved in sport for development? How can sport for development NGOs such as Right to Play survive without the support of the private sector? What is the role of government?

6. How do organizations like the Maquila Solidarity Network contribute to sport for development?

CHAPTER 17

International Sport Law

James T. Gray, JD
Marian University, Wisconsin, USA

David L. Snyder, JD
State University of New York College at Cortland, USA

Chapter Objectives

After studying this chapter, you will be able to do the following:

- Define international sport law
- Describe the legal and regulatory framework of international sport
- Explain the complexities and challenges of applying laws, rules, and regulations across national boundaries
- Understand the advantages and disadvantages of litigation, arbitration, and mediation in resolving international sport disputes
- Identify the holdings in several significant international sport law cases
- Discuss current issues and future trends concerning international sport law

The various stakeholders in the sport industry are always searching for innovative ways to increase the number of revenue streams flowing into their organizations. Improvements in mass transportation and electronic communication have created fertile new economic opportunities for sport enterprises in the global marketplace. During the last 30 years, international sport has emerged into a multibillion dollar industry. The enormous amount of income generated through international sport has caused various disputes to arise, ranging from contract enforcement litigation to drug-testing challenges. Because of these developments, a legal framework was established for dealing effectively with these disputes and protecting the rights of the parties involved. This chapter provides an overview of the parameters of international sport law practice to provide those interested in the field with a basic knowledge and understanding of the legal and regulatory framework of international sport. Further, this chapter is designed to cultivate an appreciation of some of the complexities of international sport law.

More specifically, this chapter first examines what constitutes international sport law. Second, approaches to conflict resolution in international sport are identified, including the circumstances in which international sport-related disputes can be resolved internally and without the assistance of court intervention. Also included in this discussion is the role of alternative dispute resolution in the form of arbitration as it pertains to the interpretation of athletic rules and regulations by sport-based administrative and arbitral bodies. Third, this chapter considers the role of agents and athlete rights in the global sport arena. This section particularly focuses on the effect labor and competition laws have had in establishing the legal rights of players to market their skills on a free and open global marketplace. Fourth, this chapter examines the legal implications of the sport-for-all movement in international sport. This section includes an investigation of the legal aspects of doping, gambling, violence, terrorism, and other forms of misconduct in international sport.

International sport law deals with a wide range of issues, such as human rights, ambush marketing, media rights, licensing, piracy of intellectual property, and sweatshop labor practices, among others that were deliberately not addressed in this chapter because they are included in other parts of this book. If you are interested in learning more about topics and issues in sport law, see the list of additional resources at the end of this chapter.

What Is International Sport Law?

At the outset, it is important to define what is meant by international sport law. As opposed to being a planned development, international sport law mirrored the growth of international sport by evolving organically, defining itself along the way. The rapid growth of international sport law has been driven, in general, by the economic potential of international sport. During the last 15 years international sport law has specifically addressed the legal rights of aggrieved athletes, particularly when their economic livelihood and competition eligibility were at stake. Because of these dynamic factors, international sport law has emerged as a hodgepodge tapestry of national and international laws, administrative rules and regulations, and arbitration decisions. In addition, some politics and policy are applied, or perhaps misapplied, depending on one's perspective. Consequently, the reality is that no easily identifiable body of laws can be referred to as constituting international sport law. Rather, what emerged from this process is a tangled imbroglio of sport-based laws, rules, regulations, procedures, and policies that can be challenging for even the most competent international sport lawyer to comprehend.

One of the complexities that arise in international sport law is the issue of which law to apply to a given situation. The branch of law that attempts to reconcile issues that arise when multiple jurisdictions are involved in a dispute is referred to as **conflict of laws**. When applying conflict of laws principles, **choice of law** rules have been established to attempt to provide a means for resolving what substantive and procedural laws should govern a particular dispute (Snyder, 2003). After it is determined that a court, whether a judge or a judge and a jury, and not a sport-created arbitration process, is the proper method by which to settle a particular sport-related dispute, the plaintiff must show that the court selected has jurisdiction over the defendant.

The term **jurisdiction** is defined as "the authority by which courts and judicial officers take cognizance of and decide cases" (*Black's Law Dictionary*, 2004).

Choice-of-forum rules address which court or arbitrator should hear a particular case. Another concept associated with conflict of laws is **comity**, which refers to the voluntary and informal decision of a court in one jurisdiction to give deference to the laws, judicial decisions, and arbitral determinations from another jurisdiction (Snyder, 2003).

Another example of the types of issues that can arise given the convoluted, multitiered nature of international sport law concerns the unauthorized practice of law (UPL). Each nation has legislation that has defined the notion of what exactly constitutes the unauthorized practice of law. These UPL provisions apply to lawyers and to nonlawyers alike. Further, these laws prohibit people from engaging in the practice of law except where they are licensed or otherwise qualified and authorized to practice law (Cohen, 2009).

Previously, jurisdictional restrictions on law practice were not a significant issue because most client legal matters were confined to a single geographical setting and a lawyer's familiarity with that law was a qualification of utmost client importance. But since the 1960s, the issue of globalization of national economies and the internationalization of business has challenged the wisdom of traditional UPL concepts. Modern international and comparative law and increasing client demands require an ever-growing number of lawyers, who in the past were considered legal generalists, to concentrate in specialized areas of law, such as sport law. Also, attorneys may be requested to provide legal services outside the jurisdiction where they are admitted to practice law. For example, suppose a lawyer who is licensed in New York represents a basketball player playing in Italy, but the attorney is not licensed to practice law there. As discussed in detail later in this chapter, issues of the unauthorized practice of law also arise among nonattorneys who perform what are, arguably, legal services for their clients. Despite these relatively common scenarios, attorney regulation has not evolved with the rapid growth of international sport law practice to respond effectively to these situations. For the unwary, this could result in unintended consequences such as jail time, fines, forfeiture of fees, and attorney sanctions.

Conflict Resolution in International Sport

Disputes that arise within the context of international sport are resolved in a variety of forums, ranging from national court holdings to administrative determinations to arbitration decisions. **Arbitration** is an alternative form of dispute resolution in which a neutral third party or parties are chosen, usually by the parties involved, to resolve the matter in dispute. Arbitration offers a faster, more cost-efficient means of settling conflicts, and in specialized fields such as sport, it often offers the additional advantage of having experts in the field evaluate the merits of a case.

Limited Judicial Review and Sport-Based Dispute Resolution

In general, courts will not intervene in the internal affairs of a sport governing body and its decision-making procedures, such as arbitration. In the past, courts have held that membership in sport organizations is voluntary and that these organizations are self-regulating. Courts, however, will review the decisions of sport organization if one of the following is found:

1. The rule or regulation challenged by the plaintiff exceeds the scope of the sport organization's authority.

2. The rule or regulation challenged by the plaintiff violates an individual's constitutional rights.

3. The rule or regulation challenged by the plaintiff is applied in an arbitrary or capricious fashion or the organization abuses its discretion.

4. The rule or regulation challenged by the plaintiff violates public policy because it is considered fraudulent or unreasonable.

5. The sport organization violates one of its own rules.

6. The rule or regulation challenged by the plaintiff violates an existing law (Greenberg & Gray, 1998).

Court of Arbitration for Sport

The Court of Arbitration for Sport (CAS), which is also known by its French name, Tribunal Arbitral du Sport (TAS), was created by the International

Olympic Committee in 1984 (*20 Questions About the CAS*, 2009). The CAS headquarters, based in Lausanne, Switzerland, uses two working arbitration hearing languages—English and French (*Statutes of ICAS and CAS—A. Joint Dispositions*, 2009; *20 Questions About the CAS*, 2009). One of the major goals behind the formation of the CAS was to prevent Olympic-based legal disputes from being litigated in national courts worldwide. The IOC wanted to avoid being subject to the politics of an individual country or local jurisdiction (*CAS Origins*, 2009). Besides arbitration, the CAS has established procedures for mediation (*Organisation and Structure of the ICAS and CAS*, 2009; *20 Questions About the CAS*, 2009).

Unlike legal decisions in which the concept of precedent is universally recognized and established, the awards and opinions of the CAS are not binding on later decisions. But by providing guidance in later cases and strongly influencing later awards, previous CAS decisions and opinions have helped establish a set of rules and principles of international sport law. These are gradually evolving into a source of law commonly known as the **lex sportiva** (Nafziger, 2004). Although lex sportiva carries strong persuasive influence, prior CAS decisions do not constitute binding precedent in subsequent arbitrations.

Concerns that the close financial and political ties between the CAS and the IOC might compromise the decision-making independence of the CAS in any proceeding in which the IOC was a party led to a number of reforms to the system, which became effective in 1994. The most fundamental change was the founding of an organization, independent of the IOC, to administer and finance the CAS. This organization, called the International Council

Learning Activity

Visit www.tas-cas.org. Select a recent CAS case or one from its online archives and write a legal brief (summary) of the decision. Your legal brief should include the important facts of the decision, an identification of the issue or dispute between the parties, the rules that were applied to facts, and the conclusion or final decision associated with this dispute.

Learning Activity

Discuss how an organization, such as CAS, can function given that different countries have different sets of laws. What if CAS policies, rules, or regulations are inconsistent with the laws of a particular country? In this situation, should the law or CAS policies be applied to athletes?

of Arbitration for Sport (ICAS), is composed of 20 distinguished jurists who have agreed not to serve either as arbitrators or counsel in CAS proceedings (*The 1994 Reform*, 2009).

CAS was originally designed to hear only Olympic-related disputes, but it has expanded its jurisdiction during the last 10 years to include other competitions and events such as the Commonwealth Games and the European Football Championships (Nafziger, 2004). Further, CAS arbitration services are divided into Ordinary and Appellate divisions (*Organisation and Structure of the ICAS and CAS*, 2009). Since the mid-1990s, CAS has maintained on-site arbitration through the CAS ad hoc division, which renders expeditious decisions on issues that arise in major sporting competitions (*The Decentralized CAS Offices and the Ad Hoc Divisions*, 2009).

For CAS arbitration to occur, the parties must agree to submit their dispute to CAS-sponsored arbitration. After the parties agree to arbitration, they are required to select preapproved arbitrators from a designated list compiled by CAS and the applicable law relative to the merits of a case. Lastly, the parties must observe CAS' Rules of Procedure (*The CAS Code*, 2009). According to CAS Rules of Procedure, the applicable law to decide a dispute is that chosen by the parties, or in the absence of such a choice, Swiss law. CAS arbitration involves both written and oral arguments. In arbitrations, CAS adopts the standard of proof of the sport organization or federation whose ruling is under dispute (*The CAS Code*, 2009; *20 Questions About the CAS*, 2009).

Politics and International Sport

Sport and politics are indelibly intertwined. Even though the International Olympic Committee (IOC) is technically a nongovernmental organization that has only limited status outside the Olympics, nations recognize its authority, give deference to its decisions, and conduct diplomacy with it. The role of politics in formulating foreign policy manifested itself prominently during the "ping-pong" diplomacy between the United States and China in the 1970s, South Africa's apartheid era, the United States boycott of the Moscow 1980 Summer Olympic Games to protest the Soviet Union's invasion of Afghanistan in 1979, and the Soviet Union's retaliation boycott against the United States during the 1984 Los Angeles Summer Olympic Games (Nafziger, 2004).

Recognizing that favorable results in international sport competitions help validate a country's social and political system, East Germany engaged in a pervasive and highly successful governmental campaign to establish a prominent international sport presence. This undertaking was often done at the expense of their athletes, including subjecting them to an extensive doping program through which many East German athletes were pressured to use performance-enhancing drugs (Ungerleider, 2001). Sometimes, these drugs were introduced into an athlete's system without the person's knowledge or consent (Longman, 2004; Harding, 2005).

South African style apartheid officially commenced in 1948. Afterward, South Africa's ruling National Party banned interracial sport, including any competition with foreign teams or events whose athletes were nonwhite. Because of these measures, a group of nations threatened to boycott the Olympic Games unless South Africa was excluded from these competitions. After initially deciding to invite South Africa to participate in the 1968 Mexico City Olympic Games, the IOC rescinded its invitation because of pressure from countries who opposed South Africa's apartheid policy. Later, in 1972 and 1976, many African nations threatened to boycott the Olympic Games unless South Africa and Rhodesia (now modern Zimbabwe) were banned from these events. The Gleneagles Agreement, which sought to prevent all sporting contact with South Africa or any other country that allowed apartheid, applies to all countries in the British Commonwealth of Nations (Nafziger, 2004).

Furthermore, several African nations demanded to exclude New Zealand from Olympic competition because their national rugby team, ironically known as the All Blacks, competed in South Africa during the apartheid era. In the case of *Ashby v. Minister of Immigration*, a New Zealand court denied the plaintiff's attempt to enjoin the defendant from granting temporary permits that would allow the Springboks, the South African national rugby team, permission to enter the country to engage in competition with local teams. Although the IOC agreed to ban South Africa and Rhodesia, it did not exclude New Zealand from the Olympic Games. In reaction to this decision, 20 African countries, along with Iraq and Guyana, boycotted the 1976 Montreal Summer Olympic Games (Liu, 2007).

Likewise, the United Nations General Assembly "requested all states and organizations to suspend domestic sport competition with South Africa and with any organizations and institutions in that country that practice apartheid." The boycott of South Africa from the Olympic Games continued for 28 years until the dismantling of the apartheid system from 1990 to 1994. Nelson Mandela, the first president of South Africa, believed that Olympic sanctions contributed to the ultimate transformation of South African culture and had a "significance which goes beyond the boundaries of sport" (Liu, 2007).

Similarly, in 1980 and 1984, during the height of the cold war, 65 nations, led by the United States, refused to compete during the 1980 Moscow Summer Games because of the Soviet Union's invasion of Afghanistan. In retaliation, the Soviet Union and 14 other nations boycotted the next Summer Olympics, which were held in Los Angeles during 1984. One of the shortcomings of the United States government's compulsion of a boycott of the Moscow Olympic Games by the USOC was the unclear, and often contradictory, policy statements issued by the Carter administration. Because of the boycott of the Moscow Summer Games, a group of 25 American Olympic athletes sued the United States Olympic Committee to obtain an injunction to allow them to compete and circumvent the boycott decision (*DeFrantz v. USOC*, 1980).

In the new millennium, the use of sport-based boycotts and embargoes of teams and athletes for reasons of national politics are almost nonexistent. To prevent last-minute boycotts like those that occurred in 1980 and 1984, in 1985 the Olympic Charter was amended to provide that all NOCs must respond to the IOC's invitation to compete in the upcoming Olympics eight months before the scheduled games.

CASE STUDY

DeFrantz v. USOC
492 F. Supp. 1181 (D.D.C. 1980)

In the wake of the Soviet Union's invasion of Afghanistan, former United States president Jimmy Carter, in a liberal exercise of his executive power, compelled an American-led boycott of the 1980 Moscow Summer Olympic Games. Under President Carter's influence, the United States Olympic Committee (USOC) withdrew from the 1980 Summer Olympic Games, along with the Olympic committees of several other NATO-member nations. The USOC is a federally created private organization that exists under Congressional imprimatur through the Ted Stevens Olympic and Amateur Sports Act of 1978 (formerly known as the Amateur Sports Act), a federal statute.

In response to this boycott, several American athletes filed a lawsuit in federal court to enjoin the USOC from preventing them from competing in the Olympics. The plaintiffs cited three legal reasons in support of their claim. First, they alleged that the USOC violated its own administrative rules and regulations in issuing the boycott order. Second, they claimed that the USOC violated the terms and conditions of its charter under the Amateur Sports Act. Finally, the athletes maintained that several of their federal constitutional rights were violated. The aggrieved athletes argued that having made the United States Olympic team in their respective sports, they now had a property interest that was being denied without due process of law, which was a violation of their legal rights as protected by United States Constitution.

The court found in favor of the USOC, although much of its legal reasoning was problematic. With regard to the athletes' constitutional claims, the court determined that despite the fact that the USOC was created by a federal statute, and although their decision to boycott the Games was compelled by the president, the USOC was not a state actor. **State action**, which is a requirement under U.S. law for federal constitutional rights to apply, roughly translates as "governmental involvement." Under the nexus or entanglement test, which is the dominant test that has been articulated by U.S. courts for determining whether state action is present in a given situation, the issue of whether a quasi-governmental entity is a state actor depends on the degree of connectivity that the entity has with the government. In *DeFrantz*, the court erroneously concluded that the USOC did not receive federal funding, when, in fact, the organization received federal financial support pursuant to the Amateur Sports Act. Often, the presence of federal funding is enough of a connection with the government to have an entity declared a state actor under the nexus or entanglement test.

With regard to the due process claims, the court further held that even if the USOC were a state actor, participation in the Olympics was a privilege and not a recognized legal right. But the decision did not adequately address the issue of the USOC failure to remain politically neutral, in violation of the Amateur Sports Act, the Olympic Charter, and USOC's internal rules and regulations.

The *DeFrantz* case reveals how political influences can invade the international sport arena. The court's decision reflects a general judicial reluctance to intervene in matters involving sport organizations. The case also depicts the tension and uncertainty that can arise within the many tiers of international sport law when the ability of governing bodies, such as the IOC and USOC, to regulate sport is challenged through the legal system.

In 2006 Major League Baseball created and hosted the World Baseball Classic. Many of the significant games were to be held in the United States, including games in which the Cuban national baseball team was scheduled to compete. In response, the United States Department of the Treasury wanted to ban the Cuban national team from entering the United States in connection with the World Baseball Classic. Because of public and media criticism and lost revenue and promotion opportunities for Major League Baseball, the federal government ultimately reversed its prohibition and allowed the Cuban team to play in the games held in America (O'Brien, 2008).

Athlete Representation and Athlete Rights

Until the mid-1960s agents were rarely allowed to represent professional athletes. But during the last 50 years, the opportunity for representation of players by agents has grown dramatically, in direct correlation to the global economic expansion of the sport industry. Worldwide sport radio, television, and web broadcasting fees have increased significantly. For instance, Australian media mogul Rupert Murdoch has spent millions, and sometimes billions, in U.S. dollars to secure the broadcast rights to sporting competitions including the English Premier League and the National Football League (NFL) in America (Harris, 2009; Kaplan & Ourand, 2009). The more revenue streams that are available to sport leagues, the more money is available for allocation to player salaries, thus increasing the interest of outside representation for professional athletes.

Further, several landmark sport law decisions including the European football decision by the European Court of Justice in the *Bosman* case in 1995 (*Union Royale Belge des Societes de Football Association [ASB], Royal Club Liegois SA, and Union des Associations Europeennes de Football [UEFA] v. Jean-Marc Bosman,* 1995) and the *Messersmith and McNally* arbitration decision in Major League Baseball (MLB) in 1976 (*National & Am. League Prof'l Baseball Clubs v. Major League Baseball Players Ass'n,* 1976; *Kansas City Royals Baseball Corp. v. Major League Baseball Players Ass'n,* 1976) created free agency by holding that professional athletes were no longer bound, in perpetuity, to their clubs. After these decisions, many professional athletes were able to parlay their talents as free agents to the highest bidder, allowing them to obtain the maximum compensation possible for their services.

Lastly, the emergence of sport-based media has reflected the increasing interest, and sometimes the importance, of professional athletes to the larger society. For instance, besides being stars in their sports, athletes such as David Beckham, Yao Ming, and Tiger Woods are icons of popular culture. Given this confluence of events, agents have emerged to play a critical role in the protection of athletes' legal rights and the promotion of business opportunities for their clients.

Sport Agent Activities, Qualifications, Abuses, and Regulations

During the early years of sport agency, anyone could become an agent. All that was required was for an athlete who earned sufficient income to pay agent fees. Complicating matters further is the wide range of services such as tax advice, financial planning, and investment counseling that agents provide to athletes, often under one roof, and sometimes incompetently. In general, **sport agents** represent professional athletes during their employment contract negotiations with teams, help arrange trades or transfers from one team to another, manage athletes' financial activities, schedule personal appearances for players, and negotiate player endorsement agreements (Greenberg & Gray, 1998).

For instance, American baseball Hall of Fame legend George Herman "Babe" Ruth consulted Christy Walsh, an attorney and cartoonist, to serve as his agent and to provide financial advice during the stock market crash of 1929. When Ruth was reminded that he earned more money than United States president Herbert Hoover, he said, "I had a better year" (Greenberg & Gray, 1998).

More recently, in Europe during the 1990s unethical agent practices were highlighted in the case of Norwegian football agent Rune Hauge, who represented footballers John Jensen and Pal Lydersen regarding their transfer to the Arsenal Football Club in England. It was alleged that Hauge paid former Arsenal manager George Graham a £425,000 (US$680,000) "bung" to sign these players. Graham was found guilty by the English Football Association of accepting a kickback and was suspended for one year. In 1995 FIFA imposed a lifetime ban on Hauge's agent activities. This ban was later reduced by FIFA on appeal to two years (Collins, 2000).

European football offers significant player salaries to many young and financially unsophisticated footballers who, although they are excellent players, may not be expert in safeguarding large sums of money. As a result, player–agent relationships tend to be fraught with abuses and indiscretions, often involving financial mismanagement and fraud. In response to such shenanigans, FIFA promulgated an agent regulatory system. What is unusual about this agent regulatory system, from an American perspective, is that a player labor union did not create it. Instead, it was set up by an organization, FIFA, which represents the best interests of teams and leagues, not players. This occurred because player labor unions in Europe are relatively weak compared with their North American counterparts, and most of the power lies with the European teams, leagues, and agents. For example, Britain's Professional Footballers Association (PFA) and the International Players' Association (FIFPro) have not been able to establish any effective agent qualification standards, nor have they been able to enforce any meaningful agent regulations as effective as North American sport-based labor unions such as the Major League Baseball Players Association (MLBPA), the National Basketball Players Association (NBPA), and the National Football League Players Association (NFLPA) (*MLBPA Regulations Governing Player Agents*, 1993; *NBPA Regulations Governing Player Agents*, 1991; *NFLPA Regulations Governing Contract Advisors*, 2007).

Because of this power vacuum, FIFA established a football agent code of conduct. The most recent version of these regulations requires that agents be licensed directly by the relevant member association, which in the American context means professional leagues. These regulations include (1) the admissibility of player agent activities, (2) the acquisition and loss of player agent licenses, and (3) the rights and obligations of agents, players, and clubs to each other within professional football. Further, these regulations cover conflict resolution in connection with player–agent disputes, as well as any sanctions that may be applied to agent misconduct (*FIFA Players' Agents Regulations*, 2008).

International Player Contracts

In representing professional athletes regarding their international sport opportunities, agents have a fiduciary duty to provide effective personal counseling and sound business advice. Agents must also be knowledgeable regarding the legal aspects of contract negotiations and drafting. This item can raise concerns in jurisdictions where providing advice during contract negotiations and drafting contractual provisions may constitute the practice of law. Some nonattorney agents may be engaged in the unauthorized practice of law, and as a result some athletes may not be receiving competent representation in contract negotiations.

With regard to rendering personal counseling and business advice to young and often impressionable athletes, agents can help prepare their clients for the crucible of international competition. For instance, agents should advise clients who agree to play for an overseas team that they are often expected to carry the team to success, however unreasonable that expectation may be. Leadership skills, cultural awareness and sensitivity, tact and diplomacy, and appreciation of diversity are all skills that an athlete needs to develop to deal effectively with the inevitable adversity that will happen in a new, and sometimes strange, personal and sport employment environment. Given the unique circumstances of international sport, agents can play a crucial role in developing the personal maturity of their athlete clients. For example, imagine that a professional female American basketball player is contracted to compete in a foreign professional league. In many cases, the athlete may neither speak the native language nor be familiar with the local customs. Issues of separation from family and friends will require an adjustment for both the athlete and her new team. If possible, the agent should investigate the availability of a more established and mature player who could help mentor the younger athlete's transition. Issues such as gender expectations, race relations, transportation, accommodations, meals, and communication needs may be as critical to the athlete's success abroad as her athletic prowess. In the complex world of modern sport, helping the athlete appreciate her role in the larger society that she is becoming a part of and providing guidance in her personal growth are arguably more important than any other services that an agent provides.

Regarding specific international player contract negotiation and drafting considerations, as a general legal principle, these agreements include a promise by an athlete to tender personal and unique services to a professional team on an exclusive basis for a specific term and agreed salary and benefits. Subject to any contractual limitations or restrictions negotiated through collective bargaining, a team may remove a player from his or her position on the roster at any time, with or without cause. But the team may be required to compensate a player with monetary damages under certain circumstances, such as if the team violates the player's contract or any applicable provisions contained in a collective bargaining agreement, or is found to have acted in a discriminatory fashion toward the athlete in violation of the law.

With respect to the international player contracts, the most significant provisions include (1) the term of the agreement, (2) the services to be rendered on and off the field, (3) compensation provisions regarding base salary, (4) deferred compensation, (5) low-interest player loans, (6) signing bonuses, (7) performance bonuses, (8) award or honor bonuses, and (9) choice of law and choice of forum provisions that determine which specific law will apply and which court or arbitrator will have jurisdiction over any disputes that might arise under the terms and conditions of the contract. From the athlete's perspective, applying her or his native law to contract disagreements will be advantageous when confronted with litigation. Similarly, the athlete should negotiate, if possible, that an arbitrator rather than a judge should hear any contract dispute because the athlete can have the power to appoint an arbitrator, whereas judicial rules beyond the control of the athlete dictate the appointment of judges to specific disputes. When negotiating international sport contract provisions, athletes and agents must think strategically about protecting themselves upon termination of the contract because ultimately it will occur.

With the increased frequency of international player movement from team to team or from league to league, escape clauses have become more common in the player–team contract dynamic. These types of clauses allow a player and a team to come to a mutual agreement to terminate a contract before it expires at an agreed time and price (Greenberg and Gray, 1998). If an escape clause is absent from player employment agreements, litigation usually results. For example, *Moscow Dynamo v. Ovechkin* involved a dispute over whether a United States court should uphold a Russian arbitration ruling allowing Moscow Dynamo, which owned the contractual rights to Washington Capitals player Alexander Ovechkin, to enforce their existing contract. In this case, during the National Hockey League owner's lockout of 2004–05, Ovechkin signed to play professional hockey in the Russian Professional Hockey League with Moscow Dynamo. Afterward, Ovechkin signed another contract with a second Russian club, Avangard Omsk, which included an escape clause that allowed him to join the Capitals

upon the end of the NHL lockout. Dynamo's position was that it matched Omsk's offer, pursuant to their league guidelines, and therefore retained their rights to Ovechkin. Further, Moscow Dynamo claimed that their original contract did not have any escape clause whatsoever. In resolving this matter, an American federal court held that it did not have jurisdiction to enforce the Russian-based arbitration ruling in favor of Moscow Dynamo. Because of this decision, Ovechkin was able to continue to play and be paid a higher salary by the Capitals (*Moscow Dynamo v. Ovechkin*, 2006).

Another problem with international sport contracts arises when the playing season ends and the player is not paid the last installment of her or his salary under the terms of the contract. This circumstance can be complicated by the choice of law and choice of forum provisions in the contract. If they specify that the athlete must bring the action in the host country, using the law of the host country, then the athlete faces the difficulties of securing foreign legal counsel and negotiating an unfamiliar legal system to resolve the dispute. Also, the visa allowing the athlete to stay in the country typically expires in conjunction with the end of team employment, which is the legal basis for the athlete's presence in that country. Thus, the player often must litigate the issue from overseas. This circumstance has become so common in some European professional basketball leagues that many agents regard the last salary installment as a tax or a donation to the team. In some instances, there is almost an implicit understanding between the parties that the last installment payment of a player's contract will not be paid and will automatically be retained by the team, unless the team chooses to renew the player's contract for an additional term.

Restraints on Player Movement

Player free agency and the ability of clubs to place reasonable restraints on player movement from team to team have been ongoing issues in sport for over a century. In the late 19th century, a number of competing professional baseball leagues existed in the United States. The competition among teams in the various leagues resulted in a rise in player salaries. In response, in 1879 the owners of the clubs in one of these leagues, the National League, adopted the reserve clause.

CASE STUDY

The *Bosman* Ruling

Case C-415/93, *Union Royale Belge des Societes de Football Association (ASBL), Royal Club Liegois SA, and Union des Associations Europeennes de Football (UEFA) v. Jean-Marc Bosman,* 1995 E.C.R. 1-4921

Jean-Marc Bosman, a Belgian footballer, played professionally for RFC de Liege in Belgium. When his contract with RFC de Leige expired, the club offered Bosman a new contract at the league minimum wage, which was about one-quarter of his previous salary. After Bosman refused to agree to those terms, RFC de Leige placed him on its transfer list at such a high price that other teams were not interested in his football services. In response to these actions, Bosman requested a transfer to US Dunkerque, a French club. The transfer was never completed because RFC de Leige believed that US Dunkerque would not pay the transfer fee; RFC de Leige never requested the required approval certificate for transfer from the Belgian Football Association (ASBL). As a result, Bosman was forced to remain with RFC de Liege. The club then suspended Bosman for one year, preventing him from playing in the upcoming season.

Bosman filed a lawsuit claiming that as a European Union citizen, he possessed the right under Article 48 of the Treaty of Rome (now Article 39 of the European Union Treaty) of freedom of movement within the European Union to find employment. Bosman argued that allowing teams to impose transfer fees when players sought to switch clubs prevented him from exercising his right to freedom of movement in his desire to be employed by another European football club of his choice.

Bosman initially brought his lawsuit before a Belgian court where an interlocutory decision was entered in his favor. The case was then sent to the Cour d'Appel in Liege, which revoked the interlocutory decision regarding the interpretation of the transfer rules but upheld the order against RFC de Liege to pay Bosman and to allow him to be employed by another team without any transfer fee to be paid to the team. After reviewing the pertinent articles in the Treaty of Rome, the Cour d'Appel in Liege referred the case to the European Court of Justice (ECJ) so that they could render a final decision regarding the case.

The ECJ ruled in favor of Bosman. The court held that imposition of transfer fees for players moving from one European Union club to another whose contracts had ended violated EU **competition law**, which is designed to prohibit monopolistic practices on the theory that such conduct inhibits free trade. But the court in *Bosman* found that transfer fees could still be imposed on players who remained under contract with their clubs. The ECJ also held that quota systems were illegal and that EU clubs could sign as many players from other European Union nations as they wanted, although limits on players from outside the EU could still be imposed.

The *Bosman* decision has resulted in an increase in the salaries paid to European footballers and has created the European concept of player free agency. It has also caused some clubs to offer longer-term contracts to players, often to the detriment of smaller clubs that cannot afford to make such offers.

The **reserve clause** gave "the club the exclusive right automatically to renew the contract and that bound the athlete to the club until retirement or until the athlete was traded or released" (*Black's Law Dictionary*, 2004).

As intended, the reserve clause had a chilling effect on player salaries. Subsequently, a more equitable system for player opportunity evolved over time as courts worldwide invalidated comprehensive league restraints on player movement without the consent of the athletes affected because these restraints violated anticompetition laws. For instance, various courts in the United States, the European Union, and Australia all have found that complete bans on player free agency, as unilaterally imposed by owners and leagues, were unlawful (See *Mackey v. Nat'l Football League*, 543 F.2d 606 [8th Cir. 1976]; *Union Royale Belge des Societies de Football Association v. Bosman* [1996], 1. C.M.L.R. 645 [E.C.J.]; *Buckley v. Tutty*, 125 C.L.R. 353 [H.C. 1971]).

CASE STUDY

Efforts to Control Player Movement in Japanese Baseball

The concept of owning and playing is vividly illustrated within the context of Japanese baseball. Ever since the Masanori Murakami affair in 1965, involving a dispute between the San Francisco Giants and Nankai Hawks over the rights to Murakami, the owners in Nippon Professional Baseball (NPB) have employed various strategies to dissuade and curtail players from leaving for the Major Leagues (Cafardo, 2007). The efforts have ranged from the imposition of subtle social pressures, to implied threats of blacklisting, to formal agreements with Major League Baseball and its member clubs designed to limit player movement between clubs in the two leagues. With regard to blacklisting, it is no longer an implied threat. In 2008 the Japanese club owners announced that a two-year ban from the NPB would be imposed on any Japanese high school baseball player who signed to play overseas (Fornelli, 2008; *Japan tries to discourage amateurs from playing in MLB with ban*, 2008).

This tension is also reflected internally in Japanese professional baseball. In 2004 the Japanese Professional Baseball Players Association (JPBPA) called for a weekend strike on September 18 and 19, 2004, to protest the loss of jobs that would result from the proposed merger of two professional Japanese baseball teams, the Kintetsu Buffaloes and the Orix Blue Wave. The strike was the first in the history of Japanese baseball (Whiting, 2004). When JPBPA leader Atsuya Furuta requested a meeting with Japanese baseball owners to discuss the proposed merger of the two teams, Tsuneo Watanabe, president of Yomiuri Holdings and Tokyo's Yomiuri Giants, scornfully commented, "He's just a player, he should know his place" (Whiting, 2004). In Japanese society, negotiating a consensus is the preferred means of resolving conflict, and strikes are not frequently implemented in labor relations in Japan. Reflecting this sentiment, Furuta humbly said with regard to the strike, "I sincerely want to apologize to everyone for this, but it can't be helped" (Whiting, 2004). Ultimately, in 2005 continued financial instability resulted in the two teams merging and becoming known as the Orix Buffaloes.

One of the costs associated with the harsh practices implemented by the owners in Japanese professional baseball and their unwillingness to compete in the global arena for top talent has been the mass exodus of a number of Japan's star players, starting with Hideo Nomo in 1995. Since then, numerous other stars such as Ichiro Suzuki, Hideki Matsui, and Daisuke Matsuzaka have left Japanese baseball for the Major Leagues to maximize their career earning potential. Meanwhile, the Japanese public and media have shifted their primary focus away from professional baseball in their native land to televised Major League Baseball offerings. As a result, the NPB is facing economic uncertainty, and from the perspective of many observers it has devolved into little more than a feeder league for MLB.

But in places such as Africa, Asia, and South America, free agency is not an issue or it may be a minimal one. League or team economics do not provide sufficient revenue to create a viable leaguewide bidding system for player services. Alternatively, athlete free agency has no tradition or there may be a lack of history connected with player job security within the native culture. In other words, "owners own and players play." The globalization of sport has opened new doors for athletes from these continents to exploit the global marketplace as free agents. For example, many of the top Brazilian footballers leave for Europe to maximize their earning potential.

Learning Activity

Select a professional sport (e.g., hockey, basketball, baseball, football) and identify some of the ways that teams and leagues attempt to restrain free movement of players to competitor leagues and teams in other countries. Identify one or two specific examples and list possible legal issues and remedies that might exist for teams, leagues, and athletes.

Promoting Sport for All

The Olympic Charter encourages the development of sport for all, which in conjunction with other provisions helps establish the practice of sport as a human right (*Olympic Charter*, 2007). Outside the United States, many countries have created, by legislation, an entity known as a ministry of sport. These organizations, which are government based and taxpayer funded, promote sport, culture, and physical activity nationwide. One of the primary functions of a ministry of sport is sport for all, whereby efforts are directed to integrate sport and recreation into the lives of citizens from childhood to the senior years.

For instance, the Malta Sports Act's preamble states that its Sports Ministry will "encourage and promote sport, to provide for the establishment of a national sport council to exercise the functions relating to sport currently vested in the Department of Youth and Sport . . ." (*Malta's Sports Act—Chapter 455*, 2003). Similarly, the mission statement of Singapore's Ministry of Community Development, Youth, and Sports provides that the nation wants to develop "socially responsible individuals, inspired and committed youth, strong and stable families, a caring and active community, and a sporting people" (*Mission Statement—Singapore Ministry of Community Development, Youth, and Sports*, 2005). Likewise, the entity known as Sport and Recreation South Africa, the national governmental department responsible for sport and recreation for that nation, "strives to create an active and winning nation" as well as "to improve the quality of life of all South Africans, foster social cohesion and enhance nation building by maximizing access, development and excellence at all levels of participation in sport and recreation" (Sport and Recreation South Africa, n.d.).

Gender and Race Issues in International Sport

The Olympic Charter prohibits discrimination against any country or person based on grounds of race, religion, politics, or otherwise. Yet participation by women in the Olympics was severely limited until 1928, and even after that, progress toward gender equity in international sport competitions has been slow to evolve.

International sport has generated emerging developments not yet confronted in the United States. For instance, in *Gardner v. All Australian Netball Association* (*Gardner v. Nat'l Netball League Pty Ltd.*, 2001) a female netballer wanted to compete while she was pregnant. The national governing organization banned this athlete from competition because they did not want her to endanger the health and safety of the unborn, the mother, or other netball competitors. To be reinstated to competition, Gardner complained that the eligibility rules of netball regarding pregnant players were a violation of Section 22 of Australia's federal Sex Discrimination Act (SDA). In holding in favor of Gardner, the court pointed out that the SDA should be read narrowly to ensure the maximum protection of the rights of women.

Another emerging issue pertaining to international sport is affirmative action and race discrimination. During South Africa's apartheid era, rugby was exclusively a white man's game. After apartheid officially ended in South Africa during the 1990s, the national team faced a dilemma in terms of how it could continue to excel within international rugby competition and simultaneously integrate nonwhite players on the club. South Africa's postapartheid constitution provides for equal opportunity in all phases of society. In gauging the reaction of the country's equal opportunity legislation as applied to international rugby, South Africa's sports minister, Makhenkesi Stofile, commented, "The notion that when a black man excels, it is just a 'regstellende aksie' (affirmative action) is born of the prejudice of the mind, which assumes that no good can come out of these flat noses" (Mohamed, 2008).

Religious impediments have also imposed constraints on female athletes. In countries where Islamic fundamentalism and its interpretation of Sharia law are practiced, women are subjugated to males. Consequently, opportunities for women in those societies to participate in sport are extremely limited. But recently Muslim women have begun to emerge from the shadows of gender oppression. For instance, in 2003 Lima Azimi became the first Afghan woman ever to compete in a major international sporting event (Nafziger, 2004).

Athletes With Disabilities and Sport Law

On September 22, 1989, the International Paralympic Committee was established. This nonprofit organization was formed and organized by 162 National Paralympic Committees from five world regions and four disability-specific international sport federations. These four federations include the (1) Cerebral Palsy International Sport and Recreation Association, (2) the International Blind Sports Federation, (3) the International Sports Federation for Persons With Intellectual Disability, and (4) the International Wheelchair and Amputee Sports Federation (International Paralympic Committee, 2009).

In 2007 the United Nations' Convention on the Rights of Persons With Disabilities and its Optional Protocol was agreed upon; 82 nations signed the Convention, 44 countries signed the Optional Protocol, and one nation ratified the Convention. The Convention signals a transformation in international societal attitudes and official government policy with respect to people with disabilities. This agreement attempts to integrate people with disabilities into mainstream, or nondisabled, society. In other words, the United Nations desires to change the view that people with disabilities are objects of charity who require medical treatment and social protection. Instead, the United Nations wants people to accept those with disabilities as citizens who possess legal rights and are capable of claiming those rights and rendering decisions about their lives based on their free and informed consent. Ideally, this action will foster an acceptance of the disabled as being active

and productive members of international and domestic society (United Nations, 2006).

Given the United Nations position relative to people with disabilities generally, coupled with sport-based medical advances and improvements in technology, the distinction between those with disabilities and the "able-bodied" is becoming blurred as it pertains to international sport. This issue was confronted in the 2008 Court of Arbitration for Sport decision concerning a dispute between Oscar Pistorius, a disabled South African sprinter, and the International Association of Athletics Federations, which governs international track and field events (*CAS Arbitral Award—Oscar Pistorius*, 2008).

Integrity of International Sport

International sport law promotes the concept of *inclusiveness*, particularly when contending with issues of race, gender, and disability as applied to world competitions and athlete participation in those events. Additionally, one should also be aware of the ongoing threats to the integrity of sport, posed by various illicit activities such as gambling, doping, and violence. *Integrity of sport* means that

CASE STUDY

Pistorius v. International Association of Athletics Federations (IAAF)
CAS 2008/A/1480 Pistorius v/IAAF

South African Oscar Pistorius, a professional sprinter, uses prosthetic legs to race because he is a double amputee. The International Association of Athletics Federations (IAAF) believed that the use of these prosthetic devices gave Pistorius a competitive advantage over able-bodied athletes during elite international track events. At the time, Pistorius was approaching qualifying at the Olympic and World Games and had therefore reached the elite ranks in the world for sprinters. The IAAF sanctioned a study to evaluate this issue. Based on the findings of that report, the IAAF declared Pistorius ineligible to compete in any IAAF-sanctioned events. With this ruling, his elite international sprinting career abruptly ended.

Pistorius appealed the IAAF's ruling to the Court of Arbitration for Sport (CAS). The CAS found for Pistorius, reversing the IAAF's decision, thus allowing

Pistorius to compete in all IAAF-sanctioned sprint events. The CAS decision, however, was extremely narrow in its scope. For example, the CAS determination did not allow for the upgrade of Pistorius' prosthetics in any way. Also, the decision specifically stated that should new technology become available to allow more precise testing, then Pistorius' prosthetics should be reevaluated to determine whether any unfair competitive advantage is present. Finally, the CAS specifically pointed out that its decision "has absolutely no application to any other athlete, or other type of prosthetic limb."

Despite the limitations of this ruling, the *Pistorius* case was a watershed legal decision because it marked the first time in history that an elite athlete with disabilities was granted the right to compete against able-bodied competitors.

international sport competitions are perceived as fair, relatively speaking, and free from vice. International sport law has been applied to protect sport competitions from the potential harm that can occur from the misconduct of devious gamblers, unscrupulous dopers, and those engaging in unwarranted violent behavior.

Doping

The use of performance-enhancing drugs by athletes has become a crisis of epidemic proportions and has marred the public image of many sport leagues and sporting events. Doping undermines the integrity of sporting competitions by giving athletes who use performance-enhancing substances a competitive advantage over competitors who do not. Concerns have also been raised about the influence that the use of such substances by professional and world-class athletes might have on impressionable youth, who may admire athletes and view them as role models.

During the cold war, rumors circulated that the athletes from the Soviet Union and other Soviet-bloc nations were using drugs to improve their athletic performance. Given the political tension of those times, discerning whether the claims had any validity or were fueled by Western fear and paranoia was difficult. But ultimately, various investigative reports not only revealed those allegations to be true but also exposed that doping by athletes from those countries was the result of organized and systematic programs administered and subsidized by their respective governments (Stewart, 2006; Mehlman, Banger, & Wright, 2005).

In response to those and similar concerns, the IOC began to implement an antidoping program. The first efforts by the IOC to control and test for performance-enhancing substances occurred in 1967 (Nafziger, 2004). The overall commitment of the Olympic Movement to curtail the use of performance-enhancing substances is found in Rule 2(8) of the Olympic Charter, which states that the IOC "leads the fight against doping in sport and participates in the international fight against drugs" (Olympic Charter, 2007).

Despite the early efforts of the IOC to address the doping dilemma, problems associated with athlete doping continued to surface. The magnitude of the situation became apparent at the 1988 Summer Olympic Games in Seoul, South Korea, when Canadian Ben Johnson had his gold medal in the 100-meter sprint revoked after testing positive for use of steroids. In the aftermath of this shocking revelation, the IOC intensified its efforts to control the use of performing-enhancing drugs by Olympic athletes.

In 1999 the World Anti-Doping Agency (WADA) was formed to "promote and coordinate the fight against doping internationally" (WADA History, n.d.). The IOC incorporated the World Anti-Doping Code (WADC) into its bylaws and tasked WADA with the responsibility of administering the WADC with respect to the Olympic Games and the national and international sport federations (Nafziger, 2004). Various national antidoping agencies, such as the United States Anti-Doping Agency (USADA), were established to assist WADA in its mission (Nafziger, 2004).

As embodied in the Olympic Charter, to be eligible to compete in the Olympics, an athlete must comply with all aspects of the World Anti-Doping Code. Under the WADC, an action commenced against an athlete for doping must be brought within eight years of the alleged violation. In a doping case under the WADC, the burden of proof is on the antidoping organization making the allegation against the athlete, and the standard of proof is "comfortable satisfaction." The WADC defines *comfortable satisfaction* as "greater than a mere balance of probability but less than proof beyond a reasonable doubt" (*The World Anti-Doping Code*, 2009 [revised]). The standard of proof in a given case is the degree of certainty or assuredness that the finder of fact, usually the jury, needs to have to determine any issues in controversy. For example, in the United States, the standard of proof in civil cases for personal injury is "preponderance of the evidence," and in criminal cases it is "beyond a reasonable doubt" (*Black's Law Dictionary*, 2004).

An athlete accused of violating the doping policies has a number of due process rights under the WADC,

Learning Activity

Visit www.wada-ama.org/en. How does WADA interact with national antidoping agencies such as USADA? Has athlete drug use been reduced since the creation of either WADA or USADA? Is antidoping enforcement fair to the athletes whom it affects?

including but not limited to (1) the right to present evidence and call and cross-examine witnesses; (2) the right to be represented by legal counsel; (3) the right to a timely, reasoned written decision; and (4) the right to an interpreter at the hearing if necessary. The recommended methods for giving effect to the World Anti-Doping Code and related international standards are referred to as the models of best practice (*The World Anti-Doping Code*, 2009).

In a definitive set of opinions, the CAS developed a rule of strict liability for the presence of prohibited substances in a urine or blood sample whenever it has been detected by approved scientific procedures. Within the context of doping,

> (the) principle of strict liability means that an antidoping rule violation occurs whenever a prohibited substance (or its metabolites or markers) is found in the bodily specimen of an athlete, whether or not the athlete intentionally or unintentionally used a prohibited substance or was negligent or otherwise at fault. (World Anti-Doping Agency, 2007, 2008)

Other examples of violations of the rules under the World Anti-Doping Code include (1) aiding and abetting an athlete in violation of the code, (2) failure by the athlete to provide whereabouts information for missed tests in connection with out-of-competition testing, (3) attempting to tamper with a doping control, and (4) refusal of the athlete to provide a body fluid sample after notification. The general sanctions by the CAS for doping violations are a two-year suspension of eligibility for unmitigated violations and a termination of eligibility for recidivism (Howman, 2003; *The World Anti-Doping Code*, 2009). In doping cases, recidivism refers to repeated violations of the WADC (Howman, 2003).

Despite these efforts, at the 2007 World Conference on Doping in Sport, IOC President Jacques Rogge somberly observed, "Doping is one of the most serious threats the Olympic Movement has ever seen" (Rogge, 2007). The majority of CAS cases involve appeals of various sanctions related to doping incidents (Nafziger, 2004). The doping problem has become so pervasive that it seems almost impossible to put the genie back in the bottle.

From a legal perspective, the efforts to control doping in sport have raised numerous due process issues. **Due process** generally means that governing bodies should adhere to principles of fundamental fairness and justice when determining the rights and status of those under their review.

Establishing antidoping rules and regulations requires defining which substances are to be banned. Creating lists of banned substances could allow dishonest athletes to continue to cheat by using substances with slightly different chemical formulas that produce the same performance-enhancing results but are not on the list of prohibited substances. Establishing general, nonspecific prohibitions, such as "any substance that enhances an athlete's performance" is problematic as well. From a legal standpoint, such rules can come under attack for vagueness because athletes cannot be expected to comply with the rules and regulations if they do not know what they are. Another issue with lists of banned substances is that many commonly used medications and prescription drugs, such as cough medicine, may contain substances on the WADC banned list. Issues also arise regarding the intersection of WADA's jurisdiction and national law. Many of the substances on the WADC banned list may not be illegal to purchase or use in the country where the athlete resides. Consequently, the athlete may not be violating the laws of his or her country and may believe that taking such substances is not wrong.

Also, concerns have been raised regarding the efficacy of the doping procedures established by WADA and the various national antidoping agencies. Although WADA adopts a "best practice" rule regarding testing procedures, the 2008 CAS appeal involving American cyclist Floyd Landis demonstrates that the procedures used to test for banned substances are not perfect. Although Landis lost his appeal, the CAS acknowledged that there were "some minor procedural imperfections" in the procedures used to test Landis for banned substances. Of particular concern are issues involving sample tampering and chain of custody (*Floyd Landis v. USADA*, 2008). Chain of custody is the documentary proof of the continuity of evidence that guarantees the integrity of a sample and ensures proper identification of the provider of the sample (Soek, 2006).

Given the extremely high stakes involved in international sport for leagues, teams, players, and sponsors, an argument could be made that positive doping results should be permitted only in circumstances where it can be demonstrated that the procedures implemented were completely error free.

Third, the WADC "whereabouts" rule raises right-to-privacy issues regarding the extent to which sport governing bodies can intrude on the private and personal lives of athletes. The athlete whereabouts rule requires that information be provided by or on behalf of an athlete detailing the athlete's exact location on a daily basis to enable unannounced doping testing (World Anti-Doping Agency, 2007). In balancing the rights of the athletes against the need to control the use of performance-enhancing substances in sporting competitions, the argument could be made that such a rule is over-reaching.

Finally, doping problems are not unique to the Olympic Games. For example, in his highly publicized exposé, former Major League Baseball star Jose Canseco contended that use of steroids was prevalent among athletes in baseball during his playing career (Canseco, 2005). A string of events followed the release of Canseco's controversial memoir. Earlier, in 2003, federal investigators raided the California laboratory of the Bay Area Laboratory Co-Operative (BALCO), which was suspected of providing steroids to professional athletes. The seized documents and financial records implicated a number of high-profile athletes, including Barry Bonds. In March 2005 Mark McGwire, a former teammate of Canseco, testified before a Congressional panel that steroids were "as prevalent in . . . the late 1980s and 1990s as a cup of coffee." The *Mitchell Report*, released in 2007, indicated that use of steroids in professional baseball was "widespread." The same year, Bonds was indicted on charges of perjury and obstruction of justice (Godoy, 2007). These charges are still pending.

In the case of Major League Baseball, policies and procedures for drug testing are collectively bargained between the owners and players union as a term and condition of employment. In 2005 Major League Baseball players and owners adopted a drug-testing policy for the first time. The policy imposed a 10-day suspension for first-time offenders and allowed random, off-season testing of players, as well as one unannounced mandatory test of each player during the season (Godoy, 2007). Although these policies and procedures are collectively bargained terms and conditions of employment as part of baseball's basic agreement, Congressional pressure has been credited with having much to do with the movement in the Major League Baseball toward a more stringent drug-testing policy.

Learning Activity

Define and describe some of the due process protections that exist within the major agencies responsible for drug testing of athletes. Discuss whether the procedural safeguards that are in place are sufficient given what is potentially at stake. What, if anything, could be done to improve the drug-testing procedures? Is it important who decides which drug-testing rules to implement and which drugs should be banned from sport? Are athletes legally entitled to due process? Should they be? If so, what process should be due?

One example of Major League Baseball's drug policies being applied to foreign players involved Dominican Republic player Miguel Tejada. In 2009 Tejada pled guilty in a Houston federal district court to misleading Congress about his use of performance-enhancing drugs. According to United States Immigration and Customs Enforcement, Tejada's "guilty plea in this case may subject him to detention, deportation and other sanctions." Tejada's attorneys, however, believed that "because of the nature of the offense, considered a petty offense, not a crime of moral turpitude, we believe it will have no impact on his immigration status at all" (Associated Press, 2009).

Gambling and Corruption

Following the 1919 World Series, eight member of the Chicago White Sox, including "Shoeless" Joe Jackson and Eddie Cicotte, were accused of throwing the series to the Cincinnati Reds as part of a match-fixing scheme conducted in collusion with organized gamblers. Although they were acquitted of all criminal charges by a Chicago jury, all eight members of the so-called Black Sox were banned from organized baseball for life by newly appointed baseball commissioner Kenesaw Mountain Landis (Asinof, 2000). The Black Sox scandal heralded a dark chapter in the history of American sport that has been tainted by gambling-related allegations of match fixing, fraud, bribery, and racketeering.

In 1989 baseball's all-time career hits leader, Pete Rose, was banned from baseball for betting on games. The commissioner at the time, A. Bartlett Giamatti, described Rose's punishment as "the sad end of a sorry episode" (Reston, 1997, 306). Rose initially denied the allegations but later publicly confessed to betting on baseball games (Rose, 2004). He continues to be denied admission to the National Baseball Hall of Fame because of his misconduct.

Cricket is a huge industry in India, and the top Indian professional cricket players often make 20 times the amount of their salaries in sponsorships and celebrity endorsements (Srivastava, 2000). Introduced by British colonists more than 200 years ago, the game has thrived on the Indian subcontinent. But in 2000 a shocking match-fixing and bribery scandal rocked the sport and left the entire nation reeling. Many of India's top cricket players were implicated in the scandal (Filkins, 2000).

These vignettes reveal how fragile the sport business is and how susceptible sport is to being undermined by gambling and similar forms of misconduct. As sportscaster Curt Gowdy once remarked, the biggest concern in sports is a betting or gambling scandal or a fix. He said, "Once the public loses confidence in that sport, it's all over" (*ESPN's Sports Century: Most Influential People in Sports*, 1999).

But the players are not the only sport figures susceptible to gambling, bribes, and corruption. Numerous sport officials, judges, executives, and administrators have been compromised in their roles by promises of clandestine payments and payoffs. For example, organizers Tom Welch and Dave Johnson faced criminal charges of fraud, conspiracy, bribery, and racketeering for their activities related to the securing of the Olympic bid for the Salt Lake City Winter Olympics (Snyder, 2003). During the 2002 Salt Lake City Games, the pairs figure-skating competition was marred with controversy resulting from allegations, and a subsequent investigation, that French judge Marie Reine le Gougne conspired with her husband, Didier Gailhaguet, to trade votes during the pairs and ice-dancing competitions as part of a covert deal with the Russian Federation (Snyder, 2003).

In 2007 former NBA referee Tim Donaghy pled guilty to federal charges that he accepted payoffs from a professional gambler in exchange for tips on NBA games. Donaghy then accused NBA league officials of routinely encouraging referees to call unwarranted fouls to manipulate results while simultaneously discouraging referees from making calls against star players to keep them in games and protect ticket sales and television ratings (CBS Interactive Inc., 2008).

Former IOC vice president Un Yong Kim was stripped of his IOC membership and forced to resign from the South Korean parliament after being linked with several fraudulent financial schemes. Kim was implicated in the Salt Lake City bribery scandal, which included claims that he received millions in U.S. dollars and secured a sham position in America for his son in exchange for his vote. Kim was also found guilty by a South Korean court of embezzling millions of U.S. dollars of corporate donations given to the World Taekwondo Federation (WTF). Kim was sentenced to two and a half years of imprisonment, along with a fine of about a quarter million U.S. dollars (Guardian News & Media, 2004; IOC Ethics Commission, 2005).

Another recent legal concern facing the international sport community involves the proliferation and widespread use of Internet and offshore sport betting sites. With recent advances in technology and communication, these websites are flourishing, especially with the computer-savvy younger generation. Various countries have begun to take action to curtail the rampant presence and use of online sport betting sites. For example, in the United States several successful prosecutions have been brought against offshore Internet gambling operations. In addition, several states have introduced specific legislation designed to address offshore betting, and the U.S. Congress passed the Unlawful Internet Gambling Enforcement Act in 2006 (Humphrey,

Learning Activity

How has the Internet changed the face of sport betting? What unique legal issues arise within the context of international sport gambling? Should sport gambling be considered a public health problem similar to drug addiction? Further, should Internet gambling websites, such as www .ssp.co.uk, be subject to legal regulation? If so, how?

2006). Still, it is generally acknowledged that the long-term solution to this burgeoning problem requires global cooperation, although that resolution will likely not occur for many years.

Violence and Terrorism at Sporting Events

Increasingly, violence has crept into international sport, raising a variety of legal and ethical concerns. Sometimes, the violence is between competitors.

One of the more shocking examples of violence by one competitor toward another involved the planned attack on Olympic figure skating hopeful Nancy Kerrigan during the 1994 United States Figure Skating Championships. Skating rival Tonya Harding was implicated in conspiring to orchestrate the attack with several others. Besides criminal charges, the matter raised complex administrative law issues regarding Harding's continued eligibility to compete in future Olympic Games because of the various charges associated with the assault on Kerrigan still pending against her (Snyder, 2003).

Sometimes, player violence is directed at people other than other competitors. In 2004 an ugly incident that began as an on-court brawl between member of the NBA's Indiana Pacers and Detroit Pistons ultimately spilled into the stands. Several players went into the stands and exchanged blows with spectators (Sandoval, 2004). In 1997 NBA player Latrell Sprewell was suspended for choking and throwing punches at coach P.J. Carlesimo during a practice session (Puma, 2004). Both incidents resulted in player fines and suspensions, disciplinary arbitrations regarding the penalties imposed against the players, and civil litigation. In the case of the Pistons–Pacers foray, several of the combatants also faced criminal prosecution.

In perhaps the most extreme example of player violence affecting others besides the athletes themselves, the "soccer war" between Honduras and El Salvador during the 1969 World Cup qualifying matches escalated into border violations and all-out armed conflict between the two countries (Nafziger, 2004).

Spectator violence by British football fans is commonly referred to as hooliganism. Incidents related to hooliganism have turned what Brazilian football great Pelé called the beautiful game into an ugly nightmare for some. For instance, in 1985 an infamous tragedy involving British football fans occurred at a stadium in Brussels, Belgium. In the aftermath of the event, Britain permitted 26 of its citizens to be extradited to stand trial for inciting this violence (*Football Violence Round the World*, 1998).

In 1995, 39 fans died because of violence at the European Cup final match between Liverpool and Juventus. The incident became known as the Heysel tragedy (*The Heysel Disaster*, 2000). In response to hooliganism in football, the Council of Europe passed the European Convention on Spectator Violence (Council of Europe, 1985), a cooperative system under international law to control such violence. This agreement has led to the extradition and criminal prosecution of many people suspected of violence or other criminal misconduct at sporting events.

Violence has also been perpetrated by spectators against professional athletes. On April 30, 1993, tennis star Monica Seles suffered a knife attack from a deranged fan that derailed her career. Her attacker, Guenter Parche, was convicted of causing Seles grievous bodily harm. Because of his diminished capacity, he received a two-year suspended sentence (Lowitt, 1999).

In 1972 the world watched on television in stunned disbelief as extremists from the Black September militant group kidnapped nine Israeli athletes and coaches, and killed two others during the Munich Olympic Games. In a shootout with police, all the hostages and five of the terrorists were killed. The incident changed the face of international sport.

The tragedy induced the United States State Department to introduce a Draft Convention for the Prevention and Punishment of Certain Acts of International Terrorism. Security became a major concern at international sporting events. At the 2004 Athens Summer Olympics, approximately US$800 million was spent on security alone. The security force at the event included about 20,000 personnel, 16,000 soldiers, as well as additional standby troops from NATO (Nafziger, 2004).

Summary

International sport law regulates the economic relationships between and amongst the stakeholders of global sport. First, the law provides guidance about how the revenue that is generated by international sport is to be shared by sport governing bodies, leagues, owners, players, and agents. Second, the law has also established the contours and limitations of the authority, power, and control that any one person or entity may possess and later apply to any of the various international sport stakeholders. Gone are the days when a league or a team can unreasonably banish an athlete from pursuing employment opportunities or unilaterally exclude an athlete from competition without legal redress. The arbitrary decision making that highlighted so much of 20th century sport has been continually replaced by the parameters of a more equitable 21st century international sport law.

Politics will continue to influence and shape international sport law. As the world becomes more tolerant and accepting of racial, religious, disability, and gender differences, nations will enact legislation to ensure that sport for all will become the norm of society, not the exception. Further, international sport law provides a system for dispute resolution, either through the courts or arbitration that is available to all, so long as a person has the resources to finance litigation. The law will enjoy an ever-increasing role relative to the affairs of the international sport industry as long as the global media and spectator interest in these events remains a worldwide phenomenon. In sum, so long as people continue to argue over sport-generated revenue or believe that they have been treated unfairly by the sport industry, international sport law will persistently be applied to settle these contests.

International sport law deals with a wide range of issues, not all of which could be covered in this chapter. If you are interested in learning more about topics and issues in sport law, the list on page 378 provides resources for further reading.

? Review and Discussion Questions

1. What is international sport law?

2. Under what circumstances will courts judicially review sport organization decisions?

3. Why was the Court of Arbitration for Sport created?

4. What is meant by lex sportiva?

5. What are some of the contract problems that athletes confront while playing internationally?

6. Why was the reserve clause created?

7. Why is sport for all legally important?

8. How is athlete doping legally regulated?

9. Is free agency good for international sport? Identify the various stakeholders in this debate. What balance should be struck between the player's interest in maximizing his or her income and the team's interest in maintaining the continuity of the team?

10. Is there a point at which an athlete with a disability can have a competitive advantage over other athletes because of implants, prosthetic devices, and enhancements? How should the term *competitive advantage* be defined? For example, how do we distinguish between enhancements that enable athletes with disabilities to compete from those that give a competitive advantage (e.g., use of performance-enhancing substances)?

11. With increasing frequency, international sport gambling has pervaded worldwide society from informal office pools to government-sponsored lotteries. It appears as if gambling is everywhere and that everyone is doing "the gambling thing." Given this sport-gambling phenomenon, can international sport organizations such as the International Cricket Council or the International Olympic Committee effectively prevent sport-based gambling from occurring with their respective organizations?

Additional Readings in International Sport Law

Bale, J., & Maguire, J. (Eds.). (1994). *The global sports arena: Athletic talent migration in an interdependent world.* London: Routledge.

Blackshaw, I.S. (2002). *Mediating sports disputes: National and international perspectives.* Norwell, MA: TMC Asser Press.

Blackshaw, I.S., Siekmann, R., & Soek, J. (Eds.). (2006). *The Court of Arbitration for Sport, 1984–2004.* The Hague, the Netherlands: TMC Asser Press.

Blackshaw, I.S., & Siekmann, R. (Eds.). (2005). *Sports image rights in Europe.* The Hague, the Netherlands: TMC Asser Press.

Blanpain, R. (Ed.). (2004). *International encyclopaedia of laws. Sports law.* The Hague, the Netherlands: TMC Asser Press.

Blanpain, R. (2003). *The legal status of sportsmen and sportswomen under international, European and Belgian national and regional law.* New York: Kluwer Academic.

Caiger, A., & Gardiner, S. (Eds.). (2000). *Professional sport in the European Union: Regulation and re-regulation.* The Hague, the Netherlands: TMC Asser Press.

Fay, T.G., & Snyder, D. (2006). A North American perspective on international sport. In J.B. Parks, J. Quarterman, & L.Thibault (Eds.), *Contemporary sport management* (3rd ed.) (pp. 163–188). Champaign, IL: Human Kinetics.

Gardiner, S., James, M., O'Leary, J., & Welch, R. (2006). *Sports law* (3rd ed.). Portland, OR: Cavendish.

Jennings, A., & Simson, V. (1992). *Dishonored games: Corruption, money, and greed at the Olympics.* London: Weatherhill.

Jennings, A., & Simson, V. (1992). *The lords of the rings: Power, money, and drugs at the Olympics.* London: Simon and Schuster.

Jennings, A. (1996). *The new lords of the rings.* London: Pocket Books.

Jennings, A. (2001). *The great Olympic swindle: When the world wanted its games back.* New York: Simon & Schuster.

Johnson, P. (2008). *Ambush marketing: A practical guide to protecting the brand of a sporting event.* London : Sweet & Maxwell.

Kaufmann-Kohler, Gabrielle. (2001). *Arbitration at the Olympics: Issues of fast-track dispute resolution and sports law.* Norwell, MA: Kluwer Law International.

McArdle, D. (2000). *From boot money to Bosman: Football, society and the law.* London: Cavendish.

Panagiotopoulos, P. (Ed.). (2004). *Sports law (Lex sportiva) in the world.* Athens, Greece: Ant. N. Sakkoulas.

Panagiotopoulos, P. (2003). *Sports law: A European dimension.* Athens, Greece: Ant. N. Sakkoulas.

Parrish, R., & Miettinen, S. (2008). *The sporting exception in European Union law.* The Hague, the Netherlands: TMC Asser Press.

Parrish, R. (2003). *Sports law and policy in the European Union.* Manchester, United Kingdom: Manchester University Press.

Paine, Michael. (2005). *Olympic turnaround.* London: London Business Press.

Pound, R.W. (1994). *Five rings over Korea: The secret negotiations behind the 1988 Olympic Games in Seoul.* New York: Little, Brown.

Pound, R.W. (2004). *Inside the Olympics.* Montreal, QC, Canada: Wiley & Sons.

Siekmann, R., & Soek, J. (Eds.). (1998). *The basic documents of international sports organisations.* Boston: Kluwer Law International.

Siekmann, R., & Soek, J. (Eds.). (2001). *Arbitral and disciplinary rules of international sports organisations.* Boston: Kluwer Law International.

Siekmann, R., & Soek, J. (Eds.). (2005). *The European Union and sport: Legal and policy documents.* The Hague, the Netherlands: TMC Asser Press.

Siekmann, R., & Soek, J. (Eds.). (2007). *The Council of Europe and sport: Basic documents.* The Hague, the Netherlands: TMC Asser Press.

Siekmann, R., Soek, J., & Bellani, A. (Eds.). (1999). *Doping rules of international sports organisations.* Cambridge, MA: Kluwer Law International.

Siekmann, R., Parrish, R., Branco Martins, R., & Soek, J. (Eds.). (2007). *Players' agents worldwide: Legal aspects.* The Hague, the Netherlands: TMC Asser Press.

Simson, V., & Jennings, A. (1992). *Dishonored games: Corruption, money & greed at the Olympics.* New York: SPI Books.

Smith, A., & Westerbeek, H. (2004). *The sport business future.* London: Palgrave Macmillan.

Smith, A., & Westerbeek, H. (2004). *The sport business in the global marketplace.* London: Palgrave Macmillan.

Thoma, J.E., & Chalip, L. (1996). *Sport governance in the global community.* Morgantown, WV: Fitness Information Technology.

Ueberroth, P. (1985). *Made in America.* New York: William Morrow.

Whiting, R. (1977). *The chrysanthemum and the bat: The game Japanese play* (fifth printing). Tokyo: The Permanent Press.

Whiting, R. (2004). *The meaning of Ichiro: The new wave from Japan and the transformation of our national pastime.* New York: Warner Books.

Whiting, R. (1989). *You gotta have Wa.* New York: Vintage Books.

Wise, A.N., & Meyer, B.S. (1997). *International sports law and business* (3 vol.). Boston: Kluwer Law International.

Managing Service Quality in International Sport

David J. Shonk, PhD
James Madison University, Virginia, USA

Cindy Lee, PhD
West Virginia University, USA

Chapter Objectives

After studying this chapter, you will be able to do the following:

- Define service quality
- Describe the characteristics of a service
- Identify various types of services such as consumer, professional, and human services
- Describe the various standards, targets, and evaluators of quality in international sport
- Discuss how international sport organizations approach the concept of customer service
- Understand service quality in relation to international sport
- Discuss the issue of service failure and recovery
- Explain why organizations employ service guarantees

Key Terms

We live in a world in which our very functioning depends on the services of others (Orwig, Pearson, & Cochran, 1997). The advances of 21st century technologies have only served to increase the importance and need for services. All too often, however, we hear about the negative aspects of services or lack thereof. Sport organizations compete within a service-based economy. As sport continues to globalize and reach new international markets, the competition for high-quality service continues to exist. This chapter informs the reader about what constitutes a service and provides background about the concept of service quality from an international perspective.

What Is a Service?

To gain a better understanding of service quality in international sport, we must first have a general understanding about what constitutes a service. In this regard, we consider the following questions:

1. How is a service defined, and how does a service differ in relation to a good?
2. What are the unique characteristics of a service?
3. Are there different types of services?

Services are acts, deeds, performances, or efforts, whereas goods are defined as articles, devices, materials, objects, or things (Berry, 1980). Services have also been described as economic activities that create added value and provide benefits to the consumer (Gilmore, 2003). According to Kandampully (2002), a customer who buys a physical good acquires a title to the good, and ownership is transferred. In contrast, when a consumer purchases a service, he or she receives only the right to that service and only for a specified time.

Sport managers must have an understanding of the unique nature of a service. Four characteristics are generally used to highlight the differences between a service and a good: (1) intangibility, (2) heterogeneity, (3) inseparability, and (4) perishability. Services are deemed **intangible** in the sense that they cannot be seen, felt, tasted, or touched, in contrast to goods (Zeithaml, Parasuraman, & Berry, 1985). The **heterogeneous** nature of a service suggests that its delivery may vary from one time to the next because people are often involved in supplying it and because each customer is different (Klassen,

Russell, & Chrisman, 1998). A service is **inseparable** because it is both produced and consumed at the same time. Finally, services are **perishable** because they cannot be saved, stored for reuse at a later date, resold, or returned in the same sense that a good can (Lovelock & Gummesson, 2004). In international sport, the concept of perishability is important because after an event (e.g., football match) ends, sport managers will never have another opportunity to sell inventory (e.g., tickets, sponsorships) for that particular event again. For example, if a person had a ticket for the Opening Ceremony of the Olympics Games but could not make it to the venue, the value of the ticket and the opportunity to watch the event would be gone after it was completed.

International sport organizations may engage in a variety of different types of services. Chelladurai (2005) highlights three types of services: (1) consumer services, (2) professional services, and (3) human services. Consumer services are based on the low skill required by an employee and the routine nature of the service. A concession employee responsible for the cash register during an event at Wembley Stadium in London is performing a consumer service. Professional services require greater knowledge, expertise, and a certain competence in a specialty area on the part of the service provider. An example would be a recreation center in Hong Kong that provides participants with fitness testing and consultation. Human services are undertaken to enhance a person's well-being by altering his or her behavior, attributes, and social status. Although services in general require a high degree of involvement on the part of the consumer

Learning Activity

Break up into groups of three or four and develop a sport that would appeal to an international audience. In regard to your new sport, please respond to the following: (1) Provide a name for the sport and give a brief description of how it works; (2) develop a governing body for your new sport; and (3) list some consumer, professional, and human services that could be offered by the governing body.

(Grönroos, 2001), human services require the most human involvement of any of the three types of services discussed. In regard to human services, the raw materials are human beings, who are variable in terms of their age, gender, and general level of fitness. For example, coach Gregory Shipperd of the Delhi Daredevils, a cricket team in the Indian Premier League, provides the players with a human service when he instructs them.

Service Quality in International Sport

To address the differences between good and services, scholars in the early 1980s began to integrate the literature on quality management in manufacturing and applying it to services (Kandampully, 2002). Thus, the study of services marketing highlights the unique characteristics of a service in comparison with a good. In the marketing of a service, much of what the customer is buying is the labor or human acts of performance (Rafiq & Ahmed, 2000). A widely studied topic within the services marketing literature is the concept of service quality. **Service quality** is defined as the gap between the customer's expectations of a service and the customer's perceptions of the service received (Grönroos, 2001; Parasuraman, Zeithaml, & Berry, 1988, 1985).

Evaluating Service Quality in International Sport

Because of the broad nature of the term *quality*, sport managers need to understand what should be evaluated in terms of service quality. Scholars have advanced two perspectives of service quality, referred to as the Nordic perspective and the American perspective, after the researchers who proposed them (Brady & Cronin, 2001; Kandampully, 2002). More recent conceptualizations have also highlighted the multidimensional nature of service quality.

Grönroos (1984) is credited with developing the Nordic perspective, which perceives service as the result of a consumer's view of a bundle of service dimensions. The Nordic model conceptualizes service quality as primarily two dimensional, consisting of technical quality and functional quality. Technical quality answers the question about what the consumer actually receives. It is the technical result of a service production process and has to do with buyer–seller interactions such as contacts that the consumer has with various resources and activities of the firm. Functional quality answers the question about how the consumer receives the service. Evaluating functional quality is more difficult than evaluating technical quality because the former is perceived in a subjective way. To help in understanding technical and functional quality, consider a ski vacation to Innsbruck, Austria. As a consumer, you may buy a ski package that includes lodging, airfare, ski equipment rental, and lift tickets, which would be representative of technical quality (i.e., what you receive). Now consider booking this ski vacation through a travel agency. You return home to tell the travel agent that you had a wonderful time in Austria, that almost every element of the trip was enjoyable, and that your experience had no major conflicts. In this respect, how you receive the service is equally important and interactions with the travel agent become part of the functional quality of the service.

The five-dimensional American model of service quality, conceptualized by Parasuraman, Zeithaml, and Berry (1988), is termed SERVQUAL. This perspective describes quality in terms of characteristics about how the service is delivered related to

- tangible elements (physical facilities, equipment, and appearance of personnel),
- reliability (ability to perform the promised service dependably and accurately),
- responsiveness (willingness to help customers and provide prompt service),
- assurance (knowledge and courtesy), and
- empathy (caring and individualized attention) of the service personnel.

The SERVQUAL model assumes that quality is the result of gaps between a customer's expectations and her or his perceptions of service performance. The first gap is the difference between consumer expectations and management perceptions of consumer expectations. The second gap is the difference between management perceptions of consumer expectations and service quality specifications. The third gap is the difference between service quality specifications and the service actually delivered. The fourth gap is the difference between service delivery and what is communicated about the service to consumers.

Our example from the Nordic model of a consumer traveling for a ski trip to Innsbruck, Austria, can also be applied within the context of the American model. For example, tangible elements may include the ski lodge and equipment. Reliability would include the services provided by various employees at places such as the hotel, restaurants, and ski lodge in Innsbruck, in addition to the travel agent's satisfactory booking of all travel arrangements. In the same way, representatives of these organizations would be responsive when they helped the customer contact a taxicab or provided assurance that the flight would arrive in time.

More recent conceptualizations of service quality recognize that multiple dimensions are needed to evaluate the concept of quality. Brady and Cronin's (2001) model of service quality had three primary dimensions: interaction quality, physical environment quality, and outcome quality. Each of these dimensions was found to have three subdimensions. Interaction quality refers to the perceptions of the customer concerning the interpersonal interactions that take place during service delivery. The subdimensions of this dimension suggest that an employee's attitude, behavior, and expertise help to shape a customer's perceptions of interaction quality. Physical environment quality focuses on the influence that the surrounding environment or physical facilities have on the perceptions of the customer. Customers' perceptions of the facility design, ambient conditions, and social conditions of the physical facility directly influence their perception of the quality of the physical environment. Outcome quality refers to a customer's perceptions of what he or she is left with after the service is rendered. Subdimensions of outcome quality include perceptions of waiting time, tangibles, and valence.

We know that quality of the outcome, interactions with service personnel, and the physical environment play an important role in the delivery of quality service in sport. Which factors are most important, though, varies by the type of service provided and the age and background of the consumer. For example, a study of service quality in a major league All-Star Game in the United States revealed that the quality of the contest was the most important factor for most in attendance (Shonk

& Chelladurai, 2009). Another study found that children attending a sport camp in Greece cited interactions or relationships with coaches as a vital factor (Costa, Tsitskari, Tzetzis, & Goudas, 2004). A study of Australian rules football found that older spectators attending a game placed greater importance on aspects of the physical environment (i.e., the stadium) that make them feel at home, whereas younger fans were more concerned with the sounds and smells of the game (Westerbeek, 2000). In a study of two major college football games in the United States, Wakefield, Blodgett, and Sloan (1996) indicated that one of the most significant factors affecting spectators was whether they felt crowded or cramped because of limited access and space in the stadium.

Consumer Perceptions of Quality in International Sport

Through the years, quality has taken on a variety of definitions, and consumer perceptions of quality may vary significantly. Therefore, sport managers must have an understanding of consumer **standards of quality**, which are the specific criteria applied by the sport consumer when judging quality (Chelladurai & Chang, 2000). From an international perspective, consumer standards of quality may be different around the world based on factors such as the norms or level of a sport; geographical, cultural, and religious considerations; and political factors. As mentioned earlier, service quality entails an understanding about what should be evaluated. In this regard, Chelladurai and Chang (2000) cite three **targets of quality** evaluations in sport, which are the features of a product being subjected to evaluations of quality. In sport these include (1) the core service, (2) the physical context such as the physical facilities and equipment in which the service is provided, and (3) the interpersonal interactions in the performance of the service.

Learning Activity

Select an international sporting event (e.g., Tour de France). Research the event and create a presentation that outlines the (a) standards and (b) targets of quality evaluations for the event.

Core Services

The core service relates to the performance of the promised service such as the contest itself, expert coaching, or fitness instruction. Within the context of spectator sport, managers have little to no control over the outcome of the game and thus the core service. Consumer perceptions of the core service may vary depending on a variety of factors such as the level of play, location, and cultural norms. In terms of the level of play, consumers attending a high school baseball game will have lower expectations concerning the outcome of the game than will spectators attending a professional contest. In the same manner, consider the expectations of a consumer at a high school game in comparison with the expectations of a spectator who purchases tickets at the Dallas Cowboys new venue, which boasts a retractable roof, retractable end zone doors, exclusive club seats, and a colossal video board as large as two basketball courts (Dallas Cowboys, 2010).

Likewise, consider the expectations of parents and young children in various places. In some parts of the world equipment and facilities are well developed. In other parts of the world, however, equipment and facilities are not well maintained. For example, Yaro (2010) reports that a lack of sporting equipment and facilities are seriously hampering sport activities in the Upper East Region of Ghana, where some sport stadiums are falling apart. Thus, parents and children may differ in terms of their expectations of facilities and equipment based on culture and socioeconomic factors.

Physical Context

The physical context dimension is described as the quality of the facilities, their location, the equipment and tools used in the production of the service, the amenities provided to the clients, the accessibility of the facilities, and the ease of use of the equipment. Although the contest may be the core service in spectator sport, a number of other goods and services are often bundled around the core service. For example, in the case of spectator sport, other goods and services may include concessions, merchandise, ticketing, parking, and sponsorship services. These goods and services may be referred to as a **consumer benefit package**, which Collier (1994) described as a "clearly defined set of tangible (goods-content) and intangible (service-content) attributes the customer recognizes, pays for, uses or experiences" (p. 63).

The consumer benefit package will differ among spectator sport, participant sport, fitness, and recreation because of the needs of the client. We noted earlier that the standards of quality may differ from an international perspective based on a variety of factors. Although the core service (i.e., the contest) does not vary from region to region, the targets of quality or the breadth of the consumer benefit package will vary based on the number of targets to be evaluated. For example, because sport facilities are more developed in many parts of North America than they are in Africa, consumers will evaluate a greater number of targets of quality. A North American stadium may include parking services, sophisticated food and beverage vendors, luxury seating, and multiple sponsors that will be subjected to evaluation by consumers. In contrast, stadiums in many underdeveloped or developing countries may not include the number or sophistication of such services.

Also, consider how consumer expectations for concession food may vary from region to region because traditional types of food eaten in various parts of the world differ. In some cases, consumers in various localities may not eat some types of food because of religious convictions. Consumers attending a baseball game at Camden Yards, home of the Baltimore Orioles, may have different expectations than do consumers in Tokyo, Japan, in terms of what constitutes value, what meets their needs, and what exceeds expectations. For example, Maryland crab cakes may be found on the menu at the stadium in Baltimore, whereas fried octopus could be on the menu in Tokyo. The case study explores how the Arsenal Football Club in North London is both shaping and responding to changing consumer expectations at their stadium.

Stadium Services and the Arsenal Football Club Spectator Experience

Arsenal Football Club is an English professional football club based in Holloway, North London. They play in the Premier League and are one of the most successful clubs in English football. They play a high level of football and strive to provide a high-quality experience at the stadium so that fans enjoy a good time even if the team does not win.

Detailed Transportation Information

Efforts to enhance the fan experience start even before the game begins. The Arsenal website (www .arsenal.com) provides detailed transportation and parking information. The interactive website allows a visitor to select items such as which entrance to use and how to have a specific need met, such as use of wheelchair vehicle. In addition, for people with disabilities, the website provides information regarding various public transportation options accessible to them.

Stadium

Stadium atmosphere and amenities are important influencing factors on fan experience. For about a century, sport stadiums and arenas in Europe have evolved slowly. Seating was dreadful or nonexistent, and concessions were antiquated. Conditions started to change in the 1980s after several disasters in football stadiums, which were partially attributed to the practice of making spectators stand for an entire game. New seats and private boxes were added, and many new stadiums and arenas were built in the last 10 to 15 years (Romanuk, 2007).

In 2000 Arsenal proposed to build a new stadium, which was completed in July 2006. Emirates Airlines purchased the naming rights by signing a lucrative sponsorship deal worth about £100 million (US$180 million) (BBC Sport, 2004). Emirates Stadium is a beautiful state-of-the-art venue that sells out all 60,000 seats each match day.

The stadium is user friendly for people with disabilities. Stadium Tour, Arsenal Museum, and banqueting and meeting facilities are fully accessible to people with disabilities. Some of the amenities include lift access from car park or podium level, wheelchair accessible toilets, and induction loops for people with hearing impairments.

After the game, Arsenal broadcasts the coach's postgame news conference on the in-house video system to entice fans to stay longer in the stadium (Romanuk, 2007). The postgame news conference (providing comments about game strategies, selection of players, and so on) is an effort to extend the fan experience within the ballpark to strengthen the connection with the team. This is also an attempt to imitate the American model, maximizing revenue by changing spectator culture. When fans spend extended time at the stadium, they might spend more money.

Various Food Choices and Concession

Cultural differences play a role in regard to concession. In the United States, many people arrive at a stadium or arena to have a tailgating party and enjoy watching pregame practice.

In Europe, friends traditionally meet for drinks or dinner at a pub or bar and head off to the stadium or arena just before the game is due to start. But more Europeans are now eating at the stadium before or after the sporting event, although this practice is still in its early stage compared with what occurs at some major North American venues. Concession service is thus more important than ever, and the concession business is one of the fastest growing areas of sport business in Europe. To give a reason for people to come early and stay late, Arsenal offers discounted beer prices before and after the game, inducing fans to stay longer at the stadium. Another interesting aspect that shows cultural differences concerns the rules for beer consumption, which are different in some European countries compared with the United States. France does not allow any alcoholic beverages in the venue except in VIP areas, and in the United Kingdom spectators can drink only in concourses and out of sight of the playing surface. In contrast, Germany and Switzerland allow alcohol in the seating areas.

Emirates Stadium offers four restaurants to VIP customers that range from a self-service buffet to white tablecloth, fine dining. Four bar areas offer beer, liquor, wine, and premium foods. Private box holders can order anything from a traditional afternoon tea to full meal service. The various hospitality packages and menus are explained on the website (www.arsenal.com/hospitality/events). For general admission seating, major efforts are concentrated on improving the quality of basic customer service by decreasing wait time and enhancing employee friendliness and food quality. By eliminating long lines and educating concession clerks, Arsenal expects to increase fan satisfaction.

Arsenal Museum

Before the game or during days, fans can visit the spectacular Arsenal museum at a minimum cost.

The museum includes various exhibitions of medals, memorabilia, and shirts worn by famous players. With its long and successful football history, Arsenal uses the museum to connect fans with the team. The facility also features an impressive Legends Theatre and more than a dozen fully interactive sections based on Arsenal's proud history.

Interpersonal Interactions

The interpersonal interactions dimension refers to the helping orientation and behavior of employees, courtesy and care toward clients, and the prompt delivery of individualized attention. From an international perspective, consider how people in various parts of the world evaluate interpersonal interactions differently. Consider the Olympic Games, which will be held in London, England, in 2012, and in Sochi, Russia, in 2014. The bidding phase for hosting these megaevents started nine years earlier. Spectators from all over the world will attend these games and stay in hotels, ride public transportation, visit various sport venues, and visit attractions around the destination. These types of services are being provided to a wide range of people who will have varied expectations regarding interactions with contact personnel. In addition, how the people in hosting countries greet and interact with visiting tourists for the Olympics will influence the overall perceived experience. To provide a better experience to visiting tourists, public campaigns are sometimes launched to educate citizens of the host country about global etiquette. For example, China launched a "self-improvement campaign" to educate its citizens about public manners before the Beijing Olympic Games (Yardley, 2007). The case study on the Australian Open explores how organizers of this event provided services to meet the needs of international and local visitors to the event.

Who will evaluate the standards and the targets of quality within the context of international sport? According to Chelladurai and Chang (2000), the **evaluators of quality** may include clients, service providers, and organizations. From an international perspective, clients may include spectators attending a sporting event in China, a sport participant competing in the Senior Olympics in North America, or someone buying a shoe from a sporting goods store in Europe. Service providers may be involved with a number of different kinds of organizations. From an international perspective, these may include organizations such as multinational corporations like Nike, governing bodies such as the International Olympic and Paralympic Committees, or events such as the Tour de France.

Service Failure and Recovery in International Sport

When a sport organization experiences a breakdown in the service process, such as a merchandise or food vendor who ignores a consumer, the service organization experiences a **service failure**. Today's sport manager refers to every occasion in which a consumer comes into contact with the organization as a touch point. These **touch points** have also been referred to as moments of truth (Grönroos, 1990). Consider the touch points in relation to attending a sport event. The consumer may come into contact first when purchasing a ticket (which may be online, over the phone, or in person). Next, he or she travels to the contest and may arrive to discourteous parking attendants or be unable to find a parking spot. The consumer enters the stadium or arena and may find dirty restrooms and a rude usher. Finally, the spectator's team may lose the contest. Based on the preceding scenario, note that sport managers have virtually no control over the contest itself. In this regard, a sport marketer cannot control the level of play on the court or field. But the sport manager has control of key personnel such as ushers and ticket takers and directs their interpersonal interactions with consumers. In the same manner, sport managers can control unpleasant aspects of the physical environment such as dirty restrooms and offensive odors.

For many organizations, a **service guarantee** is an effective way to improve or jump-start quality

Australian Open: Key Service Elements at an International Sport Event

First held in 1905, the Australian Open is the first of the four Grand Slam tennis tournaments. The tournament is held in January at Melbourne Park, which is the home of Tennis Australia and the Australian Open. The Australian Open has been successful in terms of attendance. In 2009 it hit the highest single-day attendance for any Grand Slam tournament of 66,018. The overall attendance has increased by about 80,000 from 2004, totaling 603,160 in 2009 (www.australianopen.com). In 2009 attendees from all over the world benefitted from the following services, many of which were planned to help fans feel welcome.

• *State-of-the-art facilities.* This state-of-the art venue has 22 outdoor courts, including 3 show courts, and 4 indoor courts. The A$25 million (US$19 million) revamp of the Melbourne Park facilities in the mid-1990s created a carnival-like atmosphere. The Centre Court is named Rod Laver Arena. Opened in 2000, Hisense Arena (formally known as Vodafone Arena) is a multipurpose venue. Both stadiums have retractable roofs so that players can continue their games irrespective of weather. Given that the Australian Open is held in the middle of summer, retractable roofs relieve spectators from excessive heat, helping them to enjoy games more in inclement weather.

• *Friendly website.* The website of the Australian Open (www.australianopen.com) provides a variety of information from tennis rules to transportation to activity information. By simply browsing the website, visitors can obtain a lot of useful information regarding the Australian Open. The site also provides tour information about Melbourne, including city attractions, shopping, and ethnic restaurants, in various languages such as English, Chinese, Korean, and Japanese. Thus, potential visitors from many countries would have no problem getting necessary information before their trip to the Australian Open.

• *Connection with fans in new ways.* The 2009 Australian Open offered fans an official fantasy tennis competition (i.e., Super Tennis) free of charge. In Super Tennis, participants take the role of coach and select the ultimate team. The selected players score points based on their actual performance until they are knocked out during the two-week competition. The contest is customized to a new generation of technology-savvy fans who can enjoy the thrill of competition at home anywhere in the world. Fans can also download the official iPhone app for the Australian Open Tennis Championships, which allows fans to follow live action during the game period. In addition, by using social media such as Facebook and Twitter, the Australian Open aims to connect with fans all year round.

• *Live entertainment.* The Australian Open doubled spectator space at the event for its citizens and visitors in 2010 with the introduction of Grand Slam Oval. In this space, visitors can enjoy tennis on two big screens, visit a variety of bars, listen to live music, and enjoy various free entertainment. This expansion of the site is an effort to provide a better spectator experience at the event. By offering a variety of activities, the Australian Open provides a festival for visitors and citizens. In addition, Fan Zone, an autograph stand, Nintendo spaces, and a photo booth were set up to meet visitors' needs.

• *Transportation services.* Considering that fans come from all over the world to see the Australian Open, providing convenient transportation services to the site is useful in enhancing the overall experience of the spectators from the beginning. On the official website of the Australian Open, a potential visitor can search and book a flight ticket through the Virgin Blue fare finder. In addition, to help the planning of each spectator's trip, an online journey planner was provided showing a step-by-step route and available transportation, which can be beneficial for international travelers who are not familiar with the area. After spectators reach the site, free shuttle trams are available to all holders of valid game tickets.

• *Volunteer training.* The Australian Open uses numerous volunteers in the areas of officiating, court services and operations, and office administration. One of the requirements for volunteers is that they commit to attending compulsory training sessions, which may include how to run to a ball to pick it up properly (i.e., ball kid) and how to interact with spectators from different countries and cultures (i.e., court service). By mandating volunteer training, the Australian Open attempts to provide a high-quality service to spectators.

Learning Activity

Think of a recent international sporting event and discuss the various touch points consumers would have encountered during that event. What kind of service failures can occur in these touch points, and how would they be recovered?

initiatives, to maintain superior quality levels, and to signal high quality to consumers (Wirtz, Kum, & Lee, 2000). A service guarantee helps build marketing muscle and forces a firm to ensure that its basic delivery system meets standards, and it encourages the firm to examine the fail points and work toward their elimination (Wirtz, 1998). Although many products (e.g., a car, microwave) are purchased with a warranty or guarantee that the product will work, Hart (1988) suggested that

CASE STUDY

Government Involvement to Improve 2010 South Africa World Cup Visitor Experiences

South Africa became the first African country to host the FIFA World Cup in 2010. The World Cup took place in 10 stadiums in nine host cities located in eight of the nine provinces in South Africa. For this truly international event, the South African government made 17 guarantees to FIFA in relation to the delivery of the 2010 World Cup including spending R600 billion (US$78 billion) on infrastructure development including building and upgrading stadiums and improving public transportation and communication services for visitors. To make this historic event happen, the South African government invested heavily and provided a variety of services for visiting tourists. During the event, coordinated by various government departments, South Africa provided smoothly connected services in the areas of transportation, accommodation, safety and security, communication, and entertainment for better experiences for World Cup visitors.

For the first time in the history of the FIFA World Cup, the host country offered an event visa for tourists who purchased FIFA match tickets. Therefore, visitors to South Africa did not need to go through a cumbersome procedure to get a visa to enter the country. In addition, the Ministry of Communications set up telecommunication infrastructures conforming to FIFA's requirements for wired and wireless national and international telephone, data, audio, and video exchanges. The Ministry of Finance waived customs duties, taxes, costs, and levies on the import and export of goods belonging to the FIFA delegation, its commercial affiliates, the broadcast right holders, the media, and spectators.

To ensure the safety of players and visitors, a special security plan was developed and implemented in conjunction with the Organizing Committee. More than 41,000 specially trained officers were deployed during the event. In terms of infrastructure, R170 billion (US$25 billion) was invested in the transport system in the period 2005 through 2010 to accommodate the increased travel demand created by the World Cup.

Lastly, the Department of Tourism provided information about graded accommodation establishments in and around the host cities, attraction points for its national parks and heritage sites, emergency services including health and medical services, and various entertainment opportunities (World Cup, 2010).

Because of these efforts made by South Africa, the 2010 South Africa World Cup was evaluated as a success. One of the issues in the 2010 World Cup was the use of the vuvuzela—a plastic blowing horn that produces a loud and distinctive sound. A unique scene in the stadiums of the South Africa World Cup was spectators (especially South Africans) blowing vuvuzelas. Their constant use during the 2010 World Cup caused some communication problems among players and broadcasters. Some spectators found the sound annoying because of its high noise level. FIFA, however, refused to ban the use of vuvuzelas, stating that they were a symbol of South Africa and the way in which South Africans enjoyed football, just as Brazilian fans use samba drums and Switzerland fans use cow bells.

many business executives believe that, by definition, services cannot be guaranteed because they are delivered by human beings who are less predictable than machines. Within sport services, the quality of souvenir merchandise items such as shirts can be guaranteed, and the item can ultimately be replaced in the case of a defect. But other features of a sport service such as a consumer's satisfaction with the outcome of the contest (i.e., win or loss) or with the overall experience are difficult to guarantee because subjective perceptions are involved.

We can define **international sport services** as those services that apply to sport and reach beyond the national boundaries of a nation. Although providing a comprehensive list of the most important issues related to service failure and recovery within the context of international sport is difficult, we can highlight some factors that may be important for sport organizations to consider. These factors include travel, accommodations, cultural and religious differences, and sport customs. Even the rules of sport and the norms of what is called a sport may vary from place to place, and sport managers must consider these variations. For example, walking or jogging may be classified or defined as sport in some European countries, whereas it is a leisure activity for most people in the United States. In spectator sport, the rules differ as well. For example, FIBA (Fédération Internationale de Basketball Amateur), the world governing body for basketball, states that teams play four 10-minute quarters, whereas the National Basketball Association in the United States adheres to four 12-minute quarters.

Issues concerning security and the political climate in a specific region also affect service quality.

If attendees at an event feel unsafe a service failure can occur, so sport managers must consider security issues. The 1972 Summer Olympics in Munich, Germany, and the 1996 Olympics in Atlanta are prime examples of the need for security. During the 1972 Olympics, 11 Israeli athletes were taken hostage by Palestinian terrorists, and during the 1996 Olympics in Atlanta, Georgia, 2 people died and 111 were injured in a pipe bomb attack at Centennial Olympic Park. For international megaevents, government involvement is often needed to facilitate travel for international fans and create the needed infrastructure for the event. The case study on page 389 describes how these issues were dealt with at the 2010 World Cup.

Summary

As the management of sport continues to evolve and become more complex, the concept of providing high-quality service becomes more important. Many sport organizations compete for competitive advantage based on the quality of services provided. Within the context of international sport, managers must understand how the standards and targets of quality vary from region to region based on a variety of factors unique to each region. In addition, managers must consistently monitor the level and quality of services being provided by the organization. Managers must train employees how to handle service failures and to be aware of the various touch points where the customer may be in contact. In the end, high-quality service leads to satisfied customers who are loyal and make repeated purchases from the organization.

? Review and Discussion Questions

1. What are the key characteristics that distinguish a service from a good? Define and describe each of the four characteristics highlighted in this chapter.

2. The authors provide a case study featuring the Arsenal Football Club and the organization's efforts to improve the fan experience. Can you think of any targets of quality listed in the case study? Would the standards of quality differ between a spectator at an Arsenal Football event and one attending a Major League Soccer event in North America?

3. Do sport organizations need to be concerned about service quality? If so, why are these important concepts?

4. When attending a sporting event, what are some important touch points that a sport manager must be concerned about to create the best fan experience?

5. Can you provide an example of a recent service failure in which you were the consumer? How did the organization resolve the problem, and were you satisfied with the result?

Part V
International Sport Business Strategies

Portugese-born football star Cristiano Ronaldo in a Barclays Premier League game between Manchester United and Arsenal. The logos that the players wear are a common form of sponsorship in European professional sport leagues. Manchester United has been rated one of the world's most valuable sport franchises.

CHAPTER 19

International Sport Marketing

R. Brian Crow, EdD
Slippery Rock University, Pennsylvania, USA

Kevin K. Byon, PhD
University of Georgia, USA

Yosuke Tsuji, PhD
University of the Ryukyus, Japan

Chapter Objectives

After studying this chapter, you will be able to do the following:

- Understand marketing concepts and apply them to a global setting
- Recognize characteristics of global sport consumers
- Appreciate the scope of branding in the global sport industry
- Explain marketing and branding as they relate to global sport organizations and events
- Discuss international sport marketing and branding trends

Key Terms

Global market development and expansion is extremely important for the success of the sport industry. Consider the following issues, seemingly unrelated to each other, and think about how each addresses themes central to international sport marketing:

◆ Is India the last great untapped sport market? Its sponsorship market is estimated to be US$250 million per year, TV rights are worth over US$350 million per year, and both are growing fast. And cricket is not the only sport; football, Formula One racing, golf, and tennis are emerging sports in India, which has nearly one-sixth of the world's population (Campbell, 2008).

◆ Manchester United from England's Premier League (EPL) recently negotiated the most lucrative shirt sponsorship deal in the league's history. The partnership, with U.S.-based Aon Corporation, is believed to be worth £80 million (US$132 million) over four years. This partnership raised eyebrows among the 5,400 London-based Aon employees who had pension benefits cut because of the recent economic downturn (McCullagh, 2009).

◆ Kobe Bryant, NBA superstar and four-time champion, is a hero in China. He is the rare American star athlete with international credentials, having lived in Italy and being fluent in both Italian and Spanish. Chinese fans love him for his basketball skills as well as his philanthropy. His star power in China also benefits Nike, one of Bryant's main sponsors, which lists China as its number two market behind the United States (Paul, 2009).

This far into the textbook, you have no doubt begun to understand the far-reaching scope of sport in the global marketplace. Global sport marketing plays a big role. For example, leading insurance company American Insurance Group (AIG), which posted a loss of US$99 billion when it suffered a liquidity crisis in 2008 (Ellis, 2009), was also arguably one of the world's largest sport sponsors and most recognizable brands. The company's portfolio included an annual deal of approximately US$20 million with Manchester United of the EPL (*AIG Ends*, 2009). As you will see throughout the remainder of this chapter, sport marketing on a global scale can help create worldwide superstars, turn locally popular teams into global icons, and form international partnerships. Global sport marketing will shape the future of sport for many years to come.

The purpose of this chapter is to build on the foundation of knowledge that you have developed relative to global sport by reviewing established sport marketing principles, introducing characteristics of sport consumers, and exploring the importance of international sport brands. The focus of this chapter is on global brand development and sponsorship in international sport. In addition, we provide information on sport consumers and how they are discovered, reached, marketed to, and influenced by global sport brands. The chapter will encourage you in your study of global sport to read information beyond this text. You will be able to get a feel for the current state of sport marketing by reading periodicals such as Street and Smith's *SportsBusiness Journal* and *SportsBusiness Daily*, *Sport Business International*, and academic publications such as the *International Journal of Sports Marketing and Sponsorship* and the *International Journal of Sport Management and Marketing*. Our goal is to encourage you to explore the ever-changing world of global sport with an understanding of proven marketing principles.

The study of marketing and branding from an international perspective is important for a variety of reasons. First, there is increased opportunity for students to gain meaningful employment in the sport industry when crossing national borders. Second, sport consumers and organizations operate differently in countries around the world, so exposure to a global perspective is crucial. Finally, the contents of this chapter are important for the evolution of the continued study of sport marketing and branding from a global perspective.

From a marketer's perspective, international growth and expansion is a way to attract more fans, either in person or through media. Nearly every sport organization in North America, from MLB to the NFL to the NBA has reached across national borders to showcase its players and realize additional business opportunities. For instance, the official MLB website is now offered in five languages (English, Spanish, Japanese, Korean, and Chinese) to attract people from all over the world. The 2008 NBA All-Star Game was televised in more than 215 countries in 41 languages (National Basketball Association, 2008). Furthermore, about 53 percent of the Internet audience for NBA.com was from outside the United States, and 20 percent of those were in China alone (National Basketball Association,

2008). In some cases, completely new and unique competitions like the World Baseball Classic (WBC) have been created to take advantage of the global marketplace (Fullerton, 2007).

Sport organizations worldwide have sought to expand to international markets. Since the first cricket game was held in England in the 16th century, the sport has grown to become the second most popular sport in the world after football. The International Cricket Council (ICC) has 104 member countries (International Cricket Council, 2010). The ICC has made an effort to pursue membership globally, and two new countries, Bangladesh and Zimbabwe, have joined since 1990. Taekwondo, a Korean martial art, has its headquarters, called Kukkiwon, in South Korea. As one of the famous martial arts, taekwondo became an official part of the Summer Olympic Games in 2000 and is now practiced by over 50 million people in 162 countries (Kukkiwon, 2010).

In several cases, ownership extends across borders. American Malcolm Glazer, owner of the NFL's Tampa Bay Buccaneers, purchased the EPL's Manchester United team for $1.5 billion in 2005. Michael Lerner, owner of the NFL's Cleveland Browns, bought the EPL's Aston Villa team in 2006 for $100 million. George Gillett Jr., former owner of the Montreal Canadiens, and Tom Hicks, former owner of the Texas Rangers, purchased the Liverpool football team for $300 million. In October 2010 the Liverpool team was sold for $484 million to New England Sports Ventures, which is owned by John Henry, current owner of the Boston Red Sox.

These teams were attractive because of high match-day attendance, potential for global branding and merchandising, and significant television revenues (Chadwick, 2007).

Many of the seemingly complex issues discussed in this chapter will be more easily understood by

Learning Activity

Identify the team or sport organization with which you most closely identify (i.e., your favorite team). List the top five reasons why you identify with this team. How might these reasons change or stay the same if you lived in a different country? Compare and discuss your notes with classmates.

keeping this notion in mind: In the context of sport, a global marketer is essentially trying to identify and reach a specific class of consumer, create or enhance a product or service to meet that consumer's needs or wants, and develop brand loyalty so that the consumer becomes a lifelong fan by maintaining contact through various touch points.

Marketing Principles and Terms

Several terms and principles need to be examined at this point in the chapter. Marketing has been defined as the process of creating, communicating, and delivering the value of a product, service, or idea to the consumer (Mullin, Hardy, & Sutton, 2007). Sport marketing is defined as meeting the needs and wants of sport consumers through various exchange processes, either by the marketing of sport (the product or service) or marketing through sport (using sport as a marketing vehicle for nonsport goods and services) (Mullin et al., 2007). But what makes the marketing of sport unique from the marketing of nonsport goods and services? Funk (2008) distinguished **sport marketing** from traditional marketing in terms of 10 aspects:

1. Sport organizations must both compete and cooperate with one another.
2. Sport consumers are often experts of the products that they use or consume.
3. The supply of sport products is high, and demand fluctuations are common.
4. Sport products are intangible.
5. Sport products are simultaneously produced and consumed.
6. Sport facilitates socialization.
7. Sport products are inconsistent in nature.
8. Maintaining control over the core sport product is difficult.
9. Ancillary products remain important to sport.
10. Sport is difficult to price.

These unique characteristics make sport marketing both challenging and rewarding, often to a greater extent in a global setting.

To help you apply these unique aspects and other global characteristics to an international level, we often refer to marketing-related terms, so you should familiarize yourself with these concepts before moving forward.

◆ Brand, in terms of sport, refers to the name, logo, and symbols associated with the sport organization that serve to provide a point of differentiation from similar products in the marketplace (Fullerton, 2007).

◆ Promotion is generally considered any activity designed to stimulate interest in, awareness of, and purchase of a product. It can include price discounts, sweepstakes, giveaways, advertising, personal selling, public relations, and sponsorship (Fullerton, 2007).

◆ **Sponsorship** can be defined as acquiring rights to affiliate or associate with a product or event for the purpose of deriving benefits related to that affiliation or association, including retail opportunities, purchase of media time, entitlement, or hospitality (Aaron, 2008).

◆ Licensing is the granting of rights to a third party that desires to associate itself commercially (for profit and not for profit) with an institution by using trademarks, names, logos, symbols, and slogans (Collegiate Licensing Company, 2009).

To illustrate how closely related sponsorship and licensing can be, consider the case of global manufacturer Adidas and the international governing body of football, FIFA (Fédération Internationale de Football Association). Adidas is the official licensee and supplier of the FIFA World Cup 2010 and 2014, and as such it has exclusive rights to many partnership opportunities with the organization (FIFA, 2008).

Four basic elements are central to marketing. These are known as the marketing mix, or the four Ps of marketing. The marketing mix consists of product, place, price, and promotion. Product is what the seller provides for the buyer, and it can be an item, service, or idea. Place (distribution) is how the seller gets the product to the buyer or where the service takes place. Price is what the seller charges the buyer for the product, service, or idea. Promotion is the method that the seller uses to advertise the product, service, or idea to potential buyers (Mullin et al., 2007). For example, if a family goes to a baseball game after seeing a family-night game advertised on television, the product is the game and any food or merchandise bought at the ballpark;

the place is the ballpark; the price is the amount of money that the family pays for the game, parking, food, and souvenirs; and the promotion can be the TV ad, a giveaway at the game, or coupons left on the seat for each fan.

The International Sport Consumer

To understand why sport marketing is important, we must first identify and understand the consumer. A consumer is a person who uses products and services and to whom the marketing efforts are directed (Peter & Olson, 2008). A **sport consumer** is different from a consumer in traditional marketing because the sport consumer deals with sport products and services, which are fundamentally different from general business products and services. Aaron (2008) defined a sport consumer as "an individual, who purchases sporting goods, uses sport services, participates or volunteers in sport and follows sport as a spectator or fan" (p. 35).

Taking into consideration these unique aspects, Aaron (2008) differentiated sport consumers into four types, including (a) sporting goods consumers, (b) sport services consumers, (c) sport participants and volunteers, and (d) sport supporters, spectators, and fans. Sporting goods consumers are those who purchase tangible sport products such as sporting equipment, licensed merchandise, and sport memorabilia. Sport services consumers are those who use sport-related services such as sport education, coaching clinics, and medical services offered by leisure and recreation centers. Sport participants and volunteers are consumers who are actively involved in sport activities as participants or unpaid employees. Lastly, sport supporters, spectators, and fans are those who consume sporting events passively through game attendance, watching sport events on television or other media, and reading about sporting events online or in print.

Although all the previous types of consumers are important and relevant in a global setting, the next few paragraphs focus on sport spectators, who often represent many of the characteristics seen in all four types of sport consumers.

The field of sport consumer behavior has been a popular area of study in sport management. Definitions, concepts, and theories developed in marketing and psychology have been applied to advance understanding (Funk, Mahony, & Havitz, 2003). In the field of general consumer behavior, Peter and Olson (2008) defined consumer behavior as "the dynamic interaction of affect and cognition, behavior, and the environment by which human beings conduct the exchange aspects of their lives" (p. 5). In other words, consumer behavior is a process of understanding how consumers think, feel, and react to products and services generated by an organization. Additionally, it is an understanding about how a social environment (e.g., reference groups, geographic locations, culture, subculture, cross-culture, and social setting) can influence a consumer's thoughts, feelings, and behavior. Within the field of sport management, Funk (2008) defined sport event consumer behavior as "the process involved when individuals select, purchase, use, and dispose of sport and sport event related products and services to satisfy needs and receive benefits" (p. 6). Understanding this process allows sport marketers to position their sport products and services to satisfy targeted consumers' needs, wants, and desires.

Applying the previous definition to international sport consumers requires caution because of the influence of culture (McCracken, 1986), defined as the fundamental values and distinctions used to understand and categorize the world. More specifi-

cally, culture has to do with values, attitudes, and behaviors that may differ from one place to the next. Therefore, what is most relevant in one culture may be insignificant in another. For instance, Western culture (e.g., the United States and the United Kingdom) is traditionally known as an individualistic society that emphasizes separateness and individualism. On the other hand, Eastern culture (e.g., China and Korea) is regarded as a collectivistic society that focuses on connectedness and social bonding. Sport marketers should be aware of these basic cultural differences despite the fact that the world is becoming homogenized because of new communication technologies. In a collectivistic society, a national brand (e.g., the national team) is more popular than an individual or regional brand (e.g., a regional team), which is more popular in an individualistic society.

But as Funk (2008) argued, the sport marketing environment is dynamic, and sport consumers' needs are constantly changing. Therefore, sport marketers need to make a continued effort to investigate the factors that influence sport consumers to consume sport products and services, such as attending live sporting events, purchasing licensed merchandise, watching sporting events on television or the Internet, and reading sport-related magazines.

CASE STUDY

National Basketball Association

The NBA, headquartered in New York City, started with 11 teams and played its first game in Toronto, Canada, in 1946. Today's NBA has little resemblance to its forerunner in terms of number of teams, player salaries, media coverage and exposure, and, most important, global reach. In the early 21st century, the NBA has taken the lead in expanding beyond the geographical borders of its member teams.

Perhaps the most visible mark of the NBA's globalization is the number of non-American players on NBA rosters. The 2010–2011 season began with 84 rosters spots filled by players born in 38 countries outside the United States (National Basketball Association, 2010a), an increase of nearly 100 percent since 2000–2001. In addition, the NBA created and continues to manage its Basketball Without Borders

program, a global community outreach program that uses basketball to unite young people in foreign lands (National Basketball Association, 2010b).

The NBA is considered an industry leader in globalization. Its games, according to NBA president of global business partnerships and international business operations Heidi Ueberroth, are broadcast in 215 countries and in 41 languages (Swangard, 2008). The NBA is on the cutting edge of developing international relationships for its previously North American–only brand. NBA commissioner David Stern recognized this opportunity ahead of most others and focused on international expansion decades ago. Because sport is unique in its ability to bridge cultures and bring people together, having a strategy to grow outside the United States is

(continued)

(continued)

important if sport is to continue to be relevant (Swangard, 2008, p. 185).

Ueberroth cited three reasons why the NBA has been successful in this endeavor: (1) Basketball is an easy game to learn and understand, (2) little infrastructure or equipment is required, and (3) basketball promotes fitness, teamwork, and a healthy lifestyle. In addition, the NBA has international revenue from television rights, digital media, marketing partnerships, merchandise, and global events (Swangard, 2008). Although the globalization of the game itself is evident, the aspects important to a sport manager are the international marketing, sponsorship, and business growth of the NBA. For example, although Americans have become owners of European football teams (see chapter 17), the NBA is the first North American sport league to have one of its teams owned by a foreign businessperson. Russian Mikhail Prokhorov purchased 80 percent of the New Jersey Nets in 2010, which precipitated the league's opening of a Moscow office (Emmett, 2010). The NBA also has an office in Johannesburg, South Africa, and six offices in Europe (Emmett, 2010).

The NBA has perhaps the largest global licensing portfolio of any sport league in the world. Licensees number over 200 worldwide, 60 of which are in Europe (Emmett, 2010). Although media rights still make up the largest percentage of NBA revenue, licensing and sponsorship (including global partners) are not far behind. In fact, Spanish banking conglomerate BBVA recently agreed to become the official bank of the NBA, WNBA, and NBA Developmental League (Emmett, 2010). This partnership is evidence that non-U.S. entities are using sport, in particular basketball, to reach the North American market.

To date, the NBA has staged 93 games outside the United States and Canada in 31 cities in 16 countries and territories. Madrid hosted the Boston Celtics in 1988 as part of the McDonald's Open in one of the first international games featuring an NBA team (National Basketball Association, 2009). Spain hosted NBA Europe Live games in 2006 through 2009, and the NBA visited Madrid in 2007 when the Toronto Raptors and Memphis Grizzlies played Real Madrid and Estudiantes, respectively (National Basketball Association, 2009).

The NBA has also reached into China and other Asian countries, and is now starting to focus on India. Fans in these countries can connect with the NBA brand now only through media and licensed products, but in the future they hope to see exhibitions or regular season games, much like the Nets–Raptors

games to be played in London's O$_2$ Arena in March 2012 (Emmett, 2010).

Beginning in 1992 when the "Dream Team" cruised through the Summer Olympics, kids from around the world have longed to play in the NBA. Perhaps the most important of the league's international players for overseas ventures is Yao Ming of China, who plays for the Houston Rockets. His importance, like his physical size, cannot be underestimated. China, and its 1.3 billion citizens, is considered the final frontier for professional basketball (Larmer, 2005). The target market for the NBA—the hip, trendy, and cool crowd—exists in China, which until recently was an untapped market. When NBA commissioner David Stern first approached Chinese officials in 1989 about broadcasting NBA games there, he was turned away (Larmer, 2005). Stern knew that for the Chinese people to embrace the league, they would need to see one of their own become a success. Enter Yao Ming. In 2004, while his Houston Rockets games drew viewership of nearly 1 million fans in the United States, they regularly drew up to 30 million viewers in China (Larmer, 2005).

The NBA recently announced the formation of NBA China, a new entity that will conduct all the league's businesses in greater China with partners the Bank of China, China Merchants Investments, ESPN–Disney, Legend Holdings, and the Li Ka Shin Foundation, who invested $253 million to acquire 11 percent of the new company. Commissioner David Stern stated,

> The strategic investment from these companies will allow us to continue working with the General Administration of Sports and the Chinese Basketball Association to grow our sport and emphasize, in both rural and urban Chinese communities, its contributions to fitness, healthy lifestyle and an appreciation of teamwork. (Swangard, 2008)

At the same time, Chinese companies such as Lenovo and Haier are beginning to expand their brands in the United States (Swangard, 2008).

What then is the future for the NBA globally? According to Ueberroth, Europe will have a division of the NBA before 2020 (Swangard, 2008). The NBA is clearly the front-runner among U.S.-based sport leagues in reaching a global audience. The NBA has taken a leadership position by taking a sport league into the global marketplace. As you develop into a leader in the sport industry, you must lead your organization into this arena as well.

Generally, these factors can be categorized into two broad categories: (*a*) internal factors and (*b*) external factors. Internal factors are related to psychological variables that predict what sport consumers purchase, whereas external factors are related to variables within the social environment that influence sport consumers' decision making.

Internal Factors Affecting Sport Consumption

Motivation and identification have been consistently identified as the two most important factors influencing sport consumption behavior. These two psychological factors interact with each other, indicating that true sport consumption behavior can be understood when two factors are considered simultaneously. Several scales have been developed to measure spectator motivation by considering factors such as achievement, aesthetics, affiliation, drama, escape, knowledge, and social interaction.

Briefly defined, achievement in spectator motivation refers to vicarious achievement. The aesthetics motive refers to the artistic appreciation associated with the sport (Fink, Trail, & Anderson, 2002). The affiliation motive concerns the inherent desire of people for affiliation with some entity such as a sport team. The drama motive refers to spectators' excitement about an uncertain outcome until the last minutes of a game. Escape has to do with the spectator's desire to get away from her or his ordinary life. Knowledge concerns the need to acquire information associated with a particular sport or sport team. Finally, social interaction refers to spectators' needs for socialization opportunities through spectatorship.

Although studies on motives and identification affecting sport consumption have been conducted mostly in the context of North American sport, the factors listed earlier have been consistently found to be important dimensions in international sport settings. For instance, Neal and Funk (2006) found that several motive factors, including vicarious achievement, player interest, entertainment value, drama, and socialization influenced spectators to attend Australian football games. Spectator motive was also found to be an important driving force for fans of the Japanese Professional Football League (Mahony, Nakazawa, Funk, James, & Gladden,

2002). Recently, researchers found that motive positively influenced both Korea and U.S. spectators to watch mixed martial arts events (Kim, Andrew, & Greenwell, 2009).

Vicarious achievement is a noteworthy contributor to sport fan motivation. The idea behind vicarious achievement is that sport fans are motivated to consume sport, whether attending an event or watching an event on television, because by doing so they feel a sense of accomplishment through the success of their team or a specific player, thus bringing feelings of arousal and pleasure. Cialdini and his associates (1976) coined the term *basking in reflected glory* (BIRG) to explain this phenomenon, which states that people tend to associate themselves with a successful sport entity (team or player) to enhance their self-esteem. For instance, during the 30 days of the 2002 Korea–Japan FIFA World Cup football games, supporters of the Korea national team formed a sea of red throughout South Korea by wearing red-colored T-shirts. In this case, national identity could be an important additional factor that accounts for why the phenomenon occurs when it comes to rooting for a national team.

On the opposite end, Snyder, Lassegard, and Ford (1986) coined the term *cutting off reflected failure* (CORF) to refer to a tendency for people to cut themselves off, or distance themselves, from an unsuccessful sport entity to protect their self-esteem. This effect can be seen when fans of losing teams stop wearing apparel displaying the team's logo while a losing streak continues. Spectatorship suffers as well; for example, the Detroit Lions of the NFL, en route to a winless record in 2008, had the lowest average attendance in the league. The Collegiate Licensing Company (CLC) rankings for the 2007–2008 fiscal year revealed that the schools that led the nation in the sale of licensed merchandise were among the most successful programs in the country (Hughes, 2009). The effect of a losing record on licensing revenue can have even broader effects as teams gain a larger international fan base.

Knowledge is another internal factor affecting sport consumption. The acquisition of knowledge associated with a particular sport or sport team allows people to exhibit their affiliation with the team to others. Fink et al. (2002) defined the knowledge motive as "learning about the sport, team, or players through social interaction and media consumption that include reading the box scores and watching the sport news on television" (p. 159). This motive is clearly related to sport consumption behavior, including game attendance (Holt, 1995) and television viewing (Gantz & Wenner, 1991). Recently, Seo and Green (2008) in their examination of online sport users indicated that acquiring knowledge to share with other sport fans in an online community can be a motivating factor influencing sport consumption.

A primary reason that cricket, the national pastime for most South Asian nations, including India, Pakistan, Sri Lanka, and Nepal, is not popular in North America is likely related to the lack of knowledge of the sport. Simply put, many people in North America do not know the rules, players, or teams. According to the escalator model developed by Mullin, Hardy, and Sutton (2007), a consumer must be aware of products or services to become a heavy user or loyal customer. Thus, marketing strategies should be implemented to enhance consumer awareness and increase consumer knowledge about once unknown international sport products and services. This idea also applies to companies that use sport to reach sport fans. For instance, global beverage marketer Coca-Cola heavily promoted its products during international cricket matches to enhance consumer awareness in South Asian markets.

External Factors Affecting Sport Consumption

According to Mullin et al. (2007), there are two types of sport products: (*a*) core products and (*b*) peripheral products. The core product in spectator sport is the game or competition itself. As such, the core product is the essence of the sport organization. Zhang, Pease, Hui, and Michaud (1995) found that several elements of the core product affect sport consumption behavior. These elements include, but are not limited to, the following: home team performance, presence of star players on the home team, quality of home team players, opposing team performance, quality of opposing team, opposing team history and tradition, closeness of competition, duration of the game, skill level, ticket price, ticket affordability, quality of seating, direct mail and notification, publicity, game time, and game schedule for the season.

One of the unique characteristics of sport marketing is that sport organizations earn significant revenue by selling not only the core product but also peripheral products, such as parking, concessions, and stadium services, that support the provision of the core product (Gillentine & Crow, 2005). The peripheral products are sometimes referred to collectively as service quality (covered in chapter 18), which is one of the most frequently studied areas within the fields of marketing and sport management (Parasuraman, Zeithmal, & Berry, 1988). One global example of revenue production from a peripheral source is the selling of sponsorship space on team jerseys, a practice popular in European, Asian, and South American sport organizations. Although other factors influence sport consumer behavior, they are beyond the scope of this chapter. Refer to the articles listed in the reference section for a more detailed discussion of these factors.

Learning Activity

Write down at least five reasons why you have consumed (or would like to consume) sport globally. Discuss your reasons among your classmates. Address how you think sport management students in other countries would answer this question.

Marketing and Sponsorship in a Global Economy

Because of significant advancements in technology and communication, sport consumers in the 21st century can enjoy a wide variety of sport offerings. Executives within sport organizations now have the ability to reach a much broader marketplace. Many professional sport organizations continue to eye foreign markets, realizing the potential for new fans and opportunities. For example, NFL fans in London got to watch the San Francisco 49ers defeat the Denver Broncos in 2010, marking the fifth time that the NFL had held a regular season game outside North America since 2005, in an event known as the International Series. The demand was high; 45,000 tickets were sold in 90 minutes, and in the second round of ticket sales, 15,000 seats were sold in just half an hour (National Football League London, 2010). Apostolopoulou and Papadimitriou (2005) stressed the importance of targeting foreign markets by mentioning that "international markets have become a source of substantial revenue for the professional leagues, and U.S. professional leagues consider international expansion the cornerstone for their future growth" (p. 173). As in any market, sport marketers must understand targeted consumers' behavior for effective market selection decisions, which include segmenting, targeting, and positioning (Shank, 2009).

The Giro d'Italia, a long-distance road bicycle stage race, is Italy's biggest annual sporting event. More than 7 million people in Italy view it live (Connolly, 2010). The Giro is an example of a sport event in the process of building an international presence. Its history dates back to 1909 when a local newspaper company, in hopes of increasing its circulation, started the event (Connolly, 2010). The event has since grown, but how can this event go global and rival the popularity of the Tour de France? To begin, event organizers attracted top cyclists to participate, which in turn increased the reach of the event to casual observers who tuned in through increasingly interested global media outlets such as ESPN (Connolly, 2010). Second, the race included an international section through the Netherlands, attracting nearly 1 million Dutch spectators. As more foreign fans watch the event, more foreign sponsors can be solicited (Connolly, 2010). True success will not come from being exactly like the Tour de France but from making the Giro d'Italia its own world-class event.

Sport organizations are not the only entities that are trying to reach a global audience. Corporations, in an effort to expand internationally, often look to collaborate with sport properties to help grow their businesses. We need look no further than the list of sponsors for the International Olympic Committee (IOC) or FIFA. For example, the IOC developed the Olympic Partner (TOP) Programme in 1985 to give fewer than a dozen major partners exclusive rights to Olympic marks, events, and programs. Partners include Coca-Cola (a sponsor since 1928), watch manufacturer Omega from Switzerland, and Panasonic (a full list of TOP sponsors can be found at www.olympic.org).

In the case of FIFA, its sponsorship program (FIFA Sponsorship Programme 2007–2014) provides three tiers of partnership. The top tier, FIFA Partner, enjoys the highest level of association with FIFA activities such as its competitions, special events, and development programs. For example, Dubai-based Emirates Airlines signed a US$195 million deal to become a FIFA Partner, with rights to all FIFA events including the 2010 and 2014 FIFA World Cups (FIFA, 2009a). With the World Cup matches held in Germany in 2006 and South Africa in 2010 and slated for Brazil in 2014, and countless qualifiers held in numerous countries, the reach of this global partnership is significant. FIFA also has marketing partnerships with Sony (Japan), VISA (United States), Adidas (Germany), Coca-Cola (United States), and Hyundai–Kia Motors (Korea) (FIFA, 2009b). Second- and third-tier partnerships are FIFA World Cup Sponsor and National Supporter, which are limited in their rights and activities. A FIFA World Cup Sponsor receives global opportunities such as category exclusivity and brand associations but is limited to the FIFA World Cup. A National Supporter receives benefits in the host country only.

Although IOC sponsors and FIFA Partners may have disparate product lines, they share one characteristic: a desire to align with a powerful sport property to enhance their global branding strategy. To acquire the rights, the TOP sponsors and FIFA Partners (per product category) paid approximately $100 million and $44 million each, respectively. Those figures cover just the rights fees. Generally, sponsoring companies spend at least three times the rights fees to leverage the sponsorship rights.

Learning Activity

Do some research and create a list of the top 10 global sport sponsors in terms of money spent in 2000. Next, create a list using the same criteria from the past year. Identify the companies that have remained on the list, those that have fallen off it, and those that have recently made it. In class or on a web-based discussion board, discuss the changes.

Given the expense involved, what motivates companies to become involved in sponsorship? What unique benefits do companies gain from association with international megaevents? One possible answer would be exposure and visibility to international audiences. According to several industry reports, the cumulative global TV audience for the 2006 FIFA World Cup Germany was 26.3 billion, and the 2008 Beijing Summer Olympic Games Opening Ceremony drew 34.2 million viewers in the United States (Basu, 2010; Landreth, 2008). Increasing **brand awareness** through association with international megaevents like Olympic Games is the first and foremost step for consumer product adoption (Shank, 2009).

International Brand Management

A brand is something that distinguishes a company from its competition (Couvelaere & Richelieu, 2005). Brand components can be marks, symbols, signs, logos, slogans, color schemes, or a combination of the preceding. A brand is a promise to the consumer to meet established expectations. Brand expression, made up of elements (positioning, identity, and personality) within the marketer's control, is distinguished from brand perception, in which the brand expression has been altered by the viewpoint of consumers (van Gelder, 2004). In

CASE STUDY

Komatsu Limited

Komatsu Ltd., the world's second largest manufacturer and supplier of construction, mining, and utility equipment, has strategically used sport to increase its brand awareness and brand image in the global community. To create a global presence, Komatsu used former MLB player Mike Piazza as an endorser when he played for the Los Angeles Dodgers in the mid-1990s ("MLB Stars," 1996). Piazza appeared in several advertisements for Komatsu (Johnson, 1998).

To enhance its brand awareness and image further, Komatsu decided to sign Hideki Matsui as a global ambassador in 2003, the year when Matsui decided to play for the New York Yankees (Komatsu Japan, 2003). The rationale for Komatsu's move was that they saw several characteristics in Matsui that they believed they mutually possessed. Matsui, one of the premier Japanese baseball players in MLB, was considered a major figure on the global stage, the same direction in which Komatsu was headed. Also, Matsui's strong work ethic and desire for excellence aligned well with Komatsu. Another reason that Matsui was a good fit was the fact that Matsui's father and grandfather had previously worked for Komatsu (Komatsu Japan, 2003).

Through this contract, Matsui has appeared in advertisements for Komatsu on television and radio, and in newspapers, magazines, and point-of-purchase posters. Komatsu purchased signage on the right field upper deck of Yankee stadium during Matsui's tenure with the Yankees (Komatsu Japan, 2003). With Matsui's move to the Angels in the 2010 season, Komatsu relocated its sponsorship, placing its logo in a similar location in that team's stadium (Chunichi Sports, 2010). Furthermore, Komatsu has been an official sponsor of MLB in Japan since 2003, providing commemorative memorabilia (calendars, caps, golf balls, towels, and so on) each season (MLB International, n.d.).

In a similar fashion, subsidiaries of Komatsu have used sponsorships to reach their target markets, focusing especially on car racing. Komatsu America Corporation has sponsored Tony Pedregon, a two-time National Hot Rod Association (NHRA) world champion (Komatsu America, 2010), and has been a presenting sponsor in the Canadian Tire Series (Komatsu 300 at Riverside Speedway in Nova Scotia), now owned by NASCAR (Riverside Speedway, 2010). They have also sponsored Bobby Labonte of Phoenix Racing in the NASCAR Sprint Cup Series (Breaking Limits, 2010). Other notable sponsorship includes Komatsu Australia Pty. Ltd.'s sponsorship of Triple Eight Race Engineering in the V8 Supercar Series (Komatsu Australia, 2008). It remains to be seen whether Komatsu's pursuit of global business through athlete endorsements and corporate sponsorship has been effective, and whether it should continue in the future.

other words, marketers create an expression and hope that consumers will perceive it as anticipated. This goal is difficult to achieve in a sport setting because marketers rarely have control over the core product—the game—or its outcome. Therefore, sport marketers focus on touch points such as game environment, safety, security, in-game entertainment, parking, food service, facility cleanliness, and customer service, all areas that affect brand perception and over which they have control.

Defining International Branding

To develop a definition of international (or global) branding, we must look to the academic marketing literature. Most researchers in this field, and likely marketing practitioners as well, assume that consumers and students believe branding to be nothing more than logos or distinguishing marks of a product or service (Onkvisit & Shaw, 1989). Others have discovered an international brand-planning process composed of both the core essence of the brand and its execution (de Chernatony et al., 1995). Basically, many assumptions are made in the understanding of international branding, in what both researchers and consumers believe.

An issue to be considered when determining whether a product or brand is global is the degree to which marketing strategies differ from the home country to global markets (Whitelock & Fastoso, 2007). Researchers have not reached a consensus on the process of international branding and its components. A narrow view of **global branding** refers only to the brand name and related decisions on a global level. To illustrate, think of the NFL's showcasing of its product internationally by playing games between two of its teams in Europe, as has been done once a season since 2007. This approach to globalization, a regularly scheduled game, has been well received.

On the other hand, a broad definition of international branding emphasizes developing the product, service, or brand globally to appeal to the attitudes, likes, and perceptions of the target market (Whitelock & Fastoso, 2007). Think in terms of the now-defunct NFL Europa (previously the World League of American Football, or WLAF, often pronounced "we laugh"). In this instance, the NFL took its game, with its rules, to an overseas local target, placing teams in Frankfurt, Berlin, and Hamburg, Germany, as well as Barcelona, Spain, among others. This approach was seen as forcing a truly American sport on Europeans. Although the effort was remotely successful, it was often seen as a developmental minor league and not as appealing as the NFL product.

With that in mind, the following definition of international branding (to which you may add *sport* before every occurrence of the word *brand* or *branding*) was proposed: **International branding** is a field within international marketing concerned with the challenges that companies (sport organizations) face when their brands cross national borders. These challenges relate to the essence of the brand in terms of brand name, brand visual (e.g., logos and colors) and sound elements (e.g., jingles, music), and brand personality (Whitelock & Fastoso, 2007, p. 266).

Building an International Sport Brand

So now that we know what an international brand is, let us apply that to the sport industry. Because FIFA was previously used as an example, we will use it again in a branding sense. FIFA is a global brand, and as such it has developed a mission statement, "Develop the game, touch the world, build a better future," to reflect its brand promise, "For the Game. For the World" (FIFA, 2010). It should be no surprise that professional sport organizations try to position themselves as brands and build what is known as brand equity, or the attributes associated with a particular brand within a product category (Fullerton, 2007). Obviously, marketers want brand equity to be positive, but it can be negative. For example, the Pittsburgh Pirates of MLB, at this writing, are on the verge of setting the record for most consecutive nonwinning seasons by a professional team. The equity with the Pirates' brand is not positive.

Other teams, such as Manchester United, the New York Yankees, the Dallas Cowboys, and the New Zealand All Blacks, have positive brand equity. Notable attributes contributing to this positive brand equity are winning, history, and team identification, which is a psychological connection to a team (Wann & Branscombe, 1993). Of course, not everyone is a fan of those teams, but they have built, through brand management, a level of positive equity that leads to brand loyalty. **Brand loyalty**, in the context of sport, can be thought of as the ability of a sport brand to survive, even when on-field performance is mediocre, and it can lead to additional revenues (Couvelaere & Richelieu, 2005). Targeting international fans would require a carefully tailored strategy to foster team or player identification. As mentioned earlier, sport organizations that seek to expand their target market must consider cultural factors. As referenced in this chapter's case study, the NBA is developing itself as a global brand. Building a brand on an international scale requires a significant commitment of time, money, and human resources, but the rewards can be great. Expanding into foreign countries means that marketers must know, appreciate, and respect the customs of the land and build a strategy accordingly.

For example, in some countries it may be against the law or considered in bad taste to play games on Sunday or show beer advertisements during a television broadcast. Marketers must be cognizant of regional differences when creating a global marketing and branding strategy. Norms and conventions related to sport can vary widely between cultures. Consider the sport of buzkashi. This Central Asian tradition involves teams of players vying to see who can grab a goat or calf from the ground while riding a horse at full gallop. The goal of a player is to grab the carcass of a headless goat or calf, get it clear of the other players, and then pitch it across a goal line or into a target circle. From a branding perspective, how do you think this would be received in another region? Though this sport is popular, it would probably have difficulty expanding to other parts of the world because of people's reactions to

the use of the dead calf. It would not be an easy sell in most foreign marketplaces. Using an artificial prop such as a sandbag in place of the dead calf might help, but the original imagery might still generate a strong reaction in people outside the sport's native region. Hence, recognizing cultural differences is vital to making sure your brand is accepted globally.

Branding, however, is not a guaranteed solution to creating global influence. In fact, some believe that branding is harmful to creativity, ingenuity, and quality. Lucas Conley, in his book *Obsessive Branding Disorder*, claims that we focus too much on creating brands when we should be creating quality products and delivering superior service (Conley, 2008). Nevertheless, sport organizations must be willing and able to expand beyond national borders to survive and thrive in the 21st century and beyond.

Summary

We have introduced the concepts related to global sport marketing and international branding in the sport industry. Marketing is a critical component in any organization's strategic plan, but it is often hindered in the sport industry by lack of control over the product on the field, pitch, track, or court. Therefore, marketers look to enhance the product components that they can control.

We are all sport consumers, and as such we rely on a variety of factors in developing loyalty and affinity for a sport organization. These factors, whether used independently or in combination with each other, form the basis for sport consumption decision making. Whether we buy Nike shoes and apparel exclusively, or buy season tickets to our favorite teams, or watch the FIFA World Cup Finals regardless of which countries are playing, we are showing our level of commitment to a brand.

Brand management is the act of purposefully creating an image or perception in the mind of the customer related to a product, service, or team. Expanding that image globally requires careful consideration and planning, but the reward of successful international marketing is worth the risks and challenges.

Learning Activity

Think of your favorite sport team or league. What is its brand image? Does it have positive or negative brand equity? If you were a top administrator, what strategies would you implement to make positive changes in the perception of the brand?

? Review and Discussion Questions

1. Which non-U.S. sport league has the strongest global presence? Why?
2. Define brand equity and explain how it can be achieved globally.
3. Describe the global strategy of the National Basketball Association and evaluate its effectiveness.
4. Name several athletes with global popularity. Explain how they achieved their fame.
5. Name several sports with global appeal and awareness. Explain how they achieved that status.
6. Name several sports that have been unable to achieve international popularity and explain the obstacles that they faced in globalization.

New Media and International Sport

James Santomier, PhD
Sacred Heart University, Connecticut, USA

Joshua A. Shuart, PhD
Sacred Heart University, Connecticut, USA

Artur Costabiei, MA
Tourist Board Kronplatz, Italy

Chapter Objectives

After studying this chapter, you will be able to do the following:

- Understand and discuss the nature and dynamics of new media and the relevancy of new media technologies for the sport industry worldwide
- Understand the relationship among new media technologies, sport content, and the globalization of sport
- Understand and identify the most important parameters for developing, implementing, and managing new media projects
- Identify and discuss important new-media-related challenges, dimensions, and issues facing sport enterprise managers worldwide
- Understand that new media is central to the future of the global sport industry

Key Terms

The integration of new media technologies within the global sport industry has resulted in radical changes in the production, distribution, and consumption of sport entertainment. As competition for consumer attention intensifies in a complex and networked global business environment, the challenge for sport enterprises is to deliver value to consumers and manage their brands effectively. Competition for the attention of consumers has become a major tenet for the development and implementation of new media initiatives within the sport industry. The result has been enhanced global access to sport content for consumers and more business opportunities for media enterprises, federations, leagues, franchises, and individual athletes and coaches worldwide.

The synergistic relationship between sport and new media that has developed over the past 10 years is the result of the increasing complexity of the global sport industry, additional demand for sport content by media, and convergence of consumer needs worldwide. Therefore, sport managers must understand the conceptual and practical dimensions of developing and implementing new media projects as well as the significance of new media for the future of sport business. Sport managers at all levels should be prepared to identify new media opportunities that are relevant to their specific sport enterprises. This chapter addresses the relationship between sport content and new media technologies and discusses the central issues and challenges related to developing and implementing new media projects from the local to the global level.

What Is New Media?

New media is a term that refers to the convergence of telecommunications, computing, and traditional media, and it includes any media production that is digitally distributed and interactive. New media includes websites; audio and video content streaming on the Internet and mobile devices; audio and video content on demand (VoD); chat rooms, blogs, and e-mail; social media such as Facebook, MySpace, and Twitter; digital marketing by e-mail and text messages; viral marketing; DVD and CD-ROM media; virtual reality environments; video games; Internet telephony; digital cameras; and mobile technologies such as smartphones using 3G and 4G technology to access the Internet. New media technologies that are most significant for

the global sport industry include (1) broadband, (2) high-definition TV (HDTV), (3) interactive TV (iTV), and (4) **3G and 4G** (third- and fourth-generation) wireless technologies.

Two characteristics distinguish new media from "old" media. The first relates to how digital content is transmitted and accessed. New media technologies integrate text, graphics, pictures, video, and sound content. The content is then distributed, for example, by high-speed always-open broadband Internet connections directly to digital platforms, such as computers, PDAs, or mobile phones, where consumers access it. The second distinguishing characteristic of new media is interactivity, which is most significant for future sport-related digital content development. The availability of broadband access to the Internet and to mobile smartphones is increasing rapidly and now exceeds cable TV penetration in most consumer markets worldwide. With increased broadband access and mobile connectivity, consumers (also referred to as *prosumers*, those who simultaneously produce and consume products and services outside the monetary economy in the digital era) are able to access sport news and event coverage through their digital platform of choice whenever (time shifting) they want and wherever (geo shifting) they are.

The Internet, which is the core of new media, emerged through scientific research conducted primarily by the U.S. Department of Defense's Advanced Research Projects Agency (DARPA) and the Advanced Research Projects Agency Network (ARPANET) project, which involved the University of California at Los Angeles in cooperation with several other U.S. universities. The Internet is literally the underpinning of the digital revolution. It consists of host computers (servers) linked together by dedicated **broadband** connections capable of transmitting and exchanging large amounts of

Learning Activity

While attending a professional, intercollegiate, or community sport event, identify any new media technologies that may be integrated into the production of the event. After the event, visit the website of the team or teams and identify and document any additional new media initiatives.

data. These broadband connections, referred to as backbone or trunk lines, are dedicated, which means that they are always open, or accessible, as long as an Internet connection is available. Information transmission is possible in part because all the linked computers use the same hypertext markup language, or HTML—the authoring and editing language used to develop "pages" on the World Wide Web. The World Wide Web (WWW), or simply the web, is an extensive distributed hypertext document library that is carried by the Internet framework. Documents, graphics, and other multimedia content reside on the web in the form of small "packets" that can be retrieved and viewed by anyone with access to the Internet.

Some analysts have used the term *web 2.0* to describe how the commercial use of the Internet has grown and evolved. Web 2.0 is a concept that emerged after the dot-com bubble burst in 2001. It came into common usage after the first O'Reilly Media Web 2.0 conference in 2004. During an interaction between Tim O'Reilly and web pioneer Dale Daugherty, Daugherty argued that the web was more important than it was before the dot-com bubble burst because it contained inherently more interesting and useful applications and websites. Although some argue that the term is meaningless, others contend that the term describes the changing trends in the use of specific web technologies and design elements that focus on enhanced creativity, secure information sharing, collaboration, and functionality.

Web 2.0 concepts have led to the development and evolution of web-based communities and hosted services, such as social-networking sites, video-sharing sites, wikis, and blogs. Although the term suggests a new version of the web, it does not refer to any technological updates but rather to changes in how software developers and end users employ the web. The term *web 2.0* is now part of Internet lexicon; it has more than 9.5 million citations in Google. According to Tim O'Reilly, "Web 2.0 is the business revolution in the computer industry caused by the move to the Internet platform and an attempt to understand the rules for success on that new platform."

New Media Technologies

New media, or **digital technologies**, have four broad functions in the context of international sport. These include (1) information gathering, sorting, and searching through services such as Google and Bing; (2) sport content production, which is specific to a particular digital platform such as the Internet, HDTV, or mobile devices; (3) sport content distribution through ISPs and specific sport content websites such as ESPN3.com or cbssports.com; and (4) content access and display through specific digital platforms such as computers, mobile phones, PDAs, and so on. All four of these functions are now commonly incorporated into a variety of digital platforms, such as computers, PDAs, mobile phones using 3G or 4G technology, digital and audio recorders, and digital video and still (megapixel) cameras.

For example, the 3G and 4G technology currently used in most smartphones (a mobile phone offering advanced capabilities, often with PC-like functionality) allows significant interactivity, such as online gaming, and incorporates advanced features such as live streaming video. The continued development of mobile gaming will have a significant effect on companies such as Electronic Arts, which has a large library of sport video games. Other new media technologies include global positioning satellite (GPS) devices and immersive, 3D, and omni-directional sensors and acquisition tools. All these technologies are used effectively by sport media enterprises such as ESPN, CBS Sports, NBC Universal Sports, and international media companies such as BBC Sport, Eurosport, and Switzerland-based In Front Sports & Media to enhance the production and distribution of sport content through their websites and high-definition TV (HDTV) channels.

With respect to content production, the most important technological development contributing to the adoption of new media by sport enterprises worldwide is digital image compression technology. This technology allows live video streaming on the Internet and smartphones and is the key technology of web cameras because the compressed video file size is small enough to stream rapidly through a network line of the Internet or local area network (LAN). As an example of the options that this technology opens up for sport content, Major League Baseball's Advanced Media (MLBAM) initiative, MLB.TV Mosaic, allows consumers to view up to six games on a computer screen simultaneously while selecting the audio, retrieving statistics from a custom list of players, and tracking and receiving alerts from games throughout the MLB schedule.

Ensequence, a leading provider of software and services for interactive TV, makes the software required to access Mosaic. After consumers log in, download, and launch the player, they can select among various Mosaics and view as many as six games. When consumers click on a selected game being streamed, the audio for that game is played. MLB now offers more than 2,000 games in high definition online through Mosaic with full DVR-like functionality, including pause and rewind.

Another new media technology, object-oriented multimedia, is made up of clickable, or interactive, objects that may be placed in a sport video, for example. In an object-oriented system, objects can be overlapped but still accessed individually. Also, object-oriented images benefit from high-quality output devices. The higher the resolution of a monitor or HDTV, the sharper an object-oriented image will look. What this technology means for sport is that viewers of digital sport content are able to view additional objects that may be embedded in the video. That is, every element in a digital video can contain additional content. For example, a digital video broadcast of a sport event may include linear narrative, images of the game action, and additional content that may be available on demand. While viewing the sport broadcast, the consumer may use a mouse, remote control stick, or voice command using speech recognition technology to access the video details or biographies of specific players, previous plays or game highlights, or promotions for licensed merchandise. From a content and revenue perspective, the broadcaster is able to layer in much richer content and information than is originally captured, thereby enhancing the value of the sport broadcast.

Broadband

Broadband is vitally important to new media and to the development of the global sport industry because it provides two-way access to the Internet. With the increasing availability of broadband worldwide, consumers are able to receive (download) and transmit (upload) digital content (data) at extremely high speeds. The rapid development of the interactive capabilities of the Internet and the concomitant development of websites using that capability have transformed the web into a global platform for engaging, entertaining, and informing consumers. Sport consumers worldwide may not only view live streamed or **video on demand (VOD)** sport content but also participate in fantasy sport leagues and engage in online betting, e-commerce, social networking, and file sharing. VOD, or AVOD (audio video on demand), allows consumers to select the time and place they access (i.e., watch or listen) sport content. An important distinction to be made is that, unlike national and regional broadcasting networks, the Internet operates across international boundaries, which distinguishes it from other forms of media. The global rollout of wireless fidelity (Wi-Fi) networks with broadband access has provided millions of place-shifting and time-shifting sport consumers with seamless connectivity to the Internet, allowing them instant access to the websites of their favorite teams worldwide.

Broadband subscription prices are dropping because of increased competition and bundling of services (combining television, broadband, and telephone services) by cable TV and traditional telecommunications companies. The rapid penetration of broadband has enabled some sport enterprises to increase their global fan base and revenue significantly. For example, Manchester United has more fans in Asia than it does in Europe and the United States combined. Besides profiting from subscription services through cable, DSL, satellite, and mobile technology, broadband-related revenues are derived from digital advertising, sponsorship, e-commerce, content syndication, pay per view, fantasy sports, and gaming.

Broadband technology, however, also complicates the sale and distribution of sport broadcast rights. Media enterprises are finding it difficult to retain sport content and necessarily are adopting more flexible rights strategies as sport leagues, federations, and franchises exercise greater autonomy and control over their content distribution. Minority, or niche, sports, such as professional bowling, lacrosse, fencing, and indoor football, previously overlooked by mainstream broadcasters, will now be able to provide content through their websites directly to fans worldwide. Many sport content distributors, unable to compete with the spending power of larger media companies, will now be more interested in the content of minority sports in their efforts to develop a discernible profile within the sport media marketplace.

For large sport enterprises, such as the Football League in the United Kingdom, online commerce can be significant. FL Interactive, the online business unit of the Football League, provided record financial distributions of more than £3 million (US$6 million) to European football franchises for the 2007–2008 season. The distribution represented a 50 percent increase over the previous year (Glendenning, 2008). FL Interactive manages and develops Internet and mobile rights for 78 official U.K. football club websites, including 65 Football League clubs, 7 Premier League clubs, and 6 clubs from the Football Conference. Sites are viewed by more than 4.1 million unique users per month.

"This new generation of websites will keep our clubs at the forefront of football's online media market, whilst also giving clubs greater flexibility to manage their websites at a local level so that supporters can enjoy a first class service from their club," said FL Interactive chairman Ian Ritchie. Among the new services, each of the 78 new official club websites will offer a comprehensive range of free video, including daily football news and goal clips, and substantial enhancements to subscription video services (Glendenning, 2007).

In addition to broadband, the increasing availability of **bandwidth**, a term used to describe the amount of data transferred to or from a website or server within a prescribed period (in bits per second), is critical to the successful distribution of and access to digital sport content worldwide. In another context, the term *bandwidth* is used to refer to the amount of monthly data transfer consumed by an Internet user. Transmission speed and video quality are paramount to bridging the gap between the quality of video on the Internet and that is currently available by television. Without continued upgrades to speed and quality, consumers would opt not to view sport broadcasts online.

Distribution of digital content may be through asymmetric digital subscriber lines (ADSL, or more briefly, DSL) often provided by telecommunications companies, cable modem technology often provided by local or regional cable TV providers, digital cellular telephony, and finally, advanced wireless networking, including low-earth orbital (LEO) and direct-to-home broadcast satellite (DBS) technology. Telecommunications companies providing ADSL services may have a difficult time competing with cable, satellite, and terrestrial broadcasters in the future because HDTV, VoD, and other high-level digital services require significantly more bandwidth than current ADSL providers are capable of

delivering (Santomier & Shuart, 2008).

Access and display of digital content continues its rapid development through such devices as personal digital assistants (PDAs), electronic books, tablet PCs, smartphones, wearable computers, and high-definition TV (HDTV) technology. These platforms are continually improving, becoming increasingly thin and light, providing enhanced resolution and color rendition, and, perhaps more important, becoming more affordable. The next generation of digital display technologies will be increasingly portable, high resolution, intuitive in design, and with an increasingly transparent user interface. Frequently, several digital functions are integrated into a single device. Integrated multifunctional devices such as smartphones are capable of receiving and transmitting data, pictures, and voice.

Mobile technologies include a multitude of wireless devices, such as mobile handsets, personal digital assistants (PDAs), and wireless fidelity (Wi-Fi) "hotspots," which have enabled the untethering of laptop computers. Advances in mobile technologies, ubiquitous in modern life, have made a range of new and enhanced data services available to consumers. The number of mobile phones worldwide reached 2.5 billion in 2009, and the most recent feature-rich handsets, or smartphones, include Internet access, multimedia messaging (MMS), touch screens, Java-based applications, music capability, and integrated digital cameras, as well as numerous specific applications that are either free to subscribers or can be purchased. A recent study has indicated that many consumers with smartphones are now accessing the Internet more frequently and for longer periods with their handheld devices than with their computers.

The popularity of mobile devices for accessing the web has been driven in part by the availability of wireless networks. A WLAN (wireless local area network) is an extension or replacement of traditional fixed-line LANs. Multiple users are able to access the Internet as long as they are within the WLAN area, which typically extends for up to 100 meters, and are connected to the network. An increasingly larger number of stadiums and arenas have adopted this technology to provide their own information services to licensed holders within their grounds or to provide value-added digital services to consumers. Wi-Max is similar to Wi-Fi, but it allows multiple users to access the Internet at high speeds and provides a much wider potential footprint—up to 30 miles (48 km). Wi-Max has developed much slower than anticipated, and many Wi-Max projects in U.S. cities have been dropped for a variety of reasons.

Cisco Systems built a wireless network into the recently completed Yankee Stadium. The new network allows for everything from in-game replays to concessions, providing what Cisco considers a new fan experience. The network, which cost between US$15 and US$16 million, integrates voice, video, and data and provides HD video throughout the stadium as well as a high level of interactivity. Cisco installed 1,100 high-definition IP monitors in luxury suites, restaurants, bars, and the restrooms to ensure that consumers do not miss any of the game. After the game the monitors direct spectators to the nearest exits and provide them with traffic and subway information. Spectators sitting in the luxury suites are able to change the view of the game on their high-definition IPTV, call-up instant replays, and order food and beverages right from a Cisco IP phone in the suite.

Mobile technologies represent an effective way for sport brands to reach new consumers and provide value-added components to their loyal consumers (Barnes, 2005). The almost universal availability of mobile phones and significant market penetration worldwide provide sport brands with an opportunity to reach a large and often specifically targeted audience. For example, in countries such as Brazil, China, and India many consumers do not have landline phone service but do have mobile phone service. Those consumers with smartphones and the willingness to pay for and view sport events on the small screen as opposed to the big screen provide significant revenue to the sport industry and to mobile service providers such as Verizon, AT&T, Vodafone, Orange, and others.

Besides offering live sport event video streaming and video on demand (VOD), SMS (short messaging services), and MMS (multimedia messaging services), mobile network operators, in cooperation with their broadcast partners, are able to offer unique sport-branded ring tones, wallpapers, interactive games, ticketing, voting, and competitions, sometimes as dimensions of specific sport sponsorship activation.

Mobile sport content has proven revenue streams because of a large consumer base that subscribes

Learning Activity

View a live streamed international professional sport event on your computer or, if possible, on your mobile phone. Evaluate the quality of the production. Visit the websites of several international sport events, teams, or federations and (1) evaluate the website, (2) identify how the organization communicates with its consumer base, and (3) determine whether opportunities are available for user-generated content (UGC).

to sport-related services. For sport rights holders, mobile technologies provide new opportunities to enhance the relationship with consumers. For mobile operators, the technology is an essential part of their content offering, providing opportunity for subscriber upgrades. The rights to sport content are used to create mobile video packages, typically offering customers video match highlights, previews of games, archive footage, premiership round-ups, audio bulletins, near-live picture messages, and match scores.

In 2007 the English Premier League received approximately US$150 million (£74 million, or €109 million) over three years from the sale of its mobile and Internet clips. Just before the FIFA 2006 World Cup, Italian mobile phone company 3 Italia became the first company to roll out 3G mobile video using the direct video broadcasting handheld (DVB-H) protocol. DVB-H is one of several protocols developed to provide high-quality broadcast television over handsets. After acquiring the national license as digital TV operator in 2005, the following June 3 Italia launched the first digital mobile TV based on DVB-H technology in the world, broadcasting on a mobile exclusive basis in Italy all the matches from the FIFA World Cup 2006. 3 Italia also provides a wide array of multimedia, video communications, and Internet services, as well as entertainment, music, information, cinema, sport, and mobile TV.

High-Definition TV

High-definition TV (HDTV) is perhaps the most significant digital technology in sport broadcasting because HDTV provides at least four times better picture quality than conventional TV, resulting in

CASE STUDY

Integration of New Media Into the 2006 FIFA World Cup

FIFA has made a significant commitment to new media, and until the 2008 Beijing Olympics, the 2006 FIFA World Cup was the most advanced global sport event relative to the integration of digital broadcast production and distribution technologies. FIFA, with its media partner Host Broadcasting Service (HBS), provided more content, more delivery capacity through more systems and devices, and a larger variety of digital platforms than any previous sport event. HBS produced a "new media content package" that consisted of an extensive range of material and services specific to new media. The content reflected the demands of new media licensees and allowed them to deliver sport content directly to their customer base, whether online or through mobile networks, while limiting unilateral end-to-end production costs.

HBS provided the primary broadcast feed in 16:9 HDTV digital format for all 64 games, which required the deployment of 25 widescreen HDTV cameras, high-motion cameras (which take 300 frames per second), stump cameras (small cameras placed in devices used for the action), and super slow-motion cameras. The HDTV feed from all venues was delivered directly to the new media unit at the International Broadcasting Center (IBC) in Munich, where a dedicated new media package was produced so that licensees had no need to edit it extensively. Innovations such as pan and scan technology, which was developed to reduce movies to the smaller format TV screen, were used to allow editors to zoom in and capture key action such as a specific goal, producing a picture that was much more dramatic and relevant for the smaller mobile screens.

Besides the broadcasting of all 2006 FIFA World Cup games in HDTV, other important new media innovations included (1) the involvement of consumers in user-generated content (UGC), which included

photo and video sharing as part of the social media experience, and (2) the availability of World Cup content through mobile phones, which was most popular in Italy, the tournament winners.

The 2006 FIFA World Cup website was at the time one of the most successful sport event websites in history, garnering more than 4.2 billion page views (Hefflinger, 2006). Regarding the website, FIFA president Sepp Blatter stated,

> We are offering a one-stop destination for all information on and around the FIFA World Cup in nine languages. The unparalleled coverage produced by 50 FIFA editors coming from 20 different countries and the wealth and depth of content on FIFAworldcup.com have been recognized by sport lovers around the world as the best place to follow the event online.

The website was jointly produced, marketed, and hosted by FIFA and U.S.-based technology company Yahoo! Inc. Yahoo experimented with corporate sponsorships for each of the separate features of its website. Sportswear maker Adidas AG sponsored a goal counter, Emirates Airline sponsored a game time chart, Global Gillette sponsored the online voting for the Best Young Player Award, and McDonald's Corporation sponsored the website's fantasy football game.

The 2006 FIFA World Cup provided new elements of user-generated content (UGC) for sport consumers and broadcasters, which included (1) new ways of experiencing sport events; (2) participation and involvement through self-production of videos and pictures, blogs, forums, games, file sharing, and message boards; (3) the ability of sport enterprises to test what consumers want, what advertisers will buy, and how to filter the right UGC content into their websites; and (4) the ability of the sport enterprise to keep its content germane to the consumer.

---

dynamic realism and immediacy. HDTV also has an improved aspect ratio (the ratio of the width of a picture relative to its height), which refers to the shape of the screen. Non-HDTVs have an aspect ratio of 4:3, whereas HDTVs have an aspect ratio of 16:9, the ratio found on most movie theater screens.

Besides improved resolution and immediacy, HDTV has significantly better audio quality because the Dolby digital format used in digital broadcasts provides 5.1 separate channels of digital surround sound, which enhances the viewing appeal of all sports, especially football (soccer) and hockey.

Sport has consistently played an important role in helping to attract consumers to new technologies, and HDTV is especially suited for broadcasting sport. It addresses the need for enhanced picture quality and sound, and viewing sport on HDTV is a new and energizing experience for many consumers. Images can also be produced in HD quality for Internet streaming and video on demand (VoD), as well as mobile networks. Innovations for viewing on mobile technologies, such as pan and scan technology, originally developed to reduce movies to the smaller format TV screen, have been used to allow editors to zoom in and capture key action, thus producing a picture that is much more dramatic and relevant for mobile-sized screens.

The availability of HDTV in homes, sports bars, and outdoor viewing venues likely contributed to the increased viewing audience for the 2010 World Cup. Over 700 million people viewed the final game between Spain and the Netherlands. In addition to continued penetration of HDTV worldwide, some sport events are now broadcast in 3D. For example, ESPN broadcasted 25 of the 2010 World Cup games in 3D. Although 3D is neither as readily accepted nor as widely viewed as HD, it is another platform that will contribute to enhanced viewing experiences for sport consumers. In fact, ESPN's launch of its ESPN 3D network in conjunction with its coverage of the World Cup games is perhaps the primary driving force behind the heightened awareness of 3DTV. Consumers have found, however, that viewing sport events on 3D TV does not compare with the experience of viewing 3D movies in the theater (Santomier & Costabiei, 2009).

Interactive TV

Interactive TV (iTV) services employ digital technology. Therefore, the potential for iTV depends on the deployment of digital television platforms, which are dispersed across cable, satellite, and terrestrial delivery systems. The transmission of television by broadband Internet (IPTV) may offer an additional boost to interactive TV services, which are broadcast together with the video feed and are instantly accessible by consumers. **Interactive TV (iTV)** encompasses all interactivity conducted through digital TV networks, whether free or revenue generating, and whether linked to a specific program or not. Increased distribution of interactive digital TV platforms will determine the extent of interactive sport TV, which will be in the form of an added service for pay TV subscribers as well as a vehicle for generating new revenues. A primary growth area will likely be in transactional services that are based on sport, such as competitions, gaming, information, voting, and participation.

NDS, a News Corporation company, creates the security and enabling technologies as well as the interactive applications that allow operators to generate revenue by delivering digital content to TVs, set-top boxes (STBs), digital video recorders (DVRs), PCs, mobile phones, portable media players (PMPs), removable media, and other devices. A leader in sport iTV, NDS created a complex and interactive application specifically for the 2002 FIFA World Cup. While watching a World Cup game, consumers engaged in interactive activities such as voting for their favorite team, choosing multiple camera angles, accessing match statistics, and viewing match highlights. For example, subscribers in Argentina, Mexico, and Venezuela had access to voting options for their favorite players and teams while viewing real-time statistics. The application also was developed with advertisers in mind because it was capable of supporting country-specific screens, which allowed advertisers to broadcast regional advertisements during game breaks. U.S.-based digital service providers such as DirecTV have also continued to emphasize user interactivity.

New Media and Sport Content

New media is a dynamic and commercially viable component of sport entertainment worldwide, and sport enterprise managers are finding it necessary to create or revise organizational objectives and make operational and financial decisions in an increasingly competitive and technologically complex business environment. Therefore, they must understand the unique dimensions, issues, and challenges associated with developing, implementing, and managing new media initiatives within the sport enterprise.

Digital sport content is an asset that, if managed properly, should increase in value, generate significant revenue, and attract new consumers, sponsors, and partnerships. The integration of new media within the sport industry has enhanced the value of sport content because it offers a broad range of new channels of distribution (platforms), as well as unique and dynamic ways of connecting with sport consumers. As a direct result of the integration of new media technologies, many sport enterprises are now maintaining their broadcast rights, leveraging their digital content, enhancing their brands, and generating significant broadcast revenue.

Manchester United, one of the world's most valuable sport franchises and the most popular sport franchise online, attracted 2.2 million unique visitors to its website during March 2007. Approximately 60 percent, or 1.3 million of Manchester United's 2.2 million monthly visitors, reside outside the United Kingdom. As stated previously, new media platforms allow sport consumers worldwide to access their favorite teams wherever and whenever they want, and this example shows that millions of fans are taking advantage of this access. Other popular football teams online are Liverpool (1.5 million global unique visitors), Arsenal (1.4 million), Real Madrid (1.1 million), Barcelona (1.05 million), Chelsea (1.0 million), and AC Milan (0.8 million) (PRNewswire, 2007).

Commercial opportunities in digital content fall into two categories—production and distribution. Most sport broadcasters partner with sport content producers because they do not own rights to the content. But in many cases, after purchasing rights, broadcasters are able to develop content-related opportunities for consumers to generate their own content (UGC). U.S.-based sport leagues, such as the NFL, NBA, MLB, and NHL, as well as the IOC, FIFA, the Premier League, and the Bundesliga, to name a few key enterprises, distribute rights on a worldwide basis.

The types of digital sport content that consumers are most likely to access by new media vary widely, but some of the more common types of information accessed are highlights, general information, and specific event or game-day information.

◆ *Highlights.* Sport event highlights are a much shorter type of content and are often more appropriate for mobile devices. Short clips (usually between three and five minutes long) can be distributed to any kind of media platform and usually are in high demand. One of the most interesting international content distribution agreements was the National Football League's deal in Japan, which was part of the league's internationalization strategy. The NFL and Sports Marketing Japan (SMJ) provided NFL fans in Japan with daily video highlights and interview footage on their mobile phones. This arrangement marked the first time that NFL highlights were available to wireless phones in Asia. Off-field content such as interviews, press conferences, daily practice sessions, reports, and player profiles can be produced either by a media company or by the sport rights holder and then distributed. These elements represent additional content for consumers who want to know more about their team or events and are interested in what happens in and around their favorite players.

◆ *General information.* The history, statistics, roster, schedules, and scores of a sport franchise are particularly popular on websites and mobile devices. This type of content requires constant updating to keep consumers current and to ensure that they feel connected to the franchise. Increased access to information by fans around the world can play a role in building an international market; the more information that fans have about their favorite team and its players, the more likely it is that they will have high levels of fan identity, which leads to higher purchasing activity. Team songs, pictures, and other downloadable content such as wallpaper and ring tones are attractive as well.

◆ *Game-day information.* Game-day or event-day content may be in the form of stadium or arena information, event history, contacts, parking, weather, team lineups, and finally live video feeds of the event itself. This type of content is important for consumers because they want to have easy and fast access, which may be particularly appropriate for mobile devices. Having easy access to value-added content can make an event more enjoyable for consumers before, during, and after the event, even if they were not in attendance at the event itself.

◆ *Sponsorship content.* New media has emerged as a significant dimension of branding and global sport sponsorship because of its ability to communicate with consumers worldwide across a multitude of digital platforms. Global brands are taking advantage of these compelling economic, consumer, and media trends by using the emotional impact of sport to connect with consumers. As competition among brands continues to intensify, sport content—teams, leagues, federations, events, athletes, and celebrity causes—delivered to consumers online, on-site, uploaded, downloaded,

CASE STUDY

Union of European Football Associations (UEFA) Media Committee

In 2008 UEFA established a media committee to address all media issues relating to UEFA and sport. The establishment of the committee probably was related directly to the issues UEFA addressed with the European Newspaper Publishers' Association (ENPA) regarding "the proposed restrictions on the use of online photography and the amount of access given to non-rights holders beyond the match stadiums" (Sports City, 2008a, p. 1). Ultimately, the ENPA was given more freedom to publish digital photos, and UEFA lifted all restrictions in reporting from nonmatch venues.

The primary role of the UEFA Media Committee is to advise UEFA "on determining the organizational requirements for media work at UEFA events, on collaborating with organizations covering UEFA events, and on public relations work" (UEFA, 2008, p. 1). In addition, the committee monitors issues related to accreditation at UEFA events, fosters cooperation with international media organizations, surveys developments in the media sector, and makes proposals for addressing new challenges.

The Euro (Union of European Football Associations) 2008 Championship website, www.euro2008 .com, launched in February 2008, recorded over 1 billion page views by June 24, 2008. Over 42 million visitors from over 200 countries accessed text, multimedia, and video coverage of the Euro matches in June 2008, and up to 4.3 million visitors accessed the website on a single day of the tournament. The 2008 website traffic represented an increase of 250 percent compared with the traffic at euro2004 .com. The website, which was available in seven European languages and three Asian languages,

was launched 100 days before the start of the competition. The key feature of the website before the beginning of the tournament was the ability to view video on demand (VoD) of 130 prior matches in the history of the tournament. After competition started, the website featured live video streaming of the 16 competing teams; video, audio, text, and photo content; and a forum for user participation that allowed consumers to leave comments and opinions on blogs and photo blogs as part of the Fanzone section.

All of the Euro 2008 content was distributed from one central location, which provided video, audio, text, and photo content needs. In addition, the website offered three types of video coverage: live match simulcast in collaboration with UEFA broadcast partners, video on demand offering individual matches, and highlights and free videos produced as "vodcasts." UEFA also offered a video service and a Euro2008 Pass, which included all 31 matches in the tournament as well as reruns and highlights.

Regarding the sale of media content rights going forward, UEFA made major changes in the rights sales format for the 2009–12 cycle of the UEFA Champions League, UEFA Super Cup, and UEFA Europa League. TEAM Marketing AG, the exclusive marketing partner of UEFA for these competitions, manages the process now. The most interesting of the changes is that media content rights will be granted on a platform-neutral basis, which means that successful bidders for live match rights will also benefit from exclusivity across all media platforms, including TV, Internet, and mobile, during the live match.

---

broadcast, narrowcast, or podcast, will continue to increase in value. A synergistic relationship has emerged between new media and sport sponsorship primarily because new media enables brands to communicate more effectively and more often with consumers, develop brand awareness rapidly in new markets, and provide new communications platforms and content opportunities. This content may include video commercials, pictures, graphics, logos, and so forth that are displayed on a variety of screens by sponsors.

New Media Challenges

Among the many new-media-related challenges facing sport management are developing and implementing multiplatform new media projects, which require many unique skills. Dynamic strategic planning is needed for developing and integrating mission-critical new media into the systems and operations of sport enterprises. Most important, managers of sport enterprises must realize that although new media is complex, with intelligent and rational strategic planning and e-business implementation, it allows for maximum adaptation to business environment changes worldwide.

Marketing

Probably the most significant opportunity for sport enterprises presented by new media is its ability to develop deeper relationships with consumers. The opportunity to increase the distribution of sport content, generate new audiences, connect with highly identified consumers, and create dynamic communities is extremely valuable and will, in the long term, result in significant financial value. Interactivity, niche information, and personalization are core elements of almost all new media initiatives, and as new media technologies evolve, they will provide increased distribution of specific sport content. In addition, customer relations management (CRM) software tools provide marketers with consumers' identities, addresses, purchasing habits, and intimate information.

The key to integrating new media successfully into the sport enterprise ultimately depends on the ability of specific sport content to aggregate a sufficient number of consumers over multiple digital platforms. The ability to aggregate, identify, and track large numbers of consumers enables the sport enterprise to satisfy its specific needs through mass tailoring on an individual basis. Therefore, the challenge for sport brands is to integrate social media and niche marketing as well as enhance their brands. Sport managers should understand the dynamics and strategies of social media and viral marketing. For example, online communication allowed the entire world to share in the sudden increase in interest surrounding David Beckham's move to U.S.-based Major League Soccer (MLS). Although sport enterprises should leverage the Internet for branding, marketing campaigns should be part of an integrated strategy that is benchmarked using diverse metrics and multiple media platforms including TV and print. The key value proposition of new media is that it allows consumers to engage visual and textual information more easily, which often results in increased revenue. For example, Manchester United's website can be navigated in languages other than English. Consumers who speak Spanish, Arabic, Chinese, Japanese, or Korean can thus easily interact with the team, share experiences with other fans, and purchase licensed merchandise.

Managing New Media

Although new media offers many opportunities, developing and integrating new media into the sport enterprise presents a number of challenges, including (1) identifying the objectives and opportunities for integrating new media, (2) determining what specific new media technologies are appropriate, (3) developing (or finding) relevant new media management skills, (4) creating new financial resources to maintain existing levels of media expenditure and funding, (5) developing necessary production skills within the enterprise to capture and store digital content and use it effectively and efficiently, and (6) sourcing the technology skills that will enable all the previous challenges to be met.

The following brief summary, adapted from Briggs (2003), should provide sport managers with a basis from which to develop, implement, and manage new media projects. All successful new media projects share a number of characteristics:

(1) they are relatively simple conceptually; most websites worldwide are similar in structure, varying primarily in the specific sport content; (2) revenue is considered during the development phase of the project, which requires identifying a revenue model that may vary from one project to another as well as from one country to another; (3) revenue is maximized by a repeatable format, which means that subsequent versions of the format should appeal to all audiences over time; (4) formats include viral elements and possibly a format that allows consumers to contribute material (UGC) or opinions, or to vote on specific sport topics, an aspect that appeals to fans worldwide; (5) consideration is given to the strengths and weaknesses of specific new media platforms, knowing that success is more likely if a multiplatform approach is selected; and (6) a cultural fit is present that may include significant local adaptation for targeted international audiences and on prevailing and emerging trends and attitudes.

To ensure that the new media project is developed and implemented effectively, sport managers may want to consider the following:

1. Assembling a core team to assist in the development of the new media initiative.

2. Brainstorming specifically about content and technology opportunities to take the concept beyond the initial idea. For example, does the project have international appeal? If so, how will that affect the development and implementation of the project?

3. Market testing the concept with a representative audience or focus group—selecting appropriate consumers worldwide to test-drive the concept.

4. Developing appropriate financing, budgeting, and revenue analysis. As stated earlier, revenue sources may be different from one country to the next depending on the nature of the project.

5. Addressing country-specific and enterprise-specific legal and rights issues.

6. Planning the integration of specific technologies within the enterprise.

7. Developing a prototype or beta version if feasible.

8. Ensuring quality control.

9. Addressing distribution and marketing issues as they relate to both international and local markets.

10. Coordinating on-going management and maintenance.

User-Generated Content

User-generated content (**UGC**) describes a variety of new sources of online information that is created, initiated, and circulated by consumers intent on educating each other about products, brands, services, personalities, and issues. UGC refers to any number of online or social media vehicles including but not limited to consumer-to-consumer e-mail, postings on public Internet discussion boards and forums, consumer ratings of websites or forums, blogs (short for weblogs, or digital diaries), moblogs (sites where users post digital images, photos, or movies), social-networking websites, and individual websites.

The growth of UGC, however, may pose challenges and opportunities for sport enterprises, primarily because some UGC content may be potentially negative for sport brands. For example, blog posts about the outcome of a specific contest or a specific athlete or coach may reflect negatively on the sport enterprise. For example, Tiger Woods' worldwide "friends" on Facebook were not outraged by his behavior as much as they were by the fact that he stopped communicating with them.

From a content distribution perspective, sport enterprises should develop an appropriate strategy for managing and integrating appropriately selected UGC with traditional sport content. Generally, content such as videos, blogs, and photos is developed and posted by users (consumers). But some sport content may be made available to consumers so that they can create their own services. In some instances, users may collect sport content from a variety of digital feeds and create their own services, or mash-ups—a video, blog, and so on. In this case, the sport enterprise is in the position of determining what specific sport content will be made available to users for self-production. The Eurosport Group, for example, launched an innovative Facebook application that was available in five languages: English, French, German, Spanish, and Italian. The Eurosport online team focused on exchange and interactivity between the Eurosport platform and sport fans worldwide by offering its users cutting-edge online products within the world of sport. The Eurosport Group is the leading multimedia platform in Europe with Eurosport, eurosport.com, and Eurosportnews.

The pan-European channel Eurosport, available in 18 languages, reaches 98 million homes and 220 million viewers across 54 countries. Available in five languages, eurosport.com is now clearly established as one of the leading pan-European sport websites, generating up to 85 million pages viewed per month. Eurosportnews provides up-to-date worldwide sport news and is transmitted to 18 million homes in seven languages in more than 70 countries.

Digital Rights

Sport rights holders have an opportunity to exploit the high demand for sport content either by selling their rights or by distributing the content themselves. This is one of the more important issues regarding new media applications. Any sport enterprise that is able to capture its digital images can also broadcast those images, which ultimately allows it to provide information and entertainment (either audio or video) directly to consumers. This capability increases the control that the sport enterprise has over broadcast revenues and other extraneous factors that were previously controlled by cable enterprises and television networks. Broadband distribution drastically reduces the influence that TV networks hold over sport by allowing teams and leagues to offer games and other services directly to consumers (examples include www.mlb .tv, www.nba.tv, www.mutv.com, and www.nfl.tv).

Before the emergence of new media, media enterprises had more power over sport rights holders. Today, even though global media enterprises often still drive strategies, sport rights holders can choose what to do with their content. New media provides not only more options for sport enterprises but also more options for users on interactive and video levels; price is therefore less of an issue. Sport is one of the key drivers for generating vital revenues for both sport and media enterprises worldwide. The key to success is cooperation between media and sport enterprises to create benefits for both by providing the best available content. High-quality sport content not only satisfies consumers but also attracts investors and advertisers, who will facilitate the growth of the sport business.

Media fragmentation, as well as consumer fragmentation worldwide, has resulted in significant issues within the broadcast industry. The numerous ways that content can now be viewed seriously affect its value. Broadcast enterprises worldwide confront the need to protect their digital assets. For sport enterprises, the central intellectual property issue is how to monetize digital rights, develop a brand, and at the same time remain open to some degree to grassroots, consumer-driven interactive efforts such as blogging, video posting, and UGC (Fisher, 2008a). This goal is becoming more daunting by the day as video-sharing sites proliferate on the Internet: "In the age of Beckham and Rooney, Ronaldo and Zidane, the attempt to commercially control both images and information around sport has never been so great" (Haynes, 2007, p. 1).

The Digital Millennium Copyright Act (DMCA) provides safe harbor for websites that remove copyright-infringing content on request from the copyright owner. The DMCA, although a United States copyright law, implements two 1996 treaties of the World Intellectual Property Organization (WIPO). The DMCA criminalizes the production and dissemination of technology, devices, or services intended to circumvent measures (commonly known as digital rights management, or DRM) that control access to copyrighted works.

Policing websites, however, takes an enormous amount of time and effort. In 2007 the English Premier League sued Google Inc.'s YouTube for copyright infringement. The lawsuit, filed in the United States, charged that YouTube "deliberately encourages massive copyright infringement on its website to generate public attention and boost traffic. This has resulted in the loss of valuable content." Lawyers for Google contended that the plaintiff misunderstood the Digital Millennium Copyright Act. Google and YouTube, in contrast, argued that they were entitled to "safe harbor" protection under federal copyright law because they had insufficient notice of the particular alleged infringements. The Premier League and coplaintiff Viacom lost the case because the judge ruled that the defendants were in fact entitled to safe harbor protection "against all of the plaintiff's claims for direct and secondary copyright infringement." A sport enterprise's broadcast rights are its most important asset, and sport organizations are now taking important steps to protect them.

New Media Dimensions

New media technologies already have changed the way in which fans consume sport and interact with each other. Interactivity is at the forefront of nearly

Additional Readings in Sport and New Media

New media technologies are constantly evolving, and their roles in the sport industry are changing as a result. Consulting sport websites, such as these, can help you keep abreast of changes in the world of sport and technology:

www.sbrnet.com

The website of the Sport Business Research Network. This subscription-based service provides sport marketing and business information, as well as updates on sporting goods and new media.

www.sportbusiness.com

Provides comprehensive coverage of breaking sport news, technology information, and sport-related technology improvements.

www.sportsbusinessdaily.com

Publishes up-to-date information on sport marketing, sponsorship, and new media.

www.sports-city.org

Provides information related to sport events worldwide by providing the latest sport business news, tenders, jobs, and market reports.

www.sportsmarketing20.com

This site is a digital think tank for sport marketers in the web 2.0 world.

www.sportsbusinessradio.com

Addresses the issues and people that directly impact the world of sport business.

Learning Activity

Visit Sports Business Research Network (www.SBRnet.com). If your university subscribes to SBRnet.com, search for articles related to new media in the Search All Publications section of the website. Make a list of some recent new media ventures or technology developments within the global sport industry. Find one that interests you and prepare a brief presentation on it for the class.

every new media endeavor. Several key dimensions of new media have enabled sport enterprises worldwide to enhance their relationships with consumers and their brands.

New media is a rapidly changing area. In addition to the topics discussed in the sections below, the sidebar provides a few additional resources that can help you develop an understanding of new media in sport and keep up with this rapidly changing area.

Social Media

Social media include applications, platforms, and media that focus on facilitating interaction, collaboration, and sharing of content. Most social media are Internet-based applications (which can also be accessed through mobile devices) that manage textual information, such as blogs (Blogger, Wordpress), microblogging (Twitter, Pownce), wikis (Wikipedia), forums, or social networks (Facebook, MySpace, LinkedIn). Other social media Internet applications allow users to share more than text, such as photo-sharing tools (Flickr, Picasa), video-sharing tools (YouTube, Vimeo), livecasting (Ustream), or audio- and music-sharing applications (last.fm, ccMixter, FreeSound). More recent social media includes virtual worlds (Second Life), online gaming, game sharing (Miniclip.com), and mobile social media such as Nomad social networks, in which users share their current position in the real world. Most sport enterprises are incorporating social networking in their new media strategies because it is a magnet for advertising and sponsorship. In fact, social networks usually collect a large quantity of personal data, which sport enterprises can use to target specific audiences.

Despite the rapid development and integration of social media into the marketing strategies of sport brands worldwide, many have neither developed a social media measurement strategy nor determined how well social media compares with other digital marketing initiatives. For the most part, the data focused on by marketing professionals to evaluate social media ROI or ROO include:

(1) internal sales and distribution data; (2) consumer behavior studies—for target identification; (3) media channel data—for media consumption information; and (4) buzz data—related to buzz or viral marketing.

Gaming

Online Game Market forecasts that the worldwide market for online games will grow from $3.4 billion in 2005 to more than $13 billion in 2011. Gaming is helping to increase the number of consumer Internet subscription services, and the use of the game delivery method of online digital distribution has helped contribute to an increasing acceptance of in-game advertising. A prime example of this is Blizzard Entertainment's World of Warcraft (WoW), which is a massively multiplayer online roleplaying game (MMORPG) played by over 11 million people worldwide. WoW was expected to generate over US$100 million in each of several different markets in its first year alone. These games not only allow consumers to do what current online games do but also add a large number of capabilities such as user-generated dynamic content, large community involvement, variations in the game itself, and other capabilities that only broadband can facilitate.

Sport is one of the major themes in gaming. Leading production enterprises such as Electronic Arts (EA) are constantly seeking new opportunities to generate revenue. Sport enterprises are attempting to create partnerships or even to offer online games on their own. Capcom Software, for example, acquired the rights to publish a MotoGP game on PlayStation. MotoGP is the international premier championship of motorcycle road racing and is currently divided into three distinct classes: 125cc, Moto 2 (the 250cc was replaced by the new Moto2 600cc class in 2010), and Moto GP. The game is likely to feature all the top riders and teams including Honda, Yamaha, Suzuki, and Ducati. The goal of MotoGP goal is to deliver high-quality entertainment that matches the core values of the MotoGP brand.

Fantasy Sports

One of the most popular activities for consumers in the sport industry is fantasy games. Approximately 15 million people are willing to pay more than $1.5 billion on fantasy sports, and marketers are willing to play along by sponsoring fantasy leagues or displaying ads on fantasy web pages. Although fantasy sports were born of paper, pencil, and calculator, the preferred venue to trade players and trash-talk is now online through live drafts, message boards, and instant messaging. The 15 million consumers engaged in fantasy sports each year are worthwhile targets for advertisers. Although a marketer used to be able to buy into fantasy football with a low six-figure deal, today's main sponsorships command seven figures, and smaller sponsorships run around the half-million dollar mark. Online fantasy sports is a relatively new but important service that can engage and connect consumers and, as previously stated, generate significant revenues through subscription and sponsorship.

Although several media companies offer fantasy games through their websites, leagues have started their own fantasy tournaments and games. Many allow consumers to acquire management skills. For example, in the NFL-sponsored Financial Football, consumers answer finance-related questions to earn points. Another example is the NBA's Salary Cap Challenge, which allows consumers to trade players and make virtual money out of their deals. Other forms of games such as predicting results or drafting games also are becoming popular. The most common type of fantasy game is the traditional manager game, in which consumers build their own teams by picking the league's players and earning points according to the performance of the real players. Fantasy games and services are often offered through mobile devices, which keep consumers up to date 24/7.

Gambling

New media has set benchmarks for the gambling industry because gaming websites and mobile devices allow creation of new services that the sport industry is learning to apply. Live video streaming and closer interaction with consumers will increase opportunities to incorporate "in-running" betting (live betting while the event takes place). Also having significant potential is online gambling that integrates broadband video with a "bet and watch" facility. Gamblers will have the opportunity to watch an event and have the betting board on the screen at the same time while at the computer or when using a mobile device. Partnerships between gambling and sport enterprises are more common than one might think; in fact, the Austrian company BWIN is AC Milan's main sponsor. The football team's website offers live betting through BWIN and features several links and services.

The primary international issue related to gambling laws is that they vary drastically from one country to another. In the United States, for example, laws at the federal, state, and local levels regulate "gaming" and gambling. Regardless, gambling and betting online have increased exponentially. Gambling-Law-US.com presents, explains, and analyzes the patchwork of state and federal gambling laws that apply to the boom. The International Masters of Gaming Law is a nonprofit association of gaming attorneys, regulators, educators, executives, and consultants from around the world who are dedicated to education and the exchange of professional information and advice.

Summary

New media is a rapidly changing area of business development within the sport industry. The integration of new media will continue to affect all business units of the sport enterprise, from internal operations such as customer relations management (CRM) to social media and viral marketing. New media also will provide sport enterprises with new opportunities to enhance their brands and generate revenue. Developing and implementing mission-critical new media initiatives are a significant undertaking that requires sport managers to have a variety of unique skills. Most important, sport managers should recognize that although new media is complex, with intelligent and rational strategic planning and effective e-business implementation, it allows for maximum adaptation to dynamic changes in the business environment.

? Review and Discussion Questions

1. It has been stated emphatically that the development of international sport is driving the development of new media technologies and vice versa. What new media technologies are most likely to be employed in the near and foreseeable future by sport enterprises worldwide?

2. Identify and explain three new media strategies that sport enterprises worldwide could choose to develop and implement to increase their consumer base.

3. Identify the most significant new media challenges facing sport enterprise managers worldwide.

4. Why is it critical for sport enterprises worldwide to integrate their marketing and media efforts strategically? What is the role of social media in sport marketing and promotion?

5. What dimensions of the sport industry stand to benefit the most from new mobile technologies and applications?

Sport Facilities Management

Robin Ammon Jr., EdD
University of South Dakota, USA

Babs Surujlal, PhD
Vaal University of Technology, South Africa

Chapter Objectives

After studying this chapter, you will be able to do the following:

- Differentiate between different types of facilities
- Demonstrate an understanding of the procedures, principles, and current trends in managing a facility, including operational philosophies and mission statements
- Understand the various management options that may be used for a sport and recreation facility
- Analyze why sustainability and "green" facilities have become important to the facility management industry
- Recognize how a variety of issues will affect the quality of service at a facility
- Identify potential risks associated with facilities and know how a crowd and alcohol management plan will assist in reducing those risks

Key Terms

This chapter is intended for practitioners working in a facility environment, academics, and students from a variety of majors, including sport management, who will be seeking opportunities to work with facilities. What competencies should key facility personnel possess? What factors should be considered when designing a facility? What are the steps that can be taken to minimize the risk (or improve the safety) associated with a facility? This chapter answers these questions and others, and provides examples pertaining to facility management and risk management. Both areas of facility management are unique, but they share elements to the point that identifying which skill set is being performed at any one time is often difficult. In fact, in many situations both occur simultaneously. A symbiotic relationship exists between facility management and risk management.

Sport and entertainment facilities have experienced an exponential increase since the early 1990s. Facilities today are subjected to greater intensity of use than they were 20 years ago. The globalization of sport has resulted in a dramatic increase in the construction, maintenance, and renovation of sport facilities worldwide. In many instances spectators' and athletes' experiences of the sport event hinges on the sport facility that was used. Spectators and athletes may feel unenthusiastic about being involved in certain events because they do not feel safe or comfortable with a particular sport facility. For example, violence at several Italian football matches in 2008 resulted in the cancellation of a few Serie A games. Therefore, careful thought must be given to every aspect of a facility—its design, location, safety features, ambience, maintenance, and management.

The structure of sport facilities has evolved over time. In the past sport events took place in open-air arenas in facilities constructed for the entertainment of various stakeholders. In recent years, however, many facilities have been constructed with the prime purpose of hosting large-scale events. In the last 40 years sport facilities have evolved dramatically. The United States has been the leader in terms of the breadth and diversity of new facilities in the world, and this phenomenon has spread internationally. The greatest growth in the 21st century has occurred in Japan (which hosted World Cup football with Korea in 2002) and Greece (Fried, 2005). The costs involved in building facilities are phenomenal. For example, the largest stadium in the world, May Day stadium in Pyongyang, North Korea (capacity 150,000) cost US$525.32 million. The stadium hosts a variety of events such as football. The stadium is also the site of large Arirang Festivals, in which thousands of performers hold up cards depicting a variety of scenes. Thousands of gymnasts and other performers accompany these scenes. France spent US$1.5 billion for the 1998 World Cup, and China spent approximately US$3.5 billion on 37 stadiums to host the 2008 Olympic Games and an additional US$1.94 billion on an Olympic village. The final cost for the 10 stadiums built or renovated for the 2010 FIFA World Cup was around US$2 billion, which was double the original estimate. These figures highlight the magnitude of international sport and recreation facility growth and the costs incurred (Van Wyk, 2008).

The increase in the range and demand of sport and recreation facilities has led to greater focus on facility planning, design, and management. Consequently, employees in these facilities need to have better skills, which will be discussed later, but first it is important to know about the various types of facilities found within the sporting world.

Types of Facilities

The number and types of sport, entertainment, and recreation facilities have increased dramatically. Many of these facilities are as diverse as the events that they host.

◆ *Single purpose facilities.* Facilities designed for only one sport are **single-purpose facilities**. Among these facilities are tennis courts, golf courses, skate parks, bowling alleys, motor sport tracks, and water parks.

◆ *Multipurpose facilities.* Communities experience considerable difficulty trying to maintain and sustain single-purpose facilities. For that reason, **multipurpose facilities** capable of hosting a variety of events such as concerts, ice shows, collegiate and professional sporting events, circuses, and recreational vehicle shows have been built. Awareness of the flexible options offered by multipurpose facilities is increasing.

◆ *Indoor facilities.* During the past 25 to 30 years numerous covered stadiums and large arenas have been built. These facilities have movable stands and convertible floors that enable them to accommodate a variety of events, from small gatherings to large concerts, extravaganzas, conventions, sport events, and festivals. Many of these facilities house high-tech equipment such as large video screens and video monitors that provide close-ups, instant replays, and special features to enhance the entertainment experience of their spectators. Some traditional outdoor sports, such as football and lacrosse, can be played in these indoor facilities.

◆ *Outdoor facilities.* Not all sport and entertainment facilities are enclosed within roofs and walls. Outdoor facilities such as golf courses and ski areas are also classified as sport and entertainment facilities (Ammon & Stotlar, 2011). Because of the nature of such facilities, seating areas for spectators may be limited or nonexistent. Spectators can, however, view the activities in a variety of ways.

◆ *Country clubs.* In most instances, country clubs are exclusive organizations that offer a few sports such as tennis, golf, and swimming for their members. In addition, country clubs also provide dining and accommodation facilities to their members and guests, and they frequently host catered events like weddings, awards functions, and sport banquets. Country clubs are usually membership-driven organizations.

◆ *Gymnasiums.* A gymnasium is a typical feature for virtually all universities, colleges, and high schools, as well as most middle schools and many elementary schools. These facilities are used for physical education, intramural sport, and interscholastic athletics.

◆ *Nontraditional facilities.* The appeal of activities such as indoor climbing, inline skating, skateboarding, and snowboarding has resulted in the growth of nontraditional facilities.

Regardless of the size or type of the facility or the kinds of events that it hosts, one factor remains consistent: To maintain a safe and enjoyable environment, proper management of the facility and event is of paramount importance.

Facility Personnel

Most facilities employ a diverse number of personnel including, among others, a facility director, food and beverages manager, event coordinator, director of operations, marketing manager, guest services manager, and public relations officer. Among them, the facility director, the director of operations, and the event coordinator have significantly more responsibilities than other personnel. They therefore need various administrative skills to operate facilities efficiently and effectively.

The **facility director** is directly responsible for most sport and entertainment facilities. This person is mainly responsible for the creation of the **standard operating procedures** (**SOPs**) of the facility. These procedures are the guidelines for how the facility operates. For example, does the event host only sport events, or does it host a variety of events such as concerts and community events? Additional SOPs include the issues of whether alcohol is served at events or whether a pat-down or visual search is used as fans enter the venue. The facility director ensures that these procedures are administered correctly and coordinates the employees that fall directly under him or her. A facility manager's duties depend on the size of the facility and the number of employees in the facility.

The **director of operations** reports directly to the facility director and is responsible for all personnel, procedures, and activities related to the facility. This person has a variety of responsibilities such as defining the roles, responsibilities, and authority of facility staff; recruiting personnel to coordinate the various areas of the facility; coordinating personnel, policies and procedures, and activities within the facility; evaluating facility operations; and making recommendations to the facility director.

The **event coordinator** is traditionally responsible for managing the individual events, which vary greatly from entertainment events to political rallies and sport events. The event coordinator's responsibilities usually include transporting, assembling, erecting, and storing equipment as directed; establishing a control system for venue and equipment logistics (e.g., inventory management, storage,

Learning Activity

Search online and find two or three sport facilities in each of North America, Europe, Asia, South America, Africa, and Australia. Describe each facility using the categories described in this section.

transportation of equipment); recruiting, training, and supervising specific event personnel; assisting in maintaining venues and equipment throughout the event; facilitating ticketing and ticket distribution at venue sites; and evaluating venue and equipment operations.

Management Structure Options

A variety of management structure options may be used for a sport and recreation facility. These options depend on the social and financial outcomes desired.

Direct Management

In this instance the owner, sometimes a local government authority, is directly involved in the administration of the facility. The owner may employ a facility manager but will be responsible for all aspects of the facility's operation including operating policies, financial performance, and asset maintenance. The facility owner has complete control over venue operations. Raymond James Stadium, home to the Tampa Bay Buccaneers of the National Football League, is an example of a venue operated in this management style. The Tampa Bay Sports Authority manages the stadium for the city of Tampa.

Contract Management

In this instance the owner contracts the management of the facility to an individual manager, an organization, or a facility management company. The responsibilities of the owner and contractor are set out in a formal contract for a fixed period. The owner has less administrative responsibility. Normally, the owner is responsible for major building maintenance and any loan repayments, unless the contract states otherwise. The contractor negotiates an operating budget and is responsible for financial performance in return for greater freedom in operating policies. The facility operates independently of the owner. If an operational surplus is realized, the contractor normally receives a percentage of the profit. Additional financial incentives are often built into the contract to encourage the operator to succeed. Contracting offers a number of advantages including greater expertise, increased productivity and efficiency, improved service quality and customer satisfaction, increased accountability, and shared risks.

Examples of public assembly facility management companies include Spectacor Management Group (SMG), Global Spectrum, Anschutz Entertainment Group (AEG), and VenuWorks. These companies manage and operate theaters, event centers, convention centers, arenas, and stadiums throughout the world. For example, Suncorp Stadium in Queensland, Australia, is managed by AEG. Other contracted venues are listed in table 21.1.

Lease Management

In this option a formal lease detailing the rights and responsibilities of the owner (lessor) and the operator (lessee) is adopted. The structure of the lease agreement determines the degree of control that the facility owner has over facility operations. The lessee normally has full property rights and is responsible for financial performance, asset maintenance, and

Table 21.1 Examples of Sport Venues Run by Facility Management Companies

Company	Facilities
AEG	• Brisbane Entertainment Centre, Brisbane, Australia • Sprint Center, Kansas City, Missouri • Shanghai World Expo Performing Arts Center, China
Global Spectrum	• John Labatt Centre, London, Ontario • University of Phoenix Stadium, Glendale, Arizona • Singapore National Stadium, Singapore
SMG	• Reliant Stadium, Houston, Texas • The Palladium, Dubai, United Arab Emirates • Oslo Spectrum Arena, Oslo, Norway
VenuWorks	• Cedar Rapids Ice Arena, Cedar Rapids, Iowa • Swiftel Center, Brookings, South Dakota

operational policies. The lessor receives an agreed rental income (or a percentage of the net surplus) but has no direct control over day-to-day management. The lease is usually set for a medium to long term. The owner has no day-to-day administrative responsibility and reduced financial risk.

Shared Management

A growing number of facilities have recently been developed as multiuse or multipurpose facilities. These facilities generally allow a number of groups to use a single area or building for their activities. The idea is to broaden access to the facility, maximize usage, and apportion operating costs to get the best possible value from the facility. Administration of these facilities may be complex. The advantages of shared-use facilities include less duplication and maximum use of facilities and services; shared operating costs; opportunities to share services, resources, and expertise; improved relationships between participating organizations; and increased community ownership of facilities. Shared facilities should be centrally located in highly populated areas, provide safe and convenient access, be flexible in design to accommodate a range of activities, and provide adequate administration and storage areas. Management agreements for shared-use facilities should be comprehensive, detailing all cost sharing and legal and access arrangements, so that responsibilities and usage rights are clear. Although management agreements for shared facilities are essential, the key elements of a successful partnership are flexibility, trust, open communication, and a spirit of cooperation. Many YMCAs around the world use this type of management. They lease out part of their building to a variety of community groups including educational institutions, sport organization offices, day care centers, community centers, churches, community health centers, health clinics, and art and entertainment events.

Whichever management structure is adopted, a well thought out management plan that includes performance indicators, financial goals, customer service objectives, future considerations, marketing objectives, and an evaluation component should be prepared. This kind of plan will enable management to improve the effectiveness and efficiency of a facility. A well-developed management plan could be used to educate staff, community groups, and decision makers about a facility; gain support; and attract funds. A plan provides a sound reference document with policies and procedures.

Issues in Facility Management

Facility management is a profession that embraces a variety of disciplines such as planning, designing, leasing, space planning, project management, capital management, property management, facility marketing, building and operation management, and event management (Fried, 2005).

Most facility owners do not have the luxury of continually being able to inject large amounts of money into sport and recreation facilities that are not seen to be successful. As facilities become more sophisticated and elaborate, they are expected to be more efficient and effective and less financially draining. Facility personnel must therefore have the competencies to manage the facility effectively and efficiently. Careful consideration should be given to issues such as staffing, security systems, booking procedures, financial management, and health and safety issues to ensure smooth day-to-day management of the facility.

The management of a sport facility can either encourage or discourage people's active involvement in the facility. Facility managers need various administrative skills to operate facilities efficiently and effectively.

Fan safety and crowd control are important considerations in facility management. In April 2001, 43 fans were killed and 160 were injured in a stampede during a football match at Ellis Park Stadium in Johannesburg, South Africa. Twelve years previously, in 1989, a football disaster occurred at Hillsborough Stadium in the United Kingdom when 96 Liverpool fans were killed as the result of a huge crowd crush. The incident was the deadliest in British football history. See the sidebar for more on this tragedy and the new guidelines for sport facilities that came about as a result. More recently, in March 2009, 22 spectators were killed and over 130 were injured when a crowd stampeded during a World Cup qualifying match in Côte d'Ivoire. Thousands of spectators were trying to push their way into the stadium when security forces fired tear gas into the crowd. These tragedies forever changed the way that facilities are managed. Customer service and safety, although considered important before these three events occurred, are now utmost priorities for facility managers. These types of issues must be of paramount concern for today's facility managers when planning, administering, coordinating, and evaluating the day-to-day operations of a facility.

The mission statement of a facility provides guidelines that outline the parameters for operating the facility. It provides the roadmap that guides the path for the facility. It should provide direction for all facility personnel and encompass the goals and objectives critical for the success of the facility. The goals and objectives should be realistic, achievable, motivating, and specific and should state the end result envisioned by the facility owners. Here is an example of a mission statement, one used by Vanderbijl Health and Fitness Centre in Gauteng, South Africa:

> At Vanderbijl Health and Fitness Centre we will strive to offer the most innovative, comprehensive, unique, distinctive and energetic health programs and fitness services. It is our mission to contribute to an improved quality of life among members through health and fitness services utilizing state of the art equipment and practices as well as the most knowledgeable staff.

Other issues facing sport facility managers have to do with the impact of the facility on the community and environment. Facility sustainability and legacy are important current topics in facility management; these are discussed in detail in the following sections.

Facility Sustainability

Sustainability is simply a comprehensive philosophy in which a variety of environmentally friendly materials and procedures are used to help reduce energy expenditures. The concept of social responsibility pertaining to environmental matters is paramount for today's facility managers. Therefore, within the last decade many individuals and organizations in the sport and entertainment industry have begun to focus on sustainability. The Philadelphia Eagles and Lincoln Financial Field are recognized as one of the earliest organizations to become involved in "green" facilities.

Stadiums, arenas, and other sport and entertainment facilities leave a large carbon footprint. A **carbon footprint** is "a measure of the impact our activities have on the environment, and in particular climate change. It relates to the amount of greenhouse gases produced in our day-to-day lives through burning fossil fuels for electricity, heating and transportation, etc." (*What is*, 2008, p. 1). In addition, whenever thousands of people gather in a confined space, such as a stadium or arena, vast quantities of garbage are produced. Aluminum beer cans, plastic beverage cups, popcorn containers, food wrappers, peanut shells, partially eaten food, and discarded game programs all contribute

Reserved Versus Open Seating and Spectator Safety

One major step that sport facility managers have taken to protect against dangerous crowd control issues has been to use reserved seating for events. Reserved seats prevent people from rushing to be the first to reach the best viewing spots and from stampeding across open standing-room viewing areas. Many facilities throughout the world use reserved seats during events, but this has not always been the case in all sport stadiums. Terraces, or tiered flat standing-room-only areas, were permitted in most European stadiums for many years. In fact, some stadiums in various parts of the world still use terraces for their fans, despite the potential crowd control dangers associated with open seating or standing-room areas.

Great Britain's Premier League, however, has not allowed terraces since the late 1980s. As previously mentioned, this decision came about because of the 1989 Hillsborough disaster. Thousands of football fans flocked to Hillsborough Stadium in April 1989 to watch the FA Cup semifinal between Liverpool and Nottingham Forest. Unfortunately a crushing of fans occurred because too many people were allowed into an already full terrace at one end of the stadium. Ninety-six people were killed or received fatal injuries. Lord Justice Taylor (a member of the British Parliament) headed an investigation into the disaster, which resulted in a document called the *Taylor Report*. This report mandated that all Premier League stadiums eliminate terraces and provide reserved seating for their fans. Terraces are still allowed, however, in the lower divisions.

to the vast amount of waste produced at sporting events.

Understanding the effect that sustainability has on the proverbial bottom line, architects and facility planners are aware that "the focus on energy depletion, energy costs, the costs of operation and the impact on the environment that buildings bring is going to shape building design for quite a while" (Henricks, 2007, p. 37).

Thus, one trend in facility construction definitely involves building green facilities. Dick (2007) defined a **green facility** as "a structure that is designed, built, renovated, operated, or reused in an ecological and resource-efficient manner" (p. 1). This concept has begun to receive a great deal of publicity and will continue to be a growth industry for many years.

Facility Legacy

The London 2012 Games have made "legacy" (the use of venues after an event is completed) a high priority during their planning phase for the Summer Olympics. The 2010 World Cup in South Africa had similar concerns. In many instances, however, sport facilities have been built for large-scale events with little thought given to how the facility will be used after the event. Numerous venues built for the 1976 Summer Olympics in Montreal, the 2000 Sydney Olympics, and the 2004 Athens Games have suffered the fate of becoming white elephants. Incredible financial burdens have been placed on governments as well as Olympic organizations.

Some sport organizations, however, have ensured sustainability of their facilities. The Chelsea Football Club Stadium in Stamford Bridge (London, England) has hotel rooms similar to those contained in the Rogers Centre in Toronto, Ontario. West Ham United, another team in England's Premier League, has converted its luxury suites into hotel rooms that can be rented to the general public. Some international stadiums have become involved in the scheduling of nontraditional events. The new 60,000-seat indoor stadium near Essen, Germany, has a retractable roof and a sliding field. The field was used when Germany hosted the 2006 FIFA World Cup. The Ellis Park Stadium (capacity 60,000 spectators) in South Africa, accredited by FIFA for football and IRB for rugby, has a Sony Jumbotron screen, an advertisement scroll, a medical surgery

> ### Learning Activity
>
> The Veltins Arena football stadium in Gelsenkirchen, Germany, was one of several stadiums used to host the 2006 FIFA World Cup. Research the stadium online and discuss its design and layout. Comment on the steps that were taken to make the stadium appealing to the public and the ways in which the stadium was made multifunctional to ensure its sustainability.

unit, and a media center. The stadium hosts both international and domestic events.

Aspects of Service Quality

For any sport or entertainment event to be a success, the quality of service provided must meet the needs of the customers. The operation of sport facilities has become a highly competitive industry, and service excellence has become a prerequisite for survival and success. Services are intangible because they cannot be touched, smelled, seen, or heard before the actual experience. As a result, patrons rely on tangible cues, or physical evidence, to evaluate a service before its purchase. Chapter 18 provides an in-depth look at the factors that influence service quality in international sport.

Customer service, guest relations, and fan services are terms used to describe the relationship that exists between the event (or facility) management and the people who attend the event (Ammon & Stotlar, 2011). A customer's estimation of the value of a service is largely influenced by the relationship that an organization is able to nurture because these relationships ultimately denote the core competence of the service package (Kandampully & Duddy, 1999). Facility managers must therefore nurture and sustain positive relationships with their customers to attract and retain them as well as to maintain a competitive advantage.

Ammon and Stotlar (2011) described the customers or guests as the fuel that the sport and entertainment industry relies on. Without customers neither the events nor the facilities to house them would be necessary. Building long-term relationships with customers has become a critical issue in sport organizations (Shank, 2003). Sport organizations know that to be successful in the competitive environment of sport, they must be able to implement effective customer relationships. Developing long-term relationships with customers enables organizations to add value to their offerings (Shani & Sujana, 1992). Customer relations needs to begin with top management in an organization and filter down through every level of employees in the facility.

The quality of customer service can be measured through surveys or by the use of secret shoppers (i.e., people who attend the events and pose a variety of scenarios to venue employees to determine the effectiveness of the customer service plan). The results are then presented to venue managers, who implement the necessary changes. The facility manager should therefore clearly define expected standards for customer service, programming, facility and equipment maintenance, marketing, human resource management, and financial management.

Parking

Access to the facility and safe on-site parking contribute greatly to a patron's decision to attend an event at a particular facility. Clearly demarcated parking areas that provide a smooth flow of traffic may enhance a patron's experience of a facility. Therefore, careful consideration should be given to the design of the facility. As with every plan, the various stakeholders, including the local police, must provide their input. The facility manager can ensure the safety of patrons by employing various means at his or her disposal. A well-trained staff and strategically placed closed-circuit television cameras in the parking lots are ways to accomplish this goal. Providing emergency access lanes for police, fire, and medical personnel may avert dangerous situations. Intersections with higher than normal accident rates must be identified, and extra officers should assist out-of-town fans through these problem areas. Posting adequate signs on major thoroughfares to direct arriving spectators also decreases potential problems (Ammon & Stotlar, 2011).

In addition, the number and location of parking spaces for people with disabilities will affect the quality of their experience. After fans have found places to park, an unobstructed pathway to the venue is important. Fans with visual impairments will have different needs from those with mobility impairments.

Parking space availability may enhance fans' overall event experience. Excessive time spent searching for parking or walking to the stadium may frustrate some low-tolerance or task-oriented individuals, thereby leading to dissatisfaction with the facility experience.

Aesthetics

Facility aesthetics refers to the interior and exterior appearance of the facility and includes architectural design; landscaping; color of the facility walls, facades, and seats; the presence of sponsor signage; and artifacts from the team's past. Many new stadiums with historical architectural designs are springing up to increase game attendance. Facility aesthetics contributes to the attractiveness of the facility, which in turn influences its appeal to patrons.

Scoreboard Quality

One of the specific interior design considerations that contribute to a positive fan experience is the quality of the scoreboard. The scoreboard in some stadiums is seen as the focal point of the interior. Throughout the game fans continually monitor the scoreboard for updates on scoring, player statistics, instant replays, highlight videos, and other form of entertainment, such as contests, cartoon animations, and music videos. In sport venues modern graphic scoreboards can be used to generate excitement in between innings or periods.

Seating

A facility management issue is the quality of seats available to spectators. Seating comfort refers to the perceived comfort of the seating and the spacing of seats relative to each other. Seating comfort is affected by both the physical seat and the space between the rows of seats (also known as knee space). Seating comfort will vary because of design or conditions (new versus deteriorating, padded versus unpadded, bench seats versus seats with backs). Proximity to other seats also has an effect; spectators may be physically and psychologically uncomfortable if they are forced to sit too close to other spectators.

Fans who have been fortunate enough to view a game from a luxury box recognize the effect that the location of seats has on their enjoyment of a game. An additional type of seating option is club

Learning Activity

Think of a sporting event that you attended recently and your experience at that event. In what ways did aspects of facility design such as parking or transportation, aesthetics, scoreboard, and seating positively or negatively affect your experience? If you had been attending an international sport event such as the Olympics or a World Cup game, how would your expectations or needs have been different?

seats. These seats typically offer the padded seats found in private suites without the privacy. Club-level seating commonly includes wider seats, more knee space, access to food and beverages stands and climate-controlled lounges specifically for club-seat owners, and parking benefits. Seating for people with disabilities must also be a concern for sport venue operators. Since the mid-1990s the design and construction of sport facilities in the United Sates has taken into consideration the needs of people with disabilities. Providing accessible seats with adequate sight lines throughout a sport facility has become of paramount importance.

Layout Accessibility

Layout accessibility refers to the freedom that patrons have to move freely about the facility. An effective layout provides ease of ingress and egress. Proper signage to direct patrons to ancillary service areas such as concessions, restrooms, and merchandise stands may reduce confusion and contribute to a positive experience of the facility. Within the leisure and sport industry context, layout accessibility may also refer to the way in which furnishings and equipment, service areas, and passageways are arranged.

Maintenance

Careful consideration should be given to the maintenance of a facility, and adequate funding should be devoted to this function. Failing to maintain a facility could lead to unnecessary costs such as replacement, premature failure of equipment, shortened lifespan of equipment, building code violations, lower productivity, and excessive repair costs. Some facilities believe that renovating an older facility is cheaper than constructing a new one. The National Football League's Lambeau Field (Green Bay, Wisconsin) and Soldier Field (Chicago, Illinois) are two such American football stadiums that decided to remodel rather than rebuild. Others of note include Fenway Park (Boston Red Sox, Boston, Massachusetts) and Lord's Cricket Grounds (London, England).

Risk Management

Risk management has been defined as controlling the financial and personal injury losses from sudden, unforeseen, and unusual accidents and intentional torts (Ammon, 2010). These risks can be physical or financial in nature. Risks that injure spectators (such as trip and fall hazards) as well as losses that are a result of financial risks (for example, vandalism and theft) must be controlled. But eliminating all risks is not possible. Some of the risks are inherent, meaning that they are part of the activity itself. For example, an inherent risk of skiing is falling, and an inherent risk of swimming is drowning. The following are some potential risks and hazards associated with a sporting event or facility:

- Spectators invading the field or court
- Poor signage
- Fights in the crowd
- Traffic congestion
- Intoxicated spectators
- Terrorist attacks
- Poorly trained security
- Poorly designed facility
- Inadequate parking lot lighting
- Trip and fall hazards

Risk management has been used to combine the facility manager's interest in limiting financial risk with the patrons' interest in being safe. When a good risk management plan is implemented, the potential for litigation diminishes. Spectators at sport events will not tolerate inappropriate fan behavior or unsafe facility conditions, and facility managers must develop an awareness of the hazards for which they will be held accountable. An effective risk management plan will help to control and diminish the risks that confront today's recreation or sport managers (Ammon, 2010).

Every sport facility, no matter the size, should have a current risk management plan. The steps used in creating this plan will be similar in all types of organizations. Thus, managers at golf courses, aquatic centers, ski areas, skateboard parks, and park and recreation departments use the same basic principles. Developing a risk management plan consists of a variety of separate steps. The identification stage is one of the key aspects of developing a successful risk management program. If a facility manager wants to control risks in the venue, those risks must be identified. Each venue has primary and secondary factors that must be addressed to reduce the possibility of losses. These factors should be included in the standard operating procedures (SOPs) of every organization, and risk managers must consider them when trying to reduce risks (Ammon, 2010).

The second step in developing an effective risk management plan is to classify the risks. The purpose of the classification stage is to determine the likelihood that the risk will occur and the severity of the potential loss that will arise from the risk.

The final stage in developing the risk management plan is to determine a treatment to reduce or control the risks. Note that a facility manager will be faced with both financial and personal injury types of risks. The facility manager may avoid the risk, transfer the risk to another party, retain the risk, or reduce the risk. The type of treatment that a risk manager uses for the identified and classified risks depends on the nature of the risk and the likelihood that the risk will occur. Avoiding the risk means that the identified activities should not be included within the content of a program or that they should be discontinued if they are presently offered. Transfer is the shifting of the liability or responsibility for loss from the service provider to another party. The most utilized type of transfer is through insurance. When a risk is retained the organization keeps the risk and assumes financial responsibility for certain injuries or financial losses that may occur. Reduction involves trying to reduce or restrict the risk, therefore diminishing the number of lawsuits. Hiring and training quality staff, employing appropriate signage, and inspecting the facility for potential risks are all examples of effective reduction techniques (Ammon, 2010).

Risk management is a necessity for sport facility managers. Although many risks can be identified,

Learning Activity

Many sport federations in Europe try to present popular events at smaller-sized venues to attract new markets. Imagine that you work at a small sport facility in Amsterdam. One of these federations has approached you to organize a handball event. After a three-week evaluation period you determine that one of the biggest weaknesses is lack of a proper risk management plan. None of the staff in the sport federation that approached you knows anything about risk management. How would you effectively communicate the concept to them so that you can put on the event? Identify and classify two facility risks and one equipment risk for the event.

classified, and treated, some hazards will still exist and accidents will occur. Expecting a risk manager to eliminate all injuries and financial losses is unrealistic. Therefore, risk management plans must evolve and fluctuate; they are never static.

Crowd Management

Most sport facilities need a crowd management plan. If a facility manager wants to provide a safe, enjoyable, and secure environment for as many patrons as possible, then crowd management is a necessity. Crowd management has been defined as a tool to help facility or event managers provide a safe and enjoyable environment for their guests by implementing the facility or event policies and procedures (Ammon & Unruh, 2010). A crowd manager's duties include managing the movement and activities of the guests, assisting in emergencies, and assisting guests with specific concerns related to their enjoyment of the event by communicating with them in a polite and professional manner. To develop an effective crowd management plan, issues such as the capacity of the venue, the location of the venue, the demographics of guests, and the type of event must be researched. An important concept to remember is that every employee needs to be aware of her or his role in the plan, however small (Ammon & Unruh, 2010).

An effective plan includes five components. The first is to hire and then train the staff properly. This staff consists of ticket takers, searchers, and peer-group security. It may also include uniformed law enforcement officers hired to provide additional security. The second major component in a crowd management plan is to prepare for emergencies that may take place during the event. Examples include dangerous weather (hailstorms or tornadoes), medical situations (heart attacks or seizures), fires, bomb scares, or terrorist activities. A third component pertains to dealing with ejections. Actions that may result in an ejection include intoxication or disruptive behavior, a fight between fans, or throwing an object on the field. An effective communication network is the fourth component of an effective crowd management plan. Such a network usually consists of multichannel radios that allow the crowd management staff to work efficiently and cooperatively to handle situations as they occur. Representatives from facility management,

Learning Activity

Read the case study on risk management at Ellis Park Stadium. In a small group, list three to four main risks involved in conducting a similar event at the venue. Organize your list by how frequently each risk might occur and how severe the consequences would be if it did occur. Then, propose at least one step that you would take to reduce the identified risks at your event.

CASE STUDY

Risk Management at Ellis Park Stadium in South Africa

A variety of calamities can potentially occur during daily operations at sport facilities. Many of the potential risks are similar in most countries, but some are specific to particular events or facilities. Cultural differences between how spectators behave in different countries and when watching different sports may come into play. For example, many fans in the United States socialize before sport events by bringing food and drink to tailgate parties. South Africa football fans are a little more rowdy. They blow trumpets, wave banners, and wear team merchandise, such as shirts, headgear, and masks. In contrast, rugby and cricket fans prefer to have barbecues and beer but are much more subdued at matches.

Stadium disasters are not a new phenomenon in South Africa. In January 1991, 40 fans were trampled to death and 50 were injured in a stampede when fighting broke out before a preseason "friendly" between Orlando Pirates and Kaiser Chiefs at the Ernest Oppenheimer Stadium in Orkney. In April 2001, 43 fans were crushed to death, 160 were injured, and many more were traumatized at a football match between the same two teams at the Ellis Park Stadium in Johannesburg. Fans tried to enter the stadium even though the event was sold out. Ellis Park Stadium is regarded as one of South Africa's prime stadiums and is accredited by both SAFA and FIFA for football and by SARFU and IRB for rugby. Kaiser Chiefs and Orlando Pirates have among the biggest fan bases in South Africa, and it is still unclear why the authorities allowed a second match (less than four months after the first disaster) to take place at a stadium that was considered too small for their collective fan bases. A neighboring stadium was available and could have comfortably accommodated double the number of spectators.

A disaster report on the Ellis Park tragedy identified numerous risk management problems that led to the disaster. Future events must eliminate these issues to ensure a safer event. Some of these concerns include inaccurate estimation of the number of people attending the match, failure to learn from the previous disaster, overcrowding, inappropriate and inadequate response by security staff, use of tear gas, failure to identify and designate areas of responsibility, failure to adhere to FIFA and SAFA guidelines, unacceptable spectator behavior, corruption and dereliction of duty, an inadequate public address system, unsatisfactory attitude of private security companies, poorly managed ticket sales, and failure to provide a big screen for fans outside the venue who were unable to buy tickets to watch the match.

medical, security, and law enforcement should be part of this communication network. The fifth and final component of a crowd management plan is the use of signage. Signage is an underutilized tool in risk and crowd management. Adequate signage provides spectators with directions to important locations outside the venue such as roadway exits, parking areas, facility entrances, and the ticket office. Inside the facility signs indicate the location of concession stands, first-aid rooms, telephones, restrooms, smoking areas, and exits (Ammon & Unruh, 2010).

Alcohol Management

Alcohol has been linked with sporting events for many decades in many countries (Nelson & Wechsler, 2003), and its use is common practice in many countries. McDaniel, Kinney, and Chalip (2001) argued that it would be unusual to view a sporting event without seeing some form of event signage or a commercial for an alcohol product.

The consumption of alcohol at athletic events is often blamed for injuries that produce litigation. Intoxicated patrons may injure themselves or innocent third parties, and this concern has prompted some sport facility administrators to eliminate alcohol sales, thus forgoing a revenue source. Alternatively, they may contract alcohol sales to an outside vendor or gamble that any litigation pertaining to alcohol sales will be manageable or covered by insurance.

International football organizations such as FIFA and UEFA ban alcohol sales at some events, although the venue operators can still sell alcohol at certain locations during FA Cup Finals (Fried & Ammon, 2009). Scotland's government went so far as to ban the sale of alcohol at all football matches in 1980. In 2004 Russia went a step further by banning alcohol consumption in all public places, including stadiums, with the only exception being restaurants. Even with alcohol bans at most European facilities, fans often drink before an event and may already be intoxicated when they arrive at the facility. In the United States, sport fans participate in tailgate parties held in venue parking lots before games. The availability of alcohol allows fans to become intoxicated before they even enter the facility. After fans are inside, however, most U.S. sport venue managers allow them to buy only two alcoholic drinks at any one time. At some venues

in Europe, fans are able to purchase as many as four drinks per transaction (Fried & Ammon, 2009).

Many spectators consume excessive levels of alcohol at events, and most of the problems at events are associated with such overindulgence. Many events in Europe (specifically football matches) have witnessed unruly fan behavior because of intoxicated fans. In many instances overindulgence accentuates the presence and effect of hooliganism at these matches. The National Football League has struggled with large numbers of intoxicated fans at their games. Oftentimes these drunken spectators ruin the game for sober fans. These incidents can cause public relations problems for the NFL. Before the 2008 season the NFL and its 32 teams agreed to a fan code of conduct, which states the following:

> When attending a game, you are required to refrain from the following behaviors: behavior that is unruly, disruptive, or illegal in nature, intoxication or other signs of alcohol impairment that result in irresponsible behavior, foul or abusive language or obscene gestures, interference with the progress of the game (including throwing objects onto the field), failing to follow instructions of stadium personnel, and verbal or physical harassment of opposing team fans. (McCarthy, 2008, p. 1–3)

The league wanted to send a stern message to fans who abused alcohol during the games. Decreasing the number of intoxicated fans entering the stadiums was a major goal of the code. The NFL also wanted to put their season ticket holders on notice that they would be responsible for the conduct of anyone using their tickets and occupying their seats. Violators of the code face various penalties that may include ejection and revocation of season tickets if the behavior is judged sufficiently detrimental (McCarthy, 2008).

Training people who serve alcohol or handle intoxicated patrons is an important facet of a successful alcohol management strategy and crowd management plan. Two programs in the United States have received recognition for their positive effect on alcohol-related situations. Training for Intervention Procedures by Servers of Alcohol (TIPS) and Techniques for Effective Alcohol Management (TEAM) provide successful training pertaining to effective alcohol management.

A sport facility manager should employ a comprehensive risk management plan containing extensive crowd management strategies as well as alcohol management policies. Therefore, an effective alcohol management plan, similar to a crowd management plan, must consider the facility's patrons and their safety. Providing an attractive and safe environment will motivate fans to return to the venue, thus ensuring a steady stream of revenue. The following elements will assist facility managers when serving alcohol at a facility:

1. Every person attempting to purchase alcohol should have his or her identification checked.

2. No more than two beers should be sold during an individual transaction.

3. The size of each serving should be no larger than 12 ounces (360 ml).

4. Beer sales must end at a specific point during the event.

5. Trained crowd management should be stationed at the facility entrances to prohibit intoxicated individuals from entering the facility as well as to prevent patrons from entering the facility with alcoholic beverages.

6. Implementing a designated driver program will provide a popular service by building rapport with event patrons while reducing the chances that intoxicated patrons will drive home.

Summary

FIFA's World Cup, the Australian Open, concerts, and high school basketball games all have two common denominators: They take place in some type of facility, and they are events. These facilities and the events held in them need managers. An event also requires a knowledgeable manager to be successful. This manager is usually designated as the event coordinator (or similar term). The event coordinator needs a broad understanding of the various components involved in managing an event. Items such as the type of seating, crowd management, alcohol policies, and event evaluation must be carried out to produce an effective event.

A variety of management options may be used for a sport and recreation facility. These options depend on the social and financial outcomes that the facility hopes to achieve. These options include direct management, contract management, lease management, and joint management.

Sustainability has become a buzzword in the facility management industry. The effect that sport and entertainment venues have on the environment needs to be recognized and monitored. The concept of social responsibility pertaining to environmental matters is important for today's facility managers. Venue operators and owners must understand how these initiatives will affect their ability to maintain their profitability while satisfying the concerns of their stakeholders.

A customer's estimation of the value of the services provided by a venue operator is often influenced by the relationship between the stakeholder and the sport organization. To entice paying customers to return to the facility, facility managers must nurture and sustain positive relationships with their customers. Without these ticket-buying fans the sport industry would disappear. The quality of customer service is often affected by items such as parking, appearance of the facility, quality of seats and scoreboard, and patrons' ability to move freely around the venue.

Because of worldwide terrorism, risk management has become a tremendously important responsibility for all personnel working with facilities and events. The terrorist attacks on September 11, 2001, forever changed the facility and event management industry. Sport venue and event managers who can anticipate potential areas of loss and injury and can take action to decrease them are in high demand. An effective crowd management and alcohol management plan is vital to reducing the potential risks that a facility manager faces.

Some areas of sport have downsized because of a variety of factors, such as changes in the economy, corporate mergers, and corporate bankruptcies that affected Chrysler, General Motors, and others. Because of these various events, the future of facility and event management is not as clear as it once was. As revenues have slowed, profit margins have narrowed. The influence of this domino effect on facility and event management needs to be continually monitored.

? Review and Discussion Questions

1. Describe the difference between single-purpose and multipurpose facilities. Name some examples of venues of each type around the world.

2. What is a mission statement? Give examples of appropriate items to note in a mission statement for a sport facility.

3. Describe the responsibilities of the facility director, director of operations, and event coordinator at a sport facility.

4. Name the four types of facility management discussed in the chapter. Discuss which one would be the most beneficial for a multipurpose stadium.

5. Currently, several companies privately manage more than 300 facilities nationally and internationally. List these companies. Why would a facility choose to contract with one of these companies?

6. Explain the difference between facility sustainability and legacy. Are they both necessary? Why or why not?

7. Facility aesthetics is purported to be valuable for spectators who attend events. Which of the examples discussed in the chapter would be the most important to you if you were attending an event at an arena to watch a basketball competition?

8. Why is employing trained people to reduce facility risks a less expensive alternative than reacting to potential disasters or litigation without such people? How can most litigation be avoided?

9. Suppose that you are attending an international football match in Italy. Name some specific components of crowd management that you would expect to see.

International Sport Tourism

Douglas Michele Turco, PhD
Drexel University, Pennsylvania, USA

Kamilla Swart, EdD
Cape Peninsula University of Technology, South Africa

Chapter Objectives

After studying this chapter, you will be able to do the following:

- Describe the components of the sport tourism industry
- Define key terms in sport tourism
- Differentiate the three main segments of the sport tourist market
- Describe the economic, sociocultural, environmental, political, and legacy impacts of sport tourism
- Identify constraints to travel and sport tourism for persons with and without disabilities
- Introduce the steps and considerations for strategic sport tourism planning

Key Terms

W hat and where do you want to play today? Cricket in Delhi? Surfing in Maui? Skiing in New Zealand or catching the football match in Liverpool? What about a yacht race in Valencia or Formula One in Abu Dhabi? The wide world of sport tourism awaits you and millions of sport enthusiasts. Sport is big business. Cities wager millions of dollars to stage an Olympic Games, Formula One races, World Cup events, and other sport events. In return, cities expect millions from sponsors, developers, and visitors. Although global sponsorship spending slowed in 2008 after reaching US$30 billion in 2007, the top 12 Olympic sponsors spent US$866 million to sponsor the Beijing Olympic Games, nearly one-third more than they did for Athens. Coca-Cola spent an estimated US$70 million and millions more to sponsor the controversial torch relay (Khan, 2008). Street and Smith's *SportsBusiness Journal* estimated the size of the U.S. sport industry at US$213 billion in 2007, more than twice the size of the U.S. auto industry (www.sportbusinessjournal.com).

Tourism is also big business. World tourism arrivals are projected to reach over 1.6 billion by 2020, and long-haul travel is growing at a faster pace than intraregional travel (WTO, 2008). Associated global tourism spending is estimated to be in the region of US$4.5 trillion (Sport Business, 2006). Sport tourism is a niche market segment that is contributing to this growth, and it appears as if sport-related travel will continue to increase. Sport tourism can account for about 25 percent of tourism receipts in some regions (Sport Business, 2006). Even when global economic growth slows, the desire to travel remains high for many people.

People travel for a variety of reasons: to visit friends and relatives, to conduct business, and to engage in leisure. Sport tourism is a major segment of the broader leisure travel market. Sport tourism resides at the intersection of the sport and tourism industries and is dynamic and filled with intrigue, challenges, and opportunities for research and business practice (see figure 22.1). Sport tourism combines the best and worst of both the sport industry and the tourism industry. Sport is a universal language, involving competition, conflict, emotion, and often entertaining drama. Tourism by its nature is invasive, involving host–guest interactions and impacts. Tourism is not always about happy tourists and their spending; at times it leads to crowding,

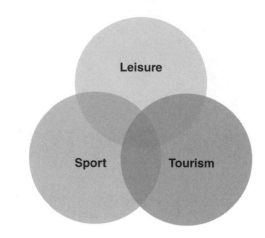

Figure 22.1 Sport and tourism intersection.

queuing, environmental degradation, price gouging, and resentment by locals.

Sport, tourism, and leisure are closely related concepts. Broadly, **leisure** can be defined as that portion of a person's time that is not directly devoted to work or work-connected responsibilities (Kraus, 2001, 38). Sport as a ludic physical activity, spectator consumption of this activity, and tourism as pleasure-based travel can be considered subsets of leisure (Hinch, Jackson, Hudson, & Walker, 2006). **Sport tourism** is defined as leisure-based tourism that takes people temporarily outside their home environment to participate in or watch physical activities, or venerate attractions associated with physical activities (Gibson, 1998).

Sport tourism as an academic discipline has evolved considerably in the past two decades. Textbooks, academic conferences, undergraduate and graduate degree programs, and a scientific journal, *Journal of Sport and Tourism*, now exist. This chapter examines the current body of knowledge devoted to sport tourism and identifies patterns of sport tourist behaviors, impacts, issues, and future areas for best practice and further study. Focus areas covered include event economic impacts, serious sport tourists, prestige-worthy sport tourism, social impacts, residents' perceptions of events, and watching friends and relatives. Through this analysis and knowledge sharing, it is intended that sport tourism studies will continue to prosper for the next 20 years.

Core Principles and Terms

Some debate continues about the definitions of the words *sport* and *tourism*. For example, what length of stay, distance travelled, and trip purpose make someone a tourist? Those issues, however, are not addressed in this chapter. For the sake of this chapter, a tourist is defined as a visitor for at least one night but not more than six months and whose main purpose of visit is other than the exercise of an activity remunerated from within the place visited. Similarly, what is and is not sport will not be argued in this chapter, although these arguments can be made (e.g., Is Greco-Roman wrestling a sport and arm wrestling not? Horseracing versus rodeo? Pairs ice dancing versus ballroom dancing?). For purposes of this chapter, assume that sport involves physical activity, competition, and agreed-upon rules of performance, and is considered sport by its participants.

Sport tourism is defined simply as travel to a destination to experience sport. Sport tourists are visitors to a destination for the purpose of participating, viewing, or celebrating sport (Turco, Riley, & Swart, 2002). **Visiting friends and relatives (VFRs)** are tourists nonresident in the host community whose primary motive is to visit friends or relatives. In sport tourism, **watching friends and relatives (WFRs)** are VFRs with associates who are participating in a sport event. The sport tourism industry involves all the people, places, and things that support, influence, and are affected by sport tourists. It is the collection of businesses, institutions, resources, and people servicing sport tourists. Included are tourists, host residents, and providers of goods and services in the broad tourism categories of transportation, accommodations (e.g., hotels, bed and breakfasts, resorts, and eating and drinking places), and shopping. Sport serves as either the focal or the secondary attraction.

Figure 22.2 illustrates the sport tourism system—the interactions of the sport tourism industry in the marketplace. Natural resources often form the basis of the sport tourism system. Many participatory and event-based sport tourism experiences occur in natural resource settings. Fishing, nautical, marine, and aquatic sports are enjoyed on water; climbing, snowboarding, and skiing on mountains; and Nordic skiing, snowshoeing, snowmobiling, and hunting in forests and fields. The demand for and finite supply of natural environments for sport present challenges to sport and destination managers, and is a growing area of research investigation. The natural environment adds to the challenge and

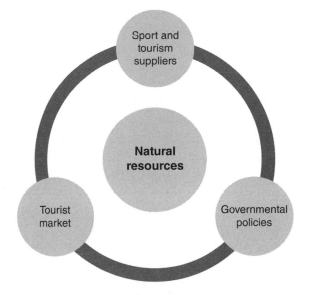

Figure 22.2   Sport tourism system and its interactions with the marketplace.

allure of a sport tourism attraction. For example, the extensive red sandstone formations have made Moab, Utah, a mountain biking mecca. Colorado's rarified air and mountainous terrain make the Leadville Trail 100 Ultramarathon extremely difficult and thus more prestigious for its finishers. The tourism infrastructure of transportation, communication, accommodations, and attractions is built on natural resources. Governmental policies including immigration and travel requirements, security, trade, tariffs, currency values, and international relations influence the tourism supply and tourist demand. Communication of sport and tourism information is critical because people obviously do not travel to places that they do not know about. Destination marketing organizations (convention and visitors bureaus, governmental travel offices) and sport and tourism suppliers (sport tourism attractions such as museums, halls of fame, and stadiums; sport organizers; managers, tour operators, and travel agents) use an array of methods and mediums to communicate to potential and current travelers, including websites, trade shows and events, periodicals, and advertisements.

Types of Sport Tourists

Three primary types of sport tourists have been identified: participatory, event based, and celebratory. Participatory sport tourists travel to destinations to play sport. They may include golfers playing a round at Royal St. Andrew's Golf Club in Scotland, skiers at St. Moritz in Switzerland, runners in the Berlin Marathon, or those mountain bikers at Moab. Participatory sport tourists may be elite professionals or rank amateurs; the qualifiers for participatory sport tourists are that they are visitors to the host destination and that they are engaged in sport.

Some participatory sport tourists play a dual role in the sport tourism industry. As visiting sport competitors they require transportation, accommodations, and other tourist services, and simultaneously they serve as the attraction for event-based sport tourists. Event-based sport tourists are those who travel to a destination to watch others participate in sport. Examples of sport events witnessed by tourists (and researched by scholars) range from A to Z: America's Cup to the Zagreb Open tennis tournament. Consider the Little League World Series in tiny Williamsport, Pennsylvania. Held annually in August, the Little League World Series (LLWS) is the pinnacle of athletic achievement for boys up to 13 years of age. Teams from around the world compete in round-robin and elimination play, attracting over 500,000 spectators and live television coverage worldwide on ESPN. Lodging accommodations are sold out within a 100-kilometer radius of the city. The athletes, coaches, and officials are participatory sport tourists to Williamsport for the 10 days of the LLWS. Parents, friends, and relatives of the participants are event-based sport tourists.

Celebratory sport tourists travel to destinations to visit halls of fame, museums, stadiums, and other places of remembrance (see table 22.1). They may travel to experience the festive sport atmosphere surrounding a sport event. Numerous celebratory sport tourism attractions exist. At the 2006 FIFA World Cup in Germany, thousands of people congregated in city fan parks to have fun, to participate in the festivities, and to celebrate football even though they did not have tickets to a match. Thousands of people each year pay their pounds to tour an empty Wimbledon Tennis Centre. The Beijing Organizing Committee for the Olympic Games (BOCOG) reported that in the two months following the 2008 Olympic Games, 200,000 people paid to tour the National Olympic Stadium, known as the Bird's Nest. The Basketball Hall of Fame in Springfield, Massachusetts, attracts 250,000 visitors each year, 20 percent of whom are from outside the United States. The Hillerich & Bradsby Company, makers of the iconic Louisville Slugger baseball bat, receives 200,000 paying visitors annually to see the manufacturing process in its factory.

A crowd of sport event spectators contains distinct market segments with respect to consumer behavior. Their places of origin and local spending influence the economic impact of the event. Among sport event spectators, several distinct market segments were identified by Preuss (2005): runaways, changers, casuals, time switchers,

Table 22.1   Halls of Fame and Their Locations

Hall of fame or sport museum	Location	Website
Hockey Hall of Fame	Toronto, Ontario	www.hhof.com
National Baseball Hall of Fame and Museum	Cooperstown, New York	www.baseballhalloffame.org
International Tennis Hall of Fame	Newport, Rhode Island	www.tennisfame.com
Negro Leagues Baseball Museum	Kansas City, Missouri	www.nlbm.com
Pro Football Hall of Fame	Canton, Ohio	www.profootballhof.com
International Boxing Hall of Fame	Canastota, New York	www.ibhof.com
International Swimming Hall of Fame (ISHOF)	Fort Lauderdale, Florida	www.ishof.org
Motor Sports Hall of Fame	Novi, Michigan	www.mshf.com
National Sports Museum	New York, New York	www.sportsmuseum.com
Canada Olympic Park	Calgary, Saskatchewan	www.canadaolympicpark.ca
Gilles Villeneuve Museum	Montréal, Quebec	www.villeneuve.com
Olympic Museum	Lausanne, Switzerland	www.museumolympic.org

Learning Activity

Select a hall of fame, sport museum, or other celebratory sport tourism attraction and research the trends in visitor demand over the past 10 years. Who are the primary consumer markets in terms of their geographic and demographic characteristics?

avoiders, extensioners, eventers, and home stayers (see table 22.2). **Casual tourists** are visitors who attend a sport event but were in the host community primarily for other reasons, such as to visit friends or relatives, or to conduct business. Day trippers, or **excursionists**, are visitors who do not stay overnight in the host community. **Primary sport event tourists** are those who visit the host community specifically because of the sport event in question. Residents are sport event attendees in their home community. Resident spending represents a switching of transactions from one local business, that is, a restaurant, cinema, theatre, or other experience, to another, in this case the sport event. **Time switchers** are those who purposely schedule their visit to coincide with the sport event but who would have visited at another time anyway. Runaways are residents who purposely leave the host city during the event because of the event.

Homestayers are residents who purposely stay in the host city during the event because of the event. Preuss and Schutte (2008) suggested that primary sport event tourists spend at higher levels than the overnight visitors whom they displace in hotels and other paid accommodations. In such cases, the value-added of primary sport event tourists must be factored into this crowding-out effect. See chapter 14 for more about the economic impacts of attendance at sport events.

Serious Sport Tourists

Serious sport tourists take sport participation to another level. They are focused and highly committed to participating in their sport. Serious sport tourists demonstrate a strong commitment to sport participation, a dedication that borders on obsession according to those less committed. Elite gymnasts and their families sacrifice normalcy for specialized and intense training, often accompanied by high social, psychological, and financial costs. For these children, the rigors of daily training and diet can make sport a worklike obligation. Serious youth sport tourists are often accompanied to competitions by their serious parents. They spend more money on sport-related goods and services, travel more frequently, stay longer, and spend more per night than other tourists do (Getz, 2008). For those reasons, the Walt Disney World Company built the Wide World of Sports complex in Orlando in 1997 (www.disneysports.com).

Table 22.2 Sport Event Spectator Market Segments and Description

Segment	Description
Extensioners	Tourists who would have come anyway but stay longer because of the event
Eventers	Persons who travel to the host city because of the event
Home stayers	Residents who opt to stay in the city during the event and spend their money at home rather than on a vacation somewhere else at some other time in the year
Runaways	Residents who leave the city and take a holiday elsewhere
Avoiders	Tourists who stay away but would have come without the event; can be either "cancellers," tourists who cancel their trips entirely, or "pre- or postswitchers," tourists who will come earlier or later
Changers	Residents who leave the city and take their holidays at the time of the event rather than at some other time in the year
Casuals	Tourists who would have visited the city even without the event
Time switchers	Tourists who wanted to travel to the city but at another time

Also included by Preuss are residents of the host city who attend the event.

Adapted from Preuss (2005).

Serious sport tourists need not be elite athletes. In fact, most are amateurs. Consider these examples of sport events that draw both elite and amateur competitors:

◆ The physical demands to prepare for and compete in an Ironman Triathlon imply a serious commitment to sport. To earn the title of Ironman finisher, the participant must swim 2.4 miles (3.9 km), cycle 112 miles (180 km), and then run a marathon (26.2 miles, or 42.2 km). Most of the 22 Ironman races held worldwide have a capacity of 2,000, although some accept as many as 2,500 athletes. The demand is so high for some Ironman events that entries sell out on the first day of open registration. Countries that hosted Ironman events in 2008 included Australia, Brazil, China, Germany, Japan, Malaysia, South Africa, Spain, New Zealand, the United Kingdom, and the United States.

◆ The 50-States Marathon Club is made up of runners who have completed a marathon in each state in the United States. Besides the serious time, financial, and physical demands that must be met to run a marathon, the added time, travel, and accommodation costs to run in every state demonstrate the high level of commitment that these athletes have toward their chosen endeavor.

◆ A marathon is not long enough for some sport enthusiasts; ultramarathoners want to run twice the distance or more. The Badwater Ultramarathon is recognized globally as the world's toughest foot race. The event pits up to 90 athletes against one another and extreme conditions. The race covers 135 miles (217 km) nonstop from Death Valley to Mt. Whitney, California, in temperatures up to 130 °F (55 °C). A person obviously does not wake up in the morning and decide to run the Badwater; the event requires years of dedicated endurance training.

Serious leisure is the

> systematic pursuit of an amateur, hobbyist, or volunteer core activity that people find so substantial, interesting, and fulfilling that, in the typical case, they launch themselves on a leisure career centered on acquiring and expressing a combination of its special skills, knowledge, and experience. (Stebbins, 2007, p. 3)

Serious leisure participants distinguish themselves by the (1) need to persevere at the activity, (2) availability of a leisure career, (3) need to put in effort to gain skill and knowledge, (4) realization of various special benefits, (5) unique ethos and social world, and (6) an attractive personal and social identity (Stebbins, 2007). Serious leisure can be contrasted with casual leisure; a key defining characteristic is that serious leisure provides a sense of social identity (Green & Jones, 2005). Traveling to participate in serious leisure may include serious sport tourism.

Many who are serious about leisure are competitors in nonprofessional sports, as Shipway and Jones (2007) found among distance runners. They operationalized serious sport tourism as travel to pursue serious leisure sport interests. Green and Jones (2005) suggested that sport tourism can provide serious leisure participants with (1) a way to construct or confirm their leisure identity, (2) a time and place to interact with others sharing the ethos of the activity, (3) a time and place to parade and celebrate a valued social identity, (4) a way to further their leisure "career," and (5) a way to signal their career stage. A person's serious leisure lifestyle communicates and forms the basis for personal and communal identity.

Serious sport tourists also include spectators who follow their favorite teams to attend away matches. In some cases, visiting sport event tourists outnumber (and outcheer) home fans, negating the home-field advantage. Consider the legions of Manchester United fans who travel throughout the year to witness their team in action. Tour operations have been established on the club's website to offer sport travel packages to serious sport fans. When Manchester United qualified for the May 2008 Champions League finals in Moscow, the club was allocated 21,000 tickets, most costing either £67 (US$132) or £117 (US$231). Add a £95 (US$188) Visa charge and accommodation costs in one of the most expensive cities in the world, and financing the football expedition would top £1,000 (US$1,975) per person.

Sport Tourism Suppliers and Consumers

Figures 22.3 and 22.4 (adapted from Turco et al., 2002) provide an illustration of sport tourism suppliers and consumers based on the level of intensity with which people partake in sport tourism. Those most involved are the athletes, competitors, and participants as well as the officials, organizers, coaches, and coaching staff. These sport tourists are required for most forms of sport tourism to occur. Fans and

> ## Sport Tour

ING New York City Marathon

The ING New York City Marathon is one of the largest participant races in the world. More than 37,000 runners participate, 2.5 million spectators line the streets of New York, and the worldwide television audience exceeds 300 million. The marathon is known for the diversity of its participants—80 percent of the runners are from outside New York City and nearly 50 percent come from outside the United States. An impact study found New York to be the beneficiary of US$188 million from the marathon (Fickenscher, 2009), making it the highest-grossing single-day sporting event in New York. Study results were based on surveys of 1,000 participants in the 2005 race. Marathon participants and spectators spent US$65 million on hotels, US$44 million on food and beverages, US$41 million on retail merchandise, US$15 million on entertainment, US$13 million on transportation, and US$10 million on running and fitness gear at the ING New York City Marathon Health and Fitness Expo. The study also reported that runners are likely to spend more money than the average tourist because they view the race as a commemorative event. Half of runners from abroad stay in the city for an average of six days.

general spectators are less involved because they may have alternative activities that can draw their attention, interest, and time away from the sport tourism activity. Spectators can also participate in sport tourism incidentally if they travel to a destination for other leisure-related purposes.

The range of sport tourism suppliers is presented next. Note that participants are demanders and suppliers of sport tourism services, because without them there will be no one to organize or observe (Turco et al., 2002). Sport museums and halls of fame also serve as primary attractions. The organizers,

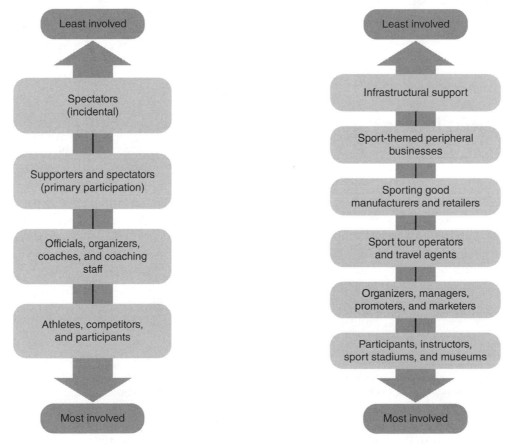

Figure 22.3   Sport tourism consumers.

Figure 22.4   Sport tourism suppliers.

managers, and marketers of sport tourism opportunities serve as the link between the sport and other tourists. They are directly involved in the production of the sport attraction, and include sport associations, sport commissions, and government sport ministries. A **sport commission** is an organization created to promote sport in a particular community, often with the goal of improving economic development. Sport tour operators and travel agents provide travel and hospitality services to the sport tourist. Sporting goods manufacturers and sport retailers of equipment, apparel, and memorabilia are found at the next level because they are not directly involved in promoting travel opportunities. But they could also serve as primary attractions or secondary attractions if their factories or stores are set up to draw sport tourists (for example, the Louisville Slugger factory and Niketown). Sport-themed restaurants are peripherally involved in the supply of sport tourism services because their revenue is mainly generated by nonsport tourist clientele. Government, at all levels, provides basic infrastructure such as transport and health and safety services. In addition, governments could provide sport tourism policy planning and financial support, and they often maintain the natural resources required for many sport tourism activities. They are less involved but are a significant supplier of sport tourism.

Economic Impact of Sport Tourism

Because sport tourism involves a wide variety of consumer activities, interests, and behaviors, its economic impact is varied and complex. Major international sport events (e.g., the Commonwealth Games) are often presented as making multibillion dollar contributions to an economy. Although major sport events have a significant economic impact, the exact impact is not easy to quantify because of the complexity surrounding how to account for consumer spending. Evaluating the economic impact of sport tourism involves the study of varied spending behaviors of different types of sport tourists and consideration of the issue of destination branding, whereby a sport tourism event can play a role in shaping perceptions of a place well into the future.

Measuring the Economic Impact of Events

Economic impact studies are one of the most common forms of evaluating megaevents such as the Olympic Games and the FIFA World Cup. Studies have been conducted on a wide range of events using a variety of methods, from automobile racing (Burns, Hatch, & Mules, 1986) to World Cups (Maennig, 2007; Lee & Taylor, 2005; Baade & Matheson, 2004). Despite widespread use, skepticism is growing about sport event economic impact research, in part because of faulty studies and overinflated findings (Crompton, 2006; Baade, Baumann, & Matheson, 2006). Inaccuracies occur for several reasons, including purposeful falsification. Crompton (2006) argued that some event studies are inflated for political reasons, perhaps to sell or justify public investment in sport, to improve public relations, or to advance an election campaign. For example, it was estimated that the economic impacts of the 2010 FIFA World Cup would be R14.75 billion (US$1.9 billion), contribute R66.75 billion (US$8.5 billion) to GDP, and generate an additional R19 billion (US$2.4 billion) in government taxes to demonstrate the event's value to taxpayers (Grant Thornton, 2008). In 2008 and 2009 organizers of the 2012 London Olympic Games faced strong protest from residents about cost overruns and taxpayer financing of the Games during the global recession.

Megaevents are bid on primarily for the expected value added to the host city. An economic impact study essentially measures how much value the event adds to the city. Put another way, what would be missing from the economy without the event? One can visualize a giant hand pulling an event from a city and ponder how much money would be extracted. A sport tourism event's pull or drawing power is measured by its ability to attract nonresidents and induce consumer spending at and near the event venue (Yu & Turco, 2000).

Visitors drawn by a major sport event may displace others who would have visited but did not because they could not secure accommodations or because they were not willing to deal with the crowds attracted by the event. Other tourists and residents avoid the megaevent or are priced out. In turn, the host city loses money that would have otherwise been spent. Crompton (2006, 76) contended that "if each of these visitors merely replaces another

Learning Activity

Research and analyze a (relatively) large sport event from a tourism perspective. How many overnight stays were attributed to the event? What were the tourist impacts on the host city?

potential visitor who stayed away from the community because of the congestion associated with the tourism event, there is no new economic impact."

There is a tendency to compare event economic impact totals as if a larger amount implies greater import or success. Events vary by edition. Host cities change, economies change, and competitors change, as do spectators. Turco et al. (2011) compared visitor spending at the 2007 and 2003 Cricket World Cups. The 2003 Cricket World Cup (CWC) took place in South Africa, Zimbabwe, and Kenya, and the 2007 edition was in the West Indies. Fifty-eight percent of the net benefit to South Africa arose from spending by foreigners, who spent an average of R1,400 (approximately US$190) per day for an average of 16 days. But per day visitor spending figures for the 2003 CWC and 2007 CWC were nearly identical (US$190 for 2003 and US$191 in 2007). The 2003 CWC matches in South Africa were attended by 626,845 people, whereas the 2007 CWC sold more than 672,000 tickets and recorded the highest ticketing revenue for a CWC. The average length of stay of a foreign visitor for the 2003 CWC was 16 days, which was slightly longer than the average stay of a non-CWC foreign visitor (12 days). Visitors who came specifically for CWC 2003 stayed the shortest, whereas those who had timed their holiday to coincide with the event ended up staying more than 22 days. This trend was also evident in the Guyana segment of CWC 2007. Although the patterns across events spanning years and continents are consistent in per capita spending, caution should be used when comparing economic impact figures from event to event. Despite a plethora of prior studies, the need remains for a refined and agile model that can predict the economic impact of a sporting event. Many studies fail to account for variances in consumer behavior among spectator market segments and the crowding-out effect. Distinguishing sport event tourists by their spending behaviors (as Preuss and others have done) will lead to more accurate economic impact estimations. See chapter 14 for more on ways to analyze the overall economic impact of sport events.

The case study illustrates the importance of cricket in several countries and the level of investment necessary to host the thousands of athletes and spectators at a Cricket World Cup and reap the consequent economic and social benefits of hosting these kinds of sport tourism events. The case also points to the future of cricket and the lengths that some will go to maximize the sport's potential as a commodity. It also demonstrates that economic impacts cannot be viewed in isolation and that the political ramifications of sport tourism should further be considered.

CASE STUDY

Preparing for Visitors to the 2007 and 2011 Cricket World Cups

The International Cricket Council (ICC) Cricket World Cup tournament is one of the world's largest sporting events. Cricket World Cup (CWC) matches officially began in 1975 in England, with eight teams: the six Test playing nations (England, Australia, New Zealand, West Indies, India, Pakistan) along with Sri Lanka and South Africa. The tournament has been taking place every four years since then, participated in by major teams all over the world. The ICC awarded the West Indies the right to host the 2007 CWC, marking the first time that the West Indies would host a major international sporting event. Through a process of bidding, eight territories—Antigua and Barbuda, Barbados, Grenada, Guyana, Jamaica, St. Kitts and Nevis, St. Lucia, and Trinidad and Tobago—were selected to host the main matches. Each of these eight Caribbean territories upgraded its cricket stadium, airport, and hospitality facilities to meet the criteria set by the ICC and to cater to the thousands of visitors expected to witness the matches. Australia bested Sri Lanka to win the 2007 CWC.

(continued)

(continued)

The CWC is one of the world's most viewed sporting events. As an indicator of its worldwide appeal, 2007 CWC matches were televised in 200 countries to over 2.2 billion viewers. Television rights for the 2011 and 2015 World Cups were recently sold for over US$1.1 billion, and sponsorship rights were sold for a further US$500 million (cricinfo.com, 2007). Attendance for the entire 2007 Cricket World Cup averaged 11,176 per match (www.icc-cricket .com). This television presence both helps to drive future sport tourism and allows hosting countries the opportunity for destination branding.

Stadium deals associated with the 2007 Cricket World Cup reveal the sport's global financial network. Stadium construction in Guyana was financed in part by the Government of India. Guyana built a new 16,000-seat stadium at a cost of US$25 million to host the Super Eight matches. In 2003 India's ruling government promised a US$20 million loan for the building of the stadium. But when the Congress Party won the Indian general election, a shift in policy occurred. Guyana re-signed for a US$6 million loan from India's government, under the previous terms, and a US$19 million commercial loan from the Import Export Bank of India. Guyana will not pay off the new loan agreement until at least 2024. Indian architects designed the stadium, and 85 percent of the spending on the building work was to go to Indian companies. Similarly, Chinese and Taiwanese governments made significant investments for stadiums in Barbados and St. Kitts and Nevis. Of the eight venues constructed or refurbished for the 2007 World Cricket Cup, China assisted in the construction of five, providing more than 1,000 workers and more than US$140 million in financing. China, where cricket is currently played by about 1,000 of the country's 1.3 billion people, aims to have 150,000 players, its own league, and a competitive national team by 2020 (Sheringham, 2007). In St. Kitts and Nevis, the Taiwan government funded the construction of Warner Park Stadium, an US$8 million investment (Erikson & Wander, 2007), and a Taiwanese construction company helped build facilities in St. Vincent and the Grenadines, where Cricket World Cup warm-up matches were played. The establishment of this infrastructure for the event helped to establish the event's legacy and created the potential for future income from use of these facilities.

An example of the lengths to which some will go to improve cricket in the West Indies and globally is in Antigua, where Texas billionaire Sir Allen Stanford invested over US$100 million to prepare the island to host its 2007 CWC matches. In October 2008 Stanford invited England to play the Stanford 20/20 Stars at Stanford Cricket Grounds for a US$20 million prize in front of a worldwide television audience (Stanford's team bested England). Since then, Stanford has been charged by the U.S. Securities and Exchange Commission (SEC) for financial fraud of over US$8 billion. Allegedly, he operated a Ponzi scheme similar to that run by disgraced New York financier Bernard Madoff. In February 2009 the English and Wales Cricket Board severed all ties with Stanford.

A global battle for supremacy is occurring in the world of cricket. The balance of power in cricket appears to have shifted from the Commonwealth countries (England, the West Indies, and the South Pacific islands) to Asia, in particular India, Pakistan, Sri Lanka, and the United Arab Emirates (UAE). The next Cricket World Cup champions will contribute to the debate about cricket's regional balance of power.

The recent terrorist attacks in India, however, could have significant repercussions for cricket in the region. A number of international cricket events were cancelled, a significant setback because 70 percent of the world's cricket revenues are generated in India. Moreover, some contend that these attacks may create a crisis of confidence in sport tourism in India and the region (sportbusiness.com). India and Pakistan are scheduled to cohost the 2011 Cricket World Cup, but Pakistan's participation is in jeopardy following the recent attacks on the Sri Lankan cricket team in Pakistan. South Africa will host the Champions Trophy because both Sri Lanka and Pakistan were ruled out. Pakistan was originally scheduled to host the one-day international competition, but the ICC postponed that event after several teams voiced concerns about security.

Economic Behaviors of Sport Tourists

How much does the average sport event tourist spend per trip? The answer depends on the nature of the sport event, the spectator market, and the characteristics of the host economy.

The spatial proximity of sport tourists to the host economy influences their spending, as does whether they are first-time visitors. Event visitors from communities near the host economy typically spend less money than those who come from greater distances. International visitor groups to the 2005 Little League World Series spent, on average, US$700 more in the

Williamsport economy than domestic visitor groups did, after adjusting for group size and length of stay (Scott & Turco, 2007). As the geographic origins of event spectators change from year to year, so too will their economic impact on the host economy. The residential location of the competing athletes influences who and how many will travel to watch the competition and how much they will spend (Tang & Turco, 2001). Greig and McQuaid (2004) conducted spectator interviews at two one-day rugby international matches in Edinburgh, Scotland (Scotland versus England and Scotland versus France), to estimate the economic impact on the region and city. The researchers found that the origin of spectators differed between matches, naturally reflecting the origins of the visiting teams, and they noted a clear association between the distance that spectators come to watch the match and the amount that they spend. Likewise, sport spectators who travel longer distances to attend an event spent more in the host community. Holding all other variables constant, Tang and Turco (2001) found that for every 100 miles (160 km) a visitor group traveled, they spent on average US$26.08.

The prestige of a sport tourism experience as perceived by the sport consumer also influences the size of the visitor group and their spending. Competing in a world championship is for most athletes a once-in-a-lifetime opportunity, and these events often attract large numbers of spectators who are relatives or friends of the athletes. The Olympic Games and World Cups are the most prestigious events in the world for the sports that they cover because of their global nature, scale, and scarcity. Grand Slam events in tennis (Australian, French, and U.S. Opens and Wimbledon) and golf (Master's, British and U.S. Opens, PGA Championship) are more prestigious than others. For other sports, events may change in perceived prestige over time. The Little League World Series is a once-in-a-lifetime opportunity for 12-year-old baseball players, because age restrictions will not allow them to compete the following year. The family and friends of the ballplayers who attend the event spend at significantly higher levels than other visitors do. This finding is consistent with what Turco (1997) found among high school basketball championship spectators, whose spending levels corresponded to their perception of the event's prestige. Fans who assigned more prestige to the event spent more than those who perceived the event to be less prestigious. History, prize money, media coverage, scarcity, and the field of competitors influence perceived prestige. The prestige of the Moscow (1980) and Los Angeles (1984) Olympic Games was diminished because of the boycott absence of teams representing the rival super powers, the United States and the USSR. The composition of a tournament field and its "star power" influence media attention, gallery size, and its economic impact. An annual event such as the U.S. Open golf championship may experience significant fluctuations in attendance, spectator market segment proportionality, and spending from year to year. For example, when Tiger Woods is in contention for a tournament victory, all these factors increase. In 88 tournaments since 2003, Woods finished in the top five 54 times, pushing the final-round television rating share to a 4.4 average. The other 34 events averaged a 3.4 share—a 29 percent difference. This disparity is known as the Tiger Woods effect. In 2007 weekend ratings were 58 percent higher in tournaments in which Tiger played (Sandomir, 2008).

Much is made in marketing literature about attracting repeat consumers, but first-time sport tourists spend more money than repeaters do. The novelty of the destination and not knowing which local businesses provide the best value are reasons why first timers spend more than repeat visitors do. Repeaters have "been there, done that" and do not feel the need to do "that" again, that is, purchase souvenirs or attend another attraction. Tang and Turco (2001) showed that repeat visitor groups to a sport event spent US$189.56 less than first-time visitors did.

Learning Activity

Because recurring events are different each time, choose a recurring event (e.g., Wimbledon, Calgary Stampede) and research how sport tourism consumer spending patterns change from one edition to the next.

Destination Branding

The overall impression that the destination creates in the minds of tourists can be described as the destination brand (Chalip & Costa, 2006). Sport tourism events are a critical component for the branding of destinations as desirable locations for

Watching Friends and Relatives

Relatively little attention has been devoted to tourists who travel to watch relatives or friends participate in sport events. As previously alluded to, spectator research at the Little League World Series found that player association makes a difference in terms of sport tourists' spending, length of stay, and game attendance (Scott & Turco, 2007). Spectators with a player association spent more time and money in the local economy. In fact, they spent nearly three times as much, mostly in travel, lodging, and souvenirs. Most teams qualify for the World Series a few weeks before the event, so expenditures are often made at the last minute, without the benefit of advance purchase discounts. The researchers surmised that for some visitors in this category, watching a friend or relative in the Little League World Series was a once-in-a-lifetime experience and they were willing to spend money on the event accordingly. They may have realized that they should experience all that the Little League World Series has to offer, including attending most games, purchasing souvenirs, staying for the whole time that their child plays, and eating out instead of consuming budget meals. A comparison of consumer behavior among domestic and international WFRs and other tourist consumers at the Little League World Series is provided in table 22.3. Note that domestic WFRs spent nearly three times as much money as spectators in other market segments did.

As WFRs travel more frequently to attend competitions, they adjust their spending behavior. Turco (1997) noted that parents of young athletes who frequently traveled to competitions became adept at cost-saving strategies, thereby minimizing the impacts on the host economy. Ride sharing, bringing prepared meals and snacks, and taking motor homes or camper trailers are among the practices used by parents who travel with their young athletes to competitions. Although Scott and Turco found no difference in spending among repeat and first-time visitors with player associations, further research is warranted. Repeat participation in the Little League World Series is rare for athletes. As with the consumer behavior of repeat visitors, per trip spending by WFRs is likely to diminish as they attend additional sporting events in which their friends and relatives participate.

Table 22.3   Characteristics of WFR and Other Tourists at the 2005 Little League World Series

Behavior	Domestic WFR sport tourist	Domestic sport tourist
Travel party size	3 persons	4 persons
Sessions attended	6 sessions	4 sessions
Length of stay	7 nights	3 nights
Spending	US$2,377; US$1,215 for travel	US$668; US$175 for travel
Behavior	International WFR sport tourist	International sport tourist
Travel party size	4 persons	2 persons
Sessions attended	9 sessions	6 sessions
Length of stay	11 nights	7 nights
Spending	US$4,550; US$1,600 for travel	US$3,200; US$700 for travel

Domestic and international WFR sport tourist data adapted from Scott and Turco (2007).

tourism and investment. Not surprisingly, marketers are increasingly using sport tourism events (and the associated attractions and activities) to enhance the destination brand of the host city (or region or country) and or use it as a differentiating strategy.

One way of doing this is through cobranding, that is, by pairing the event brand with the destination brand to reinforce or change a brand image. The 2010 FIFA World Cup is a case in point. Because the FIFA World Cup is a global brand, South Africa was in a position to leverage its association with this brand and consequently to enhance its tourism and investment profile and stature. Similarly, FIFA used the opportunity to improve its global footprint and image by hosting the first World Cup in Africa. For this positive transfer to take place, however, a properly managed event communication strategy was required. Higham (2005, 154) noted that "the role of the media is critical to achieving destination branding outcomes." This task was particularly challenging for South Africa (and Africa generally) because the destination is often associated with negative images. Dimeo and Kay (2004), using the 1996 South Asia Cricket World Cup as a case, cautioned that developing countries are less able to control images projected by the media because of preconceived notions and prejudices of the Western media. Thus, working with event promoters, sponsors, and media becomes critical to ensuring that the destination is portrayed in the desired way.

Sport can create immediate name brand recognition for its host and vice versa. When sport and destinations are highly successful at cobranding, it is nearly impossible to think of one (sport) without the other (destinations). Consider the following: Innsbruck and Lake Placid (Winter Olympic Games), Indianapolis (Indy 500), Pamplona (San Fermin Festival, Running of the Bulls), and Dakar (Rally). Chalip and Costa (2006) argue that some brands are so closely associated with the host destination that it goes beyond cobranding. The sport tourism event can be viewed as an extension of the destination brand. It is contended that the Cape Argus Pick n Pay Cycle Tour, which has attracted about 35,000 cyclists to Cape Town annually since 1978, can be considered a brand extension. The race route features 104 kilometers of the scenic Cape Peninsula.

An element that seems to receive little attention in the success of building destination brands is community support for the event. In fact, this aspect was rated the single most important determining factor among destination and event marketers in Australia (Chalip, 2005). A portfolio of sport tourism events is required to sustain the impact of events on the destination brand and to enhance the reach and frequency of destination-specific messages. But only sport tourism events most suited to building the destination brand should be included (Chalip & Costa, 2006). Furthermore, other sport tourism attractions and activities that complement events in the overall destination marketing communications mix should also be considered (Chalip, 2005).

The perceived attractiveness of the host community (alternative attractions, climate, culture, nightlife, shopping, proximity to relatives and friends, and so on) elicits larger visitor groups and stimulates relatively more spending from sport tourists. A sport event destination may not possess warm, sunny weather, snow-capped mountains, or white sand beaches, but other regional attractions, in aggregate, may encourage sport tourists to extend their stays. For example, aside from the Little League World Series, Williamsport, Pennsylvania, is not known for or marketed as a tourism destination. The area boasts no distinguishing natural resources or other unique attractions. Little League officials have staged a parade and developed a self-contained entertainment complex with a museum, conference facility, recreation center, park, and lodging accommodations, in addition to the sport stadiums and practice and training facilities, to keep visitors longer.

Social Costs and Benefits of Sport Tourism

As revealed in table 22.4, generic survey statements explore a range of social costs and benefits attributed to events: entertainment, economic benefits, community pride, regional promotion, use of public funds, disruption to locals, community injustice, loss of access to public facilities, development and maintenance of public facilities, poor behavior, and environmental impacts. Fredline et al. (2003) have developed sound, reliable testing instruments to measure sport tourism social impacts.

Crime (or the perception of crime) is a major deterrent to sport tourism and can be linked to the regional showcase element. The stakes were high for South Africa and the 2010 FIFA World Cup as the country sought to combat crime and the perception of crime. Government officials and business leaders wagered that a successful event would bring thousands of tourists, economic prosperity, and social cohesion to the country postapartheid. To remedy its high crime image and protect its financial investment in advance of 2010, the South African government developed a comprehensive safety and security plan. Key elements included working with international agencies to gather intelligence, focusing

Table 22.4   Measures to Assess Residents' Perceptions of Sport Event Social Impacts (Responses: Agree, Disagree, Don't Know)

Impact	Statement
Entertainment	The EVENT gave REGION residents an opportunity to attend an interesting event, have fun with their family and friends, and interact with new people.
Economic benefits	The EVENT was good for the economy because the money that visitors spend when they come for the event helps to stimulate the economy, stimulates employment opportunities, and is good for local business.
Community pride	The EVENT made local residents feel more proud of their city and made them feel good about themselves and their community.
Regional showcase	The EVENT showcased REGION in a positive light. This helps to promote a better opinion of our region and encourages future tourism or business investment.
Public money	The EVENT was a waste of public money; that is, too much public money was spent on the event that would be better spent on other public activities.
Disruption to local residents	The EVENT disrupted the lives of local residents and created inconvenience. While the event was on, problems like traffic congestion, parking difficulties, and excessive noise were worse than usual.
Community injustice	The EVENT was unfair to ordinary residents, and the costs and benefits were distributed unfairly across the community.
Loss of use of public facilities	The EVENT denied local residents access to public facilities; that is, roads, parks, sporting facilities, public transport, or other facilities were less available to local residents because of closure or overcrowding.
Maintenance of public facilities	The EVENT promoted development and better maintenance of public facilities such as roads, parks, sporting facilities, and public transport.
Bad behavior	The EVENT was associated with some people behaving inappropriately, perhaps in a rowdy and delinquent way, or engaging in excessive drinking, drug use, or other criminal behavior.
Environmental impact	The EVENT had a negative impact on the environment through excessive litter or pollution or damage to natural areas.
Prices	The EVENT led to increases in the price of some things such as some goods and services and property values or rental costs.

Adapted from Fredline, Jago, & Deery (2003).

on border security at ports of entry, providing route security, establishing key football tourist nodes in host cities, acquiring state-of-the-art information and communication military technology, and deploying a dedicated force of 41,000 officers (GCIS, 2008). Moreover, R665 million (US$85 million) was spent on procuring special security equipment, and R640 million (US$82 million) was spent on deploying officers specifically for the event.

Price inflation may occur in cities hosting megaevents well before the event begins (Beard, 2008). Property values in London's boroughs where Olympic venues will be sited are expected to rise 3.3 percent (Kavetsos, 2009). On another note, a sport megaevent may provide entertainment for many locals (in addition to tourists) and elevate civic pride. In advance of Canterbury's hosting of the Tour de France Stage 1 race, Bull and Lovell (2007) found that the vast majority of Canterbury residents were aware of the event and that many planned to watch the race or participate in related activities. Despite the potential for various negative impacts, support for the decision to host the event was overwhelming.

Learning Activity

Considering the 2010 FIFA World Cup in South Africa, discuss the role and influence of media coverage and perceptions of crime on a potential sport tourist's decision to visit a host city.

Residents and Mega Sport Events

Residents in host cities experience firsthand the impacts of megaevents during the event lifecycle: application and bidding, preparation, operation, and legacy stages. For an Olympic Games, residents may have encountered sport tourists directly or been affected indirectly by their presence during the Games. Following the Games, residents may use new or improved transportation systems, accommodations, and other infrastructure in the host city or region. They are therefore in a unique position to evaluate the event as taxpayers, hosts, consumers of infrastructure, and possible consumers of Olympic sport venues. Residents may experience sport side by side with sport participants and spectators. For example, among the 40,000 runners in the Berlin Marathon are a mix of Berliners and visitors.

Previous studies of residents and major sport events include the America's Cup (Soutar & McLeod, 1993), Formula One (Fredline & Faulkner, 2002), and the Olympic Games (Preuss, 2004; Cashman, 2003; Mihalik, 2003; Ritchie, 2000), among other events (Turco, 1998). With respect to the Olympic Games, patterns of residents' perceptions are remarkably consistent across decades, continents, and cultures. Resident surveys implemented after an Olympic Games report reductions in negative responses regarding concerns expressed before the Games. Longitudinal studies (1991–1994) at the national (Norway) and local (Lillehammer) levels surrounding the 1994 Lillehammer Winter Olympics found responses preceding the Olympic Games to be unfavorable (55 percent and 50

percent respectively). Postevent research found significant increases in positive evaluations (80 percent national, 88 percent local). Unlike Torino, Lillehammer had a substantial number of residents opposed to the bid (30 percent). Before the 1996 Atlanta Summer Olympic Games, residents expressed concerns over traffic, inflation, and excessive costs. After the Games the responses were more positive. The sole exception was security, given that the event was marred by an attempted attack in Centennial Olympic Park. In the landmark study by Ritchie and Aitken (1984, 1985) and extended by Ritchie and Lyons (1990), residents were asked before the 1988 Winter Olympic Games whether they thought in general that it was a good idea for Calgary to host the event. Nearly 85 percent responded positively, a figure that increased to 97.8 percent after the Games.

The megaevent lifecycle includes bid (application and candidacy), preparation, operation, and legacy stages. The length of each stage varies considerably: Two years for bidding, seven years for preparation, 17 days of operation, and a lifetime for the legacy. Public perceptions of the event shift across the lifecycle, from elation and euphoria at the bid stage; concerns over readiness, costs, anxiety, and "wait and see" in the preparation stage; relief and joy during operations; and pride, appreciation, and satisfaction following the Games. This rollercoaster pattern of resident perceptions is illustrated by Guala and Turco (2007) in their study of residents in relation to the 2006 Winter Olympic Games in Torino (see figure 22.5). Torino residents were

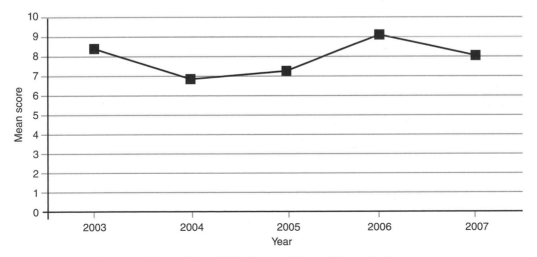

Figure 22.5 Residents' perceptions of the 2006 Torino Winter Olympic Games.

asked between 2003 and 2007 to evaluate the overall experience of hosting the Olympic Games. Residents assigned highly favorable ratings at the outset but offered less positive opinions in 2005 and 2006. After the Olympic Games, evaluations were most favorable, and they remained high one year later. The ups and downs of a megaevent as perceived by residents of the host city over the event's lifecycle are consistent across several Winter and Summer Olympic Games, spanning continents, cultures, and time.

As the sport event evolves, so too do the opinions of host residents toward the event. Therefore, it behooves the sport event organizing committee to conduct periodic assessments of residents across the event lifecycle.

Impacts in Nonhost Cities

Although much is made of the primary host cities for an Olympic Games, FIFA World Cup, or UEFA Euro Cup, other cities serve as hosts for preliminary matches, training, or team base camps. Hosting a megaevent often requires the unique natural resources, sport venues, or accommodations of neighboring cities. For the 2008 Beijing Olympic Games, equestrian events took place in Hong Kong, sailing events were held in Qingdao, and preliminary football matches were played in Shanghai, Tianjin, Shenyang, and Qinhuangdao before the finals in Beijing. The impacts of a mega sport event may be more pronounced in these satellite cities because of their relatively small size and the large numbers of spectators that they must host. For major international football competitions, teams often establish base camps away from major cities to prepare for matches and avoid the distractions of larger cities. England's national team chose the famous Buhlerhohe Schlosshotel, located in the mountains above Baden Baden, as their home away from home during the finals of the 2006 FIFA World Cup. Wives and girlfriends (WAGs), fans, and media followed in droves. Spreading the benefits beyond the host cities for the 2010 FIFA World Cup was a strategy used by various regional governments. For example, the Western Cape government embarked on base camp bids, planned public viewing areas in smaller towns like Stellenbosch and George, and promoted other locations as satellite accommodation areas.

Sport Tourism and Universal Accessibility

A potential growth segment for sport tourism is people with disabilities. About 30 percent of the world's population is made up of persons with temporary or permanent disabilities (Cuyas, 2002). About 53 million people in the United States have disabilities, of which 125,000 are active in competitive sport (McGough, 2002). United States disabled travelers spend more than $13 billion a year on travel-related services (including more than 17 million hotel visits) (Lloyd, 2003). The 1990 Americans with Disabilities Act (ADA) and other similar policies globally have enabled people with disabilities to travel more as well as lead more physically active lifestyles. Similarly, senior participation in leisure activities such as travel and sport is increasing (Delpy Neirotti, 2003). Besides the elderly and those who are clinically disabled, parents with children benefit from a more accessible environment. Their presence creates a more diverse audience. An inaccessible event may have lower attendance, causing an adverse effect on the event organization and host community economically. Sport tourism managers must therefore consider accessibility issues when planning a sport tourism event.

Examples of universal accessibility initiatives taken to enhance inclusivity are highlighted next. Because 7 to 8 percent of spectators to the 2012 Summer Olympic Games in London are expected to have disabilities (Waterman & McGrath, 2007), the Disabled Persons Transport Advisory Committee introduced a five-point plan to enable people with disabilities to get to the Games on time and without difficulties (DPTAC, 2005). The plan includes a strong legal basis, commitment from the top, adequate human and financial resources, involvement of disabled people at every level, and binding commitments to inclusive design.

Key functional areas that require policies for special accessibility needs were identified by the Special Operations Committee for the Olympic Games. These included ticketing, workforce training, technology, communications, catering, merchandise, sport presentation, and spectator services. By implementing successful universal accessibility strategies and measures, a destination will be able to attract future sport tourism events that cater better to universal accessibility in general and disabled

Sport Tour

Deaflympics

The Deaflympics has been staged every four years since 1924 and is the second longest-running multisport event in the world after the Olympics. The event in Melbourne (2005) attracted over 3,000 competitors. The 21st Summer Deaflympics was held in Taipei from September 5 through September 19, 2009. Taipei was the first city in Asia to host the Deaflympics Games. About 4,000 athletes from 80 nations competed in 20 sports: athletics, badminton, basketball, bowling, cycling, football, handball, orienteering, shooting, swimming, table tennis, tennis, volleyball, beach volleyball, water polo, freestyle wrestling, Greco-Roman wrestling, karate, judo, and taekwondo. Additional information on the Deaflympics is available at www.2009deaflympics.org. Learn more about Taipei as a tourist destination at www.taipeitravel.net.

---

sport in particular. A number of events such as the Commonwealth Games, Deaflympics, Special Olympics, and Olympics and Paralympic Games cater to many athletes with disabilities and become possibilities for future business. Moreover, a focus on accessibility can position the host city or region as an accessible tourism destination. Improvements to accommodations, facilities, transportation, and infrastructure will encourage general tourism among people with disabilities in the future. This, in turn, will also positively affect the residents of a host destination by creating a more knowledgeable and supportive society for people with disabilities.

Legacy Effects of Sport Tourism

Sustaining sport tourism is a primary management challenge in the face of finite natural resources, financial market uncertainty, and fierce competition from other destinations and competing leisure interests, such as casino gambling. The bidding process for major sport events can generate a great deal of excitement, but legacy effects are important to consider. Some events lead to "flow-on" investments, increased tourism, relocation of headquarters by associations and corporations, or mitigation of social problems in the community. Such impacts may not materialize until years after the event. Indianapolis developed a strategy involving sport as a catalyst for economic development in the late 1980s and has adhered to its plan of establishing itself as the U.S. capital of amateur sport. Several national sport governing bodies, including the National Collegiate Athletic Association (NCAA),

were lured to Indianapolis. Enduring sport and destination image and brand are also components of a sport tourism legacy. As noted earlier, sport and destinations may become inextricably linked. For example, Manchester, England, is linked to Manchester United Football Club, Kenya to distance running, and Brazil to football.

Legacy is no longer a desirable extra but an essential priority for any host destination, sport federation, or organizing committee responsible for bidding, winning, and delivering a major sport tourism event. Preuss (2007, p. 86) defined legacy as "all planned and unplanned, positive and negative, tangible and intangible structures created for and by a sport event that remain longer than the event itself." Examples of planned legacy structures may be museums or halls used for meetings or exhibits after the event; an unplanned structure would be a terrorist attack that tarnished the city's tourism image. What constitutes a positive or negative legacy structure may be in the eye of the beholder. An increase in the number of visitors may be positive for tourist-dependent business owners but negative for residents who deplore mass tourism and its consequences. Some legacy structures are long lasting, take years to develop, and occur during the buildup to an event (e.g., infrastructure). Others may occur during the event, such as viewers' impressions of Chinese culture gained from watching the Opening Ceremony of the 2008 Beijing Olympic Games.

Sport tourism event planners may have a range of legacy imperatives such as improved accessibility for persons with disabilities, youth sport development, improved tourism image, environmental neutrality, and economic stimulus, among others.

From a universal accessibility perspective, the Australian Sports Commission (1998) predicted the following legacies from the Paralympic Games in Sydney 2000:

◆ Raised awareness and appreciation of athletes and all peoples with disabilities

◆ A greater number of trained officials

◆ Improved infrastructure

◆ Improved capacity to meet the needs of large numbers of travelers with disabilities

For Beijing and the 2008 Olympic Games it was about portraying a green event and being a more open, modern society that embraced the world. The organizing committee for the 2008 Beijing Olympic Games adopted the motto "One World, One Dream" to convey an Olympic ideal shared by all. The motto may also apply to China's ambition to be the world's economic superpower. Judging by its strong foreign trade position and financial stability relative to other nations, China is in a strong position to capitalize on the 2008 Olympic Games for years to come. But the extent to which China continues to make improvements in air quality, sustainable clean energy, and recycling now that the Beijing Olympic Games are over remains to be seen.

In a developing country such as South Africa where opportunity costs are more pronounced, a legacy manager was employed as part of the organizing committee—a first for FIFA. The legacy for the 2010 FIFA World Cup goes beyond the borders of South Africa because it was the first event of its kind on the continent and the event has embraced an Africa-wide legacy program as well.

The global financial crisis that began in the fourth quarter of 2008 sent shockwaves through the sport industry. Companies cancelled or cut back on sport event sponsorships. The credit crunch made it more difficult to obtain stadium financing. For example, the British government conceded in 2008 that the 2012 Olympics budget was £500 million (US$1 billion) short of private-sector money because of the credit crunch (O'Connor, 2008), and that they had depleted half of the £1 billion (US$2 billion) contingency funds intended for emergencies. Consumers also curtailed their leisure travel and spending.

Many major corporations have devised social responsibility efforts as management and public relations strategies, including conservation and recycling programs to address positive legacy impacts. Supporting such efforts while sponsoring gas-guzzling, ear-rattling Formula One or NASCAR racing would appear to be a contradiction in corporate social responsibility. At some point, a consumer backlash against automobile racing may occur because of its profligate energy usage. Consumer resentment may cause corporate sponsors to back away from motor sport events. This forecast is not to imply that the Indianapolis 500 will eventually restrict its field to Toyota Prius hybrids or that motor sport will die, only that the contradictions will not be lost on the sport tourist as consumer.

Sport Tourism Planning and Evaluation

Major cities prepare years in advance to vie for the most coveted events in sport: the Olympic Games, World Cups, the Commonwealth Games, and so forth. Smaller cities compete for relatively smaller events including the World Games, Deaflympics, the Ryder Cup, and the World Figure Skating Championships. Some have argued (Naughright, 2004) that the playing field is uneven and stacked against developing countries that apply to host the megaevents. Africa has never hosted an Olympic Games, and the FIFA World Cup has not been to South America since Argentina hosted, and won, the 1978 tournament. Under FIFA's new rotation system, Brazil was the sole bidder for the 2014 World Cup. The country is setting aside nearly US$1 billion to update its stadiums, including the Maracanã in Rio de Janeiro, which hosted the 1950 World Cup final. Developing countries that are attempting to level the playing field can initiate joint bids, as India, Pakistan, and Sri Lanka did in their successful bid to host the 1996 Cricket World Cup. But event organization across borders brings about additional complexities to developing countries that are already competing in an uneven global political economy. Nevertheless, developing countries have not been deterred from entering the race. India hosted the 2010 Commonwealth Games and will host the 2011 Cricket World Cup. Rio de Janeiro will host the 2016 Olympics, and in 2008 Durban announced its intention to apply for the 2020 Olympic Games.

Despite the potential that sport tourism offers, cases of strategic planning in sport tourism are rare

Learning Activity

Review the bid specifications for a major sport event from the website of a sport governing body (e.g., FIFA, Olympic Games, UEFA, Formula One, ICC). Which city in your country would be most suited to host the event and why?

(Higham, 2005), probably because the focus is on the short-term gains that result from hosting sport tourism events rather than the long-term consequences for a host destination. Sport tourism planning includes planning for sport tourism events and event-related infrastructure as well as planning for other sport tourism facilities such as halls of fame and museums. Sport tourism planning has generally been geared to the tourist, and little attention has been paid to local use. Planning for sustainable sport tourism development must take into account the interests of local residents. Planning for dual use is further exacerbated by the fact that sport and tourism policy and planning usually reside in different government departments. Institutional arrangements therefore affect how sport tourism is planned at respective destinations.

Because substantial funds, especially public funds, are invested in bidding and hosting sport tourism events, significant accountability is required. Monitoring and evaluation of sport tourism initiatives should include triple bottom-line assessments (economic, social, and environmental) as well as evaluation of sponsorship effectiveness, marketing effectiveness, and media impact.

Summary

We have introduced sport tourism, defined its industry segments, described its impacts, and offered examples of sport tourism practices. This section summarizes the key points made earlier in the chapter and offers suggestions for future study in sport tourism.

Participatory sport tourism stimulates event-based sport tourism and, subsequently, celebratory sport tourism. To what extent does celebratory sport tourism influence participatory and sport event tourism, if at all? For example, are those who visit the National Basketball Hall of Fame in Springfield, Massachusetts, more (or less) likely to travel to watch or compete in basketball events? Are those who visit Wimbledon or Old Trafford more (or less) likely to watch or compete in tennis and football events? Similarly, to what extent does sport event tourism influence participatory sport tourism? For example, are visitors to the U.S. Open Golf Championship more (or less) likely to travel to play golf? Are residents who witness the Cape Argus Pick n Pay Cycle Tour more (or less) likely to participate in the Argus or travel to other cycling events around the world? During Lance Armstrong's record string of seven consecutive Tour de France victories, bicycle sales in the United States rose 27 percent.

What inhibits or constrains people from experiencing sport tourism? How do they negotiate these constraints? Typically, the constraints are lack of time, money, opportunity, or self-concept. The vast body of knowledge already existing on constraints to leisure (Jackson, 2005) can be extended to sport tourism environments. Constraints to sport tourism for persons with disabilities, which include the aforementioned constraints as well as transportation and architectural barriers, inaccessible communications, inflexible sport rules, and lack of adaptive sport equipment, offer another intriguing research opportunity.

Serious sport tourists were introduced as those who travel to pursue their leisure sport "careers." Further understanding of serious sport tourists is warranted to gain insights into their sport involvement, time and financial management priorities, and consumer behavior. The commitments of time and financial resources for elite and less skilled serious sport tourists may be compared. Elite athletes are hypothesized to spend less time and money on training and equipment because their exceptional skills and performance are sufficient for success, whereas less skilled athletes attempt to compensate by investing in training and expensive equipment.

Event-based sport tourism involves sport participants as the focal attraction and typically includes spectators, some of whom may be visitors to the host city. Most research on sport tourism focuses on megaevents in developed countries. Relatively little research has focused on events in developing countries, in part because they have not been chosen as hosts by sport governing bodies. Countries previously excluded have recently been more aggressive and competitive in their event bidding. South Africa was awarded the 2010 FIFA World Cup, and Brazil was chosen to host the event in 2014. India (Delhi) hosted the 2010 Commonwealth Games and will host the Cricket World Cup in 2011. Sport event tourism managers in developing countries, including Central European countries new to democracy, market-driven economics, and sport governance systems, face unique challenges. Their communities often lack appropriate sport venues, adequate transportation systems, and sufficient accommodations at various star ratings for large numbers of fans. They may have limited capital, be politically unstable to some degree, be oriented to a single sport, and have a male-dominated culture. One may argue that all countries are developing or redeveloping because of globalization, population shifts, immigration, changes in political ideology, adaptation to a market economy, diminishing supplies of food and water, imbalances in supply and demand for oil and energy, and climate change. Each of the aforementioned factors presents a unique research avenue for scholars interested in sport tourism in developing countries.

Some sport events appear to attract high-end consumer groups because of the relative cost of entry (e.g., America's Cup yacht race, Masters Golf Tournament, Singapore Formula One), and others draw thriftier visitors (Yu & Turco, 2000). Per day and per capita spending would presumably be higher among spectators and participants who attend upscale events, but this is not always the case. Investigations into the sport lifestyles of the rich and famous (as well as the poor and unnoticed) may shed light on this question. Few published studies have provided glimpses into the sporting involvement of the super rich in polo, yachting, fox hunting, and so on, likely because of participant privacy issues.

Lastly, the watching friends and relatives market at sport contests should be studied in relation to event prestige. Because WFRs are often seasoned, repeat consumers of sport events, they have devised ways to keep travel costs in check. A reasonable hypothesis, however, is that greater event prestige will negate the decreasing spending effects associated with repeat visitors.

? Review and Discussion Questions

1. What activities do participatory, event-based, and celebratory sport tourists engage in?

2. What distinguishes serious sport tourists from other participatory sport tourists?

3. List examples of the suppliers and consumers of sport tourism. Which individuals are both suppliers and consumers? Explain.

4. How would you count the number of sport tourists visiting a ski resort community for the season? Attending a Winter Olympic Games?

5. Think of a recent international sport event. Did publicity surrounding the event show an attempt to create a destination brand for the city or country where the event was held? In what ways?

6. What are some of the possible negative impacts on residents because of sport tourism?

7. If you were planning a sport tourism event to be held in your community, what legacy effects would you predict for the event? What measures would you take to ensure a positive legacy?

References

Chapter 1

AFP. (2008, 18 May). *Japanese baseball joins fight against global warming*. Retrieved February 27, 2009, from http://afp.google.com

Amis, J., & Cornwell, B. (Eds.) (2005a). *Global sport sponsorship*. New York: Berg.

Amara, M., Henry, I., Liang, J., & Uchiumi, K. (2005). The governance of professional soccer: Five case studies—Algeria, China, England, France, and Japan. *European Journal of Sport Science*, 5(4), 189–206.

Amis, J., & Cornwell, B. (2005b). Sport sponsorship in a global age. In J. Amis and B. Cornwell (eds.), *Global sport sponsorship*. New York: Berg.

Appadurai, A. (1990). Disjuncture and difference in the global cultural economy. *Theory, Culture, & Society*, 7(2/3), 295–310.

Associated Press. (2009, 25 May). *US, Iran could meet—on soccer field*. Retrieved July 22, 2009, from http://kdrv.com/page/120772

Baghdadi, G. (2009, 17 July). *Non-aligned nations vow to keep up "self-determination."* Retrieved July 25, 2009, from www.cbsnews.com/blogs/2009/07/17/world/worldwatch/entry5177137.shtml

Bairner, A. (2001). *Sport, nationalism, and globalization*. Albany: State University of New York Press.

Baker, W., DeTienne, K., & Smart, K. (1998). How Fortune 500 companies are using

electronic resume management systems. *Business Communication Quarterly*, 61(3), 8–19.

Baker, W. (2007). *Playing with God: Religion and modern sport*. Cambridge, MA: Harvard University Press.

Baxter, K. (2010, 14 June). World Cup: FIFA to fans—buzz off. *Los Angeles Times* (internet edition). Retrieved June 25, 2010, from http://latimesblogs.latimes.com/sports_blog/2010/06/world-cup-fifa-to-fans-buzz-off.html

Baxter, L., & Montgomery, B. (1996). *Relating: Dialogues & dialectics*. New York: The Guilford Press.

Beck-Burridge, M., & Walton, J. (2001). *Sports sponsorship and brand development*. Hampshire, United Kingdom: Palgrave.

Blanchard, K. (2000). The anthropology of sport. In J. Coakley and E. Dunning (Eds.) *Handbook of sport studies* (pp. 144–156). London: Sage.

Bluedorn, A., & Denhardt, R. (1988). Time and organizations. *Journal of Management*, 14(2), 299–320.

Bourhis, J., Adams, C., Titsworth, S., & Harter, L. (2004). *Selected material from human communication*. New York: McGraw-Hill Custom.

Cantelon, H., & Letters, M. (2000). The making of the IOC environmental policy as the third dimension of the Olympic Movement. *International Review for the Sociology of Sport*, 35(3), 294–308.

Carpenter, J. (2000). *Legal concepts in sport: A primer* (2nd ed.). Reston, VA: American Association for Active Lifestyles and Fitness.

Chalip, L. (2006). Towards social leverage of sport events. *Journal of Sport & Tourism*, 11(2), 109–127.

Chalip, A. Johnson, & L. Stachura (Eds.), *National sports policies* (pp. 23–38). Westport, CT: Greenwood Press.

Championing environmental legacies. (2009, 18 April). Retrieved July 22, 2009, from www.vancouver2010.com

Chernushenko, D., van der Kamp, A., & Stubbs, D. (2001). *Sustainable sport management: Running an environmentally, socially, and economically, responsible organization*. Nairobi, Kenya: United Nations Environment Programme.

Coakley, J. (2003). *Sport in society*. New York: McGraw-Hill.

Coakley, J., & Donnelly, P. (1999). *Inside sports*. London: Routledge.

Cober, R.T., Brown, D.J., Blumental, A.J., Doverspike, D., & Levy, P. (2000). The quest for qualified job surfer: It's time the public sector catches the wave. *Public Personnel Management*, 29, 479–494.

Collina, P. (2003). *The rules of the game*. London: Macmillan.

Condie, S. (2009, 28 April). *Richest English Premier League clubs deep in debt*. Retrieved July 28, 2009, from http://sports.yahoo.com

Coplin, W., & O'Leary, M. (1983). *Introduction to political risk analysis*. Croton-on-Hudson, NY: Policy Studies Associates.

Dagas, S., & Benn, T. (2006). Young Muslim women's experiences of Islam and physical education in Greece and Britain: A comparative study. *Sport, Education and Society*, 11(1), 21–38.

Dewey, J. (1916). *Democracy and education: An introduction to the philosophy of education*. New York: Free Press.

DiMeglio, S. (2008, 27 August). LPGA hopes language policy makes players more accessible. *USA Today*. Retrieved July 17, 2009, from www.usatody.com/sports/golf/lpga/2008-08-26-languge-policy_N.htm

Dolles, H., & Söderman, S. (2008). Mega-sporting events in Asia—impacts on society, business and management: An introduction. *Asian Business & Management*, 7, 147–162.

Doob, L. (1971). *Patterning of time*. New Haven, CT: Yale University Press.

Dowd, A. (2010, 3 February). *Vancouver gets climate change bronze.* Retrieved June 23, 2010, from www.reuters.com/article/idUSTRE61247N20100203

Egan, A. (2008, 7 August). *The world's most expensive stadiums.* Retrieved July 28, 2009, from http://sports.yahoo.com

English Rugby. (2009, 19 February). *RFU sets up credit crunch hotline.* Retrieved June 23, 2010, from www.scrum.com/scrum/rugby/story/92159.html

ESPN.com News Services. (2009, 18 May). *Report: U.S. government may subpoena as many as 104 MLB players.* Retrieved July 25, 2009, from http://sports.espn.com/mlb/news/story?id=3401868

Feldman, D. (1976). A contingency theory of socialization. *Administrative Science Quarterly, 21,* 433–452.

FIFA. (2009). *Our mission.* Retrieved July 17, 2009, from www.fifa.com/aboutfifa

Finn, G. (1991). Racism, religion and social prejudice: Irish Catholic clubs, soccer, and Scottish society. *International Journal of the History of Sport, 8*(1), 72–95.

Finn, G. (1994). Faith, hope and bigotry. Case studies of anti-Catholic prejudice in Scottish soccer and society. In G. Jarvie & G. Walker (Eds.), *Ninety minute patriots? Scottish sport in the making of the nation* (pp. 91–112). Leicester, United Kingdom: Leicester University Press.

FIA. (2009). *Make cars green.* Retrieved July 27, 2009, from www.makecarsgreen.com

Flanagin, A., & Waldeck, J. (2004). Technology use and organizational newcomer socialization. *Journal of Business Communication, 41,* 137–165.

Flyvbjerg, B., Bruzelius, N., & Rothengatter, W. (2003). *Megaprojects and risk.* Cambridge, United Kingdom: Cambridge University Press.

Foster, K. (2005). Is there a global sports law? *Entertainment and Sports Law Journal* [online journal], 2(1).

Friedman, J. (1990). Being in the world: Globalization and localization. *Theory, Culture & Society, 7,* 311–328.

Gems, G., Borish, L., & Pfister, G. (2008). *Sports in American history: From colonization to globalization.* Champaign, IL: Human Kinetics.

Giulianotti, R., Bonney, N., & Hepworth, M. (1994). *Football, violence and social identity.* London: Routledge.

Goldenbach, A. (2007, 28 September). After NFL's first prayer, religion touched down. *Washington Post.* Retrieved July 22, 2009, from http://washingtonpost.com

Gratton, C., Shibli, S., & Coleman, R. (2005). Sport and economic regeneration in cities. *Urban Studies, 42*(5/6), 985–999.

Gronewold, N. (2009, 18 February). Beijing Olympics met or exceeded green goals. *Scientific American.* Retrieved June 23, 2010, from www.scientificamerican.com/article.cfm?id=beijing-olympics-met-or-e

Hall, E. (1983). *The dance of life: The other dimension of time.* Garden City, NY: Anchor Press.

Hanvey, R. (1976). *An attainable global perspective.* Denver, CO: Center for Teaching International Relations.

Hargreaves, J. (2002). Globalisation theory, global sport, and nations and nationalism. In J. Sugden & A. Tomlinson (Eds.), *Power games: A critical sociology of sport* (pp. 25–43). London: Routledge.

Harris, P., & Moran, R. (1991). *Managing cultural differences* (3rd ed.). Houston, TX: Gulf.

Harris, P., Moran, R., & Moran, S. (2004). *Managing cultural differences: Global leadership strategies for the 21st century.* Oxford, United Kingdom: Butterworth-Heinemann.

Hersey, P. (1984). *The situational leader.* Escondido, CA: Center for Leadership Studies.

Higgs, R. (1995). *God in the stadium: Sports & religion in America.* Lexington: University Press of Kentucky.

Hoffman, S. (1992). Evangelicalism and the revitalization of religious ritual in sport. In S. Hoffman (Ed.), *Sport and religion* (pp. 111–125). Champaign, IL: Human Kinetics.

Horne, J. (2004). The global game of football: The 2002 World Cup and regional development in Japan. *Third World Quarterly, 25*(7), 1233–1244.

Horne, J. (2006). *Sport in consumer culture.* New York: Palgrave.

Horne, J., & Manzenreiter, W. (Eds.) (2004). *Japan, Korea and the 2002 World Cup.* London: Routledge.

Houlihan, B. (1991). *The government and politics of sport.* London: Routledge.

Jablin, F.M. (1985) Task/work relationships: A life-span perspective. In M. Knapp & G. Miller (Eds.), *Handbook of interpersonal communication* (pp. 615–654). Beverly Hills, CA: Sage.

Jablin, F. (1987). Organizational entry, assimilation, and exit. In F. Jablin, L. Putnam, K. Roberts, & L. Porter (Eds.), *Handbook of organizational communication: An interdisciplinary perspective* (pp. 679–740). Newbury Park, CA: Sage.

Jablin, F. (2000). Organizational entry, assimilation, and disengagement/exit. In F. Jablin & L. Putnam (Eds.), *The new handbook of organizational communication: Advances in theory, research, and methods* (pp. 732–818). Thousand Oaks, CA: Sage.

JCN Newswire. (2008, 3 July). *Mazda to provide electricity for Japanese pro baseball's 2008 All-Star Games.* Retrieved February 27, 2009, from http://allbusiness.com

Jenkins, G. (2008, 18 December). *Rugby looks to sidestep the credit crunch.* Retrieved June 23, 2010, from www.scrum.com/scrum/rugby/story/88610.html

Katz, D., & Kahn, R. (1978). *The social psychology of organizations.* (2nd ed.) New York: Wiley.

Keys, B. (2006). *Globalizing sport: National rivalry and international community in the 1930s.* Cambridge, MA: Harvard University Press.

Kolb, D. (1984). *Experiential learning: Experience as the source of learning and development.* Englewood Cliffs, NJ: Prentice Hall

Leonard, T. (2008, 21 July). West Ham fans brawl with Columbus Crew as football hooliganism hits the US. *Telegraph.* Retrieved July 14, 2009, from http://telegraph.co.uk

Leys, C. (2001). *Market-driven politics.* London: Verso.

Lindsey, I. (2008). Conceptualizing sustainability in sports development. *Leisure Studies, 27*(3), 279–294.

Maffesoli, M. (1996). *The time of the tribes.* Thousand Oaks, CA: Sage.

Magdalinski, T., & Chandler, T. (2002). *With God on their side: Sport in the service of religion.* London: Routledge.

Magnússon, G. (2001). The internationalization of sports: The case of Iceland. *International Review for the Sociology of Sport, 36,* 59–69.

Maguire, J. (1999). *Global sport: Identities, societies, civilizations.* Oxford, United Kingdom: Polity Press.

Maguire, J., Poulton, E., & Possamai, C. (1999). Weltkrieg III? Media coverage of England versus Germany in Euro 96. *Journal of Sport & Social Issues, 23*(4), 439–454.

Matchett, S. (1999). *The mechanics tale: Life in the pitlanes of Formula One.* London: Orion Books.

Matchett, S. (2005). *The chariot makers: Assembling the perfect Formula 1 car.* London: Orion Books.

Matsuda, G. (2010, 17 February). *Overwhelming outrage about NBC's Winter Olympics coverage should move IOC to end exclusive TV rights deals.* Retrieved June 23, 2010, from http://frozenroyalty.net/2010/02/17/overwhelming-outrage-about-nbcs-winter-olympics-coverage-should-move-ioc-to-end-exclusive-tv-rights-deals/

McCormack, G. (2002). Things more important than football? Japan, Korea and the 2002 World Cup. In J. Horne and W. Mazenrieter (Eds.), *Japan, Korea and the 2002 World Cup* (pp. 29–42). London: Routledge.

McHenry, J. (1980). The use of sports in policy implementation: The case of Tanzania. *Journal of Modern African Studies, 18*(2), 237–256.

Mead, G. (1934). *Mind, self, & society from the standpoint of a social behaviorist (volume 1).* Chicago: University of Chicago Press.

Nafziger, J. (1992). International sports law: A replay of characteristics and trends. *American Journal of International Law, 86*(3), 489–518.

Naisbitt, J. (1994). *Global paradox.* New York: Avon Books.

Nederveen Pieterse, J. (2003). *Globalization and culture: Global mélange.* Lanham, MD: Rowman & Littlefield.

Noble Wilford, J. (2007, 18 September). World's languages dying off rapidly. *New York Times.* Retrieved July 25, 2009, from www.newyorktimes.com/2007/09/18/world/18cnd-langauge.html

Oberjuerge, P. (1998, 21 June). *World Cup: U.S. eliminated from Cup after 2-1 loss to Iran.* Retrieved July 22, 2009, from www.soccertimes.comworldcup/1998/games/jun21.htm

O'Donnell, C. (2001, May). *Breaking down language barriers—how hockey teams cope with team members who speak different languages.* Retrieved July 17, 2009, from http://findarticles .com/p/articles/mi_m0FCM/is_7_29/ai_73023295

Ohmann, S., Jones, I., & Wilkes, K. (2006). The perceived social impacts of the football World Cup on Munich residents. *Journal of Sport and Tourism, 11*(2), 129–152.

Olympic Day spreads Olympic values worldwide. (2010, 11 June). Retrieved June 22, 2010, from www.olympic.org/en/content/Olympism-in-Action/At-grassroot-level/Olympic_Day_spreads_Olympic_values_worldwide

Payutto, P. (1998). *Buddhist economics: A middle way for the market place.* Bangkok: Buddhaddhamma Foundation.

Perry, N. (2005). *Close encounters of another kind: Nationalism, media representations and advertising in New Zealand rugby.* In S. Jackson and D. Andrews (Eds.), Sport, culture, and advertising: Identities, commodities and the politics of representation (pp. 154–171). New York: Routledge.

Pfahl, M. (2002). Buddhism and systems thinking: A conceptual framework for management actions in Thailand. *Journal of Global Business Review, 1*(1), 46–55.

Pfahl, M., & Bates, B. (2008). This is not a race, this is a farce: Formula One and the Indianapolis Motor Speedway tire crisis. *Public Relations Review, 34*(2), 135–144.

Plamintr, S. (1994). *Getting to know Buddhism.* Bangkok, Thailand: Buddhadhamma Foundation.

Price, J. (2001). *From season to season: Sport as American religion.* Macon, GA: Mercer University Press.

Reuters. (2001, 28 September). *Hancock turns up pressure on IOC.* Retrieved June 23, 2010, from www.sportbusiness.com/news/130713/hancock-turns-up-pressure-on-ioc

Reuters. (2009, 28 April). *Serie A—Juventus lose racism appeal.* Retrieved July 25, 2009, from http://uk.eurosport.yahoo.com

Ritzer, G. (1993). *The McDonaldization of society.* Newbury Park, CA: Pine Forge.

Ritzer, W. (2007). *The McDonaldization of society.* Thousand Oaks, CA: Sage.

Schmidt, C. (2006). Putting the Earth in play: Environmental awareness and sports. *Environmental Health Perspectives, 114*(5), A286–A295.

Senge, P. (1994). *The fifth discipline: The art and practice of the learning organization.* New York: Doubleday Business.

Sewart, J. (1987). The commodification of sport. *International Journal for the Sociology of Sport, 22*(3), 171–190.

Shropshire, K., & Davis, T. (2003). *The business of sports agents.* Philadelphia: University of Pennsylvania Press.

Siegfried, J., & Zimbalist, A. (2000). The economics of sport facilities and their communities. *Journal of Economic Perspectives, 14*(3), 95–114.

Simson, V., & Jennings, A. (1992). *The lords of the rings: Power, money, and drugs in the modern Olympics.* London: Simon & Schuster.

Sklair, L. (2002). *Globalization.* Oxford, United Kingdom: Oxford University Press.

Sorek, T. (2002). The Islamic Soccer League in Israel: Setting moral boundaries by taming the wild. *Identities: Global Studies in Culture and Power, 9,* 445–470.

Stahl, H., Hochfeld, C., & Schmied, M. (2004). *Green goal: Legacy report.* Retrieved June 15, 2009, from www.fifa.com

Stewart, R. (2007). *Sport funding and finance.* Oxford, United Kingdom: Butterworth-Heinemann.

Stone, D., Stone-Romero, E., & Lukaszewski, K. (2006). Factors affecting the acceptance and effectiveness of electronic human resource systems. *Human Resource Management Review, 16,* 229-244,

Sustainability. (2009). *About sustainability.* Retrieved July 22, 2009, from www.london2010.com/plans/sustainability/index.php.

Taylor, F. (1911). *The principles of scientific management.* New York: Harper.

Thoma, J., & Chalip, L. (1996). *Sport governance in the global community.* Morgantown, WV: Fitness Information Technology.

Thurow, L. (1996). *The future of capitalism: How today's economic forces shape tomorrow's world.* New York: Penguin Group.

Tomlinson, A. (2002). Theorizing spectacle: Beyond Debord. In J. Sugden and A. Tomlinson (Eds.), *Power games: A critical sociology of sport* (pp. 44–60). London: Routledge.

Tomlinson, J. (1999). *Globalization and culture.* Chicago: University of Chicago Press.

Tribunal Arbitral du Sport. (2009). *20 questions about the CAS.* Retrieved July 25, 2009, from www.tas-cas.org/20question

UPI. (2009a, 5 April). *Button wins the Malaysian Grand Prix.* Retrieved July 17, 2009, from www.upi.com

UPI. (2009b, 26 February). *Report: NBA takes out $200 million loan.* Retrieved July 28, 2009, from http://upi.com

Vancouver Olympic Games. (2008, 8 September). *Demand for 2010 Olympic sponsorship strong after Beijing 2008 Olympic Games.* Retrieved July 25, 2009, from http://vancouver2010.comen/news.

Vancouver Olympics. (2010a). *Environmental assessment.* Retrieved June 23, 2010, from www.vancouver2010.com/more-2010-information/sustainability/reports-and-resources/environmental-assessment/

Vancouver Olympics. (2010b). *Vancouver debrief comes to an end.* Retrieved June 23, 2010, from www.olympic.org/en/content/Olympic-Games/Vancouver-2010/Vancouver-2010/?articleNewsGroup=-1&articleId=91389

Wakeford, N. (2003). The embedding of local culture in global communication: Independent Internet cafés in London. *New Media & Society, 5*(3), 379–399.

Walseth, K. (2006). Young Muslim women and sport: The impact of identity work. *Leisure Studies, 25*(1), 75–94.

Watts, J. (2008, 29 July). Olympics environment: Beijing shuts all building sites and more factories to clear the smog. *Guardian.* Retrieved July 22, 2009, from www.guardian.co.uk/sport/2008/jul/29/olympicgames2008.china

Willenbacher, E. (2004, Fall). Regulating sports agents: Why current federal and state efforts do not deter the unscrupulous athlete-agent and how a national licensing system may cure the problem. *St. John's Law Review.* Retrieved July 25, 2009, from http://findarticles.com/p/articles/mi_qa3735/is_200410/ai_9478272

Wise, A., & Meyer, B. (1997). *International sports law and business.* Boston: Kluwer Law International.

Withers, T. (2009, 24 May). *Cavs sign ownership deal with China group.* Retrieved July 11, 2009, from http://sports.yahoo.com

Zwick, D., & Dieterle, O. (2005). The [e-]business of sport sponsorship. In J. Amis & T. Cornwell (Eds.), *Global sport sponsorship* (pp. 127–146). New York: Berg.

Chapter 2

Britcher, C. (2002, May). Major leagues seek foreign field. *Sportbusiness International,* pp. 48–51.

Brown, M. (2008, September 4). *Complete listing: NFL broadcasting in 231 countries and territories.* Retrieved March 30, 2009, from www.bizoffootball.com/index.php?option=com_content&view=article&id=312:complete-listing-nfl-broadcasted-in-231-countries-and-territories&catid=40:television&Itemid=57

Chen, M. (1999). *Taiwan: Fitness equipment, industry sector analysis.* Washington, DC: U.S. and Foreign Commercial Service and U.S. Department of State.

Daft, R., & Marcic, D. (1998). *Understanding management* (2nd ed.). Forth Worth, TX: Dryden.

Gladden, J.M., & Lizzandra, M. (1998). International sport. In L.P. Masteralexis, C.A. Barr, & M.A. Hums (eds.), *Principles and practice of sport management* (pp. 208–242). Gaithersburg, MD: Aspen.

Joining forces: Yankees, Man Utd announce joint marketing deal. (2001, February 6). Retrieved June 16, 2008, from http://sportsillustrated.cnn.com/soccer/news/2001/02/06/yankees_united_ap/

Kaplan, D. (2002, May 12–19). SFX sports in Russian alliance. *Street and Smith's Sportbusiness,* p. 5.

Lefton, T. (2009, March 2). WBC touts regional sponsors for 2009 event. *Street & Smith's SportsBusiness Journal.* Retrieved March 30, 2009, from www.sportsbusinessjournal.com/article/61698

Lombardo, J. (2003, June 14–21). Rockets think globally, act locally for arena name. *Street and Smith's Sportbusiness*, p. 34.

NFL Europa closes. (2008). Retrieved June 16, 2008, from www.nfl.com/news/story?id=09000d5d801308ec&template=without-video&confirm=true

Roberts, E.B., & Mizouchi, R. (1989). Inter-firm technological collaboration: The case of Japanese biotechnology. *International Journal of Technology Management, 4*(1), 43–61.

RNCOS. (2008, July 1). *Skills and low-cost benefits underpinning China footwear industry.* Retrieved October 8, 2008, from www.global-production.com/footwear/news/

SGB (Sporting Goods Business). (2008, September) *Update: First L.L. Bean store to open in China.* Retrieved October 9, 2008, from www.sportinggoodsbusiness.com

SGB (Sporting Goods Business). (2008, November) *Update: Adidas to sponsor Russia Football Union.* Retrieved December 1, 2008, from www.sportinggoodsbusiness.com

SGB (Sporting Goods Business). (2000, March 27). *Ajay makes golf franchise deal in South Africa.* Retrieved October 9, 2008, from www.sportinggoodsbusiness.com

Tedeschi, M. (1997, April 14). *Report blasts Nike factory conditions; company vows changes in contract plant.* Sporting Goods Business, p. 46.

Thorne, G. (2009, March 29). 2009 WBC: A tournament to remember. *USA Today.* Retrieved March 30, 2009, from www.usatoday.com/sports/baseball/columnist/thorne/2009-03-29-thorne-column_N.htm

Chapter 3

Allen, D.G. (2006). Do organizational socialization tactics influence newcomer embeddedness and turnover? *Journal of Management, 32*(2), 237–256.

Breitenecker, R.L. (1992). The Caribbean Basin Initiative—an effective U.S. trade policy facilitating economic liberalization in the region: The Costa Rican example. *Law & Policy in International Business, 23,* 913–949.

Cable, D.M., & Parsons, C.K. (2001). Socialization tactics and person-organization fit. *Personnel Psychology, 54,* 1–23.

Carte, P., & Fox, C. (2004). *Bridging the culture gap: A practical guide to international business communication.* London: Canning.

Chaney, L.H., & Martin, J.S. (2004). *Intercultural business communication* (3rd ed.). Old Tappan, NJ: Prentice Hall, Pearson Education.

Chun, S., Gentry, J.W., & McGinnis, L.P. (2004). Cultural differences in fan ritualization: A cross-cultural perspective of the ritualization of American and Japanese baseball fans. *Advances in Consumer Research, 31,* 503–508.

Dawson, L. (2008). Building the bird's nest. *Architectural Review, 223*(1337), 96–97.

Dunning, E. (1989). Multinational enterprises and the growth of services: Some conceptual and theoretical issues. *Services Industries Journal, 9,* 5–39.

Hall, J.C., & Leeson, P.T. (2007). Good for the goose, bad for the gander: International labor standards and comparative development. *Journal of Labor Research, 28,* 658–676.

Hofstede, G. (1980). *Culture's consequences: International differences in work-related values.* Beverly Hills, CA: Sage.

Hofstede, G. (1991). *Cultures and organizations. Software of the mind.* London: McGraw-Hill.

Hofstede, G., & Bond, M.H. (1984). Hofstede's culture dimensions: An independent validation using Rokeach's value survey. *Journal of Cross-Cultural Psychology, 15,* 417–433.

Jackson, S.J., Brandl-Bredenbeck, H.P., & John, A. (2005). Lost in translation: Cultural differences in the interpretation of commercial media violence. *International Journal of Sport Management and Marketing, 1*(1/2), 155–168.

Lombardo, J. (2010, May 24). After two years, NBA China on steady course. *Street & Smith's SportsBusiness Journal.* Retrieved August 20, 2010, from www.sportsbussiness-journal.com

LPGA.com, (n.d.). *KOLON–LPGA cross-cultural professional development program.* Retrieved September 10, 2010, from www.lpga.com/content_1.aspx?pid=20082&mid=2

MacIntosh, E., & Doherty, A. (2008). Inside the Canadian fitness industry: Development of a conceptual framework of organizational culture. *International Journal of Sport Management, 9*(3), 303–327.

Maguire, J., & Bale, J. (1994). Introduction: Sports labour migration in the global arena. In J. Bale & J. Maguire (Eds.) (pp. 1–21). *The global sports arena: Athletic talent migration in an interdependent world.* London: Fran Cass.

Maguire, J., Jarvie, G., Mansfield, L., & Bradley, J. (2002). *Sports worlds. A sociological perspective.* Champaign, IL: Human Kinetics.

Martin, J. (1992). *Cultures in organizations: Three perspectives.* New York: Oxford University Press.

Rabotin, M. (2008, July). Deconstructing the successful global leader. *American Society for Training and Development,* pp. 54–59.

Samiee, S. (1999). The internationalization of services: Trends, obstacles and issues. *Journal of Services Marketing, 13,* 319–328.

Schein, E.H. (1985). *Organizational culture and leadership.* San Francisco: Jossey Bass.

Schaub, C., & Schindhelm, M. (2008). *Bird's nest: Herzog & de Meuron in China* [Motion picture], Brooklyn, NY: Icarus Films.

Shenkar, O., Luo, Y., & Yeheskel, O. (2008). From "distance" to "friction": Substituting metaphors and redirecting intercultural research. *Academy of Management Review, 33*(4), 905–923.

Smith, D.C. (2008). Pulling the plug on culture shock: A seven step plan for managing travel anxiety. *Journal of Global Business Issues, 2*(1), 41–46.

Sofka, J. (2008, October 27). Any company's China strategy must account for obstacles. *Street & Smith's SportsBusiness Journal.* Retrieved August 20, 2010, from www.sportsbussinessjournal.com

Stempler, R.H. (1991). Costa Rica: A Nirvana for export manufacturers? *Transnational Lawyer, 4,* 202–252.

Wilson, R. (2008, September 3). LPGA's English-only rule backfires, could lead to lost sponsors. Retrieved September 10, 2010, from http://golf.fanhouse.com/2008/09/03/lpgas-english-only-rule-backfires-could-lead-to-lost-sponsors/

Chapter 4

AAUSports.org. (2008). *About AAU.* Retrieved November 20, 2008, from http://aausports.org/default.asp?a=pg_about_aau.htm

Barr, C. (2009). Collegiate sport. In L.P. Masteralexis, C. Barr, & M. Hums (Eds.), *Principles and practice of sport management* (pp. 205–232). Sudbury, MA: Jones and Bartlett.

Berry, R.C., Gould, W.B., & Staudohar, P.D. (1986). *Labor relations in professional sports.* Dover, MA: Auburn House.

Bloom, M., Grant, M., & Watt, D. (2005). *Strengthening Canada: The socio-economic benefits of sport participation in Canada.* Ottawa, ON: Conference Board of Canada.

British Colleges Sport. (n.d.). *Competition programme.* Retrieved July 13, 2010, from www.britishcollegessport.org/competitionprogramme/tabid/184/default.aspx

Brunt, S. (2009, April 22). Crunch time for Cohon in Ottawa and Toronto. *Globe and Mail,* p. S1.

Canadian Football League. (2009). Retrieved July 30, 2009, from www.cfl.ca

Canadian Heritage. (2002). *The Canadian sport policy,* Ottawa, ON: Minister of Public Works and Government Services.

Cazeneuve, B., Habib, D., Menez, G., Syken, B., Woo, A., & Schecter, B. (2004, December 27). Teams on the move. *Sports Illustrated,* p. 101. Retrieved October 29, 2009, from: http://vault.sportsillustrated.cnn.com/vault/article/magazine/MAG1115122/index.htm

Center for Negro League Baseball Research. (2006). *Barnstorming teams.* Retrieved July 12, 2010, from www.cnlbr.org/DefiningNegroLeagueBaseball/BarnstormingTeams/bid/56/Default.aspx

CFL Drug Policy at a glance. (2010). Retrieved February 7, 2011, from www.cfl.ca/article/cfl-drug-policy-at-a-glance

Chappelet, J.L., & Bayle, E. (2004). *Strategic and performance management of Olympic sport organizations,* Champaign, IL: Human Kinetics.

Chelladurai, P. (2001). *Managing organizations for sport & physical activity.* Scottsdale, AZ: Holcomb Hathaway.

Church, A.G. (2008). *Pressure groups and Canadian sport policy: A neo-pluralist examination of policy development.* PhD dissertation. University of Western Ontario, London.

Collins, S. (2006). National sports and other myths: The failure of U.S. soccer. *Soccer and Society, 7*(2–3), 353–363.

Condotta, B. (2010, February 22). US–Canada hockey game most-watched sporting event in Canadian history. *Seattle Times.* Retrieved September 21, 2010, from http://seattletimes.nwsource.com/html/talkofthegames/2011156169_us-canada_hockey_game_most_wat.html

Cousens, L., & Slack, T. (2005). Field-level change: The case of North American major league professional sport. *Journal of Sport Management, 19*(1), 13–42.

Cox, A.E., Noonkester, B.N., Howell, M.L., & Howell, R. (1985). Sport in Canada, 1868–1900. In M.L. Howell & R. Howell (Eds.), *History of sport in Canada.* Champaign, IL: Stipes.

Croset, T., & Hums, M. (2009). History of sport management. In L.P. Masteralexis, C. Barr & M. Hums (Eds.), *Principles and practice of sport management* (pp. 205–232). Sudbury, MA: Jones and Bartlett.

Danylchuk, K., & Maclean, J. (2001). Intercollegiate athletics in Canadian universities: Perspectives on the future. *Journal of Sport Management, 15*(4), 364–379.

De Knop, P., Engstrom, L.M., Skirstad, B., & Weiss, M.R. (1996). *The organizational network: Worldwide trends in youth sport.* Champaign, IL: Human Kinetics.

Dobuzinskis, A. (2010, April 9). *Tiger Woods comeback draws record golf audience.* Reuters. Retrieved July 23, 2010, from www.reuters.com/article/idUSTRE6384CV20100409

Edrington, C., DeGraaf, D., Dieser, R., & Edrington, S. (2002). *Leisure and life satisfaction* (4th ed.). New York: McGraw-Hill.

Epstein, D. (2008, September 10). Money changes everything. *Sports Illustrated,* p. 18.

Fairley, S., Lizandra, M., & Gladden, J. (2008). International sport. In L.P. Masteralexis, C. Barr, & M. Hums (Eds.). *Principles and practice of sport management* (p. 184). Sudbury, MA: Jones and Bartlett.

Fort, R. (2000). European and North American sports differences. *Scottish Journal of Political Economy, 47*(4), 431–455.

Galant, H., Renick, L., & Resnick, B. (2005). Labor relations in professional sports. In B. Parkhouse (Ed.), *The management of sport organizations* (pp. 301–333), Boston: McGraw-Hill.

GHSA. net. (2006). *General information.* Retrieved November 23, 2008, from www.ghsa.net/general

Gillion, L. (2008). Recreational sport. In L.P. Masteralexis, C. Barr, & M. Hums (Eds.), *Principles and practice of sport management* (p. 462). Sudbury, MA: Jones and Bartlett.

Granatstein, J.L., & Hillmer, N. (2000, September 4). The coach: James Naismith. *Maclean's, 113*(36), p. 35.

Hinckley, D. (2003, March 27). Road work the season between seasons chapter 28. *New York Daily News*, p. 75. Retrieved July 13, 2010, from www.lexisnexis.com. proxygsu-gso1.galileo.usg.edu/hottopics/lnacademic/

Houlihan, B. (1997). *Sport, policy and politics: A comparative analysis*. London: Routledge.

Hums, M.A., & MacLean, J.C. (2004). *Governance and policy in sport organizations*. Scottsdale, AZ: Holcomb Hathaway.

ICN Sportsweb.com. (2010). *History of modern sports*. Retrieved July 12, 2010, from www.icnsportsweb.com/history-modern-sports-insight.html

Ifedi, F. (2008). *Sport participation in Canada, 2005*. Ottawa, ON: Culture, Tourism and the Centre for Education Statistics.

Johnson, E.L. (1979). *History of YMCA physical education*. Chicago: Association Press.

Kinder, T.M. (1998). *Organizational management administration for athletic programs* (4th ed.). Dubuque, IA: Eddie Bowers.

Kaburakis, A. (2008). International comparative sport law—the US and EU systems of sport governance: Commercialized v. socio-cultural model competition and labor law. *International Sport Law Journal*, 3(4), 108–127.

Lally, P.S. (2008). Sport in Canadian educational institutions. In J. Crossman, *Canadian sport sociology* (2nd ed.) Toronto, ON: Thomson-Nelson.

Leitch, K.K., Bassett, D., & Weil, M. (2006). *Report of the expert panel for the Children's Fitness Tax Credit*. Ottawa, ON: Department of Finance Canada.

Macintosh, D., Bedecki, T., & Franks, C.E.S. (1987). *Sport and politics in Canada: Federal government involvement since 1961*. Montréal, QC: McGill–Queen's University Press.

Macintosh, D., & Whitson, D. (1990). *The game planners: Transforming Canada's sport system*. Montréal, QC: McGill–Queen's University Press.

Major League Soccer. (2011). *2011 MLS roster rules*. Retrieved February 7, 2011, from www.mlssoccer.com/2011-mls-roster-rules

Masters, M. (2009, April 22). Colts president eases fears of NFL invasion; Bill Polian; Indianapolis to play one game in Toronto. *National Post (Canada)*, p. S4.

Masteralexis, L.P. (2009). Professional sport. In L.P. Masteralexis, C. Barr, & M. Hums (Eds.), *Principles and practice of sport management* (pp. 205–232). Sudbury, MA: Jones and Bartlett.

McAllister, M.P. (2010). Hypercommercialism, televisuality, and the changing nature of college sports sponsorship. *American Behavioral Scientist*, 53(10), 1476–1491. Retrieved July 17, 2010, from http://abs.sagepub.com/content/53/10/1476.abstract

McLean, D.D., Hurd, A.R., & Rogers, N.B. (2007). *Recreation and leisure in modern society*. Retrieved November 22, 2008, from http://aausports.org/default.asp?a=EVENTS/pg_BA_EventListing.htm

Metcalfe, A. (1987). *Canada learns to play: The emergence of organized sport, 1807–1914*. Toronto, ON: McClelland and Stewart.

Millson, L., & Sekeres, M. (2008, December 4). CFL watches, waits; league owners maintain united front against first regular-season NFL game to be played in Canada. *Globe and Mail*, p. R9.

MLB.com. (2008). *History of the game*. Retrieved November 22, 2008, from http://mlb.mlb.com/mlb/history/

MLNSports.com. (n.d.). *MiLB. National League: About the farm*. Retrieved July 14, 2010, from www.mlnsports.com/baseball/affiliated/farms/NLfarm.htmlDistinctive

Nafziger, J.A. (2008). A comparison of the European and North American models of sports organisation. *International Sports Law Journal*. Retrieved July 14, 2010, from www.thefreelibrary.com/A+comparison+of+the+European+and+North+American+models+of+sports..-a0212546233

NCAA.org. (2008). *About the NCAA*. Retrieved November 14, 2008, from www.ncaa.org/wps/ncaa?ContentID=2

NCAA.org. (2009). *Men's basketball attendance: Division I summary*. Retrieved July 29, 2009, from www.ncaa.org/wps/ncaa?key=/ncaa/ncaa/sports+and+championship/general+information/stats/m+basketball/attendance/index2.html

Nelson, M. (2005). Sports history as a vehicle for social and cultural understanding in American history. *Social Studies*, 96(3), 118–125.

NHL.com. (2010). *Stanley Cup Playoffs attract largest audience ever*. Retrieved September 21, 2010, from www.nhl.com/ice/news.htm?id=531630

NIRSA.org. (2008). *About us*. Retrieved November 23, 2008, from www.nirsa.org/AM/Template.cfm?Section=About_Us

Noll, R.G. (2003). The organization of sports leagues. *Oxford Review of Economic Policy*, 19(4), 530–551.

19cbaseball.com. *The game*. Retrieved November 18, 2008, from www.19cbaseball.com/game.html.

NSGA.org. (2010). *Sports participation*. Retrieved July 16, 2010, from www.nsga.org/i4a/pages/index.cfm?pageid=3346

Olympic.org. (2010). *Vancouver 2010*. Retrieved September 21, 2010, from www.olympic.org/en/content/Olympic-Games/All-Past-Olympic-Games/Winter/Vancouver-20101/

Palm Bay Parks and Recreation. (2010). *Adult programs*. Retrieved July 15, 2010, from www.palmbayflorida.org/parks/index.html

PGA.com. (2008). *The PGA of America*. Retrieved November 24, 2008, from www.pga.com/pgaofamerica/history/

Popular culture: From baseball to rock and roll. (2005, December). John Bull & Uncle Sam, Four centuries of British-American Relations. Library of Congress. Retrieved July 12, 2010, from www.loc.gov/exhibits/british/brit-7.html

Priestner, Allinger, C., & Allinger, T. (2004). *Own the podium—2010: Final report*. Ottawa, ON: Independent Task Force for Winter NSOs and Funding Partners.

Ralph, D. (2002, April 30). Tagliabue to Toronto: "I don't see expansion on the horizon": What CFL offers "should be preserved," NFL boss says. *National Post (Canada)*, p. S4.

Reiss, S.A. (1998). Historical perspective on sport and public policy. *Policies Study Review, 15*(1), 3–15.

Robinson, M.J. (2005). Sport governance. In B. Parkhouse (Ed.), *The management of sport organizations* (pp. 96–110). Boston: McGraw-Hill.

Royal Commission on Learning. (1995). *For the love of learning*. Vols. 1–4. Toronto, ON: Queen's Gate Printer.

Sandomir, R. (2007, June 30). N.F.L. pulls the plug on its league in Europe. *New York Times*, p. 1.

Schwartz, J. (2010, March 5). The world's top sports events. *Forbes*. Retrieved July 15, 2010, from www.forbes.com/global/2010/0315/companies-olympics-superbowl-daytona-worlds-top-sports-events.html

Siegfried, J. (1995). Sports player drafts and reserve systems. *Cato Journal, 14*(3), 443–452.

SBJ Report. (2008). [Electronic version]. *Street & Smith's Sports Business Journal, 16*. Retrieved November 11, 2008, from http://web.ebscohost.com/ehost/detail?vid=10&hid=9&sid=8a217a18-679a-4979-a9f5-c1664093562b%40sessionmgr7&bdata=JnNpdGU9ZWhvc3QtbGl2ZQ%3d%3d#db=sph&AN=34554406

Shilbury, D. (2000). Considering future sport delivery systems. *Sport Management Review, 3*, 199–221.

Simeon, R., & Robinson, I. (2004). The dynamics of Canadian federalism. In J. Bickerton & A.G. Gagnon (Eds.), *Canadian politics* (4th ed.) (pp. 101–126). Toronto, ON: Broadview Press.

Smith, R. (1990). *Sports and freedom: The rise of big-time college athletics*. New York: Oxford University Press.

Sport Canada. (2009). *Organization of sport in Canada*. Retrieved July 30, 2009, from www.canadianheritage.gc.ca/pgm/sc/mssn/org-cdn-eng.cfm.

Sport Matters Group. (2009). *What is the Sport Matters Group?* Retrieved July 30, 2009, from www.sportmatters.ca/Content/SMG/About%20Us/About%20the%20Sport%20Matters%20Group.asp?langid=1

Starr, M. (1999, October 25). Blood, sweat and cheers. *Newsweek 134*(17), pp. 42–45.

Sutton W.A., McDonald, M.A., Milne, G.R., & Simperman, J. (1997). Creating and fostering fan identification in professional sport. *Sport Marketing Quarterly, 6*(1), 15–22.

Thibault, L., & Harvey, J. (1997). Fostering interorganizational linkages in the Canadian sport delivery system. *Journal of Sport Management, 11*(1), 45–68.

USATF.org. (2010). *2010 National championships and international team qualifying events*. Retrieved July 15, 2010, from www.usatf.org/events/2010/USAOutdoorTFChampionships/

Washington, M., & Ventresca, M. (2008). Institutional contradictions and struggles in the formation of U.S. collegiate basketball, 1880–1938. *Journal of Sport Management, 22*(1), 30–49.

Weiss, M.R., & Hayashi, C.T. (1996). The United States. In P. De Knop, L.M. Engstrom, B. Skirstad, & M.R. Weiss (Eds.), *The organizational network: Worldwide trends in youth sport* (p. 43). Champaign, IL: Human Kinetics.

Whitson, D., Harvey, J., & Lavoie, M. (2000). The Mills Report, the Manley subsidy proposals, and the business of major-league sport. *Canadian Public Administration, 43*(2), 127–156.

Chapter 5

Aidar, A.C., Bueno de Almeida, C., & Miralla, R.G. (2004). Recent history of Brazilian soccer. In R. Fort & J. Fizel (Eds.), *International sports economics comparisons* (pp. 245–261). Westport, CT: Praeger.

Antunez, M. (2008). Mary Teran: Cautiva del deporte o mujer politica? *Fazendo Genero 8-Corpo, Violencia e Poder*. Retrieved November 25, 2008, from www.fazendogenero8.ufsc.br/sts/ST54/Marta_%20Antunez_54.pdf

Arbena, J.L. (1991). Sport, development, and Mexican nationalism, 1920–1970. *Journal of Sport History, 18*(3), 350–364.

Arbena, J. (1999). Significado y alegría en el deporte en América Latina. *Efdeportes, 4*(17). Retrieved November 6, 2008, from www.efdeportes.com

Arbena, J.L. (2002). The later evolution of modern sport in Latin America: The North American influence. In J.A. Mangan & L.P. DaCosta (Eds.), *Sport in Latin American society* (pp. 43–58). London: Frank Cass.

Arbena, J.L., & LaFrance, D.G. (2002). Introduction. In J.L. Arbena & D.G. LaFrance (Eds.), *Sport in Latin America and the Caribbean* (pp. xi–xxxi). Wilmington, DE: Scholarly Resources.

Archetti, E.P. (2005). El deporte en Argentina (1914–1983). *Trabajo y Sociedad: Indagaciones sobre el empleo, la cultura y las prácticas políticas en sociedades segmentadas. 7* (VI). Retrieved November 25, 2008, from www.unse.edu.ar/trabajoysociedad/Archetti.pdf

Asociación de Fútbol Argentino. (2009). *Asociación del Fútbol Argentino*. Retrieved February 24, 2009, from www.afa.org.ar

Associated Press (2008, September 13). *Los estadios de béisbol en Puerto Rico nuevamente tienen público en sus gradas. Pero ahora es para ver partidos de fútbol*. Retrieved January 6, 2009, from www.prsoccer.org/index.php?option=com_content&task=view&id=135&Itemid=2

Azul Azul S.A. (2008). *Oferta de acciones de primera emisión*. Santiago, Chile: Author.

Bairner, A. (2001). *Sport nationalism, and globalization: European and North American perspectives*. Albany, NY: SUNY Press.

Barraza, J. (2006). Historia de la CONMEBOL. In H. Mayne-Nichols Secul (Ed.), *Historias Sudamericanas en la Copa del Mundo 1930–2006* (pp. 8–10). Asunción, Paraguay: CONMEBOL.

Bayle, E., & Robinson, L. (2007). A framework for understanding the performance of national governing bodies of sport. *European Sport Management Quarterly, 7*(3), 249–268.

Big Count. (2006). *Statistical summary report by association*. Fédération Internationale de Football Association. Retrieved July 25, 2010, from www.fifa.com/mm/document/fifafacts/bcoffsurv/statsumrepassoc_10342.pdf

Bravo, G. (1996). Sport administration in Chile through its sports structures. In J.L. Chappelet & M.H. Roukhadze (Eds.), *Sport management. An international approach* (pp.39–52). Lausanne, Switzerland: International Olympic Committee.

Bravo, G. (2011). CONMEBOL. In J. Nauright & C. Parrish (Eds.), *Sports around the world: History, culture, and practice*. Santa Barbara, CA: ABC-Clio.

Brewster, K. (2005). Patriotic pastimes: The role of sport in post-revolutionary Mexico. *International Journal of the History of Sport, 22*(2), 139–157.

Bustillo, M. (April, 1999). A Cuban mix of muscles and ideology. *UNESCO the Courier,* 32. Retrieved January 20, 2008, from www.unesco.org/courier/1999_04/uk/dossier/txt23.htm

Cardoso, F.H. (1977). The consumption of dependency theory in the United States. *Latin American Research Review, 12*(3), 7–24.

Carrión renuncia y se destapan casos de corrupción en Min. Deportes. (2008, December 3). *Hoy.com.ec.* Retrieved June 17, 2010, from www.hoy.com.ec/noticias-ecuador/ministro-de-deportes-dimite-a-su-cargo-321923.html

CARICOM. (2003). *Report: Second meeting of the Human Resource Development (HRD) in Sport Committee.* Retrieved December 9, 2007, from www.caricom.org/jsp/community_organs/cubanmodelsportdev.pdf

Cary, P. (2007). Where ball players are born and made. *US News and World Report.* Retrieved February 2, 2008, from www.usnews.com/usnews/news/articles/070318/26baseball.htm

Chappell, R. (2002). Sport in Latin American from past to present: A European perspective. In J.A. Mangan & L.P. DaCosta (Eds.), *Sport in Latin American society* (pp. 159–180). London: Frank Cass.

Chase-Dunn, C. (1982). A world-system perspective on "dependency and development in Latin America," *Latin American Research Review, 17*(1), 166–71.

Chiarini, A. (2002, May 19). Industria do esporte movimenta R$25 bilhoes e empraga 300 mil. *O Estado de Sao Paulo.* Retrieved November 10, 2007, from http://br.geocities.com/cesaras/104htm

Chiledeportes. (2006). *Memoria seis años de deporte 2000–2006.* Santiago, Chile: Instituto Nacional del Deporte.

Chiledeportes: Bachelet anuncia estrictas medidas para erradicar corrupción. (2006, October 30). *El Mercurio online Chile.* Retrieved June 12, 2010, from www.emol.com/noticias/nacional/detalle/detallenoticias.asp?idnoticia=234522

Claro, J. (1999a). *Programa para la modernización del fútbol chileno. Anexo 1: índices de concentración del fútbol chileno* (pp. 1–16). Santiago, Chile: Author.

Claro, J. (1999b). *Programa para la modernización del fútbol chileno. Anexo 3: evolución histórica de las recaudaciones y la asistencia a los estadios del fútbol chileno.* (pp. 21–36). Santiago, Chile: Author.

Colombia Presidencia de la República. Secretaría de Prensa. (2008, August 4). *Invertidos $21 mil millones en preparación y participación de Colombia en Olímpicos de Beijing.* Retrieved November 25, 2008, from http://web.presidencia.gov.co/sp/2008/agosto/04/14042008.html

Comisión Nacional del Deporte. (2001). *Plan nacional de deportes 2001–2006.* Centro Nacional de Información y Documentación del Deporte. México, D.F. Retrieved October 21, 2007, from www.conade.gob.mx

Comitê Olímpico Brasileiro. (n.d.). *Lei Agnelo/Piva. Sobre O COB.* Comitê Olímpico Brasileiro. Retrieved November 11, 2007, from www.cob.org.br/

Comitê Olímpico Brasileiro. (2008). *Demonstração da aplicação dos recursos provenientes da Lei Agnelo Piva 2007.* Retrieved November 11, 2008, from www.cob.org.br/downloads/downloads/2007/lei_agnelo_2007.zip

Comité Olímpico de Puerto Rico (COPUR). (n.d.). *Visión y desarrollo.* Retrieved January 30, 2008, from www.olimpur.com/olimpur_html/vision_y_desarrollo.htm

CONCACAF.com. (n.d.). *The Confederation of North, Central America and Caribbean Association Football.* Retrieved October, 21, 2007, from www.concacaf.com/

CONADE. (2007). *Antecedentes.* Consejo Nacional de Cultura Física y Deporte. Retrieved October 21, 2007, from www.conade.gob.mx/paginas_07/historia.asp

Confederación Sudamericana de Fútbol. (2009). *Confederación Sudamericana de Fútbol.*

Retrieved February 24, 2009, from www.conmebol.com

Consejo Nacional del Deporte de la Educación. (2007). *Historia del CONDDE.* Consejo nacional del deporte de la educación. Retrieved October 21, 2007, from www.condde.org.mx/modules.php?name=Content&pa=showpage&pid=1

Contecha, L. (1999). La educación física y el deporte en Colombia. Una historia. *Efdeportes, 4*(17). Retrieved November 6, 2008, from www.efdeportes.com

Contecha, L. (2003). La educación física como profesión en la universidad Colombiana. Aproximación histórica. *Efdeportes, 9*(63). Retrieved November 6, 2008, from www.efdeportes.com/

Cornejo, A. (1999). Historia de la educación física y el deporte en El Salvador. In H. Vederhorts (Ed.) *Geschichte der Leibesubunsen,* 6 (pp. 1070–1078). Berlin: Batelz & Wernitz.

Corrupción secretaría de deportes Republica Dominicana. (2008, October 19). *Nuria investigación periodística.* Retrieved June 9, 2010, from www.youtube.com/watch?v=zLViQAhRR4Y

Corruption and sport: Building integrity and preventing abuses. (2009). Transparency international. Working paper 03/2009. Berlin. Retrieved June 18, 2010, from www.transparency.org/publications/publications/working_papers/wp_03_2009_sport_and_corruption_9_september_2009

DaCosta, L.P. (1996). The state versus free enterprise in sports policy: The case of Brazil. In L. Chalip, A. Johnson, & L. Stachura (Eds.), *National sports policies* (pp. 23–38). Westport, CT: Greenwood Press.

DaCosta, L.P., & Miragaya, A. (2008). Estado da arte do conhecimento sobre legados de megaeventos esportivos no exterior e no Brasil. In L.P. DaCosta, D. Correa, E. Rizzuti, B. Villano, & A. Miragaya (Eds.), *Legados de megaeventos esportivos* (pp. 33–45). Brasilia, Brazil: Ministério do Esporte.

Dakar. (2009). *Dakar 2009.* Retrieved February 23, 2009, from www.dakar.com

Departamento de Recreación y Deporte de Puerto Rico. (n.d.). *LIDEA.* Retrieved January 28, 2008, from www.gobierno.pr/DRD/Inicio/Destacamos/Interescolar.htm

Deporte Como Expresión Cultural de un Pueblo (n.d.). *Fundación Puertorriqueña de las humanidades.* Retrieved December 20, 2007, from www.fphpr.org/pdfs/programas/esp/seg_temp/g_e_deporte.pdf

DIGEDER. (1987). *Análisis diagnóstico y formulación de una estrategia de desarrollo para el fútbol chileno.* Dirección General de Deportes y Recreación. Santiago, Chile: Author.

Doig, A. (1995). Mixed signals? Public sector change and the proper conduct of public business. *Public Administration, 73,* 191–212.

Domenech, L. (2003). *Historia y pensamiento de la educación física y el deporte.* Río Piedras, PR: Publicaciones Gaviotas.

Duke, V., & Crolley, L. (1996). Football spectator behaviour in Argentina: A case of separate evolution. *Sociological Review, 44*(2), 272–293.

ECLAC. (2008). *Preliminary overview of the economies of Latin American and the Caribbean 2008.* Economic Commission for Latin American and the Caribbean. Santiago, Chile: Author.

Economía y Negocios Online. (2006, June). *Colo Colo. Blanco y Negro SA. Descripción de la empresa.* Retrieved September 17, 2007, from www.economiaynegocios.cl/mercados/empresas.asp?simbolo=COLO%20COLO

Ettedgui, H., & Fuenmayor, A. (2002). *La hazaña del siglo.* Caracas, Venezuela: Radio Deporte.

Fabri, A. (2006). *El nacimiento de una passion: Historia de los clubes de futbol.* Buenos Aires, Argentina: Capital Intelectual.

Federación Argentina de Pato. (2008). *El Deporte.* Retrieved November 20, 2008, from www.pato.org.ar/

Federación Mexicana de Fútbol Asociación. (2007). *Introducción.* Retrieved October 28, 2007, from www.femexfut.org.mx/portalv2/(tb35l0iv1rwxhrmgiohpaab0)/default.aspx?s=135

Ferrarese, M.S. (2008). El pato: De juego social a deporte de elite. *Recorde: Revista de historia do esporte, 1*(1), 1–13. Retrieved February 17, 2009, from www.sport.ifcs.ufrj.br/recorde/pdf/recordeV1N1_2008_19.pdf

Ferreira, M., & Bravo, G. (2007). A multilevel model analysis of professional soccer attendance in Chile, 1990–2002. *International Journal of Sports Marketing & Sponsorship, 8*(3), 254–271.

FIFA.com. (2010). *FIFA/Coca Cola World Ranking 2010.* Fédération Internationale de Football Association. Retrieved August 15, 2010, from www.fifa.com/worldfootball/ranking/lastranking/gender=m/fullranking.html#confederation=0&rank=187

Foldesi, G.S. (1991). From mass sport to the "sport for all" movement in the "socialist" countries in Eastern Europe. *International Review for the Sociology of Sport, 26*(4), 239–257.

Frias, A. (2006, October 11). Carlos Orlando Ferreira Pinzón: La imagen del dirigente moderno. *El Universal.* Retrieved November 20, 2008, from www.patincolombia.com/noticias/entrevistaferreira.html

Frydenberg, J., & Di Giano, R. (2000). El futbol de la Argentina. Aproximaciones desde las ciencias sociales (VI). Entrevista a Carlos Altamirano. *Efdeportes, 5*(27). Retrieved November 30, 2008, from www.efdeportes.com

Fundamentação Sobre o Sistema Nacional de Esporte e Lazer (2006). *Texto II. II conferencia nacional do esporte.* Brasilia, Brasil: Ministerio do Esporte. Retrieved December 10, 2007, from http://portal.esporte.gov.br/arquivos/conferencianacional/textoII_fundamentacao_sobre_sistema_23_01_06.doc

Gems, G. (2005). Puerto Rico: Sport and the restoration of national pride. *International Journal of Regional and Local Studies, 1*(1), 107–120.

Gilbert, A. (2007). From dreams to reality: The economics and geography of football success. In R.M. Miller & L. Crolley (Eds.), *Football in the Americas: Fútbol, futebol, soccer* (pp. 52–72). London: Institute for the Study of the Americas.

Gómez, A., & Parra, L. (1986). *Historia de la educación física en Colombia como profesión, 1936-1986.* Bogotá, Colombia: Universidad Central Bogotá.

González, M. (1998). El Nuevo modelo deportivo nacional. In *Proceedings of the VII Congreso Nacional de Educación Física, Deporte y Ciencias Aplicadas* (pp. 1–8).Caracas, Venezuela: CONICIT.

Guadalajara 2011. (n.d.). *Medallero general acumulado (1951–2007).* Portal oficial de los XVI Juegos Panamericanos Guadalajara 2011. Retrieved October 26, 2011, from www.guadalajara2011.org.mx/esp/02_juegos/resulta-dos_generales.asp

Graca, A., & Kasznar, I. (2002). *O esporte como industria: Solucao para criacao de riqueza e emprego.* Rio de Janeiro, Brazil: Confederacao Brasileira de Voleibol.

Grassi, D. (2008, January 24). *Baseball ill-equipped for global politics.* Retrieved August 5, 2010, from www.sportscolumn.com/2008/01/24/baseball-ill-equipped-for-global-politics/

Gratton, C., & Taylor, P. (2000). *Economics of sport and recreation.* London: Routledge.

Gregory, S. (2010, July 26). Struck out by béisbol. In the Dominican Republic, teens become prey to big-league dreams. *Time, 176*(4), 44–49.

Grindle, M. (2010). *Constructing, deconstructing, and reconstructing career civil service systems in Latin America.* Faculty Research Working Paper Series. Harvard Kennedy School.

Guttmann, A. (1994). *Games and empires. Modern sports and cultural imperialism.* New York: Columbia University Press.

Hill, C.W. (2003). *International business. Competing in the global marketplace.* New York: McGraw-Hill.

Heineman, K. (2005). Sport and the welfare state in Europe. *European Journal of Sport Science, 5*(4), 181–188.

Houlihan, B. (1994). *Sport and international politics.* New York: Harvester Wheatsheaf.

Houlihan, B., & White, A. (2002). *The politics of sport development: Development of sport or development through sport?* New York: Routledge.

Howard, D.R., & Crompton, J.L. (2004). *Financing sport* (2nd ed). Morgantown, WV: Fitness Information Technology.

Huertas, F.R. (2006). *Deporte e identidad. Puerto Rico y su presencia deportiva internacional (1930–1950).* San Juan, PR: Terranova. Centro de Estudios Avanzados de Puerto Rico y El Caribe.

Impacto Economía. (2006). *El impacto de la industria de Major League Baseball (MLB) en la República Dominicana.* Fundación Global Democracia y Desarrollo. Retrieved January 28, 2008, from www.funglode.org/Funglode-App/Articulo

Instituto Nacional de Deporte. (2005). *Manual de implementación unidades educativas de talento deportivo.* Caracas, Venezuela: Author.

IBOPE Mídia. (2001, March). *Pesquisa sobre futebol.* Retrieved December 5, 2009, from www2.ibope.com.br/CalandraKBX/filesmng.nsf/Opiniao%20Publica/Downloads/fut%20cons%20Interact.pdf/$File/fut%20cons%20Interact.pdf

IPSOS World Monitor. (2002). *Couch and field: Eight sports' global draw.* First quarter, 45–52.

Iriarte, M.L. (2009, October 10). El 66% de equipos de fútbol del mundo en bolsa tienen retornos positivos en 2009. *Diario La Tercera.*

Keegan, W., & Green, M. (1997). *Global marketing.* Lebanon, IN: Pearson Prentice Hall.

Kennedy, J. (2008). The sporting dimension to the relationship between Ireland and Latin America. *Irish Migration Studies in Latin America, 6*(1), 3–14.

Key, J. (1998). El modelo de organización del deporte Venezolano. In *Proceedings of the VII Congreso Nacional de Educación Física, Deporte y Ciencias Aplicadas* (pp. 174–186).Caracas, Venezuela: CONICIT.

Klein, A.M. (1989). Baseball as underdevelopment: The political-economy of sport in the Dominican Republic. *Sociology of Sport Journal, 6,* 95–112.

Klein, A.M. (1991). *Sugarball: The American game, the Dominican dream.* New Haven, CT: Yale University Press.

Krich, J. (2002). *El béisbol: The pleasures and passions of the Latin American game.* Chicago: Dee.

LAC Databook. (2009). Latin America and the Caribbean: Selected economic and social data. Washington, DC: U.S. Agency for International Development. Retrieved October 25, 2009, from http://pdf.usaid.gov/pdf_docs/PNADQ200.pdf

Liga Venezolana de Béisbol Profesional. (n.d.) *Condiciones del campeonato. Temporada 2009–2010.* Retrieved November 10, 2009, from www.lvbp.com/scripts/home/condiciones.asp

López de D'Amico, R. (2006). Organization of sport in Venezuela. In J. Parks, J. Quaterman, and L. Thibault (Eds.), *Contemporary sport management* (pp. 330-331), Champaign, IL: Human Kinetics.

López de D'Amico, R., & Guerrero, G. (2007). Recursos humanos para la actividad físico-deportiva. In J.R. Prado & V. Gonzalez (Eds.). *La educación física y el deporte en la República Bolivariana de Venezuela* (pp. 95–117). Mérida, Venezuela: Universidad de Los Andes.

Lupo, V. (2004). *Historia politica del deporte Argentino.* Buenos Aires, Argentina: Corregidor.

Martinez, F. (2007, August 19). El estado es el gran sponsor del deporte Argentino. *Pagina, 12.* Retrieved November 9, 2008, from www.pagina12.com.ar/diario/ultimas/index-2007-08-19.html

McGehee, R. (1994). Los juegos de las Américas. Four Inter-American multi-sport competitions. In R. Cox (Ed.), *Sport in the global village* (pp. 377–387). Morgantown, WV: Fitness Information Technology.

McPherson, A. (2006). *Intimate ties, bitter struggles. The United States and Latin America since 1945.* Dulles, VA: Potomac Books.

Medeiros, A.M., Perez, L.C., Enout, C., Leite, S., & Renno, T. (1997). *Esportes no Brasil. Situacao atual e propostas para desenvolvimiento.* O Banco Nacional de Desenvolvimento Econômico e Social— BNDES. Retrieved October 28, 2007, from www.bndes.gov.br/conhecimento/relato/esprt-br.pdf

Miller, R. (2004). [Review of the book *Sport in the Latin American and the Caribbean*]. *Journal of Latin American Studies, 36,* 188–190.

Miller, R. (2007). Introduction: Studying football in the Americas. In R.M. Miller & L. Crolley (Eds.), *Football in the Americas: Fútbol, futebol, soccer* (pp. 1–34). London: Institute for the Study of the Americas.

Miller, R.M., & Crolley, L. (Eds.). (2007). *Football in the Americas: Fútbol, futebol, soccer.* London: Institute for the Study of the Americas.

Ministério do Esporte. (2007). *Institucional.* Brasilia: Ministerio do Esporte. Retrieved October 26, 2007, from http://portal.esporte.gov.br/institucional/historico.jsp

Modiano, P. (1997). *Historia del deporte Chileno. Orígenes y transformaciones.* Santiago, Chile: DIGEDER.

Montecinos, E. (2009). *Los juegos regionales más antiguos. Juegos deportivos centroamericanos y del Caribe.* ODE-CABE–CACSO.

Muñoz, C. (2001). *Historia de la dirección general de deportes y recreación. Las políticas estatales de fomento al deporte.* Santiago, Chile: Instituto Nacional de Deportes de Chile.

Navarro, J. (2006). *Softbol algunos aspectos históricos.* Caracas, Venezuela: Fundadonidex.

Nef, J. (2007). Public administration and public sector reform in Latin America. In G. Peters & J. Pierre (Eds.), *Handbook of Public Administration* (pp. 323–335). Thousand Oaks, CA: Sage.

ODEPA.com. (n.d.) *La Organización Deportiva Panamericana.* Retrieved October 19, 2007, from www.olimpur.com/ODEPA1.htm

ODESUR.org. (n.d.). *Organizacion Deportiva Suramericana. Historial.* Retrieved September 1, 2010, from www.odesur.org/esp/organizacion/historico.asp

Ordenan captura por escándalo de corrupción en Cali. (2010, June 11). *Caracol Radio.* Retrieved June 18, 2010, from www.caracol.com.co/nota.aspx?id=1311826

Panfichi, A., & Thieroldt, J. (2007). Identity and rivalry: The football clubs and *barras bravas* of Peru. In R.M. Miller & L. Crolley (Eds.), *Football in the Americas: Fútbol, futebol, soccer* (pp. 143–157). London: Institute for the Study of the Americas.

Patín Colombia. (2007). *El mejor legado del patinaje.* Retrieved September 2, 2008, from www.patincolombia.com/Mundial%20espana%202008/ElMejorLegadoDelPatinajeCOFP.pdf

Pettavino, P., & Brenner, P. (1999). More than just a game. *Peace Review, 11*(4), 523–530.

Pettavino, P.J., & Pye, G. (1994). *Sport in Cuba: The diamond in the rough.* Pittsburgh, PA: University of Pittsburgh Press.

Pitts, B.G., & Stotlar, D.K. (2007). *Fundamentals of sport marketing* (3rd ed.). Morgantown, WV: Fitness Information Technology.

Política Nacional do Esporte. (2005). *Texto V. II Conferencia nacional do esporte.* Brasilia, Brazil: Ministerio do Esporte. Retrieved November 5, 2007, from http://portal.esporte.gov.br/arquivos/conferencianacional/textoV_politica_nacional_esporte_18_01_06.pdf

Presidencia de la Nacion. (2008). *Deportes.* Retrieved November 29, 2008, from www.casarosada.gov.ar/index.php?option=com_confent&task=view&id=42&itemid=58

Puchan, H. (2004). Living "extreme": Adventure sports, media and commercialization. *Journal of Communication Management, 9*(2), 171–178.

Rachman, G. (2007). Beautiful game, lousy business: The problems of Latin American football. In R.M. Miller & L. Crolley (Eds.), *Football in the Americas: Fútbol, futebol, soccer* (pp. 161–173). London: Institute for the Study of the Americas.

Ramallo, S., & Aguiar, F. (2007). Marketing in Argentine football: A snapshot. In M. Desbordes (Ed.), *Marketing and football: An international perspective* (pp. 465–488). Burlington, MA: Butterworth-Heinemann.

Recasens, A. (1999). *Las barras bravas.* Facultad de Ciencias Sociales. Universidad de Chile. Retrieved July 15, 2010, from www.facso.uchile.cl/publicaciones/biblioteca/docs/libros/barras.pdf

Regalado, S.O. (2000). Latin players on the cheap: Professional baseball recruitment in Latin America and the neocolonialist tradition. *Indiana Journal of Global Studies, 8*(1), 9–20.

Riojas-Martínez, J.M. (2008). *Modelo de deporte universitario en México.* Consejo Nacional del Deporte de la Educación, A.C. Retrieved September 5, 2010, from www.ascun.org.co/eventos/pleno_2008/memorias_xix_plenoBienestar/paneles_areas/Deporte/CONDDE_Mexico.pdf

Riordan, J. (1999). The impact of communism on sport. In J. Riordan & A. Kruger (Eds.), *The international politics of sport in the twentieth century* (pp. 48–66), London: Spon.

RPC Pesquisa e Consultoria. (2004). *Pesquisa quantitativa. Perfil do voleibol nacional.* Retrieved November 21, 2007, from www.volei.org.br/newcbv/institucional/index.asp?pag=pesq-opiniao

Ruck, R. (1999). *The tropic of baseball. Baseball in the Dominican Republic.* Lincoln: University of Nebraska Press.

Sambolín, L.F., Ríos de Vásquez, C., & Stewart, R. (n.d.).*Transfondo histórico. Ochenta años de la liga atlética interuniversitaria.* Retrieved January 3, 2009, from www.universia.pr/lai/historia.jsp

SEDEFIR. (2004a). *Sobre nosotros.* Secretaría de Estado de Deportes, Educación Física y Recreación. Retrieved January 20, 2008, from www.sedefir.gov.do/nosotros.htm

SEDEFIR. (2004b). *Reglamento del PARNI.* Secretaría de Estado de Deportes, Educación Física y Recreación. Retrieved January 20, 2008, from www.sedefir.gov.do/pdf/reglamento_parni.pdf

Sermeño, F. (October, 1993). Barcelona 92: Turismo o experiencia. *Afición Deportiva, 10* (34).

Slack, T. (1982). Cuba's political involvement in sport since the socialist revolution. *Journal of Sport & Social Issues*, 6(2), 35–45.

Skidmore, T., & Smith, P. (2005). *Modern Latin America*. New York: Oxford University Press.

Smith, B.L. (2002). The Argentinian junta and the press in the run-up to the 1978 World Cup. *Soccer and Society*, 3(1), 69–78.

Sotomayor, O. (2004). Development and income distribution: The case of Puerto Rico. *World Development*, 32(8), 1395–1406.

Spagnuolo, D.L. (2003). Swinging for the fence: A call for institutional reform as Dominican boys risk their futures for a chance in major league baseball. *University of Pennsylvania Journal of International Economic Law*, 24(1), 263–287.

Stier, W.F., & Alvarez, C.C. (1991). The organizational structure of amateur sport within the country of Mexico. Five perspectives. *Physical Educator*, 48(1), 49–54.

Tesche, L., & Rambo, A.B. (2001). Reconstructing the fatherland: German turnen in southern Brazil. In J.A. Mangan (ed.), *Europe, sport world. Shaping global societies* (pp. 5–22). London: Frank Cass.

The not-so-beautiful game (2002, June 1). *Economist*, 363(8275), 12–13.

Thoma, J.E., & Chalip, L. (2003). The Olympic Movement. In *Sport in the global community*. (pp. 21–48). Morgantown, WV: Fitness Information Technology.

UNCAF.com. (n.d.). *Unión Centroamericana de Fútbol*. Página Oficial. Retrieved October 21, 2007, from http://uncaf.net/portal/modules/myhome/

UNDP. (1990). *Human development report 1990. Concept and measurement of human development*. United Nations Development Programme. New York: Palgrave Macmillan.

UNDP. (2009). *Human development report 2009. Overcoming barriers: Human mobility and development*. United Nations Development Programme. New York: Palgrave Macmillan.

Van Bottenburg, M. (2001). *Global games*. Urbana: University of Illinois Press.

Vargas, A. (2000). The globalization of baseball: A Latin American perspective. *Indiana Journal of Global Studies*, 8(1), 21–36.

Viceministerio de Deportes se hunde en acusaciones. (2010, January 29). *La Patria*. Retrieved June 20, 2010, from http://lapatriaenlinea.com/?nota=16423

Wagg, S. (2002). *British football and social exclusion*. London: Routledge.

Wiarda, H.J., & Kline, H.F. (2007). *Latin American politics and development* (6th ed.). Cambridge, MA: Westview Press.

Williamson, R.C. (1997). *Latin American societies in transition*. Westport, CT: Praeger.

Zavala, H. (2001). El fútbol en México. Reflexiones para una noche en vela. *Efdeportes. Revista Digital*, 7(39). Retrieved December 3, 2007, from www.efdeportes.com/

Chapter 6

Commissioner Goodell: Restructured Season Would Allow for more International Games. (2010). NFL Labor News. Retrieved on February 11, 2011, from http://nfllabor.com/2010/10/29/commissioner-goodell-%E2%80%9Crestructured-season-would-allow-for-more-international-games%E2%80%9D/

Committee for the Development of Sport (CDDS). (2002, August 9). *10 Years of Sprint 1991–2001*. Part II. Collected texts on sport for all policies, etc. 43. Strasbourg, France: Council of Europe.

Council of Europe. (2003, January 27). European Convention on Spectator Violence and Misbehaviour at Sports Events and in Particular at Football Matches (T-RV). Strasbourg, France. T-RV (2003) 1.

Crampton, R. (2004). Czech sport governing bodies and social capital. *International Journal of the History of Sport*, 21(5), 672–680. Taylor & Francis Ltd.

Davies, L. (1996). The future development of sport in eastern Europe. *European Journal for Sport Management* 2, 7-13.

Dimitrov, D., Helmenstein, C,. Kleissner, A., Moser, B., and Schindler, J. (2006). Die makroökonomischen Effektedes Sports in Europa, Studie im Auftrag des Bundeskanzleramts, Sektion Sport, Wien.

Fort, R. (2000). European and North American sports differences (?). *Scottish Journal of Political Economy*, 47(4).

Hoehn, T., and Szymanski, S. (1999). The Americanisation of European football. *Economic Policy*, 28, 205-240.

Jennett, N., and Sloane, P.J. (1985). The future of league football: A critique of the report of the Chester Committee of Enquiry. *Leisure Studies*, 4(1), 39-56.

Lee, M. (2006). *The race for the 2012 Olympics: The inside story of how the bid was won*. Virgin Books: London.

Premier League Season Review 2007/08. (2008) Retrieved on February 11, 2011, from www.premierleague.com/staticFiles/e2/8/0,,12306~133346,00.pdf.

Premier League Season Review 2008/09. (2009) Retrieved on February 11, 2011, from www.premierleague.com.

Ramet, S. (1992.) *Nationalism and federalism in Yugoslavia: 1962–1991, second edition*. Bloomington, IN: Indiana University Press.

Riordan, J. (1994). *Russia and Eastern Europe in the future of the modern Olympic movement. Critical reflections on Olympic ideology*. Second International Symposium for Olympic Research. Centre for Olympic Studies.

Sylt, C., and Reid, C. (2008). Keeping the wheels turning. *Financial Times*. Retrieved February 11, 2011, from. www.ft.com/cms/s/2/333268be-25c4-11dd-b510-000077b07658.html#ixzz1EKlXs4xA.

Toft, T. (2006, April). *Development in European law*. Berlin. European Commission Competition DG. Information, Communication and Media.

White paper on sport. (2007, July 11). Brussels COM (2007). 391 final. Presented by the Commission: SEC (2007) 932, SEC (2007) 934, SEC (2007) 935, SEC (2007) 936.

Chapter 7

Alegi, P. (2010). *African soccerscapes: How a continent changed the world's game*. Athens: Ohio University Press.

Alegi, P. (2006). Sport, race, and liberation before apartheid: Albert Luthuli, 1920s–1952, in C. Thomas (Ed.). *Sport and liberation in South Africa* (pp. 66–82). East London: University of Fort Hare and Department of Sport and Recreation.

Amusa, L.O., & Toriola, A.L. (Eds.) (2003). *Sport in contemporary African society: An anthology*. Mokopane, South Africa: Africa Association for Health, Physical Education, Recreation, Sport and Dance.

ASEC Mimosa Equipe. (2008). Chat en direct avec me roger ouegnin. Retrieved December 6, 2008, from www.asec.ci/index2.php?page=view_chat.

Ayieko, O. (2010). Stemming the dearth of talent after school. Retrieved March 20, 2011, from www.nation.co.ke/sports/Stemming+the+dearth+of+talent+after+school++/-/1090/1013204/-/item/0/-/q98g1fz/-/index.html.

Baker, W.J., & Mangan, J. A. (1987). *Sport in Africa: Essays in social history*. New York: Africana.

Bale, J. (2004). *Three geographies of Africa footballer migration: Patterns, problems and 'postcoloniality'*, in G. Armstrong and R. Giulianotti (Eds.), *Football in Africa: Conflict, conciliation and community* (pp. 229-246). Palgrave Macmillan, Basingstoke.

Boniface, P. (2002). *La terre est ronde comme un ballon; géopolitique du football*. Paris: Seuil.

Breasted, J. (1976). *The dawn of conscience*. New York: Scribner Book.

Burnett, C. (2006). Indigenous games of South African children: A rationale for categorization and taxonomy. *South African Journal for Research in Sport, Physical Education and Recreation 28*(2), 1–13.

Chepyator-Thomson, J.R. (1999). *Race and representation: The Kenyan factor in distance running*. North American Society for the Sociology and Sport (NASSS) conference. November, 3-6, Cleveland, OH.

Chepyator-Thomson, J.R. (1990). Traditional games of Keiyo children: A comparison of pre- and post-independent periods in Kenya. *Interchange, 21*(2), 15-25.

Confederation of African Football. (2007). Statute. Retrieved from http://www.cafonline.com/userfiles/file/CAF_statutes_english.pdf

Copnall, J. (2004). Asec's amazing run. Retrieved December 6, 2006, from http://news.bbc.co.uk/sport2/hi/football/africa/3949019.stm.

Darby, P. (2002). *Africa, football, and FIFA: Politics, colonialism, and resistance*. London ; Portland, OR: F. Cass.

Darby, P., Akindes, G., & Kirwin, M. (2007). Football academies and the migration of African football labor to Europe. *Journal of Sport & Social Issues, Vol. 31*(No. 2), 143-161.

Dreyfus, G. (2007). *Tous les africains de L1*. Retrieved September 22, 2008, from www.rfi.fr/sportfr/articles/092/article_55066.asp.

Guanqun, W. (December 16, 2010). Kenyan president pledges support for sports. Retrieved March 20, 2011, from http://news.xinhuanet.com/english2010/world/2010-12/16/c_13652309.htm.

Hokkanen, M. (2005). "Christ and the imperial games' fields" in south-central Africa–sport and the Scottish missionaries in Malawi, 1880-1914: Utilitarian compromise. *International Journal of the History of Sport, 22*(4), 745-769.

Hokkanen, M., & Mangan, J.A. (2006). Further variations on a theme: The games ethic further adapted—Scottish moral missionaries and muscular Christians in Malawi. *International Journal of the History of Sport, 23*(8), 1257-1274.

Kenyatta, J. (1938). *Facing Mount Kenya*. Nairobi, Kenya: Kenway.

Kidd, B. (2008). A new social movement: Sport for development and peace. *Sport in Society, 11*(4), 370–380.

Krotee, M.L. (2003). Global intersections—an outsider's view of sport in South Africa. In L.O. Amusa & A.L. Toriola (Eds.). *Sport in contemporary African society: An anthology* (pp. 363–375). Mokopane, South Africa: Africa Association for Health, Physical Education, Recreation, Sport and Dance.

Mazrui, A. (1986). *The Africans: A triple heritage*. London: BBC.

Mélik-Chakhnazarov, A. (1970). *Le sport en afrique*. Paris: Présence africaine.

Merrett, C. (2006). Bowl brilliantly, bat badly—and don't stay for tea. In C. Thomas, *Sport and liberation in South Africa* (pp. 66–82). East London: University of Fort Hare and Department of Sport and Recreation.

Ministry of Youth and Sport. (2011). Achievements: Participation of teams in international events. Retrieved March 20, 2011, from www.youthaffairs.go.ke/Sports/index.php?option=com_content&view=category&layout=blog&id=2&Itemid=4.

Murray, W.J. (1994). *Football: A history of the world game*. Aldershot, Hants, UK: Scolar Press; Brookfield, VT: Ashgate.

Ndee, H.S. (2010). Epilogue: Traditionalism, colonization, and modernization. *International Journal of Sport History, 27*(5), 960-983.

Nicholson, M. (2007). *Sport and the media: Managing the nexus*. Oxford, UK; Burlington, MA: Elsevier.

Nyanjom, O. (2008). *Foul play: The crisis of football management in Kenya.* Nairobi, Kenya: Africog.

Poli, R. (2002). Le football en côte-d'ivoire: Organisation spatiale et pratiques urbaines. Neuchâtel: Editions CIES.

Ricci, F.M. (Ed.) (2000). *African Football: Yearbook 2000,* 3rd edition. Rome: Prosports.

Skelton, R. (2010). *Wrestling boom sweeps Senegal.* Retrieved March 15, 2011, from http://news.bbc.co.uk/2/hi/business/8617738.stm.

Supreme Council for Youth and Sport Printing Office. (1981). *A major responsibility of sport council* (rev. ed.). Cairo, Egypt.

Thornton, G. (2003). *South African 2010 soccer World Cup bid—economic impact assessment study.* Johannesburg, South Africa: Grant Thornton Kessel Feinstein.

Van der Merwe, F.J.G. (2007). *Sport history, a textbook for South African Students.* Stellenbosch, South Africa: FJG.

Wagner, E. (1989). *Sport in Asia and Africa: A comparative handbook.* New York: Greenwood Press.

Chapter 8

Abdul Wahid, Z.A. (Ed.). (1970). *Glimpses of Malaysian history.* Kuala Lumpur, Malaysia: Dewan Bahasa dan Pustaka.

About the ASC. (2009). Retrieved from www.ausport.gov.au/about/what_is_the_asc

Abraham, C. (1988). Inter cultural management at the crossroads. *Malaysian Management Review, 24*(1), 58- 65.

Booth, D. (2002). "On the shoulders of a giant": W.F. Mandle and the foundations of sports history in Australia. *International Journal of the History of Sport, 19*(1), 151–158.

Brownfoot, J.N. (2003). "Healthy bodies, healthy minds"; sport and society in colonial Malaya. *International Journal of the History of Sport, 19*(2), 126–156.

Central Intelligence Agency: The world factbook. (2009). Appendix B—International organizations and groups. Retrieved from www.cia.gov/library/publications/the-world-factbook/appendix/appendix-b.html

Chareanpusirikul, S., & Wood, R. (2002). Mintzberg, managers and methodology: Some observation from a study of hotel general managers. *Tourism Management, 23*(5), 551–556.

Chatterjee, Samir R., & Pearson, Cecil A.L. (2003). Ethical perceptions of Asian managers: Evidence of trends in six divergent national contexts. *Business Ethics: A European Review, 12*(2), 203–211.

Chelladurai, P., Shanmuganathan, D., Jothikaran, J., & Nageswaran, A.S. (2002). Sport in modern India: Policies, practices and problems. *International Journal of the History of Sport, 19*(2), 366–383.

Chong, T. (2005). *Modernization trends in Southeast Asia.* Singapore: Institute of Southeast Asian Studies.

DeSensi, J.T., Kelley, D., Blanton, M.D., & Beitel, P.A. (1988). *Employer expectations of sports managers and evaluation of sports management programs in the United States.* Paper presented at the North American Society for Sport Management Conference, Urbana, IL.

Dickson, B. (2000). *Sports for All Programme as catalysts to the development of national sports.* Paper presented at the Sukan Malaysia 2000.

Foreman, J. (2001). *Corporate governance issues in a professional sport* [electronic version]. Retrieved from www.commerce.adelaide.edu.au/research/aaaj/apira_2001/papers/Foreman172.pdf

Green, M. (2007). Olympic glory or grassroots development?: Sport policy priorities in Australia, Canada and the United Kingdom, 1960–2006. *International Journal of the History of Sport, 24*(7), 921–953.

Hashim, M.Y. (1992). *The Malay Sultanate of Malacca.* Kuala Lumpur, Malaysia: Dewan Bahasa dan Pustaka.

History of New Zealand. (2007). Retrieved from http://en.wikipedia.org/w/index.php?title=History_of_New_Zealand

Hj. Deraman, Abd. Rahman. (2000). Sports association managerial enhancement; towards international excellence. Penang, Malaysia: Ministry of Youth and Sport Malaysia.

Hofstede, G. (2007). Asian management in the 21st Century. *Asia Pacific Journal of Management, 24,* 411–420.

Hong, F. (2002). Into the future: Asian sport and globalization. *International Journal of the History of Sport, 19*(2), 401–407.

Horton, P.A. (2002). Shackling the lion: Sport in independent Singapore. *International Journal of the History of Sport, 19*(2), 243–274.

India at a glance. (2005). Retrieved from http://india.gov.in/knowindia/india_at_a_glance.php

Kim, K.K. (1985). *Sportsmen in the days of yore.* Kuala Lumpur, Malaysia: New Straits Times.

Koehler, L.S., & Lupcho, P. (1990). *Sport management and the process of professionalisation.* Paper presented at the Fifth Annual NASSM Convention, Louisville, KY.

List of countries by GDP (PPP) per capita. (2007). Retrieved from http://en.wikipedia.org/wiki/List_of_countries_by_GDP_(PPP)_per_capita

Lizandra, M. (1993). *Sports management curricula: Identification of minimum core content areas and courses to be included in each content area for undergraduate and graduate (master's) sports management programs.* Unpublished doctoral thesis, Temple University, Philadelphia.

Lutan, R. (2005). Indonesia and the Asian Games: Sport, nationalism and the "new order." *Sport in Society, 8*(3), 414–424.

Mangan, J.A. (2003). Prologue: Asian sport: From the recent past. *International Journal of the History of Sport, 19*(2), 1–10.

Manzenreiter, W. (2007). The business of sports and the manufacturing of global sport inequality. *Business of Sports, 2*(6), 1–22.

Megat Daud, M.A.K. (2000). *The sports industry in Malaysia.* Paper presented at the 3rd ICHPER.SD Asia Congress, Kuala Lumpur, Malaysia.

Mendoza, G. (1992). *Management: The Asian way.* Petaling Jaya, Malaysia: Eddiplex.

National sport policy. (1989). Kuala Lumpur, Malaysia: Ministry of Youth and Sport, Malaysia.

Nalapat, A., & Parker, A. (2005). Sport, celebrity and popular culture: Sachin Tendulkar, cricket and Indian nationalism. *International Review for the Sociology of Sport, 40*(4), 433–446.

Ninth Malaysian plan. (2006). Putrajaya, Malaysia: Economic Planning Unit, Prime Minister's Department.

Oceania. (2007). Retrieved from http://en.wikipedia.org/w/index.pp?title=Oceania

Oceania, 8000–2000 BC. (2000). Retrieved from www.metmuseum.org/toah/ht/oc/ht02oc.htm

Overview—Association of Southeast Asian Nations. (2005). Retrieved from www.aseansec.org

Pacific Islands Forum. (2009). Retrieved from http://en.wikipedia.org/wiki/Pacific_Islands_Forum

Pacific Islands Forum Secretariat. (2009). Retrieved from www.forumsec.org/

Parks, J.B., & Quarterman, J. (Eds.). (2003). *Contemporary sport management* (2nd ed.). Champaign, IL: Human Kinetics.

Parks, J.B., & Quarterman, J. (Eds.). (1998). *Contemporary sport management.* Champaign, IL: Human Kinetics.

Radzi, W. (2000). *Challenges and future directions of sports management in Malaysia.* Paper presented at the Proceedings of the 3rd ICHPER.SD Asia Congress, Kuala Lumpur, Malaysia.

Roberts, K. (2005). *Land of new opportunity.* Sport Business.

Sepak takraw. (2007). Retrieved from http://en.wikipedia.org/w/index.php?title=Sepak_Takraw

Silk, M. (2002). "Bangsa Malaysia": Global sport, the city and the mediated refurbishment of local identities. *Media, Culture & Society, 24,* 755–794.

Smith, Aaron C.T., & Westerbeek, Hans M. (2004). "Professional" sport management education and practice in Australia. *Journal of Hospitality, Leisure, Sport and Tourism Education, 3*(2), 38–45.

Southeast Asia. (2007). Retrieved from http://en.wikipedia.org/w/index.php?title=Southeast_Asia

Sports investment, events and media to power growth in the Singapore sports industry. (2009). Retrieved from www.ssc.gov.sg/publish/Corporate/en/news/media_releases/2009/sports_investment.html

Sriboon, N. (2007). Sport and recreation activities and economic crisis in Thailand. *Asian Sport Management Review, 1*(1), 2–7.

Wilson, I.D. (2002). *The politics of inner power: The practice of pencak silat in West Java.* Murdoch University, Perth, Australia.

Chapter 9

Central Intelligence Agency. (2010). *CIA world factbook.* Retrieved from www.cia.gov/library/publications/the-world-factbook/geos/JA.html

Chehabi, H.E. (2001). Sport diplomacy between the United States and Iran. *Diplomacy & Statecraft, 12*(1), 89–106.

Cheng, P. (2006). The development of Asian sport industry. Retrieved from http://140.122.100.146/acad/ebook/9301/ld41.doc

Chinese Olympic Committee. (2009). *Official Web site of the Chinese Olympic Committee.* Retrieved July 30, 2009, from http://en.olympic.cn

Chinese Sporting Goods Federation. (2005). *Home.* Retrieved July 28, 2006, from http://csgf.org.cn/en

Chou, J. & Gao, F. (1999). A study on the concept of sports population. *Sport Science, 2,* 11-14.

D2PD.com. (2006). *The analysis and suggestions on the commercial opportunities of the Beijing Olympic Games.* Retrieved July 3, 2006, from www.d2pd.com/html/10/bencandy_2512.htm

Daly, A. & Kawaguchi, A. (2003). Professional Sport in Australia and Japan: League Rules and Competitive Balance. 29, 21-32.

Eschenfelder, M.J., & Li, M. (2006). *Economics of sport* (2nd ed.). Morgantown, WV: Fitness Information Technology.

Harada, M. (2010). Development of sport industry: Japan's experience. Paper presented at the 2010 Annual Conference of the Asian Association for Sport Management, Kuala Lumpur, Malaysia.

Hong, F. (2003). Epilogue—into the future: Asian sport and globalization. In J.A. Mangan & F. Hong (eds.). *Sport in Asian society.* London: Frank Cass.

Hu, L.K. (2006). *Culture coherence and regional economic cooperation in Northeast Asia.* Retrieved July 27, 2009, from http://faculty.washington.edu/karyiu/confer/beijing06/papers/hu_lk.pdf

Jones, R. (1999). Sport in China. In J. Riordan & R. Jones (eds.), *Sport and physical education in China* (pp. 1–19). London: Spon.

Kim, S.S. (2004). Northeast Asia in the local-regional-global nexus: Multiple challenges and contending explanations. In S.S. Kim (ed.), *The international relations of Northeast Asia.* Lanham, MD: Roman & Littlefield.

Kimura, K. (2007). *The sport industry in Japan.* Paper presented at the 2006 Annual Conference of the North American Society for Sport Management, Toronto, ON, Canada.

Korean Overseas Information Service. (2007). *Government policies.* Retrieved January 10, 2008, from www.korea.net/korea/kor_loca.asp?code=J010102

Ministry of Culture, Sport and Tourism (2006). *Physical education white book* (Korean). Seoul, South Korea: KyeMoon.

Ministry of Education, Culture, Sports, Science and Technology (MEXT). (1991). *Japanese government policies in education, science, and culture 1991*. Retrieved July 27, 2009, from www.mext.go.jp/b_menu/hakusho/html/hpae199201/hpae199201_2_005.html

Ministry of Education, Culture, Sports, Science and Technology (MEXT). (2000). *Basic plan for the promotion of sports* [Press release]. Retrieved July 27, 2009, from www.mext.go.jp/english/news/2000/09/000949.htm

Ok, G. (2007). *Transformation of modern Korean sport: Imperialism, nationalism, globalization*. Elizabeth, NJ: Hollym International.

Sasakawa Sports Foundation. (2008). The 2008 SSF national sport-life survey: Executive summary. Tokyo, Japan.

Seoul Olympic Sports Promotion Foundation. (2007). *ChongHapEopMuHyunHwang* (Korean).

Seoul Olympic Sports Promotion Foundation. (2007). *SOSFO vision*. Retrieved November 12, 2007, from http://sosfo.or.kr/english/sosfo/vision.asp

Sporting goods market in China. (2006). Retrieved from http://buyusainfo.net/docs/x_3734998.pdf

State General Administration of Sport. (2000). *2001–2010 Sport reform and development planning document*. Retrieved July 25, 2006, from www.sport.gov.cn/admin/show_info.php?n_id=456

Stevenson, C., & Nixon, J. (1987). A conceptual scheme of the social functions of sport. In A. Yiannakis, T. McIntyre, M. Melnick, & D. Hart, (Eds.). Sport sociology: Contemporary themes (3rd Edition) (pp. 23-29). Dubuque, IA: Kendall/Hunt.

The tremendous potential of the sport industry in China. (2006, July 7). *Shanghai Financial News*. Retrieved July 24, 2006, from www.shfinancialnews.com/gb/node2/node12251/node12252/node12267/userobject1ai1221635.html

United Nations Environment Programme. (2004). *Environmental indicators: Northeast Asia*. Retrieved from http://rrcap.unep.org/pub/indicator/Vertical%20North%20East%20Asia.pdf

U.S. Department of State. (2009). *Background notes*. Retrieved from www.state.gov/r/pa/ei/bgn

Web Japan. (2009). *Sports: Promoting health for people. Japan Factsheet*. Retrieved July 28, 2009, from http://web-jpn.org/factsheet/pdf/12Sports.pdf

Wolfers, J. (n.d.). The business of sports: where's the money. Retrieved from http://bpp.wharton.upenn.edu/jwolfers/Papers/Comments/The%20Business%20of%20Sports.pdf

World Taekwondo Federation. (2007). *Introduction: About the World Taekwondo Federation*. Retrieved August 31, 2007, from www.wtf.org/site/about_wtf/intro.htm

Xiong, H. (2007). The evolution of urban society and social changes in sports participation at the grassroots in China. *International Review for the Sociology of Sport, 42*(4), 441–471.

Yao, X.Z. (2000). *An introduction to Confucianism*. Cambridge, United Kingdom: Cambridge University Press.

Chapter 10

10 drug scandals. (2003, January 19). CBC Sports Online. Retrieved April 11, 2010, from www.cbc.ca/sports/indepth/drugs/stories/top10.html.

2018 Olympic candidates confirmed. (2010, August). *SportsPro, 24*, 31.

Al-Ahmed, A. (2008, May 15). Bar countries that ban women athletes. *New York Times*. Retrieved April 11, 2010, from www.nytimes.com/2008/05/19/opinion/19iht-edahmed.3.13017836.html

Alvarez, J.E. (2005). *International organizations as lawmakers*. New York: Oxford University Press.

Amnesty International. (2008, July). *China: The Olympics countdown—broken promises*. Retrieved April 11, 2010, from www.amnesty.org/en/library/asset/ASA17/089/2008/en/8249b304-5724-11dd-90eb-ff4596860802/asa170892008eng.pdf

Andersen, J. (2009, October 4). Call for action against all forms of corruption in sport, Open letter to the IOC president and the International Olympic Committee, gathered in Copenhagen, Denmark, on the occasion of the 121st IOC Session and the XIII IOC Congress. *Play the Game*. Retrieved April 11, 2010, from www.playthegame.org/news/detailed/call-for-action-against-all-forms-of-corruption-in-sport-4543.html

Anderson, Zach. (2008, August 22). London Olympics Broadcast Rights Top $1 Billion. *Brand Dunk*. http://branddunk.com/2008/08/22/london-olympics-broadcast-rights-top-1-billion

Battistoni, Peter. (2010, March 12). *No need to combine Olympic and Paralympic games, chief insists*. Retrieved March 14, 2011, from www.olympics-now.com/2010/03/12/no-need-to-combine-olympic-and-paralympic-games-chief-insists

Bay Area Laboratory Co-Operative. (2009, May 19). *New York Times*. Retrieved April 11, 2010, from http://topics.nytimes.com/topics/reference/timestopics/organizations/b/bay_area_laboratory_cooperative/index.html

BBC News. (2010, March 24). *Profile: Lee Kun-hee*. Retrieved April 11, 2010, from http://news.bbc.co.uk/go/pr/fr/-/2/hi/business/8584702.stm

Beijing 2008. (2008). Athletics. Retrieved January 2, 2008, from http://en.beijing2008.cn/cptvenues/sports/athletics/index.shtml

Bell, D. (2002). Are all Paralympic elite athletes? International Games Archive 1998-2002: 1-12.

Berkes, H. (2008, June 7). Nazi Olympics tangled politics and sport. *All Things Considered*, NPR Radio. Retrieved April 11, 2010, from www.npr.org/templates/story/story.php?storyId=91246674

Booth, D. (2003). Hitting apartheid for six? The politics of the South African sports. *Journal of Contemporary History, 38*(3), 477–493.

Brazil's decade of sport. (2010, August). *SportsPro, 24*, 54–57.

Bringing show business to the snow business. (2010, August). *SportsPro, 24,* 90–93.

British Columbia Supreme Court. (2009). Sagen v. Vancouver Organizing Committee for the 2010 Olympic and Paralympic Winter Games, 2009 BCSC 942.

Brittain, I. (2010). *The Paralympic Games explained.* London: Routledge

Burton, R., & O'Reilly, N. (2010a). U.N. role offers IOC chance to place sport amid global priorities. *SportBusiness Journal, 12*(48), 21.

Burton, R., & O'Reilly, N. (2010b). Analysis must show NHL the value of Olympic competition. *SportBusiness Journal, 13*(3), 21.

Burton, R., & O'Reilly, N. (2010c). Opportunity now for Paralympics to grab North American spotlight. *SportBusiness Journal, 13*(10), 36.

Burton, R., & O'Reilly, N. (2010d). Assessing Vancouver after the facts, accusations, shades of truth. *SportBusiness Journal, 13*(19), 21.

Carr, Susannah. (2009). Title IX: An opportunity to level the Olympic playing field. *Journal of Sports and Entertainment Law, 19,* 149.

Center on Housing Rights and Evictions Report: Fair Play for Housing Rights. (2007).

China embraces. (2009). Retrieved March 14, 2011, from http://news.xinhuanet.com/english/2009-02/26/content_10901530.htm

Christie, J. (1997, December 5). Disabled athletes get full status. Globe and Mail. A21.

Clark, J. (1992, August). Fifth wheels: The XXV Olympiad is the XXVth to exclude disabled jocks, Village Voice, p 4.

CNN/Sports Illustrated. (1999a, December 13). *Tough sell: Samaranch trying to persuade Congress that IOC is reformed.* Retrieved April 11, 2010, from http://sportsillustrated.cnn.com/olympics/news/1999/12/13/samaranch_congress_ap/

CNN/Sports Illustrated. (1999b, December 16). *On the carpet: Samaranch appears before Congress to defend reforms.* Retrieved April 11, 2010, from http://sportsillustrated.cnn.com/olympics/news/1999/12/15/ioc_congress/#more

Crary, D. (2010, February). Organizers strive to achieve inclusiveness, sustainability. *Daily Hampshire Gazette,* pp. D1–2.

Cribb, R. (2010, February 6). Canada to issue 'biological passports.' *Toronto Star.* Retrieved April 11, 2010, from http://olympics.thestar.com/2010/article/761533--canada-to-issue-biological-passports

Deford, F. (1999, December 15). Congress should let Samaranch have it. *CNN/Sports Illustrated.* Retrieved April 11, 2010, from http://sportsillustrated.cnn.com/inside_game/defordnews/1999/12/15/deford/

Donati, A. (2007, February). *World traffic in doping substances.* Retrieved April 11, 2010, from www.wada-ama.org/rtecontent/document/Donati_Report_Trafficking_2007-03_06.pdf

Donnelly, P., & Petherick, L. (2006). Worker's playtime? Child labour at the extremes of the sporting spectrum. In R. Giulanotti & D. McArdle (Eds.), *Sport, civil liberties, and human rights* (pp. 9–29). New York: Routledge.

Dryden, N. (2006). For power and glory: State sponsored doping and athletes' human rights. *Sports Lawyers Journal, 13,* 1.

Dryden, N. (2009). Supporting every child's right to play. *Canadian Journal of Volunteer Resources Management, 17,* 1.

Dubin, C.L. (1990). *Commission of inquiry into the use of drugs and banned practices intended to increase athletic performance.* Ottawa, ON: Canadian Government Publishing Centre.

Fay, T.G. (1999). *Race, gender, and disability: A new paradigm towards full participation and equal opportunity in sport.* Doctoral dissertation. University of Massachusetts at Amherst.

Fay, T.G., & Snyder, D. (2006). A North American perspective on international sport (chapter 8). In J.B. Parks, J. Quarterman, & L. Thibault (Eds.), *Contemporary sport management* (3rd ed.). Champaign, IL: Human Kinetics.

Fay, T.G, Velez, L., & Parks, J. (2011). A North American perspective on international sport. In P.M. Pedersen, J.B. Parks, J. Quarterman, & L. Thibault (Eds.). *Contemporary sport management* (4th ed.) (pp. 392–413). Champaign, IL: Human Kinetics.

Fay, T.G., & Wolff, E.A. (2009, Summer). Disability in sport in the twenty-first century: Creating a new sport opportunity spectrum. *Boston University International Law Journal, 27*(2), 231–248.

FIFA. (2009, March 24). *FIFA and UEFA reject WADA 'whereabouts' rule.* Retrieved April 11, 2010, from www.fifa.com/aboutfifa/federation/releases/newsid=1040455.html

Fisman, R. (2010, February 11). Is figure skating fixed? *Slate.* Retrieved April 11, 2010, from www.slate.com/id/2244277/

Gabriel, T. (1998, April 24). China strains for Olympic glory. *New York Times Magazine,* I 6, p. 30.

Gillis, C. (2010, March 3). *Chantal Petitclerc.* Retrieved March 14, 2011, from http://historywire.ca/en/article/20908

Goldman, T. (2010, July 10) Runner Semenya cleared after gender test.. *All Things Considered,* NPR Radio. Retrieved February 6, 2011, from http://www.npr.org/templates/story/story.php?storyId=128342113

Goodbody, J. (1995, March 2). China pledges to jail drug takers. *The Times,* Sports.

Guttmann, A. (2002). *The Olympics: A history of the modern games* (2nd ed.). Urbana: University of Illinois Press.

Hartmann, D. (2003). *Race, culture, and the revolt of the black athlete: The 1968 Olympic protests and their aftermath.* Chicago: University of Chicago Press.

Harvey, R. (1988, August 30). East Germans credit success to application of knowledge. *Los Angeles Times*, I 3, p. 1.

Hill, D. (2008). *The fix: Soccer and organized crime.* Toronto, ON, Canada: McClelland & Stewart.

Hong, F. (2006). Innocence lost: Child athletes in China. In R. Giulanotti & D. McArdle (Eds.), *Sport, civil liberties, and human rights* (pp. 46–62). New York: Routledge.

Houlihan, B. (2006). Civil rights, doping control, and the World Anti-Doping Code. In R. Giulanotti & D. McArdle (Eds.), *Sport, civil liberties, and human rights* (pp. 9128–145). New York: Routledge.

Hoy, M. (2009). Oscar Pistorius—changing our perception of disabled sport. *Play the Game.* Retrieved April 11, 2010, from www.playthegame.org/news/detailed/oscar-pistorius-changing-our-perception-of-disabled-sport-4444.html

Human Rights Watch. (2008, March 31). *China: International Olympic Committee operating in moral void.* Retrieved September 26, 2009, from www.hrw.org/en/news/2008/03/31/china-international-olympic-committee-operating-moral-void

Hums, M.A., & MacLean, J.C. (2009). *Governance and policy in sport organizations.* Scottsdale, AZ: Holcomb, Hathaway.

International Association of Athletics Federations (2008). Coverage of the Athletics events of the Games of the XXIX Olympiad 8 to 24 August (Athletics Events 15 to 24 August). Retrieved January 2, 2008, from http://www.iaaf.org/OLY08/results/byevent.html

International Olympic Committee. (2009.) Olympic marketing fact file. Retrieved February 14, 2011, from www.olympic.org/Documents/IOC_Marketing/IOC_Marketing_Fact_File_2010%20r.pdf

IOC re-elects President Jacques Rogge. (2009, October 9). Retrieved April 11, 2010, from www.olympic.org/en/content/Media/?CalendarTab=0&currentArticlesPageIPP=10&currentArticlesPage=10&articleNewsGroup=-1&articleId=73403

Jennings, A. (1996). *The new lords of the rings.* London: Pocket Books

Johnson, W.O. (1993). *The Olympics, a history of the Games.* Birmingham, AL: Bishop Books

Johnson, W.O. (1996, May 27). Olympics, 100 years of change. *TIME International*, 147(22).

Jørgensen, L. (2009, October 9). As the IOC brand gets stronger, so do the advantages of being situated in Switzerland. *Play the Game.* Retrieved April 11, 2010, from www.playthegame.org/news/detailed/as-the-ioc-brand-gets-stronger-so-do-the-advantages-of-being-situated-in-switzerland-4571.html

Kaerup, I.R. (2009a). The price of a medal is rising. *Play the Game.* Retrieved October 18, 2010, from www.uniflip.dk/online-magazines/3/21603/37879/pub/

Kaerup, I.R. (2009b). The ISL bribery system: 138 million CHF for senior officials in the Olympic world. *Play the Game.* Retrieved October 18, 2010, from www.playthegame.org/uploads/media/Jens_Weinreich_-_The_ISL_bribery_system.pdf

Kaerup, I.R. (2009c). No clear victory as China set out to improve image through Beijing 2008 Olympics. *Play the Game.* Retrieved October 18, 2010, from www.playthegame.org/news/detailed/no-clear-victory-as-china-set-out-to-improve-image-through-beijing-2008-olympics-4426.html

Katz, D. (1994). *Just do it: The Nike spirit in the corporate world.* Holbrook, MA: Adams Media Corporation.

Kelso, P. (2008, June 7). IOC acts on gambling. *The Guardian.* Retrieved April 11, 2010, from www.guardian.co.uk/sport/2008/jun/07/olympicgames2008.athletics

Kelso, P. (2009, February 4). Drug cheats in for shock as new UK anti-doping body gets approval. *Daily Telegraph.* Retrieved April 11, 2010, from www.telegraph.co.uk/sport/othersports/drugsinsport/4516129/Drug-cheats-in-for-shock-as-new-UK-anti-doping-body-gets-approval.html

Klein, J. (2008). The starting Line: Blade Runner Not Chosen for Beijing. Retrieved July 28, 2008 from http://olympics.blogs.nytimes.com/tag/oscar-pistorius/.

Legg, D. Burchell, A., Jarvis, P., & Sainsbury, T. (2009). The Athletic Ability Debate: Have we reached a tipping point? *Palaestra.* 25(1): 19-25.

Legg, D., & Steadward, R. (2011). The Paralympic Games and 60 years of change (1948-2008): unification and restructuring from a disability and medical model to sport based competition, Sport in Society, Taylor & Francis.

Legg, D., Fay, T., Hums, M.A., & Wolff, E. (2009). Examining the inclusion of wheelchair exhibition events within the Olympic Game 1984–2004. *European Sport Management Quarterly*, 9(3), 243–258.

Lewis, L. (2010, March 24). Samsung boss Lee Kun Hee regains control. *The Times.* Retrieved April 11, 2010, from http://business.timesonline.co.uk/tol/business/industry_sectors/technology/article7074275.ece

Lombardo, J. (2010). FIBA event expects revenue jump. *SportBusiness Journal*, 13(17), 6.

London 2010 budget cut by new British government. (2010, July). *SportsPro*, 23, 27.

Longman, J. (1999, December 10). Olympics; reforms are unlikely to transform the I.O.C. *New York Times.* Retrieved April 11, 2010, from www.nytimes.com/1999/12/10/sports/olympics-reforms-are-unlikely-to-transform-the-ioc.html1

Longman, J. (2010, March 30). South African runner plans return. *New York Times.* Retrieved February 6, 2010 from http://www.nytimes.com/2010/03/31/sports/31semenya.html

Longman, J. (2004, December 5). Revelations merely confirm suspicions about use of drugs, *New York Times*, 18, p. 5.

Macdonald, N. (2010, February 11). Is the judging in figure skating still rigged? *Macleans*. Retrieved April 11, 2010, from www2.macleans.ca/2010/02/11/is-the-judging-in-figure-skating-still-rigged/

Macur, J. (2009, March 23). Rule requiring drug testers to know athletes' whereabouts draws protest. *New York Times*. Retrieved April 11, 2010, from www.nytimes.com/2009/03/23/sports/othersports/23testing.html

Mickle, T. (2010a). Assessing Vancouver's legacy . . . the good-time Games. *SportsBusiness Journal, 12*(43), 1, 26–27.

Mickle, T. (2010b). FINA wants more of Olympic TV revenue pool. *SportsBusiness Journal, 12*(48), 6.

Mickle, T. (2010c). Network demise further proof of USOC culture shift. *SportsBusiness Journal, 13*(2), 1, 6.

Mickle, T. (2010d). Recalling Olympic leader's legacy. *SportsBusiness Journal, 13*(2), 7.

Mickle, T. (2010e). 25 years ago, IOC's TOP teetered, then thrived. *SportsBusiness Journal, 13* (10), 1, 44–45.

Mickle, T. (2010f). IOC ends drought, adds P & G, Dow Chemical. *SportsBusiness Journal, 13*(13), 4.

Mickle, T. (2010g). Rogge's youth games reaching the starting line. *SportsBusiness Journal, 13*(15), 26.

Mickle, T. (2010h). Blackmum: USOC's mission is to re-establish credibility. *SportsBusiness Journal, 13*(22), 1, 27.

Mickle, T. (2010i). NBC, USOC join to sell 12 package. *SportsBusiness Journal, 13*(22), 1, 27.

Mickle, T., & Durand, J. (2010a). IOC sets 14-16 media plan. *SportsBusiness Journal, 12*(43), 1, 27.

Mickle, T., & Durand, J. (2010b). IOC could go it alone on U.S. rights deal. *SportsBusiness Journal, 13*(14), 1, 28.

Montville, L. (1998, January). Wet and wild: A Chinese drug bust, *Sports Illustrated*, p. 64.

NOCs & Athletes. (n.d.). Retrieved March 14, 2011, from www.games-encyclo.org/?id=11837&L=1).

Olympic Charter. (2010, February 11). Retrieved April 11, 2010, from www.olympic.org/Documents/Olympic%20Charter/Charter_en_2010.pdf

Olympic truce. (2009). Retrieved April 11, 2010, from www.olympic.org/en/content/The-IOC/Commissions/International-relations-/Olympic-Truce/

Olympic Women. (2008). *Some early history about women and the Olympics*. Retrieved April 11, 2010, from www.olympicwomen.co.uk/Potted.htm

Olympics History. (n.d.). Retrieved March 14, 2011, from http://olympics.india-server.com/olympics-history.html

Paralympic Games Vancouver 2010. (2010). Retrieved March 14, 2011, from www.paralympic.org/Paralympic_Games/Past_Games/Vancouver_2010/index.html

Paralympian. (2009). The ability of athletes with a disability: Summary of athletes who competed in the Olympic Games brings the question of potentiality to surface., 2, 3.

Pfister, G. (2000). Women in the Olympic Games: 1900–97. In B.L. Drinkwater (Ed.), *Women in sport: The encyclopedia of sports medicine*. London: Blackwell Science, an IOC Medical Committee Publication.

Pistorius v. International Amateur Athletics Federation, CAS 2008/A.1480 (Ct. of Arb. for Sport May 16, 2008). http://tas-cas.org/d2wfiles/document/1085/5048/0/amended%20final%20award.pdf.

Pound, R.W. (2004). *Inside the Olympics: A behind-the-scenes look at the politics, the scandals, and the glory of the Games*. Toronto, ON, Canada: Wiley & Sons.

Preuss, H. (2004). *The economics of staging the Olympics: A comparison of the Games 1972–2008*. Northampton, MA: Edward Elgar.

Preuss, H. (2008). The impact and evaluation of major sporting events. Published as a special issue of *European Sport Management Quarterly*. London: Routledge.

Reuters. (2008a, March 24). *Awarding Games to China was right move: Rogge*. Retrieved April 11, 2010, from www.reuters.com/article/idUSL2413041720080324

Reuters. (2008b, July 26). *IOC's Rogge quiet on human rights for reasons of state*. Retrieved April 11, 2010, from www.reuters.com/article/idUSL632487320080726

Reuters (2008c). *Should men-only Muslim teams be barred from the Olympics?* (2008, May 21). Reuters. Retrieved April 11, 2010, from http://blogs.reuters.com/faithworld/2008/05/21/should-men-only-muslim-teams-be-barred-from-the-olympics/

Right to Play. (2010). *At a glance*. Retrieved April 11, 2010, from www.righttoplay.com/International/about-us/Pages/Glance.aspx

Rosner, S.R., & Shropshire, K.L. (2011). *The business of sports* (2nd ed.), pp. 453–476. Sudbury, MA: Jones & Bartlett Learning.

Ruibal, S. (2004, April 14). Gene alteration sets off alarm in doping fight. *USA Today*, p. 3C.

Samsung concludes contract with the International Olympic Committee to sponsor Olympic Games through 2016. (2007, April 23). Retrieved April 11, 2010, from www.samsung.com/us/news/newsRead.do?news_seq=3687&page=1

Schneider, A.J. (2006). Privacy, confidentiality, and human rights in sports. In R. Giulanotti & D. McArdle (Eds.), *Sport, civil liberties, and human rights* (pp. 146–164). New York: Routledge.

Shaw, C. (2009). Delegates approve Coventry Declaration to protect civil rights. *Play the Game*. Retrieved October 18, 2010, from www.uniflip.dk/online-magazines/3/21603/37879/pub/

Siddons, L. (1999, March 17). IOC expels all six members in Salt Lake City scandal. *The Guardian*. Retrieved April 11, 2010, from www.guardian.co.uk/Olympic scandal/Story/0,,209532,00.html

Simpson, V., & Jennings, A. (1992). *The lords of the rings*. Toronto, ON, Canada: Stoddart.

Smith, T., & Steele, D. (2007). *Silent gesture: Autobiography of Tommie Smith*. Philadelphia: Temple University Press.

Sokolove, M. (2004, January 18). In pursuit of doped excellence; the lab animal. *New York Times Magazine*, p. 28.

Sport Accord Members. (n.d.). Sport Accord. Retrieved March 14, 2011, from www.sportaccord.com/en/members/index.php?idContent=644&idIndex=32

Steadward, R. (1994). *Athletes with disabilities and their quest for Olympic inclusion*. Paper presented to the Joint Assembly of the IOC Executive Board and the Association of National Olympic Committees, Atlanta, GA.

Steadward, R. (1996). Integration and sport in the Paralympic Movement, *Sport Science Review, 5*(1), 26–41.

Team Darfur. (2008, July 22). *China's broken promises*. Retrieved April 11, 2010, from www.teamdarfur.org/node/461

Terman, Rachel. (2008, August 11). *Foul ball: Muslim women banned from participation*. Retrieved April 11, 2010, from www.wluml.org/node/4757

The Women and Sport Commission. (2009). Retrieved April 11, 2010, from www.olympic.org/content/The-IOC/Commissions/Women-and-Sport/

Ungerleider, S. (2001). *Faust's gold: Inside the East German doping machine*. New York: St. Martin's Press.

UN General Assembly A/HRC/10/7/Add.3. (2009).

United Nations. (2006). *The Millennium Developmental Goals Report 2006*. Retrieved March 14, 2011, from http://mdgs.un.org/unsd/mdg/Resources/Static/Products/Progress2006/MDGReport2006.pdf

United Nations (2007). *Convention on the Rights of Persons with Disabilities*. Retrieved March 14, 2011, from http://www.un.org/disabilities/convention/conventionfull.shtml

Wamsley, K.B. (2008, February). *Social science literature on sport and transitioning/transitioned athletes*. Retrieved April 11, 2010, from www.athletescan.com/Images/Publications/Transitioning%20Athlete%20Project/Social%20Science%20Literature%20on%20Sport%20and%20Transitioning-Transitioned%20Athletes.pdf

Whitten, P. (1995, January). China drug bust. *Swimming World*, p. 71.

Wilson, S. (2010a, January 20). *IOC recommends gender-test centers*. Associated Press. Retrieved April 11, 2010, from www.usatoday.com/sports/olympics/2010-01-20-3875669216_x.htm

Wilson, S. (2010b, February 10). *The International Olympic Committee remains vigilant against the threat of illegal betting and match-fixing at the games*. Associated Press. Retrieved April 11, 2010, from http://articles.sfgate.com/2010-02-10/sports/17872247_1_betting-ioc-match-fixing

Wolbring, G. (2008a). *Ableism, Enhancement Medicine and the techno poor disabled*. in P.Healey & S. Rayner (Eds.), *Unnatural Selection: The Challenges of Engineering Tomorrow's People (pp. 196-209)*. London, Sterling, VA: Earthscan.

Wolbring, G. (2008b). *One World, One Olympics: Governing Human Ability, Ableism and Disablism in an Era of Bodily Enhancements. in A.Miah (Ed.), Human Futures: Art in the Age of Uncertainty (Liverpool: Liverpool University Press)*.

Wolbring, G. (2008c). Oscar Pistorius and the future of Olympic, Paralympic and other sports. *SCRIPTed, 5*(1), 139. Retrieved October 2, 2008, from www.law.ed.ac.uk/ahrc/scritp-ed/vol5-1/wolbring.asp

Wolbring, G., Legg, D., & Stahnisch, F. (2010). Meaning of Inclusion throughout the History of the Paralympic Games and Movement, *The International Journal of Sport and Society, 1*(3): pp.81-94.

Women runners seek injunction. (1984, March 7). Associated Press. Retrieved April 11, 2010, from www.nytimes.com/1984/03/07/sports/women-runners-seek-injunction.html

Wong, Jan. (2010, December 3). *Chantal Petitclerc, 2004*. Retrieved March 14, 2011, from www.theglobeandmail.com/news/national/nation-builder/chantal-petitclerc-2004/article723009

World Anti-Doping Agency. (2009a). *A brief history of anti-doping*. Retrieved April 11, 2010, from www.wada-ama.org/en/About-WADA/History/A-Brief-History-of-Anti-Doping/Category.id=312

World Anti-Doping Agency. (2009b). *World anti-doping code*. Retrieved April 11, 2010, from www.wada-ama.org/Documents/Anti-Doping_Community/WADA_Anti-Doping_CODE_2009_EN.pdf

World Anti-Doping Agency. (2009c, December). *Questions and answers on the Athlete Biological Passport*. Retrieved April 11, 2010, from www.wada-ama.org/en/Science-Medicine/Athlete-Biological-Passport/Questions-Answers/

World Anti-Doping Agency. (2010, March). *Questions and answers on whereabouts*. Retrieved April 11, 2010, from www.wada-ama.org/en/Resources/Q-and-A/Whereabouts/

Zappelli, P.G. (2010, January 25). *IOC Ethics Commission decision with recommendations, No. D/01/2010*. Retrieved April 11, 2010, from www.olympic.org/Documents/Commissions_PDFfiles/Ethics/Ethics_Lee_Decision_02_10.pdf

Chapter 11

Bandini, P. (2009). *Golf and rugby sevens to be included in 2016 Olympics in Rio de Janeiro*. Retrieved from www.guardian.co.uk

BBC. (2009a, June 15). *Seven sports aim for Olympic spot*. Retrieved from http://news.bbc.co.uk

BBC. (2009b, August 13). *Golf & rugby set to join Olympics*. Retrieved from http://news.bbc.co.uk

Chen, L. (2004). Membership incentives: Factors affecting individuals' decisions about participation in athletics-related professional associations. *Journal of Sport Management, 18*(2), 153–173.

Crouse, K. (2009, July 24). Swimming bans high-tech suits, ending an era. *New York Times.* Retrieved from www.nytimes.com

Fédération Internationale de Football Association (FIFA). (2009a). *About FIFA.* Retrieved on October, 10, 2009, from www.fifa.com/aboutfifa/federation/associations.html.

Fédération Internationale de Football Association (FIFA). (2009b). *FIFA financial report, 2008.* Retrieved on October, 10, 2009, from www.fifa.com/mm/document/affederation/administration/01/03/94/23/fifa_ar08_eng.pdf

Fédération Internationale de Natation (FINA). (2009a). *FINA organizational chart.* Retrieved on October 8, 2009, from www.fina.org/project/index.php

Fédération Internationale de Natation (FINA). (2009b). *Press releases: PR58—FINA bureau meeting.* Retrieved from www.fina.org

FINA. (2010a). *FINA approved swimsuits.* Retrieved July 24, 2010, from www.fina.org

FINA. (2010b). *GR 5 swimwear, rules & regulations.* Retrieved July 24, 2010, from www.fina.org

Fermoso, J. (2008, June 6). High-tech swimsuits approved by Olympic committee promise to even the competition. *Wired.* Retrieved from www.wired.com/gadget-lab/2008/06/high-tech-swims/

Gladden, J.M., & Lizandra, M. (2004). International sport. In L.P. Masteralexis, C.A. Barr, & M.A. Hums (Eds.), *Principles and practice of sport management* (2nd ed., pp. 208–239). Gaithersburg, MD: Jones and Bartlett.

Gomez, B. (2009, July 2). Inline skaters hope to roll into 2016 Olympics. *Gazette.*

Hums, M., & MacLean, J. (2004). *Governance and policy in sport organizations* (pp. 257–294). Holcomb Hathaway.

International Association of Athletics Federations (IAAF). (2009a). *IAAF national member federations.* Retrieved from www.iaaf.org/aboutiaaf/structure/federations/index.html

International Association of Athletics Federations (IAAF). (2009b). *Home of world athletics.* Retrieved October 9, 2009, from www.iaaf.org/aboutiaaf/index.html

International Baseball Federation (IBAF). (2010a.) *Intercontinental Cup.* Retrieved from www.ibaf.org/en/tournament.aspx?id=7934f35e-3ebe-4ac9-aad6-208fbf8794f3

International Baseball Federation (IBAF). (2010b). *International Baseball Federation.* Retrieved from www.ibaf.org/en/

International Basketball Federation (FIBA). (2009a). *FIBA organization.* Retrieved October 8, 2009, from www.fiba.com/pages/eng/fc/FIBA/fibaStru/p/openNodeIDs/963/selNodeID/963/fibaCentBoar.html

International Basketball Federation (FIBA). (2009b). *Inside FIBA.* Retrieved from www.fiba.com

International Biathlon Union (IBU). (2009). *Events.* Retrieved October 31, 2009, from www.biathlonworld2.de/en/events.html?PHPSESSID=cfcee1076615d4ed74643660fc8d7d91

International Olympic Committee (IOC). (2009). *The International Olympic Committee.* Retrieved October 7, 2009, from www.olympic.org/en/content/The-IOC

International Tennis Federation (ITF). (2009). *International Tennis Federation—The world governing body of tennis.* Retrieved October 9, 2009, from www.itftennis.com

International Table Tennis Federation (ITTF). (2009). *International Table Tennis Federation.* Retrieved October 9, 2009, from www.ittf.com

Kelso, P. (2009, June 14). *Golf and rugby sevens favourites for 2016 Olympics.* Retrieved from www.telegraph.co.uk

Malcolm, D., and Crabtree, P.E. (2008). *Tom Morris of St Andrews: The colossus of golf 1821–1908.* Edinburgh, Scotland: Birlinn.

Michaelis, V. (2009, August 12). Seven sports lobbying for 2016 Olympic Games. *USA Today,* 2C.

MSNBC. (2008). *IOC: No proof China cheated in gymnastics.* Retrieved October 10, 2009, from www.msnbc.msn.com/id/26337759

Olympic Charter. (2007a). *Chapter 1: The Olympic Movement and its action.* Retrieved from www.olympic.org/Documents/Reports/EN/en_report_122.pdf

Olympic Charter. (2007b). *Chapter 3: The international federations (IFs).* Retrieved from www.olympic.org/Documents/Reports/EN/en_report_122.pdf

Olympic Charter. (2007c). *Chapter 5: The Olympic Games.* Retrieved from www.olympic.org/Documents/Reports/EN/en_report_122.pdf

Olympic Programme Commission. (2009). *Programme review.* Retrieved from www.olympic.org/en/content/The-IOC/Commissions/Olympic-Programme/

Roberts, B.S., Kamel, K.S., Hedrick, C.E., McLean, S.P., & Sharp, R.L. (2003). Effect of a FastSkin suit on submaximal freestyle swimming. *Medicine and Science in Sports and Exercise, 35*(3), 519–524.

SportAccord. (2009). *About SportAccord.* Retrieved October 23, 2009, from www.agfisonline.com/vsite/vnavsite/page/directory/0,10853,5148-175946-193164-nav-list,00.html.

Theodoraki, E. (2007). *Olympic event organization.* Burlington, MA: Elsevier Linacre.

USA Swimming Association. (2010, June 1). *Amendments to conform USA swimming open water swimsuit rules to FINA open water swimsuit rules.* Retrieved from www.usaswimming.org

Chapter 12

Amara, M., Henry, I., Liang J., Uchiumi, K. (2005). The governance of professional soccer: Five case studies—Algeria, China, England, France and Japan. *European Journal of Sport Science, 5*(4), 189–206.

Arthur, D. (2003). Corporate sponsorship of sport: Its impact on surfing and surf culture. In J. Skinner, K.

Gilbert, & A. Edwards (Eds.), *Some like it hot: The beach as a cultural dimension*, (pp. 154–168). Oxford, United Kingdom: Meyer & Meyer Sport.

Association of Surfing Professionals (ASP). (2009). *ASP history*. Retrieved April 4, 2009, from www.aspworldtour.com/about-asp/asp-history/

Baranko, J. (2008). *Resurgence of the NHL*. Retrieved January 16, 2009, from http://law.marquette.edu/cgi-bin/site.pl?2130&pageID=3690

BBC News. (2007, November 30). *India cricket rebel series begins*. Retrieved February 27, 2009, from http://news.bbc.co.uk/go/pr/fr/-/2/hi/south_asia/7120283.stm

Beamish, R. (1991). The impact of corporate ownership on labor-management relations in hockey. In P.D. Staudohar & J.A. Mangan (Eds.), *The business of professional sports* (pp. 202–221). Chicago: University of Illinois Press.

Burton, R., & Cornilles, R.Y. (1998). Emerging theory in team sport sales: Selling tickets in a more competitive arena. *Sport Marketing Quarterly, 7*, 29–37.

Daly, A., & Kawaguchi, A. (2003). Professional sport in Australia and Japan: League rules and competitive balance. *The Otemon Journal of Australian Studies, 29*, 21–32.

Edwards, A., & Skinner, J. (2006). *Sport empire*. Oxford, United Kingdom: Meyer & Meyer Sport.

Fitzsimons, P. (1996). *The rugby war*. Sydney, New South Wales, Australia: Harper Collins.

Giulianotti, R. (1999). *Football: Sociology of the game*. Cambridge, United Kingdom: Polity Press.

Hiscock, G. (2009, February 5). *Tough times for cricket's global CEO*. Retrieved March 1, 2009, from www.theaustralian.news.com.au/business/story/0,28124,25010704-5018624,00.html

Hoye, R., & Cuskelly, G. (2007). *Sport governance*. Oxford, United Kingdom: Elsevier.

International Cricket Council. (2008). Retrieved March 15, 2009, from www.icc-cricket.com

Kitchin, P. (2008). Twenty-20 and English domestic cricket. In S. Chadwick & D. Arthur (Eds.), *International cases in the business of sport* (pp. 101–113). Oxford, United Kingdom: Butterworth-Heinemann.

Lanagan, D. (2003). Dropping in: Surfing, identity, community and commodity. In J. Skinner, K. Gilbert, & A. Edwards (Eds.), *Some like it hot: The beach as a cultural dimension* (pp. 169–184). Oxford, United Kingdom: Meyer & Meyer Sport.

Law, A., Harvey, J., & Kemp, S. (2002). The global sport mass media oligopoly: The three usual suspects and more. *International Review for the Sociology of Sport, 37*(3–4), 279–302.

Lee, J. (2001, April 11). *Chairman of the board*. Retrieved January 6, 2007, from http://bulletin.ninemsn.com.au/bulletin/eddesk.nsf/6df5c28ed2c6c605ca256a1500059f03/fb66f9a95a7f08feca240007f310?OpenDocument/

Masters, R. (1997). *Insideout: Rugby league under scrutiny*. Sydney, New South Wales, Australia: Ironbark.

Meenaghan, T. (1991). Sponsorship—legitimising the medium. *European Journal of Advertising, 25*(11), 5–10.

Mills, D. (1991). The blue line and the bottom line: Entrepreneurs and the business of hockey in Canada, 1927–90. In P.D. Staudohar & J.A. Mangan (Eds.), *The business of professional sports* (pp. 175–201). Chicago: University of Illinois Press.

Morgan, M. (2002). Optimizing the structure of elite competitions in professional sport: Lessons from rugby union. *Managing Leisure, 7*, 41–60.

Noll, R.G. (2003). The organization of sports leagues. *Oxford Review of Economic Policy, 19*(4), 530–551.

Oebbecke, M. (1998). *Toward a framework of total quality management (TQM) in professional sport team organizations: Identification and validation of TQM constructs, and the development of an associated measurement instrument*. EdD dissertation. Temple University, Philadelphia.

RedOrbit. (2004, September 15). *NHL to lock out players Thursday*. Retrieved January 30, 2009, from www.redorbit.com/news/general/86504/nhl_to_lock_out_players_thursday/

Ross, S. (2003). Competition law as a constraint on monopolistic exploitation by sport leagues and clubs. *Oxford Review of Economic Policy, 19*(4), 569–584.

Sage, G. (1998). *Power and ideology in American sport*. Champaign, IL: Human Kinetics.

Shaw, S., & Amis, J. (2001). Image and investment: Sponsorship of women's sports. *Journal of Sport Management, 15*(3), 221–248.

Skinner, J., Stewart, B., & Edwards, A. (2003). The post-modernisation of rugby union in Australia. *Journal of Football Studies, 6*(1), 51–69.

Smith, A.C.T., & Stewart, B. (2010). The special features of sport: A critical revisit. *Sport Management Review, 13*, 1–13.

Stewart, B., Nicholson, M., & Dickson, G. (2005). The Australian Football League's recent progress: A study in cartel conduct and monopoly power. *Sport Management Review, 8*(2), 95–117.

Szymanski, S. (2003). The assessment: The economics of sport. *Oxford Review of Economic Policy, 19*(4), 467–477.

Szymanski, S., & Kuypers, T. (1999). *Winners and losers*. London: Penguin Books.

Tomlinson, A. (2005). The making of the global sports economy: ISL, Adidas and the rise of the corporate player in world sport. In M.L. Silk, D.L. Andrews, & C.L. Cole (Eds), *Sport and corporate nationalisms* (pp. 35–65). Oxford, United Kingdom: Berg.

Zhang, J.J., Pease, D.G., & Smith, D.W. (1998). Relationship between broadcasting media and minor league hockey game attendance. *Journal of Sport Management, 12*, 103–122.

Chapter 13

Fédération Internationale de Football Association. (2008a). *FIFA associations*. Retrieved November 15, 2008, from www.fifa.com/en/aboutfifa/federation/associations.html

Fédération Internationale de Football Association. (2008b). *FIFAU-20 World Cup Egypt qualifiers*. Retrieved November 16, 2008, from www.fifa.com/en/u20worldcup/qualifiers/index.html

Fédération Internationale du Sport Universitaire. (2008b). *Current structure. Objectives of FISU*. Retrieved November 18, 2008, from www.fisu.net/site/page_531.php

Fédération Internationale du Sport Universitaire. (2008c). *FISU history*. Retrieved November 20, 2008, from www.fisu.net/site/page_518.php

Fédération Internationale du Sport Universitaire. (2010). *FISU today*. Retrieved June 26, 2010, from www.fisu.net/en/FISU-today-517.html

International Children's Games. (2004a). *History of the ICG*. Retrieved February 17, 2004, from www.childrens-games.org/icg.html

International Children's Games. (2004b). *Cleveland welcomes you*. Retrieved February 17, 2004, from www.childrens-games.org/index2.html

International Children's Games. (2008). *42nd International Children's Games*. Retrieved November 17, 2008, from www.sficg2008.com/site3.aspx

International Children's Games. (2011). *44th Games, June 28 - July 3, 2010, in Manama, Bahrain*. Retrieved February 16, 2011, from http://international-childrens-games.org/web/index.php?Itemid=172

International School Sport Federation. (2008a). *Introduction. Objectives and limits*. Retrieved November 18, 2008, from www.isfsports.org/sports/default_abstracts.asp?id=478

International School Sport Federation. (2008b). *General assembly*. Retrieved November 18, 2008, from www.isfsports.org/sports/default.asp?id=766

Little League Online. (2008a). *The mission of Little League*. Retrieved November 17, 2008, from www.littleleague.org/Learn_More/About_Our_Organization/historyandmission/mission.htm

Little League Online. (2008b). *Structure of Little League baseball and softball*. Retrieved November 17, 2008, from www.littleleague.org/Learn_More/About_Our_Organization/Structure.htm

Little League Online. (2008c). *Little League network*. Retrieved November 17, 2008, from www.littleleague.org/Learn_More/Little_League_Network.htm

Liverpool Football Club. (2008). *Liverpool FC official membership*. Retrieved November 30, 2008, from www.liverpoolfc.tv/membership/?ncid=clubmemb_spbox_01122008

YMCA. (2008). *YMCAs in the world*. Retrieved November 7, 2008, from www.ymca.ca/eng_worldys.htm

Chapter 14

Anheuser-Busch and Manchester United. (2008, October 7). *Budweiser renews sponsorship of Manchester United* [press release]. London: Anheuser-Busch. Retrieved August 7, 2009, from www.anheuser-busch.com/press/ABchina/PressReleases/Manch-United-Eng.html

Arsenal Holdings plc. (2007, May). *Statement of accounts and annual report 2006/2007*.

Asafu-Adjaye, J. (2005). Environmental economics for non-economists (2nd ed.). Singapore: World Scientific.

Atkinson, G., Mourato, S., Szymanski, S., & Ozdemiroglu, E. (2008). Are we willing to pay enough to 'back the bid'?: Valuing the intangible impacts of London's bid to host the 2012 Summer Olympic Games. *Urban Studies*, 45(2), 419–444.

Browne, M. (2007). Sports: Industry annual 2007 report, *Global License!* 10(9), 32–33.

Cobb, S., & Weinberg, D. (1993). The importance of import substitution in regional economic impact analysis: Empirical estimates from two Cincinnati area events. *Economic Development Quarterly*, 7(3), 282–286.

Dauncey, H., & Hare, G. (Eds.) (1999). *France and the 1998 World Cup*. London: Frank Cass.

Dimitrov, D., Helmenstein, C., Kleissner, A., Moser, B., & Schindler, J. (2006). *Die makroökonomischen Effekte des Sports in Europa. Projektbericht*. Retrieved October 24, 2008, from www.sport.austria.gv.at/Docs/2006/7/14/Makroeffekte%20des%20Sports%20in%20EU_Finalkorrektur.pdf

Frank, R. (2006). *Microeconomics and behavior* (6th ed.). New York: McGraw-Hill/Irwin.

Heyne, M., Maennig, W., & Suessmuth, B. (2007). *Mega-sporting events as experience goods*. Hamburg Working Paper Series in Economic Policy, No. 5.

Korkki, P. (August 3, 2008). For nations an economic fitness test. *New York Times*.

Kurscheidt, M. (2009). *Ökonomische Analyse von Sportgroßveranstaltungen: Ein integrierter Ansatz für Evaluierung und Management am Beispiel von Fußball-Weltmeisterschaften*. Berlin: Duncker & Humblot.

Kurscheidt, M., Preuss, H., & Schütte, N. (2008). Konsuminduzierter Impakt von Sportgroßevents am Beispiel der Fußball-WM 2006—Befragungsergebnisse und Implikationen für die EURO 2008. *Wirtschaftspolitische Blätter*, 55(1), 79–94.

Mankiw, N. (2007). *Principles of macroeconomics* (4th ed.). Mason, OH: Thomson South-Western.

Milner, B. (November 7, 2006). NFL wants to play on a global field. *Toronto Globe and Mail*.

Nolan, R. (September 11, 2008). Protestors crash Berlin arena's opening party. *Spiegel Online International*. Retrieved August 7, 2009, from www.spiegel.de/international/germany/0,1518,577656,00.html

Preuss, H. (2004). *The economics of staging the Olympics. A comparison of the Games 1972–2008.* Cheltenham, United Kingdom: Edward Elgar.

Preuss, H. (2005). The economic impact of visitors at major multi-sport events. *European Sport Management Quarterly, 5*(3), 283–305.

Preuss, H. (2007). The conceptualisation and measurement of mega sport event legacies. *Journal of Sport & Tourism, 12*(4), 207–228.

Preuss, H., Kurscheidt, M., & Schütte, N. (2009). *Ökonomie des Tourismus durch Sportgroßveranstaltungen. Eine empirische Analyse zum Fußball-Weltmeisterschaft 2006.* Wiesbaden, Germany: Gabler Research

Solberg, H.A., & Preuss, H. (2007). Major sport events and long-term tourism impacts. *Journal of Sport Management, 21*(2), 215–236.

Spilling, O.R. (1999). Long-term impacts of mega-events: The case of Lillehammer 1994. In C. Jeanrenaud (Ed.), *The economic impact of sport events* (pp. 135–166). Neuchâtel, Switzerland: Editions CIES.

Stahlberg, M. (October 17, 2007). King of the back road. *Eugene Register Guard,* section B, p. 1.

Varian, H. (1990). *Intermediate microeconomics* (2nd ed.). New York: Norton.

Zenith International Ltd. (March 2006). *Zenith report on global sports drinks.* Retrived January, 24, 2009, from www.zenithinternational.com/pdf/reports/z1400GSp-Dtoc.pdf

Chapter 15

Andreff, W., & Staudohar, P.D. (2000). The evolving European model of professional sports finance. *Journal of Sports Economics, 1*(3), 257–276.

Baade, R.A. (2003). Evaluating subsidies for professional sports in the United States and Europe: A public-sector primer. *Oxford Review of Economic Policy, 19*(4), 585–597.

BBC Sport Online. (2004, November 12). *Leeds sell ground after bid fails.* http://news.bbc.co.uk/sport2/hi/football/teams/l/leeds_united/3995041.stm

Eckard, E.W. (2004). Team promotion in early major league baseball and the origin of the closed sports league. *Explorations in Economic History, 42,* 122–152.

Ennis, D. (2008, November, 28). *EU not swayed by FIFA 6+5 rule but will discuss UEFA plan.* Reuters Online. http://football.uk.reuters.com/european/news/LS513274.php

Fetini, A. (2008, October 23). *Two minute bio: Thaksin Shinawatra.* Time.com. www.time.com/time/world/article/0,8599,1853113,00.html?xid=feed-cnn-topics.

Fort, R. (2000). European and North American sports differences (?). *Scottish Journal of Political Economy, 47*(4), 431–455.

Maxcy, J., & Mondello, M. (2006). The impact of free agency on competitive balance in North American professional sports leagues. *Journal of Sport Management, 20,* 345–365.

Noll, R.G. (2002). The economics of promotion and relegation in sports leagues: The case of English football. *Journal of Sports Economics, 3*(2), 169–203.

Noll, R.G. (2003). The organization of sports leagues. *Oxford Review of Economic Policy, 19*(4), 530–551.

Parkes, R., Houlihan, A., Ingles, G., & Hawkins, M. (2007). Deloitte football money league. In D. Jones (Eds.), *Sports business group at Deloitte,* 1–34.

Rosen, S., & Sanderson, A. (2002). Labour markets in professional sports. *Economic Journal, 111*(469), 47–68.

Ross, S.F., & Szymanski, S. (2002). Open competition in league sports. *Wisconsin Law Review, 3,* 625–656.

Sky Sports Online. (2008, September 1). *City take over confirmed: Abu Dhabi United Group deal agreed.* www.skysports.com/story/0,19528,11661_4078332,00.html

Szymanski, S. (1999). The market for soccer players in England after Bosman: Winners and losers. In C. Jeanrenaud & S. Kesenne (eds.), *Competition policy in professional sports: Europe after the Bosman case.* Antwerp, Belgium: Standard Editions.

Szymanski, S., & Valletti, T.M. (2005). Promotion and relegation in sporting contests. *Rivista Di Politica Economica, V-VI,* 3–39.

Van Riper, T. (2009, January 13). *The most valuable teams in sports.* Forbes.com. www.forbes.com/2009/01/13/nfl-cowboys-yankees-biz-media-cx_tvr_0113values.html

Whiting, R. (1990). *You gotta have Wa.* New York: Macmillan.

Chapter 16

Adidas Group. (2007). *Giving 110%: Our efforts to be a responsible business in 2007.* Retrieved April 25, 2009, from www.adidas-group.com/en/sustainability/_downloads/social_and_environmental_reports/2007_adidas-Group_printed_report.pdf

Babiak, K., & Wolfe, R. (2006). More than just a game? Corporate social responsibility and Super Bowl XL. *Sport Marketing Quarterly, 15,* 214–222.

Babiak, K., Tainsky, S., & Juravich, M. (2008). *Professional athlete philanthropy: Walking the talk?* Paper presented at the 23rd Annual North American Society for Sport Management Conference (NASSM), Toronto, ON, Canada.

Basketball Without Borders. (2008). *Basketball without borders Africa.* Retrieved May 4, 2009, from www.nba.com/bwb

Bhanji, Z. (2008). Transnational corporations in education: Filling the governance gap through new social norms and market multilateralism? *Globalisation, Societies and Education, 6*(1), 55–73.

Blowfield, M., & Frynas, J.G. (2005). Setting new agendas: Critical perspectives on corporate social responsibility in the developing world. *International Affairs, 81*(3), 499–513.

Breitbarth, T., & Harris, P. (2008). The role of corporate social responsibility in the football business: Towards the development of a conceptual model. *European Sport Management Quarterly, 8*(2), 179–206.

Canada, Industry Canada. (2009). *Corporate social responsibility.* Retrieved April 19, 2009, from www.ic.gc.ca/eic/site/csr-rse.nsf/eng/home

Capdevila, G. (2007, July 6). UN: Global Compact with business "lacks teeth"—NGOs. *Inter Press News Service.* Retrieved May 5, 2009, from www.corpwatch.org/article.php?id=14549&printsafe=1

Changemakers, Inc. (2007). *Sport for a better world competition.* Retrieved May 4, 2009, from www.changemakers.net/en-us/competition/sports

Chauhan, P.S. (2008). *Stakeholder approach to understanding the role of the Olympic Games in social development.* Unpublished thesis. University of British Columbia.

Coakley, J., & Donnelly, P. (2004). Sport in Society: Issues and Controversies (1st Canadian edition). Toronto, Canada: McGraw Hill Ryerson.

Cole, C.L. (2008). Nikes especially for American Indians: Noble gesture or savage racism? *Journal of Sport and Social Issues, 32*(1), 3.

Cole, C.L., & Hribar, A. (1995). Celebrity feminism: Nike style. Post-Fordism, transcendence, and consumer power. *Sociology of Sport Journal, 12,* 347–369.

Cooper, A.F. (2007). Politics and diplomacy: Beyond Hollywood and the boardroom. *Georgetown Journal of International Affairs, 8*(2), 125–133.

Esteva, G., & Prakash, M.S. (1998). *Grassroots post-modernism: Remaking the soil of cultures.* London: Zed Books.

Frisby, W. (2005). The good, the bad and the ugly: Critical sport management research. *Journal of Sport Management, 19*(1), 1–12.

Frisby, W. (2006). Understanding sport management research. In J. Parks, J. Quarterman, & L. Thibault (Eds.), *Contemporary sport management* (3rd ed.) (pp. 441–460). Champaign, IL: Human Kinetics.

Guelke, A., & Sugden, J. (1999). Sport and the "normalizing" of the New South Africa. In J. Sugden & A. Bairner (Eds.), *Sport in divided societies* (pp. 73–96). Brighton, United Kingdom: Meyer and Meyer Sport.

Hayhurst, L. (2009a). *Manufacturing sport for development interventions: Exploring the discourses and dangers of Global Corporate Social Engagement (GCSE) programs.* Paper presented at the Bodies of Knowledge Conference, University of Toronto, ON, Canada.

Hayhurst, L. (2009b). The power to shape policy: Charting sport for development policy discourses. *International Journal of Sport Policy, 1*(2), 203–227.

Himmelstein, J.L. (1997). *Looking good and doing good: Corporate philanthropy and corporate power.* Bloomington: Indiana University Press.

Homeless World Cup, (2008). *About us.* Retrieved April 11, 2008, from www.homelessworldcup.org/content/about-us

Hopkins, M. (2006). *Corporate social responsibility and international development: Is business the solution?* London: Earthscan.

Houlihan, B., & White, A. (2002). *The politics of sports development: Development of sport or development through sport?* London: Routledge.

Hudson's Bay Company (HBC). (2007). *Acting with a global mind: HBC global social responsibility report.* Retrieved April 19, 2009, from www.hbc.com/hbc/socialresponsibility

Hums, L., Lyras, A., Wolff, E., Hamakawa, C., Peachey, J.W. (2008). *The Olympic Movement and social responsibility: Organizational best practices which can bring about social change.* Paper presented at the 23rd Annual North American Society for Sport Management Conference (NASSM), Toronto, ON, Canada.

International Baby Food Action Network. (2010). *Breaking the Rules, Stretching the Rules.* Retrieved January 11, 2011, from www.ibfan.org/news-2010-1224.html.

Kidd, B., & Donnelly, P. (2000). Human rights in sport. *International Review for the Sociology of Sport, 35*(2), 131–148.

Kidd, B. (2008). A new social movement: Sport for development and peace. *Sport in Society, 11*(4), 370–380.

King, S. (2001). Marketing generosity: Avon's women's health programs and new trends in global community relations. *International Journal of Sports Marketing & Sponsorship, 3*(3), 267–290.

King, S. (2004). Pink Ribbons Inc: Breast cancer activism and the politics of philanthropy. *International Journal of Qualitative Studies in Education, 17*(4), 473–492.

King, S. (2006). *Pink Ribbons Inc.: Cancer and the politics of philanthropy.* Minneapolis: University of Minnesota Press.

Knight, G., & Greenberg, J. (2002). Promotionalism and subpolitics: Nike and its labour critics. *Management Communication Quarterly, 15*(4), 541–570.

Lucas, S. (2000). Nike's commercial solution: Girls, sneakers, and salvation. *International Review for the Sociology of Sport, 35*(2), 149–164.

Mallen, C., & Bradish, C. (2008). *Corporate social responsibility, corporate citizenship and innovative pedagogy in sport management.* Paper presented at the 23rd Annual North American Society for Sport Management Conference (NASSM), Toronto, ON, Canada.

Maquila Solidarity Network. (2009). *About us.* Retrieved May 5, 2009, from http://en.maquilasolidarity.org/

McGlone, C., & Martin, N. (2006). Nike's corporate interest lives strong: A case of cause-related marketing and leveraging. *Sport Marketing Quarterly, 15,* 184–189.

Millington, R. (2009). *Rebounding basketballs and (re)producing knowledges: Analyzing the dominant discourse of basketball without borders.* Paper presented at the Bodies of Knowledge Conference, University of Toronto, ON, Canada.

Misener, L. (2008). *Mega-events and corporate social responsibility: A stakeholder perspective of compatibility.* Paper presented at the 23rd Annual North American Society for Sport Management Conference (NASSM), Toronto, ON, Canada.

Nestlé Canada. (2009). *Creating Shared Value Report.* Retrieved January 11, 2011, from www.nestle.ca/NR/rdonlyres/9F537C54-FF8D-466B-803F-5C580AD76479/0/E_CreatingSharedValue.pdf.

Newell, P., & Frynas, J.G. (2007). Beyond CSR? Business, poverty and social justice: An introduction. *Third World Quarterly, 28*(4), 669–681.

Nike, Inc., (2006). *Innovate for a better world: Nike FY05–06 corporate responsibility report.* Retrieved 11 December, 2007, from www.nikeresponsibility.com/pdfs/bw/Nike_FY05_06_CR_Report_BW.pdf

Nike Foundation. (2005). *Nike Foundation master plan.* Portland, OR.

Nike Foundation. (2008). *Home.* Retrieved June 1, 2008, from www.nikefoundation.org

Peace One Day. (2009). *One day one goal.* Retrieved May 5, 2009, from www.peaceoneday.org/football.aspx

Pearson, R. (2007). Beyond women workers: Gendering CSR. *Third World Quarterly, 28*(4), 731–749.

Polonsky, M.J., & Wood, G. (2001). Can the overcommercialization of cause-related marketing harm society? *Journal of Macromarketing, 21*(1), 8–22.

Ponte, S., Richey, L., & Babb, M. (2009). Bono's product (RED) initiative: Corporate social responsibility that solves the problems of "distant others." *Third World Quarterly, 30*(2), 301–317.

Prahalad, C.K. (2005). *The fortune at the bottom of the pyramid.* Upper Saddle River, NJ: Wharton School.

Prescott, D., & Phelan, J. (2008). *Shared goals through sport: Getting a sustainable return for companies and communities.* Retrieved August 6, 2008, from www.iblf.org/sport.

Prieto-Carron, M., Lund-Thomsen, P., Chan, A., Muro, A., & Bhushan, C. (2006). Critical perspectives of CSR and development: What we know, what we don't know, and what we need to know. *International Affairs, 82*(5), 977–987.

Rapley, J. (2007). *Understanding development: Theory and practice in the third world.* Boulder, CO: Lynne Rienner.

Right to Play. (2007). *Adidas and Right to Play kick off Red Ball Campaign.* Retrieved May 4, 2009, from www.press.adidas.com/en/DesktopDefault.aspx?tabid-16/94_read-7986/

Right to Play. (2009). *When children play, the world wins.* Retrieved May 6, 2009, from www.righttoplay.com/site/PageServer

Roy, A. (2007). In her name: The gender order of global poverty management. In A.L Cazebas, E. Reese, and M. Waller (eds.), *The wages of empire: Neoliberal policies, repression and women's poverty* (pp. 28–40). Boulder, CO: Paradigm.

Ruggie, J.G. (2003). The UN and globalization: Patterns and limits of institutional adaptation. *Global Governance, 9,* 301–321.

Sage, G. (1999). Justice do it! The Nike Transnational Advocacy Network: Organization, collective actions, and outcomes. *Sociology of Sport Journal, 16,* 206–235.

Sharp, J. (2006). Corporate social responsibility and development: An anthropological perspective. *Development Southern Africa, 23*(2), 213–222.

Smith, A.C.T., & Westerbeek, H.M. (2007). Sport as a vehicle for deploying corporate social responsibility. *Journal of Corporate Citizenship, 25,* 43–54.

SOS Children's Villages. (2009). *FIFA for SOS's Children's Villages: Sport and social responsibility in partnership.* Retrieved May 5, 2009, from www.soschildrensvillages.ca/child-charity/Corporate-Giving/corporate-partners/International-Corporate-Partners/FIFA/Pages/default.aspx

Spain, W. (2007, May 31). Nike announces new responsibility campaign. *Marketwatch.* Retrieved June 25, 2008, from www.marketwatch.com/news/story/nike-vows-change-labor-practices/story.aspx?guid=%7BBB75224B-7826-49A3-98BC-16FC914BED2F%7D

Sport for Development and Peace International Working Group (SDP IWG). (2006). *Sport for development and peace: From practice to policy.* Retrieved June 12, 2006, from www.righttoplay.com/site/DocServer/Right_to_Play__From_Practice_to_Policy_book.pdf?docID=3061

UNHCR. (2005). *Designers on a mission: Dressing refugee girls for sports.* Retrieved April 2, 2008, from www.unhcr.org/cgi-bin/texis/vtx/news/opendoc.htm?tbl=NEWS&page=home&id=42cbed364

United Nations Global Compact (UNGC). (2007). *The Global Compact Network.* Retrieved August 10, 2008, from www.unglobalcompact.org/ParticipantsAndStakeholders/index.html

University of Toronto. (2001). *Athletic apparel, uniforms and equipment code of conduct.* Retrieved May 6, 2009, from www.trademarks.utoronto.ca/code.html

Visser, W. (2008). Corporate social responsibility in developing countries. In A. Crane, A. McWilliams, D. Matten, J. Moon, & D.S. Siegel (eds.), *The Oxford handbook of corporate social responsibility* (pp. 474–499). New York: Oxford University Press.

Vodafone. (2009). *Corporate responsibility.* Retrieved April 19, 2009, from www.vodafone.com/start/responsibility.html

Watts, M. (2005). Righteous oil? Human rights, the oil complex, and corporate social responsibility. *Annual Review of Environment and Resources, 30,* 373–407.

Willis, O. (2000). Sport and development: The significance of Mathare Youth Sports Association. *Canadian Journal of Development Studies, XXI*(3), 825–849.

World Federation of Sporting Goods Industries (WFSGI). (2009). *Members' CSR profiles.* Retrieved April 19, 2009, from www.wfsgi.org/articles/128

Zadek, S. (2007). *The civil corporation.* London: Earthscan.

Chapter 17

20 questions about the CAS. (2009). Retrieved June 21, 2009, from www.tas-cas.org/en/20questions.asp/4-3-214-1010-4-1-1/5-0-1010-13-0-0/

Asinof, E. (2000). *Eight men out: The Black Sox and the 1919 World Series.* New York: Holt.

Associated Press. (2009, February 11). *Tejada pleads guilty to lying about steroid use.* Retrieved July 23, 2009, from http://nbcsports.msnbc.com/id/29123151/

Black's law dictionary (8th ed.). (2004). St. Paul, MN: Thomson West.Cafardo, N. (2007, August 1). Masanori Murakami was Japanese trailblazer to the major leagues. *Baseball Digest, 66*(6), 29.

Canseco, J. (2005). *Juiced: Wild times, rampant 'roids, smash hits, and how baseball got big.* New York: William Morrow.

CAS Arbitral Award—Oscar Pistorius, CAS 2008/A/1480/Pistorius v/ IAAF (Court of Arbitration for Sport (CAS) May 16, 2008).

CAS origins. (2009). Retrieved June 21, 2009, from Court of Arbitration of Sport (TAS–CAS) website, www.tas-cas.org/history

CBS Interactive Inc. (2008, July 29). *Game over for crooked ex-NBA ref.* (C. I. Inc., Producer) Retrieved June 21, 2009, from CBS News website, www.cbsnews.com/stories/2008/07/29/sports/main4301832.shtml

Cohen, M.M. (2009). Ethics in the multijurisdictional practice of admiralty lawyers. *Fordham International Law Journal, 32,* 1135.

Collins, R. (2000, March 18). Rune Hauge, international man of mystery. Retrieved June 21, 2009, from *The Guardian,* www.guardian.co.uk/football/2000/mar/18/newsstory.sport1

Council of Europe. (1985, August 19). *European Convention on Spectator Violence and Misbehaviour at Sports Events and in Particular at Football Matches.* Retrieved June 21, 2009, from the Council of Europe's official treaty website, http://conventions.coe.int/Treaty/EN/Treaties/Html/120.htm

DeFrantz v. USOC, 492 F. Supp. 1181 (D.D.C. 1980).

ESPN's sports century: Most influential people in sports (1999). [Motion picture].

FIFA players' agents regulations. (2008). Retrieved June 21, 2009, from the Fédération Internationale de Football Association (FIFA) website, www.fifa.com/mm/51/55/18/playersagents_en_32511.pdf

Filkins, D. (2000, June 2). Innocence has met its match in cricket scandal. *Los Angeles Times.*

Floyd Landis v/USADA, CAS 2008/A/1394 (Court of Arbitration of Sport (TAS-CAS). June 30, 2008).

Football violence round the world. (1998, June 15). Retrieved June 21, 2009, from BBC News Online, http://news.bbc.co.uk/2/hi/sport/football/112863.stm

Fornelli, T. (2008, October 7). *International pastime: Japan imposes ban on players returning from U.S.* (T. Fornelli, producer). Retrieved June 21, 2009, from MLB

Fanhouse, http://mlb.fanhouse.com/2008/10/07/international-pastime-japan-imposes-ban-on-players-returning-fr/

Gardner v. Nat'l Netball League Pty Ltd. (2001). 182 ALR 408; [2001] FMCA 50.

Godoy, M. (2007, December 13). *Timeline: Key moments in baseball's doping probe.* Retrieved June 21, 2009, from National Public Rado (NPR), www.npr.org/templates/story/story.php?storyId=17220752

Greenberg, M.J., & Gray, J.T. (1998). *Sports law practice* (2nd ed.). Charlottesville, VA: Lexis Law.

Guardian News & Media. (2004, January 9). *Olympic Games: Top Korean Un Yong Kim caught in bribery row.* Retrieved June 21, 2009, from Buzzle.com, www.buzzle.com/editorials/1-9-2004-49267.asp

Harding, L. (2005, November 1). Forgotten victims of East German doping take their battle to court. *The Guardian,* p. 9.

Harris, N. (2009, February 7). £1.78bn: Record Premier League TV deal defies economic slump. *The Independent.* www.independent.co.uk/sport/football/premier-league/163178bn-record-premier-league-tv-deal-defies-economic-slump-1569576.html

Howman, D. (2003, November 12). *Sanctions under the World Anti-Doping Code.* Retrieved June 21, 2009, from World Anti-Doping Agency website, www.wada-ama.org/rtecontent/document/LEGAL_sanctions_howman.pdf

Humphrey, C. (2006, October 13). *Unlawful Internet Gambling Enforcement Act of 2006: Internet gambling funding ban.* Retrieved June 21, 2009, from Gambling Law US, www.gambling-law-us.com/

IOC Ethics Commission. (2005, February 4).

International Paralympic Committee. (2009). *About the IPC.* Retrieved June 21, 2009, from www.paralympic.org/release/Main_Sections_Menu/IPC/About_the_IPC/index.html

Japan tries to discourage amateurs from playing in MLB with ban. (2008, October 8). (A. Press, Producer). Retrieved June 21, 2009, from ESPN.com, http://sports.espn.go.com/mlb/news/story?id=3632083

Kansas City Royals Baseball Corp. v. Major League Baseball Players Ass'n, 532 F. 2d 615 (8th Cir. 1976).

Kaplan, D., & Ourand, J. (2009, May 18). NFL close to extensions with Fox, CBS. *Street & Smith's SportsBusiness Journal,* p. 1.

Liu, J.H. (2007). Lighting the torch of human rights: The Olympic Games as a vehicle for human rights reform. *Northwestern University Journal of International Human Rights, 5,* 213.

Longman, J. (2004, January 26). Drug testing; East German steroids' toll: "They killed Heidi." *New York Times,* p. D1.

Lowitt, B. (1999, October 7). Disturbed fan stabs top-ranked Seles. *St. Petersburg Times*.

Mackey v. Nat'l Football League, 543 F.2d 606 (8th Cir. 1976).

Malta's Sports Act—Chapter 455. (2003, January 27). Retrieved June 21, 2009, from Malta Ministry of Education, Culture, Youth & Sport website, www.education.gov.mt/ministry/doc/pdf/acts/sports_act.pdf

Mehlman, M.J., Banger, E., & Wright M.W. (2005). Health Law Symposium: Doping in Sports and the Use of State Power, *St. Louis Law Journal, 50*, 15.

Mission statement—Singapore Ministry of Community Development, Youth, and Sports. (2005, February 18). Retrieved June 21, 2009, from Singapore's Ministry of Community Development, Youth, and Sports website, http://app.mcys.gov.sg/web/corp_mission.asp

MLBPA regulations governing player agents. (1993, December). Retrieved June 21, 2009, from Sports Lawyers Association (SLA) website, www.sportslaw.org/

Mohamed, A. (2008, February 4). *Stop racial discrimination or else—Stofile*. Retrieved June 21, 2009, from IOL: News for South Africa and the World, www.iol.co.za/index.php?set_id=6&click_id=4&art_id=vn20080204061849269C492123

Moscow Dynamo v. Ovechkin, 412 F. Supp. 2d 24 (D.C. Dist. Ct. 2006).

Nafziger, J.A. (2004). *International sports law* (2nd ed.). Ardsley, NY: Transnational.

National & Am. League Prof'l Baseball Clubs v. Major League Baseball Players Ass'n, 66 Labor Arbitration 101 1976 (Messersmith and McNally Grievances) (1976).

NBPA regulations governing player agents (as amended). (1991, June). Retrieved June 21, 2009, from Sports Lawyers Association (SLA) website, www.sportslaw.org

NFLPA regulations governing contract advisors (as amended). (2007, March). Retrieved June 21, 2009, from National Football League Players' Association (NFLPA) website, www.nflplayers.com/images/pdfs/Agents/NFLPA_Regulations_Contract_Advisors.pdf

O'Brien, J. (2008). Political balk: Opening the door for U.S.–Cuba policy reform via diplomatic blunder at the World Baseball Classic. *Villanova Sports and Entertainment Law Journal, 15*, 213.

Olympic Charter. (2007, July 7). Retrieved June 21, 2009, from the website of the Olympic Movement, http://multimedia.olympic.org/pdf/en_report_122.pdf

Organisation and structure of the ICAS and CAS. (2009). Retrieved June 21, 2009, from Court of Arbitration of Sport (TAS-CAS) website, www.tas-cas.org/en/infogenerales.asp/4-3-238-1011-4-1-1/5-0-1011-3-0-0/

Puma, M. (2004, December 10). The *"choke" artist*. Retrieved June 21, 2009, from ESPN Classic website, http://espn.go.com/classic/s/add_sprewell_latrell.html

Reston, J.J. (1997). *Collision at home plate: The lives of Pete Rose and Bart Giamatti*. Lincoln: University of Nebraska Press.

Rogge, J. (2007). Speech by Dr. Jacques Rogge, president, International Olympic Committee. *World Conference on Doping in Sport* (p. 5). Madrid, Spain.

Rose, P. (2004). *My prison without bars*. Emmaus, PA: Rodale Books.

Sandoval, G. (2004, November 23). Charges to be filed in Pistons–Pacers brawl. *Washington Post*, p. D7.

Snyder, D.L. (2003). International sports law. In D.J. Cotten & J.T. Wolohan (Eds.), *Law for recreation and sport managers* (3rd ed., pp. 34–43). Dubuque, IA: Kendall Hunt.

Soek, J. (2006). *The strict liability principle and the human rights of athletes in doping cases*. The Hague, the Netherlands: TMC Asser Press.

Sport and Recreation South Africa. (n.d.). *2008–2012 Strategic Plan—Sport and Recreation South Africa*. Retrieved June 21, 2009, from www.srsa.gov.za/ClientFiles/SRSA%20Strategic%20Plan%202008-2012%2012%20May%2008.pdf

Srivastava, S. (2000, April 20). *Scandal damages Indian cricket*. Retrieved June 21, 2009, from BBC News, http://news.bbc.co.uk/2/hi/south_asia/720880.stm

Statutes of ICAS and CAS—A. joint dispositions. (2009). Retrieved June 21, 2009, from Court of Arbitration of Sport (TAS–CAS) website, www.tas-cas.org/statutes

Stewart, Laura S. (2006). Comment: Has the United States Anti-Doping Agency gone too far? Analyzing the shift from "beyond a reasonable doubt" to "comfortable satisfaction." *Villanova Sports & Entertainment Law Journal, 13*, 207–243.

The 1994 reform. (2009). Retrieved June 21, 2009, from Court of Arbitration of Sport (TAS–CAS) website, www.tas-cas.org/en/infogenerales.asp/4-3-236-1011-4-1-1/5-0-1011-3-0-0/

The CAS Code. (2009). Retrieved June 21, 2009, from Court of Arbitration of Sport (TAS–CAS) website, www.tas-cas.org/d2wfiles/document/281/5048/0/3.1%20CodeEngnov2004.pdf

The decentralized CAS offices and the ad hoc divisions. (2009). Retrieved June 21, 2009, from Court of Arbitration of Sport (TAS–CAS) website, www.tas-cas.org/en/infogenerales.asp/4-3-240-1011-4-1-1/5-0-1011-3-0-0/

The Heysel disaster. (2000, May 29). Retrieved June 21, 2009, from BBC News Online: http://news.bbc.co.uk/2/hi/uk_news/768380.stm

The World Anti-Doping Code. (2009 [revised], January 1). Retrieved June 21, 2009, from World Anti-Doping Agency website, www.wada-ama.org/rtecontent/document/code_v2009_En.pdf

Ungerleider, S. (2001). *Faust's gold: Inside the East German doping machine*. New York: St. Martin's Press.

Union Royale Belge des Societes de Football Association (ASBL), Royal Club Liegois SA, and Union des Associations Europeennes de Football (UEFA) v. Jean-Marc Bosman, Case C-415/93 (1995).

United Nations. (2006, December 13). *Convention on the Rights of Persons with Disabilities.* Retrieved June 21, 2009, from UN Enable, www.un.org/disabilities/default. asp?navid=12&pid=150

WADA History. (n.d.). Retrieved June 21, 2009, from World Anti-Doping Agency website, www.wada-ama.org/en/ dynamic.ch2?pageCategory.id=253

Whiting, R. (2004, September 29). *The fans in Japan: Why they're happy when baseball players go on strike.* Retrieved June 21, 2009, from Slate Magazine, www.slate.com/ id/2107321

World Anti-Doping Agency. (2007, May 18). *Anti-doping glossary.* Retrieved June 21, 2009, from World Anti-Doping Agency website, www.wada-ama.org/rtecontent/ document/Anti-Doping_Glossary_En.pdf

World Anti-Doping Agency. (2008). *Q&A: Strict liability in anti-doping.*

Chapter 18

BBC Sport. (2004, October 5). *Arsenal name new ground.* Retrieved February 17, 2011, from http://news.bbc. co.uk/sport2/hi/football/teams/a/arsenal/3715678.stm

Berry, L. (1980). Services marketing is different. *Business Forum, 30* (May–June), 24–29.

Brady, M.K., & Cronin, J.J. (2001). Some new thoughts on conceptualizing perceived service quality: A hierarchical approach. *Journal of Marketing, 65* (July), 34–49.

Chelladurai, P. (2005). *Managing organizations for sport and physical activity: A systems perspective* (2nd ed.). Scottsdale, AZ: Holcomb Hathaway.

Chelladurai, P., & Chang, K. (2000). Targets and standards of quality in sport services. *Sport Management Review, 3*, 1–22.

Collier, D.A. (1994). *The service quality solution: Using service management to gain competitive advantage.* Milwaukee, WI: ASQC Quality Press.

Costa, G., Tsitskari, E., Tzetzis, G., & Goudas, M. (2004). The factors for evaluating service quality in athletic camps: A case study. *European Sport Management Quarterly, 4*, 22–35.

Dallas Cowboys. *Be a part of Dallas Cowboys football history.* Retrieved June 23, 2010, from http://stadium.dallascowboys.com/suites/suiteInfo.cfm.

Gilmore, A. (2003). *Services marketing and management.* Thousand Oaks, CA: Sage.

Grönroos, C. (1984). A service quality model and its marketing implications. *European Journal of Marketing, 18*(4), 36–44.

Grönroos, C. (1990). *Service management and marketing: Managing the moments of truth in service competition.* Toronto, ON, Canada: Lexington Books.

Grönroos, C. (2001). A service quality model and its marketing implications. *European Journal of Marketing, 18*(4), 36–44.

Hart, C.W.L. (1988, July/August). The power of unconditional service guarantees. *Harvard Business Review,* 54–62.

Kandampully, J. (2002). *Services management: The new paradigm in hospitality.* Frenchs Forest, NSW, Australia: Pearson Education Australia.

Klassen, K.J., Russell, R.M., & Chrisman, J.J. (1998). Efficiency and productivity measures for high contact services. *Services Industries Journal, 18*(4), 1–18.

Lovelock, C., & Gummesson, E. (2004). Whither services marketing: In search of a new paradigm and fresh perspectives. *Journal of Service Research, 7*(1), 20–41.

Orwig, R.A., Pearson, J., & Cochran, D. (1997). An empirical investigation into the validity of SERVQUAL in the public sector. *PAQ*, 54–68.

Parasuraman, A., Zeithaml, V.A., & Berry, L.L. (1985). A conceptual model of service quality and its implications for future research. *Journal of Marketing, 41*–55.

Parasuraman, A., Zeithaml, V.A., & Berry, L.L. (1988). SERVQUAL: A multiple-item scale for measuring consumer perceptions of service quality. *Journal of Retailing, 64*(1), 12–40.

Rafiq, M., & Ahmed, P.K. (2000). Advances in the internal marketing concept: Definition, synthesis and extension. *Journal of Services Marketing, 14*, 449–462.

Romanuk, P. (2007, Feb. 5). New venues bring needed change to Europe. *SportBusiness Journal.* Retrieved August 1, 2010, from www.sportsbusinessjournal.com/ index.cfm?fuseaction=article.preview&articleID=53821

Shonk, D.J., & Chelladurai, P. (2009). Service quality in event sport tourism: Development of a scale. *International Journal of Sport Management and Marketing, 6*, 292-307.

Wakefield, K.L., Blodgett, J.G., & Sloan, H.J. (1996). Measurement and management of the sportscape. *Journal of Sport Management, 10*, 15–31.

Westerbeek, H.M. (2000). The influence of frequency of attendance and age on "place"—specific dimensions of service quality at Australian rules football matches. *Sport Marketing Quarterly, 9*(4), 194–202.

Wirtz, J. (1998). Development of a service guarantee model. *Asia Pacific Journal of Management, 15*, 51–75.

Wirtz, J., Kum, D., & Lee, K.S. (2000). Should a firm with a reputation for outstanding quality offer a service guarantee? *Journal of Services Marketing, 14*(6), 502–515.

World Cup Government Services. (2010). Retrieved June 28, 2010, from www.sa2010.gov.za/en/node/2850

Yardley, J. (2007, April 17). No spitting on the road to Olympic glory, Beijing says. *New York Times.* Retrieved June 26, 2010, from www.nytimes.com/2007/04/17/ world/asia/17iht-web-0417china.5314587.html

Yaro, B.K. (2010). *Ghana: Lack of sports equipment affecting sporting activities in Upper East.* Retrieved June 23, 2010, from http://allafrica.com/stories/200908140723.html

Zeithaml, V.A., Parasuraman, A., & Berry, L.L. (1985). Problems and strategies in services marketing. *Journal of Marketing, 49*, 33–46.

Chapter 19

Aaron, C.T. (2008). *Introduction to sport marketing*. Oxford, United Kingdom: Elsevier.

AIG ends soccer sponsorship. (2009). CNNMoney.com. Retrieved March 2, 2009, from http://money.cnn.com/2009/01/21/news/international/uk_soccer/

Apostolopoulou, A., & Papadimitriou, D. (2005). Global sport industry. In A. Gillentine & R.B.Crow (Eds.), *Foundations of sport management* (pp. 169–183). Morgantown, WV: Fitness Information Technology.

Basu, S. (2010, June 11). 10 weblinks to catch the football fever at FIFA World Cup 2010. Retrieved January 20, 2011, from www.makeuseof.com/tag/10-weblinks-catch-football-fever-fifa-world-cup-2010/

Breaking Limits. (2010, October 26). *Komatsu America Corp. and Tractor & Equipment Company partner with Phoenix Racing at Talladega*. Retrieved November 16, 2010, from http://news.blmarketing.affinigent.net/NewsArticles/tabid/85/ItemId/581/Komatsu-America-Corp-and-Tractor-Equipment-Company-Partner-with-Phoenix-Racing-at-Talladega.aspx

Campbell, S. (2008, July 10). *India: Opportunities in the business of sport*. Retrieved November 10, 2010, from www.sportbusiness.com/products/reports/india-opportunities-in-the-business-of-sport-167993

Chadwick, S. (2007, June). The Americans are coming. *Sport Marketing Quarterly, 16*(2), 123–124.

Chunichi Sports. (January 21, 2010). *Komatsu in Angel stadium*. Retrieved November 7, 2010, from www.nikken-times.co.jp/new/20100121.0/1264031405.html

Cialdini, R.B., Borden, R.J., Thorne, A., Walker, M.R., Freeman, S., & Sloan, L.R. (1976). Basking in reflected glory: Three (football) field studies. *Journal of Personality and Social Psychology, 39*, 406–415.

Collegiate Licensing Company. (2009). *Licensing information*. Retrieved January 3, 2009, from www.clc.com/clcweb/publishing.nsf/Content/get+licensed.html

Conley, L. (2008). *Obsessive branding disorder*. New York: Public Affairs.

Connolly, E. (2010, September). Turning a race into an event. *SportsPro Magazine* (25), pp. 98–101.

Couvelaere, V., & Richelieu, A. (March, 2005). Brand strategy in professional sports: The case of French soccer teams. *European Sport Management Quarterly, 5*(1), 23–46.

de Chernatony, L., Halliburton, C., & Bernath, R. (1995). International branding: Demand- or supply-driven opportunity? *International marketing review, 12*(2), 9–21.

Ellis, D. (2009). *U.S. takes another crack at AIG rescue*. CNNMoney.com. Retrieved March 2, 2009, from http://money.cnn.com/2009/03/02/news/companies/aig/index.htm

Emmett, J. (2010, November). The NBA's global game. *SportsPro Magazine* (27), pp. 63–66.

FIFA. (2008). *About FIFA partners*. Retrieved November 23, 2008, from www.fifa.com/aboutfifa/marketingtv/partners/adidas.html

FIFA. (2009a). *Emirates: A first class partner*. Retrieved June 1, 2009, from www.fifa.com/aboutfifa/marketing/partners/emirates.html

FIFA. (2009b). FIFA brand—our commitment. Retrieved June 15, 2009, from www.fifa.com/aboutfifa/federation/mission.html

FIFA. (2010). *Sponsorship Programme*. Retrieved November 5, 2010, from www.fifa.com/worldcup/organisation/marketing/index.html

Fink, J.S., Trail, G.T., & Anderson, D.F. (2002). Environmental factors associated with spectator attendance and sport consumption behavior: Gender and team identification differences. *Sport Marketing Quarterly, 11*, 8–19.

Fullerton, S. (2007). *Sports marketing* (2nd ed.). New York: McGraw-Hill/Irwin.

Funk, D.C. (2008). *Consumer behavior in sport and events: Marketing action*. Oxford, United Kingdom: Elsevier.

Funk, D.C., Mahony, D.F., & Havitz, M.E. (2003). Sport consumer behavior: Assessment and direction. *Sport Marketing Quarterly, 12*, 200–205.

Gantz, W., & Wenner, L.A. (1991). Men, women, and sports: Audience experiences and effects. *Journal of Broadcasting & Electronic Media, 35*, 233–243.

Gillentine, A., & Crow, R.B. (2005). *Foundations of sport management*. Morgantown, WV: Fitness Information Technology.

Holt, D.B. (1995). How consumers consume: A typology of consumption practices. *Journal of Consumer Research, 22*, 1–16.

Hughes, D. (2009). *The collegiate licensing company names top selling universities and manufacturers*. Retrieved February 4, 2009, from www.clc.com/clcweb/publishing.nsf/Content/Fiscal+Year-End+Rankings+July+1%2C+2007+-+June+30%2C+2008

International Cricket Council. (2010). *Home*. Retrieved October 1, 2010, from http://icc-cricket.yahoo.net/

Johnson, G. (June 3, 1998). Dodgers took a calculated move. *Los Angeles Times*. Retrieved November 16, 2010, from http://articles.latimes.com/print/1998/jun/03/business/fi-55910

Kim, S., Andrew, D.P., & Greenwell, T.C. (2009). An analysis of spectator motives and media consumption behavior in an individual combat sport: Cross-national differences between American and South Korean mixed martial arts fans. *International Journal of Sports Marketing and Sponsorship, 10*, 157–170.

Komatsu America. (2010, September 16). *Komatsu America partners with Pedregon racing*. Retrieved November 16, 2010, from www.komatsuamerica.com/091610-Pedregon-Racing

Komatsu Australia. (December 8, 2008). *Komatsu and Triple Eight: Different industry, same goals.* Retrieved November 7, 2010, from www.komatsu.com.au/komatsuworld/news/articles/Pages/KOMATSUANDTRIPLEEIGHTDIFFERENTINDUSTRY,SAMEGOALS.aspx

Komatsu Japan. (2003). *Komatsu adopts Hideki Matsui of New York Yankees as its image character.* Retrieved November 3, 2010, from www.komatsu.co.jp/CompanyInfo/press/2003050119280916250.html

Kukkiwon. (2010). Retrieved October 3, 2010, from www.kukkiwon.or.kr/intro.jsp

Landreth, J. (2008, August 10). *Olympics draw impressive ratings worldwide.* Retrieved January 20, 2011, from www.reuters.com/article/2008/08/11/industry-olympics-overseas-dc-idUSN1029559220080811

Larmer, B. (2005). The center of the world. *Foreign Policy,* September/October, 66–74.

Mahony, D.F., Nakazawa, M., Funk, D.C., James, J., & Gladden, J.M. (2002). Motivational factors impacting the behavior of J. League spectators: Implications for league marketing efforts. *Sport Management Review, 5,* 1–24.

McCracken, G. (1986). Culture and consumption: A theoretical account of the structure and movement of the cultural meaning of consumer goods. *Journal of Consumer Research, 13* (June), 71–84.

McCullagh, K. (2009). *Man Utd. signs football's biggest shirt sponsorship.* Retrieved June 29, 2009, from www.sportsbusiness.com/news/169581/man-utd-signs-football%E2%80%99s-biggest-shirt-sponsorship

MLB International. (n.d.). *MLB International sponsorships.* Retrieved November 15, 2010, from http://mlb.mlb.com/mlb/international/sections.jsp?feature=mlbi_sponsorship

MLB stars look for marketing success in Japan. (1996, November 11). *SportsBusiness Daily* Retrieved November 7, 2010, from www.sportsbusinessdaily.com/article/42454

Mullin, B.J., Hardy, S., & Sutton, W.A. (2007). *Sport marketing* (3rd ed.). Champaign, IL: Human Kinetics.

National Basketball Association. (2008). Harlem Globetrotters, NBA team up in international effort. Retrieved January 20, 2011, from www.nba.com/2008/news/11/24/globetrotters/

National Basketball Association (2009). *NBA's international fames fact sheet.* Retrieved February 18, 2011, from www.nba.com/europelive/fact_sheets.html

National Basketball Association (2010a). *Season opens with record 84 international players.* Retrieved February 18, 2011, from www.nba.com/news/2010-11-international-players/index.html

National Basketball Association (2010b). *Basketball without borders.* Retrieved February 18, 2011, from www.nba.com/bwb/

National Football League London. (2010). *International Series 2010: San Francisco 49ers v Denver Broncos.* Retrieved from October 5, 2010, from www.nfllondon.net/

Neal, L., & Funk, D. (2006). Investigating motivation, attitudinal loyalty and attendance behaviour with fans of Australian football. *International Journal of Sports Marketing & Sponsorship, 7,* 307–319.

Onkvisit, S., & Shaw, J.J. (1989). The international dimension of branding: strategic considerations and decisions. *International marketing review, 6*(3), 23–34.

Parasuraman, A., Zeithaml, V.A., & Berry, L.L. (1988). SERVQUAL: Multiple-item scale for measuring consumer perceptions of service quality. *Journal of Retailing, 64*(1), 12–40.

Paul, A. (2009). Kobe's next conquest: China. *Wall Street Journal.* Retrieved June 29, 2009, from http://online.wsj.com/article/SB10001424052970204556804574258222289862830.html

Peter, J., & Olson, J. (2008). *Consumer behavior and marketing strategy* (8th ed.). New York: McGraw-Hill.

Riverside Speedway. (2010). *Komatsu 300.* Retrieved November 16, 2010, from www.riversidespeedway.ca/Komatsu%20300%202010.htm

Seo, W.J., & Green, B.C. (2008). Development of the motivation scale for sport online consumption. *Journal of Sport Management, 22,* 82–109.

Shank, M.D. (2009). *Sport marketing: A strategic perspective* (4th ed.). Upper Saddle River, NJ: Prentice Hall.

Snyder, C.R., Lassegard, M., & Ford, C.E. (1986). Distancing after group success and failure: Basking in reflected glory and cutting off reflected failure. *Journal of Personality and Social Psychology, 51,* 382–388.

Swangard, P. (2008). Executive interview with Heidi Ueberroth. *International Journal of Sport Finance, 3*(4), 185–188.

van Gelder, S. (2004, September). Global brand strategy. *Brand management, 12*(1), 39–48.

Wann, D.L., & Branscombe, N.R. (1993). Sport fans: Measuring degree of identification with their team. *International Journal of Sport and Exercise Psychology, 24,* 1–17.

Whitelock, J., & Fastoso, F. (2007). Understanding international branding: Defining the domain and reviewing the literature. *International Marketing Review, 24*(3), 252–270.

Zhang, J.J., Pease, D.G., Hui, S.C., & Michaud, T.J. (1995). Variables affecting the spectator decision to attend NBA games. *Sport Marketing Quarterly, 4,* 29–39.

Chapter 20

Barnes, C. (2005). *Mobile technologies: The opportunities for sport.* London: SportBusiness Group.

Briggs, J. (2003, June 16). Managing new media projects: From conceptual development to commercial exploitation. *OTHER Media.* Retrieved August 15, 2005, from www.othermedia.com

Fisher, E. (2008a, February 4). Guarding online content. *SportsBusiness Journal*. Retrieved February 4, 2008, from www.sportsbusinessjournal.com

Glendenning, M. (2008, October 22). £3m payout to sport league clubs. *Sportbusiness.com*. Retrieved October 22, 2008, from www.sportbusiness.com

Glendenning, M. (2007, June 6). FL Interactive launches new club websites. *SportBusiness Newslines*. Retrieved June 25, 2010, from www.sportbusiness.com

Haynes, R. (2007). Sports' image rights in the new media age. *European Sport Management Quarterly, 7*(4), 361–374.

Hefflinger, M. (2006). *Yahoo World Cup site draws 4.2 billion views, streams 138 million videos*. Digital Media Wire. Retrieved June 4, 2009, from www.dmwmedia.com

PRNewswire. (2007, May 16). Top European sport clubs have global fan base. *PRNewswire*. Retrieved May 16, 2007, from www.prnewswire.com

Santomier, J.P., & Costabiei, A. (2009). New media challenges facing football in the 21st Century. In S. Chadwick, & S. Hamil (Eds.), Managing football: An international perspective. London: Butterworth Heinemann.

Santomier, J.P., & Shuart, J.A. (2008). Sport new media. *International Journal of Sport Management and Marketing, 4*(1/2).

Sports City. (2008a, October 10). FIFA and UEFA to take part in media focused workshop at Soccerex 2008. *Sports City*. Retrieved October 10, 2008, from www.sports-city.org/news

UEFA. (2008). *Media studies on agenda*. Retrieved March 3, 2008, from www.uefa.com

Chapter 21

Ammon, R., Jr. (2010). Risk management process. In D.J. Cotton & J.T. Wolohan (Eds.), *Law for recreation and sport managers* (5th ed., pp. 282-300). Dubuque, IA: Kendall/Hunt.

Ammon, R., Jr., & Stotlar, D. (2011). Sport facility and event management. In P. M. Pedersen, J.B. Parks, J. Quarterman, & L. Thibault (Eds.), *Contemporary sport management* (4th ed., pp. 293–312).

Ammon, R., Jr., & Unruh, N. (2010). Crowd management. In D.J. Cotton & J.T. Wolohan (Eds.), *Law for recreation and sport managers* (5th ed., pp. 338-350). Dubuque, IA: Kendall/Hunt.

Dick, G. (2007, November). *Green building basics*. California Integrated Waste Management Board. Retrieved June 9, 2008, from www.ciwmb.ca.gov/GreenBuilding/Basics.htm

Fried, G. (2005). *Managing sport facilities*. Champaign, IL: Human Kinetics

Fried, G. & Ammon, R., Jr. (2009). Alcohol management: Boon or boondoggle? *Journal of Crowd Safety and Security Management 1*(2), 62-80.

Henricks, M. (2007, October/November) A blueprint for building success. *Facility Manager, 23*(5), 37–39.

Kandampully, J., & Duddy, R. (1999). Relationship marketing: A concept beyond the primary relationship. *Marketing Intelligence & Planning, 17*(7), 315–323.

McCarthy, M. (2008, Aug. 6). NFL unveils new code of conduct for its fans. *USA Today*. Retrieved June 1, 2009, from www.usatoday.com/sports/football/nfl/2008-08-05-fan-code-of-conduct_N.htm

McDaniel, S.R., Kinney, L., & Chalip, L. (2001). A cross-cultural investigation of the ethical dimensions of alcohol and tobacco sports sponsorships. *Teaching Business Ethics, 5*(3), 307–321.

Nelson, T.F., & Wechsler, H. (2003). School spirits: Alcohol and collegiate sports fans. *Addictive Behaviours, 28*, 1–11.

Shank, M. (2003). *Sports marketing: A strategic approach* (2nd ed.) Upper Saddle River, NJ: Prentice Hall.

Shani, D., & Sujana, C. (1992). Exploiting niches using relationship marketing. *Journal of Services Marketing, 6*(4), 43–52.

Van Wyk, J. (2008). The 2010 FIFA World Cup in South Africa: The politics of hosting a mega international event. *World Journal of Managing Events, 2*(1) 1–9.

What is a carbon footprint? (2008). Retrieved December 29, 2008, from www.carbonfootprint.com/carbonfootprint.html

Chapter 22

Australian Sports Commission. (1999). *Vista Downunder: Proceedings from the international conference on athletes with disabilities*, P. Mayne (ed.). November 1–7.

Baade, R.A., Baumann, R., & Matheson, V.A. (2008). Selling the game: Estimating the economic impact of professional sports through taxable sales. Southern Economic Journal, 74 (3), 794–811.

Baade, R.A., & Matheson, V.A. (2004). The quest for the cup: Assessing the economic impact of the World Cup. *Regional Studies, 38*(4), 343–354.

Beard, M. (2008, November18). Fears over legacy in the "forgotten Olympic borough." *Evening Standard*. Retrieved from www.standard.co.uk

Bull, C., & Lovell, J. (2007). The impact of hosting major sporting events on local residents: An analysis of the views and perceptions of Canterbury residents in relation to the Tour de France 2007. *Journal of Sport & Tourism, 12*(3/4), 229–248.

Burns, J.P.A., Hatch, J.H., & Mules, T.J. (1986). *The Adelaide Grand Prix: The impact of a special event*. Adelaide, Australia: Centre for South Australian Economic Studies.

Cashman, R. (2003). *Impact of the Games on Olympic host cities*. Barcelona, Spain: Centre d'Estudis Olympics.

Chalip, L. (2005). Marketing, media and place promotion. In J. Higham (ed.), *Sport tourism destinations: Issues, opportunities and analysis* (pp. 162–175). Oxford, United Kingdom: Elsevier.

Chalip, L., & Costa, C. (2006). Building sport event tourism into the destination brand: Foundations for a general theory. In H. Gibson (ed.), *Sport tourism concepts and theories* (pp. 86–105). London: Routledge.

Crompton, J.L. (2006). Economic impact studies: Instruments for political shenanigans? *Journal of Travel Research, 45*(1), 67–82.

Cuyas, E. (2002). *White paper on accessibility: Investigative study 1998–1999*. Lausanne, Switzerland: International Olympic Committee.

Delpy Neirotti, L. (2003). An introduction to sport and adventure tourism. In S. Hudson (ed.)., *Sport and adventure tourism*. New York: Howarth Press.

Dimeo, P., & Kay, J. (2004). Major sports events, image projection and the problems of "semi-periphery": A case study of the 1996 South Asia Cricket World Cup. *Third World Quarterly, 25*(7), 1263–1276.

DPTAC. (2005). *Government accessibility advisor predicts Olympic victory for disabled people*. Retrieved February 23, 2011, from www.dptac.gov.uk/pn/051019.htm

Erikson, D. P., & Wander, P. (2007). China: Cricket 'champion.' *Inter-American Dialogue*. Retrieved February 23, 2011, from www.thedialogue.org/page.cfm?pageID=32&pubID=274

Fickenscher, Lisa. (2006). Marathon brings NYC $188 million; Race adds more to city economy than any other single-day sporting event. *Crain's New York Business*. Retrieved February 23, 2011, from http://goliath.ecnext.com/coms2/gi_0199-5850246/Marathon-brings-NYC-188-million.html

Fredline, L., Jago, L., & Deery, M. (2003). The development of a generic scale to measure the social impacts of events. *Event Management, 8*(1), 23–37.

Fredline, E., & Faulkner, B. (2002). Variations in residents' reactions to major motorsport events: Why residents perceive the impacts of events differently. *Event Management, 7*, 115–125.

GCIS. (2008). *South Africa 2010*. Retrieved from www.sa2010.gov.za/safety-and-security

Getz, D. (2008). *Serious sport event tourists*. Presentation at the European Association for Sport Management Congress, September 13, Heidelberg, Germany.

Grant Thornton. (2008). 2010 World Cup set to contribute R55 bn to SA's GDP. Press briefing, November 27.

Gibson, H. (1998). Sport tourism: A critical analysis of research. *Sport Management Review, 1*(1): 45–76.

Green, B.C., & Jones, I. (2005). Serious leisure, social identity and sport tourism. *Sport in Society, 8*(2), 164–181.

Greig, M., & McQuaid, R. (2004). *Determinants of visitor expenditure at a major sports event*. At European Regional Science Association Conference, August 25–29, 2004, University of Porto, Portugal.

Guala, A., & Turco, D.M. (2007). *An analysis of Turin's Olympic legacy*. Paper presented at the European Association for Sport Management Congress, Turin, Italy.

Higham, J.E.S. (2005). Sport tourism destinations: Issues, opportunities and analysis. Oxford, United Kingdom: Elsevier.

Hinch, T. Jackson, E.L. Hudson, S., & Walker, G. (2006). Leisure constraint theory and sport tourism. In H. Gibson (ed.), *Sport tourism concepts and theories* (pp. 10–31). London: Routledge.

Jackson, E. (2005). *Constraints to leisure*. State College, PA: Venture.

Kahn, Huma. (2008, August 7). Sponsors Win Big With Coveted Olympic Partnerships. *ABC News*. Retrieved February 23, 2011, from http://abcnews.go.com/Business/China/story?id=5526570&page=1

Kavetsos, G. (2009). *The impact of the London Olympics announcement on property prices*. London: Cass Business School.

Kraus, R. (2001). *Recreation and leisure in modern society*. Toronto, ON, Canada: Jones and Barlett.

Lee, C.K., & Taylor, T. (2005). Critical reflections on the economic impact assessment of a mega-event: The case of the 2002 FIFA World Cup. *Tourism Management, 26*, 595–603.

Lloyd, A. (2003). Travel trends: Disable travel. *Hemispheres, 11*, 30–32.

Maennig, W. (2007). *One year later: A re-appraisal of the economics of the 2006 soccer World Cup, Hamburg*. Contemporary Economic Discussion, No. 10.

McGough, S. (2002). Facilities for people with disabilities. In *Architecture and international sporting events: Future planning and development*, Proceedings of the 2nd Joint Conference organized by the International Olympic Committee and the International Union of Architects Sports and Leisure Programme. Lausanne, Switzerland, June 8–9.

Mihalik, B.J. (2003). Host population perceptions towards the 1996 Atlanta Olympics: Benefits and liabilities. In M. De Moragas, C. Kennett, & N. Puig (eds.), *The Legacy of the Olympic Games, 1984–2000* (pp. 339–345). Lausanne, Switzerland: International Olympic Committee.

Nauright, J. (2004). Global games: culture, political economy, and sport in the globalized world of the twenty-first century. *Third World Quarterly, 25*(7), 1325-1336.

O'Connor, A. (2008, October 24). Credit crunch robs Olympic Games of £500m private sector money. *The Times*. Retrieved from www.timesonline.co.uk/tol/sport/olympics/london_2012/article5003605.ece

Preuss, H. (2004). *Economics of staging the Olympic Games: A comparison of the Games 1972–2008*. Cheltenham, United Kingdom: Elgar.

Preuss, H. (2005). The economic impact of visitors at major multi-sport events. *European Sport Management Quarterly, 5*(3), 281–301.

Preuss, H. (2007). The conceptualisation and measurement of mega sport event legacies. *Journal of Sport and Tourism, 12*(3/4), 207–227.

Preuss, H., & Schutte, N. (2008). *Football tourists and their contribution to the economic impact—evidence from EURO 2008 in Austria/Switzerland.* Paper presented at the 2008 European Association for Sport Management Conference, Heidelberg, Germany.

Ritchie, J.R.B. (2000). Turning 16 days into 16 years through Olympic legacies. *Event Management, 6*(2), 155–65.

Ritchie, J.R.B., & Aitken, C.E. (1984). Olympulse I: The research program and initial results, *Journal of Travel Research, 22*(1), 17–25.

Ritichie, J.R.B., & Aitken, C.E. (1985). Olympulse II: Evolving resident attitudes toward the 1988 Olympic Winter Games. *Journal of Travel Research, 23*(3), 28–33.

Ritchie, J.R.B., & Lyons, M. (1990). Olympulse VI: A post-event assessment of resident reaction to the XVth Olympic Winter Games. *Journal of Travel Research, 28*(3), 14–23.

Sandomir, R. (2008, June 18). How big is "Tiger Effect"? Networks will soon learn. *New York Times.* Retrieved June 18, 2008, from www.nytimes.com/2008/06/19/sports/golf/19sandomir.html

Sheringham, S. (2007). China splurges on Caribbean cricket in quest to isolate Taiwan. *Bloomberg.* Retrieved February 23, 2011, from www.bloomberg.com/apps/news?pid=newsarchive&sid=ajv47UQW6sq8

Scott, A.K.S., & Turco, D.M. (2007). VFRs as a segment of the sport event tourist market. *Journal of Sport and Tourism, 12*(1), 41–52.

Shipway, R., & Jones, I. (2007). Running away from home: Understanding visitor experiences and behaviour at sport tourism events. *International Journal of Tourism Research, 9,* 373–383.

Soutar, G., & McLeod, P. (1993). Residents' perceptions on impacts of the America's Cup. *Annals of Tourism Research, 20,* 571–582.

Sport Business. (2006). *The business of sport tourism* (August). Retrieved from sportbusiness.com/reports/160251/the-business-of-sport-tourism

Stebbins, R.A. (2007). Serious leisure: A perspective for our time. New Brunswick, NJ: Aldine/Transaction.

Tang, Q., & Turco, D.M. (2001). A profile of high-value event tourists. *Journal of Convention and Exhibition Management, 3*(2), 33–40.

Turco, D.M. (1997). Measuring the economic and fiscal impacts of state high school sport championships. *Sport Marketing Quarterly, 6*(3), 49–53.

Turco, D.M. (1998). Host residents' perceived social costs and benefits towards a staged tourist attraction. *Journal of Travel and Tourism Marketing, 7*(1), 21–30.

Turco, D.M., Ally, S.A., Cox, M., & McAlmont, C. (2011). A look at the watching friends and relatives market at the 2007 Cricket World Cup. In Jordan-Miller, L.A., Tyson, B., Hayle, C. & Truly, D. (Eds) *Sport Events Management: The Caribbean Experience.* Ashgate Publishing.

Turco, D.M., Riley, R.W., & Swart, K. (2002). *Sport tourism.* Morgantown, WV: Fitness Information Technology.

WTO. (2008). *Long-term prospects: Tourism 2020 Vision.* Retrieved from http://world-tourism.org/market_research/facts/market_trends.htm

Waterman, T., & McGrath, R. (2007). *2012 Olympic and Paralympic transport plan question time.* Retrieved from www.c-london.co.uk/files/pdf/2012%20transport%20plan%20summary%20v3.pdf

Yu, Y., & Turco, D.M. (2000). Issues in tourism event economic impact studies: The case of the 1995 Kodak Albuquerque International Balloon Fiesta. *Current Issues in Tourism, 3*(2), 138–149.

Index

About the Contributors

Gerard Akindes, PhD, is an assistant professor in sports administration at Ohio University, USA. He received his doctorate in media arts and studies from Ohio University. He is the cofounder of Impumelelo, an interdisciplinary electronic journal of African sport, and cofounder and coordinator of the Sports in Africa conferences at Ohio University. His research interests include the economic aspect of the migration of African football players and sport as a tool of development.

Robin Ammon Jr., EdD, is an associate professor in the department of kinesiology and sport science at the University of South Dakota, USA. He earned his EdD in sport administration from the University of Northern Colorado, USA. His research areas include legal liabilities in sport, risk management in sport and athletics, and premises liability. Dr. Ammon has written extensively with sixteen articles in refereed journals, fifteen chapters in sport management books, and four textbooks in print. He has presented over 60 times at local, regional, national, and international conferences on topics including facility, legal, crowd management, and security issues. He has consulted for various events such as the NFL Super Bowl, 2011 NHL Winter Classic, and collegiate athletic events. Dr. Ammon is the 17th president of the North American Society for Sport Management.

Elesa Argent, PhD, is a senior lecturer of leadership and enterprise at the London Metropolitan University Business School in the United Kingdom. In addition to her academic role, Dr. Argent is also vice president of the International Federation of American Football and head of research for the British Universities American Football League.

Willie Burden, EdD, is an associate professor of sport management as well as undergraduate program coordinator at Georgia Southern University, USA. His research interests include sport marketing, management of sport organizations, and student athlete welfare. He has coauthored several book chapters and written journal articles in publications such as the *International Journal of Sport Management*,

Sport Marketing Quarterly, and *International Sports Journal*. He has directed a successful NCAA Division 1 intercollegiate athletics program and played professionally in the Canadian Football League for eight seasons. His professional affiliations include the North America Society for Sport Management, and the American Alliance of Health, Physical Education, Recreation and Dance.

Kevin K. Byon, PhD, is an assistant professor in the sport management and policy program at the University of Georgia, USA, where he teaches undergraduate and graduate sport marketing. He received his PhD in sport management from the University of Florida. His primary research interests concern sport consumer behavior and sport tourism. Dr. Byon has published 13 peer-reviewed research articles and has made over 50 national and international presentations. His published research articles have appeared in numerous journals, including *Sport Management Review, International Journal of Sports Marketing & Sponsorship, International Journal of Sport Management, Marketing Intelligence & Planning,* and *Journal of Vacation Marketing*. Dr. Byon is originally from South Korea.

Li Chen, PhD, is professor in sport management and chairperson of the department of sport and recreation management at Delaware State University, USA. He has published more than 60 research papers and proceedings in research journals including the *Journal of Sport Management* and presented nearly 60 research presentations at international and national conferences. He has served as an invited editor for the *International Journal of Sport Management and Marketing* and on the editorial board for five research journals. His research interests are in human resources management and consumer motivation.

Anthony G. Church, PhD, teaches in the school of sports administration in the Faculty of Management at Laurentian University in Sudbury, Canada. His primary research areas are related to policy, governance, and strategic decision making in sport organizations. He received his PhD in sport policy from the University of Western Ontario, Canada, and teaches undergraduate and MBA courses in sports administration, facility management, policy and governance, international sport management, and leadership and ethics in sport organizations. He also consults for sport councils and executive boards and works with other researchers aligned with the Institute for Sport Marketing at Laurentian University.

Artur Costabiei, MA, is currently a marketing and communications manager at the Tourist Board Kronplatz/Plan de Corones, Italy, representing one of the most important ski resorts in the country. Taking advantage of his international experience, he implements marketing strategies for the European market. Prior to this position, he was active in athlete management, focusing in particular on public relations and media. He has a MA in sport management from the University of Florence, Italy.

R. Brian Crow, EdD, is a professor of sport management at Slippery Rock University in Slippery Rock, Pennsylvania, USA. Crow has held faculty positions at the University of Southern Mississippi and Hampton University. His research interests include intercollegiate athletics, studying guest service at sport venues, and hazing among athletes. Dr. Crow is also the president and CEO of GameDay Consulting.

Nikki Dryden, JD, is a two-time Olympic swimmer from Canada and a human rights and immigration attorney in New York, USA. Dryden competed at the 1992 and 1996 Olympic Games and covered the 2004 and 2008 Olympics for SwimNews Magazine. Dryden has worked in Kenya and Sri Lanka and currently works on legal issues at the nexus of sport and human rights. She has spoken at such conferences as Play the Game, the World Conference on Women and Sport, and the International Sports Law and Business Conference. Dryden is an athlete ambassador for several organizations including Right To Play.

Adel Elnashar, PhD, is a former professor of sport management at the University of Bahrain. He was the previous associate dean for graduate studies and research and head of the department of sport management at Minia University, Egypt. His research interests include international and comparative sporting structures and systems along with cooperative and competitive group structuring. He is a reviewer for the *Journal of Research for*

the International Council for Health, Physical Education, Recreation and Dance (ICHPER•SD) as well as the *International Journal of Sport Management*. He is secretary general of ICHPER•SD.

Mosaad Ewies, PhD, is a professor and head of the department of recreation in the Faculty of Physical Education at Helwan University, Egypt. His research interests cover the areas of sport for all and physical education in universities and schools. In addition to being an editor of several sport-related cultural books on addiction struggle, citizenship, leadership, and recreation, Dr. Ewies is the president of Sport Syndicated in Egypt and the vice president of the ICHPER-SD for the Middle East.

Ted Fay, PhD, is a professor and former chair of the sport management department at the State University of New York at Cortland, USA. He has focused much of his scholarly work in social and public policy, sport governance, and sport for development and strategic management. Dr. Fay has an extensive background in international sport including experience with the Olympic and Paralympic Movements. Over the span of 30 years, he has worked with or for a number of national and international sport governing bodies including the International Paralympic Committee. Dr. Fay has been actively involved in nine winter Paralympic Games, from 1980 through 2010.

James T. Gray, JD, is assistant professor and the director of the Sport and Recreation Management Program at Marian University, Wisconsin, USA. He is a 1986 graduate of Temple University in Philadelphia, Pennsylvania, and a 1990 graduate of Marquette University Law School in Milwaukee, Wisconsin. He formerly served as assistant director of the National Sports Law Institute of Marquette University Law School. Gray is coauthor of the second edition of a two volume textbook entitled *Sports Law Practice*, and he is the sole author of the third edition of the same text, which is considered one of the seminal books for sport law practitioners.

Lyndsay M.C. Hayhurst, MA, is a doctoral candidate in the Faculty of Physical Education and Health, the Collaborative Graduate Program in Women's Health, and the Comparative Program on Health and Society at the Munk School of Global Affairs at the University of Toronto, Canada. Her research interests include postcolonial feminist approaches to international relations; sport for development and peace, gender, and health; and corporate social responsibility as it pertains to international development. Her publications have appeared in *Third World Quarterly*, *Progress in Development Studies*, *International Review for the Sociology of Sport*, *International Journal of Sport Policy*, *Sociology of Sport Journal*, and *European Sport Management Quarterly*.

Kevin Heisey, PhD, is associate professor in the department of sports management at Liberty University, Virginia, USA. His primary research interest focuses on the economic effects of sport megaevents on host economies.

Brad R. Humphreys, PhD, is a professor in the department of economics at the University of Alberta in Canada, where he holds the chair in the Economics of Gaming. His research on the economic impact of professional sports, the economics of intercollegiate athletics, and competitive balance in sport leagues has been published in academic journals, including the *Journal of Urban Economics*, the *Journal of Policy Analysis and Management*, the *Journal of Economic Behavior and Organization*, the *Journal of Sports Economics*, and *Contemporary Economic Policy*. In 2007, he testified before the United States Congress on the financing and economic impact of professional sport facilities.

Megat A. Kamaluddin, MSC, is a faculty member in the Faculty of Education at the University of Malaya, Malaysia. He received both his undergraduate and graduate degrees in sport management from St. Thomas University, Florida, USA. He was instrumental in establishing the first sport science (specifically sport management) undergraduate academic program in Malaysia in 1995. He is also the founding member and current president of the Malaysian Association for Sport Management (MASMA) as well as the vice president of the Asian Association for Sport Management (AASM). His research interests are sport industry management and the economics of sport.

Bruce Kidd, PhD, is professor in the Faculty of Physical Education and Health at the University of Toronto, Canada. A former dean, he writes and teaches about the history and political economy of Canadian and international sport. He has frequently served as a policy advisor to governments and sport organizations and chairs the Commonwealth Advisory Body on Sport, which advises the Commonwealth Secretariat and member governments on sport policy, especially sport for development and peace. He also chairs the Maple Leaf Sport and Entertainment Team Up Foundation, which enriches opportunities for disadvantaged children and youth through sport and physical activity.

Kazuhiko Kimura, MS, is professor in sport management and associate dean for academic affairs of the Faculty of Sport Sciences at Waseda University in Tokyo, Japan. His recent interests of research are sport event management and sport tourism. He is a board member of the Japanese Society of Management for Physical Education and Sport and serves on the Central Council for Education of Japan's Sports and Youth Subcommittee. He coauthored *Sport and Health Tourism* (2009) and has written more than ten books related to sport management including two translation books.

Yong Jae Ko, PhD, is an associate professor in the department of tourism, recreation, and sport management at the University of Florida, USA. His primary research line focuses on sport and event marketing and consumer behavior. More specifically, he has been involved in a variety of research projects focused on sport consumers' psychological and behavioral patterns. Dr. Ko's research has resulted in numerous peer-reviewed articles in journals including, but not limited to, *Managing Service Quality*, *Journal of Marketing Management*, *Journal of Sport Management*, *International Journal of Sports Marketing and Sponsorship*, *Annals of Tourism Research*, and *Sport Marketing Quarterly*.

David Legg, PhD, is an associate professor in the department of physical education and recreation at Mount Royal University in Calgary, Canada. He is actively involved as an educator, researcher, and volunteer in sport management and adapted physical activity. In 2004, David was a visiting professor at Dalhousie University in Halifax, Canada, and in 2008 to 2009 at Deakin University in Melbourne, Australia. As a volunteer, Dr. Legg is the president for the Canadian Paralympic Committee, board member of Toronto 2015 Pan ParaPam American Games, director for Sport Alberta, and chairperson of the Alberta Youth Olympic Symposium.

Cindy Lee, PhD, is an assistant professor in the department of sport sciences at West Virginia University, USA. Her research interest lies in applying the principles of consumer behavior and psychology to the sport context, which helps understand and explain how and why sport spectators and fans behave in certain ways. She is a member of the North American Society of Sport Management (NASSM) and has presented her research at the NASSM, Sport Marketing Association, and Association for Consumer Research conferences.

Rosa López de D'Amico, PhD, teaches at Universidad Pedagógica Experimental Libertador in Maracay, Venezuela. She acts as the coordinator of the research center on studies in physical education, health, sport, recreation, and dance. Dr. López de D'Amico obtained her PhD in sport management at the University of Sydney in Australia, where she also completed a Ewing Postdoctoral Fellowship. Her primary areas of research are: sport management, pedagogy, and gender issues. She is the current president of the Latin American Association for Sport Management, and she also serves on the board of ISCPES, IAPESGW, and ICSSPE. She is a guest professor at West Virginia University, USA, and the University of Macau, in China. From 2009 to 2011, she was the president of the Aragua State Institute of Sport in Venezuela.

Joanne MacLean, PhD, is dean of the Faculty of Applied Health Sciences and associate professor of sport management at Brock University, Canada. Her research interests involve human resources and organizational behavior in nonprofit sport organizations, with specific interest in understanding effective management of community sport organizations worldwide. She has participated in 3 FISU Games, as a coach in Fukuoka, Japan (1995); an assistant chef de mission in Palma de Mallorca, Spain (1999); and as Canada's chef de mission in Daegu, Korea (2003). MacLean has authored or coauthored three books and published extensively in sport and management journals. She is a research fellow of the North American Society for Sport Management.

Jaime Orejan, PhD, is an assistant professor of sport management at Winston-Salem State University in North Carolina, USA. His research interests are management and marketing of soccer in the areas of sponsorship, foreign markets, and Hispanics.

His secondary area of research is in international education, particularly cultural issues in management and marketing of sports. He has published and presented his research at both the national and international level and has recently authored a book on the history and development of soccer worldwide.

Michael E. Pfahl, PhD, is an assistant professor in sports administration at Ohio University, USA. Prior to this, he was on the International College faculties at Yonok College (Thailand) and Bangkok University (Thailand) teaching management and marketing. Additional sport experiences include various management and sales positions with the Cleveland Cavaliers and the Cleveland Lumberjacks as well as cofounder and president of Players Management, Inc., a sport marketing and athletic representation firm. Dr. Pfahl's current research interests are primarily conducted from a qualitative perspective and include the convergence of media, technology and sport, environmentalism and sport, and human resource issues in sport organizations.

Holger Preuss, PhD, is professor in sport economics and sport sociology at the Institute of Sport Science in the Faculty of Social Science, Media, and Sport at Mainz University, Germany. His research interests are in economic aspects of mega sport events and the impact of sport on the German economy. He is associate editor of the *Journal of European Sport Management Quarterly* and the *Journal of Sport and Tourism*. He is also a member of the editorial board of the *Journal of Sport Finance*, the *Sport Management Review*, *International Journal of Sport Policy*, and the *Journal of Scandinavian Sport Studies*. He has written seven books and published more than 60 articles in sport management. Dr. Preuss is also professor at the University Molde in Norway, guest professor at the University of East London in the United Kingdom, and international scholar at the State University of New York at Cortland in the United States.

Wirdati M. Radzi, MSA, teaches sport management at the University of Malaya Sport Centre in Malaysia. After completing her legal studies at the International Islamic University Malaysia, she continued with her graduate education in the premier master of sports administration program at Ohio University, USA. She is currently working on her PhD in sport management, focusing on the

Malaysian sport management experience. She is involved in sport management consultative works with several public sport agencies as well as the national sport governing bodies in Malaysia. Her research interests range from legal aspects of sport to sport governance.

James Santomier, PhD, is a professor in the marketing and sport management department in the John F. Welch College of Business at Sacred Heart University, Connecticut, USA. He also is a visiting professor at the University of Bayreuth, Germany. He received a BA and MA in physical education from Montclair State University, New Jersey, USA, and a PhD in physical education from the University of Utah, USA. His research interests include sport marketing and sponsorship, new media, and the sociology of sport.

David J. Shonk, PhD, is an assistant professor of sport and recreation management at James Madison University in Harrisonburg, Virginia, USA. His research interests are related to services marketing, interorganizational networks, and business strategy in sport. He is a member of the North American Society of Sport Management and has had affiliations with the National Association for Sport and Physical Education, Sport Marketing Association, and the Sport Management Association of Australia and New Zealand.

Joshua A. Shuart, PhD, is an associate professor and chair of the marketing and sport management department at Sacred Heart University, Connecticut, USA. He completed his PhD in sport management at the University of Connecticut, where he worked as a research associate in the Laboratory for Leisure, Tourism, and Sport. His research interests include new media, sponsorship, and athlete endorsements.

James Skinner, PhD, is associate professor in sport management and head of the department of tourism, leisure, hotel and sport management at Griffith University, Australia. His research interests are in culture, strategy, leadership, and change in sport; drugs in sport; sport and social capital; and sport governance and policy. His work has appeared in leading sport management journals such as the *Journal of Sport Management, European Sport Management Quarterly, Sport Management Review,* and the *International Journal of Sport Management and Marketing.*

He has conducted consultancies for international and national sport governing bodies, professional sporting organizations, and the Australian Sports Commission.

David L. Snyder, JD, is a professor in the sport management department at the State University of New York at Cortland, USA, and a part-time professor in the sport management program at Tompkins Cortland Community College, New York, USA. He has served as president of an international sport marketing company headquartered in Tokyo, Japan. His two primary areas of research interest are the business of Japanese baseball and legal issues in Major League Baseball. He is chair of the Asian Baseball Committee for the Society for American Baseball Research and interviews editor of the *International Journal of Sports Marketing and Sponsorship.*

Kamilla Swart, EdD, is an associate professor in the Faculty of Business and heads the Centre for Tourism Research in Africa at the Cape Peninsula University of Technology in South Africa. Her research interests include sport and event tourism, with a specific focus on the 2010 FIFA World Cup, and event policies, strategies, and evaluations. Dr. Swart has published on varied topics related to the bidding and impacts of sport tourism events in South Africa.

Babs Surujlal, PhD, is a research professor in the Faculty of Management Sciences at Vaal University of Technology in Vanderbijlpark, South Africa. He earned his PhD in sport management.

Minoo Tehrani, PhD, is a professor of management in the Gabelli School of Business at Roger Williams University, Rhode Island, USA. Her PhD is from Arizona State University, USA, with specialization in the areas of strategy and international management. She serves as the director of the international business major at Roger Williams University. Dr. Tehrani has published in several journals, including *Organization Management Journal, Journal of Business and Economic Studies,* and *Journal of American Academy of Business.*

Yosuke Tsuji, PhD, is an assistant professor of marketing in the department of industrial management at the University of the Ryukyus in Okinawa, Japan. His research focuses on sport consumer behavior, especially on corporate brand awareness and corporate brand images in sport sponsorship activities. His secondary focus is on effectiveness of sport event management. He has published in several journals, including *Journal of Sport Management* and *Sport Marketing Quarterly*.

Douglas Michele Turco, PhD, is associate professor of sport management at Drexel University, Pennsylvania, USA. He has authored over 40 journal articles in such journals as *Sport Marketing Quarterly, International Journal of Sport Management, Journal of Travel Research,* and *Journal of Sport and Tourism.* Dr. Turco consults on sport and tourism planning, event economic impacts, and consumer market research for organizations worldwide. He is also on the faculty at the Rajiv Gandhi Indian Institute of Management in India, IMC FH-Krems in Austria, and National Taiwan Sport University.

Wayne Usher, PhD, is a faculty member of the School of Education and Professional Studies at Griffith University, Australia. His research interests surround current international and national trends associated with social media (also known as web 2.0 and web 3.0) and mobile applications (such as for iPads and smartphones) and how these technologies impact various health and sport settings. Predominately, Dr. Usher's research areas include the role of the Internet and social media and how they impact early 21st century health care professionals and sport managers. His research settings include health, fitness, education, business, and e-sport marketing.

Luisa Vélez, PhD, is an assistant professor in sport management at the State University of New York at Cortland, USA. Her research interests are in minority representation in sport and issues in international sport. She is a board member of the Latin American Association for Sport Management.

Sharianne Walker, PhD, is chair and professor of sport management in the School of Business at Western New England College, Massachusetts, USA. She is the author of two books focusing on the principles of managing successful sport organizations. She has also written several journal articles,

chapters, and book reviews in the areas of sport marketing, strategic management of international sport organizations, sport facility management, and the finance of sport organizations. She has presented at both international and national sport management and business conferences. Dr. Walker continues to maintain an active consulting practice that works with sport organizations and leaders in both the for-profit and nonprofit sectors.

Nicholas M. Watanabe, PhD, is an assistant teaching professor of sport management in the department of parks, recreation and tourism at the University of Missouri, USA. His research interests are in sport economics and finance as well as international sport management. He is working with colleagues in universities across Asia on research and educational projects in sport management and is one of the contributors to the *International Journal of Sport Finance* blog.

Di Xie, PhD, is general manager of the Active Sport International Co., Ltd., a sport marketing company that specializes in promoting running events in China. She received her doctorate in sport management from the Ohio State University, USA, in 2005 and subsequently taught sport management at Western Illinois University, USA, from 2005 to 2009. Her research interests include revenue generation and fund-raising for running events and operation of sport business at the global level. She is an enthusiastic marathon runner and guest professor of the Central University of Finance and Economics in Beijing, China.

Chia-Chen Yu, EdD, is professor and director of the sport management program in the department of exercise and sport science at the University of Wisconsin-La Crosse, USA. She has published 15 peer-reviewed journal articles in the areas of international sport marketing and computer application in sport management and presented at over 30 national and international conferences. She has served on the editorial board of the *Journal of Sport Management Education* and as an invited reviewer for numerous journals including the *International Journal of Sport Management and Marketing* and *European Sport Management Quarterly.*

About the Editors

Ming Li, EdD, is professor in sports administration and chair of the department of sports administration in the College of Business at Ohio University, USA. Li received his doctorate in sport administration from the University of Kansas. His research interests are in financial and economic aspects of sport and management of sport business in a global context.

Li is a former president of the North American Society for Sport Management (NASSM) and currently is serving as commissioner of the Commission on Sport Management Accreditation (COSMA). He is a member on the editorial board of the *Journal of Sport Management* and *Sport Marketing Quarterly* and has coauthored two books in sport management. He is guest professor of six institutions in China, including the Central University of Finance and Economics and Tianjin University of Sport.

Li served as an Olympic envoy for the 1996 Atlanta Olympic Games. He also served as a consultant for the 2010 Guangzhou Asian Games Organizing Committee.

Eric W. MacIntosh, PhD, is an assistant professor in the faculty of health sciences, School of Human Kinetics at the University of Ottawa, Ontario, Canada. He earned his doctorate at the University of Western Ontario with a specialization in sport management.

His research interests include the study of organizational behavior particularly within the context of the Canadian fitness industry. He also focuses on sport marketing principles within sport systems and events.

MacIntosh has published his research in many sport management journals, including the *Sport Marketing Quarterly, Sport Management Review, European Sport Management Quarterly,* and the *Journal of Sport Management.* He has also presented his research at sport management conferences, such as the North American Society for Sport Management and the European Association for Sport Management.

Gonzalo A. Bravo, PhD, is an assistant professor of sport management at West Virginia University, USA. A native of Santiago, Chile, Bravo completed a master's degree in sport administration from Penn State University and a PhD in sport management from Ohio State University. Before joining academia, he worked as sport director in a large sport organization in Chile.

His research interests focus on issues in organizational behavior and sport management as an academic discipline. His work has been published in the *International Journal of Sport Marketing and Sponsorship, Sport Management Education Journal,* and the *Journal of Sport Management.* He has presented invited lectures and keynote speeches in Brazil, Chile, China, Japan, Mexico, and Venezuela.

Bravo is a member of the North American Society for Sport Management and the North American Society for the Sociology of Sport. He also serves as the vice president for the Latin American Association for Sport Management and scientific director for the Latin American Association for Socio-Cultural Studies in Sport.